John Ireland
AND THE AMERICAN
CATHOLIC CHURCH

John Ireland, Archbishop of St. Paul, 1908 (Photo by B. C. Golling; MHS)

John Ireland

AND THE AMERICAN CATHOLIC CHURCH

Marvin R. O'Connell

MINNESOTA HISTORICAL SOCIETY PRESS
ST. PAUL · 1988

MINNESOTA HISTORICAL SOCIETY PRESS
St. Paul 55101

Copyright 1988 by the Minnesota Historical Society
All rights reserved
Manufactured in the United States of America
10 9 8 7 6 5 4 3 2 1
International Standard Book Number 0-87351-230-8

Library of Congress Cataloging-in-Publication Data
O'Connell, Marvin Richard.
John Ireland and the American Catholic Church / Marvin
R. O'Connell.
p.   cm.
Bibliography: p.
Includes index.
ISBN 0-87351-230-8 : $34.95
1. Ireland, John, 1838–1918.   2. Catholic Church —
United States — Bishops — Biography   3. Catholic
Church — Minnesota — Biography.   4. Minnesota —
Church history.   I. Title.
BX4705.I7048 1988
282'.092'4 — dc19
[B]   88-18828
CIP

IN MEMORIAM
Patrick Henry Ahern
1916–65

Contents

Illustrations

Acknowledgments

EVERYBODY HAS two grandfathers, and so does this book. Archbishop John R. Roach of St. Paul and Minneapolis, John Ireland's fifth successor, suggested the need for a new biography and generously offered the resources of the archdiocese to defray some of the costs involved. Russell Fridley, former director of the Minnesota Historical Society and long notorious as a friend of historians and historical scholarship, enthusiastically endorsed the project in a similarly open-handed manner. I am deeply grateful to them both for their confidence in me.

My best thanks are due also to the National Endowment for the Humanities, which awarded me a Fellowship for Independent Study and Research so that I might be freed for a year from my ordinary academic duties and devote myself entirely to writing this book.

Much of this work is based upon archival research, in deposits located both in this country and abroad. I owe a debt to those who either opened their materials to me or helped me to use them intelligently. Among these are Charles Burns, Scott Jesse, Deborah Kahn, Josef Metzger, O.M.I., M. Felicitas Powers, R.S.M., Wendy Clauson Schlereth, W. Thomas White, and Robert J. Wister.

Many other people helped me in various ways. I hesitate to name them lest I inadvertently leave someone off the list. But that is a chance I must take, and I ask forgiveness ahead of time for any such omission. I warmly thank Florence D. Cohalan, Joseph B. Connors, R. Emmett Curran, S.J., Louis Delahoyde, Vincent P. DeSantis, Jay P. Dolan, Henri DuLac, John Tracy Ellis, Robert E. Faricy, Gerald P. Fogarty, S.J., Kay Gutzmann, Ambrose V. Hayden,

Thomas D. Jardine, James Kellen, Robert L. Kerby, Ralph McInerny, Frances Panchok, Jaroslav Pelikan, William L. Portier, John D. Root, Daniel Sheerin, Marguerita Smith, O.P., Marina Smith, Robert Taft, S.J., Robert Trisco, Anthony Vito, and Ronald Weber.

I am grateful as well to Jean Brookins and her staff at the Minnesota Historical Society Press. If this were a well-ordered universe, every author would have the benefit of an editor as able and as sensitive as Ann Regan. Whatever infelicities remain in this book are my fault, not hers.

My friend and colleague, Professor Philip Gleason, read the entire work in typescript. There is no way I can adequately state my appreciation to this wise and witty man for sharing with me his unmatched understanding of nineteenth-century American Catholic history and for steering me away from shoals whenever they threatened.

Finally, the dedication of this book pays a personal and professional debt of long standing.

Marvin R. O'Connell
Notre Dame, Indiana

I drank a little and talked with the priest about Archbishop Ireland who was, it seemed, a noble man and with whose injustice, the injustices he had received and in which I participated as an American, and of which I had never heard, I feigned acquaintance. It would have been impolite not to have known something of them when I had listened to such a splendid explanation of their causes which were, after all, it seemed, misunderstandings. I thought he had a fine name and he came from Minnesota which made it a lovely name: Ireland of Minnesota.

Ernest Hemingway, A Farewell to Arms

Few deserve a biography, and to the undeserving none should be given.

John Ireland, Introduction to The Life of Father Hecker

Prologue
1899

THEY HAD COME to Paris only a few days before from Orléans, where the archbishop had scored another of his many oratorical triumphs, this one a panegyric of Joan of Arc, delivered in the florid French he had learned as a seminarian almost half a century before. Five thousand persons of quality had packed the cathedral to hear him, while a similar number, unable to find even standing room inside, had spilled out through the portico and down the steps into the adjacent square. He had not disappointed them, the eloquent *archevêque américain;* for two hours—the powerful voice rising and falling, the rounded phrases and learned allusions blending into one another—he had eulogized the Maid of Domremy as a statesman, soldier, woman, and saint, as one who "in her whole life . . . was the embodiment of patriotism and religion. Her life and her death spoke love of country and love of Church."[1] It was the archbishop's most familiar theme, one he had expounded from a thousand platforms and pulpits—so much so that it had become identified with him and, through him, with the vibrant Catholic church in the United States. At Orléans the huge congregation had listened to this Americanist message again, enraptured, most of them, with the preacher's "refined figure, charming and strong, in which sweetness seemed mirrored in intelligence."[2]

Now, on this May morning in the last year of the century, they walked purposefully out of the Tuileries Gardens, turned right across the corner of the vast Place de la Concorde, and right again into the Rue de Rivoli—the archbishop and his young priest-secretary taking their constitutional, unmistakably American in their suits of somber black broadcloth, with starched white Roman

1

collars at their throats and soft felt hats, the brims turned up, set squarely on their heads. The archbishop, at sixty, was stout and silver-haired, with a celtic cream-and-ruddy complexion. He was of medium height, though he looked taller as he strode vigorously along, his thick shoulders thrown back and his massive jaw thrust upward and outward. The younger man had difficulty keeping pace with him.

The glitter and symmetrical elegance of the new Paris created by Baron Haussmann crowded in around them, as did the splendid symbols of nineteenth-century pride and achievement: behind them, up the broad Champs-Élysées, loomed the Arc de Triomphe, and across the river stood Monsieur Eiffel's celebrated tower of iron, erected only ten years before. There were signs as well of present concerns: they passed a newsvendor's kiosk and could see that the most prominent name displayed in the headlines of the papers was that of Alfred Dreyfus.

But the archbishop stared blankly straight ahead and seemed oblivious to his surroundings, as had been so often the case since this European journey had begun the previous January. They had gone first to Rome, and then, with the spring, to Naples and a holiday on the coast. By mid-April they were in Turin, and on May 8 the archbishop had preached his sermon in Orléans. Ahead on the schedule were a series of lectures in Paris, dinner with the King of the Belgians in Brussels, two weeks of receptions and luncheons in London as guests of the Duke of Norfolk, and finally a visit to the archbishop's native County Kilkenny and a speech to a temperance rally in Cork City. The archbishop had plunged into all the public activities with his accustomed zest, and the secretary had no doubt that he would continue to do so. But in between ceremonial engagements, at odd, unoccupied moments, a cast of weariness came over his eyes, and a moody silence enveloped him.

They turned left into the Rue Castiglione and walked past the smart shops and restaurants which, at this early hour, were shut up tight. When they crossed the Rue Saint-Honoré and approached the entrance to the Place Vendôme, the archbishop suddenly stopped. The secretary, a few steps behind and slightly out of breath, drew abreast of him and followed his gaze up at the statue of Napoleon I, garbed in a Roman toga, atop the obelisk in the center of the square.

"Did you know," the archbishop said, "that the base of the obelisk was constructed out of the cannon captured by Napoleon at the Battle of Austerlitz? In 1805."

"No, your Grace," the secretary said.

"One of his greatest victories. It is called the battle of the three emperors. French, Austrian, Russian."

The secretary nodded. Accumulating military lore was one of the archbishop's favorite diversions.

The archbishop spoke again, his voice now sharper, almost gravelly in tone. "When we were in Rome," he said, and paused. "Do you know what they asked me in Rome? At the Vatican?"

"No, your Grace."

"They asked me," the archbishop said, his shoulders hunching forward, "they asked me if I believed in the divinity of Christ."

With that John Ireland straightened and set off briskly across the Place Vendôme, the imperious eye of the great Napoleon upon him.[3]

"Beggar's Gabardine"

1838–50

T HOMAS CARLYLE went to Ireland in the summer of 1849 as though driven "by the point of bayonets at my back. Ireland really is my problem; the breaking point of the huge suppuration which all British and all European society now is. Set down in Ireland, one might at least feel, '*Here* is thy problem. In God's name, what wilt thou do with it?' " At the end of his trip he described Ireland in the wake of the Great Famine as an "ugly spectacle: sad health, sad humour; a thing unjoyful to look back upon. The whole country figures in my mind like a ragged coat; one huge beggar's gabardine, not patched or patchable any longer."[1] Carlyle's sense of guilt mingled with impotence and condescension was not untypical of the parade of observers who crossed over from Britain and were plunged immediately into a misery so profound, so ancient, so pervasive that solutions to it seemed beyond human capacity. A few years earlier young Mr. Gladstone, in a letter to his wife, evoked a gentler, if not less despairing image: "Ireland, Ireland, that cloud in the west, that coming storm!"[2] But for the earthy Carlyle Ireland was an enormous boil, bulging with putrid matter and ready to burst.

In July 1849, he visited Kilkenny City, a "gray, old, dilapidated town," and on a "day dreadfully hot" he toured the local workhouses: one an abandoned brewery "filled to bursting with some eight thousand (?) paupers"; another a "huge chaos," where "one or two thousand great hulks of men [were] lying piled up within brick walls. . . . Did a *greater* violence to the law of nature ever before present itself to sight, if one *had* an eye to see it?" Outside, lounging everywhere, were "idle people, . . . sitting on street curbstones, etc.; numerous in the summer afternoon; idle old city; can't well think how they live." What Carlyle's sharp eye observed could have been seen, with infinite unhappy variations, all over the island, not just in the southeastern portion of it where County Kilkenny lay; and the fact was that the crowning disaster, which began in 1845, decreed that many of the Irish could not survive any longer in their ancestral homes: more than a million of them died during the Famine and more than a million others went away.[3] The next day Carlyle followed the usual tourist's route, down the county by rail to Thomastown and by carriage beyond, where he saw "squalid hamlets, ditto cottages by the wayside, with their lean goats and vermin; I have forgotten the details of them."[4]

The train upon which Carlyle traveled that July morning passed within a few miles of the village of Burnchurch, a gaggle of cabins under the shadow of the ruins of a castle that had once guarded the east-west road between the market towns of Callan and Gowran. Tradition had it that soldiers had once upon a time burned down a church located on the site, and the local Catholics, no philologists, insisted that the culprit had been bloody Cromwell, whose army had indeed camped there in 1650 on its way to imposing obedience to the Commonwealth on Callan and then on Kilkenny City.

The countryside round about, typical of County Kilkenny, rolled gently, but was "seldom so precipitous or severe as to preclude the operations of the plow."[5] It was upland, to be sure, damp and cool, with swift, lowering clouds and spatters of rain a commonplace, but the steep hills that were visible from Burnchurch on a fine day rose in County Carlow, to the east. The oaks stood sturdy, as did some pine, though there were also many stunted trees bent over by winds from the sea scarcely thirty miles away. The foliage was so lush, so wild, that it seemed poised to repossess at any moment the land which human labor and ingenuity had wrung from it. One sign of that labor was the grid of stone fences that marked off the fields and pastures from one another.

Travelers through the district were often struck by the sharp clarity of the air, which called to mind the old Kilkenny doggerel: "Fire without smoke, earth without bog,/Water without mud, and air without fog."[6] A lovely, lilting land it could have been, in its multiple shades of green, and fertile enough that upwards of 20 percent of it was given over to the cultivation of grain, the cash crop with which tenants paid their rents. There were marble quarries, too, and even modest deposits of coal. It should have been a moderately prosperous place, and instead it was a cockpit of malnutrition and disease and unarticulated hatreds. Kilkenny was not so desolate perhaps as counties to the west and northwest, not quite so dependent for the survival of its people upon the potato. But it was no less victimized by a tiny ascendancy class, alien to the populace in race and religion, more often than not absentee landlords who spent their money abroad, and for the sake of whom the world's greatest power imposed a mindless system of exploitation that denied dignity, economic well-being and opportunity, and even the minimum of physical decencies to eight men and women out of ten. For all practical purposes Ireland was a garrison state; on the eve of the Famine there were more British troops stationed there than in the whole sub-continent of India.[7] On the eve of the Famine Kilkenny, though in theory as much a constituent part of the United Kingdom of Great Britain and Ireland as English counties like Yorkshire or Surrey, teetered on the brink of social dissolution.

Tradesmen and professional people scarcely existed outside Kilkenny City. Almost everyone worked in the fields, so much so that the dark blue smocks worn by the peasantry were practically emblematic of the county. Casual labor went for a shilling a day, but a man was lucky to find a job for one or two days in the week.[8] Even those who possessed specialized skills had to give priority to tending their patches of potatoes to feed their families, and of wheat to pay their rent to the landlords' agents — so undercapitalized and primitive was the Irish economy. Such was the case of Richard Ireland, who had learned the carpenter's trade from his father.[9]

The surname "Ireland," common enough in Ulster, was rare in the southern counties. It is probable that Richard's ancestors had emigrated to England, most likely to Devonshire, toward the end of the Middles Ages. Then, at the time of the Tudor dynasty (1485–1603), when surnames came into ordinary use, many families found it convenient to assume a name that designated the place of their more or less remote origins. Thus there came to be a considerable number of English Irelands, some of whom gained notoriety, like William Ireland, a Jesuit executed in 1679 on the evidence of Titus Oates, and John Ireland, who died as Anglican Dean of Westminster in 1842.[10] In 1612 a gentleman from Devon established a plantation near Belfast and brought settlers with him from his home county, among whom was at least one man named Ireland. The family flourished and multiplied in the north, and by the beginning of the nineteenth century one member of it had migrated south to County Kilkenny. There Richard Ireland was born in 1803.[11]

He was by all accounts a man of remarkable intensity. Tall, lean, and raw-boned, he walked quickly, and with a jerky, awkward motion. When he spoke, the words rushed pell-mell from his mouth, almost out of control. His whole manner testified to a deep, inner impatience. Though he had had hardly any formal education, he was clever at mathematics and possessed a vast fund of native lore: his children never forgot the tales he told them of Ireland's heroic kings and warriors.[12] They remembered, too, that he was a stern disciplinarian, an unbending patriarch, who expected and received obedience from his extended family. Harder for them to discern, perhaps, were Richard Ireland's restlessness, his ambition, and his resentment at the lot that had fallen to him as an Irishman.

He was a widower with a three-year-old daughter when, in 1836, he married Judith Naughton. The Naughtons, originally a clan from County Galway, had been settled around Burnchurch since the middle of the eighteenth century. Judith, who preferred to be called Julia, was a severely handsome woman with dark hair and a wide mouth, whose natural playfulness — so the family tradition had it — acted as a wholesome foil to her husband's often grim demeanor. She was typical of the Irish peasant women of her generation whose straitened circumstances and conventional piety had to sustain them through the horrors of the Famine and, in Judith's case, through the hardly less searing experience of emigration. She did not know what reserves of courage she would shortly have to find within herself when Richard Ireland brought her as a bride to his home in Burnchurch.

The cottage was sturdier than most, for Richard Ireland was a personage of relative substance, a tenant indeed, but one who belonged to the class of "twenty-acre men."[13] That set him off from the wretched mass of his contemporaries, who grew their potatoes on an acre or two and lived in one-room hovels without chimney or windows, their children squatting with the pig around the peat fire, a dung heap festering just outside the door.[14] Ireland's house, by contrast, was built of stone, with a wall around it and a pretentious iron gate leading into the foreyard, and in that house Judith Ireland bore her first child on September 11, 1838. The baby boy was taken to the nearest Catholic chapel, in Danesfort, a mile and a half away, baptized, and given the name John.[15] There followed between 1842 and 1849 the births of Ellen, Eliza, Richard, and Julia, who, with their half-sister Mary Ann, brought the total complement of children in the household to six.

The times were harsh for everyone indeed, but especially for children, and John Ireland seldom reminisced about them. He attended a local school where he could not have learned much more than the rudiments of letters and arithmetic.[16] The parish priest at Danesfort taught him enough Latin to serve mass. It does not seem likely that he was allowed as much time for play as for chores. Nor can one calculate with any precision the effect upon the mind and feelings of an impressionable child to be surrounded on all sides — in Burnchurch itself, in Danesfort, in Kells, in Kilree, in Dunnamaggon, all within a few miles' radius — by the ruins of churches, castles, monasteries, which gave mute witness to the defeat of his religion and his race.

Surely he saw often enough another destructive sign of that defeat, the drunkenness in which so many despairing Irish men and women indulged. On this matter he kept one memory as green as the Kilkenny countryside. "When I was a very young boy," he recalled in 1890, "Father [Theobald] Mathew [the Franciscan temperance preacher] came to my native town to administer the pledge. I served his mass, and he asked me to attend him. He went about everywhere, giving the pledge, and everywhere he administered it, I took the pledge. He used to introduce me sometimes as his little teetotaler; I was not then seven years old."[17]

Father Mathew began his crusade against strong drink the year John Ireland was born, and it achieved early dramatic results. Hundreds of thousands heeded the priest's appeal and pledged to abstain entirely from alcohol. That a good many of them kept their promise helps explain why the production of Irish whisky fell from more than twelve million gallons in 1839 to five and a half million in 1844.[18]

The "national curse" against which Father Mathew strove was at once a cause and an effect of the degradation in which the Irish masses had to live. "Now I confess," the bishop of Ossory told Alexis de Tocqueville in 1835, "that the people has some of the characteristics and, unfortunately, some of the defects of savage people. This people has all the virtues dear to God; it has faith; there is no better Christian than the Irishman. Their morals are pure; premeditated crime is very rare. But they basically lack the civil virtues. They have no foresight or prudence. Their courage is instinctive; they throw themselves at an obstacle with extraordinary violence and, if they do not succeed at the first attempt, give it up. . . . But," the bishop asked his French visitor, "whose fault is it, if not theirs who have reduced [the Irish] to this state by bad government? What became of the Greeks under the Turks? Before 1792 we could have no schools, we could not be called to the bar, the magistracy was closed to us, we could not possess land."[19] The bishop and his fellow Catholic clergymen had much to contend with in their "savage people," who were badly instructed, prone to superstition, not without strong traces of anticlericalism, and ever ready to turn a saint's day observance or a wake into a drunken orgy. Before the Famine, probably around 40 percent attended Sunday mass or received Easter communion.[20] The Irish Catholicism John Ireland knew as a child was a far cry from that marvel of regularity and discipline it was to become late in the nineteenth century and to remain throughout the twentieth.

The Famine, that watershed event, put a check upon Father Mathew's activities.[21] About the time he was carrying his crusade into the villages of Kilkenny, the disquieting news that blight had appeared in the potato crop began to circulate throughout the district. The first reports, in September 1845, came out of Wexford and Waterford.[22] Soon the disease turned up in other counties where severe shortages quickly developed. There was considerable concern about this visitation, though most people learned of it with stoical acceptance; the Irish, cruelly dependent upon the potato, not as the staple but as the exclusive element in their diet, were all too accustomed to local failure of a crop and the resultant suffering.[23]

Indeed, a government commission estimated that one-third of the population lived in semi-starvation *every summer* before the new crop came in, even in years when the potatoes were abundant.[24] And hardly anyone was sophisticated enough to understand the worried agronomists who pointed out that the partial blight of 1845 represented a strain of plant disease unknown before and who puzzled over how to treat it.[25]

The summer of 1846 was damp and the hottest in memory. The blight struck at the potatoes again, but this time it ravaged the crop all over Ireland. Fields green and luxuriant were transformed in a day into black stubble. The cost of potatoes went from two shillings a hundredweight to seven and then to twelve, until they were unavailable at any price. And without potatoes to eat, there was nothing to eat. A starving people awaited the harvests of 1847 with foreboding. The disease duly reappeared, but not universally, and some dared to hope that the worst was over. The year 1848, however, was a repetition of 1846; the whole potato crop rotted in the fields, and a calamity of unprecedented proportions descended upon unhappy Ireland.

A second apocalyptic horseman followed close upon the heels of the first. Typhus in various forms was not a stranger to Ireland, but in the midst of pervasive hunger it became a raging pestilence. Its easy victims were a people chronically ill-nourished and now literally starving, whose sanitary conditions, primitive to begin with, had deteriorated to the vanishing point, who wore the same filthy, louse-infested rags day after day and huddled together in any warm place, thus infecting one another. In its more virulent form the disease caused profuse bleeding from the nose and other hemorrhaging; scurvy-like, it was often complicated by jaundice, so that the whole body assumed an eerie orange-brown color and was caked in dried blood.

Reports of rampant starvation in Kilkenny were heard as early as April 1846, combined with the horrible vision of hungry children mysteriously gone bald and whiskered, so that they looked like monkeys or aged dwarfs. Even before that the fever struck John Ireland's home county, but it was worse in the west where the incidence of hunger was higher. Hordes crowded into the roads east searching for food and joining other thousands who had been evicted from their pathetic little farms for default of rent. Many of them died in the ditches by the roadside, but others, less severely infected or in remission, completed their trek to the eastern towns and so guaranteed that the epidemic spread to every corner of the island. Terror more often than compassion greeted these slouching, emaciated, yellow-faced legions and their "road fever."[26]

The intensity of suffering during the Great Famine reached a level that beggared the imagination. At the end of 1846 a local magistrate described in a letter to the *Times* of London the scene in one rural area with which he was familiar. Finding the village apparently deserted, he entered a hovel where he saw "six famished and ghastly skeletons, to all appearances dead, . . . huddled in a corner on some filthy straw, their sole covering what seemed a ragged horse cloth and their wretched legs hanging about naked above the knees." On closer inspection they proved to be alive, four children, a woman, "and what once had been a man." Soon two hundred "such phantoms" surrounded him, most of whom were delirious from hunger or fever. "Their demoniac yells are still ringing in my ears, and their horrible images are fixed upon my brain." In a cabin nearby he found two frozen corpses, half devoured by rats. In another there were seven people lying together, one of them dead, the others without sufficient strength to move themselves or the corpse. He saw a woman, crazed by fever, drag out of her cabin the naked body of her dead daughter, aged about twelve, and leave it in the yard, half-covered with stones.[27]

Such scenes by 1848 had become a grisly commonplace. Attempts at relief by private agencies failed for lack of resources, while the British government, hesitant at best and hampered by Malthusian and laissez-faire ideology, provided too little too late. The bitter spectacle of ships loaded with Irish grain sailing out of Irish ports in the hallowed name of free trade, while crowds of starving people watched from dockside, burned itself into the Irish national consciousness.

The choice for the masses quickly narrowed down to that between flight and death. To be sure, the partial blight of 1845 did not materially affect the character of Irish emigration, which for forty years had been a carefully planned venture, undertaken by those of middling means and never embarked upon during the stormy autumn and winter sailing seasons or without sufficient resources to sustain the emigrants through the voyage and immediately after. But the disastrous harvest of 1846 changed all that, and during the last six months of the year the poorest of the poor, the cottiers, who had seen their rows of potatoes go black and rotten almost overnight, fled to the seaports in headlong panic. By January 1847, these dregs of the vicious Irish land system were joined by multitudes of the more stable classes—ten- to twenty-acre men, artisans, small merchants—ruined by the universal blight of 1846, just as sick and hungry as the cottiers, jamming into the ports of embarkation for North America—Sligo, Limerick, New Ross, Queenstown, Liverpool—pleading for passage on any vessel, however small, however filthy. "For the first time thousands risked their lives upon a winter crossing, ready, it was said, to undergo any misery, 'save that of remaining in Ireland.' "[28] There were not enough ships at first to service them, so they waited during damp, cold weeks in shantytowns of tents and lean-tos, through which swept new waves of typhus and related fevers. By the end of the 1847 sailing season 230,000 persons had managed to flee Ireland for the New World, of whom forty thousand died at sea or in quarantine camps shortly after disembarking.

The relatively better harvest of 1847 checked the emigration somewhat. So did news about the horrors of the passage and about the economic difficulties experienced by the survivors on the other side of the Atlantic. But the totally diseased potato crop of 1848 unleashed the flood of hysteria again, so that the numbers who embarked for America in the winter of 1848–49—to say nothing of the uncounted thousands who poured into the slums of Liverpool and London—were as high as, if not higher than, those of two years earlier. Among them were Richard Ireland, his unmarried sister, Nancy, and his nephew, Thomas Howard.

There were four Howard children who, when their parents died during the early stages of the Famine, moved into their mother's brother's stone cottage in Burnchurch.[29] These added responsibilities may have contributed to Richard Ireland's decision to leave his native country. But at a deeper level, that decision, shared by hundreds of thousands of Irishmen similarly circumstanced, testified to how devastating a tragedy the Famine was. They had been disposed at first to hang on in hopes that things would at least be no worse after the blight had gone away than before. But their stoicism was tested to its limits; four ruined harvests in a row broke their will. The Famine was hardly less a psychic calamity than a physical one, bringing in its train not only starvation, pestilence, and death for a million and a half Irish, but engendering also a destruction of the spirit of a whole people. The accumulated injustices and deprivations of centuries reached their climax with a misfortune so complete that storekeepers and twenty-acre men and craftsmen like Richard Ireland had no heart left, and in their despair they were ready to endure the hardships and indignities of refugees. Between 1845 and 1851, the total population of Ireland fell a staggering 20 percent, the rural population 25 percent. More than two million people left Ireland permanently during the decade after 1845, three-quarters of them during the blight years (1846–50).[30]

Richard Ireland, his sister, and his nephew landed in Montreal in late 1848 or early 1849.[31] Thomas Howard remained there with another aunt who had emigrated a year or two earlier. The conditions among the Irish dumped into Quebec province were appalling; thousands died in the Grosse Isle quarantine camps, and other thousands were shipped inland from the St. Lawrence during the coldest months of the Canadian winter. Richard and Nancy, like the huge majority of the refugees, wanted no part of British North America. They departed for the United States as soon as they had passed quarantine and settled in the nearest town of any consequence, Burlington, Vermont, where Ireland found work doing odd jobs and some carpentry. Meanwhile, Judith Ireland remained in Burnchurch with the other nine children awaiting her husband's call to join him. That call came in the late summer of 1849 — probably a month or two after Thomas Carlyle had passed by on the train from Kilkenny City to Thomastown.

The Atlantic voyage of the emigrant ships took about five weeks, and testimony abounds that it was a hideous experience — how hideous for a peasant woman in charge of nine children, one an infant, can hardly be exaggerated. Only seven pounds of food were provided the passengers, and the drinking water often grew putrid within a few days of departure. Unscrupulous masters and brokers routinely sold more space than the ships possessed; one ship, for example, had thirty-six berths to accommodate 260 persons. Most of the vessels used by the fleeing Irish were merchantmen with no passenger berths at all; men, women, and children were indiscriminately packed into the holds like bales of cotton or like the African slaves of a generation earlier, without adequate air or light or sanitary facilities. The Irish emigrant ships were floating cesspools, and dysentery and cholera killed one in five who sailed on them. American customs officers upon boarding one such vessel discovered pigs and people lying together on deck in "filth and feculent matter."[32]

Somehow Judith and all the children survived the voyage to Montreal where Richard and Nancy met them, and where Thomas Howard was reunited with his siblings and his cousins. Then all of them set out for Burlington where John Ireland probably celebrated his eleventh birthday. They spent nearly two years there and learned many of the harsh lessons reserved for the uprooted at all times and places.

At least once during the sojourn in New England Richard Ireland went to Boston and took some of the children with him. He showed them Bunker Hill and Concord Bridge and, in his familiarly emphatic manner, his big right hand stabbing awkwardly at the air, he told them stories of the American Revolution, much as he had told them at Burnchurch of the Irish heroes of old.[33] The distinction could not have been lost upon his elder son whom hardship had already matured beyond his years. The minutemen of '75 had stood their ground and fired at the whites of their enemies' eyes, until they had won their struggle and created a nation. The tales of Irish patriots, by contrast, always ended in defeat — a host of fallen minstrel boys who could prevail neither by the harp nor by the sword. Young John Ireland, who in later life proved to be a romantic but never a sentimentalist, turned away from Erin's isle without regret and without nostalgia. Even then he sensed that America offered him freedom and dignity and a fair chance to try his manhood. America was the future.

~ II ~
L'Étoile du Nord
1838–52

T HE TRIP TO BOSTON and Bunker Hill may have resulted from
Richard Ireland's hopes to find work in a larger market than
Burlington. If so, he was disappointed—perhaps not surprisingly.
The waves of immigrants had already begun to arouse Yankee ap-
prehension, which often manifested itself in the famous addendum
to employment notices: "Irish need not apply."[1] The thirteen
Irelands and Howards, in any case, departed New England for the
west after the winter of 1851.

In so doing they represented a decided minority among their fellows: more than three-quarters of the Irish who settled in the
United States during the Famine years remained in the cities of the
east and northeast, content to duplicate as best they could in bleak
urban neighborhoods the village life they had left behind. The lure
of the west was the lure of cheap land, and the Irish, peasants
though most of them had been, proved to be, among all the immigrant nationalities, the least attracted to farming. John Ireland
would have to contend with this reluctance later on, when he had
become a promoter of western colonization. But the unvarnished
fact was that most of the Irish had brought with them from the old
country only bitter memories of a vicious and exploitative land system. They had no capital and few of the skills necessary to compete
in the highly individualistic and competitive agriculture practiced in
America. Their fund of boldness had been used up by the harrowing
Atlantic crossing, and the availability of menial jobs, at wages un-
dreamt of back home, gave them reason enough to stay where they
were.[2]

Not reason enough, however, for the restless Richard Ireland.

By the autumn of 1851, he had led his large brood as far west as Chicago, then a bustling town of some forty thousand, just beginning the sustained expansion that was to make it, within a few decades, the metropolis of America's heartland.[3] But the Irelands were not destined to play a role in that growth; they stayed in Chicago only a few months, even though the boom in construction must have provided opportunities for a journeyman carpenter like Richard Ireland. The older children went to school, John to the extravagantly titled University of St. Mary of the Lake, which had been opened by the Catholic bishop in 1844.[4] Stories about the brief interlude in Chicago were told much later within the family circle. One of them recalled that John, on his way to school one morning, missed the ferry on which he customarily rode across the river; in midstream the boat unaccountably foundered and sank, and everyone on board was drowned. Thus was John Ireland preserved for the struggles and achievements of the future.[5]

A rather more credible family tradition was that Richard Ireland met "by chance" a fellow Kilkenny man named John O'Gorman on a Chicago street, and the two of them decided to pool their meager resources and go off to the Minnesota frontier.[6] Why they chose to gamble on so raw and remote a place to settle is unclear, but perhaps they had been beguiled by the pages of the *Minnesota Pioneer,* copies of which were routinely dispatched south and east with the intention of attracting new residents. James Madison Goodhue, who had founded the paper in 1849, waxed lyrical about the glories of the Minnesota Territory, about its "fresh, bracing climate," about its "lands as fertile as the banks of the Nile," about the unparalleled possibilities for economic development now that the native Indians were "fading, vanishing, dissolving away."[7] Goodhue's sentiments shortly came to be emblazoned on the Minnesota state seal, which showed a farmer plowing his field and an Indian brave galloping away, all under the inscription, "L'étoile du nord" — the Star of the North.

Whatever the sources of their information, Ireland and O'Gorman were sufficiently convinced to put their families — O'Gorman had a wife and four young sons — on the trail west one more time.[8] In April 1852 they traveled by foot and wagon, all nineteen of them, across northern Illinois to Galena, where they caught the Missis-

sippi steamer *Nominee* on its first run upstream of the season. The
great river, vast and muddy brown in its spring flood, stretched out
before them and all around them. The paddleboat chugged slowly
up through the majestic valley, past Dubuque on the western shore
and Prairie du Chien on the eastern, carried them over the shimmer-
ing bosom of Lake Pepin, and, at the end of the voyage, almost to
the guns of Fort Snelling, which stood sentinel at the strategic junc-
tion of the Mississippi and Minnesota rivers. On May 19, 1852, the
Nominee sailed around the bend at Dayton's Bluff and docked at the
levee at the foot of Jackson Street. The *Minnesota Democrat,* in a small
news item, welcomed two "respectable and intelligent Irish families" to their new home in St. Paul.[9]

What they saw when they stepped off the boat was a frontier village of perhaps fifteen hundred inhabitants,[10] who lived and
worked in a hodgepodge of log and frame buildings hugging the
east bank of the Mississippi; or rather one part of the village, the so-
called Lower Town, separated by steep bluffs covered with elm and
cedar from the Upper Town a mile or so upstream, which clung to

*The corner of Sixth Street and Wabasha Street, St. Paul, in 1857. The third
Cathedral of St. Paul is under construction at center. (MHS)*

a levee of its own and catered to the occasional steamer traffic coming off the Minnesota River. They heard as much French spoken along the muddy streets as they did English, for St. Paul had begun its existence, hardly more than a decade before, as a center of a fur trade still dominated by flamboyant coureurs des bois, whose ancestors had worked for the great Canadian companies, the North West and the Hudson's Bay, and who themselves now did business in beaver pelts and buffalo robes with John Jacob Astor's American Fur Company. Indeed, the high point of the summer season in St. Paul, as it was to continue to be for many years after 1852, was the arrival each July of the creaking caravan of wooden ox carts, loaded with furs and driven by colorfully garbed bois brûlés from the Red River Valley, four hundred miles to the northwest.[11]

The new arrivals found shelter all together for a while, in a shack hastily thrown up not far from the river—one long windowless room with only partitions of bed sheets to separate Irelands and Howards from O'Gormans. During the summer each family secured a lot and built a house for itself. The Ireland home, on Pearl Street (now West Fifth), was a double-level wooden dwelling, simple in the extreme, composed of a ground floor of kitchen, parlor and bedroom, with two more bedrooms upstairs. The O'Gormans lived a block away, while Nancy Ireland, who now took charge of the Howard children, occupied another house nearby.[12]

Small, ugly, and treeless as it was—treeless because of the pressing need for building materials and for fuel to survive the savage winters (what Goodhue had euphemistically called the "fresh, bracing climate")—the Lower Town where John Ireland spent a short portion of his boyhood was not without charm or bright promises for the future. Frontier St. Paul was a natural depot, standing at the head of navigation on the Mississippi, and therefore its economic viability, in an era when inland trade followed the great river systems, was assured. Not far away, at the Falls of St. Anthony— around which a settlement, eventually to be incorporated into the city of Minneapolis, had already formed—lay a secure source of water power and hence a guarantee of permanent industrial capacity. Fort Snelling, a federal military post, was close at hand, though any need to protect white setters from the native Dakota and Ojibway had long since ceased. All around the riches of nature abounded. To the west and southwest rolled the seemingly endless prairie, thick, black earth, millions of fertile acres of it, virtually stolen from the Indians through a series of shameful treaties and available for $1.25 an acre to the squatters who would farm it. To the north were almost limitless timber reserves, and to the northeast, not far beneath the ground, immense deposits of iron ore, the existence of which was unknown in 1852.[13]

As for charm, St. Paul possessed that variety of it proper to a community of pioneers set on the edge of a wilderness. Everything was new, every hope seemed possible of fulfillment, every day promised a different adventure. The harsh living conditions were smoothed over by the egalitarianism of the frontier, which offered opportunity as well as discomfort to everybody. A certain cultural tension was, to be sure, inevitable: the people of St. Paul had all come from somewhere else, all intent on fashioning a better future for themselves, and yet self-consciously committed to being agents of a civilization created in the past.

At the time the Ireland family was settling into its modest new house on Pearl Street, the town had neither a hospital nor a cemetery nor a jail; the citizens tended to agree that the most compelling need was for a jail. Five churches, served by clergymen of five different Christian denominations, had been built by 1852. Four doctors plied their somewhat primitive craft, and fourteen lawyers had hung out their shingles. Richard Ireland undoubtedly noted that St. Paul already boasted of eighteen carpenters. Four contentious newspapers competed for a limited readership — these were among eighty-nine published in Minnesota during its brief territorial history (1849–58). There was a "shaving saloon" on Third Street, and only a few doors away an ice cream parlor. Corn cost fifty cents a bushel and eggs nineteen cents a dozen. A bottle of whisky could be bought for a quarter. An active chapter of the Sons of Temperance could not prevent the proliferation of taverns and a high incidence of drunkenness. The local Irish celebrated St. Patrick's Day with a "supper," at which as many as eighteen toasts might be drunk. Two months after the Irelands' arrival a man, "while in a fit of jealousy and drunkenness, shot his wife through the heart with a pistol." (The culprit was arrested but escaped, due, no doubt, to the lack of a proper jail.) The town had yet to be fully incorporated, but, since St. Paul was the territorial capital, politicians were much in evidence; the most eminent of them, even at that early date, were Alexander Ramsey and Henry H. Sibley, who between them would dominate public life in Minnesota for many years to come. When young John Ireland had his first sight of St. Paul from the deck of the *Nominee,* there was as yet no capitol building for him to see and no city hall.[14]

But there was a cathedral.

A cathedral always houses a *cathedra,* the throne of a bishop, the chair from which the bishop teaches and rules his flock with the authority of the apostles. One of the five clergymen in St. Paul in 1852 was indeed a Roman Catholic bishop, and the church in which he presided was a cathedral, the second cathedral, in fact, of the year-old Diocese of St. Paul. The bishop was Joseph Cretin, a short, balding, corpulent Frenchman of fifty-three, who had for his ecclesiastical jurisdiction the whole of the Minnesota Territory, from Iowa to Canada, from Wisconsin to the Missouri and White Earth rivers in the Dakotas — 166,000 square miles in all. To assist him in his ministry he had a handful of priests and seminarians, all of them (save one eccentric Italian) Frenchmen like himself. The people whom he was charged to serve included, in his own laconic words, "3000 catholiques, 1000 hérétiques, 27,000 infidèles."[15]

The presence of the bespectacled, diffident, and yet tough-minded Joseph Cretin on the Minnesota frontier was testimony to the remarkable revival of French Catholicism, which lasted through much of the nineteenth century and which exerted so powerful an influence on John Ireland's life and career. In the field of Christian education, in the foundation of new religious orders and the reform of old ones, in the development of a lively popular piety and a vigorous religious press and new modes of political and economic thought, the "eldest daughter of the church" displayed a vitality astonishing to the many who had presumed her demise in the wake of the Revolution of 1789. But there was no more striking sign of her renewed strength than the contribution she made to worldwide evangelization. "No matter where the traveller rests his feet," Ireland later observed in his biography of Cretin, "in whatever part of the globe tribes and peoples are awaiting the announcement of the Gospel of Christ, the French missionary greets him." And he added,

Bishop Joseph Cretin (MHS)

grandiloquently, thinking of Cretin and his companions: "Heaven-lit pages in the history of France, which no shortcomings along other lines of action, however grievous now and then these may seem to be, can ever throw into obscurity, are those that tell of its contributions to Catholic missions in foreign lands."[16]

Cretin came from bourgeois stock—his father had been a prosperous baker in Montluel, Department of Ain, a few miles from Lyon. Joseph, born in 1799, was the youngest of three surviving children. His only sister, Clemence, who never married, was his life-long confidante: "Her devotion to her brother . . . in all the circumstances of his career," Ireland noted, "was remarkable in its fervor and its disinterestedness." The family was staunchly Catholic and, as a result, suffered much from the excesses of the Revolution. An uncle of Monsieur Cretin was guillotined during the Terror, and Madame Cretin, "with an infant child in her arms," was imprisoned briefly, because she had "protested aloud against the persecution to which Catholics were subjected." Napoleon Bonaparte, for reasons of his own, stopped the persecution, and Joseph never remembered a time when mass could not be said in the open; but the altar the Cretins had kept hidden during the penal days remained in their home, an honored symbol of what the family had suffered for the old faith and of the value they placed upon it.

Such fierce loyalty had its effect upon Joseph Cretin's religiosity. By the time he began his formal schooling, at thirteen, under the tutelage of the local priest, he was already keeping a spiritual diary and writing down carefully "what defects of character he was to correct and what virtues he was to cultivate." He passed naturally from the little school in the presbytery to the petit séminaire in Meximieux a few miles away. He stayed there three years, till 1817, and then moved on to more advanced studies at similar institutions in Argentière and Alix. So far he followed a classical course which, though under clerical auspices, involved no commitment for the future. His father grew impatient. "You know very well," Monsieur Cretin told his son, "that I never urged or forced any vocation upon you. I have left you entirely free; you are free yet. But [now] . . . it is time to declare . . . whether you have consecrated yourself to the ecclesiastical state or chosen another profession. Your mother and I are most anxious to know this." However much this question was discussed within the Cretin household, the definitive answer to it came in a letter to Montluel from Paris in October 1820: "At last I have put on the cassock, never to put it off."

To have been sent for his theological studies to Saint Sulpice, the premier grand séminaire in France and, for that matter, in the Catholic world, was itself a tribute to young Cretin's industry and piety. He was no deep thinker, then or ever, but in fact the training offered by the seminary had as much, if not more, to do with steeling the will as with cultivating the intellect. The strict regimen, with its careful and elaborate schedules, its exclusiveness, its often petty preoccupation with detail, suited him perfectly. "I am entirely at home," Cretin wrote to his family. "It seems to me that all I see, all I hear of the clerical spirit, of the ecclesiastical life, is of my very nature." He applied himself with dogged perseverance to the task at hand, methodical and regular in his habits, abstemious in his tastes. He set down in a little notebook — which lay, well-thumbed, at his bedside when he died thirty-five years later in far-off Minnesota — a list of personal rules: "To remember that God is my beginning and my last end. . . . To ask often of myself, when I pass from one exercise to another, what ought I do? What am I doing? Why and to what intention? . . . To perform the present act as if it were the last of my life. To act as if there were on earth only God and myself. . . . To examine myself carefully after each act, . . . and should I be obliged to acknowledge guilt, to humble myself before God, crave pardon from Him, and impose upon myself some penitential act of self-denial. To beg from God that he make me more humble, more void of myself[,] that he extirpate within me all love of myself."[17]

Sentiments like these, it must be remembered, were typical among diocesan clergy trained under Sulpician direction or inspiration—and virtually all the clergy were so trained during the nineteenth century, since the Sulpician model was adopted nearly everywhere. Foreign or even distasteful as they may sound to modern ears—too introspective, it might be argued, too individualistic and self-indulgent, with more than a hint of Jansenism about them—these techniques of spiritual formation, nurtured within the serene precincts of the seminary and idealized into norms of conduct for a lifetime, go a long way toward explaining how quite ordinary men found the inner strength to endure the hardship, physical and emotional, which was the common experience on the missions. The missionaries were products, to be sure, of a romantic generation, as eager to prove themselves in the religious arena as their contemporaries were in the political or scientific or artistic; for some the barricades, for others cathedrals in the wilderness. But perhaps loneliness is more bearable for him who acts as if there were on earth only God and himself; pain and discomfort may be more readily taken in stride by him who has worn a hair shirt, as Joseph Cretin did at Saint Sulpice. Whatever else their education did, it prepared the French missionaries for a life of action in which they could display their own version of that prized quality called élan.

Cretin, however, was thirty-eight years old and fifteen years a priest before his turn on the missions came. Meanwhile he served with distinction in the parochial ministry of his native Diocese of Belley. Upon his ordination at the end of 1823, his bishop assigned Cretin to Ferney, a town tucked away in the northeast corner of the diocese, virtually a northern suburb of Geneva. Young Abbé Cretin first acted as curate and then, after a few years, became curé himself. His work at Ferney covered the whole range of pastoral activities. He built a new church, and paid for it, largely by soliciting funds outside his more or less moribund parish; he did not scruple, then or later, to beg support for his enterprises. He established a convent of cloistered Carmelites in the town, and also invited in an active order of nuns to operate a girls' school. He opened a presbyteral school of the kind he had himself attended in Montluel. This latter he expanded into a boarding school for boys—the "Pensionnat" of Ferney—which he supervised and in which he taught. He exhibited great love and considerable talent for music; he played the flute passably well, and often spent his recreation in songfests with the pupils of the pensionnat. Under his direction the parish soon came to be known for the gusto of its congregational singing, in both Latin and French.

Cretin was always punctilious in observing, down to their smallest rubrical details, the ceremonials of the church. He visibly enjoyed the pomp of the liturgy, which he considered an important source of edification, especially in a town like Ferney, full of Protestants and lapsed Catholics. His concern for the material needs of the poor became legendary, as did his reputation for personal austerity. He appeared shy to his parishioners, and somewhat rigid, but still urbane in his manner (he had come to Ferney, after all, from Paris) and elegant in his speech. During the Revolution of July 1830, he also impressed them with his courage. When an anti-clerical mob, which had already put the Carmelite nuns to flight (they never returned), approached the pensionnat, Abbé Cretin, with only a few boys at his back, confronted the rioters, "and in strong words bade them not dare come further." They did not.[18]

At least once during his tenure in Ferney Cretin had requested permission from his bishop to go to the missions in China. The bishop had refused, pointing out gently that the curé could find plenty of pagans to convert in the Department of Ain. But in 1838 the bishop changed his mind and, rather grudgingly, granted Cretin a temporary leave of absence from the Diocese of Belley. The leave became in due course permanent, and the crucial factor in securing it seems to have been the intervention of Mathias Loras.

Loras was another representative of that striking renaissance of religious fervor — with all its pietistic and romantic overtones — that gripped French Catholicism after the Revolution. He belonged to an old and prominent family, active in the business life of Lyon for three centuries. During the bloody days of the Convention, the Lorases, like the Cretins in nearby Montluel, paid dearly for their loyalty to the faith; Mathias's father was executed in 1793. The younger Loras determined to be a priest, and in the early years of his training he was a schoolfellow of Jean Marie Vianney, later the celebrated curé of Ars. From 1814 to 1823 Loras was teacher and then superior in the petit séminaire at Meximieux, where Joseph Cretin was his pupil. In 1829 he went to the missions in the United States.[19] "He was a gentleman of the old French school," John Ireland said of Loras much later. "He was most polite in manner, without giving room to the smallest suspicion of affectation, . . . scrupulously exact in his attire, which often betrayed poverty but never meanness or untidiness, always dignified in bearing, even when stooping to apparently menial tasks that circumstances of the time commended to his spirit of zeal and humility."[20] Loras had to stoop to menial tasks often during his labors in the backwoods of Alabama, but his enthusiasm and dedication never wavered. Late in 1837 he was consecrated bishop of the newly created Diocese of Dubuque, "comprising all the western part of the territory commonly called Wisconsin, that is, the area lying between the western bank of the Mississippi River and eastern bank of the Missouri."[21]

Even before he traveled up the Mississippi to visit his new see, Bishop Loras sailed to France in search of money and priestly recruits. He centered his activities, naturally enough, in Lyon, his old home. During the spring of 1838 he visited Ferney and invited Joseph Cretin to join him in America. This time the bishop of Belley raised no objections, and Cretin began to prepare for his departure.

He did so with almost pathological secrecy. About August 1 he warned his sister Clemence to prepare her "heart for a severe trial." Two weeks later the feast of the Assumption of the Virgin was celebrated at Ferney, as usual, with music and fireworks that lasted late into the evening. Very early the next morning, August 16, the now former curé of Ferney, without a word to anyone, crept out of the presbytery and fled to Geneva, where he boarded the stage for Paris. Not even a message, received a day or two earlier, that his aged father was gravely ill in Montluel and would probably die, could deter him. In Paris he joined Loras and the four senior seminarians whom the latter had succeeded in recruiting, and on the evening of August 18 the whole party set out for Le Havre and the ship that would carry them across the Atlantic. From Le Havre Cretin sent Clemence a letter which demonstrated that even high nobility of purpose is not always without its self-serving side.

> My dearest sister, I beseech you in the name of the faith in your heart, do not blame me for what I have done; do not sorrow too much over my departure. Console my father, or rather refrain from telling him of my absence. . . . For a long time I have been preparing myself for this great sacrifice, foreseeing and weighing all circumstances, and striving to overcome all the obstacles nature was putting in my way. . . . I am quite tranquil, because my conscience is my witness that I have followed upon the ways of God. . . . Yes, I am to be a missionary in a country where there is a large number of savages to be converted. I do not go there to search for gold, or to make scientific discoveries, or military expeditions. Were these my purposes, men would applaud my departure from my native land. . . . Rejoice that your brother is perfectly resigned to the sacrifices, however heavy, that God may require of him. . . . At the break of day I escaped [from Ferney] as a fugitive. I had not the strength to make resistance to manifestations of sorrow and sadness; the sorrow and sadness should have weighed even more heavily upon myself. That is why I did not make known my intentions to you or go to see you. Your letters, your tears, would have been desolation of soul.[22]

At least he had the good grace not to quote the ninth chapter of the Gospel of St. Luke.[23]

Inclement weather delayed departure for several weeks. Finally the seven of them — Bishop Loras, Cretin, another, much younger priest, and four subdeacons — boarded the American brig *Lion,* which set sail on September 17, 1838. (As the *Lion* cleared the harbor, Judith Naughton Ireland, at Burnchurch, County Kilkenny, watched over her first-born son, now six days old.)

Joseph Cretin served in the immense Diocese of Dubuque for twelve years, until, in 1851, the northwest portion of it was de-

tached and given to him as a diocese of his own. In the course of
those years he ran through the whole gamut of the missionary's enterprise, "an uninterrupted racing," John Ireland admiringly called
it, "summer and winter, to points hundreds of miles apart, that
sacraments be administered, that the word of God be heard by
Catholics and non-Catholics. It was the mass and the sermon in the
shelter of the grove, beneath humble cabin roof, in school house or
village hall; it was the dogmatic conference that Catholics be
strengthened in their faith, that non-Catholics, if not brought
within the fold, lose their prejudices and learn to esteem their Catholic fellow-citizens; now one thing, now another—always incessant, tireless [sic] work."[24] It was well for Cretin that at heart he always remained a prosaic sort of man, for there was little glamor in
the existence he had chosen for himself. Loras named him vicar
general, a heady title indeed, but in a sense every missionary priest
was a vicar general, so often was he alone and separated from his
bishop by enormous distances. Though most of the time he kept a
residence in Prairie du Chien, Cretin had to be often in Dubuque,
Potosi, Galena, Fort Snelling, and Mendota (which he called "St.
Peter's," the name used before 1852), up and down the river, in the
camps of the Winnebagoes, whose extremely difficult language he
finally mastered, better, perhaps, than he did English. He was, like
all frontier clergymen of all denominations, essentially a circuit
rider: sixty or seventy miles a day astride his little black pony, and
in the evening—after hearing a confession or two, witnessing a
marriage, baptizing a mixed-blood baby—a bed of skins spread out
on the dirt floor of a fur trader's shack.

Each season presented its own perils. In the summer he walked
in perpetual fear of rattlesnakes, "particularly near the rivers," he
explained to Clemence in 1845, "where at every step one hears the
rattling of the tail of this frightful reptile"; and, even worse, the
mosquitoes, "myriads" of them, maddening the horses and blacken-
ing the sky: "I am devoured by them, . . . without having a moment's rest, day or night. . . . I wear silk gloves, I put on my
boots, I cover my face with gauze to avoid the sting of this troublesome insect, but during mass it settles on my crown, which is then
defenseless, and my head swells immediately half an inch at least for
half a day." And nothing could have prepared one born and raised

in the valley of the Rhone for the long midwestern winters of numbing cold, impassable heaps of snow, and, with the Mississippi frozen solid for five months, even more pronounced isolation and loneliness. Travel attempted during the winter, though it may have provided some companionship, was particularly hazardous. On one occasion a priest riding cross-country with Cretin fell and broke his arm when his horse shied on the slippery ground; with no medical help available for scores of miles in every direction, Cretin had to set the bone, and it took him five attempts before he succeeded, while the injured man lay in a snowbank, shrieking with pain.[25]

But it never crossed Joseph Cretin's mind that the deprivations he suffered were in vain. He and his colleagues watched the slow growth of the Catholic community with justifiable satisfaction. Conversions, to be sure, were disappointingly few, and Protestant hostility toward the Catholic missionaries was never far beneath the surface. For his part Cretin considered Protestants simply "hérétiques"; he liked them no better than he had in Ferney, and he habitually treated them with stiff reserve. But immigration, especially into what came to be the states of Iowa (1846) and Wisconsin (1848), included significant numbers of Catholics, and this necessarily altered the status of the missionaries.

It was a fateful shift in emphasis. If the missionaries had originally come from France to convert and "civilize" the Indians — "these poor savages," as Cretin invariably called them — demographic reality imposed upon them a different set of priorities. It was part of Cretin's creed that the ever-increasing, white Catholic immigrants needed and were entitled to the ministrations of the missionary priests, whose time and energy were not unlimited. And such ministrations appeared to mean duplicating European parochial and institutional structures. So property was purchased, and permanent churches were built, and rude little schools were opened — presbyteral schools, to begin with, of the kind Loras and Cretin had attended in France. Nuns and monks were exhorted to found modest establishments within the diocese. Cretin brought a printing press to Prairie du Chien — he was always fascinated by machinery of any kind — and cranked out on it pious treatises, tracts, prayer-cards, even dim pictures of Jesus and the saints. He employed music in his ministry with the same zest as he had in Fer-

ney. "I play the organ," he told Clemence, "which I can push from
my room to the choir loft which is on a level with my room. I have
mounted it on wheels." He arranged a harmonized version of the
litany of the Blessed Virgin similar to the one he remembered hearing when he was a boy; "We often sing it here," he said wistfully.

As early as 1841 Loras was in contact with colonization bureaus
in New York, and throughout their careers both he and Cretin
campaigned vigorously in the eastern press to induce Catholics to
settle in the Midwest. In this they were precursors to John Ireland,
and in another vitally important activity as well. Drunkenness, they
quickly discovered, was the universal bane of the frontier and, of
more direct relevance to them, the single greatest obstacle to the development of the stable Catholic family and parochial life they presumed to be the ideal. They consequently became strong temperance crusaders, apostles of total abstinence from alcohol—Loras
even to the point of declining to drink the choice wines served at
his brother's table in Lyon.[26]

Strictly speaking Bishop Loras's jurisdiction was limited to the
lands west of the Mississippi River, but in fact he and his little band
of missionaries ministered regularly to places like Galena and Prairie du Chien, which were subject by church law to the bishops of
St. Louis and Detroit respectively.[27] Canonical niceties did not signify much on the frontier; the priests went where there were people
who wanted their services, and it appeared sensible to all concerned
that the settlements on the upper reaches of the river should depend
upon Dubuque for clerical personnel.

In April 1840 Loras sent Father Lucien Galtier up the Mississippi to establish a permanent mission at Mendota, the site of a trad-
ing post of the American Fur Company. Mendota was just across
the Minnesota River from Fort Snelling, but, like the fort, on the
west bank of the Mississippi and therefore technically part of the
Diocese of Dubuque. Galtier, one of the subdeacons Loras had
recruited in France in 1838, had been ordained a priest only a few
months before his arrival in Mendota. He was a handsome, dark-
eyed man of twenty-nine, who proved to be more sensitive than
most missionaries and more prone to depression as well. Some
years later he recalled his first sight of his new field of labor.

The boat landed at the foot of Fort Snelling, then garrisoned by a few companies of Regular soldiers under the command of Major PLYMPTON. The sight of the Fort, commanding from the elevated promontory the two rivers, the Mississippi and the St. Peter [the Minnesota], pleased me; but the discovery, which I soon made, that there were only a few houses on the St. Peter [Mendota] side, and but two on the side of the Fort, surrounded by a complete wilderness, and without any signs of fields under tillage, gave me to understand that my mission and life must henceforth be a career of privation, hard trials and suffering, and required of me patience, labor and resignation.[28]

These gloomy expectations were amply fulfilled. Through his first year Galtier endured loneliness, primitive accommodation, severe illness ("bilious fever and ague"), and — perhaps most enervating of all — boredom. There were five Catholic families in Mendota and six at the fort, with the broad Minnesota River separating the two groups; these and a handful of soldiers were the young priest's only charges, and their number diminished rather than increased during his tenure.

On the other (east) side of the Mississippi, however, and downstream a few miles, lay a nameless little settlement composed mostly of squatters expelled some years before from the federal lands that formed part of the Fort Snelling military reservation. Here there lived about twenty families of which thirteen were Catholic, and to this more or less cohesive community, in which French was the dominant language, Galtier — though the area was outside his canonical responsibility — gradually turned the bulk of his attention.

In the autumn of 1841 it was determined that a church should be built on the east bank. Several sites were available, and, "after mature reflection," Galtier decided on

the nearest spot to the head of navigation, outside the [military] reservation line. . . . In the month of October, 1841, I had, on the above stated place, logs cut and prepared, and soon a poor log church, that would remind one of the stable of Bethlehem, was built. The nucleus of St. Paul was formed. On Nov. 1st, 1841, I blessed the new *Basilica,* smaller indeed than the Basilica of St. Paul, in Rome, but as well adapted as the latter for prayer and love to arise therein from pious hearts. The church was thus dedicated

The chapel of St. Paul, about 1855 (Photo by Joel Whitney; MHS)

to St. Paul, and I expressed a wish that the settlement should be known by no other name. I succeeded. I had, previously to this time, fixed my residence at St. Peter [Mendota], and as the name PAUL is generally connected to that of PETER, and the gentiles being well represented in the new place in the persons of the Indians, I called it St. Paul.[29]

The little chapel took less than a week to construct. All materials and labor were contributed. It stood twenty-four feet long by eighteen feet wide by ten feet high, with the ridge of the roof extending five feet higher. The walls were built of oak logs, the rafters of tamarack, and the roof and floor of pine slabs. There were two windows three feet square and a door seven feet tall. A crude wooden cross was wedged into the roof just above the door. One who, as a young man, had participated in the building project, estimated long afterward that, given labor costs in 1841, the chapel must have been valued at about sixty-five dollars.[30]

In 1847 an addition approximately doubled the chapel's floor space. By that time, however, Galtier had gone away, not without bitterness, and Augustin Ravoux, another of the group of subdeacons who had accompanied Bishop Loras from France in 1838, had taken his place. Galtier had fallen victim to the privations of his frontier apostolate, about which he complained ceaselessly. He grew increasingly quarrelsome, and his relations with Loras became so strained that he went back to France, intending, it seems, to remain there. But the lure of the missions coursed through Galtier's blood and could not be denied. He returned to America in 1847, though not to the jurisdiction of the bishop of Dubuque; he was adopted instead into the new Diocese of Milwaukee where he served honorably until his death in 1866.[31]

Father Ravoux proved a rather more hardy specimen. Before he took up residence in Mendota in 1844 Loras had assigned him as missioner to the Dakota, whose language he learned and for whom he prepared a catechism and prayer book (printed on Joseph Cretin's press in Prairie du Chien). It was a harsh existence, traveling from encampment to encampment, with few visible consolations. But Ravoux did not give in to discouragement at the small number of converts he made, nor did he ever lose interest in the Indians, even after other duties had come to preoccupy him. (A grisly testimonial to the high regard in which they held the French "black-robe" was to be given in 1862 when thirty-one of the thirty-eight Dakota condemned to death for their part in the bloody conflict of that year asked for baptism at Ravoux's hands.[33])

Ravoux was a shrewd, somewhat cantankerous man whose strong convictions made him more than a match for his rough environment. He spoke his mind with utter frankness, sparing neither the moral sluggards in his own flock nor local Protestant worthies "who vomited now and then their pestiferous poison,"[34] nor even, when the mood was on him, the lapses of his own ecclesiastical superiors. He was especially vexed at the bishops of Dubuque and Milwaukee who failed, in Ravoux's mind, to appreciate the need to send more missionaries to serve the growing Catholic population under his charge. "Bishop Henni [of Milwaukee, now responsible for St. Paul, on the east bank of the Mississippi]," he complained to Loras, "is not sending anyone to St. Paul. I am very far from judging

him guilty before God, yet if your Grace would like to inform him
that his children in Jesus Christ at St. Paul and the neighborhood,
to the number of eleven or twelve hundred, have been begging for
several years that he deign to help them immediately, you would be
performing a great act of charity."[35]

A solution to this particular concern was at hand. Minnesota
Territory was created March 3, 1849. A few months later the Catholic bishops of the United States, assembled in council in Baltimore,
petitioned Pope Pius IX to set up "a new episcopal See in the town
of St. Paul, in the Territory of Minnesota, to be co-terminous with
that Territory in its jurisdiction."[36] The moment, however, was not
propitious for a swift implementation of such a request. In the wake
of the Revolution of 1848 the pope had fled into the Kingdom of
Naples, and during the sixteen months of his exile the Roman curia
operated with considerably less than its wonted efficiency. Pius IX
did not return to Rome until April 1850.[37] On the following July
19 a papal brief formally established the Diocese of St. Paul, and
four days after that Joseph Cretin was named its first bishop.

Ravoux's joy at this news was tempered by a letter from Cretin
in which the latter expressed hesitancy about accepting the appointment. In his reply Ravoux, with characteristic candor, argued that
such diffidence was misplaced, "that things were in such a condition
in this new territory that, according to my opinion, [Cretin] was
obliged, *sub grave*,[38] to give his consent to bear the load imposed
upon him by Divine Providence." Cretin, still undecided, sailed for
France where his old superior, the bishop of Belley, having persuaded him to lay aside his ill-defined scruples, consecrated him a
bishop, January 26, 1851.[39]

Once he had put his hand to the plow Joseph Cretin never
looked back. He arrived at his see city aboard the steamer *Nominee*
on a bright July day in 1851, accompanied by the six clerics he had
recruited for his diocese and with a purse containing the modest
amount of money he had managed to collect before his departure
from France.[40] "To describe the pleasure I felt at their arrival,"
Ravoux recalled, "would be a difficult task. I had been for seven
years without any brother priest." He escorted the bishop from the
boat and conducted him on a tour of his new domain—a short tour
indeed, which culminated at Galtier's weather-beaten little chapel,

now a cathedral, squatting forlornly upon a bluff above the great river.[41]

When, ten months later, the same *Nominee* docked again at the Lower Levee, fourteen-year-old John Ireland stepped ashore and into the moral world created by the French missionaries. They were to be his heroes, his models: Loras, Cretin, Ravoux, even the flawed Galtier. Two of them he would come to know personally, and all of them would be the subjects of his continuous study and reflection. Toward the end of his life he began a full-scale biography of Cretin. Ravoux was at first his mentor, then his colleague, and finally, as the erstwhile apostle of the Dakota sank into senility, his charge. Loras he considered a "saint," and the memory of Galtier a "benediction." They possessed qualities that appealed strongly to Ireland's frank, romantic temperament. Their faith had a manly simplicity and directness about it, a certainty into which no doubts intruded and which endowed their smallest actions with nobility and purpose. They consistently displayed immense physical courage, indifference to danger and discomfort. They had forsaken stable homes and promising careers and had traveled across half the world to minister to "savages" and rogues. They were celibate indeed, but no one, John Ireland least of all, would question the masculinity of men who braved every hardship, endured every privation, risked death at every turn of the wilderness trail. And in the midst of their labors, despite their shabby surroundings and chronic shortage of means, they never ceased to be gentlemen, conscious as they always were of their station and their ancient breeding: Loras, poor as a churchmouse but always fastidious about his dress; Cretin, the artist performing on flute and organ; Ravoux, author and orator in three languages. What impressed itself most sharply upon Ireland's mind—and, perhaps more important, upon his imagination—was that these men treated a religious calling as a noble cause, as an opportunity for greatness. They did so without affectation or pretense; but still there clung to them the aura of knights-errant, of banners snapping in the breeze, and of armor glittering in the sun.

Not that Ireland was blind to their shortcomings. Loras he knew to have been a notoriously inept administrator. Cretin remained in many ways a pedantic little man who fretted constantly over his bulging waistline.[42] Ravoux, with the passage of years, grew ever more eccentric and acerbic, ever more resentful that his past accomplishments were not duly appreciated.[43] "But," as Ireland observed at Ravoux's funeral in 1906, "what were these but the merest accidents." In all that really mattered the French missionaries had strode across an unknown land like giants.

III

"Ireland, Jean, des États Unis"
1852–61

BISHOP CRETIN'S new diocese could not boast of much material means in 1851. But thanks to the canny Augustin Ravoux it had already attained a significant endowment for future expansion. During the period of uncertainty, when Cretin had gone to France still unsure whether he would accept the appointment to St. Paul, Ravoux had seized an opportunity to buy twenty-one lots in what was to be the commercial heart of the city for eight hundred dollars, and a twenty-second for one hundred dollars more. "I considered the purchase of the twenty-two lots a very good bargain for the church," he observed with satisfaction in 1890, and "the event proved I was not deceived in my expectation."[1] Ravoux of course had no cash to complete the transaction, but as soon as Cretin arrived in July 1851, the bishop promptly paid the nine hundred dollars with money he had brought with him from abroad and took possession of the deeds.

Among the parcels of real estate thus made available to the diocese was one on Sixth Street and Wabasha, and Cretin immediately determined to construct there a multi-purpose building to serve as a cathedral, a clergy residence, a seminary, and a boys' school. The facility was ready for use by November 1851, at a total cost of about five thousand dollars. Galtier's log chapel, dismissed by an unsentimental Cretin as little better than a shack, was converted into a temporary convent-school for girls, staffed by four Sisters of St. Joseph whom Cretin had persuaded to come to Minnesota from their mother-house in Carondolet, Missouri.[2] So began, modestly enough, the association between the bishops of St. Paul and this group of religious women, a relationship that was to be, without

The second Cathedral of St. Paul, about 1880, when it was used as the bishop's residence. The door at lower left marks the meeting room for the Crusaders, a temperance society founded by John Ireland. (MHS)

question, the most important the diocese ever entered into.

Cretin pleaded, usually in vain, with superiors of other religious orders to send priests, nuns, and brothers to work in his diocese, but—except for the Benedictine monks who established a priory near St. Cloud in 1856[3]—his invitations went unheeded; superiors were understandably hesitant to risk their limited personnel in ventures on the unsettled frontier. During the harsh winter of 1851 the Josephite sisters—two of them Frenchwomen and a third a creole born in Louisiana—may have appreciated that reluctance: they lived and labored under the most primitive conditions imaginable. But in the spring Cretin built them a small, snug, brick house, and here, in September 1852, St. Joseph's Academy opened its doors to eighty-seven pupils, among them ten-year-old Ellen Ireland.[4] Galtier's chapel provided one more service to the people of St. Paul — in 1854 the sisters used it as a dispensary to nurse victims of a cholera epidemic — before it was torn down.[5]

The new brick and limestone cathedral on Sixth Street seemed a grand edifice in contrast to the old. Bishop Cretin lived on the second story, along with the handful of seminarians, mostly French, whom he had managed to recruit. A small room was also reserved there for the visits of Father Ravoux, now vicar general and pastor at Mendota. On the ground floor was the church proper. In the basement, besides a kitchen, dining room, and parochial library, Cretin built several classrooms, because, predictably, he intended to set up a school for boys as soon as practicable.[6] Here John Ireland matriculated in the autumn of 1852.

The education he, John O'Gorman's eldest son Thomas, and perhaps forty or fifty other boys received was rudimentary at best. Their first teachers were two of Cretin's young French priests whom most of them had great difficulty understanding. Another schoolmaster, a seminarian from New York, found the job more than distasteful. "What am I doing, do you think?" he wrote to a friend. "I am teaching the Catholic school — my mission is among the dirty little ragged Canadian and Irish boys. Every day . . . I practice patience with these wild little fellows — try to teach them who God is, and then to instruct them in the mysteries of A, B, C. . . . To take the charge of these impudent and insulting children of ungrateful parents was the greatest mortification I ever underwent."[7]

Joseph Cretin, however, apparently discerned positive qualities in at least two of the "dirty little Irish boys." Early in April 1853 the bishop singled out, almost literally from the schoolyard, John Ireland, fourteen years old, and Thomas O'Gorman, barely eleven, and proposed to send them to France and enroll them in a seminary where they could prepare themselves for the priesthood. As O'Gorman reconstructed the scene a half-century later, Cretin led the two boys into the church, placed their hands on the altar, and said: "I put you under the protection of God and His Blessed Mother; you are the beginning of my diocesan seminary, the first seminarians of St. Paul."[8] In this somewhat melodramatic fashion Cretin expressed his resolve to fulfill the first obligation of a Catholic missioner, the provision of a native clergy. Externs brought in from France and elsewhere could sustain the local church only so long.

No record survives as to the bishop's negotiations with the Ireland and O'Gorman families, but it can be assumed that the prospect of a continental education for their sons, at no cost to themselves, was not displeasing to them. Nor would they, as pious Catholics, have been anything but flattered at the venerable bishop's suggestion that their boys might be worthy to be priests. Aside from purely religious considerations — and these are impossible to measure with the evidence at hand — the Irelands and O'Gormans recognized the priests they had known as persons of standing and distinction, well-educated and relatively cultivated men who enjoyed an automatic esteem within their community. This had been the social reality in the old country, and it was just as clearly manifested, if not more so, among the rootless immigrants along the American frontier. The lads would have to be told that they were free at any time to terminate the arrangement; Joseph Cretin, who remembered his own parents' delicacy in this regard, would have seen to that.[9] But there is no reason to suppose that Richard and Judith Ireland would have tried to dissuade their clever son from trying a vocation they believed would assure him prestige and security in this world and a rich reward in the world to come. The bishop's proposal was therefore accepted, and on September 20, 1853, John Ireland and Thomas O'Gorman boarded a river steamer bound for Galena and the distant horizons beyond. They never saw their patron again.

Joseph Cretin spent the balance of his days striving to organize his frontier diocese along traditionally hierarchical lines. He was, for all practical purposes, the parish priest for the whole city of St. Paul until 1855, when a congregation for German-speaking Catholics was separated from the cathedral. But he was responsible also for the new parishes and stations springing up across Minnesota Territory, the need for them increasing as the immigration increased. Never a pushy or belligerent man, Cretin nevertheless made clear his own authoritative position: "When you preach," he told one of his motley band of clergy, "always bear in mind that you represent the Bishop, and speak as you think he would speak." His style of life and ordinary routine remained starkly simple. "He made his bed, swept and dusted his room and, when necessary, took up the loose strips of carpet, shook them out of the window and put them down again. . . . He generally split his own wood and carried it to his room himself."[10] He said mass every weekday morning, winter and summer, at five o'clock, and at seven on Sundays. Of the four confessionals in the church the one closest to the Blessed Virgin's altar was the bishop's, and he occupied it for many a wearing hour. He was a familiar sight carrying the Eucharist to the sick along St. Paul's muddy streets. His flock grew at the same unruly pace as the Territory and the town, so much so that he decided to build still another cathedral — the third in a diocese only five years old — larger and more grandiose, for which he laid the cornerstone on July 27, 1856.[11] He did not live to see it completed.

Bishop Cretin traveled round his diocese often, performing mostly simple, priestly tasks; but the black pony was gone now, and the distances he was able to cover were less than when, at the prime of life, he had first arrived in America. One sign that an episcopal visitation had occurred in a particular parish was the heightened enthusiasm there for hymn-singing in which Cretin continued to take such delight. "Long after his death, some old Irish settler might be heard humming in pretty good French, 'En Ce Jour, O bonne Madonne.' "[12] He carried all the burdens of a pioneer bishop, especially the chronic shortages of priests and money. He maintained his crusade against strong drink and the saloon trade, and one of his proudest boasts was the formation in Minnesota of a Catholic Total Abstinence Society.[13] His concern for the Indians in his diocese did not diminish, but he could do little to convert them, due in part to his own inability to furnish qualified personnel and in part to growing religious hostility; he engaged in seemingly endless quarrels with government Indian agents and Protestant missionaries. Cretin's years in St. Paul coincided with the meteoric rise and fall of the nativist Know-Nothing party and its platform of ethnic and religious bigotry. The bishop never gave an ideological inch to the "hérétiques," though his personal relationships with non-Catholics became more amiable than they had been before.[14]

Cretin dedicated himself, in sum, to a principle he never articulated because it was, to him, so obvious. Humanly speaking the Catholic church has flourished or, in hard times, has survived only in those places where it has succeeded in creating or maintaining the ordinary structures of parish and benevolent institution.[15] The bishop, however poor he may have been, however distracted, however, on occasion, morally or intellectually flawed, has acted as the nucleus around which the local Catholic community has coalesced. Joseph Cretin took it for granted that the genius of Catholicism has always expressed itself in a visible organization, a complex of physical sites in which to worship and learn and minister, a discernible system of authority, a predictable cycle of feast and fast. To put together such an institutional framework was equivalent, in Cretin's mind, to planting the Catholic seed in the good ground of the American Upper Midwest.[16]

By Christmas 1856 Bishop Cretin knew he was dying. Always sensitive about his girth, he had to bear the added cross that the dropsy he suffered now puffed up his body even more. He said mass for the last time on January 26, 1857, the sixth anniversary of his episcopal consecration. After that he scarcely left his bed, though he slept hardly at all. Just before he died, on the morning of Sunday, February 22, he said to those gathered in his mean little room: "In my life I have asked neither for health nor sickness, for riches nor poverty, for success nor failure; but only that the will of God be done. In the long nights when I cannot sleep I always pray for you."[17]

CRETIN had asked Augustin Ravoux to escort his two young seminarians to France. Their journey took about a month, and the tedium of it, as Ireland liked to recall in his old age, was lightened by various boyish pranks and mishaps which much discomfited the strait-laced chaperon. In Paris, for example, Ravoux confiscated a bottle of wine given the boys by their boardinghouse landlady and put it into his own valise, where it broke, saturating his personal effects.[18] It was with some relief that in mid–October 1853 the vicar general delivered his charges to the rector of the petit séminaire of Meximieux, Department of Ain, and turned to the other, more congenial duties the bishop had assigned him while in France, the pre-

Petit Séminaire de Meximieux, Department of Ain, France (from Marx, "O'Gorman")

dictable ones of soliciting funds and seeking priestly recruits for the Diocese of St. Paul.

Meximieux, a town of two or three thousand, lay along the great post road linking Lyon and Geneva, only a short distance north and east of Joseph Cretin's birthplace at Montluel. On the eastern outskirts of Meximieux, set into the flank of a gently rising hill, stood the seminary complex — one large U-shaped building, four and five stories tall, or rather a group of interconnected buildings whose markedly diverse architectural styles indicated haphazard additions over the years, and, nearby, several smaller, special-purpose structures, along with a series of little plazas, galleries, and terraces, thick clusters of trees, and gardens sweeping down toward the highway.[19] Here, on a bright October afternoon, John Ireland and Thomas O'Gorman walked shyly into the refectory where their new schoolmates, curious to see what backwoods Americans looked like, had gathered to meet them.[20]

Meximieux, Cretin's own alma mater (1814–17), was one of two "minor" or "preparatory" seminaries[21] maintained by the bishop of Belley. That a diocese of middling size should have had the resources to support two such institutions was testimony to the dramatic reversal of fortunes experienced by the Catholic church in France during the first half of the nineteenth century. Indeed, the very existence of the diocese was indicative of the profound change, because, though of ancient foundation, Belley had been suppressed at the time of the Revolution and restored only in 1822.[22] Its energetic bishop, Alexandre-Raymond Devie—the same man who had ordained Cretin, had given him license to go to America, and finally had consecrated him bishop—offered his brother of St. Paul, as a contribution to the missions, free seminary education for those young men whom Cretin judged suitable.[23]

The institution to which Ireland and O'Gorman came was a far cry from the petit séminaire as it had existed in penal times, when classes met secretly in barns outside Meximieux. The apparent rebound from those bad old days continued and accelerated during the Second Empire (1852–70), the first eight years of which coincided with John Ireland's residence in France. Statistical growth was prodigious. The number of French secular priests, for example, rose to nearly sixty thousand, the number of female religious quadrupled, the number of male religious multiplied by a factor of ten.[24] Schools, missions, church-sponsored institutions of all kinds flourished as never before. The enigmatic emperor, Napoleon III, himself an unbeliever and a notorious philanderer, sensed that public opinion, especially among the rural masses, still adhered more or less to the tenets of the old religion, and he therefore courted ecclesiastical support by, among other things, increasing substantially that portion of the national budget devoted to religious purposes and by employing French troops to keep at bay the forces of the Italian Risorgimento that lusted after the temporal domain of the pope.[25] His policy was not consistent or even coherent, but by and large the French bishops, not without some hesitation and reluctance, endorsed the empire and urged their people to uphold it. Dissenting voices, to be sure, were raised within the Catholic community, a few liberal Cassandras who predicted that the church would rue the day it had embraced an authoritarian regime doomed by its own moral ambivalence.[26] Their prophecies were fulfilled in 1870 when the fall of Napoleon III unleashed a generation of fierce anticlericalism. John Ireland had long been home in Minnesota by then, and it is unlikely that during his sojourn in France he paid much attention to the erastian issues and debates—certainly not as a teenager at Meximieux. Yet, later, the collapse of the only variety of church-state union he had known firsthand, however casually, could not but have influenced the development of his views on that subject.

Ireland spent four years at Meximieux, and he was supremely happy there. He cherished all his life "la douce image de ma jeunesse," an image that never failed to raise his spirits, to console him, as he put it in 1891, amidst his labors and sorrows. "It awakens in my soul memories of peace and happiness; it speaks to me of virtue and truth."[27] And at the end of his life, writing of himself in the third person, he "refuse[d] to pass over the name of Meximieux without a . . . fond salute. . . . The years of his residence [there] were years of unalloyed happiness—years too of precious fruitage that has stood well by him in the long career of his priesthood. The influences of Meximieux have never faded from his mind and heart; his gratitude to Meximieux has never had a moment of interruption."[28]

The minor seminary Ireland remembered so fondly was a school for the intellect indeed, but also a setting designed to train the will. The masters, all priests of the Diocese of Belley, were moral monitors as well as pedagogues. They resided on the premises with the students from the second week in October till the end of July. The daily routine, calculated to inure the students to good, regular habits, varied only on Sundays and major feasts when elaborate liturgies occupied the time ordinarily spent in the classroom and when more recreation was allowed. At 5:30 A.M. a clanging bell awakened the seminarians in their dormitories. They were expected to rise promptly, recite to themselves three Hail Marys, wash, and dress with due modesty. They were especially enjoined not to dawdle in bed, because "there is no time so dangerous to repose"—one of several euphemisms employed to warn adolescent boys against sexual fantasies and self-indulgence. The students then gathered in the chapel for vocal prayers and fifteen minutes of "meditation"—silent reflection based upon some mystery of the gospel, the virtues of a saint, or a similar source of inspiration. Devotional manuals were supplied to help them perform this difficult species of prayer, but, even so, many a young seminarian was startled awake by the pull of the book slipping out of his hands. This taxing exercise completed, low mass was celebrated, also, in accord with the liturgical norms then in force, a quiet time, during which the students were encouraged to follow the priest's mostly inaudible Latin with missals printed in the vernacular. Consistent with the then common Catholic practice, they received the Eucharist about once a month.[29]

Classes took up six mornings a week and four early afternoons. Shortly before the noon meal the students repaired to the chapel for a five-minute "particular" examination of conscience, intended to focus the individual seminarian's attention upon his "particular" or overriding fault—bad temper, sloth, impatience, or whatever flaw he discerned within his own character—and upon the concrete steps he had taken (or had failed to take) to correct it since the self-inquiry of the previous day. Recreation began at mid-afternoon (at noon on Wednesdays and Saturdays) and consisted of organized games, walks through the town or countryside, and, not infrequently, manual labor to keep the seminary grounds neat and to maintain the gardens and orchards. The emphasis in any event was on the physical exercise that conventional wisdom said lively boys needed to preserve the health of their souls and their bodies. Communal recitation of the rosary came just before supper, and the evening hours were taken up with study and review of the lessons of that day. After a brief night prayer, which included a "general" examination of conscience and an Act of Contrition, the lights went out at half-past nine or ten o'clock.

The domestic arrangements at Meximieux were supervised by the Marist Sisters, whose convent stood on the edge of the seminary compound.[30] The food they served was plain but ample and nourishing, though young Ireland and O'Gorman had appetites typical of adolescents and feasted whenever they had the opportunity on gifts of fruits in season—apricots, strawberries, cherries—and, with special zest, on chocolate and other sweets.[31] The promotion of basic cleanliness was also the nuns' responsibility, and they did the best they could in a community of 160 boys and men.[32] But they offered no frills; if John Ireland wanted his shirts ironed and his socks darned—and he did—he had to look elsewhere, he had to look down the post road toward Montluel.[33]

Clemence Cretin, the bishop's unmarried sister, still resided in the old family home. Her means were more than adequate to sustain a simple style of life, which centered in the care of her aged mother and in a doting relationship with her nieces and nephews. Her piety was genuine, uncomplicated, and deep, and, intertwined with it, was the dedication to her missionary-brother whom she adored and for whom she was ready to do any service. When he sent to nearby Meximieux his two "dirty little Irish boys," she immediately took charge of them.

Pious spinster Clemence Cretin may have been, but she was no shrinking violet. Although she was careful not to intrude upon the prerogatives of the seminary authorities—indeed, she collaborated closely with them—she assumed a strong and independent line of her own. "Guard your vocation well," she warned Ireland and O'Gorman[34] early in 1854, and then added a few weeks later: "Be faithful to your sublime vocation, and my brother will be happy to have made sacrifices for your happiness in procuring an excellent education for you."[35]

Mademoiselle Cretin kept a sharp eye on more mundane matters as well. Winter in the valley of the Rhone was benign compared to the frigid upper Mississippi, but when the boys complained nevertheless of cold and damp she dispatched to each of them a woolen comforter and told them, "You will keep on your knitted jackets during the night." Throughout their stay at Meximieux she lavished care on them, but not without a stiff dose of admonition. "You are to try on the new shirt and tell me if it fits well and you like it. Others of the same kind will be made if there is nothing to change in this." "You are to order from the tailor the trousers you need." "You have received your clothes. They cost a good deal. Take care of them. Do not soil them or wrinkle them." "I am sending you the box of pens you asked [for]. . . . Take care of them. They are very expensive."[36]

She addressed them as her "dear children," and signed herself as "she who loves you as a mother." Increasingly she took on the maternal role. "I have told you," she wrote Ireland, "that I wished to replace your mother, who, perhaps, cannot now render you the services of which you have need. If it gives you pleasure that I have for you the feelings and the care of a mother, prove it to me by the conduct of a good son."[37] And like natural mothers since the world began, Clemence Cretin knew instinctively how to exact the tribute of filial submission and how to alternate the carrot with the stick, the caress with the rebuke. "Be diligent in all your duties, humble, docile, fervent, and I will always have for you the tenderness of a very devoted mother." "I will come to see you soon, and I will give you something in behalf of my brother." "If you are very good, I will ask if you might be permitted to come and spend a day with me." "No doubt you await our visit with impatience. . . . We will bring you your New Year's gifts. Have patience." The bishop had asked her again "to fill all your needs, which I have always done with pleasure. Then, be very grateful, very affectionate, very pious."[38]

Little Thomas O'Gorman she found pliable enough, but John Ireland, at a more difficult age, was a harder case. He got into scrapes at Meximieux due to impulsiveness and disobedience to the rule. None of the infractions was serious or untypical of a boy straining toward manhood, but Mademoiselle Cretin swooped down to deliver him from "the demon who inspires only pride and lies." If you are remiss, she wrote him sternly at the beginning of his second year at the seminary, "confess your fault. . . . Humiliate yourself; ask for pardon. . . . I do not wish to remind you of the trouble you have given me. I have told you that I have forgotten everything, because I hoped that this year you would correct yourself and become better. That is my wish." And if such implications of ingratitude were not enough to shame him into compliance, she was prepared to employ a gentle mockery. When she thought he was "a Saint, a young man filled with piety, with all sorts of virtues," she prayed merely for his perseverance; "now that I know your faults, I often add my tears to the prayers which I renew more often." Minor failings, like his rudeness and personal slovenliness, Clemence Cretin could more or less serenely attribute to Ireland's age and sex, and his bad language, too, though she could not refrain "from remarking to you my astonishment at having heard you pronounce certain words not at all fitting in a virtuous young man who has received a good education." What worried her most, however, was that John Ireland had not grasped as quickly the religious devotion proper to a missionary as he had, apparently, the coarser elements of the French idiom and the subjects taught in the classroom. "Virtue is better than knowledge," she said flatly.[39]

That message was not, perhaps, a bad one for a gifted but raw youth, thousands of miles from home, to listen to. Hectoring in any case did not dominate Mademoiselle Cretin's relationship with John Ireland. In fact she treated him with real affection. She was directive, to be sure, and never bashful in reminding him of the debts he owed her and her brother. Yet clearly discernible behind all her endeavors in Ireland's and O'Gorman's behalf, her endless kindnesses to them as well as her strictures, lay the one ambition which gave meaning to her life. "I am impatient to see you go to second the zeal of my brother who finds himself crushed under the weight of his charge. The business, the cares, the work, the needs multiply as the population [in Minnesota] grows." Not even the terrible blow of Joseph Cretin's death distracted her from the goal that his chosen two must be holy missionaries in the Diocese of St. Paul. "My brother loved it so much that he gave his life for it."[40]

If Ireland and O'Gorman thus had a substitute mother dwelling in Montluel, they also acquired a sister there. Marie Cretin, Clemence's (and the bishop's) niece, was her aunt's frequent companion on visits to Meximieux — "I will have many things to tell you," she wrote Ireland just before one such visit early in 1857, "and we can chat entirely at our ease" — and during the summer vacation, which the boys invariably spent with Clemence, Marie was in almost constant attendance. She reflected often on those happy times. "[My aunt and I] talked of you, of our travels, of that which amused us all so much during these last holidays. . . . It is with pleasure that I recall our charming evenings, always so gay, and above all the lessons in English, which I have forgotten a little." The tone of her letters to Ireland was less admonitory than her aunt's, but hardly less pietistic. She particularly liked to describe, at length, religious ceremonies of which she had been a witness. "Do not forget your sister during your retreat," she wrote in November 1855. At the beginning of the next year she recommended that she and her "very dear John" observe Lent with special fervor as a sign of their unity.[41]

Marie treated O'Gorman with the indulgence proper to a grown woman dealing with an occasionally mischievous small boy. "I am very angry with Thomas. He has caused M. Perrier [a seminary professor] and my aunt trouble. Tell him this for me. I embrace him just the same. I hope that he will correct himself."[42] But sometimes a hint of more-than-sisterly affection crept into the confidences she shared with Ireland.[43] This was most strikingly evident toward the end of 1856 when she passed through a period of some unspecified depression. "I suppose," she wrote, "you received the note in which I told you that I went to Ars[44] because of my trouble. Oh, if you knew how tormented I am, and how bored, you would redouble your prayers." But he was not to imagine that her "trouble," whatever it was, had changed her attitude toward him. "I promise to do everything in my power to give you every possible joy, as I have in the preceding years." She brightened at the prospect of an approaching meeting with him. "I am awaiting that day with keen impatience. I will have so many things to tell you, and the thought of the pleasure of being near you, and of recalling our last holidays, makes me wish for it even more anxiously."[45]

It was not, however, the feminine associations, important as these may have been, which lingered longest in John Ireland's memories about his time at Meximieux or which left the deepest impression upon him. The seminary, after all, exuded a starkly masculine, not to say misogynist, atmosphere; there Ireland joined a comradeship of young men who, while they struggled, as youth always does, to discover an adult definition of themselves, took it for granted that they would never be husbands and fathers. Ireland was to live his life in an exclusively male world, to act invariably within the confines of the "clerical culture."[46] No wonder he looked back upon Meximieux, not only as an institution where he obtained his basic professional training, but also as his first spiritual home.

That home, moreover, offered him a stability he had never known before. Ireland's boyhood had passed in a turmoil of horror and uncertainty. The seminary, by contrast, with its regular round of activities, was a place as solidly predictable as the rising and setting of the sun. Ireland bridled sometimes at the conformity imposed on him, but for the most part he willingly paid that price in exchange for a secure and settled environment in which to prepare himself for a career.[47]

There existed no standardized curriculum for a French petit séminaire, but a pattern naturally emerged that reflected the institution's pre-professional character.[48] Language and literature took primacy, somewhat surprisingly, over any formal study of religion. Latin was the fundamental subject, both because it was considered the core of a classical education and because it served as the official language of the church, in the liturgy, the canon law, and the theological sciences to be studied later in the grand séminaire. Students routinely translated Cicero, Horace, and Vergil, and they were expected to develop skills in Latin composition and versification. The French classics — La Fontaine, Bossuet, expurgated versions of Racine and Molière — formed the other major area of concentration. Bossuet, the great ecclesiastical orator of the seventeenth century, became Ireland's favorite author.[49] The study of Greek received more lip-service than serious attention in most minor seminaries, and, due to its difficulty, it was usually reserved for the ablest students (among whom at Meximieux Ireland was one). Geography and history (at which O'Gorman proved adept) were haphazardly taught together. Science and mathematics were usually treated as curricular step-children, on the grounds, as one preacher put it, that such inquiries tended to dry up the fervent heart. Yet at Meximieux Ireland followed courses in algebra, geometry, and physics, excelling in the latter.[50] Indeed, Meximieux appears to have stood several cuts above the average minor seminary in the breadth of its offerings and in the quality and pedagogical attainments of its half-dozen professors — *"maîtres hommes,"* a nostalgic Ireland called them, who insisted more upon "forming the intelligence and creating a sustained love of study" than in simply cramming their pupils' memories.[51]

Ireland displayed from his first days as a student in the petit séminaire the facility, as O'Gorman recalled it, of being "mentally quick and mentally deep at the same time." But more important in the educative process than mere intellectual capacity — and more significant a clue to the years ahead — was the drive of a powerful will: in Ireland's case, O'Gorman added, "to want to learn a thing was to learn it."[52] And he wanted to learn, everything, anything. Knowledge was a citadel to be stormed and captured. He hurled himself into his studies with a "passion for work" that astonished his classmates.[53] The initial obstacle he had to overcome was perhaps the most daunting. In the autumn of 1853 John Ireland arrived in France ignorant of the language (except for a few phrases picked up from Bishop Cretin and Father Ravoux) and thus entirely dependent upon the one professor who knew some English.[54] Less than three months later he wrote a long letter in French to Clemence Cretin who warmly congratulated him for his effort, "since you find it so difficult." Late in 1855 Marie Cretin told him that her uncle the bishop "was very much pleased with your letters. He sees with satisfaction that you write French correctly."[55] Where there was a will, there was a way.

Ireland never stood quite at the head of his class, but on prize day — which occurred each July, at the end of the academic year, and which was marked by a school play[56] and other festivities — he accumulated enough seconds and thirds to earn the reputation of a good scholar among his peers.[57] But he was not satisfied only with accomplishments in the classroom; his obsession with self-improvement led him to take on extra study-projects, often of a most elaborate kind.[58] None of this furious activity seems to have put off Ireland's schoolmates or to have induced them to dismiss him as a drudge. On the contrary, they admired his competitiveness and his determination to succeed. They wearied a little at his self-conscious boasting about the grandeurs of America.[59] They smiled condescendingly at his insistence upon signing his name, with a size and sweep reminiscent of John Hancock, "Ireland, Jean, des États Unis."[60] And they chided him on occasion for his malicious conversation and for his habit of placing the worst construction upon their quite innocent remarks.[61] But, these peccadillos aside, most of his French schoolmates liked John Ireland, were impressed by him, and at least one of them emigrated to Minnesota and served with him as a priest in the Diocese of St. Paul.[62]

Clemence Cretin's nagging worry that her protégé's prowess as a student came at the expense of his piety seemed belied by the awestruck pilgrimage he made, in her company, to the curé of Ars.[63] His induction, early in his time at Meximieux, into the seminary's sodality (congrégation) pointed to the same conclusion. This organization — an elite group which included the best students and those judged by the priest in charge to possess outstanding qualities of leadership[64] — centered its activities in special devotions to the Virgin Mary, as well as in meetings at which members openly discussed one another's faults and the means to correct them. Ireland no doubt spoke as frankly as the others, but whether he enjoyed these sessions of mutual recrimination has gone unrecorded. He took away at any rate an element of "piety" from the sodality's exercises: his reverence for the Virgin remained steadfast, if conventional, all his life.[65] It may have been, however, that the peculiar charm of the seminary sodality lay as much in its exclusiveness, in its character as an honors fraternity or even a kind of secret society open only to initiates. And it may have been, as later events suggest, that even at beloved Meximieux Ireland encountered certain aspects of nineteenth-century French religiosity that did not attract him. Clemence Cretin might not have been altogether wrong.

As early as the summer of 1856 Ireland was pondering the next stage of his ecclesiastical education. He was eighteen by then, and he believed himself ready, after another year of classics, to move on to philosophical and theological studies. At first the faculty at Meximieux resisted this "ambitious design," and urged him "to stop and stay in humanities" two more years.[66] But Ireland argued that by the end of the 1857 academic year he would have fulfilled most of the requirements of the ill-defined minor seminary program, and that, besides, he had demonstrated by independent work an industry and a maturity that merited promotion. He got his way.

The other part of his plan, however, went awry. He had set his heart on doing his philosophy course at Strasbourg, where he could also learn German. Then he would return to the Diocese of Belley, enroll as a theology student in its grand séminaire, located in Brou, and thus be reunited with his Meximieux classmates. This idea ran into early trouble. In October 1856 Ireland told Marie Cretin "with sorrow" that the following year he would go not to Strasbourg, as he desired, but to Our Lady of Montbel, the Marist scholasticate near Toulon. "I despair of ever going to see you in that city," she replied.[67]

Nevertheless the decision appears not to have been final at that date, or at least Ireland managed to keep the matter open. "When you receive my letter," wrote one of the professors at Meximieux ten months later, "you will have resolved the problem of your future situation for next year. According to what you have said [to] me about your desires, I may conclude Strasbourg has been chosen.

I do not oppose. . . . There you will be able to learn Dutch [German], to follow a good course in philosophy, and together to keep, or rather to strengthen, the feelings and virtues that become to [*sic*] a future priest. With the last respect, Montbel, perhaps, would have been to prefer [*sic*], but since there are true reasons to go to Strasbourg let us hope God will supply our good Mother's protection over you as well there as at Montbel."[68] Whether out of parochial rivalry or for some more substantive cause, the same professor ruled out another possible alternative—a transfer to the other diocesan petit séminaire, in Belley, which had a philosophy faculty.

In the end Ireland was disappointed in his hopes and went dutifully off to Montbel where he did four years of philosophy and theology. Economic reasons seem to have been decisive. Bishop Devie of Belley was dead. The founder of the Marists, who, like Devie, had pledged free education for Bishop Cretin's students, was prepared to honor that commitment, even though Cretin too was now dead. John Ireland had to set aside his "ambitious design" and to swallow the bitter pill that he was, after all, a pauper, a charity case.

But he could not be made to like Montbel, and clearly he did not. Nothing is more striking about Ireland's recollections of his student days in France than the contrast between his life-long enthusiasm for Meximieux and his utter silence about Montbel. "Today," he wrote in 1891, "I offer the best tribute of love I can to my seminary of Meximieux, by striving to reproduce it in the seminary of St. Paul which I desire to leave to Minnesota as the monument of my episcopate."[69] What he contemplated when he expressed this sentiment was the establishment not of a petit but of a grand séminaire, not of another Meximieux—he had already set up a classical collège on the minor seminary model—but of another Montbel, an institution offering professional training in philosophy and theology. The St. Paul Seminary duly opened its doors in 1894, yet its founder two decades later still invoked "la douce image" of Meximieux: "The highest tribute of praise and affection to be coveted by a school is given, when, in their later years, after experiences of men and of things have been plentiful, those who had once been its pupils thank Heaven that their early mental and religious formation has been entrusted to its sheltering wings. This tribute the writer gives today, in absolute whole-heartedness, to the seminary of Meximieux."[70]

When he visited France during his middle and elderly years, he seldom failed to call at Meximieux, but he never went to Montbel. When, at the height of the church-state crisis shortly after the turn of the twentieth century, the French government closed both institutions, Ireland had no tears to shed for Montbel. But the passing of Meximieux grieved him deeply. "Alas! the fatal moment came in 1905 . . . when the mandate was read . . . that the seminary was national property and should hurry its inmates into the frosts of a wintry morning, away from their beloved harbor of sanctity and learning. . . . One day the Government of France will repent of its injustices; once more the Seminary of Meximieux will be lifted into its former splendors."[71]

One can only speculate why John Ireland disliked Montbel. Certainly its physical locale was not calculated to prejudice him in its favor. The scholasticate was a large, plain, three-storied building, with a modest neo-gothic chapel attached to one end, set in the bleak and isolated rural commune of La Crau, some fourteen miles east of Toulon and five miles northwest of the fishing village of Hyères. The scattered stucco houses, with roofs of red tile, hinted at the proximity of the Mediterranean, as did the tall umbrella pines, the palm and cork trees, the lowering skies and mild temperatures that prevailed throughout the winter months. But the commune was upland and circled all around by squat hills, which blocked off the sight and even the scent of the sea. Indeed, La Crau was a drab stretch of countryside, especially when compared to the breathtaking natural beauty near at hand in every direction. The site of Montbel, hardly a cannon-shot from the grandeur of the Riviera, had none of the bright clarity and airiness and vivid color that lit up the coast from Hyères east to St. Tropez and Nice, nor did it display the lush, green, rolling landscape characteristic of the valley of the Rhone. Meximieux was a far prettier and livelier place.

Yet it seems unlikely that John Ireland was so much affected by his physical surroundings between the ages of nineteen and twenty-three as to banish acknowledgment of that period of his life from his consciousness a half-century later. Nor is it likely that because he had not been allowed to attend the seminary of his choice he ignored forever after the existence of the seminary he actually attended. A more plausible explanation suggests itself, one which

rings true in the light of Ireland's mature convictions and which can
be discerned in his consistent devotion to Meximieux. There the
professors had all been diocesan priests. "There our masters exhibited all the piety and regularity which distinguish the better
communities of religious. But, at the same time, priests themselves
of the diocese in which their pupils would later serve, they were
more devoted to the pupils' genuine interests and better equipped
to show the proper paths to those aspirants to the priesthood."[72]
Ireland's later notorious antipathy toward religious orders is surely
reflected in these remarks. The question remains — an unanswerable
question indeed — whether that antipathy began in the seminary of
Montbel, operated by and for a religious order, or whether his dis-
taste for religious orders, arrived at afterward on other grounds,
was read back, so to speak, into his seminary experience.

The Society of Mary — the Marists[73] — traced its remote origins
to the grand séminaire of Lyon just after the conclusion of the
Napoleonic wars. There a group of eleven like-minded young men
determined to establish a new religious order consecrated to the
special service of the Virgin Mary and to the rebuilding of a
Catholicism shattered by the Enlightenment and the Revolution. As
it turned out, only four of them persevered, but one of them, Jean-
Claude Colin (1790–1875), proved to be extraordinarily zealous in
the cause and also to be a masterful organizer. Ordained a secular
priest in 1816, Colin found himself, more or less by accident,
within the precincts of, and therefore subject to, the Diocese of Belley when it was restored in 1822. So it was that he became for a time
a confrere of Joseph Cretin.[74] Devie, the forceful bishop of Belley,
looked kindly upon Colin and encouraged his ambitions, with one
important condition: the bishop insisted that Colin's projected congregation function as a strictly diocesan institute and thus remain
under his own control.[75] Indeed, as Colin gathered disciples around
himself, the bishop put them all to work preaching missions in the
countryside and staffing various diocesan facilities (including, till
1845, the petit séminaire at Belley).

But Colin had a different and a grander vision. He wanted his
Society of Mary to take its place within the Catholic world on a par
with the older religious orders, universal in its apostolate and not
confined within the boundaries of a single diocese. In 1836 the Holy

See[76] formally granted his petitions, approved the constitution drawn up by Père Colin—as he was now called[77]—and assigned to the Marists as their own mission field the islands of the western, central, and southern Pacific ("Oceania"). This did not mean, however, that the order was to be inactive elsewhere, and soon Marist houses opened across France and in Belgium, Italy, and Spain.[78] Bishop Devie, overruled by his Roman superiors, accepted the decision with good grace, and the Marists continued to exert much influence within the Diocese of Belley, not least at Meximieux.[79] By 1852 the young order had grown to 280 priests and lay brothers.[80]

That same year a rural entrepreneur named Blaise Aurran, who lived near Hyères, Department of Var, offered Colin a tract of two hundred acres in the commune of La Crau, and offered further to build upon it a scholasticate—roughly equivalent to a grand séminaire for religious—in which aspiring Marists could be trained in philosophy and theology. Aurran explained that he wished thus to make amends for his irreligious and anti-clerical youth, and also to honor his wife who, after many years of happy but childless marriage, had, with his consent, retired to a convent.[81] Colin gratefully accepted this proposal, and the result was the speedy construction, supervised personally by the donor himself, of Our Lady of Montbel. Fittingly, Aurran spent his last days there as a lay brother.

John Ireland was apparently unmoved by the charming details connected with Montbel's foundation. He formed no strong attachments either to the place or to its people. When he arrived he found at least one former schoolmate from Meximieux,[82] but O'Gorman he had had to leave behind—a circumstance, however, that may have been as much a relief to him as a deprivation.[83] During Ireland's years at the scholasticate (1857–61) the number of students varied between twenty-five and thirty-five. All but one or two of them were Marists, many destined for the missions in the South Seas and a few destined for martyrdom there.[84] Among the most notable of Ireland's contemporaries was an Irishman of about his own age named Francis Redwood, who became a Marist missionary in New Zealand and eventually archbishop of Wellington. Many years later he and Ireland corresponded fitfully, and Redwood even visited St. Paul. But there was no old school tie between them; they regarded one another as fellow prelates rather than alumni of the same seminary.[85]

Ireland found the regimen at Montbel little different from what he had experienced at Meximieux; all seminaries—petit and grand, diocesan and religious—adopted pretty much the same daily round of study and prayer-exercises in accord with the model developed so successfully by the Sulpicians. Père Colin was no enemy to pious routine and certainly no innovator. And though he was far from seeing the intellectual life as an end in itself, he did insist that the Marist theological schools offer a respectable academic program, one that was solid, thorough, and unadventuresome.[86] The curriculum at Montbel reflected the founder's convictions, and indeed those of most Catholic Frenchmen of the middle of the nineteenth century: conventional, conservative, polemical, ultramontane,[87] free of any taint of the liberalism spawned by the Revolution. The newly ordained priest had to enter an essentially perverse and hostile environment, and he needed intellectual as well as moral weapons if he were to triumph over the enemies of the faith.

There is no reason to suppose that young John Ireland quarreled with this point of view.[88] But all that can be said with certainty about his time at Montbel is that he exhibited there the same "passion for work" that had distinguished him at Meximieux. The only documents of this period to survive are five 8-by-15-inch notebooks and fragments of a sixth—a total of about 375 longhand pages—in which Ireland set down a record of studies he undertook more or less related to his seminary course.[89]

One of these booklets he labeled "Theologie, Philosophie, histoire, Politique, etc., no. 22,"[90] something of a grab-bag, which included in its fifty-nine pages investigations as various as the church-state problem from medieval to modern times, the validity of secession from the American Union, the place of consecrated virginity in the life of the church, the right of the pope to depose secular rulers, the relationship between Catholicism and works of charity—a collection of topics, mostly controversial, that a priest might be expected to address from the pulpit or in the lecture hall. The inclusion of secession in the list is noteworthy for its timeliness and as an indication that Ireland, far away as he was, kept track of the travails through which his adopted country was then passing.

Each of the other five notebooks was devoted to a particular theological inquiry or "tract": on revelation (eighty-one pages); on the incarnation and grace (seventy-one pages); on justice and rights (eighty-six pages); on the place of the Virgin Mary in the economy of salvation (seventy pages); and on the nature of the church (only ten pages survive). To these matters Ireland applied a consistent methodology throughout. He began by copying out, or summarizing, in Latin, the salient points raised in a standard scholastic textbook, like that of the prominent Jesuit theologian, Giovanni Perrone.[91] Then often, though not always, he entered on the facing page brief corroborative statements, in French, English, or Latin, on the same subject. These were not infrequently anecdotal in character. Thus, in arguing "the necessity for Christians of studying the Jewish religion or Old Testament," Ireland related how Mendelsohn, the composer, "being urged to embrace Christianity, answered: 'What do you think of a man who, when a fire breaks out on the ground floor, takes refuge in the upper story?' Mendelsohn was a Jew, wavering in his faith on account of attacks against the Old Testament." Ireland cited no source for this story, nor did he as a rule concern himself with elaborate documentation. He leaned heavily on Perrone, referred to Orestes Brownson[92] with some frequency, to Bossuet almost as often, and, more surprisingly, to the eminent Protestant divine, William Paley.[93] Otherwise he was content to leave his sources unacknowledged or to employ a citation code intelligible only to himself.

For the notebooks represented a practical, not a speculative, exercise. They were meant to be deposits of information which Ireland could call upon once the responsibilities of preaching and teaching had been entrusted to him. On the same principle he occasionally pasted into the notebooks cuttings from *The Pilot*, a Catholic newspaper published in Boston. These were not numerous, but their variety indicated how wide-ranging were Ireland's interests: "The Civilization of the Japanese" ("That civilization which does not assist men in the attainment of the *end* for which they are created is not a blessing but a curse. . . . The Catholic Church is the only source of true civilization"); a "Letter to the Prince of Wales" ("[The Irish] people under such a government have an inviolable right, and are under a solemn moral obligation, to break its yoke"); and a wry criticism of the American Tract Society, an evangelical group, allegedly a guardian of public morals and yet afraid to take a stand against the wicked slave-trade ("The principle of expediency . . . has always been popular among Protestants. . . . The American Tract Society has proved itself worthy [of that principle] . . . by its readiness to condemn dancing and its modest discretion about calling the trade in human beings a sin").

Not all of this material was entered into the notebooks at the same time. The Latin core text was written at Montbel, but at least some of the supporting quotation and anecdote was added later.[94] Ireland treated the notebooks as workbooks; he returned to them often, inserting this, underscoring that, refining something else. He practiced, in other words, what he was to preach later to his own seminarians: a priest must acquire early the habit of reading with a pen in his hand, because sustained and methodical study was a serious obligation for one who ventured to instruct others.[95]

No more is known about Ireland's departure from Montbel than about his arrival there four years earlier. Predictably he saved his last fond farewells for Meximieux, which received him on July 18, 1861. The members of the seminary sodality assembled in his honor and presented him with a medal of the Virgin Mary "which he kissed and placed . . . on his heart. . . . [Then he] embraced one after the other all his brothers, without saying a word."[96] An ordained deacon by this time, with only the order of the priesthood left to be conferred upon him once he returned to St. Paul, he promised to say mass for them all in America.[97] On July 23 he left for Le Havre and the ship that would carry him across the Atlantic.[98]

The Battle of Bull Run had been fought in Virginia two days before.

IV

"You Were with Me at Corinth"

1861–63

THE MINNESOTA to which John Ireland returned in the late summer of 1861 was not so much the rude frontier he had left eight years before. Development had been slower, to be sure, and less spectacular than promoters had hoped and, in many instances, had promised. Nevertheless, the territory, detached from its westernmost portions, had been admitted to the Union in 1858 as the thirty-second state. Its white population stood at a little more than 170,000, a figure which disappointed boosters and real-estate speculators—enormous paper fortunes had been lost when land values plummeted after the bank panic of 1857—but which still represented an increase of 2,500 percent in less than a decade. Of this total, fifty-nine thousand had been born outside the United States, thirteen thousand in Ireland.[1]

Most Minnesotans lived in the southeastern third of the state, and most of them were farmers: eighteen thousand farm families worked nearly three million acres of wheat, oats, corn, barley, vegetables, and pasturage. Their existence was harsh and full of care, especially during the long and brutally cold winters. But the soil was deep and rich, and it blossomed under their hands; lavish gardens grew in the wilderness, and, as the pioneers took root themselves, they assumed a sturdy, even a belligerent, self-regard. Meanwhile, to the west and north of them, the bewildered Indians, driven from their ancestral homes, cheated and lied to by unscrupulous speculators, nourished within themselves the seeds of hatred. A bitter harvest, for Indians and white settlers alike, lay just ahead.[2]

St. Paul in John Ireland's absence had grown into a lively town of eleven thousand. Some of its early promise had already been fulfilled. More than a thousand steamboat dockings were recorded at its levees in 1861, and the volume of freight moved on and off its busy wharves had multiplied many times over in a few years. There was as yet no rail link to the east; ten miles of lonely and un-used track, running west to St. Anthony and optimistically called the St. Paul and Pacific, did nothing to dissipate a keen sense of iso-lation from the rest of the country among people who could depend upon river transport only from April to November. The comple-tion of a telegraph line in 1860 was therefore a great event, which, among other benefits, enabled the local press to compete success-fully for world and national news with the *New York Tribune,* up till then the most widely read paper in the state.

The gaudy, often evanescent trappings of civilization had come, as they always do, in the train of economic expansion. Minnesota's first home-grown college graduates received their degrees two years before John Ireland's return from France. By that time almost five hundred schools were in operation in the state, providing evi-dence, incidentally, of the prevalence of the double standard: female teachers earned on an average thirteen dollars a month, males twenty-one dollars. As early as 1857 St. Paul supported three professional theatrical companies, a minstrel show, a circus, a tent show, and an amateur dramatic society. *Il Trovatore* was produced locally in 1859. Other forms of entertainment were also available for those with less refined tastes: in March 1860, several thousand St. Paulites gathered in a yard next to the new jail and watched the hanging of a woman who had poisoned her husband. A jail had in-deed been built by the time Ireland came back, and a state capitol, and a city hall, and a dozen more churches, and—thanks to the Sis-ters of St. Joseph—a hospital.

Serious illness—pneumonia, diphtheria, tuberculosis, even on occasion the dreaded cholera—was a constant reminder to town and countryside of the fragility of the human condition. Richard Ire-land, Jr., a child of eight, died of typhoid while his elder brother was studying overseas.[3] But many people migrated to Minnesota because of what they perceived to be its relatively salubrious climate, among them a physician named William Worrall Mayo, who came to St. Paul in 1854 in flight "from the malarial hell of the Wabash Valley in Indiana."[4] Later he would move on to Rochester, in the southern part of the state, where he and his brilliant sons would create one of the great medical complexes in the world. The incidence of disease remained in any event part of the gamble of life, and the pioneers had little choice but to accept it as such. Meantime they seized the opportunities a growing city and state offered them. Richard Ireland, for example, did not allow mourning for his little son to prevent him from plying his carpenter's trade with diligence, or, for that matter, from dabbling in politics — though in this latter activity he was less successful than his friend John O'Gorman.[5] Opportunity knocked on some doors in a very casual fashion. In the summer of 1856 James Jerome Hill, a young man from Ontario, born the same year as John Ireland, "took a notion to go and see St. Paul."[6] He stayed there for the rest of his remarkable life, this builder of empires.

Another new resident of St. Paul, less eager to be there than most others, was its new Roman Catholic bishop, the Right Reverend[7] Thomas Langdon Grace, of the Order of Preachers. He had been born in 1814 in Charleston, South Carolina, of Irish immigrants who, however, had sprung from much more genteel stock than the Irelands had.[8] As a child he moved with his family to Ohio where he fell under the influence of the Dominican friars — white-clad members of the famed Order of Preachers[9] — who were so prominent as missionaries in that state and also in Kentucky and Tennessee.[10] At seventeen Grace joined the Dominican order, and in 1838 his superiors sent him to Italy for his theological training. He spent nearly seven years there, mostly in Rome and Perugia. The quality of clerical education available in the Italy of the 1830s and 1840s was not particularly good, but it compared favorably with what a young friar might have received among his poverty-stricken religious brethren in Ohio.

In 1846, a year after his return to the United States, Grace, at the behest of the Dominican bishop of Nashville, took up his ministry in Memphis. He remained there thirteen years, built a fine church, a school, and an orphanage, and gained the esteem of the whole community, which he left only with the greatest reluctance. "Your zeal, your example, and your eloquence," his parishioners declaimed on the eve of his departure, "have done much to awaken and preserve the faith of those entrusted to your pastoral care, and to command the respect of our fellow citizens who are not of our communion."[11]

For a Catholic priest to have won such plaudits in a southern city where the nativist movement had flourished during the 1850s was no mean accomplishment, and it may have led Father Grace to respond without enthusiasm to the call of the north; or perhaps he envisioned the upper reaches of the Mississippi Valley as frozen wastes, inhabited only by primitives. At any rate, when the papal bulls came from Rome appointing him bishop of St. Paul, Grace sent them back, accompanied by a Latin letter, written in his crabbed hand and filled with conventional platitudes and pieties. "I have tried in vain to bend my will, after much prayerful consideration, to accept so great an apostolate." However, his "own incapacities, which are enormous," together with much work still undone in Memphis, led him to "implore humbly" that due consideration be taken of his "unworthiness" and that he be allowed to decline the appointment.[12] But Rome was having none of it,[13] and by mid-summer, 1859, the public press was reporting that, since "the Holy Father [had] insisted on his acceptance, . . . the dutiful son [had] acquiesced." On July 24, in the age-old rite conducted this time in the Cathedral of St. Louis, Thomas Grace was elevated to the order of bishop. In attendance was the indefatigable Augustin Ravoux who, after the ceremony and the modest festivities following it, conducted Grace upriver aboard the *Northern Belle* to his see-city, where, as one who witnessed his arrival put it, he received "a heartfelt, enthusiastic welcome, such a one as would prove that our hearts are none the colder for a residence in this northern clime."[14] The new bishop found his diocese comprised of fifty thousand Catholics served by twenty-seven priests in ninety towns and settlements — prodigious growth since Joseph Cretin had first come to St. Paul.[15]

Two years later the bishop also found John Ireland, literally on his doorstep. On his way home from France the young deacon traveled overland as far as the railroad would take him, to Prairie du

Chien. He attended mass there on the last Sunday in August 1861 and, too shy to introduce himself to the officiating priest—who might well have been Lucien Galtier—he paced along the riverbank through the afternoon until it was time to board the steamer north.[16] His arrival in St. Paul caused little stir except among his own family, smaller now than when he left, since his brother Richard had died and his sister Ellen had become a nun (as had his cousin, Ellen Howard[17]). He was soon settled into rooms in the three-storied clergy residence, where the bishop also lived, next to the cathedral on West Sixth Street—both buildings new to him— there to await Grace's pleasure with regard to ordination to the priesthood and assignment.

The wait was rather more prolonged than he might have expected. At the moment Ireland reported for duty the bishop was away, visiting the settlements in the lower Red River Valley, the far northwest corner of his diocese.[18] When he returned to St. Paul in late September, he put Ireland to work as a part-time secretary, while he satisfied himself as to the candidate's intellectual, moral, and liturgical preparation for the ecclesiastical state. He finally set the date for the ordination: the fourth Sunday of Advent, December 22, 1861.[19] Thomas Langdon Grace was not one disposed to hurry.

Grace, in his forty-seventh year when John Ireland first met him, was a portly, round-faced man whose small-lensed spectacles gave him a permanently startled expression, to which a corona of frizzed hair thick around a balding pate added a somewhat Pickwickian flavor. His placid temperament belied a shrewd and discerning mind. Moreover, his extended European experience lent Grace a cosmopolitan and scholarly air, which he wore with unaffected ease all his life and which stood him in good stead among his various frontier constituencies.

Such an aura would have profited Grace little in a rough-and-tumble world had he not been a genuinely cultivated man. In his case, reputation did not outrun fact. Thomas Grace displayed a refinement, a polish, an elegance of manner and speech that helped earn him the regard of his contemporaries, including non-Catholics, as "one of the ablest prelates in America."[20] For a community vital and expanding, and yet self-consciously aware of its own crudities, the presence of this cultured and bookish clergyman offered a measure of reassurance, a token, so to speak, of its own respectability.[21] Habitually courteous and amiable, Grace got on well with most people, even with the likes of the often prickly Ravoux, whom he made vicar general, a gesture calculated to soothe the feelings of the no longer dominant French group within the diocese. Vulgarity, however, he could not abide and would not tolerate; once, when a pastor in Minneapolis placarded the town with posters advertising the dedication of his new church, Bishop Grace, who was scheduled to perform the ceremony, stonily refused to attend.[22]

There was nothing flashy about him. On the contrary, his strength lay in the careful, understated manner in which he fulfilled the humdrum obligations of his office. He was cautious, balanced, always civil, never hasty in his judgments.[23] Above all, he possessed a serene appreciation of his own worth, which kept him preserved from the least pang of jealousy; the success of others did not trouble or threaten Thomas Grace. This quality proved crucial in his relationship with Ireland. Grace was never a leader who initiated projects, but neither would he obstruct a subordinate who did. John Ireland's restless genius, with all its rough edges, thus found an ideal superior in Grace, who benevolently gave his gifted younger colleague free rein and always bestowed credit where credit was due. The result was a fruitful partnership that lasted nearly a quarter of a century.

The partnership began modestly and predictably enough when the newly ordained Ireland was assigned as assistant pastor in the cathedral parish. To secure enough priests to minister to his diocese's burgeoning Catholic population was Grace's first and constant anxiety.[24] But circumstances determined that the bishop would lose, at least for a time, the services of this new curate. The war of the slaveholders' rebellion[25] overshadowed all other considerations, even on the far-off Minnesota frontier.

On St. Patrick's Day, March 17, 1862, Ireland preached from the pulpit of the cathedral the first of his sermons to attract public notice, an address "which in point of fervor, historical research, patriotic feeling, and genuine piety has not been excelled in our memory."[26] A legible text of the sermon has not survived, but it is safe to say that the "patriotic feeling" expressed in it was not un-

John Ireland, 1862 (MHS)

related to efforts, started shortly after the bombardment of Fort Sumter, to raise a regiment composed of Irishmen settled in Minnesota.[27] These efforts had so far been unavailing.

Meanwhile, even before Lincoln's initial call for seventy-five thousand volunteers to enlist for three months, Governor Alexander Ramsey had pledged to the president a levy of one thousand Minnesotans to fight in defense of the Union; out of this original enthusiasm was formed the First Minnesota Regiment, destined for bloody immortality at Gettysburg. After the stunning Unionist defeat at Bull Run on July 21, 1861, the federal government expanded the mobilization to a half-million men. Minnesota's quota was 5,457 volunteers, most of whom were to be organized into five regiments of infantry.[28] Eventually, by the end of the war in 1865, eleven infantry regiments had been recruited or drafted in Minnesota, together with smaller units of cavalry, artillery, and sharpshooters.[29] St. Paul supplied fifteen hundred men for the colors—a large percentage of the town's voting population—of whom 124 died during the course of the conflict.[30]

The organization of the Fifth Regiment, Minnesota Volunteer Infantry, commenced on December 19, 1861, a few days before John Ireland's ordination. The recruiting process dragged on for three months, a sign perhaps that the intensity of patriotic ardor had cooled somewhat with the prospect of a long war. The regiment had hardly filled its complement, in late March 1862, when three of its ten companies were detached for garrison duty at the western Minnesota forts that guarded the Indian reservations. So it was that Companies B, C, and D of the Fifth Minnesota were blooded, the following summer, not by rebels in butternut grey but by brightly painted Dakota warriors.[31]

The rest of the regiment spent two months in drill and training at Fort Snelling before it departed for the battle zone in west Tennessee on May 13. Some time before that Bishop Grace formally inquired of Governor Ramsey as to the provision of care for the spiritual needs of Catholic soldiers from Minnesota, and he offered a priest to perform this task, if the priest were accorded official status. The bishop pointed out that at least one-third of the roster of the Minnesota Fifth professed the Catholic religion, and that considerable numbers of Catholics were scattered throughout the other state units as well.[32] He did not need to point out that attempts to organize an exclusively Irish Catholic regiment had failed. Nor did he deign to mention that his willingness to deplete his slender store of clergy by assigning one of them to a chaplaincy in the Union army would help quiet the murmurs heard around St. Paul that he, Charleston-born and a long-time resident of Memphis, was at heart a Confederate sympathizer.[33]

The governor, who put no stock in such rumors, was highly embarrassed by the bishop's request. For though Grace always remained carefully apolitical, he was the most prominent member of a group that numbered as much as 25 or 30 percent of the electorate, and he could not be taken lightly. But in the face of federal regulations, there was little Ramsey could do. The War Department stipulated that "there shall be allowed to each regiment one chaplain who shall be appointed by the regimental commander on the vote of the field officers and company commanders on duty with the regiment at the time the appointment shall be made."[34] On May 17, the officers of the Fifth Minnesota elected as chaplain a Methodist minister from Minneapolis named James F. Chaffee. But a few days later the canny governor found a solution of sorts for his political problem by appointing John Ireland chaplain to the Catholics of all Minnesota units serving in the western theater of operations.[35]

It was an anomalous position, as Ireland himself remembered it: "The chaplain's commission was from the State of Minnesota—not formally recognized by the U. S. Government. The duty of the State Chaplain was to go from one Minnesota regiment to another—the letters of the Governor securing for him from the federal authorities protection and liberty to travel."[36] By the time this "peculiar" and, as it shortly proved to be, impracticable appointment was made public, the Fifth Minnesota Volunteers had set off from St. Paul down the Mississippi to St. Louis and beyond, then had steamed up the Ohio as far as Paducah, and finally, after eleven days cooped up in the broiling hot paddle boat, had disembarked at Hamburg on the Tennessee River, a mile or so south of Pittsburgh Landing and the battlefield of Shiloh. In all likelihood John Ireland had gone with them.[37]

On May 24, 1862, the regiment assumed position in the Second Brigade, First Division, Army of the Mississippi, commanded by

General John Pope.[38] This force, together with General Ulysses S. Grant's Army of the Tennessee and General Don Carlos Buell's Army of the Ohio, was now part of the huge host — more than one hundred thousand effectives — under the overall command of General Henry W. Halleck. After the terrible blood-letting at the Battle of Shiloh (April 6-7, 1862), the Confederates had fallen back to the environs of Corinth, Mississippi, some twenty miles to the southwest. Their commander, General P. G. T. Beauregard, put them to work constructing a complex of fortifications and entrenchments to guard the approaches to Corinth, as though he were determined to hold the place at all costs. No one expected him to do otherwise. The logistical wisdom expressed in the famous quip often attributed to another Confederate general, Jubal Early — to win a battle "you got to git thar fustest with the mostest" — translated during the American Civil War into the use made by both sides of rivers and railroads. Victory hung not so much upon personal courage or generalship or even stamina — before the end both sides displayed those qualities in abundance — as it did upon the ability to transport troops and matériel swiftly and effectively. Corinth, an important rail center, an intersection of major north-south and east-west lines, was therefore a prize worth keeping or winning.

Though he outnumbered his Confederate counterpart by roughly two to one, Halleck followed Beauregard slowly and cautiously — caution, indeed, was Halleck's byword. After nearly a month's advance the Union army was just beginning to probe at Corinth's defense perimeter from the north and east when, on May 28, the Fifth Minnesota came under fire for the first time. Two or three rebel brigades struck Pope's outposts near the village of Farmington, a few miles due east of Corinth. During the twenty-minute fight that followed, the green soldiers acquitted themselves as green soldiers usually do, and one grizzled veteran later twitted the Fifth for having "shown its feathers" at Farmington.[39] But the regiment, however shaky its debut, stayed in formation and sustained its share of casualties, killed and wounded.[40] Thus, barely two weeks after they had left St. Paul, the farm boys and clerks — as well as the young priest only months removed from his French seminary near the Riviera — were introduced to the realities of war.

Beauregard had military realities to contend with, too, notable among them that he was outmanned and outgunned. He responded by doing the unexpected. The attack at Farmington proved to be merely a feint, part of an elaborate ruse that included the mounting of dummy cannon and dummy riflemen on the Corinth breastworks, and the chugging back and forth of locomotives to persuade the Unionists that reinforcements were arriving in the town. All this activity was in fact designed to cover a general withdrawal, and by the evening of May 28 the Confederates, having blown up the stores they could not move, were retreating in a not altogether orderly fashion south along the Mobile and Ohio railroad. Halleck, hesitant as ever, ordered a tentative pursuit, but he was unwilling to commit his whole force or to risk a major engagement.

So Pope's command followed Beauregard over a zigzag course for forty miles until June 9, when the halfhearted effort was abandoned. Many observers were to blame Halleck for adding a year to the war by allowing Beauregard to escape.[41] The Union commander, however, blandly announced a great victory[42] to the War Department and declared himself content for the time being to occupy west Tennessee and northern Mississippi and to control the railroad system from Memphis to north-central Alabama.

As for the men of the Fifth, "fresh from the exhilarating atmosphere of Minnesota," they "ever retain[ed] a vivid recollection" of the fruitless pursuit of Beauregard, "of those terrible marches under the scorching rays of the Mississippi sun." By mid-June the regiment had settled into quarters at Camp Clear Creek, near Corinth, a place remarkable (contrary to its name) for putrid water, bad food, stifling heat and humidity, lice, flies, and a variety of incapacitating diseases.[43]

John Ireland recalled thirty years afterward that he "joined the Fifth Minnesota, at Camp Clear Creek, Mississippi, shortly after the Battle of Pittsburgh Landing [Shiloh] and began his ministry."[44] His memory failed him here as to chronological details, but it was at Clear Creek that his position in the army was regularized. Reverend Chaffee, who apparently succumbed to one of the illnesses rampant in that unhealthy place, resigned the regimental chaplaincy on June 23, 1862, and Father Ireland succeeded him the next day.[45] Governor Ramsey's fanciful title of state chaplain for the whole

western theater thus went by the boards, which was just as well, because, though the Fourth Minnesota Volunteers were bivouacked
in the vicinity of Corinth, the Second and Third regiments were a
hundred miles and more away in central and eastern Tennessee (and
on July 13 the Third surrendered en masse to the celebrated Confederate cavalryman, Nathan Bedford Forrest).[46]

Catholic chaplains were by no means common in the Union
army, nor had there been, before the war, a tradition of Catholic
chaplaincies within the military establishment. Massive mobilization, however, which eventually totalled nearly a million men, of
whom a significant proportion was Catholic, made it necessary for
the federal authorities to open chaplaincies to any "regular ordained
minister of a Christian denomination."[47] Even so, only forty-three
priests were attached to the many hundreds of regiments raised in
the northern states during the Civil War, and most of them, like Ireland, served a relatively brief time. Undoubtedly one reason for
such a small number was that the regimental officers, who elected
the chaplain, represented classes that were overwhelmingly non-
Catholic and, in many instances, anti-Catholic. Ireland himself
blamed the timidity of the Catholic bishops who "wo[e]fully
neglected . . . a grand opportunity . . . to the Church in
America. . . . Priests, of course, were scarce enough in the country: but better have left two parishes to be taken care of by one pastor, and to have followed to [the] field the heroes of the country."[48]

Civil War chaplains did not enjoy the privileges of rank, because,
strictly speaking, they were civilians, not commissioned officers.
They were paid, however, first at a rate equivalent to that received
by captains of cavalry and, later, a little less. Ireland earned $118 a
month in salary and allowances, which must have seemed to him a
princely sum.[49] He did not wear a uniform of federal blue, though
a uniform of sorts for chaplains did evolve in the course of the war:
a coat of black broadcloth which reached to the knee and which had
nine black cloth-covered buttons down the front, three on each cuff,
and four at the hem, with standing collar but without shoulder straps
or insignia. A plain black hat, decorated only by a cord of the same
somber color, completed the outfit. John Ireland never felt obliged
to dress in this fashion, and at least once his office went unrecognized
when he was among soldiers who did not know him.[50]

The War Department defined the duties of the chaplain only in the broadest terms. He had to report four times a year to his regimental commander on "the moral and religious condition of the regiment" and to offer "such suggestions as may conduce to the social happiness and moral improvement of the troops." Apart from fulfilling this largely formal and infrequent obligation, and from the duty of presiding at a public service for any deceased member of the regiment,[51] young Father Ireland was left pretty much to his own devices. As he recalled his experiences much later (and, to be sure, romanticized them), they followed a predictable pattern.

In accord with the very nature of Catholicism, the sacramental ministry had to be Ireland's first concern. Administration of the Eucharist, penance, and extreme unction took precedence over exhortation. Not that he neglected to exhort. "So sweet," he remembered, "to console sick and wounded — So sweet to sit around campfires with the 'boys' — So sweet to chide one and encourage another." But what gave Chaplain Ireland unique importance in the eyes of Catholic soldiers — young men away from home for the first time, afraid, their idealism eroded by the physical and moral degradation all around them — was their conviction that he could do what no one else could do: shrive them of their sins on the eve of battle, feed them the body of Christ, anoint their senses with the holy oil should the worst befall them. So Ireland said mass on Sundays, and kept his sermons short and simple.[52] He heard confessions regularly and, when there were rumors of impending action, for hours on end. He "gave time and labor to all those within reach of which he came — visiting them — visiting hospitals — riding ten, twenty and more miles across country, alone, to reach a hospital."

Out of snippets of memory[53] John Ireland drew a more or less conventional picture of a zealous chaplain going about his work: a hardened sinner, who kept a promise to his mother to recite a Hail Mary daily, was brought back to the fullness of the faith just before he died; two soldiers, both Protestants, fell victim to smallpox, were banished from the camp and from their comrades, and found their only succor in the ministrations of the Catholic chaplain; a desperately wounded man, "youthful in years, about 22 years old, innocent in face, and in soul," sensed the presence of a priest outside the hospital tent in which he lay, called for him, and received from him the final consolations of the church; "An officer, . . . shot in the face, blood pouring out, . . . wrote on a slip of paper, 'Chaplain,' and the slip, red with blood, . . . was handed to me. I hurried: the man was conscious—dying fast. 'Speak to me,' he said, 'of Jesus.'. . . There was no time to talk of Church. I talked of the Savior, and of sorrow for sin. The memory of that scene has never been effaced from my mind."[54]

The tapestry thus stitched together does not tell a false tale, but it does not tell a complete one, either. And what was forgotten over the interval of thirty years, during which other interests, other anxieties pressed upon his mind, may be as important in understanding John Ireland as what was remembered. He came to the regiment, after all, hardly older or more seasoned than the soldiers to whom he ministered, hardly more than a boy. For all practical purposes he learned how to be a priest while choking on the dust—the summer of 1862 was abnormally dry in northern Mississippi[55]—and fighting off the flies at Camp Clear Creek. He could not but have achieved a higher level of maturity during those ten months of soldiering. If he remembered the gallantry he witnessed, the nobility of the cause, the poignant death-bed conversions, and not the waste, the brutality, the spiritual failures, it is neither surprising nor blameworthy. He took pride, and understandably so, in having been tested in that uniquely masculine world, an army on campaign. "We were soldiers of Abraham Lincoln," he told a group of veterans in 1897. "This the praise we covet; this the memory we yearn to transmit to the coming years."[56] The Irish immigrant boy, a refugee from his homeland, now belonged to the greatest military machine so far created in the annals of man. The French seminarist, accustomed to the hushed murmur of the cloister, was now Lincoln's soldier who heard the rattle of drums, the crash of artillery, the shrieks of maimed and dying men, the whine of the minié ball, the blood-curdling "rebel yell" of charging Confederate infantry. In after years, at innumerable encampments of the Grand Army of the Republic, John Ireland proudly took his place among the million men who, in their youth, had rallied to save the Union. Like them he had earned the right to wear the badge of an American patriot.

By the middle of the summer of 1862 the strategic situation in the western theater had shifted dramatically. The dispirited Confederate army that Beauregard had led out of Corinth at the end of May found new life under a new commander, General Braxton Bragg. Boldly seizing the initiative, Bragg moved his troops north and east, concentrating them in Chattanooga and employing them to maneuver the Unionists out of middle and east Tennessee. His colleague, General E. Kerby Smith, on August 11, mounted a raid-in-force into Kentucky. The remarkable success of this expedition encouraged Bragg to follow with a full-scale invasion of that state early in September. Cries of dismay were raised across the north; the roads to Louisville and even Cincinnati lay open to rebel columns at the very moment when General Robert E. Lee had driven his way into Maryland and threatened Washington, Philadelphia, and Baltimore. Back in Mississippi semi-independent commands under Generals Sterling Price and Earl Van Dorn operated out of reach of the federals. Neither force was large enough to pose a serious threat by itself, but a combination of the two could be formidable. And there was always the chance that they might slip away to the north and provide a heavy reinforcement for Bragg.

Meanwhile, the federal command structure had undergone drastic change. Halleck's enormous army had been broken up, and Halleck himself was dispatched to Washington as administrative chief of all the Union armies. Pope had been promoted to the eastern theater and there received such a thumping from Lee (August 30) that he was promptly demoted to Minnesota, to deal with the Indian war that had broken out there. Buell had been given an army of his own and sent into east Tennessee, toward Chattanooga, but his dilatory tactics there proved no match for Bragg and Smith. U. S. Grant, finally, was assigned to the District of West Tennessee, which stretched from Cairo, Illinois, into western Alabama. His subordinates were Generals William T. Sherman, headquartered at Memphis, Edward O. C. Ord at Jackson, Tennessee, and William Starke Rosecrans, who guarded a front astride the Memphis and Charleston Railroad eighty miles long, from Corinth east to the outskirts of Decatur, Alabama.[57]

Under this reorganization, Rosecrans — "voluble, highly critical, cocksure, competent"[58] — commanded four divisions totaling about twenty-three thousand men. The Fifth Minnesota Volunteers belonged to the Second Division under General David S. Stanley. At first the new arrangement made little difference to the Fifth, which continued to languish through the blinding heat at Camp Clear Creek. Rosecrans did, however, set in motion dietary and medical improvements which substantially reduced the incidence of disease among the troops stationed there. In August the Fifth took up position in the vicinity of Tuscumbia, Alabama, and for the next month patrolled a section of the Memphis and Charleston. It was for the most part uneventful duty, enlivened once or twice by raids of guerrillas endeavoring to cut the line. "The surroundings near Tuscumbia," noted one soldier, "were more favorable [than at Clear Creek]. The country was healthy, and abounded in supplies that in a large measure supplanted, or at least relieved, the monotony of the historical hardtack and side bacon."[59]

On August 29 Rosecrans heard rumors that Van Dorn and Price had begun to move, perhaps toward Bolivar, in southernmost Tennessee. Four days later, Grant, unsure of the enemy's intentions, ordered Rosecrans to pull all units stationed in Alabama back into his main force around Corinth. The Fifth Minnesota accordingly broke camp and withdrew slowly westward. A week and more of tense waiting followed, during which Rosecrans became convinced that Price, at least, was preparing to slip through the Unionist lines and head for Kentucky.

The wily Price was indeed on the prowl, but his objective was not what his adversaries expected. He concentrated his little army southeast of Corinth, and on the morning of September 13 his cavalry attacked the railroad town of Iuka, Mississippi. The Unionist brigade garrisoned there repulsed the first assaults, but then, abandoning a large quantity of stores (three thousand dollars' worth, according to John Ireland), it disengaged and retreated toward Corinth. The Fifth Minnesota had arrived in Iuka the day before. "We had not the good fortune," Ireland reported, "of coming into contact with the enemy [there], although we remained waiting for him in trenches for upwards of twenty hours." Instead the regiment participated in the withdrawal, marching "fearlessly through a hostile country, in the rear of the brigade, the most dangerous position being assigned to us, as the fitest [sic] to hold it."[60] Colonel Lucius Hubbard, the new commandant[61] of the Fifth, described the action more prosaically: "In leaving Iuka the Fifth Minnesota acted as rear guard, and was charged with the duty of keeping at bay any pursuing force. It had no trouble with the enemy in the discharge of this duty, but was nearly overwhelmed and almost trampled into the earth by a mob of 5000 or more [Negro] contrabands with their worldly effects, who crowded the column on flank and rear, in their eager efforts to escape the dangers of rebel pursuit."[62]

Price brought all of his forces into Iuka on September 14. Then, Confederate intelligence being no better than federal, it was his turn to wait. Grant resolved to crush him in a pincers between Rosecrans from the southwest and Ord from the northwest. Fighting commenced on the afternoon of September 19 and continued until nightfall. Price's divisions were badly cut up, but confusion on the Unionist side prevented the jaws of the pincers from closing, and the Confederates succeeded in getting away to the south. Grant blamed the excitable Rosecrans for Price's escape, and thus began the antagonism between the two generals, which lasted throughout the war and beyond.[63]

The Battle of Iuka was an extremely bloody affair, with a percentage of casualties as high as that of any engagement fought during the war. The Fourth Minnesota suffered three killed and forty-four wounded. The Fifth, however, remained once again unengaged, and once again its chaplain employed his exuberant prose to explain the reason: "The dark clouds of night closed too soon over the battle-ground to afford us an opportunity of showing of what materials we are composed." He recalled hearing confessions all through the night of September 18–19: "Are you sorry for your sins? said I to a hard case kneeling before me. Sorry, Father, is it? Don't you hear the rattle of musketry along the picket lines?"[64]

Price found Van Dorn at Pontotoc, Mississippi, by September 22, and placed his forces under the latter's command. Six days later this enlarged Confederate army—twenty regiments of infantry, five batteries, and about a thousand cavalrymen, roughly equivalent in numbers to the troops at Rosecrans's disposal—passed through Ripley on its way north.[65] Grant and his lieutenants were reasonably sure that an assault on Corinth was imminent, but Van Dorn's jerky line of march, skillfully obscured by a cloud of cavalry, could have meant that he was headed farther north or west. So the federal units remained stretched out to meet whatever eventuality. Stanley's division, including the Fifth Minnesota, encamped again near Clear Creek, six miles southwest of Corinth.

On October 1 Van Dorn was reported to have crossed the state line into Tennessee. At dawn the next day the federals at brigade strength encountered intense pressure ten miles north of Corinth, pressure that continued on them all that day and relentlessly pushed them back toward the town. In the morning, October 3, the attack began again, clearly in force, and Van Dorn's intentions were now revealed: he had marched his men in a great loop, feinting toward various possible objectives in Tennessee, in order to come at Corinth from the north and to deal with Rosecrans before Ord could arrive in support.

Rosecrans lost no time in deploying three of his divisions to re-sist the Confederate advance, while keeping Stanley's division as an overall reserve within Corinth itself. The Fifth Minnesota, how-ever, did not even get to the town.[66] As Stanley moved forward early in the morning of October 3—a Friday—the Fifth was un-ceremoniously detached from the division and left behind to guard a bridge about four miles southwest of Corinth. There the regiment stayed throughout that blisteringly hot day—at noon the thermom-eter read ninety-four degrees—and listened to the gunfire, which grew louder with every passing hour. Colonel Hubbard was not told why holding the bridge was important; he could only speculate that the Unionists might have to retreat across it if they were driven out of Corinth.[67]

The inactivity and uncertainty rubbed the nerves of Hubbard and his men raw. By late afternoon the sound of the battle seemed to have shifted from the north to the west of Corinth, and Hubbard began to worry that if the Confederate attack swung farther in that direction the Fifth might be cut off from the main body of the Un-ion army. It also occurred to him that his insignificant command— an understrength regiment of seven companies with practically no battle experience—might simply have been forgotten in the midst of all the excitement.[68] He sent his quartermaster, Lieutenant Wil-liam B. McGrorty, into Corinth, ostensibly to secure rations but really to inquire whether anyone in authority remembered the little Fifth Minnesota and its lonely vigil at the bridge. Hubbard later de-scribed the next events.

"The night was pitchy dark" when McGrorty returned with a cavalry escort and orders to retire into the town. The regiment, muffling all sound, followed a road that twisted through a "dense growth of timber" to "within a few rods of the right flank of the rebels" whose campfires flickered nearby. The Fifth reached Corinth some time after eight o'clock and bivouacked on the northwest edge of the town, "in a reserve position near the Mobile and Ohio railroad depot." There the men lay on their arms, with the forward Confederate line a scant six hundred yards away. A bright full moon rode high across the sky.[69]

As dawn approached on October 4, and Van Dorn prepared to renew the battle, the problem that confronted him was simple and unenviable. The brilliant maneuver that had enabled him to get between Ord and Rosecrans, and the hard fighting of the day before, had earned him a dubious reward—or, to put the matter another way, had revealed the flaw in his plan. His success heretofore had placed him in the situation a field commander most wanted to avoid. Now, in order to win a decisive victory, he had to strike directly at an enemy waiting for him behind defensive works. For Rosecrans was facing him from within a rough semi-circle of entrenchments and fortifications originally constructed by Beauregard in the spring and immeasurably strengthened since by new batteries, strings of rifle pits, and an abatis of felled trees all along the front. The prospect looked bleak to Van Dorn who, nevertheless, had no tactical choice but to press forward; and many young men in blue and in butternut would pay the price that day with their lives.

"Long before the first grey streaks of dawn began to lighten the horizon," Hubbard remembered, the Fifth Minnesota Volunteers had a rude awakening. The first shell of a massive Confederate bombardment "exploded not a dozen feet" from where they lay sleeping, and one of them was severely wounded.[70] Ireland thought "the Tishomingo Hotel [adjacent to the depot], with its lighted windows, and a smoldering fire in a corner of the square where the Fifth was encamped, were inviting targets and [therefore] received the first fire of the enemy."[71] Soon the federal guns were responding with barrages of their own, and the artillery duel raged on unabated for nearly two hours. "It was grand," said a Union officer with a romantic turn of mind. "The different calibers, metals, shapes, and distances of the guns caused the sounds to resemble the chimes of old Rome when all her bells rang out."[72]

About seven o'clock the cannon on both sides ceased firing, and, except for the intermittent pop-pop of sharpshooters exchanging rifle shots, an eerie silence fell over the town, the trenches, and the woods nearby. The Fifth Minnesota stood nervously at the ready along the Mobile and Ohio tracks, facing west, at almost the exact center of the Unionist defense perimeter but still five or six hundred yards behind its most salient point. Just before nine o'clock the regiment was reduced to six companies when Stanley ordered Company A detached and to the right for scouting and skirmishing duty.[73] A few minutes afterward "the rebel batteries opened [again] and the earth seemed convulsed by the incessant discharges of artillery that followed. . . . Soon the deafening roar of musketry plainly indicated the enemy was assaulting our lines."[74] Van Dorn, two hours later than he had intended,[75] was indeed hurling his infantry forward in a double staged attack, first to the right-center of the federal line and then to its left. The first blow almost succeeded.

Hubbard never forgot the "stentorian yell" of the rebel columns as they smashed their way into the square adjoining the railroad station. And John Ireland, forty-five years after the event, called it "a scene . . . never to be forgotten, rising as vividly now before my mind as on the historic morning of October 4th, 1862 — Union soldiers from battery and from infantry rushing wildly across the square, at the opposite side from the railroad track along which was deployed the Fifth, and the Confederates soon appearing in hot pursuit. We were no more than three hundred feet from the enemy, who, seemingly not noticing us, continued to thicken their line and hasten across the square, with the apparent intent of reaching at once the center of the town."[76] Nor had Ireland's memory played tricks on him; the young chaplain recorded pretty much what the old archbishop recalled. "Suddenly a strange commotion arises behind us. We turn around, and great is our surprise. At the lower end of the square the artillery are skedaddling with an astounding rapidity; the infantry rush in through every inlet; the citizens and all idle gazers-on disappear in a second; the Butternuts emerge from the streets leading into the square. It was a solemn moment."[77]

It was the crucial moment. If the break in the line were not closed, the Confederates could take the federal entrenchments from the rear, and Corinth would be lost, if not Rosecrans's whole army. Stanley galloped into the mêlée, shouting orders through the smoke and noise, as did Rosecrans himself. "I had the personal mortification," the Unionist commander said later, of seeing "our weary and jaded troops . . . scattering among the houses."[78] Hubbard saw them, too, and behind the fleeing Unionists "the eager Confederates were already entering the streets of Corinth, driving themselves like a human wedge through the opening they had made."[79]

Now Stanley ordered Hubbard to support a beleaguered battery right and front. In the brief time it took the little regiment to swing obediently ninety degrees and to trot forward about a hundred yards toward the proper position, the battery was swept away by the rebel advance. But that pell-mell advance had exposed the Confederate column's right flank. With the coolness of a veteran Hubbard told his men to halt and to come into formation. "I see them now," John Ireland said from across the years, "a straight line, reaching across the square, . . . rifles clinched [*sic*] in firm hands awaiting anxiously the order to fire. Nor did the order come in a hurry. Colonel Hubbard, under perfect self-control, waited until the line of the enemy had strung itself fully across the square, until opposite every rifle of the Fifth there were Confederates to be stricken down." The first volley cut a great swath through the rebel ranks. The men of the Fifth reloaded and fired again. "The effect was tremendous, instantaneous. The Confederates fell, staggered, turned back."[80]

Or perhaps they paused long enough to lose their momentum, long enough to give a respite to the federal units that, moments before, had been "scattering among the houses." The Confederates at any rate stopped their rush across the square long enough to shoot back at the little regiment on their right flank, and in that instant the whole tenor of the battle changed. Resistance stiffened on the rebel left, and, from the other side, Hubbard, even as his men began to fall around him—seven were killed and sixteen wounded in a few minutes—continued methodically to direct upon the Confederates a murderous fire.

"Oh, what an admirable spectacle," cried Chaplain Ireland, "to gaze then on our brave boys! With what unanimity, with what rapidity, what visible coolness and unflinching courage, they poured in volley after volley into the ranks of their opponents!" Encountering pressure now all along their front, the Confederates fell back, slowly and stubbornly at first, contesting every foot of ground. Then they broke, "and hotly were they pursued through a narrow street until they reached the limits of the town, and concealed themselves in the woods."[81] The Fifth followed them as far as the crest of a ridge along which ran the original line of entrenchments. Under the shelter of the timber they regrouped, and then came one more time, raising the shrill rebel yell and running through the tangle of felled trees toward the muzzles of the federal guns. "I at once opened upon [them] a hot fire," Hubbard reported, "which, with the fire from along the line upon my right, which had now rallied and was reforming, arrested [their] progress and soon drove [them] back under cover of the timber."[82]

Repulsed on the right center, Van Dorn played his second, and last, card. At eleven o'clock drums and bugles and a volcano of rifle and cannon fire announced the Confederate assault upon the federal left and upon the anchor of defensive works there, a cluster of artillery and of rifle pits called Battery Robinett. In the vanguard were Colonel William P. Rogers and his sharpshooters from Texas and Arkansas. John Ireland, still in the square near the railroad station, was a witness to the prodigies of wasted valor accomplished by the Confederates in that bloody hour: "[I] had full opportunity to watch the Texan [*sic*] Rangers under Colonel Rogers charging valiantly upon Fort Robinett."[83] At the time he wrote a fevered tribute: "We were all in ecstasy, seeing the rebels charging upon Fort Robinette [*sic*], hurrying through the woods at the right, following up, with a firm step, the road leading from the edge of the wood towards the fort, and then under the galling fire of our infantry which outflanked them, in spite of all the terrible discharges of cannister and grape which thinned their ranks to a frightful extent, leaping over the parapets or trying to turn around to find the entrance to the fort."[84] Driven back once with ghastly loss, the Confederates stormed Robinett a second time, seized it for a moment, only to have the full fire-power of three of Stanley's regiments turned upon them. Rogers, waving the Stars and Bars from the battery's parapet, was shot dead, and what remained of his command streamed back in disorder to the woods from which the attack had been launched. That night a Unionist soldier wrote in his diary: "Such bravery has never been excelled on any field as the useless assaults on Robinett."[85]

But that bravery had not been enough, and shortly after noon Van Dorn, gathering together what Hubbard called, with pardonable exaggeration, "the wreck of his army,"[86] ordered a general retreat. He conducted it with a skill reminiscent of his march upon Corinth, and though large federal contingents menaced him on every side he managed to elude them.[87] The Fifth Minnesota joined in the fruitless pursuit, chasing Van Dorn, as Ireland put it, "over hills and vales, under sunshine and rain, by the most circuitous route, for over the distance of a hundred miles."[88] But it was all in vain, and by the middle of October the regiment was back in the familiar confines of Camp Clear Creek, and its chaplain was making his priestly rounds among the hospital tents.[89]

John Ireland's military career after the Battle of Corinth was something of an anti-climax. He ministered to the men of the Fifth Minnesota until the following spring, an interval during which he shared with them the soldier's ordinary lot of drudgery, boredom, dirt, loneliness, bad food, and sickness. He never saw another battle, hardly even a skirmish. During the course of those gloomy months the regiment was posted to central Mississippi, back to Tennessee, then to Arkansas and Louisiana. Nothing could have been less glamorous than the twenty-four-hour marches it was ordered to undertake through cold rain and biting wind, "without," Hubbard recalled, "much fighting," and without, so far as any of the soldiers could see, much purpose. Nothing could have been more futile than "standing in the water up to one's knees and delving in the mud with a spade," in order to build a system of canals which would, in effect, redirect the Mississippi around the Confederate fortresses guarding the river's passage.

This last enterprise—"The men regarded [it]," Hubbard said, "the most menial, and, as the event proved, it was the most unprofitable service they were called upon to perform during the war"[90]—was an early stage of Grant's fateful campaign against Vicksburg, but by this time John Ireland had had enough. In his let-

ter of resignation he explained that his bishop needed him back
home, and explained further "that in this regiment the number of
those belonging to the Catholic church (of which church I am a
minister) is comparatively so reduced, as not to warrant any more
the continual attendance of a clergyman of that church." The letter
was dated Helena, Arkansas, March 19, 1863.[91] A week later, as
Grant reorganized his divisions and shifted their locale, the Fifth
moved downriver as far as Duckport, Louisiana. There on April
3 — the day the Fifth Minnesota received its new assignment to
Sherman's Fifteenth Corps — John Ireland was mustered out of the
service.[92]

Experience of war never leaves a man unmarked, and Chaplain
Ireland could not have been an exception. Yet it remains difficult to
determine specifically how his participation in the Civil War
affected him. Too little is known about him before he joined the
Fifth Minnesota Volunteers to say with any confidence that he went
into the conflict this sort of person and emerged from it that sort.
Moreover, his own memory of the events combines with the later
perceptions of others to blur the picture. Take, for example, the
matter of his resignation. In 1892 he stated flatly that "ill health"
was his sole reason for leaving the army.[93] No doubt he believed
this to be true when he said it, but, in fact, it was not true. Certainly
he was ill periodically during his months in the south, but then
nearly all the strong young men in the regiment were similarly or
worse afflicted due to extreme physical exertion in an unfamiliar
and inhospitable climate and under very unhealthy living conditions.[94] Ireland's brief tenure should not itself have been something
he needed to explain away; short-term enlistments were the norm
in the early years of the war. Perhaps he unconsciously regretted
that after he left it the Fifth Minnesota went on to establish a brilliant record, covering itself with glory from Vicksburg to Nashville
to Mobile. While John Ireland was ministering to the good people
of the cathedral parish back in St. Paul, Lucius Hubbard was being
decorated for "conspicuous gallantry" and brevetted a brigadier
general.[95] There was at any rate a note of fantasy as well as poign-
ancy in the words with which Ireland concluded his 1892
memoir — "My years [*sic*] of chaplaincy were the happiest and most

Ireland reminiscing with Commissioner James Tanner, Adjutant General Tweedale, and Judge Loren W. Collins of the Grand Army of the Republic, about 1903. (Photo by Luxton; MHS)

fruitful years of my ministry"[96] — since, in fact, he exercised that ministry for less than ten months.

Surely the most arresting passage in Ireland's contemporary depiction of the Battle of Corinth is that, quoted above, describing the Confederate attack on Battery Robinett: "We were all in ecstasy" watching Colonel Rogers and his comrades as they plunged through sheets of flame and clouds of grapeshot toward certain death. Indeed, the whole account throbs with an unabashed *joie de bataille*. And it is revealing in other respects. It possesses not the slightest hint of religious sensibility, not even, until the very end, a conventional invocation of the deity, who is then heralded as "the God of armies." Nor does it display any appreciation of the nobility or high moral purpose of the Unionist cause. The accent is entirely upon the manliness, the vigor, the courage of the soldiers, particularly, of course, those of the Minnesota Fifth. "We soldiers of the

Fifth have a special right to pride ourselves in what has been accomplished. . . . Great is our renown in this army. The other regiments fully appreciate our valor; our praise is on every tongue."[97] The audience for whom Ireland wrote this piece—it appeared in a secular newspaper in St. Paul—may to some degree explain its jingoistic tone. But the sentiments expressed in it may also provide a genuine measure of the man who, in future years, seemed to be raised to ecstatic heights by the battles he engaged in.

Given the strategic situation in the fall of 1862, the Unionist victory at Corinth was not unimportant. Such a restrained judgment, however, did not satisfy John Ireland who, as the years passed, convinced himself that but for Corinth the North would have lost the war.[98] He similarly exaggerated the part played in the battle by the Minnesota Fifth. "I am happy to bear witness," the Fifth's divisional commander, General Stanley, had reported, "to the gallant fight of this little regiment. . . . Few regiments on the field did more effective killing than they."[99] Ireland seized upon Stanley's remark, quoted it approvingly,[100] and gradually interpolated it into a kind of awkward syllogism: the victory at Corinth saved the Union; but the Fifth "saved the day" at Corinth; therefore, the Fifth Regiment, Minnesota Volunteer Infantry, saved the Union.

It is this perspective that makes the story of the cartridges so intriguing. Some twenty-five years after the war, published accounts in various parts of the country[101] described Ireland, during the fight at the Corinth railroad depot, when the men of the Fifth were running short of ammunition, passing along the line with a box of cartridges across his shoulders and shouting above the din of the battle, "Here are cartridges for you, boys! Here are more cartridges!" Other legends about Ireland's intrepidity came and went—perhaps the least plausible had the tone-deaf chaplain, a recent graduate of French seminaries where the Revolution of '89 was anathema, singing the *Marseillaise* as he urged the troops forward[102]—but the tale of the cartridges persisted until his death.[103]

Ireland himself never referred directly to the incident, though on some public occasions he went out of his way to stress his role in the war as that of a non-combatant.[104] Yet it was significant that the story appeared in his own diocesan weekly without note or comment.[105] And the reluctance to deny it explicitly raises the possibility that at times, and in private, Ireland may have reworked his syllogism into a narrower and more personal conclusion: the Union was preserved at Corinth, and the Fifth Minnesota won the victory there, and Chaplain Ireland, passing out fistfuls of cartridges, kept the Fifth on the firing line. Not an incongruous accolade, it might have seemed, for a man widely praised, and damned, as an Americanist.

After Corinth William S. Rosecrans was rewarded with command of the Army of the Cumberland in place of the ineffective Don Carlos Buell. Over the next eleven months he won some hard-fought victories and gained a reputation as a general who took care of his men. "He [also]," said Lucius Hubbard, "gave evidence on many fields of skill, sagacity, and courage, not excelled by any of his contemporaries of the Civil War."[106] But disaster overtook him and his army at Chickamauga, Tennessee (September 19–20, 1863), and Rosecrans never really recovered from the severe Unionist defeat that occurred there. The War Department refused him any other command of importance, and, thanks largely to the unrelenting enmity of U. S. Grant, virtually put him on the shelf. After the war he engaged in various business enterprises, was briefly minister to Mexico (an appointment quashed by Grant as soon as the latter was inaugurated president), served a couple of terms in Congress, worked in the federal bureaucracy. But he seemed to lack the stability of character and the simple good luck to achieve the success his otherwise considerable talents might have earned for him.

Rosecrans was a Catholic,[107] and there were those who thought religious animosity had contributed to the failure of his military career. John Ireland did not share this view — "prejudices exist where Catholics give cause for them, and seldom elsewhere"[108] — but his regard for his old commander was certainly not lessened by their common faith. The Battle of Corinth had been a high point in both men's lives. So, in 1889, when Ireland asked General Rosecrans to address a message to a reunion of the Fifth Minnesota Volunteers, the latter responded warmly: "My dear Friend and Comrade, yes, you were with me at the Battle of Corinth. . . . We were . . . the patriots, dying and living, who offered up their best that this nation might live."[109]

V

"Father Mathew of the Northwest"

1863–73

THE PRIEST, young Father Ireland, had finished his sermon at the 10:00 A.M. mass, celebrated in the Cathedral of St. Paul on Sunday, July 26, 1863. Instead, however, of returning to the altar and continuing the service—the ordinary practice—he began to speak again.[1] "My dear friends," he said, "at the request of the Right Reverend Bishop, I shall before leaving the pulpit make a few remarks on a subject which has become one of the most engrossing topics of the day." The parishioners in attendance leaned forward a little, wondering what, after forty-five minutes of learned discourse, their assistant pastor had yet to tell them. They saw a man twenty-four years old who stood about five feet nine inches tall. He had a lanky, big-boned frame, its contours softened somewhat by the liturgical vestments he was wearing. His coarse black hair, which he parted on the left side, grew thick over the tops of his ears and around to the nape of his neck. The slate-colored eyes, the wide, severe mouth inherited from Judith Naughton, the jutting jaw line, the high, angular cheekbones—all these features combined to give his face an expression perpetually alert or even wary. He employed the quick gestures reminiscent of his father's, though the thrust and parry of his hands had more grace and more calculation in them. The most memorable thing about him—or at any rate the physical characteristic most arresting upon a first encounter—was the timbre of his voice: vibrant, resonant, powerful enough to be heard in the farthest corner of the largest hall, honeyed thunder sometimes and sometimes a throaty growl, but always loud, dominant, moving.

The tone Ireland adopted on this occasion was grave. "In order to restore peace to the country, our Chief Magistrate has thought [it] necessary to make a new levy of men, and, to obtain the requisite number, the system of Conscription is to be resorted to."[2] No doubt, he continued, the draft will take effect soon in St. Paul, "and it behooves your Pastors to remind you of your duty in such circumstances." "True Catholics" always obey the law, and he was confident that "never by your conduct will you disgrace that Church we all love so tenderly." Those required to take an oath in this connection must remember that "to swear to a falsehood is a heinous mortal sin." "Riots" had occurred elsewhere in the country as a means of resistance to the draft.[3] "We presume there is no probability of such occurrences taking place in our city." Nevertheless, "[rumors] that some dissatisfaction towards this measure of the government has been expressed have reached our ears. And it is well to tell you that the Church emphatically condemns such proceedings." The priest looked down over the silent congregation, and then the booming voice rang out again. "If a riot should occur amongst us, or any public demonstration against the execution of the laws, we here beforehand repudiate all Catholics who would, by word or deed, partake in or give aid to or countenance the proceedings. Until they would have made retraction of their conduct, the sacraments of the Church would be refused to them, and were they to lose their lives by means of the riot, they would not obtain the benefit of a Christian burial." Then, more softly: "Take care, my dear friends. Ranting politicians, under the thick cloak of hypocrisy—through an apparent interest in your welfare but in reality to satisfy their own lust for power and riches—may breathe amongst you words of discord. . . . Be led by no one; consult your own consciences, and I know you will do what is right, because your own natures never prompt you but to good and noble actions." With that he stepped out of the pulpit and strode purposefully across the sanctuary and up to the altar. The mass continued with the recitation of the creed: "Credo in unum Deum."

This was the John Ireland who first became a familiar figure in St. Paul—and, it would appear, a commanding figure from the start. When he died in 1918 a few old residents recalled how he had returned from the war in the spring of 1863[4] and had settled into the bishop's house next to the cathedral on West Sixth Street. During the more than fifty tumultuous years in between it had become scarcely possible to think of St. Paul without thinking also of Ireland, so closely intertwined were the man and the city. And difficult to appreciate that before 1863 Ireland had hardly had a home in any but the most superficial sense of the word. His life had been, up till then, a series of abrupt dislocations — goodbye to County Kilkenny and to a childhood lost to the ravages of famine and pestilence, and hello in turn to a half-dozen other places and to the indignities and uncertainties that naturally befall the refugee, the alien, the soldier on campaign.

These harsh rites of passage were mostly behind him now, but they had done much to mold and toughen him. He had been tried and not found wanting, with the result that he had already accumulated a good deal of self-esteem. And though there still remained some hard lessons to learn and a maturing process to complete, the moment had arrived for John Ireland to enter upon a man's estate and to take on, for the first time, permanent responsibilities and a set of stable relationships. One sign of this coming of age was the young priest's punctiliousness about his dress — around the environs of the church a Roman cassock buttoned from throat to shoe-top, and on the streets of the town a sober black suit with clerical collar. Propriety, not fashion, was his concern. Clemence Cretin had taught him the importance of clean linen and ironed shirts; his own instinct taught him that the leader of an impoverished and often heedless people needed to look the part.

And to sound the part, with little diffidence or reserve. Ireland's strong stand on the conscription question, his first venture into the public arena, presaged a long career of declamations, which he delivered authoritatively and which he expected to be listened to and obeyed. From the beginning he assumed it was his right to exercise leadership within the community. No priest, however young and inexperienced, had to earn the deference of his people, though of course by his own personal or professional failings he could lose it. Ireland came to his post with the conviction — bolstered by the accepted theology and by the economic and social realities of the day — that a priest deserved to rule and, if he were up to the mark, to lead. A priest was better educated than his people; a priest was single-mindedly dedicated to the service of the common good (a dramatic symbol of which was the celibate life he led); above all, a priest was set aside to dispense the mysteries of God and, if need be, to withhold them, as Ireland threatened to do to draft resisters.

On this issue, to be sure, he was following Bishop Grace's directive, but he spoke unabashedly in his own name, too, and in the name of all the clergy who shared the bishop's ministry. Some grumbling was heard among the flock—"Father Ireland won't support the families if the men go to war," one woman bitterly observed[5]—but by and large the Catholic people of St. Paul heeded their priest's injunction. The priest knew best. Certainly the priest knew better than any "ranting politicians." For one as capable as John Ireland—sublimely confident of his own powers, bubbling over with original ideas and projects, robust in health, articulate, energetic, strong willed—the automatic submission he received as he stood in the pulpit gave him an immense advantage over others similarly gifted. He could demonstrate, without a lengthy internship, that the deference given him was not ill placed.

In another sense, however, Ireland did play the role of the apprentice during these post-war years. This was the time he learned about Catholicism not simply as a creed or as a collection of abstract precepts but as a living system. The heart of Catholic life beat in the daily regimen of the parish. The round of priestly duties performed there—the celebration of mass, the hearing of confessions, preaching, visiting and ministering to the sick, catechizing, charitable endeavors, counseling the troubled, christenings, weddings, funerals—gave substance to that life. There was little drama in this kind of service. On the contrary, it readily turned into deadly routine. Yet without it the Catholic ideal went aglimmering, and the priest himself lost the central meaning of his life. Indeed, the Catholic people struck a bargain of sorts with their priests: a privileged position among them in exchange for regular sacramental ministration. No grandiose or spectacular activity could substitute for it, not even heroism on the battlefield. John Ireland, who had stood bravely upon a battlefield and who, later, would engage in many a grandiose and spectacular activity, never forgot this home truth.

Ireland's companions in the residence on Sixth Street were Bishop Grace, Father Ravoux, the vicar general, and two young

Priests attending the annual retreat of 1870. Bishop Thomas Grace is at center left, wearing a cross; to the right of him is Augustin Ravoux; to the right and below Ravoux is John Ireland. Thomas O'Gorman sits to the left and in front of the man in white. In the front row, Louis Caillet is second from left; James McGolrick is at the center and slightly higher than the others. (MHS)

French priests recruited during Bishop Cretin's time, Louis Caillet and Anatole Oster, both of whom were to serve the diocese of St. Paul with distinction over many years. Father Caillet, a gentle, self-effacing man, who had a following among the Irish immigrants as well as among the dwindling number of French, was pastor of the cathedral parish and hence John Ireland's immediate superior. The presence of the bishop in the house, however, made the difference in rank less significant, and in any case Ireland succeeded Caillet as pastor in 1867.[6]

The residence was more a missionary headquarters than an ordinary presbytery. The bishop was often gone on diocesan visitations and confirmation tours, while the other priests took duty wherever and whenever they were needed. Ireland traveled over much of the southern part of Minnesota during the early years of his ministry, to Mankato, Belle Plaine, Rochester, Winona, and, more frequently, to nearby Minneapolis.[7] He recalled later a walking trip from Waverly Mills to Watertown, west of Minneapolis, in the summer of 1866 during which he "got lost on crosspaths and trails. . . . Going on and really not knowing where, he began to feel rather perplexed and stood still in the midst of a cool, shady wood. Wiping his brow and trying to find his bearings, he thought he heard the tune of a church song, . . . real French church psalmody, well known to him from his years of study in France." He followed "the angelic sounds" through the woods and thickets until he came to a newly erected frame building. "There was a Catholic congregation gathered together without a priest, praying and singing psalms" in celebration of the feast of Corpus Christi. Father Ireland listened outside for awhile, and then, armed as he always was on these journeys with his suitcase and mass kit, entered the little church and conducted a eucharistic service for the astonished congregation.[8]

The bulk of Ireland's time and energy, however, was spent in St. Paul. After 1855 there was a separate parish, staffed by Benedictine monks, to serve German-speaking Catholics in the city, which meant that the clergy attached to the cathedral had for their charge the French- and English-speaking people. The latter were overwhelmingly Irish, and their numbers grew steadily, though not spectacularly, until 1890. At first Oster and Caillet tended to the

French portion of the congregation and Ireland to the Irish. This division of labor was by no means absolute. Ireland could preach in French if need be, and his two colleagues grew increasingly proficient in English as the years went by. Indeed, Caillet left the cathedral in 1867 to found an English-speaking parish in Lower Town. But for the most part the Irish looked upon Father Ireland as peculiarly their own, certainly an understandable attitude on their part and one perfectly congenial to the young priest, who showed early on a capacity to touch the celtic heart. "Tears indeed suffuse [Erin's] eyes," he told the crowd in the cathedral on St. Patrick's Day, 1869, "for they rest on the ivy-mantled ruins of [her] palaces and basilicas, on the fertile fields no longer the demesnes of [her] chieftains and their clans, on the emigrant ship, sailing from every port laden with the bravest and purest of [her] children, to be cast helpless on foreign strands."[9]

About 22 percent of the nearly thirteen thousand people who lived in St. Paul during the 1860s were of Irish extraction.[10] They may not have been "cast helpless" upon the strand of the Upper Mississippi, but their socio-economic position within the community was a very humble one. Most of them were day laborers, with a sprinkling of artisans and small shopkeepers. A significant proportion of the latter maintained saloons on infamous Minnesota Street, establishments largely patronized by their indigent countrymen. The Irish were concentrated in a squalid neighborhood known as "New Dublin" or simply "the patches." Their names appeared with embarrassing regularity on the police dockets. They might begin the celebration of St. Patrick's Day by attending mass, but not infrequently they ended it by being arrested as drunk and disorderly—arrested often, ironically enough, by other Irishmen who made up as much as one-third of the police force.[11]

These were the people among whom John Ireland first demonstrated his gifts for leadership. The influence he increasingly wielded over them sprang from many sources, not least from the priestly demeanor he developed and idealized during these years. It was clericalism of the loftiest kind and, as events were to prove, not inappropriate for its time and place. He later mused over the public virtues his early experience in St. Paul had taught him.[12] A priest must "take an interest in people, in their efforts to lift themselves up"; he must "teach the poor economy: our masses are in many regards no credit to us, [filling as they do] jails [and] poor-houses." He should "be affable" to all, "wish to see all, [not] putting them off" or turning them from the door on the plea that there "[is] no time now." Special care had to be taken of the poor and sick. Ireland insisted that a priest should "*re*visit them. The sick [deserve] no mere mechanical ministering, . . . even if [they are] not seriously sick": one should "talk, exhort, instruct, console. . . . A priest attentive to [the] sick is loved." But an avaricious priest, one who "counts [his] population by the number of those who pay," would earn their abiding dislike. A priest must be polite to everybody, and especially to the poor.

Yet Ireland did not mean that compassion for the poor involved antipathy toward the upper classes. The wise priest was "not so democratic as to despise the rich and persons of influence. The church needs such." Indeed, the priest himself must be a gentleman, exhibiting "good manners," avoiding all extravagance in dress and style of life. The priest's house ought to be a center of "order [and] simplicity." He should combine affability and approachableness with gravity. Ireland paraphrased Ecclesiasticus: "The clothing of the body, the laughter of the teeth, and the gait of a man tell what he is." The priest's commitment was to be expressed in "truthfulness, politeness; gravity in administering the sacraments; slowness in saying mass; punctuality; . . . dignity." There should be "no card playing" for the priest, "no bycling [*sic*], no cigar in [the] mouth before and after mass, . . . no gold chains" around his neck. Above all, priests must avoid gossiping, especially about each other and especially in the presence of the laity. They must cultivate mutual esteem and "not [be] jealous of one another," lest the bitter old proverb be fulfilled: "Wolves don't eat one another. Priests do."

But no priestly virtue or combination of virtues came to assume such importance in young Father Ireland's mind as studiousness. "How much depends on our teaching!" he later exclaimed. "Now God does not work miracles to fit us. . . . We must work and study. Take preaching; study [is] the remote and absolutely necessary preparation. We must be full of a subject to preach upon it. And this filling is not instantaneous. A living fountain, giving water to thousands, fed itself by sources scattered far and wide." And what about the confessional, that awesome place of healing and judgment? "It is fearful to think of so many souls depending for very life upon unskilled physicians." Ireland's conviction that the priest had to be first and foremost a teacher may have been nurtured in the contemplative quiet of a French seminary, but it bore fruit in the mean streets of a backwoods American town. "Children should know the catechism *litteratim,* and then understand it." There should be "private instruction for ignorant adults." In America, where there existed so much misinformed hostility to Catholicism and where secular newspapers loomed so large, the priest had a duty to "make use of the public press to instruct, [to] contradict false statements, [to] frighten maligners"; he should "let nothing pass" and never "object to having [his] sermons published." But neither child nor adult, neither rough mechanic nor prospective convert nor favored soul in need of special direction could gain anything from the priest who had "no time" to study. No editor in his right mind would publish the blatherings of a man who had "no time" to study. "How much time is lost," Ireland asked rhetorically, "[reading] newspapers, smoking, card-playing, sleeping?" It was no excuse for one to say he had "no taste for it. Study," Ireland said, "brings taste." A priest should build up a good library and subscribe to good reviews; reading more than one newspaper was a waste of time. Worthwhile books should "be gone through systematically" with notes taken down. "[To] preach well [is] to honor God's revelation," and in order to preach well a priest must make himself capable of "deep researches," without which there could be "no fullness, no freshness, no variety."

Ireland, as curate and pastor, learned something else that bore directly upon the leadership issue: "People flock to hear a priest who has something to say." The bulk of Ireland's influence came no doubt through the spoken word. Sunday after Sunday he held forth from the pulpit in the cathedral, and, as his reputation grew, so did opportunities to deliver lectures in various public halls around the town. He paid his audiences several compliments. First of all, he prepared his addresses with the greatest care, writing them out in longhand and going back over them to rephrase this thought and to clarify that. Secondly, he took pains not to talk down to his congregations. He appeared determined that his speeches should never sound like one peasant addressing other peasants. The result was edifying, to be sure, but also undoubtedly confusing on occasion to the simple and largely uneducated men and women in the pews, as when he told them that "the supernatural state [is] a gratuitous gift"[13] or that the union of Christ with the church is "a species of assimilation."[14] Nor did he deal with trivial subjects; the list of the extant sermons preached before 1875 reads like the headings of a theological manual.

He scrupulously abided by the formalities then in vogue. He always began with a scriptural quotation and then addressed his hearers as "My dear Brethren." He usually employed the first person plural, thus identifying himself with the congregation — a device recommended by all the books on homiletics; but when the occasion demanded he did not hesitate to shift to the first person singular, nor to use direct commands like "you should know" or "understand that." He regarded his sermons as "instructions," and he labored diligently to make them effective teaching instruments. Like most preachers of his generation he seldom spoke for fewer than forty-five minutes.

As to subject matter, understood in the broad sense, Ireland's sermons were almost all lessons in "Apologetics — the defense of religion."[15] Apologetics is a term that has come into some disrepute, and so it is necessary to appreciate what Ireland meant by it.[16] The act of faith, not itself an act of human reason, nevertheless cannot be unreasonable, that is, cannot fly in the face of the evidence which the human mind is capable of accumulating. Thus to believe in the resurrection of Christ — the central, and the most difficult, Christian mystery — is indeed a leap in the dark, as every act of faith must be. But it would be a grave sin of imprudence for the believer to fail to investigate insofar as he can the reasons why taking such a leap is consistent with his rational nature. Most believers have neither the training nor the leisure to explore these *praeambula fidei,* as the theologians called them, these explanations that demonstrate, not the reasonableness of the resurrection, but the reasonableness of believing in it. So the "apologetic" preacher sets before his congregation the text of the New Testament, not as a divine book now but as a source for the history of the first century, a source that examines the evidence of the empty tomb on the first Easter Sunday and the testimonies of witnesses over the next forty days. So John Ireland from the pulpit of the Cathedral of St. Paul in 1871:

> It is to history I appeal. Jesus lived in one of the most luminous historical ages—that of Augustus. . . . The facts concerning him, his declarations, his works, the events subsequent to his death, are transmitted to us by monuments differing from those which attest all past events only in this much—that they are by far more incontestably authentic and truthful, clear and precise.[17]

This conviction of the historicity of the gospels was a constant in Ireland's early sermons and a kind of bedrock beneath them.[18] From it he argued to the founding and nature of the church,[19] the indwelling of the Holy Ghost in the church,[20] and the necessity of dogma and a rule of faith.[21] The failure, as he saw it, of the Protestant churches to provide such a rule was sufficient proof that they did not teach the fullness of revelation.[22] Ireland was relentless in his public opposition to Protestantism, but he took care to keep his arguments theological and historical and not to vilify Luther, Calvin, or Henry VIII—a common enough practice among Catholic preachers and pamphleteers of the time. Similarly, though he engaged in controversy toe-to-toe with local Protestant divines, he avoided indulging in personalities. On at least one occasion, indeed, he even sounded wistful, if not ecumenical, about the divisions among Christians—and at the same time paid muted tribute to an Episcopal bishop, one of Minnesota's most revered religious leaders. "The object of the Fraternity Course [a series of lectures sponsored by the St. Paul Protestant churches] was to devise if possible some means of union. The necessity of union itself was beautifully set forth by Bishop [Henry B.] Whipple. . . . A blessed thought it was which B. Whipple gave as the keynote of the course—union. But in applauding the thought I grieved that all these efforts would be in vain, pursuing as they were a road that never could lead to unity. I felt I should tell them so."[23]

Like other great preachers of the nineteenth century—like Newman at St. Mary's, Oxford, or like Lacordaire at Notre Dame de Paris—Ireland framed his sermons in large measure to meet the perceived needs of his congregations. The rigidly anti-Protestant stance he assumed reflected, of course, his own honest view of the matter, but it also took into account the condition of his audience, immigrants and the children of immigrants, who had to live in a culture hostile—often militantly so—to their religion. The result was a homiletic tone often strongly negative.[24] But this was by no means always the case. The same objective could be achieved if Catholics could be persuaded to take pride in the church to which they belonged. Ireland spared no effort to get them to see themselves as specially blessed even if they did occupy the lower strata of society. "This church, as she exists today," he told a congregation of laborers in Minneapolis, probably in 1873,

> is the most stupendous organization on the face of the earth. She is the most complete, perfect organization, possessing, in a supereminent degree, all the elements of corporate life, a well-defined constitution, a powerful hierarchy, clearly-stated laws binding together into one solid body the governing and the governed. Her children number over two hundred millions; she has extended her power over every continent and every isle, [even] the most remote, and, while widespread, still remains everywhere the same, so wondrous is her unity, professing everywhere the same creed and acknowledging everywhere the same governing power.[25]

Here was reason for the humblest hod-carrier to straighten his back and look the world straight in the eye.

Not that Father Ireland encouraged him or any one else to compromise with that world. "We are in an age of the most materialistic tendencies," he warned.[26]

> We know, of course, the boasts of our disciples of modern progress: liberal, progressive laws; the great strides of industry; the prodigious development of science; the vast diffusion of general knowledge. The circumstances in which man today is placed are altogether different from those of past ages; with his new surroundings he is a new being.
>
> I certainly am not going to undervalue laws, science and industry; in their own place they merit and receive our plaudits. But to make them the means of man's real progress, to call them progress is the sheerest of follies. They are all outside of man, and do not reach the root of his evils, his own heart.[27]

One of the causes of pride in this "stupendous organization" was its changelessness amidst the vagaries of the world. "The church has no preference for any age," Ireland proclaimed in 1865, "for she remains unchanged in every age, and does for each precisely that which she did for the ones that went before it."[28]

Father Ireland could exchange scriptural quotations with the toughest controversialists. He was capable of a sophisticated use of statistical material to prove a point.[29] Though he seldom listed the sources he employed in putting together his arguments, he clearly read widely and carefully—following his own monitum about the need for a priest to study—in preparation for his pulpit performances.[30] Sometime after 1870, when the first Vatican Council defined the dogma of papal infallibility, he set down in a notebook the citations from the fathers of the church and the ancient councils usually brought forward in the support of the definition.[31] In this instance and others the scholarship was basically sound, if somewhat partisan, and, though it now and again gave off a schoolboy ring, it usually avoided a descent into pedantry. In commenting, for instance, upon Christ's command in the Sermon on the Mount to refrain from angry name-calling, Ireland observed: "As to the precise signification of the hebrew [*sic*] word raca, it neither is clearly understood, nor is it material that it should be. Suffice it to know that it was in the language of the Jews expressive of reproach."[32]

Ireland's brand of moral exhortation grew naturally out of his concern to instruct. It also reflected his own and his culture's sturdy individualism. Ireland never considered the sermon as part of a larger corporate experience in the liturgy of the mass. Indeed, while he admitted that fleshly human beings needed to give external expression to their worship, he remained suspicious of "pompous appearances" and placed most of his emphasis upon the cultivation of internal religion.[33] It certainly never would have occurred to him to describe the liturgy, in the words of a later pope—who, incidentally, was to be on other grounds no favorite of Ireland's—as "the indispensable source of the Christian spirit."[34] Ireland tended rather to judge the matter the other way around: a person who approached the altar on Sunday ought to have acted decently during the preceding week.[35] The fulfillment of duty was his constant theme, along with the virtues that enhanced the soul in the eyes of God.

We in our short sightedness may fancy that the important facts in history are the births and downfalls of republics, kingdoms, and empires, the development of arts and sciences, battles and conquests, wars of independance [*sic*] and of defense. But in the eye of Him who brings all these things to pass and who rules in his might all occurrences, the great events, the only ones to be remembered, are the souls saved and and cared for.[36]

The process of salvation began with God's favor, to be sure,[37] but it continued with the individual's practice of those natural virtues like courage and temperance upon which a genuinely supernatural order could be built.[38]

Ireland was similarly austere in the forms of piety he recommended. He gave clear primacy of place to devotion to the person of Christ, discoverable in the historically verifiable pages of the gospels.[39] He had little or nothing to say about peripheral matters like indulgences or pilgrimages. He thought the veneration of the saints ought to be more a matter of practical imitation of these giants of virtue than of prayers or shrines.[40] He gave due honor to the Virgin Mary, but he usually did so within a doctrinal context — an explanation, for example, of the recently defined doctrine of the Immaculate Conception in its relation to original sin — and he appeared to have little interest in the great revival of popular marian devotion so marked among Catholics in the nineteenth century.[41] He urged his people to recite the rosary and, typically, justified his support for this pious practice by an appeal to its history; but he took pains also not to exaggerate its importance. "The Rosary is not a dogma we are obliged to believe under the penalty of being treated as heretics; it is not a necessary practice to which we must submit under penalty of sin. Martyrs have been crowned, confessors and virgins have been received into the celestial courts without knowing or practicing the Rosary, at least in its actual form; and yet the road to heaven is unrestricted even for those who would not be addicted to this devotional exercise. The Rosary is among the free devotions of the Church."[42]

From the point of view of style Father Ireland's early sermons were very much the product of their time. Their language was often overripe, their imagery elaborate. Sometimes the preacher was guilty of verbal extravagance. "Let the name [of Jesus]," orated Ire-

land in 1871, "be as a nosegay culled from the gardens of Bethlehem
and Calvary, resuming [*sic*] all the sweet fragrance of the Incar[na-
tion]."[43] Sometimes his search for the unusual word led to bizarre
results, as when he called the little boat Jesus and his disciples used
to cross the Sea of Galilee a "frail embarcation."[44] But lapses of this
sort were exceedingly rare, and, though he showed an overfondness
for certain standard phrases and interjections—"inhabitable globe,"
"swelling bosoms," "our homages," and "well!" or "oh!" or "alas!"
placed after rhetorical questions—Ireland's pulpit prose was by and
large clear, well ordered, no doubt compelling and persuasive to the
audiences who listened to it, and not infrequently quite beautiful.
"Whatever the teaching of science may be," he said in 1866,

> we find deeply instilled in mankind the idea, or the instinct, that
> the heart is connected with our inward affections; that it is warm
> in the kind and loving and cold in the selfish and ungenerous; that
> it is hard in the oppressor, fluttering in the anxious, faint in the
> cowardly, calm in the virtuous. To speak of the heart is to speak
> of the passions, the emotions, the sympathies of man; it embodies
> our ideas of tenderness, of compassion, of gentleness, of forgive-
> ness, of long-suffering, of every sweet variety of love. The par-
> ent, the spouse, the friend finds his specific kind of holy affection.
> It is the well-spring whence they all gush out, and manifest them-
> selves in action and in word: "for out of the abundance of the
> heart the mouth speaketh." The heart then is the source, at least
> the symbol, of love; to think of the heart of Jesus is to think of
> his love; to honor his heart is to honor his love.[45]

And if the preacher tarried long in the pulpit, his congregation
could always look forward to one of his flashes of wit, as when he
criticized English and American travel books for their anti-Catholic
prejudices: "I would have been timid to place in this category
Dickens' 'Notes from Italy'—you would have been loathe to credit
him with prejudice—had not his 'Notes from America' satisfied you
that the eye of the great satirist can be closed upon good which
might exist outside of Albion."[46]

Ireland was careful to keep non-religious topics out of the pulpit. His warning to his parishioners about abiding by the conscription laws of 1863 was exceptional (and he gave it only after he had
finished his regular Sunday sermon). Indeed, he seems at times to

have gone to surprising lengths to maintain this rule; for example, in a sermon on anger and reconciliation with one's enemies, preached in 1864, he avoided any mention of the war.[47] Lectures delivered outside the church were of course a different matter. Thus in 1867 he spoke freely about the political crisis in Italy and its bearing upon the temporal power of the pope. He expected that, thanks to Piedmontese "craft and force," Pius IX would be driven into exile, driven "to crave a refuge from a foreign potentate upon a distant strand." The pope might then be subject to "a thousand annoyances," but, Ireland predicted, "history will repeat itself": the pope's temporal independence may be lost "for awhile, even for many years, but not forever."[48]

St. Patrick's Day sermons and speeches were exceptions, too.[49] When he spoke to his fellow countrymen on their feast, Ireland ranged over a wide variety of subjects, from romanticized versions of celtic antiquities and standard accounts of British oppression to contemporary politics and economics, and he also indulged in some of his purplest prose. "Hail, then, green flag," he exclaimed on one of these occasions, "hail to thee, within God's consecrated temple. Thou hast taken, this morning, the place that belongs to thee of right—close to the altars of religion. No flag, save the yellow and white of papal Rome, would be here more at home."[50] And on another:

> My dear Brethren, you wish me to speak to you this morning of Ireland, the land of your birth, the land of your forefathers. To speak of Ireland, the lovely isle of the ocean, whose beauty and merits have been the favored theme of so many poets, orators, and sages, whose very name is inspiration, so glorious and precious the memories that cluster around it—to speak of Ireland must ever be, especially for those who fondly claim her as their mother, a pleasurable task. I enter, with delight, upon the duty which your presence imposes.[51]

There followed each time a stirring evocation of St. Patrick's ministry and of the conversion of Ireland to Catholicism—"Ireland has never for a moment deviated from her allegiance; her faith is pure, unspotted, virginal"[52]—and an indictment of British malevolence—"Nor would I slight thee, dear isle, because thou art poor and downtrodden. It is not thy fault if thy children are compelled to flee to foreign shores. Thy hills and plains teem with plenteousness, but the oppressor is ever gnawing at thy substance and consuming thy life."[53] Usually these themes blended simply into a conventional appeal to the members of the congregation to practice their faith and to be good citizens of their adopted country—but not always. In 1871, for example, recently returned from a visit to the "old sod," Ireland reported that conditions were improving, that "Irish voters have learned, despite landlord tyranny, to exert more potent influence." He pointed to the disestablishment of the Protestant state church as "one of the most remarkable signs" of amelioration. Still, he said, without a protective tariff to promote industrialization, and without a dissolution of the political union with Great Britain, the future of Ireland remained dubious.[54]

But it was in 1865 that John Ireland preached his longest—forty manuscript pages—and most significant St. Patrick's Day sermon. Its significance lay not in the praise for "the darling little isle" or in the harsh denunciation of the penal laws—standard components of his March 17 orations—but in the candor with which he described the problems of the Irish Americans sitting in front of him, problems, he said gently, to some degree of their own making. "Dispirited and broken-hearted" by persecution and exile, some Irish "have been almost necessarily unmanned; they have lost somewhat the pride which is the essential ingredient of manhood; among some of our people there is too great an absence of what is termed respectability—they do not care enough about external decorum." Why must Irishmen be "impulsive, irritable and noisy? Another unsatisfactory feature of the Irish character is their [*sic*] hasty and passionate disposition." They quarrel endlessly among themselves, he charged, and, what is especially foolish, they have brought their old-country quarrels to this new land.[55] The Irish need to cultivate greater self-control to refine their "warm celtic race."

"I think," he went on, "there is in our character room for more energy and readiness to devise and undertake projects for our individual and social advancement, and for more perseverance in what we have undertaken. . . . We let our enthusiasm cool down; we fall back if we do not carry our point at the first assault." Ireland addressed his listeners directly: the successful person, consistent in applying himself to the task at hand, gives outward evidence of his status; therefore, "wherever you are, be sober, quiet, industrious." This new country has given you a second chance, so you should "take a lively interest in all public affairs." But "avoid excess in politics," and never stoop to selling your precious vote.[56] "Seek every means of instructing yourselves," because in America the informed and educated win the prizes. Above all, do not let yourselves be permanently "unmanned." "Be ambitious, seek to elevate yourselves, to better your lot; too often we are too easily satisfied. When a man is poor, let him live in a hovel. I esteem him; at any moment I tend him the right hand of fellowship; but if by labor, by energy, he can secure to his family comfort and respectability, and does not, then I despise him."[57] Thus did one young Irish priest, cast upon a "foreign strand," bear witness to the American dream.

One other message was common to these St. Patrick's Day orations. "There is one fault—I am not comparing [us] with other nations—it exists with us. It has done us fearful harm. Intemperance. The foe to your race today [as the British were in olden times] is the saloon keeper. [There are] over sixteen hundred Irish saloon keepers in Chicago. The remedy is total abst[inence]."[58] No conviction came so strongly upon John Ireland during the early years of his priesthood than that the consumption of strong drink was a universal and unmitigated wickedness. He began then a crusade that would last a lifetime.

Bishop Cretin, despite his upbringing in a wine-drinking country, decided early in his missionary days in America to endorse the cause of teetotalism.[59] He was genuinely shocked by the ravages caused on the frontier by whisky, among Indians and whites alike. One of the first organizations he formed after he took up residence in St. Paul was a Catholic temperance society. He lent his prestige to the movement that sought legislation to prohibit the manufacture or sale of intoxicating liquors (save for "medicinal purposes") within Minnesota Territory; such a law was duly passed by the territorial legislature in 1852 and approved by a referendum, but shortly afterward it was declared unconstitutional by the courts.[60] Cretin's own temperance society, after the initial enthusiasm, did not prosper either, and by the time the bishop died in 1857 it had ceased to function.

His successor, Thomas Grace, showed no interest in reviving it or indeed in fostering any kind of organized resistance to the liquor traffic. He attended the national council of Catholic bishops held in Baltimore in 1866 and presumably subscribed to its decree that pastors, "for the love of Jesus Christ, . . . labor with all possible care and energy for the extirpation of the vice of drunkenness," and, to this end, encourage total abstinence and form temperance societies.[61] But Grace's natural diffidence and his hesitancy to appear to impose upon his people any obligation that was not strictly and universally applicable kept him from initiating any projects in this regard. He was a man who shrank from even the faintest hint of fanaticism, which was a quality often ascribed to temperance-workers. He worried, too, about the close association in the public mind between agitation for temperance and certain varieties of evangelical Protestantism.[62]

Even so, what the bishop did not choose to do himself he would not prevent one of his subjects from doing, and the temperance cause in the Diocese of St. Paul did have its rebirth. Many years later Ireland told, with suitably dramatic flourishes, how it happened.

> Seven good, generous—too generous—men were assembled together on [a] Friday evening in a very popular saloon on Minnesota Street. They drank and treated one another; but a gleam of good christian sense dawned upon their minds and one said: "We ought to stop lest we be ruined." Another said: "Let us go and see Father Ireland, and organize a temperance society"; and a petition with seven names upon it was actually gotten up in that saloon, and candidly the keeper of the saloon was one of the signers. The writing was a little tremulous. One was commissioned to bring me the petition, and as he opened the door of my room he was not very steady on his limbs, and he nearly fell, but he soon recovered himself and said: "I have a petition for you." I read the petition and without a moment's hesitation said: "Yes, a society will be organized."

At four o'clock on the following Sunday afternoon an organizational meeting was held in the cathedral clubrooms. "Fifty men signed the pledge, and the Father Mathew society was born."[63]

Ireland used to say that his interest in the temperance question was first aroused at Meximieux, where Bishop Loras of Dubuque was proposed to the students as a model because of his heroic struggles against the baneful effects of alcohol.[64] Loras, like Cretin, was a strong total-abstainer. Otherwise, aside from his childhood encounter with Father Theobald Mathew, the famed Irish apostle of temperance, Ireland gave no public indication before 1869 that he planned war to the knife with demon rum. Yet the conviction must have been growing upon him for years. Even when he was a boy he could not but have seen what others saw among the Irish immigrants in "New Dublin": "None of [the people there] were working," one visitor observed, "and everyone I called to see had plenty of whiskey in the shanty. They were a good-natured people until they got drunk, and let me tell you by that time a stranger had better remove himself from the patches."[65] And though he did not refer to it, Ireland's experience in an army of soldiers as famous for their drunkenness as for their valor must have led him to similar conclusions about the destructive nature of insobriety. A more proximate cause of his willingness to form a temperance organization was perhaps the work he did with the cathedral's St. Vincent de Paul Society, whose task was to dispense charity to the poor members of the parish. Home visitations on these missions of mercy often revealed the close relationship between poverty and drink.[66]

Once the battle was joined, at any rate, he never looked back. Nothing during his long life absorbed him as much as did the cause of total abstinence. He placed all his gifts at its disposal, all his energies. In the course of the struggle he displayed all the best facets of his character: his straightforwardness, his determination, his vigor, his utter fearlessness, his genuine concern for the well-being of his fellows. No means to achieve the end of general sobriety were beneath him or beyond him. Charm and even humor were useful in dealing with some, high-toned oratory worked with others, and grim threats of hell-fire with still others. Sometimes Father Ireland took his stick to the drunkards in "New Dublin" and chased them from shanty to shanty. He brooked no compromise with the principle that all liquor, whether fermented or distilled or brewed, was poisonous. He accepted no halfway position. "Remember," he said once, "if you are what is called a temperate man who takes a glass but never exceeds, your example is worse than that of a drunkard."[67] And to the Irishman who would, teary eyed, drink a toast to his native land, the priest said this: "Alcohol [is] the bane and curse of [your] country and countrymen; but for it Ireland might today be free and an honored member of the sisterhood of nations; but for it Irishmen would be better, truer, nobler members of society. The man who talk[s] about Ireland and her wrongs with a glass of whiskey in his hands [is] an enemy to his country for he [is] using that which ha[s] been her curse and ruin."[68]

The Father Mathew Society of St. Paul had as its object "to encourage total abstinence, and to provide for the temporal relief of its members in certain cases. All persons over fifteen years of age who are willing to abide by its laws and who promise 'with the divine assistance to abstain from all intoxicating liquors' are eligible to membership."[69] At the preliminary meeting officers were elected and a constitution and bylaws approved. Ireland assumed the title of spiritual director. Before adjournment forty-two men (not fifty, as Ireland remembered it) took the total abstinence pledge. (Though the word "persons" was used in the society's constitution, the Catholic temperance movement in Minnesota remained exclusively male until 1876 when Ireland, by then a bishop, casually mentioned in a speech that perhaps the pledge should be offered as well to the ladies in the audience: "He barely mentioned his idea [when] they all sprang to their feet, and with one full [*sic*] swoop he made teetotalers of our mothers, wives and sisters to the utter astonishment of the strangers present.")[70]

The new society met every Sunday evening in the basement of the cathedral, which soon came to be called "Temperance Hall." The spiritual director usually opened the session with reading and commenting on a chapter of a biography of Father Mathew. There followed an hour of fellowship during which future social events were planned and candidates for membership were discussed. The society offered mutual support in dealing with a critical problem, and it grew prodigiously: within three months it boasted of three hundred members and $125 in its treasury. The initiation fee of one dollar and the monthly dues of twenty-five cents provided three dollars a week to sick members during their illness and up to twenty-five dollars, to help defray funeral expenses, to the beneficiaries of brethren who died. The manner of admission to the society was simplicity itself. A candidate was proposed by someone already a member, and, unless five negative votes were cast, the candidate assumed full status. All members were committed to report any violators of the pledge; the latter could be expected to be fined or expelled, depending on the seriousness of the infraction.[71]

The first public appearance of the Father Mathew Society came on St. Patrick's Day, 1869, when its members, wearing white rosettes in their lapels, marched in the annual parade, sat together as a body at mass in the cathedral, and later joined the other Irish societies of the city in paying a formal call of courtesy on Bishop Grace. The bishop, as was his wont on these occasions, delivered a short speech in which he complimented the Irish of St. Paul and their organizations. Then he turned to the teetotalers and said: "I refer to one [especially], and I am grateful for its success. I mean the Father Mathew Total Abstinence Society. Long may it continue to grow and flourish. I hope every one of you will make yourself an apostle of temperance. In proportion as temperance spreads sin and wretchedness and poverty will disappear."[72] Grace did not hesitate to endorse happy results.

Not every one, however, rallied to that cause. Some of the Irish resented the society, because its very existence seemed to them an admission of guilt and therefore a blot on their collective reputation. The German Catholics stood aside, saying, with barely veiled contempt, that they — moderate beer-drinkers all — did not need to belong to an organization, as the Irish did, to avoid drunkenness. The local liquor interests, concentrated along Minnesota Street, were understandably alarmed at the prospect of a successful temperance movement in St. Paul and could be expected to resist it strongly. Father Ireland himself was often reminded of the formidable reputation for political clout enjoyed by the saloon lobby. Once, about this time, when visiting the cathedral school, he asked a pupil what a capital was, and she answered that it was a place where laws were made. He then asked her to name the capital of her home state, and the little girl replied: "Minnesota Street." On another occasion one of his parishioners shook his fist in the priest's face and shouted at him: "You can't touch Minnesota Street!"[73] This was not altogether untrue, or at any rate Ireland was not prepared at this early stage of the movement to confront the powerful liquor interests head-on. When in May 1869 a petition was circulated seeking support for an ordinance to close the saloons on Sunday, Ireland, acting for the Father Mathew Society, refused to sign it.[74] Voluntarism, not legal intervention, was, he argued, the preferred way to proceed. In later years, after he had changed his tune considerably, he grimly recalled how on this occasion Minnesota Street had praised him for the "sanity" of the stand he had taken on Sunday closing.[75]

But in the spring of 1869 voluntarism appeared to be working well enough. Temperance groups, in imitation of the Father Mathew Society (and more often than not using that name), sprang up all over the southern part of Minnesota.[76] In every instance the impetus came from the local priest. In April John Ireland set out on the first of many tours around the southern counties urging parishes to found total abstinence societies.[77] Back in St. Paul, on the Fourth of July, the parent society participated formally in the town's Independence Day celebrations; the Catholic teetotalers marched in the parade beneath their new four-hundred-dollar-banner, "7 feet high and 5 wide," green on one side and sky-blue on the other, "made of rich . . . silk and beautifully surrounded with heavy gold lace fringe and bullion, with neat cords and tassels," and an "excellent representation of Father Mathew, the Apostle of Temperance."[78] After mass the members and their banner—it took four men to carry it—proceeded to the outskirts of the town to join in the gaiety of the dry parish picnic. About seven o'clock, "a party of five or six rowdies, partially intoxicated," started a fight in an adjacent picnic grounds where the Lutherans were celebrating the Fourth of July. "A messenger ran to the Catholic picnic and gave the alarm, but by much effort Father Ireland . . . induced the men to remain." Ireland himself and two policemen ran to the scene and managed to stop the "bloody and disgraceful melee," which eventually involved more than a dozen men fighting with clubs and knives. At least two of the original half-dozen culprits were drunken Irish Catholics. "It was . . . fortunate," commented the newspaper report of the fight, "that the Catholic picnic was a strictly temperance affair or otherwise it would have been impossible to have controlled them [sic] and a much more fearful scene might have ensued."[79]

It was about this time that Ireland began to be referred to as "the young Father Mathew of the Northwest," a mantle he readily, almost greedily, put around himself. He made room for many able co-workers, clerical and lay, but no peers. Notable among the lay-men was Dillon O'Brien, a cultured, peripatetic native of County Roscommon, twenty years John Ireland's senior and the latter's close auxiliary in a variety of endeavors until his untimely death in 1882.[80] The priests included Thomas O'Gorman, who had come home from France in 1865 and, four years later, was pastor of the Catholic parish in Rochester, Minnesota.[81] Ireland's closest mature associations and friendships began within the total abstinence movement and lasted throughout his lifetime. Agitation against drink, locally first and then nationally, often provided the occasion for other initiatives in other areas. The squad of young diocesan pri-ests he enlisted in the early days of the movement remained Ireland's coadjutors — his staff officers, so to speak — and, when he came into a position to do so, he carefully nurtured their careers.[82] His first contact with the Paulist Fathers, with whom he would share many causes in future years, occurred when a group of them came to Min-nesota from New York in the mid-1870s to preach total absti-nence.[83] He met John J. Keane of Washington — a staunch ally in the later battles over the parochial schools, the Catholic University, the Knights of Labor, the establishment of the apostolic delegation, and Americanism — when the two of them worked together in the na-tional Catholic temperance movement.[84] Indeed, this issue, in all its ramifications, ran like a thread through Ireland's life, binding to-gether all sorts of otherwise disparate persons and events.

How much the fledgling movement in Minnesota depended on Ireland became apparent in October 1869, when he departed for a seven-month tour of Europe. The men of the St. Paul society presented him with a purse of $750, and he promised to bring back from Ireland a genuine blackthorn cane, to be presented to the member enrolling the largest number of recruits during his absence. He kept them in his thoughts and wrote back, in the third person, about the Irish woman he met who operated an apple stand on the New York docks and who offered him a bottle of whisky to pre-serve him from seasickness. "He looked aghast. You would have said he dreaded lest some St. Paul temperance detectives were around, and in a minute he had sent the poor woman adrift with the solemn admonition: 'I never use such poison.' So far all right; your correspondent, however, will keep his eyes upon him, and woe to him if he touches or tastes." And then he added, more wistfully: "Father Ireland just now whispers that about this time of the evening the Temperance Society of St. Paul are in session, and he tells me to send his love to them."[85]

But such long-distance reassurances did not substitute for Ireland's active presence. During the winter and spring the drive to organize Catholic temperance groups outside St. Paul and Minneapolis visibly flagged. Leakage in the St. Paul society grew so pronounced that a full-scale canvass of all the city's wards was mounted, but the number of new recruits was trifling—apparently the promise of the blackthorn stick had only limited appeal. On St. Patrick's Day, 1870, two hundred Father Mathew-men gathered in the cathedral where Bishop Grace testily warned them to avoid political involvement and to stop quarreling among themselves. Ireland's return, on May 14, came none too soon for the fortunes of the total abstinence movement. Two weeks later, at a Memorial Day observance, he declared himself more determined than ever "to speak for war" against the ravages of drink (the horrors of which he had recently seen for himself in the Irish slums of New York City), and to carry on the fight "until every town and county in the state be enrolled under the banner of temperance."[86]

Ireland took to the stump that summer and fall, and, though the reception he received in some places was cool, overall the movement quickened again under his charismatic hand.[87] He encouraged the parish societies to be mindful that they competed for patronage with the local saloon which, by offering free lunches and other recreational inducements, too easily lived up to its claim to be "the poor man's club room."[88] Consequently the temperance societies began to expand their activities, opening circulating libraries and reading rooms and inviting lecturers to speak about subjects other than merely the evils of drink. This emphasis upon popular education and self-help bore the stamp of Ireland's influence, as well as his notion of how service organizations within a parish ought to function. Such steps by no means put the saloons to rout, but they helped to restore much of the temperance movement's self-confidence and morale. By late January 1871, when a giant rally was held in St. Paul to protest the Italian seizure of the last remains of the Papal States—"the most imposing religious demonstration which has ever taken place in this city"[89] — the temperance societies came out in force. During the spring a half-dozen more local temperance groups were formed around the diocese, and by May Ireland was ready to launch the next phase of the campaign. At a meeting of the St. Paul teetotalers he proposed that the level of enthusiasm for their cause had reached a point that justified the organization of a state Catholic total abstinence league.[90]

The membership quickly endorsed the idea and put out an invitation to the societies around the state to meet in plenary session sometime in the autumn. The response was tepid at best, and when the autumn came nothing had been done. The discouraged officers of the St. Paul group accordingly declared that the time was not ripe for a statewide organization. But their spiritual director was adamant, and he overrode all opposition. Upon his insistence a convention was called for January 10, 1872, the third anniversary of the founding of the cathedral's Father Mathew Society.

It lasted all day, from the high mass in the morning to "the most sumptuous supper" at nine o'clock in the evening. Twelve of the fifteen Catholic total abstinence societies in Minnesota were represented. All the notable leaders took their turn at the podium — Dillon O'Brien, Thomas O'Gorman, and many others — but it was John Ireland's "brief address" that gained the most attention from the press. "A wonderful impetus," he said, "has been given the temperance cause throughout the whole country," and Minnesota was "moving simultaneously with other parts of the country." He urged upon his listeners the need for coordinated action within the state and the formal association of the local cause with the national. He then "made an eloquent appeal in behalf of temperance itself . . . and spoke eloquently of the evils of intemperance and the fearful results which follow its indulgence, of the tears of the widow and orphans, of the fortunes wrecked, the religion scandalized and their country shamed, which lurked in the glass of sparkling liquor." Much of the rest of the day was occupied in drawing up a constitution and in selecting committees and officers. It must have been with some relief that the four hundred participants finally sat down to their repast in Ingersoll Hall. "After the supper, an hour or two was spent in an intellectual entertainment of wit, humor, speeches and a general good time."[91]

The convention of January 1872 marked a turning point in John Ireland's career as a temperance reformer. From that time on he had behind him a stable state organization, which boasted a thousand members and which, within a month, became formally associated with the Catholic Total Abstinence Union of America.[92] His own efforts in the cause began to be directed more and more toward a national audience. Not that he neglected his home base or failed to realize the necessity of refining the local movement as it grew in numbers. He was particularly concerned with the formation within the parish societies of "Cadets" and "Crusaders"—respectively boys of seven to fourteen years of age who took the pledge for five years and prayed daily for the reclamation of drunkards, and young men of sixteen to thirty who sported a uniform of blue sash, hat and plume, who abstained totally from "alcoholic liquors, wines, cordials, beer, bitters, cider, tonics or any drink whatsoever of an intoxicating nature," and who cultivated "entertainment and amusement" appropriate to their age.[93] But when he attended his first national convention late in 1873 and was promptly elected first vice president of the Union, the signal was given that the "Father Mathew of the Northwest" was about to move to a larger stage.[94] He did so with a genuine sense of accomplishment. As he wrote jubilantly to his Minnesota confreres early in 1874:

> Are we not a different people than we were five years ago? How many homes have been made happy? How many wives and children today bless us and pray for us? How many men once forgetful of their manhood and their religion are now redeemed from the thralldom of sin and with prosperity in this world are among the most devoted and earnest children of the Church? If our movement is to be judged by its fruits, by the blessings that have everywhere followed in its wake, we can truly say that the favor of heaven is with us.[95]

~ VI ~

Romanità

1867–75

DESPITE all the time and energy he expended upon it, the cause of total abstinence was by no means John Ireland's sole preoccupation during his years at the Cathedral of St. Paul. The ordinary parochial duties took precedence, of course, and related to these were activities as various as outings for the altar boys,[1] parish excursions, and series of Sunday evening lectures on topics like "The Roman Catacombs" and "The Church and the Enlightenment."[2] He continued to reside in the bishop's house next to the cathedral where he found the atmosphere congenial. The other members of the staff, Fathers Louis Caillet and Anatole Oster, agreed with Ireland on most of the large issues of the day,[3] and, because both of them had been total abstainers since Bishop Cretin's time, they sympathized also with the great cause, though they had departed for other assignments by the time the movement began in earnest in 1869.

Before they left, however, there occurred an incident rich in irony. An Irishman named Timothy Mehegan had brought his wife and two small daughters to Minnesota in 1850, two years before the Ireland family settled there. He was a dreamy, self-taught man, a tailor by trade, whose failures to make a living in Ireland and later in New York had led him to try his luck in the West. But he enjoyed no better success on the frontier. With his little shop standing forlornly empty, he tried dabbling on the side in St. Paul real estate, but he failed in that, too, and, on Christmas Eve, 1854, he suddenly died, just one of the legion of luckless pioneers. His widow and children, left virtually penniless, turned for support to the priests and nuns of the infant Diocese of St. Paul. Joseph Cretin came to their aid, as did Augustin Ravoux, and, after his arrival from France in 1855, Louis Caillet gradually took on the role of special guardian to the Mehegan family.[4] The two little girls enrolled in the "academy" opened by the Sisters of St. Joseph, where they were the schoolmates of John Ireland's sisters.

Mary Theresa Mehegan was eight years old when her father died. She grew up to be a pretty, grave, self-possessed young woman of independent mind, hard-working—at sixteen she was a waitress in the dining room of the Merchants Hotel—and fiercely devoted to the tenets of her religion. Among the regular patrons of the Merchants Hotel who found her attractive was James Jerome Hill, who had come to St. Paul from Ontario in 1856 and who, though only in his mid-twenties, already enjoyed the reputation of an up-and-coming businessman with a brilliant future. Late in 1863 Hill asked Mary Mehegan to marry him, and she accepted.[5]

It proved to be a long engagement. During the course of it Louis Caillet, Mary's confidant, earned the regard of her fiancé as well. Though he was not a Catholic, Hill intimated vaguely that he might become one some day (he never did), and in the meantime he was more than content that his wife's religion should also be the religion of his household. Caillet, for his part, urged upon Mary the need to prepare herself to become the helpmeet of a man who, the priest shrewdly predicted, was destined in a few years to be one of the leading citizens of St. Paul. "Your life may not be an easy one," he told her, "but you must continue to educate yourself to be his companion." The result was that Mary went off to Milwaukee and enrolled in St. Mary's Institute, a kind of Catholic finishing school, where the nuns taught her needlework, French, and the demeanor of a middle-class lady. Hill thoroughly approved of this arrangement and indeed helped pay for it. During the winter and spring of 1864–65 he spent most Sundays in Milwaukee, walking with Mary, properly chaperoned, along the bluffs above Lake Michigan and sharing with her his dreams of future accomplishment.

On August 17, 1867, Hill took out the marriage license and reserved the parlor of the Catholic clergy house (the ordinary locale in those days for "mixed" marriages) for mid-morning two days later. He also asked John Ireland to inform Father Caillet that the young couple expected the latter to witness their exchange of vows.

James J. Hill, 1863, and Mary Theresa Mehegan, undated (both MHS)

When the appointed time arrived, a red-faced Ireland came to the parlor and confessed that he had forgotten to deliver the message and that Caillet was out of the city and unavailable. Ireland then offered to perform the ceremony himself, but Mary Mehegan frostily refused, and asked for Father Oster instead. Thus the first recorded encounter between two giants of their time and place was an inauspicious one. And James J. Hill may have been quietly amused at the snub his bride gave the bumptious young priest, for he was certainly aware that Ireland not long before had denounced the steamboat trade — Hill's business of the moment — as demeaning and morally dangerous to his parishioners.[6]

The day would come when John Ireland would need and eagerly solicit Hill's support, but for the time being he needed the good opinion of only one person, Thomas Langdon Grace. The bishop readily and generously accorded it to him. He gave the younger man free rein in those areas — like temperance and, later, colonization — in which he took little direct interest himself. Ireland, as though in compensation, threw his restless energy behind projects dear to the bishop's heart. The partnership worked remarkably well.

Bishop Grace from his earliest days in St. Paul had urged upon his people the necessity to promote Catholic journals and newspapers. The "value and importance" of the press, he wrote in his first pastoral in 1859, "can hardly be exaggerated. . . . It is wielded unsparingly and incessantly against the truth of our religion. We need the same power in defense of that truth. . . . If we will have a press such as the necessities of the times demand, a press that will demand the attention not merely of Catholics but of the public at large, we must offer such inducements as will engage and remunerate the best talent and ability."[7] The sentiment was characteristic of Grace, who was always devoted to the merits of literary argument, but characteristic, too, was his failure to do anything to implement it. The practical task was left to Ireland.

In 1866 a printer and retired army officer named John C. Devereux, whom he had known in the war, was persuaded by Ireland to undertake a canvass of the Catholics of Minnesota to determine whether sufficient support existed for a Catholic newspaper. The results of the canvass were modest enough — fewer than seven hundred potential subscribers willing to pay three dollars a year — but, with the editorial assistance of the ever-present Dillon O'Brien, Devereux launched the *Northwestern Chronicle* and kept it afloat for nine years. Despite Bishop Grace's heady talk about "inducements" to "talent and ability," the diocese contributed nothing to the venture save free office space. In 1875 Devereux sold the paper outright to Ireland for two thousand dollars, which left the founding publisher a net profit of exactly eighteen dollars. The *Chronicle,* under a succession of clerical editors, continued to be published in St. Paul until 1900.[8]

So, thanks to the efforts of his young colleague, Bishop Grace got his newspaper, and a useful platform it proved to be for both men. Ireland also enlisted in another of the bishop's favorite causes, though this time with limited enthusiasm. Grace, like his predecessor, was a harsh critic of government Indian policy.[9] He himself had served on numerous civil panels of inquiry, and in 1868 he arranged that Ireland should be appointed, along with several non-Catholic clergymen, to the presidential board overseeing the distribution of federal scrip, in accord with prevailing treaties, to the Ojibway Indians.[10] Ireland did his duty in this regard, but without any notable passion. He entered more zestfully into another of his superior's complaints about treatment of the Indians, namely, the alleged easy access that Protestant missionaries enjoyed to the reservations in comparison to their Catholic counterparts. When a Catholic Ojibway was quoted saying that Episcopal Bishop Whipple was the most influential Christian missionary, more effective than any priest, it was Ireland who took up the cudgels. "I am confident no Catholic made [this] statement," he wrote. The Indians preferred the ministrations of Catholic priests, "but their wishes in this respect have not been regarded by the government. The Episcopalians have the advantage of simply being placed by the government in charge of the Indians at White Earth [Reservation], and this constitutes whatever success they may appear to have beyond the Catholics."[11] It was not an ecumenical era.

Nor was it an era when the primacy of the fabled little red schoolhouse went unchallenged. Nothing weighed as heavily among Thomas Grace's pastoral priorities as his conviction that "there is more danger in the public schools for the faith of the Catholic children than in all else beside."[12] An assertion of this sort was not calculated to win friends within the ruling circles of St. Paul, nor did it lend much comfort to the overwhelmingly lower-class Catholics who had to pay taxes to support the state schools and yet, if their bishop was right, dared not allow their children to attend them. Once again, it was left to John Ireland to try to find a solution.

In 1867, and again more elaborately in 1869, Ireland offered a proposal for which he claimed precedent in various parts of the country and which, he said, would protect the rights of the community while granting equal educational opportunity to Catholic students. "Fully one-half of the children of St. Paul," he wrote to the school board early in June 1869, "can derive no benefit from the present system of public education." Monies allocated by the state for support of the city schools reflected the total student population, Catholic and non-Catholic alike. "But as those schools are, the conscientious convictions of Catholic parents do not permit them to send their children there." In the name of equity Ireland offered to turn over to the school board, rent-free, the two Catholic school buildings in the city — that of the cathedral and of the German parish of the Assumption — and guaranteed also to maintain equipment and to pay for general upkeep. Teachers in both schools would be subject to the same requirements and supervision as those in the public system. No religious instruction would be given during the regular school day. In return the Catholic teachers would be paid out of school board funds. "We have school houses, teachers, and scholars," Ireland concluded. "What is needed in order that our schools be recognized by your Board?"[13]

The board responded to this communication by appointing three of its members to a committee charged to examine the matter and to report its findings in two weeks. Actually what amounted to negotiations between the committee and Ireland dragged on for most of the summer. Finally, in mid-August, the committee made a favorable recommendation to the full board. The dominant force on the committee proved to have been its chairman, General Henry H. Sibley — first governor of Minnesota — who was friendly with Ireland and with the Catholic community generally.[14] Sibley argued strongly that "the proposition offered by Rev. Mr. Ireland and others on behalf of the Catholic Church, or the schools under the care of that church, are [sic] designed to meet all legal or educational objections hitherto raised to the adoption of the Catholic schools by this Board." But not even advocacy from so prestigious a source could save the motion: it was defeated by a vote of ten to four.[15]

The problem did not thereby go away. It smoldered like a peat fire, flaring up now and then as at a school board meeting in February 1872, at which a Catholic member denounced a public school teacher for reading the Protestant Bible in his classroom, or at a St. Patrick's Day celebration a few weeks later, at which Bishop Grace labeled public education as "dangerous" to Catholic children.[16] As for Ireland, he kept the pot boiling by leaking the news that he might seek the office of superintendent of public instruction.[17] It seems unlikely that he seriously considered such a course of action, and even less likely that Grace, for all his usual forebearance, would have permitted it. Ireland at any rate did not forget his proposal of 1867 and 1869; he was to advance essentially the same one twenty years later for the town of Faribault and to provoke an even greater storm of controversy.

A lesser man than Thomas Grace might have grown weary of

his subject's ever-growing prominence, particularly since Ireland began his career as Bishop Cretin's protégé, not as Grace's. He might understandably have been nettled at reading in the daily press that when the two of them shared the same platform his words were "received with enthusiasm," while Ireland, speaking last (in the place of honor), was "greeted with a storm of applause."[18] He might well have seized upon Ireland's glaring weakness for notoriety and headlines and rebuked him in the same terms used by one of the secular newspapers: "Father Ireland, . . . by the way, rushes into print a little too easily."[19] He did nothing of the sort. Instead he acted the part of the truly enlightened administrator and allowed his gifted subordinate ever more scope to do what he was anxious to do and capable of doing. Grace leaned upon Ireland more and more, trusted him more and more. And in the autumn of 1869, he gave an especially solemn sign of that trust: he named Ireland his proctor at the forthcoming general council in Rome.[20]

Grace had traveled to Rome in 1867 for the celebration of the eighteen hundredth anniversary of the martyrdom of St. Peter, and he had no desire to return again so soon. He had to have papal permission, however, to absent himself, and Pope Pius IX, anxious to have as large an attendance as possible at this first meeting of the universal Catholic hierarchy since the sixteenth century, granted such permission only grudgingly. Grace pleaded to remain home "on account of the pressing cares of the Diocese," but he was kept in suspense for many months and learned of his exemption only days before he was scheduled to depart.[21] Ireland, who had been designated to accompany the bishop in any event, left St. Paul without him on October 18 and sailed from New York aboard the *France* on Saturday, October 23, 1869.[22]

John Ireland was a witness to, not a real participant in, the First Council of the Vatican. It would be far-fetched to suppose that a thirty-one-year-old priest from a remote missionary diocese, who enjoyed no legal status within the council — the position of the proctors ranged in the end from the ambiguous to the nugatory[23] — could have affected in any way its deliberations or decisions. The impact, indeed, was all the other way. This was Ireland's first trip to Rome, his first exposure to *romanità,* that peculiar magic worked by the eternal city upon the visitor, especially if that visitor is from a northern land. Thomas Grace, who as a student had spent many years there, no doubt intended Father Ireland to have that experience and, in the process, perhaps to make a useful contact or two: ecclesiastical promotion, after all, was ultimately in the gift of the pope and his officials. The bishop—who as an old Roman hand could have guessed that the proctorship would amount to nothing—might simply have wanted his young colleague to enjoy a well-deserved holiday; if so, his kindly intention was amply fulfilled. Not that the council itself assumed minor proportions in Ireland's mind. The color and drama associated with it were precisely calculated to appeal to his powerful imagination. The coming together of more than seven hundred bishops representing every continent and every culture served to reassure the priest from the American frontier and to confirm his favorite boast, that he and his people belonged to "the most stupendous organization on the face of the earth."[24]

To have shared the conciliar ambience, even for a little while and even from the sidelines, with the likes of Giacomo Cardinal Antonelli, the adroit papal secretary of state, and with Archbishop Henry Edward Manning—the austere Englishman who for his temperance work was a special hero of Ireland's—was an experience not soon to be forgotten. Less dramatic perhaps but important for Ireland in both the long and the short term was the opportunity the council afforded him to rub elbows with most of the American bishops, who came to Rome in extraordinary numbers.[26] Though nobody wrote down such relatively trivial happenings, this must have been the occasion when Ireland first met James Gibbons, then vicar apostolic of North Carolina,[27] and also his bête noire of later years, the irascible bishop of Rochester, Bernard McQuaid. One of Ireland's fellow proctors was Isaac Hecker, whose name would be inextricably linked with his own in many a future controversy.[28]

The passage of the *France* from New York to Queenstown and Liverpool was rough and stormy. "It is all very well," Ireland wrote to the people back in St. Paul, "to sing in a warm parlor, on sound *terra firma*, 'The sea, the sea, is the place for me.' . . . But let the musician be where I am now, and sea sick!" Among the passengers were two American bishops on their way to the council and other distinguished persons—"a miniature world," Ireland observed, "a most gregarious gathering"—but "a look into the steerage, where I spend an occasional stray hour," revealed the people there to be two-thirds Irish, "on their way to the old land. 'Why are you going home?' I asked an old woman of eighty. 'To die,' was the reply." She had been happy in the United States, "but her heart was bent on one thing—to be buried under the green sod, with the cross and the shamrock o'er her." On Sunday, "at an early hour, Protestantism gave sign that it would take possession of the saloon—we have ministers aboard. Catholicity prepared to move forward towards the steerage. 'The poor have the Gospel preached unto them.' . . . We all devoutly said together our morning prayers," and Ireland read the gospel passage appointed for the liturgy of that day—a very appropriate text describing Jesus and his disciples caught in a storm at sea. "The literal signification, the audience, I assure you, could, in their present situation, easily understand."[29]

Ireland arrived in Rome about November 19, 1869,[30] and probably settled into lodgings at Santa Maria sopra Minerva, headquarters of the Dominican Order, near the Pantheon, where Dominican Thomas Grace had resided as a student and where he stayed on his Roman visits. During the next six months Ireland was to send the *Northwestern Chronicle* reports of his experiences, describing in rich detail the conciliar pomp: the decoration and architecture of St. Peter's, the seating of the bishops and council, the subjects of the paintings on the walls. "A grand sight it is," he wrote, "to view the vast gathering, . . . the purple robes of the sacred College, . . . the magnificent copes of the Latin Prelates, . . . the gold-covered mantles and tiaras of the Orientals."[31]

He also displayed a knack for describing the more prosaic side of the council's day-to-day business. He explained the preliminary work the theologians had done in preparing an agenda. He defined within the conciliar context terms like "congregations," "commissions," and "elections." "Latin, of course, is the language spoken. It [had] been said that the bishops would understand each other with difficulty, as each nation has a peculiar pronunciation in the Latin tongue." But the problem had not developed. "On hearing the prelates, you would never think that they are from every tribe and every language under the sun; it would seem as if the days of old Rome had dawned again, so glorious is the unity of the Church in everything, in her language as well as in her faith and sacrifice!" Such was his enthusiasm that he could scarcely conclude any description without an exclamation point.

Indeed, edified himself by the council's external splendor and its apparently smooth-running procedure, Ireland seemed intent above all upon edifying his readers in Minnesota. "View [the conciliar scene]," he exclaimed, "and I will ask you, where is, if not there, the Catholic Church, the Church of all ages and all nations. . . . View [the scene], and you will find faith easy; for before you there is visible, tangible proof." What he witnessed and reported about the First Council of the Vatican was a large dose of the triumphalism that was so central to his own religious sensibilities. But of the struggles and rivalries that raged within the council he said not a word. Those who read his accounts could not have guessed that the proposal to define the personal infallibility of the pope had divided the council fathers into bitter factions, which hurled accusations of bad faith at each other.[32] Ireland himself expressed no opinion about the issue. Perhaps he had none. More likely, he learned early on that his opinion did not matter.

Ireland was one of three American priests designated by a particular bishop to act at the council in that bishop's name.[33] Shortly after its arrival in Rome the American delegation had petitioned the council's credentials committee to allow these proctors to attend the conciliar sessions, without enjoying the right to speak or vote. This request had been ignored. Early in January 1870, Ireland and Hecker renewed the petition, again without result. So strict were the conciliar rules of secrecy that exclusion from the general sessions meant that the proctors were also denied access to the meetings, held a couple of times a week, of their national delegation. The American bishops decided to get around the problem by declaring their own deliberations open to a proctor if he were named theological adviser to some bishop. Hecker took advantage of this provision, but Ireland for some reason did not, and so found himself reduced to the status of a tourist.[34]

He did not seem to mind. On occasion, to be sure, he displayed mild irritation that others failed to honor the rules of secrecy as scrupulously as he did himself: it was wearisome to preface even the most innocuous gossip with the saving phrase, "I am told." He was rather more severe with the journalists and pamphleteers who were fighting their own wars of words in the lobbies of the council. "Were I to follow the example of [the] English and French correspondents," Ireland protested, "I would tell you minutely all that is said to happen in these [conciliar] congregations; but I know for certain that all those who talk of the Council are mere guessers, and as a rule are mistaken."[35] Meanwhile he sent home no message that could possibly be offensive to pious Minnesota ears, and he reveled in the celebration of what proved to be the last Christmas of old papal Rome.

"For the last week," he wrote on January 2, 1870, "I have done little else in Rome than visit churches and admire the magnificence and pomp of the religious ceremonies that have taken place." On the afternoon of December 24, he assisted at a mass celebrated in Armenian at a convent chapel; the next morning, hurrying towards St. Peter's, he recalled that Vatican Hill was once covered with the "gardens of Nero, that the tyrant was wont to illumine with the burning bodies of the martyrs, and which is now crowned with the first Church of the world!" He attended the pope's mass at dawn, a simple affair, charming, nostalgic, the vast church filled with sleepy children and echoing to the sentimental sounds of Italian carols. But the solemn mass at 9:00 A.M. was "truly a grand spectacle: the mere curious might well prefer it to the triumphs of ancient Rome." For a clericalist like John Ireland, the scene savored of a fantasy come true. The soldiers and guards, the brilliantly dressed Roman nobility, all took their stand in and around the basilica; the prelates and the pope entered in a procession to the blare of trumpets; and mass commenced "on the very altar on which Peter celebrated, and on which his successor alone celebrates. It is true that the very splendor of the ceremonies prevents, to some extent, the calm piety which was so easily experienced at the [early] morning Mass."

In the afternoon Ireland assisted at a vesper service held in the Basilica of St. Mary Major and venerated the fragments of the manger of Bethlehem said to be preserved there. That evening he went to the Church of the Ara Coeli, where the Romans traditionally gathered at the end of Christmas Day for a special memorial to "il divino Bambino." "A little pulpit is erected near the altar," Ireland reported, "and the children, from seven to ten years of age, boys and girls, ascend in turn and deliver, with all the composure of old preachers, with perhaps more grace and simplicity, their exhortations to anxious crowds. Of course the 'Bambino' is the subject they all adopt."[36]

These Christmas festivities of 1869 were the high point of Ireland's sojourn in Rome, and he was fortunate to have been present when they were celebrated in their fullness for the last time: by the next Christmas the thousand years of papal rule had come to an end. It is doubtful that he intended to remain in Rome very long into the new year, doubtful, that is, that he ever expected his proctorship to give him a meaningful role in the work of the council; his family expected him home for Easter, in mid-April, long before the council was scheduled to adjourn.[37] But Bishop Grace had told him not to hurry, and he determined to seize the opportunity, which might not come again soon, to see some sights. Early in February 1870, he departed Rome for the south of Italy. After a leisurely tour of the ruins of Herculaneum and Pompeii, he "stood on the slope of Vesuvius, [his] eye resting on Naples Bay and the fields of Campania—a ravishing spectacle."[38] By March 16 he was in Paris, in time to learn of the death of the liberal Catholic leader, Charles de Montalembert, and to attend the great man's funeral at Ste. Clotilde. "Religion," he wrote in the *Northwestern Chronicle,* "has just lost one of its ablest and most intrepid defenders, France one of its brightest literary glories, and Catholic Ireland one of her truest and most distinguished friends."[39] From France he went to Ireland, to Kilkenny City first—"My heart [was] . . . thrilled, and my soul was . . . wrapt in ecstasy . . . when I looked around from the summit of that old round tower that has for ages stood sentinel on the banks of the Nore"—then to a "warm welcome" and homecoming at Burnchurch, then to Blarney Castle where he ritually kissed the fabled stone of that name, and finally, during the last days of April, to Dublin.[40] His ship docked in New York on May 7 or 8, and he spent a few depressing days in the city, touring Blackwell's Island and Bellevue, where he found three-quarters of the inmates afflicted with drunkenness. "I then made a vow," he recalled later, "that so long as I had the power I would speak for war against intemperance."[41] By May 14 he had arrived in St. Paul armed with the Irish blackthorn cane he had promised to whichever member of the

Father Mathew Society registered the most recruits during his absence.[42]

John Ireland therefore had resumed his ordinary duties for fully two months before the First Council of the Vatican, in the midst of a tremendous thunderstorm, defined the doctrine of papal infallibility and then adjourned, sine die.[43] The next day France declared war on Prussia and ordered home the French troops stationed in Rome, thus removing the last prop to the little that remained of the pope's temporal power. On September 20, 1870, after a brief bombardment, the forces of the Kingdom of Italy occupied the eternal city, and Pius IX, withdrawing his court behind the Leonine walls, declared himself "Prisoner of the Vatican."[44]

In far-off Minnesota these resounding events made little practical difference. The fall of Rome to united Italy was a foregone conclusion. Indeed, three years earlier Ireland had predicted that the pope, thanks to the machinations of the Piedmontese and the French, would be driven into exile, without, however, sacrificing a whit of his spiritual authority.[45] But the evident satisfaction with which the non-Catholic world greeted the pope's discomfiture — only a prelude, many said confidently, to the complete destruction of the papacy — moved the American Catholic minority, including John Ireland, to manifest support for the beleaguered Holy Father.

It was an era that loved rallies and parades, and on January 22, 1871, seven thousand men braved a driving snowstorm and marched through the streets of St. Paul — "the procession was the largest and most imposing that has ever taken place in this city or State," reported one newspaper — to protest the seizure of the pope's temporal domain. They jammed into the cathedral, "filling every nook and corner [of that] immense building," but, even so, many had to remain outside in the snow. They were harangued by speaker after speaker, clerical and lay, in English and in French, until, at the climactic moment, John Ireland, the memories of romanità still fresh in his mind, stepped to the podium. "We have fallen upon strange times," he cried. "Today ideas of right, justice, honor, seem to be obliterated from the minds of men. Material force and self-convenience are the principles that rule. Witness this very fact that has called you together: the spoliation of the Holy See, the most glaring of modern international crimes." And instead of decrying

this perversity, "peoples and governments applaud [it]. Alas, for
honor and justice." Among the Americans who applauded were
"men who a few years ago thundered the most fiercely against rebellion in the South and British interference in its favor. I did not
most assuredly blame them then, but I blame them now, because
having had one rule for themselves, they have a different one for
Pius IX." No pope, he went on, can be placed "under the sway of
an earthly power, be it that of a monarch or of a sovereign people. . . . [We Catholics] shall not allow it, and, what is our
greatest source of hope, God is with us, for it is the cause of the
Church. Once more we shall all meet within the walls of this Cathedral, then to chant a song of triumph when Pius IX will again be
the independent monarch of Rome."[46] His prediction, of course, did
not come true, but the issue of the pope's temporal power long out-
lived Pius IX, as John Ireland was to learn to his dismay.

The definition of papal infallibility posed no serious intellectual
problem for Ireland. Before the conciliar decree, he kept his opinions to himself; and once the council had proclaimed the doctrine,
he certainly went through none of the soul-searing pain that
afflicted, among others, the archbishops of St. Louis and Cincinnati.[47] Characteristically he set down in a notebook the historical
"proofs" of the doctrine, as these were to be found in standard theological manuals.[48] Also characteristically, he judged it his duty, as
part of his leadership function, to respond to attacks upon the papal
prerogative.[49]

But the quarrels of the great world outside still took second
place to the day-to-day activities of a busy parish priest who involved himself as much as possible in local affairs, and, so far as the
total abstinence movement was concerned, in national affairs as
well. On a Sunday evening in mid-January 1874, for example, Ireland delivered a stirring address at the cathedral, titled "Plain Talk
on Temperance," after which "fifty men walked up to the altar and
signed the pledge."[50] During the balance of that year he was busy
as Bishop Grace's agent in securing property (and in raising money
to pay for it) on the east bank of the Mississippi, midway between
St. Paul and Minneapolis, to be used as the site of an industrial
school for homeless Catholic boys.[51] Along with his ordinary
duties Ireland found time also to write his first piece for publication,

a memoir of Lucien Galtier.[52] But then, suddenly, the great world outside intruded itself.

The citizens of St. Paul heard the news in mid-February, 1875: "The Rev. John Ireland, Rector of the Cathedral Parish and Secretary of the diocese, has been elevated by His Holiness Pope Pius the Ninth . . . to the dignity of Vicar Apostolic of Nebraska, Wyoming, Montana and part of Dakota. . . . It is currently reported . . . that he has concluded to accept the new dignity conferred on him and that he will be accompanied to his new field of labor by his father, mother and other members of his family." There was widespread consternation, even among those elements in the community that did not always see eye-to-eye with the aggressive young priest. One editor spoke the mind of all: "While wishing the reverend gentleman every success in his future home, we must say that St. Paul can badly afford to lose his valuable services, and that it may be many years before the void he leaves here can be suitably filled."[53] Over the succeeding weeks people waited for some definitive statement, but none was forthcoming; Ireland's St. Patrick's Day address followed the routine pattern, though some in the congregation thought they discerned in the preacher's particularly warm thanks for their friendship and encouragement a sign that he would soon leave them. Then, in the last days of March, it was announced that Thomas Langdon Grace had departed for Rome, and even the dullest St. Paulite could guess the reason why.[54]

The appointment of Ireland to Nebraska proved to be part—a relatively insignificant part indeed—of a plan to reorganize the Catholic church in the Middle West. In March 1874, the suffragan bishops of the Province of St. Louis, Thomas Grace among them, met in the home of their metropolitan, Archbishop Peter Richard Kenrick.[55] Among the results of that meeting was a petition to Rome to carve out of the enormous Province of St. Louis two new ecclesiastical provinces, one in Milwaukee and another in Santa Fe.[56] The bishops also recommended that the Diocese of Chicago, which then embraced all of the state of Illinois, be divided, with a new see created in Peoria, and—of more direct consequence to Grace—that the northern two-thirds of the Diocese of St. Paul be constituted a separate vicariate. All these territorial changes were approved in Rome.

Another piece of business on the agenda of the gathering at Kenrick's house was the preparation of a slate of candidates for the Vicariate of Nebraska, whose incumbent had recently died. The right of final appointment to this post, as to all positions of episcopal rank, rested with the pope, though in fact, when he made such a decision, the pope depended entirely upon the recommendations given him by his bureaucracy. Since the United States was defined as a missionary country, the department of the Roman curia charged with overseeing American affairs was the Sacred Congregation for the Propagation of the Faith, commonly called, from its Latin name, Propaganda.[57] Candidates for American bishoprics, therefore, were screened by Propaganda before a name was finally presented to the pope. But before Propaganda could act intelligently in such an important matter, it needed information, it needed a system whereby it could decide which nominees for episcopal appointment deserved serious consideration. Indeed, it needed a system that could provide nominees. As the Catholic church grew in the United States throughout the nineteenth century, largely through immigration, the problem of finding suitable candidates for episcopal office became ever more acute. By 1870 fifty-five bishops presided over slightly fewer than four thousand ordinary priests. The latter formed the natural pool from which new bishops could be recruited when necessary, but in fact sharp tension existed between the two groups on this question: the priests with increasing stridency demanded at least a consultative role in the process of episcopal appointment—a right enjoyed by their confreres in other areas of the Catholic world—while the bishops insisted that the presentation of candidates to Propaganda was their own prerogative. Part of the difficulty and disagreement stemmed from the status of the United States as a missionary country to which, for that very reason, the ordinary norms of the universal church (canon) law need not apply. This was why activist priests campaigned relentlessly for what they considered a regularization of the situation in the United States and the establishment in this country of the conventional canon law.[58]

The quarrel raged on for years, and, like most quarrels of the sort, there were rights and wrongs on both sides. Propaganda by and large supported the bishops, though its officials grew ever more sensitive to complaints about episcopal tyranny and to charges that bishops tended to recommend to vacant dioceses their cronies and hangers-on. Nevertheless, in the spring of 1874, when Kenrick's suffragans met with him in St. Louis, the system in place securely guaranteed them the right to send a list of three names to Propaganda, along with sustaining documentation, for an episcopal vacancy within the province. The list, called a terna, was drawn up in a descending order of preference, and, though theoretically Propaganda—and all the more so the pope—could reject all the names on a terna, in practice such a conclusion to the process was rare.

Among the faults often laid at the door of the American bishops-—a maddening one to the legal-minded officers of Propaganda[59]—was the casual, even haphazard, manner in which they prepared ternae. Such apparently was the case in St. Louis in 1874, at least according to the resumé put together by one of Propaganda's clerks.[60] Kenrick and his suffragans duly submitted a terna for the Vicariate of Nebraska, but at first they nominated the same persons for the proposed new bishopric of Peoria. At the top of their list (*dignissimus*, most worthy) was Edward Hennessy, a member of the Vincentian order; next (*dignior*, very worthy) came Michael Hurley, a pastor in Peoria; and in third place (*dignus*, worthy) was John Ireland.

In effect, this amounted to the submission of three names for two positions, clearly an unacceptable procedure. So sometime later a separate terna for Peoria was sent to Propaganda, and on it were the names Frederick Wayrich, a Redemptorist from New York; John Lancaster Spalding, of the Diocese of Louisville; and John J. Kain, pastor at Harper's Ferry, West Virginia.[61] Now the prefect of Propaganda and his colleagues had the requisite six names, but, sticklers for legal niceties as they professed themselves to be, they nevertheless proceeded to treat the six in a curiously unlegal fashion, lumping them all together as they pondered their decision. Hennessy, Wayrich, and Spalding they dismissed because of unfavorable reports about their fitness for office (*"a motivo delle sfavorevoli notizie"*).[62] Kain was about to be appointed bishop of Wheeling. Hurley, as a resident pastor, was the appropriate choice for the new diocese, though his name had not appeared on the terna for Peoria.[63] That left Ireland for Nebraska. "Finally, for the Apostolic Vicariate of Nebraska, no name remains save that of the priest Ireland, about whom there is, besides, sufficient satisfactory information."[64] By mid-January 1875, the pope gave his formal approval to the appointments of Hurley and Ireland, and a month later his decision was made public.

So it was that John Ireland first attained episcopal rank through a process of elimination, and a rather sloppy process at that. But the news of his promotion had startled Bishop Grace as much as anyone else in St. Paul, and it effectively forced the hand of that usually diffident man. In April he laid siege to the huge black stone building that housed Propaganda on the edge of the Piazza di Spagna. He explained to the prefect, Cardinal Barnabò, that he had allowed Ireland's name to appear on the original terna only after his colleagues in the province assured him that the appointment to Nebraska would never come to pass. Inclusion had been intended to be a compliment to a deserving young priest, nothing more. Grace did not mince words. He expressed his personal displeasure at the turn of events. He warned that Ireland's departure would cause deep resentment in Minnesota and would lead to a host of unspecified troubles. He threatened, finally, to resign.[65]

Barnabò then put his finger on the glaring weakness in Grace's case: was Father Ireland worthy to be a bishop, or was he not? If he was, why did Grace stand in the way of the promotion? If not, why was his name placed upon the terna, when the bishop of St. Paul could easily have prevented it? Grace replied, rather lamely, that he had always intended to ask that Ireland be appointed his coadjutor.[66] Ireland, he told Barnabò on April 30, "knows intimately the state of my diocese, and is eminently qualified for episcopal rank."

Meanwhile, back in St. Paul, the object of these negotiations had his own role to play, a role carefully orchestrated with that of Bishop Grace. On April 22 Ireland wrote a Latin letter addressed directly to Pius IX in which he asked the pontiff to revoke the appointment to Nebraska. He enclosed this letter, together with the papal documents naming him a titular bishop[67] and a vicar apostolic, with another letter to Grace, to whom he wrote: "As you will perceive from reading this letter [to the pope], I enter into no details as to the reasons of my resignation, taking the liberty to refer to your statement of the case. . . . I put Nebraska entirely out of my mind and settle down quietly into my old attachment to Minnesota." Then, with a docility not altogether characteristic of him, he added: "I never by any direct acting or choosing of my own have fashioned my destiny; it has been always apparently fashioned for me, and it has been all the better with me. . . . In this whole present affair, it would be a hard task for me were I myself to decide alone what I should do. My consolation is that it is all in your hands, and not in my own."[68]

The packet containing this letter and the accompanying documents never reached the bishop, because the mail steamer carrying it was wrecked off the coast of England.[69] But the accident, as things turned out, had no bearing on the final outcome in Rome. Grace had made his case persuasively enough, and his own prestige within the curia, which stood higher perhaps than he had realized, proved enough to win the day. "There can be no doubt," read the final Propaganda report, "that Mgr. Grace has earned the favor he asks; during the sixteen or seventeen years he has ruled the Diocese of St. Paul he has consistently displayed wisdom, great zeal, and sincere attachment to the Holy See." The one legal obstacle which remained Propaganda cavalierly brushed aside: the canonical necessity for a terna could be waived in this case, the congregation decreed, because it was a matter simply of translating a vicar apostolic to another mission, a process done all the more easily since the subject had not only not taken possession but had not even been consecrated. On May 9, 1875, Pope Pius IX appointed John Ireland coadjutor bishop of St. Paul, with right of succession.

Official announcement of the appointment did not follow immediately, but rumors were rife in Minnesota within a few days. It was certain, one published report said, that Ireland would not go to Nebraska, and "more than probable" that he would be named coadjutor: "This diocese has increased so much in wealth and population within the last few years that Bishop Grace has more than he can possibly attend to."[70] When Grace arrived home, a month later, he greeted the large and enthusiastic welcoming delegation from the porch of his residence, and, in the midst of an otherwise rambling speech, he said: "My trip was undertaken mainly for matters con-

nected with the interests of this diocese, but paramount over all was
the contemplated removal of Father Ireland from the scene of his
labors in this city to a distant See. I thought and I think so
still . . . that his departure would be a loss to the interests of the
diocese and of the people who loved him so well and so truly." The
pope had listened kindly to the bishop's arguments and "had
promised that no change would take place."[71]

Not till mid-October did the official bulls of appointment arrive
from Rome,[72] and then the plans for the consecration[73] ceremony
started to be made. The date chosen was December 21, almost exactly the fourteenth anniversary of Ireland's ordination to the
priesthood. The gala day was cold, but clear and bright. The cathedral, elaborately decorated with flags and banners, was jammed an
hour before the service began. Richard Ireland and the other members of the family sat in the pews just behind the nuns and clergy.
Bishop Grace was the consecrating prelate, and among those who
took part in the long and involved ceremony was the already venerable Augustin Ravoux, as well as Caillet and Oster and several of
the young priests whom Ireland had recruited for the total abstinence movement. The preacher of the occasion was, appropriately
enough, Thomas O'Gorman, who, at the end of his sermon, turned
to his old schoolfellow and said: "Assume the burden that heaven
imposes on your shoulders. Grasp your crozier and rule the flock
committed to you."[74] It was an invitation John Ireland hardly
needed.

~ VII ~

"An Invitation to the Land"

1876–82

T HE LOT of an auxiliary bishop within the Roman Catholic system is not always a happy one. He has achieved, to be sure, a lofty spiritual status within the community of believers, since his ordination to the fullness of the priesthood has given him a standing sacramentally on a par with all other bishops, including the pope himself. But authority he has none, except what his ordinary may be pleased to delegate to him. More often than not he passes eventually to his own diocese. Even so, the interval can be long and anxious, a trying time, analogous to a term as vice president or lieutenant governor, in which loyalty to the policies of another becomes the overriding, if not the exclusive, practical virtue.

By contrast, a coadjutor bishop with right of succession, though legally no more independent than an auxiliary, enjoys the inestimable advantage of knowing that he will one day be the ordinary of the place where he is presently at work. He is the rising sun in a way in which an auxiliary can never be, and those within the diocese who think at all about their future prospects ignore him at their peril. Thus John Ireland, even in his secondary role as coadjutor to Bishop Grace for nine years, wielded much authority within the local church over which, as everyone knew, he would, in his turn, preside.

The special relationship he had developed with Bishop Grace over the dozen years before his elevation late in 1875 made his position all the more powerful. The two continued to live together in the house next to the cathedral, sharing accommodations with the priests who staffed the parish; these latter came and went, as diocesan needs dictated, but the bishops remained permanent fixtures

there, in daily communication with each other.[1] Grace, with typical
generosity, settled upon Ireland a yearly stipend of one thousand
dollars, which amounted to about half his own ordinary income.[2]
Both men would have received, in addition, offerings for the various sacramental functions they performed up to a total which,
though impossible to name precisely, would have been more than
adequate for their needs. The only luxuries Grace permitted himself
were cigars and snuff. Needless to say, the clergy house had no liquor bill.

Ireland's primary job during these years was to help Grace fulfill
the usual duties incumbent on a bishop, most of which were religiously significant and important in that sense, but not otherwise
remarkable. The coadjutor, whose appearances in the cathedral pulpit were now reduced to about once a month, regularly traveled
across the diocese to administer the sacrament of confirmation, to
dedicate new churches and schools, and to preside at other institutional functions. On these junkets he took whatever conveyance
was available, none very comfortable, and he learned to sleep in
jolting carriages and, wrapped in his overcoat, on benches in chilly
country railroad stations. Routine ceremonial activities consumed
much episcopal time and energy, for the population of the Diocese
of St. Paul continued to grow at a prodigious rate. During the years
of Ireland's coadjutorship fifty new parishes were established, and
when Grace retired in 1884, though the area of his see had been
reduced by five-sixths due to the creation of the Vicariates of
Northern Minnesota (1875) and Dakota (1879), he had subject to
his ecclesiastical jurisdiction 195 churches and 51 stations, two
hospitals, ten girls' boarding schools, five orphanages, 150 priests,
twenty-nine seminarians, members of fourteen orders of religious
women and six of men, and more than 130,000 Catholic people.[3]
Much of this growth was the natural product of the rhythms of immigration, but a significant portion of it was due directly to John
Ireland's activities as a colonizer.[4] He had worn his new miter for
scarcely a month when he issued his first invitation to the land.

Ireland had long been convinced that the ideal locale for the
Catholic immigrant, and particularly the Irishman, was the countryside. He had a Jeffersonian vision of a class of sturdy Catholic
yeomen who owned and farmed their own land and who thus

gained a measure of independence and respectability unattainable by propertyless day laborers. How he came to this position, which was not shared by most contemporary Catholic prelates, is unclear, but he came to it early. "The cities have blighted our people," he told an Irish congregation in 1865. What did the workman, lashed to the machines in mills and factories, have to show for his toil, except permanent economic uncertainty and bad health? What had immigrant labor on the railroads, the canals, and especially the steamboats led to, except broken homes, lost faith, and perverted morals?[5] Huddled together in the slums of the great eastern cities, the immigrants had exchanged one form of servitude for another. They had become the victims of unscrupulous politicians. They had fallen prey to the worst kinds of vices. What they needed if they were to experience the full promise of the American dream was land of their own. John Ireland determined to help them get it.

He could point to precedent. Both Loras and Cretin had sponsored campaigns to attract Catholics from the eastern states to settle on the fertile prairies of Iowa and Minnesota. Bishop Grace, on the other hand, apparently satisfied that the natural increase of Catholics in his jurisdiction was challenge enough, had shown scant interest in projects designed to draw in even more. But when, in 1864, young Father Ireland proposed to found the Minnesota Irish Emigration Society, the bishop, in characteristic fashion, put no obstacles in his path. Indeed, the Society, organized to establish the displaced Irish "in homes in lieu of those from which they had been compelled to flee," was incorporated in St. Paul under Grace's auspices.[6]

The Society had as its president John Ireland and, as secretary, Ireland's constant companion in good causes, Dillon O'Brien. But it hardly functioned in any serious way, largely perhaps because its president was absorbed in other activities. What little visibility it enjoyed, at any rate, was due to O'Brien, who lectured and wrote on the subject[7] and established contacts with similar bodies in various parts of the country. His efforts and those of others similarly minded brought about a national Catholic colonization convention held in St. Louis in 1869, which appointed O'Brien one of its secretaries. "Of course," a participant remembered, "there were many eloquent speeches and a string of resolutions. There was a banquet and a steamboat excursion, and everything was agreeable and harmonious down to the adjournment. And that was all. Nothing came of it. A committee had been named to carry out the design of the convention. The committee never met."[8]

The failure at St. Louis followed a pattern set decades before. During the 1840s and 1850s a variety of grandiose colonization schemes had been launched in Ireland and the United States, and all of them had come to nothing.[9] Immigrants continued to pour into the country—in 1850 there were 960,000 Irish born in the United States, 44 percent of the foreign-born total—but very few of them ventured far from the Atlantic seaboard.[10] One reason that elaborate colonization plans faltered was the opposition of Irish-American churchmen, typified by the celebrated Archbishop John Hughes of New York (d. 1864), who thought such plans "mischievous," because they disturbed "the minds of those . . . already established . . . by a gilded and exaggerated report of theoretical blessings . . . [in] the nominal ownership of . . . uncultivated land, not infrequently teeming with fever and ague," and remote from the ministrations of a parish and a priest.[11]

Hughes's strictures were probably a useful corrective to some of the visionary propaganda put forward by well-intentioned colonizers, who too often depicted farm life in the Midwest as an uninterrupted idyll. Loras and Cretin, for their part, had been careful not to disguise the difficulties settlers in their dioceses could expect, particularly in the early years. Long after the controversy had passed John Ireland was severely critical of Hughes—colonization, he said, "often met with strong opposition on the part of [men] whose position and intelligence should have promised better things"[12]—but the fact remains that no colonization plan to be applied nationwide ever gained significant support within the Catholic community. Ireland's criticism, moreover, was tinged with unintended irony, because what success the Minnesota colonies enjoyed depended to a large degree upon their modest scope and upon the tight clerical control he imposed on them.

One of John Ireland's major preoccupations during these years was, of course, the cause, local and increasingly national, of total abstinence. In this endeavor, too, O'Brien was his ally and co-worker. Gradually there formed in Ireland's mind a linkage between the two issues, a linkage pressed upon him by the older and more experienced O'Brien. To promote one of these highly desirable objectives could well be a way to promote the other. The Irish, jammed into New York and Boston tenements, supporting themselves by casual labor at a dollar or two a day, and deprived of the self-esteem that only the ownership of property could confer, were the same people victimized by the cruelties of the liquor trade. The image of the ideal Catholic farmer—secure, hard-working, independent—certainly did not suffer as far as Ireland was concerned by adding sobriety to the list of admirable virtues, and he soon came to adopt Dillon O'Brien's aphorism as his own: "Give me temperance and a healthy immigration to land as levers, and I will raise my people to the highest standards of citizenship."[13]

Ireland did not make his plan public until after his episcopal consecration, but he must have been turning it over in his mind for some time before that. In mid-January 1876 the *Northwestern Chronicle* reported that Ireland had had placed at his disposal seventy-five thousand acres of unoccupied land in Swift County, Minnesota—about 120 miles west and a little north of the Twin Cities—and a week later came the announcement that the old Minnesota Irish Emigration Society was giving way to the Catholic Colonization Bureau of St. Paul, which was to be administered by Dillon O'Brien. Ireland, it was further revealed, had signed a contract making him the exclusive agent for all the land in Swift County belonging to the St. Paul and Pacific Railroad.[14] This proved to be the first of eleven such agreements the bishop would enter into over the next five years.

Ireland's arrangement with the St. Paul and Pacific was a shrewd opening stroke, and it demonstrated that his idealism, most of the time, was carefully tempered by a hard-headed appreciation of economic realities. Earlier efforts at colonization had foundered because they had lacked the capital necessary to move people and to secure land. But Ireland's new bureau did not need any capital, so long as it acted merely as an agent in dispensing railroad property, as a middleman between the prospective settler and the corporation that owned the land. That corporation, furthermore, was very interested in that settler: "The prairie without population," James J. Hill was to observe later, "is a desert," and no railroad executive worth his salt intended the lines he built at such pain and expense to pass across an empty prairie. What he wanted along his routes were customers, thriving communities of prosperous citizens who would routinely pay for the services of his freight and passenger trains.[15]

The railroad industry had long recognized the usefulness of colonization as a way of rendering its expanding networks more profitable.[16] The Illinois Central, for example, had from the 1850s mounted a successful campaign to accelerate the process of immigration for its own commercial advantage. It opened immigrant-aid offices in the eastern United States and sent agents to selected localities in Europe to publicize the advantages of settling in the American Midwest or, more specifically, in those areas served by the Illinois Central. In 1871 alone some seven thousand Scandinavians were persuaded to cross the Atlantic and take up farming in Illinois. Railroad companies operating farther west were, if anything, more anxious to secure settlers, since the territories in which they operated were much more thinly populated than was Illinois. Thus the Northern Pacific, with its plans to push its system from the Twin Cities to the West Coast, was by the early 1870s following the Illinois Central's lead and soliciting colonists from New York to London to Amsterdam.

The nationwide financial crisis and its attendant distress, which began in 1873, changed this picture dramatically, but for John Ireland the panic opened wide the door of opportunity. Not for the last time in his colonization ventures did the bishop find himself extremely fortunate in the timing of events. The St. Paul and Pacific, in 1873 part of the larger Northern Pacific system, defaulted on its bonds on May 1. Immigration offices at home and abroad were promptly closed, orders for descriptive pamphlets and brochures cancelled. The railroad executives believed as strongly as before in the benefits to be derived from promoting colonization, but in a period of sharp retrenchment they did not have, or did not want to spend, the money to pay for it. Bishop Ireland then offered them his proposition.

Railroads like the St. Paul and Pacific had been able to encourage colonization in the first place because of the extensive property they possessed, thanks to the largesse of the federal and state governments. In Swift County, for instance, the St. Paul and Pacific owned alternate sections on both sides of its right of way for a distance of from three to five miles, up to a total of well over one hundred thousand acres. The intervening sections still belonged to the state of Minnesota and were still subject to the provisions of the Homestead Act of 1862 — which meant the land was free (save for a registration fee of fourteen dollars) to those who would live on it for five years, to the limit of eighty acres within ten miles of a land-grant railroad line or 160 acres beyond. Other adjacent public land was available to settlers who pledged to cultivate timber on the treeless prairie (ten acres of tree-plantings for every 150 acres farmed), and even tracts of state land not covered by the Homestead Act could be purchased for as little as $1.25 an acre.[17] So Ireland was not merely boasting when he said that he aimed "making a grand total of *one hundred and fifty thousand acres* open to Catholic settlement."[18]

What Ireland offered the St. Paul and Pacific was free publicity. His rank within his church — and it was not insignificant that he spoke as "Bishop" Ireland, not simply as "Father" Ireland — guaranteed that his call for colonists would receive sympathetic attention in the Catholic press all over the country and in Europe as well. The railroad executives may indeed have exaggerated the degree of influence the young coadjutor could exert in the large concentrations of Catholic population in the eastern United States, where, outside temperance circles, he was virtually unknown. But if they miscalculated on this point — they were not, after all, experts on the nuances of ecclesiastical titles — it mattered little, they soon discovered, when compared to the advantage of enlisting Ireland's single-minded determination to bring Catholic colonists to Minnesota. There was a bonus for them, too, in the equally dedicated participation in the project of a literary Irishman like Dillon O'Brien, a knowledgeable veteran of the colonization movement, who also possessed the facile gifts of a born pamphleteer.

Aside from some differences of detail, the terms that the bishop concluded with the St. Paul and Pacific were consistent with the agreements he would sign later with other railway companies. For a period of two years Ireland's Colonization Bureau was to be the sole agent for the sale of the railroad's property in Swift County. The agent received a flat 10 percent commission on all transactions.

Moreover, the railroad agreed to donate for its agent's exclusive use a generous number of lots in the towns that grew up to service the colonies. Many of these lots eventually provided sites for Catholic churches and schools, but others were put on the market by the bureau and sold at advantageous prices. Such sales, together with the agent's fees, paid the bureau's expenses. Ireland was not permitted to purchase any railroad land in his own name or for his personal use.[19]

The cost of the land to the colonist who migrated to Swift County was between five and seven dollars an acre, depending on quality and proximity to the railroad line. The down payment amounted to one year's interest at seven percent (or sixty-seven dollars on a tract of 160 acres at six dollars an acre). The balance, principal and interest, had to be paid within ten years. Ireland gained a further concession from the company, which agreed to accept at face value its own land certificates, then selling far below par, as payment; for those settlers able to take advantage of this provision the price of their tracts could be reduced to as low as $1.50 an acre.[20]

On January 26, 1876—John Ireland had been a bishop scarcely a month—the first thirty-two colonists selected their parcels. By September, eight hundred more had followed suit—75 percent of them of Irish extraction, the rest German, Polish, and French[21]—and sixty thousand acres of railroad land had been settled. So quickly did the project move forward that before the end of the year Ireland signed another contract with the St. Paul and Pacific, and eventually, in 1879, the total acreage made available by the railroad to colonists in Swift County came to 117,000. How much additional government land was taken up as a direct consequence of Ireland's initiatives cannot be said with any certainty, but it was doubtless considerable. The villages of De Graff and Clontarf gradually took shape as the east and west terminals respectively of the colony lands, and then each of them as the nucleus of a colony of its own. A little church in honor of Our Lady of Kildare was built in the former place in 1876; the pastor's name, coincidentally, was F. J. Swift. To Clontarf, seventeen miles away, Ireland dispatched his former colleague at the cathedral, Anatole Oster, who named the parish he organized there for St. Malachy, a testimony to the

Irish character of his congregation rather than to his own French sensibilities.[22]

Central to Ireland's policy was the placing of a priest in each of the ten colonies he founded. There were several reasons for this, one of them a posthumous acknowledgement of the criticisms of Archbishop Hughes. Many potential Catholic colonists, Dillon O'Brien wrote, "feared that if they came West they would be beyond the reach of church and priest." To counter this fear, the Bureau would make certain that "the resident priest and church should go in with our first settlers, be their number large or small. To this good rule we attribute, to a great extent, not alone our success in bringing settlers to our colonies, but likewise their general contentment in their new homes and brave cheerfulness in meeting the trials, hardships, and set-backs which are incident to new settlements."[23]

To Ireland's and O'Brien's credit, they did not underplay the difficulties colonists could expect, especially during the early years of settlement. "If you come from a city, you will, doubtless, feel lonely for a while, until you get accustomed to prairie life; you will miss many immediate comforts; you will have to put up with discomforts, with disappointments, with trials. The man who feels he can stand up against all such difficulties in the present, and look bravely to the future for his reward, let him come to Minnesota."[24] The presence in the colony of a priest and a church and school, however humble, would indeed guarantee the settlers spiritual solace, but would also provide them with a sense of social cohesion and of community to help sustain them during the arduous beginnings of the colony.

From Ireland's point of view the resident pastor served another important function as well. He was the bishop's agent. He acted as facilitator and adviser for the colonists. He was, in effect, an employee of the Colonization Bureau, and in that capacity he smoothed the way for the newcomers in a number of mundane ways. It was the priest who usually met the immigrants at the station, gave them the necessary initial information, put them into contact with the railroad land-office, and remained throughout their early tenure a source of encouragement and support. It was the priest, as one contemporary observer expressed it, "who manage[d] the colony for Dr. Ireland."[25] And since the priest was the bishop's subject and served only at the bishop's will, he was the ideal instrument by which Ireland and the Colonization Bureau in St. Paul were kept informed of the progress of the settlement and could, in turn, assure the railroad that the terms of the contract were being met.

The foundation of the two colonies in Swift County—De Graff and Clontarf—was followed over the succeeding five years by settlements at eight other sites in four other southwestern Minnesota counties. One of them, in a gracious gesture to the benign if uninvolved bishop of St. Paul, was named Graceville. Between 1876 and 1880 Ireland contracted altogether for about 380,000 acres of railroad land and thereby stimulated settlement on an undetermined amount of contiguous public land as well. Throughout this period the railroad companies continued to support the bishop's colonizing ventures by granting them various commercial advantages. For example, instead of insisting on conventional mortgages, they extended direct credit to the settlers by simply delaying transfer of land titles until payment was made; since they continued to be anxious to keep the lands along their rights of way productively occupied, they tended to be lenient with those who fell behind in their installments. When the Swift County colonies were short of winter fuel, the St. Paul and Pacific shipped cordwood to the colonies for sale at cost. Similarly the railroad transported free of charge saplings

"A Dull Day on the Streets of Graceville," an engraving from A Sketch of Graceville, *a promotional pamphlet published in 1887. (MHS)*

to any colonist who would plant them on his treeless farm. In response to the grasshopper plague of 1877, agricultural agents employed by the railroad were dispatched to the aid of the farmers, and the road absorbed the cost of sending to the scene the materials used in the attempt to cleanse the fields of the larvae left by the insects.[26]

All this benevolence was by no means attributable to altruism. The railroads operating in Minnesota had shared during the early 1870s the obloquy directed against the industry generally around the country. Accusations of rate fixing, tax evasion, and extortion —most of them true—had been followed by the depression of 1873, which had devastated the companies' fiscal base and had resulted in new ownership for most of the lines.[27] Here was another instance of John Ireland's good luck: just at the moment he started his colonization project, the railroads were intent upon tapping new sources of income and also upon restoring public confidence in their transactions. Promoting and, to a degree, sustaining the bishop's colonies amounted to good business, and provided as well an opportunity to restore a somewhat tarnished image. In a sense, the railroads needed Ireland almost as much as he needed them.

That this mutual dependence could have personal ramifications was demonstrated in the autumn of 1877. James J. Hill had determined to take over the insolvent St. Paul and Pacific. To do so, however, he had to attract substantial new capital, since the line's indebtedness ran to $44 million. One morning in early September, he and one of his partners took a potential backer—the president of the Bank of Montreal—on a trip along the line, so that that gentleman could see for himself the rich promise the railroad held for the future. All went well for some distance out of St. Paul, but then as the train rolled farther west, the developed farmland gave way to "wild, untenanted prairie"; the bank president shook his head gravely and remarked that no railroad could make any money in such a barren countryside. "At last," as Ireland heard the story years later from Hill's partner,

> the station of De Graff was reached. It was Sunday morning. Around a rude but good-sized structure there were crowds of people; the trails leading toward it were covered with conveyances, most of them drawn by oxen. "What is all this?" inquired

[the banker]. "Why," answered quickly his [companions], "this is but an instance of what is soon to occur along the whole line of the railroad. This is a colony opened by Bishop Ireland one single year ago. Already the settlers brought in by the Bishop are counted by hundreds, and hundreds of others are coming to join them from different parts of America and Europe. This is Sunday morning, and the settlers are going to mass."

Hill and his partner got their funding, and the latter told Ireland: "In a manner unknown to yourself, you were a friend to Mr. Hill and myself in a moment when we needed friends. Whatever I can do for you is but a return of thanks for what you and your colony once did for us."[28]

Public wrath was to rise against the railroad companies again in the 1880s, but by then Ireland's colonies were self-sustaining entities, and he himself was no longer engaged in the enterprise. He and his colonists were also fortunate in the overall economic situation they confronted during the first years, when the settlements were especially fragile. Most of the farmers devoted the bulk of their land to the cultivation of wheat, and the virgin soil responded with hearty yields. Wheat grown in western Minnesota sold at about a dollar a bushel between 1875 and 1880.[29] The expanding railroad systems made shipment to market relatively easy, and the place to which the farmers delivered their crop was, instead of Milwaukee or Chicago as heretofore, nearby Minneapolis, which soon became the flour-milling capital of the world. This is not to say that Ireland's colonists participated in an unrelieved boom, but it does mean that economic conditions were more favorable for them in 1876 than would have been the case ten years earlier or ten years later.

Ireland's original intention in mounting his colonization projects was to offer a better way of life to Catholic immigrants — particularly but not exclusively the Irish — who languished, he thought, in the slums of the large cities of the eastern United States. He did not at first advertise his colonies in, or solicit recruits from, the countries of Europe; when he altered this policy later on, the results were, at best, mixed. But his hopes to bring the very poor to his colonies were not realized either, and whatever heady ambitions he entertained about his colonization scheme somehow relieving social tensions in the crowded population centers in the East had to go by the boards.

In the first place most of the urban people whom Ireland had in mind did not, for whatever reason, want to move.[30] Perhaps the devil they knew seemed less threatening than the devil they did not know. Secondly, Ireland's Colonization Bureau was never more than a clearing house that offered a method of obtaining cheap land; it had no land of its own to dispose of. Those easterners destitute of at least minimal resources could not even get to the colonies in Minnesota, much less survive there. In the first of his immigration pamphlets, *An Invitation to the Land: Reasons and Figures* (1877), and in the succeeding ones which appeared in 1879 and 1880—folksy tracts that combined idyllic descriptions of rural life in western Minnesota with carefully researched statistical information— Dillon O'Brien candidly stated the need for the prospective colonist to possess some small fund of capital before he ventured west.

In addition to paying the railroad fare from an eastern city—for example, twenty-four dollars per person from New York or Philadelphia—he had to make ends meet until his first cash crop came in, roughly sixteen months after his arrival. "He puts up a very cheap house," wrote O'Brien, sixteen by eighteen feet, "comfortable, warm and clean—much better than a cheap lodging in a city," which cost him $38.75. Furniture, including a cooking stove at $25.00, came to $43.00, a yoke of oxen and a plow $198.00, fuel and food, including a milk cow, $130.00, adding up to a grand total of $409.75. "This sum," O'Brien warned, "[the settler] will absolutely require when he arrives on the land. To this, in his calculations, he must add his expenses coming here." A family of four, therefore, had to have, by the most optimistic projections, at least five hundred dollars in hand before it fled the steaming tenements. Nor did O'Brien's figures include a down payment on the railroad land, which could range between forty and seventy dollars. Not many of the kind of families Ireland had first envisaged as colonists could scrape together that much money. As the years passed and their experience broadened he and O'Brien necessarily revised the estimate upward until a minimum of one thousand dollars became the accepted figure.[31]

But the dream died hard. When Ireland learned, in April 1876, that Catholic farmers from eastern Minnesota were moving into Swift County and buying railroad land through the Colonization Bureau, he sternly forbade the practice on the grounds that such transactions were open only "to the poor and homeless."[32] Yet in fact most of those who eventually settled in Ireland's colonies, and stayed there, had been farmers first somewhere else, in Pennsylvania, or Indiana, or perhaps storekeepers in New England, with some money in a savings bank, and had in either case brought with them a modicum of capital and skills.[33] The people who succeeded on the Minnesota prairie were those who had a little and wanted more, not those who had nothing.

Nevertheless Ireland was always ready to lend a sympathetic ear to any plan designed to help the genuinely "poor and homeless." Early in 1877 a businessman from southern Minnesota named William O'Mulcahy proposed the formation of a joint stock company as a way of raising money for support of indigent colonists. The bishop presided and spoke at the organizational meeting of the Minnesota Colonization Company, which was formally incorporated on February 15. The new company offered for public sale twenty-five hundred shares of stock at ten dollars a share and declared its purpose to be "the buying and selling of tracts of land in . . . Minnesota and assisting needy and deserving persons in settling thereon." Ireland bought ten shares of stock (as did Bishop Grace), and for a while there was a great deal of enthusiasm about the prospects of the company.[34]

The euphoria did not last. The directors of the company could not decide whether to treat the sale of stock as a business venture or an act of charity, and their appeals to the buying public fell somewhere in between. By June 1877, they had sold only 345 shares, and two years later, when they dissolved the company, they had come nowhere near their goal of twenty-five thousand dollars. They did manage to settle twenty or thirty families on about thirty-five hundred acres of land in Swift County, but it is unlikely that many of the immigrants they assisted remained on their tracts very long. The failure of the company did not affect Ireland's Bureau, from which it was entirely distinct, a point Dillon O'Brien was at pains to stress from the beginning: "We are proud to say that we have in Minnesota a chartered stock company . . . [which] proposes to give a poor, industrious, sober man eighty acres. . . . Of course," he added carefully, "this Catholic colonization stock company scheme has no connection with our Catholic Immigration Bureau; our bureau has no capital."[35]

To have no capital proved in the long run an advantage, because it meant that the colonists who dealt with the Bureau had to invest resources of their own, however scanty, in the project, and therefore they tried harder to make it a success. This lesson John Ireland was reluctant to learn, but in 1880 some fisher folk from the west of Ireland taught it to him with bitter emphasis.

Connemara is a peninsular district jutting out of County Galway into the Atlantic. It had always been a poor place whose inhabitants eked out a living from occasional fishing and from little patches of potatoes. In 1879 the district suffered a severe food shortage, so severe that the misery in Connemara rivaled that of the famine days of the 1840s. The situation came to the attention of James Nugent, an Irish priest already well known for his charitable work in the slums of Liverpool. Nugent collected some money, visited Connemara to distribute it, and concluded that the only permanent solution to the dreadful living conditions there was the emigration of a significant proportion of the native population. He wrote to Bishop Ireland—so far had spread the fame of the Minnesota colonies—and begged him to find a place for a community of wretched Connemaras. Ireland, who had once met Nugent and revered him as a leader of the temperance movement, agreed to receive fifty families.[36]

Through a public appeal Ireland managed to raise five thousand dollars to pay for the Connemara project—a sum that proved far too small—and he persuaded the railroads to transport the refugees free of charge from the eastern seaboard to Minnesota. Meanwhile he ordered set aside for them in the Graceville colony, Big Stone County, fifty farm sites of 160 acres, upon each of which he arranged to have built a small frame house, modestly furnished, and five acres of soil broken for planting.[37] (The prairie sod was so tough that to "break" a portion of it for tillage was a settler's first and perhaps most arduous task. A farmer who broke twenty acres a year was considered to have done very well.) To these unprecedented favors were added, at the bishop's expense, a consignment of clothing, farm implements, a year's supply of seed, and credit for food at the Graceville general store.[38]

Dillon O'Brien was dispatched to Boston to meet the Connemaras and conduct them to Minnesota. They landed on June 22, 1880, 309 of them altogether, and a pitiable sight they made: "The famine was visible in their pinched and emaciated faces, and in the shriveled limbs — they could scarcely be called legs and arms — of the children. Their features were quaint, and the entire company was squalid and wretched."[39] When he saw them, the hard-headed O'Brien, as he later told his son, immediately sensed the impending disaster. "The kindly but visionary Father Nugent . . . chose . . . not the competent but the incompetent; not the industrious but the shiftless; a group composed of mendicants who knew nothing of farming, and were entirely unfitted to cope with life upon the American prairie." Indeed, most of them could not speak English.[40]

O'Brien put the best face on the situation he could, and the Connemara caravan duly detrained in St. Paul on June 26. Ireland greeted them with some ceremony. Before the main group proceeded west, the bishop found employment in the city for about seventy young unmarried adults, men and women. By the time the rest of the Connemaras arrived in Graceville some days later, Ireland had assigned to each of the fifty families a host family charged with helping the newcomers adjust to their new homes. There was still opportunity to seed the acres already broken. Established farmers in the colony were paying $1.50 or $2.00 a day for hired hands. Almost all the Connemaras had a young relative working in St. Paul, who might be expected to send regularly a little money to his parents or siblings. All in all, in the glorious summer sunshine, the prospects looked bright.

But the trouble started almost at once. The Connemaras — dirty, foul-mouthed, lazy, prone to fighting at the drop of a hat — quickly alienated the older residents. Though most of the men found work on neighboring farms, many neglected to plant a crop on their own, some because they had sold the seed. Others sold the tools that had been given them. Warnings that they must use the warm summer months to sod their little houses against the winter cold and to prepare secure storage for perishables fell on deaf ears. Reports of problems gradually filtered back to St. Paul, but Ireland, who had staked so much of his personal prestige on this project, stubbornly refused to listen to any criticisms of it. In September he toured the Graceville colony, and was only partially reassured. The Connemaras seemed to be faring well enough, but their common mutters of discontent alarmed and angered the bishop. When some of them complained about the wage rate paid for hired labor in the locality, Ireland responded by announcing that henceforth public employment in Graceville would pay a dollar a day, and that any man unhired either by a local farmer or by the community would find his credit cut off.[41]

Most disquieting to Ireland was the failure of the Connemaras to appreciate that the promise of future success would make all present sacrifices worthwhile. With the wisdom of hindsight, it is difficult to understand why he thought they would. However trying his own immigrant youth had been, he had not known the kind of deprivation familiar to the Connemaras. His father, after all, had been a twenty-acre man. But out in the far reaches of Galway they had never had one farthing to rub against another, they had never owned anything, and, as for planning for the future, in the miserable existence they had endured, survival *today* was the sole criterion of success.[42] Little wonder that they hired themselves out as casual labor, promptly spent the pittance they earned, and then remarked, with a shrug, that if trouble came, "the Bishop brought us here, and he must care for us."[43]

Trouble indeed came soon, and with a vengeance. The first blizzard of the legendary winter of 1880–81 struck Graceville in mid-October, and during succeeding months the accumulation of snow and degree of cold rivaled anything the oldest frontiersman could remember. Suffering among the Connemaras, who had neglected to insulate their shanties or dig protective cellars for their potatoes, was intense. Ireland provided them with free provisions, at a cost to him of about six hundred dollars a month, but they often proved too indolent to collect the fruits of this latest benevolence. "The Connemara men would not take the flour away [from the station], although to them it was a free gift," reported one newspaper. "Some of the other farmers, when a sum was offered them to carry the flour to the homes of the Connemara men, said that they were willing enough to make a dollar, but that they would not turn their hands to benefit such a lazy people."[44]

Investigative reporters soon got wind of the difficulties in the colony, and, when inquiries were made, the cunning Connemaras, or some of them at least, hid the food and clothing that had been given them in order to show how badly they were being treated.[45] The adverse publicity in newspapers across the country, to Ireland's sorrow and fury, reflected negatively upon his whole colonization endeavor. He sent the tireless Dillon O'Brien to Graceville, and the true story quickly emerged. In the spring, the Connemaras cheerfully gave up their farms and were transported en masse—again at the bishop's expense—to St. Paul, where Ireland secured jobs for the men, mostly in the railroad yards. They settled under Dayton's Bluff east of downtown St. Paul in a shanty town, which was known for years as "Connemara Patch."[46]

The fiasco at Graceville did the colonization movement no permanent damage.[47] The farms of the Connemaras were quickly disposed of and their cattle distributed among the colony's remaining four hundred families, none of which exhibited any resentment toward the Bureau or the bishop or any lessening of resolve to make the settlement succeed. The personal effect upon Ireland is harder to judge. A confidant of the bishop later asserted that the Connemara affair "was the greatest grief of his life,"[48] but, in the absence of direct evidence, one may be permitted to doubt that this failure, bitterly disappointing as it may have been, loomed quite so large in the firmament of a man for whom hyperbole was stock in trade.

Once he decided the Connemara experiment had foundered, Ireland cut his losses swiftly and ended it, whatever measure of grief it may have caused him. And he maintained a stiffly cheerful demeanor, at least in public. "Many thanks for the kind letter you wrote to me during my trouble with my Connemara immigrants," he told the archbishop of Baltimore, James Gibbons. "You did much by your words to cheer me up at a moment when I needed encouragement. I am glad that you at once perceived the important fact that the Connemara people are very distinct from our regular colonists. What I feared was that danger might come to our colonization movement—but this, I am sure, has not been the case. The whole trouble is over. When my 'friends' showed themselves in their true colors, I adopted treatment suited to their case, and put a quietus on their complaints."[49] Chastened by the experience he may have been, but not cured, because at the very moment the Connemaras were streaming back to St. Paul, he was lending a hand in another scheme to put a colony of indigent Irish on the land.

John Sweetman was a wealthy Irishman, a friend of Charles Stewart Parnell's, who participated in the formation of the Irish Land League in 1879.[50] He soon broke with the League, however, and determined to aid directly the distressed farmers in County Meath, where he had large properties, by a program of assisted emigration. He came to the United States in the spring of 1880 to scout out prospective sites for a colony. On the evening of his arrival in St. Paul, Friday, April 23, he called on John Ireland. The bishop received Sweetman "most cordially" and urged him to tour the Minnesota colonies and judge their merits for himself, and this he did, in the company of Dillon O'Brien.[51] After examining other possible sites in Canada and in Dakota Territory, Sweetman decided on a location near Currie, in Murray County, Minnesota, and Ireland, as agent for the railroad, arranged for a sale of ten thousand acres to him at one pound (about five dollars) per acre.[52]

By the time he brought his settlers to Currie, in the spring of 1881, Sweetman was aware of the Connemara disaster at nearby Graceville, but he hoped that the agricultural background of the people from County Meath would ease their adjustment to prairie life. Ireland secured a ten-acre plot in the village for a church and school and assigned an Irish-born priest as resident pastor. But hopes and efforts were in vain. Of the forty-one families who came to Currie in 1881 only sixteen were left two years later. Sweetman tried again in 1882, with roughly the same results. Most of his colonists fled to a city at the earliest opportunity and took menial jobs which paid eight shillings — roughly two dollars — a day, two or three times as much as they might have received at home for the same work. Altogether, in monies paid out for transportation, land, livestock, seed, tools, and housing, Sweetman lost about thirty thousand pounds in his colonization ventures.[53] He eventually recovered much of this sum by selling his Minnesota lands to French and German Catholic farmers, so that Currie indeed became a lively

Catholic colony, but not of the kind Sweetman had intended. His disappointment was shared by Ireland, who had hoped that Sweetman might have assumed direction of all the Minnesota colonies as he, Ireland, gradually withdrew from the enterprise. Instead Sweetman returned home, a sadder but wiser man: "[Settlers] taken at haphazard," he wrote toward the end of his life, "will not succeed in Western farming." He consoled himself that he would no longer have to endure the Minnesota climate, which he "hated," much preferring "our damp, cloudy atmosphere of Ireland."[54]

A short while before the double blow of Connemara and Currie, Dillon O'Brien's dream of a concerted effort at Catholic colonization on a national level was revived again. Ten years after the abortive meeting in St. Louis, on St. Patrick's Day, 1879, a "national convention" came together in Chicago to form the Irish Catholic Colonization Association of the United States. Ireland and O'Brien were in attendance, and indeed their success had been a prime source of inspiration for the conveners, prominent among whom was William J. Onahan, a Chicago business and political leader and promoter of Catholic causes.[55] Ireland and Onahan, casual acquaintances before, soon became fast friends. The convention appointed a board of directors, one of whom, at Ireland's urging, was the "energetic, enterprising" bishop of Peoria, John Lancaster Spalding.[56] This was a fateful intervention, not so much in terms of the national colonization movement, which in the end amounted to very little, but because it brought together for the first time the two most powerful personalities in the American Catholic hierarchy, who were destined over the next thirty-five years to share a close if often stormy relationship.

Between mid-April and mid-May 1879, the new association's board met several times; its major business included the election of Spalding as president and, under the laws of Illinois governing corporations, declaring itself a joint stock company with a capital of one hundred thousand dollars in shares each worth one hundred dollars.[57] The organization sounded suspiciously similar, only on a more grandiose scale, to the Minnesota Colonization Company which, Ireland must have known, was on the verge of collapse back in St. Paul. If this caused him any doubts about the present project, he kept them to himself, and at the end of May he and Spalding traveled together to New York to attend the dedication of St. Patrick's Cathedral on Fifth Avenue—and, more to the point, to drum up business for the fledgling association.[58]

Spalding took the lead, first at an informal meeting of clergy held at St. Stephen's Church in downtown Manhattan—the pastor of which was the already notable and soon to be notorious Dr. Edward McGlynn—and then with two powerful speeches, one at the Young Men's Lyceum, with McGlynn in the chair, and another, on June 4, at the Cooper Union.[59] Ireland, meanwhile, was not idle in the cause: on June 1 he spoke for an hour at St. Paul's Church on Fifty-ninth Street, a stirring address, so the local press reported, which treated of colonization and temperance and of the happy conjunction of the two in the Minnesota colonies.[60]

During the remainder of 1879 and into the next year, Ireland and Spalding toured the dioceses of the Northeast seeking support for the Colonization Association, but, their eloquence notwithstanding, the project attracted only a lukewarm response in the Catholic community. Of the modest one-hundred-thousand-dollar goal they had set for themselves, they managed to raise only eighty-three thousand dollars, which was divided ultimately between one of Ireland's colonies in Nobles County and two others, neither particularly successful, founded in Nebraska.[61] Ireland was not entirely truthful when he told Gibbons, early in March 1880, that "the [national] colonization movement so far seems to be a success. Bp. Spalding and myself secured, before we left the East, subscriptions to the stock in full [*sic*], and we have completed contracts for land in Nebraska and Minnesota." Nor was he above offering the undeclared primate of the American hierarchy[62] a small token of flattery: "Our success has been due, in very great measure, to the countenance the movement received from the foremost members of the hierarchy, to whom we are under many obligations. The one name of the Archbishop of Baltimore on our lists did more than fifty discourses from little bishops of the West."[63]

One important consequence of the colonization movement for Ireland personally was the added national exposure it gave him and the contacts it opened for him, besides those he had already established as a temperance crusader, outside Minnesota. Gibbons was not the only prominent churchman to lend him encouragement;

Archbishop John J. Williams of Boston and Bishop Stephen Ryan of Buffalo were similarly supportive, and even Hughes's successor in New York, John Cardinal McCloskey, offered a tepid endorsement.[64] Ireland clearly enjoyed his trip to New York in 1879 — he was suitably impressed by the new St. Patrick's: "an edifice marvelous in its architectural appointments and imposing beauty" — and the opportunity it afforded him to mix with his peers. He matter-of-factly informed the people back home that he had been included in a meeting of "over thirty bishops at the residence of his Eminence, Cardinal McCloskey, where a plan was devised for the . . . relief" of Archbishop John B. Purcell of Cincinnati, "who in the nobleness of his nature and little acquaintance with business details had fallen into great and distressing embarrassment."[65] His sympathy for the unfortunate Purcell was genuine, but so was his satisfaction at being consulted about the financial crisis in Cincinnati.

Ireland also, since campaigning for the Colonization Association put him frequently in the company of the bishop of Peoria, learned to hold his own with as acute a raconteur as he was ever to encounter. The formidable Spalding, "small in stature," as a daughter of William J. Onahan remembered him, "with keen gleaming eyes, . . . was a great tease, and would often poke fun at Bishop Ireland and torment him ceaselessly. Bishop Ireland would just smile and rub his hands together, a favorite gesture of his, ignore his adversary completely, until the shafts became too keen, when suddenly he would make a swift and telling retort, and there would be general laughter. Bishop Spalding would subside for a while. Then he would begin again. And so the evening would pass."[66] Such, apparently, were the social diversions of "little bishops of the West."

One reason Ireland entered so whole-heartedly into the effort to promote national colonization was his growing weariness of the burdens he bore alone in the management of the colonies in Minnesota. "Some four years ago," he wrote on August 31, 1880,

> I . . . entered single-handed upon the work of colonization. During this time I have had under my control from the St. Paul and Pacific R. R. (now the St. P[aul], M[inneapolis] and M[anitoba]) 110,000 acres in Swift County and 50,000 in Big

Stone and Traverse counties; from the St. Paul and S[ioux] C[ity] 75,000 in Nobles County, 60,000 in Murray; and from the Winona and St. Peter 45,000 acres in Lyon County. I have placed within these counties, either on government or railroad lands, 800 families in Swift, 400 in Big Stone and Traverse, 300 in Nobles, 200 in Murray, and 70 in Lyon County. I have only lately begun to operate in Lyon.[67]

He wrote these words in high summer, when the Connemara and Sweetman failures still lay ahead of him, and they recounted an achievement of which he could be proud. Yet, despite the reference to work still to be done in Lyon County, they also sounded something like a valedictory. More and more after this there appeared in his correspondence a note of irritation at the constant drain upon his time and energy and a determination to withdraw from the enterprise.[68] "I will sell almost anything I have for cash," he wrote Anatole Oster early the following year, "as I am positively determined to finish A. D. 1881 with colonization and business."[69] And a month later, as the Connemara crisis reached its climax: "I assure you, I have suffered much anxiety. . . . I hope the winter is over. How much anxiety I have suffered!"[70] Worry combined with increasing ennui to lead him to a decision he would have considered a serious ethical lapse a few years before: "Just sell the lot to Riordan [a suspected publican] without inquiring what he intends to do with it. It is not possible to have coercive measures toward drink. But we will have to use all possible moral efforts to keep people from visiting saloons."[71]

Ireland's policy of putting a resident priest in each colony, to act as pastor and guide for the settlers and as agent for the Colonization Bureau, worked well most of the time, but when it did not, the bishop faced an added problem. Sometimes he had to deal simply with sacerdotal eccentricity: "Father Swift's ways are beyond comprehension," he remarked about the first pastor of De Graff.[72] Sometimes the priest was dilatory or careless in his business dealings; when, for example, Oster put the bishop's name on a note, Ireland growled at him, "I am nearly ruined. . . . I never permit anyone to sign my name to anything!"[73] The bishop suffered more than once from the vagaries of priests whom he had adopted from other dioceses and whom he tried to work into these difficult western assignments.[74] But for the most part the resident pastors—notably Oster himself—served with distinction, and whatever success the colonies enjoyed was due in no small measure to their efforts.

Another disenchanting factor for Ireland, as the years passed and the day-to-day governance of the colonies grew more irksome to him, was the benign neglect of the bishop of St. Paul. Grace's passivity could not have been a surprise to Ireland, and indeed he knew that such passivity was the price he paid for his own authority and freedom of action. Even so, he came to feel a measure of resentment. "Regarding that debt of the Indian school," he told Oster at the end of 1883, "I think you had better try Bp. Grace. I will be most charmed if he would foot the bill."[75]

The "Indian school" at Clontarf colony, where Oster was pastor, was a special case that proved particularly troublesome to John Ireland. In 1874 the Catholic Industrial School of Minnesota was incorporated as a home and trade-school for underprivileged boys. Three years later, on a spacious tract of land between the cities of St. Paul and Minneapolis, purchased by Grace for the purpose, it began operation under the direction of the Brothers of St. Francis. It did not thrive, which pained Bishop Grace for whom it was a cherished project, and in 1879 Ireland arranged to transfer it to a site of two thousand acres near Clontarf. Religious brothers again took charge, but, finding no boys to instruct, they tried their hand at farming. In 1882, and again in 1884, they tried to launch a school, but to no avail, and in the end most of them drifted away. Eventually the federal government designated the place as a training school for Indians, and from 1885, with federal subsidies and a new staff of brothers, St. Paul's Industrial Boarding School served a largely Native American clientele until the middle of the 1890s.[76]

During the interval, however, the project hung like an albatross around Ireland's neck, despite his repeated assertions that he wanted "nothing more to do with it."[77] To maintain the brothers, both spiritually and materially, was a constant headache. He considered moving the school out of Clontarf, but he could find no other place to put it.[78] He decided at one point to mortgage the school, then changed his mind, then metaphorically threw up his hands in despair: "I kept bolstering it up until I nearly ruined myself. I can do nothing more for it."[79] But, in fact, he did a great deal more for it, spending in the process nearly fifty thousand dollars for land and buildings.[80]

Nobody, not even Oster, knew where he got this money.[81] It came from the estate of a prosperous book salesman named Michael Keegan, a Chicagoan whom Ireland had met in the early 1870s. Keegan fathered a child in his old age. In 1879, fearful — for little apparent reason — that his young wife and her relatives would somehow persuade a court to declare him incompetent before he could provide for his infant daughter, he set up a trust, whereby the child would receive all his property, to be administered prior to her majority by Ireland, and if she predeceased the bishop the property would go to him "to found an industrial school for poor boys."[82] Later that same year, in an astonishing display of human mortality, first Keegan's wife, then Keegan himself, and, on December 26, 1879, their child all died. The probate court found that no genuine trust had been set up by Keegan, and directed the property to be handed over to Mrs. Keegan's relatives.[83] But Ireland, never one to accept defeat gladly, appealed to the United States Circuit Court for Northern Illinois, which early in 1883 reversed the probate decision and awarded the estate, valued at between seventy-five and eighty thousand dollars, to Ireland.[84]

The Keegan case — during the trial of which William J. Onahan acted as Ireland's agent on the scene[85] — therefore became part of the story of Catholic colonization in Minnesota. Ireland put a large portion of what he won into the school in Clontarf, but he did not spend it all for that purpose. There is no reason to suppose that he spent any of it on himself, or that he ignored the letter or spirit of the Circuit Court's decision, which found in his favor, partly at least, from the circumstance that he did not stand to gain personally from his suit. Yet many mysteries about the funding of the colonization program remain, primarily because no set of books separate from those of the diocese was kept to monitor it.[86]

A similar paucity of records makes it difficult to know to what extent Ireland invested his own money — as distinct from that of the diocese or the Colonization Bureau — in rural real estate during these years. He was restricted by contract from purchasing any of the cheap railroad lands available to the colonists, but this did not prevent him from buying property nearby, nor from profiting when, as was invariably the case, a thriving colony increased land values substantially in the whole area. Some rural tracts he kept until the end of his life.[87] Others he disposed of when the price was right.

But Ireland's habit of employing a vigorous first person singular indifferently when speaking of a colony's business and his own often leaves an observer confused as to which was which. On occasion, to be sure, he left no doubt. "Sect. 5. 122–41 belongs to me," he told Oster in the winter of 1881. "It is for sale in whole or in parts — $5.00 per acre — at least one-half cash down. If land-hunters are not satisfied with R[ail] R[oad] land, refer them to this piece."[88] Two years later he sent Oster a check to cover the taxes on 160 acres he, Ireland, owned in Swift County, the locale of two successful colonies.[89] More ambiguous, however, was this statement: "I have sold out all my interest in De Graff, and I am very glad."[90] And this one: "I have taken the [grain] elevator [in Clontarf] *entirely* into my own hands. It is for rent or sale, on easy terms. Please have an eye on it."[91] Whether in these instances he spoke for the Colonization Bureau — which, it may be recalled, received town lots from the railroads — or for himself it is not possible to say.

Certainly his colonization work introduced Ireland to the possibilities of speculation in real estate, amd it did not limit his horizons in that regard. Early in 1883 he heard a rumor that James J. Hill was planning to construct some facilities at Devils Lake, in northern Dakota Territory, along the line of his Manitoba Railroad. He wrote Hill,

> If you do not locate at Devil's Lake City, I have nothing to say. . . . If you do locate there, I want from you the favor of giving me the first word. The parties owning the land at that point — to be candid with you — believe that you and I are not bad friends, and they have signed a positive agreement with [Ireland's agent], that in case of success, both of us will derive from the place some substantial profit. To another railroad man I would not talk as I do with you. With you I take special privileges.[92]

Though apparently nothing came of this inquiry, it indicated Ireland's wide-ranging and abiding interest in real estate speculation, an interest which garnered him considerable profits at first but which was destined to bring much trouble down on his head later on.

By 1882 John Ireland had pretty well decided that his active participation in the colonization movement should cease. The time had come to move on to other things. He could hardly have expected the sad and dramatic confirmation of this intention that occurred in the late summer of that year. On Sunday morning, September 12, Dillon O'Brien, on his way to mass at the cathedral, stopped at the clergy house next door to confer with Ireland. He never got the chance to tell the bishop what he had in mind, because, as the two men sat together in the parlor, O'Brien "suddenly and apparently without pain, and with what seemed a smile, sank back upon the seat he was occupying." Ireland cried out for Bishop Grace who quickly appeared with the sacred oils. But Dillon O'Brien lay dead,[93] literally in the arms of the priest to whom he had been so stout an ally, so reliable a tutor, so firm a friend. And for the rest of Ireland's long life no one ever took the place of the man in whose company he had issued his invitation to the land.

VIII

A Larger Stage
1883-84

D ILLON O'BRIEN's successor at the Colonization Bureau was
the highly efficient if less colorful and inspirational John P.
O'Connor, who had once managed the Sweetman colony at Currie.
Under his administration the bureau continued operations until the
end of the 1880s. But no new initiatives were undertaken during
these years, no new settlers were brought in. Consolidation, not expansion, was O'Connor's mandate, and he brought the Catholic
colonization enterprise in Minnesota to a decorous conclusion, with
the sale of the last of the town lots, for example, and the payment
of the debts incurred by the Connemara debacle. O'Connor proved
to be ideally suited for this job, and, though he always carefully invoked John Ireland's name in all the bureau's transactions, no one
doubted that he was himself fully in charge.[1] Ireland's last direct intervention was to send Anatole Oster to Devils Lake, in northern
Dakota Territory, with two hundred dollars to pay the expenses involved in conducting an unspecified number of Ojibway Indian
boys to the now federally subsidized Industrial School at Clontarf.
He instructed Oster to keep all receipts, in hopes that the travel
money could be recovered.[2]

The end of that sort of detailed concern with the colonies
marked the end also of John Ireland's young manhood. He was in
his mid-forties now, well established and widely admired in his
own community, enjoying a modest reputation elsewhere in the
United States for his continuing leadership of the temperance
movement,[3] and similarly recognized in his own country and
abroad for his work in behalf of colonization.[4] His personal financial circumstances, thanks to successful real estate speculation,

promised him security and allowed him to indulge some of his tastes: he was known, for example, as "one of the very best [book] buyers in St. Paul."[5] His interest in local history had prompted his election to the presidency of the Minnesota Historical Society in 1877, and led to a learned exchange three years later with no less a personage than the premier American Catholic historian, John Gilmary Shea.[6] He took particular satisfaction in his appointment as chaplain of the Minnesota National Guard, which honor issued from his old regimental commander, now the governor of the state. "I deem it a great privilege," Lucius Hubbard wrote, "to be able to renew in this form the official relations that formerly existed between us. . . . I ask you to regard this tender as a token of the very high esteem in which I have ever held you personally, and the profound respect I entertain for your character as a foremost representative of your Church."[7]

Yet Ireland, despite the governor's accolade, despite his own not inconsiderable accomplishments, could scarcely describe himself "a foremost representative" of his church so long as he remained a coadjutor bishop. So long as Thomas Grace continued to hold office, Ireland was technically an apprentice, no matter how free a hand his amiable master allowed him. No one as ambitious as Ireland could have endured this status for very long without pangs of impatience. But in the summer of 1884, a week after the celebration of his silver jubilee as bishop of St. Paul, Grace, aged not quite seventy, announced his resignation. He was, as always, ungrudging in his praise of his younger colleague. "Reference has been made [in earlier speeches]," Grace said at the jubilee banquet, "to the great activity in conducting the affairs of the diocese, the enlarged views, the spirit of enterprise and the energy in carrying forward works of improvement or reform. How much of this is due to one whom I need not name is not necessary to say; but I will say that in these respects the Bishop and the Diocese of St. Paul have had far more than is implied in the name of the Coadjutor." Ireland's reply was equally gracious, though the discerning listener probably put more stock in the first part of his peroration than in the second: "My past has been, through [Grace], secure and happy, and my future suggests to me no fears, because . . . he will for many and long years

be still near to inspire and direct my counsels and my under-
takings."[8]

The pope assigned to Grace in retirement the titular see of Mennith.[9] Until 1890 he lived on in his old rooms in the cathedral rectory, and after that he went into residence at St. Thomas Seminary.
On the campus of the seminary was an artificial pond around which
the venerable bishop would take his constitutional every day, accompanied by his dog. (The students, with their usual uncanny facility for nicknames, called the pond Lake Mennith.) For some years
he continued to administer confirmation and to perform other
ceremonial duties around the diocese, for which he received a stipend of twelve hundred dollars a year.[10]

But later on his health, never robust, gradually deteriorated to
the point that even such modest exertions were beyond his strength.
He was afflicted, too, during the last years of his life, by that cruelest
of spiritual maladies, scrupulosity. Late in 1896, he sought relief
from the obligation of the daily breviary. "I am now Eighty-two
(82) years of age," he wrote the apostolic delegate, "and I have great
difficulty in reciting the divine office owing to my mind becoming
feeble and the painful annoyance of scruples." He knew that in such
cases the authorities usually allowed the substitution of the rosary
for the breviary, but Grace feared "the same difficulty would attend. . . . I would therefore beg to be released from all obligations
in this respect."[11] Only a month or two before the onset of his final
illness he managed a nostalgic trip back to his Dominican mother
house in Ohio, a place he had not seen since the far-off days when
he himself had been a young friar. He returned to St. Paul in time
to celebrate his last Christmas there, and on February 22, 1897,
Thomas Langdon Grace, of the Order of Preachers, died peacefully
and in full possession of his faculties.[12] By a curious coincidence it
was forty years to the day since the death of Joseph Cretin.

The moment Grace chose for his retirement was not only an appropriate one for him personally—the end of twenty-five years as
bishop of St. Paul—but was also a characteristically generous concession to his successor. A plenary council[13] had been scheduled for
November 1884, and Grace, in stepping aside when he did, made
it possible for Ireland to attend that crucially important meeting as
a full-fledged ordinary in his own right, and not merely as someone

else's aide. There was a sense in which this handing on of the torch in St. Paul symbolized the passing away of one generation of leadership within the American Catholic community and the coming of age of another, or, as Lancaster Spalding put it rather crudely to Ireland, the end of dominance by the "old fogies."[14]

Spalding did not mean to include Grace in that category—he was genuinely fond of the retired bishop and thought him an unusually enlightened prelate.[15] But as the opening of the Third Plenary Council of Baltimore (Baltimore III)[16] approached, it became ever clearer that the Catholic church in the United States faced a number of exceedingly grave problems, and that solutions to them, if there were to be solutions, would have to be found by a new set of men. John Ireland, who was about to move with astonishing speed and effectiveness onto a larger stage, benefited, once more, by being at the right place at the right time.

Governance was Ireland's first interest and indeed his abiding and consuming passion. What happened to him in the mid-1880s in this regard was a dramatic shift away from local preoccupations to those of a national and even an international scope. The self-confidence he had manifested as a young parish priest did not diminish, nor did the industriousness, nor the charm, nor the conviction that his clerical status gave him a special license to leadership. But over the next two decades he spent himself and his gifts upon causes far removed from the vagaries of the wheat market in Swift County or the antics of the saloonkeepers on Minnesota Street. This is not to say that he neglected his local constituency; evidence abounds that, despite the growls of hostile critics, Ireland ruled his diocese conscientiously and effectively, even while he parleyed with popes and presidents. Nevertheless, his heart and mind no doubt often roamed far outside the boundaries of Minnesota, and his ambitions, too.

This altered direction in Ireland's career, this radical change of scene, was therefore due partly to his undeniable talents and aggressive temperament, partly to the independence his new status as ordinary gave him, and partly to the factor of his age—no "old fogie" he. None of this would have amounted to much, however, had not the rhythm of events opened to him opportunities for action across a wide spectrum. Ireland wanted to participate closely in giving shape to the church in America, much as he had done already — or so it seemed to him, and not without reason — in Minnesota. On the eve of the Third Plenary Council the situation appeared fluid enough to offer him a chance.

BUT BEFORE those events can be profitably examined, a word has to be said about certain speculative and practical assumptions that colored Ireland's activities, and also about certain personages with whom and against whom he labored. Little sense can be made of the commotions of the next decade and a half without bearing in mind, for example, the largely immigrant character of the nation's Catholic population, its relative poverty, its general lack of education, the suspicion it still roused in many a Protestant heart. The unspoken preoccupation of all the bishops was the maintenance of the faith among these masses and their amalgamation into the larger American culture. But fierce and often unedifying disagreements arose among them as to how this was to be done, and at what pace, and at what cost. John Ireland, an eminently successful immigrant himself, increasingly adopted the view that the peculiar political and economic circumstances in America offered the church a unique opportunity for development and, even more, a model of universal applicability. Not all his colleagues arrived at the same conclusion.

The burdens of governance were thus complicated by growing ideological rifts, and complicated further by the involvement of the egos of some truly remarkable men. The prelates of Ireland's generation call to mind the biblical saw, "Now there were giants in the earth in those days,"[17] giants whose harsh professional and personal competition was inevitable, given the arena they found themselves in, and was arguably as much a sign of their religious vitality as of their ambition or their stubbornness.

There were other factors to take into account, too. To begin with, governance of the Catholic church in the United States did not rest ultimately with American prelates like Ireland, strong-willed as they may have been; final decisions of consequence — and some trivial ones as well — were made in Rome. Ireland therefore was always an ultramontane, out of doctrinal conviction, no doubt, but also out of practical necessity. Whether he would have preferred a different constitutional arrangement is a highly speculative question; the fact was that no American bishop could accomplish anything without papal endorsement or at least papal toleration, and so Ireland's struggles in the succeeding years were played out to a large extent in the corridors of the Vatican.

There has always existed within the Catholic system a natural strain between the pretensions of the local church and those of the universal, between the individual bishop in his diocese and the pope in Rome—the pope who, with scant regard for the proprieties of metaphor, declared himself at once the bishop's brother and father. The tension was the age-old one between the king and his lords, between the monarchical and aristocratic principles—the democratic factor did not figure in the equation—only in this instance elaborated within an ecclesiastical framework. The consecrated bishop ruled his diocese, theoretically at least, with the authority of an apostle, but he had to do so in union with the pope, who represented the continuation in the church of the Petrine office. An apostle of the first century—so the theory went—could not have functioned legitimately if he had been in conflict with St. Peter. Not that the relationship needed always to be cordial: the apostle Paul, after all, had "withstood Peter to his face." But Peter's commission by Jesus to "confirm his brethren"[18] pointed to the unique authority that had been given to him, which continued to be wielded by his successors, the bishops of Rome. To understand how far this germinal idea had developed by 1884, John Ireland had only to ponder the words that stood at the head of every formal document he issued: bishop of St. Paul "by the grace of God and the favor of the Apostolic See."

The basic doctrine of the pope's primacy within the apostolic college had been routinely accepted within the Latin church over the centuries, even though theological speculation as to its precise meaning continued (and continues to this day). More to the point here, the primacy's practical ramifications had differed startlingly from one era to another. There had been times when popes were weak, and bishops in their own localities strong, and then the voice of Rome was faint and halting. Bishops then ruled their sees with little more than a casual nod toward the pope and his bureaucracy, the Roman curia. The last quarter of the nineteenth century, however, was not one of those times. Indeed, never before had the papacy's prestige among Catholics stood higher, never before had the theoretical right of the pope to "universal jurisdiction" been more effectively exercised. It was ironic—or, as some might have argued, providential—that as the temporal power of the pope first shrank and then, after 1870, disappeared, his ability to enforce his will within the ecclesiastical domain increased to an unprecedented degree.[19] The old aphorism, *"Roma locuta, causa finita est"*—"the pope has spoken, and therefore the matter is closed"—took on heightened meaning at a time when octogenarian Bishop Grace had to ask some faceless Italian clerk at Propaganda whether or not he was obliged to say the rosary every day.

If power corrupts, as that ardent foe of papal centralization, Lord Acton, said it does, then one might have expected the bureaucrats of the Roman curia with whom Ireland dealt to have been men of questionable morality. But nothing in the evidence leads to such a facile conclusion. That they made mistakes and committed sins of omission and commission goes without saying, though even saying so hardly differentiates them from the rest of humankind in any il-luminating way. In dealing with high American ecclesiastics, their most glaring fault, perhaps, was an habitual air of condescension. This stemmed partly from the hauteur exhibited by all desk men who always pretend to know more more about a problem than the agents in the field. It also resulted from the exclusively European orientation of the curialists who could hardly help arriving at judg-ments in terms of the only ecclesial model they knew. For the ordi-nary of a great see like New York or Baltimore or even St. Paul to be patronized by an obscure *minutante* (sub-secretary) of Propagan-da was an infuriating experience. But more substantive was the strong feeling that the curialists had no appreciation of the unique-ness of the American situation—in the area of church-state rela-tions, for instance—and that they believed the immigrant Catholi-cism in the United States to be simply a collectivity of the European conditions the immigrants had left behind.

Yet the Roman officials usually acted with admirable patience and cool-headedness in their day-to-day behavior toward the American bishops, who argued so violently and often indecorously among themselves. According to their own lights, and consistent with their priorities, the officials performed their jobs at a high level of professionalism and with a scrupulous regard for equity, and in doing so they displayed no less honor, no fewer good intentions than their American colleagues. They made no secret, to be sure, of their determination to concentrate major decision making at Roman headquarters. But at a moment in western history when other institutions were shaking off the last vestiges of the old feudal localism, it would have been surprising had the Catholic church not initiated its own drive toward centralization.

It seems important to make this point, because it is tempting to judge John Ireland's controversial career in terms of heroes and villains, of victories and defeats, or, what might be an even less satisfactory approach, in terms of consequences that neither he nor any other of the actors in the drama foresaw, or could have foreseen, at the time. And since the issue under dispute was usually settled by a papal decision of some kind, there is a further temptation to assign blame for the frustration of Ireland's policies on this or that occasion to an inordinate appetite for power in Rome or, more simply, to Italian cunning. Aside from the taint of racism in this point of view, the truth of the matter depends upon one's definition of "inordinate," and that the historian—for whom the assigning of blame is in any case a perilous exercise—cannot supply. Certainly the practical power of the pope, especially in the wake of the definition of his personal infallibility, had reached new heights, but neither Ireland nor his American opponents, however much they may have grumbled about its application, had any intention of repudiating that power. Instead they tried their best to manipulate it. They quarreled with each other, and then called in the curia to act as referee. When the decision came down in favor of one side, the other side murmured about the "inordinate" use of power. Such is human nature. Such is the way human institutions work. Such may have been, in this instance, the genuine corruption Acton intended to describe in his famous dictum.

A more plausible, though not unrelated, assertion—and one frequently repeated at the time—was that the Italian curialists had no real understanding of the American scene and that consequently they arrived at their decisions through ignorance or prejudice. Though this charge undoubtedly possessed a measure of truth, it was also true that the reaction of the antagonists directly involved depended, once again, upon whether a decision favored them or not: what the winner called enlightened policy, the loser ascribed to typical Italian obscurantism. And, anyway, a case could be made in the opposite sense, that the Roman officials had too much, rather than too little, information about conditions in the United States. Before 1884 they constantly badgered the American bishops for reports, statements, opinions, news of all kinds, and they complained bitterly when the Americans were slow in responding. And after 1884, when the controversies heated up, a flood of conflicting materials poured into the curia, choking the archives and bewildering, one might have thought, even the most diligent legist employed at Propaganda or at the secretariat of state. Heedless decision making in Rome was at any rate a rarity—forty years, for example, elapsed between the first papal overtures to set up an apostolic delegation in the United States and the formal establishment of that office—but, ill-considered or not, once a decision was made, it assumed an aura of sacred finality. *Roma locuta, causa finita est.*

Though from one point of view the American bishops, Ireland among them, were lobbyists competing for favor at the various Roman congregations, from another they were exceedingly—some would have said excessively—powerful men. As ordinaries in what was still technically a mission country (and hence the connection with Propaganda), they operated without the normal constraints of the canon law in force elsewhere in the Catholic world. They exercised a much more untrammeled control over their dioceses and over the lower clergy than did their brother bishops in other countries. They had no cathedral chapters[20] to contend with, nor any analogous consultative body. When they decided to form parishes or build churches or borrow money, they did so without any local limitation on their initiatives. Of course they had to account ultimately to Rome, and Rome, thanks to the steamship, the submarine telegraph, and the railroad, was closer, say, to St. Paul than it used to be. Still, in their routine administration, the American bishops ruled with little hindrance from above and none from below.

They could assign their clerical subjects to any mission they chose, and remove them or transfer them without explanation. There were no irremovable rectorships, no equivalent to the Anglican "parson's freehold." Not even the most senior and accomplished pastor of a parish enjoyed security of tenure; he served entirely at the bishop's will or whim. There existed within the American church no regular legal procedure whereby a disagreement between a priest and his bishop could be adjudicated. To pose an admittedly extreme case: if a bishop believed, even on frivolous grounds, that a priest had taken to drink or had seduced the parish organist — had succumbed to the allure of "punch or Judy," as the rough clerical patois expressed it — he could, without proving his case, transfer the priest or suspend him or send him off to do penance in a monastery. The priest in question thus lost both his mission and his reputation; his only recourse was a direct (and expensive and time-consuming) appeal to Propaganda. The resentment and bad feeling that this situation bred between the two orders was deep, especially among those priests — and they were many — who were convinced that the bishops intended to perpetuate the system, or lack of it, for their own selfish interest.[21]

But of course not all the wrong was on one side. The quality of the clergy available to the bishops for service in their dioceses was distressingly low. As the waves of immigrants, many of them Catholics, continued to flood into the country, the American bishops became understandably desperate to staff the parishes and institutions that a rapidly expanding population demanded. The development of native vocations was a depressingly slow process, and ordinaries consequently took chances on accepting into their jurisdictions priests who were neurotic or ill trained or had been in trouble elsewhere. Grace and Ireland, for example, at the behest of Archbishop Gibbons, assigned a mission to a priest who, in Baltimore, had had a drinking problem. The change of locale helped keep the unfortunate man sober for less than a year: "I am very sorry to have to tell you," Ireland wrote Gibbons early in 1881, "that Father Mahoney has fallen back into his old sin. . . . Once he tasted liquor there was no stopping. The 'spree' lasted a week, and the scandal was quite public. . . . I believe that a monastery is the only place for him."[22] At about the same time, in the notoriously ill-run Archdiocese of New Orleans, the lower clergy included in its ranks a veritable rogues' gallery, at least in the opinion of the coadjutor, who sent a list of the local disreputables to Rome: Charpentier, expelled from two religious orders, now living publicly with a

woman; Dowarlk, vagabond, who impregnated a girl; Alter, adventurer; Jusel, evil reputation; Juhel, does not work; Gouvelluz,
denounced by a nun; Glendon, drinks; Weir, drinks; Scolland,
drinks; and so the roll of dishonor continued until it totaled thirty-
five names.[23]

For many years the Roman officials had received such communications, which, if less bizarre than the one from New Orleans,
nevertheless pointed in the same distressing direction. They had
also received huge numbers of appeals from priests claiming mistreatment by their bishops. As a result, by the early 1880s some of
the high officers of Propaganda had formed a strongly unflattering
picture of the state of the clergy, high and low, in the United States.
American bishops were habitually careless, one of them wrote in
1883, in recommending candidates for promotion to the episcopacy, preferring their intimates and hangers-on to demonstrably
more worthy men. They showed a studied antipathy for candidates
trained in Rome. They had no policy in the treatment of the lower
clergy, so that priests suspended in one diocese were promoted in
another. Insubordination among the lower clergy had reached epidemic proportions, because the native priests entertained false ideas
about personal liberty, because the Europeans recruited for service
in America tended to be truculent and rebellious, and because both
groups resented the tyrannical practices of the bishops. Many of the
clergy, especially the Irish, drank too much. Bishops and priests
alike were frequently viewed by their people as money grubbers —
charging a fee at the church door, for example, and refusing to visit
the sick or to administer a sacrament without payment — and yet at
the same time they were often inept fiscal managers, running their
dioceses and parishes into foolish debts and risking bankruptcy and
civil litigation.

This bleak picture, most likely drawn by one who seldom saw
a bright side in matters American,[24] no doubt overstated the problem. But it is significant that John Ireland's friend, Bishop Spalding,
who spent the winter of 1883 in Rome, alluded to some of the same
difficulties and expressed more sympathy for the curial attitude than
for that of some his senior colleagues among the American hierarchy. Spalding found everybody he talked to in Rome, from Pope
Leo XIII on down, "most anxious to hear about America and will-

ing to do anything that may seem reasonable." He described the secretary of Propaganda, Jacobini, as "a most intelligent man" who listened attentively to all that Spalding told him. At his private audience the pope asked the bishop of Peoria to submit in writing "anything I might think it would be useful for him to know." The Roman officials, Spalding continued, "thoroughly tired" of the innumerable appeals of American priests against their bishops, had determined that there must be a plenary council in the United States; they planned to summon "three or four" American bishops "for consultation and fuller information" as a way of preparing a conciliar agenda. "There are, as you know, some old fogies in America who are opposed to this, and their opposition will have to be met."[25] Finally, Spalding assured Ireland, Rome would do anything for us "if the chaotic condition of the [American] bishops as to what ought to be done, did not keep the authorities here in a kind of labyrinth from which the way out is not easily discovered."[26]

SPALDING TRAVELED to Baltimore with Grace and Ireland and arrived there on the evening of November 6, 1884. Three days later, a Sunday, at ten o'clock in the morning, the Third Plenary Council opened with great pomp and circumstance. The weather was fine, and the crowds in attendance at the Cathedral of the Assumption were large. In the "long vested procession" from Archbishop Gibbons's residence to the cathedral walked fourteen archbishops, sixty-two bishops, six abbots, thirty-four superiors of religious congregations, eleven rectors of theological seminaries, eighty-one theologians, and twelve minor conciliar functionaries, a grand total of 220 clerics. The aged archbishop of St. Louis celebrated the pontifical mass, and the archbishop of Philadelphia, reputed to be the finest orator on the episcopal bench, preached for an hour—"finely worded," observed one of the seminary rectors, "but heavy in delivery." The ceremony lasted nearly six hours and was "impressive but tedious."[27]

Many a man of mark—John Ireland's allies and adversaries—walked in the procession of notables on that bright November day. There was crusty old Peter Richard Kenrick of St. Louis, who had been a bishop for more than forty years and who had found the infallibility decree of the Vatican Council so difficult to accept.

Nearby in the line of march was William Henry Elder of Cincinnati, who, despite his episcopal robes, looked like an unbearded Abraham Lincoln. John B. Lamy of Santa Fe, already a legend in the Southwest,[28] thin almost to the point of emaciation; stocky, bullet-headed Michael Heiss of Milwaukee, Ireland's Bavarian-born metropolitan; taciturn John J. Williams of Boston, with his heavy-lidded eyes and placid expression — all these archbishops were assigned places of honor toward the end of the line, as was the younger and strikingly handsome Patrick A. Feehan of Chicago, and, much younger still, the coadjutor of San Francisco, fresh-faced, curly-haired Patrick Riordan, who as a lad in Chicago had been, briefly, John Ireland's schoolmate.

Missing from the procession was the single American prince of the church, Cardinal McCloskey, whose ill health kept him at home in New York. But his coadjutor was there. Michael Augustine Corrigan[29] was already, at forty-five, one of the brightest stars in the episcopal firmament. Born in Newark of Irish parents, he grew up in comfortable circumstances, thanks to his father's successful food and liquor business — not necessarily a recommendation to one who held John Ireland's views on temperance. In 1859 young Corrigan went to Rome to study for the priesthood; he was among the first class to take up residence in the new American College on the Via dell'Umiltà. He carved out for himself a brilliant scholastic record over the next five years in what was, however, neither a distinguished nor a demanding course at the Urban College of Propaganda.[30] Even so, when he came back to New Jersey in 1864 a doctor of divinity, Corrigan was an accomplished linguist, a man of studious habits, and, above all, a sternly self-disciplined ecclesiastic fully imbued with romanità.

His rise was swift and his industry prodigious: theology professor, seminary director, college president, bishop of Newark at thirty-four, and, in 1880, coadjutor archbishop of New York. He had not been McCloskey's first choice, but once the appointment was made the cardinal professed himself content, particularly because Doctor Corrigan was so conversant with the procedures of the Roman curia. Corrigan toiled as unremittingly in New York as he had in Newark, and he proved himself an administrative genius in many ways — painstaking, prompt, orderly, a strong fiscal man-

Michael Augustine Corrigan, Archbishop of New York (Archives of the Archdioses of New York)

ager for whom no detail was too small and no piece of paper too insignificant. He was less successful, however, in dealing with strictly human situations. Painfully shy and diffident in manner, somewhat delicate in health, he failed to project the forceful masculine image prized by his contemporaries — one of his enemies called him "girlish."[31] Perhaps out of loneliness he tended to be secretive and to place a mask over his motives. Candor was not a virtue he practiced with any regularity, and he displayed a weakness — not unique to him by any means — for surrounding himself with second-rate functionaries who could pose no threat to him. To a degree Corrigan's rapid climb up the greasy pole of ecclesiastical preferment had done him a disservice: he had never spent a day as a parish priest, and the common touch, that indefinable sense of the aspirations of others, was entirely foreign to him. It would be hard to imagine a more marked physical and temperamental contrast than that which existed between Corrigan and John Ireland.

Unless it were that between Corrigan and the burly figure who strode up ahead in the conciliar procession, among the bishops, Bernard McQuaid of Rochester.[32] Yet appearances in this instance were deceiving, for, notwithstanding his rough and often domineering exterior, McQuaid was Corrigan's confidant, his staunchest ally, in many regards his mentor. It may have been that Corrigan's very frailty — more apparent than real — appealed to a strong

Bernard J. McQuaid, Bishop of Rochester
(*from Zwierlein,* Life of McQuaid)

personality like McQuaid, as though the younger man, sixteen years McQuaid's junior, stood in need of protection.[33] The bishop of Rochester, at any rate, had not always exhibited the vigor and toughness for which by 1884 he had become famous. Abused by a stepmother, he had spent most of his childhood in an orphanage in New York City. As a young man he was thin and consumptive-looking, and many of his bigger, healthier seminary classmates had taunted him by predicting that he would never live to be ordained, but, as McQuaid chortled when he was past eighty, "I have downed them all." He served in the relatively salubrious air of north Jersey — still part of the Diocese of New York in those days — until he went to Rochester in 1868 as first bishop. No job proved too formidable for him, no obstacle too much for his ferocious will power to overcome. He had little patience for those who complained about his one-man rule and who called him a tyrant; malingerers, he shot back at them, unwilling to work as hard as he worked himself, "a handful of priests, all foreigners, and many of them unfit for the ministry in any country." His single-minded career was to a certain extent summed up when he recalled his reaction to an especially difficult assignment he had been given: "I had one natural gift in high degree. It was not a saintly one: the more the opposition, the stronger the determination to succeed in spite of the devil and every one else." Such a man could be a dangerous enemy, as John Ireland was to find to his cost.

Near McQuaid in the ceremonial procession was the restless Spalding of Peoria, who, like Ireland, had gone to school with Patrick Riordan, but later and for a longer time, when they had been theology students together at Louvain University in Belgium. Not far away was Richard Gilmour, native of Glasgow and now bishop of Cleveland, a convert to Catholicism at the age of eighteen, a widely experienced missionary and a man known for his forthright speech. In the same group was Edward Fitzgerald of Little Rock, one of only two bishops to have voted against the decree of papal infallibility at the Vatican Council.[34] A singular sight among these dignitaries was James Augustine Healy, bishop of Portland, Maine, born on a plantation in Georgia thirty years before the Civil War, his mother a slave. Also close at hand were Ireland's near neighbors back home, neither of whom he had much regard for, Rupert Seidenbusch and Martin Marty, vicars apostolic of Northern Minnesota and Dakota Territory respectively, both Benedictine monks, the first born in Bavaria, the second in Switzerland. Ireland himself walked in company with the titular bishop of Mennith *in partibus,* who looked for all the world like a character out of Dickens.

At the head of the procession were gathered the lesser clerics, the theologians, chanters, masters of ceremonies, notaries, secretaries, and other officers of the council. Among these were James McGolrick and James Trobec, who served as theological advisers to Ireland and Grace respectively.[35] McGolrick, a pastor in Minneapolis, was fast becoming Ireland's closest confidant among the younger priests in the diocese. Both he and Trobec would become bishops in their turn, as would one of the four secretaries of the council who walked near them, Denis Joseph O'Connell, though the path O'Connell followed toward the episcopacy was far more tortuous — and more interesting — than theirs.

Of the personal and professional relationships that may be said to have begun for Ireland at the Third Plenary Council none was more important than that with Denis O'Connell.[36] Born in 1849 in Donoughmore, County Cork, O'Connell was a small child when his parents brought him and his seven siblings to Columbia, South Carolina, in the mid-1850s. His father Michael was, like Richard

Denis J. O'Connell and Serafino Cardinal Vannutelli, undated (Archdiocesan Archives, Archdiocese of St. Paul and Minneapolis)

Ireland, a carpenter by trade and a shrewd man of business, but the strongest influences within the family were clerical: three of Michael's brothers were priests, active in the Carolina missions, and a sister was a nun. By the time the Civil War began, the O'Connells were leading members of the Irish Catholic community in Columbia, a small but closely knit and not unprosperous group which, unlike its counterparts farther north, had suffered little during the nativist agitations of the 1850s. The war, however, provided an occasion for an outburst of anti-Catholic feeling, and young Denis became acquainted, in 1863, with the destructive capacity of a southern mob. But that was nothing compared to the calculated policy of General Sherman, who, marching north from Savannah, captured Columbia on February 17, 1865. One of Denis's priest-uncles tried to persuade the Unionist commander to spare the city, but to no avail: that night two-thirds of Columbia, including Michael O'Connell's house, burned to the ground.

After the war Michael O'Connell bought a farm not far from Charlotte, North Carolina, where one of his brothers was the parish priest. Young Denis received a smattering of education in his uncle's presbytery until, in 1868, he enrolled as a seminarian in St. Charles College, near Baltimore. The domicile thus established in Charlotte, fortuitous as it may have been, proved crucial in Denis O'Connell's career, because early the same year he entered St. Charles, James Gibbons had been appointed vicar apostolic of North Carolina, the jurisdiction in which O'Connell presumably would serve after his ordination to the priesthood. In Gibbons O'Connell found the first, and the most loyal and enduring, of the ecclesiastical patrons he spent his life cultivating.

During the school holidays of succeeding years the seminarian was often in the company of the young bishop—Gibbons was thirty-four at the time of his appointment—touring the vast vicariate with him and, in lighter moments, joining him on fishing trips. When Gibbons became bishop of Richmond in 1872 he arranged to have his protégé incardinated[37] into that diocese, and, as a further sign of favor, sent him off to Rome to complete his theological studies. On November 8, 1872, Denis O'Connell went into residence in the American College on the Via dell'Umiltà and began to attend classes at the Urban College of Propaganda—at both of which places Michael Corrigan had set the standards a decade before.

O'Connell's tenure as a Roman student lasted four and a half years, until his ordination in the spring of 1877. But the subject that genuinely caught his fancy during that time was the ways of ecclesiastical Rome. He learned to speak and write Italian fluently. He came to understand as few Americans ever did the convoluted protocol so prized by the officials of the Roman curia — a protocol complicated even further by the recent fall of the Temporal Power in 1870 and the consequent "exile" of the pope within the Leonine walls. In a society dominated by clerical gossip and by an old-boy network of ancient vintage, Denis O'Connell — handsome, genial, accommodating — found his true métier. He also discovered how important a part protestations of personal loyalty played in that little celibate world and indeed in the ecclesiastical world at large. When he heard, shortly before his ordination, that Gibbons had been named coadjutor of Baltimore, O'Connell wrote that he had inquired of the rector of the American College whether he, O'Connell, could swear fealty to Gibbons' person rather than to a particular diocese.

> [The rector] said no, and to satisfy me said, I could do much good for the cause of God in Virginia, and that you would consider no more my obligations to you, when you learn through himself your impotent debtor's readiness. . . . I ever cherished the hope of being able some day to repay in part the unlimited kindness you bestowed upon me, and I frequently consoled myself with the promise of passing my life under the government of the unassuming and gentle Bishop that took me to fish with him in Mr. Cox's pond, and dealt with me so familiarly in his apostolic journeys through No. Carolina's forests. I would like to be ever in your family and go always fishing with you another fish [*sic*]; but if God destines [*sic*] you for higher places, I must be content to labor unknown in the land of Virginia.[38]

O'Connell need not have worried that fate had left him to languish "unknown" in the backwoods of Virginia. He was scarcely returned from Europe and assigned to the cathedral parish in Richmond when the archbishop of Baltimore died, and Gibbons entered into his full estate as head of that primatial see. One of the rubrical duties incumbent upon the new metropolitan was to secure from the Holy See the pallium and all the appropriate archiepiscopal faculties.[39] For this task Gibbons chose O'Connell, who, by mid-October 1877, was back on shipboard, bound for Rome. He stayed there two months and carried out his assignment with the utmost punctiliousness. The diplomatic skills he had begun to develop as a student showed to good advantage on this mission which, due largely to the advanced age and poor health of the dying Pope Pius IX, involved more complications than might have been expected. O'Connell moved smoothly and cheerfully from one curial office to another, taking care to keep Gibbons informed of every step and even recommending, at one point in the proceedings, that the new archbishop spend a hundred dollars on a festive dinner for the officials of Propaganda. (Here was the first known use of a technique O'Connell was to employ often during his career.) By the new year he had brought his embassy to a successful conclusion, and on January 22, 1878, he was able to present the pallium triumphantly to Gibbons in Baltimore.

Among the prelates who witnessed Gibbons's formal investiture with the pallium was an Irish bishop named George Conroy, whom Propaganda had sent to the United States to make a formal visitation of the American church before he went on to other official duties in Canada. The absolutist American bishops, uncomfortably aware of the large number of complaints lodged against them in Rome by their lower clergy, were chronically suspicious of any intrusive curial investigation that could conceivably lead to a diminution of their powers, and so Gibbons, probably with the intention of keeping an eye on Conroy, offered him his young favorite as a companion and secretary. With Conroy's grateful acceptance, the practical education of Denis O'Connell was carried forward one more significant step. Between March and May, 1878, he traveled from St. Louis to the West Coast and back again with Conroy, a journey during which he met many influential American ecclesiastics and, at the same time, watched a seasoned papal diplomat in action.[40] Conroy, for his part, was much charmed by Father O'Connell, and it seems likely that the young priest's affability, Irish good looks, and eagerness to please left a similarly favorable impression upon the American bishops he met.[41]

In the summer of 1878 O'Connell returned to Virginia where, until 1883, he did parochial duty in Richmond and, later, in Winchester. These were, so to speak, his hidden years, and there is reason to suppose that the prosaic daily round of parish life did not altogether suit him or appeal to him.[42] But his patron in Baltimore, who discerned other useful qualities in O'Connell, had not forgotten him; as early as 1881 Gibbons recommended to Propaganda that O'Connell be made a bishop. Nothing resulted from that initiative, but two years later the archbishop summoned him from Winchester to help with the preparations for the Third Plenary Council. O'Connell, "pleased that you still remember me favorably," accepted the call with a careerist's alacrity, and, apparently without regret, shook the splendid dust of the Shenandoah valley from his feet. When he came back to the Diocese of Richmond many years later, he came with a miter on his head.

But on the day the Third Plenary Council opened, the bishop of Richmond — O'Connell's ordinary and another dramatis persona of large consequence in John Ireland's life — was a man of entirely different temper and character. John Joseph Keane[43] was intuitive rather than reflective, pious, trusting, affectionate, sentimental even, and much less comfortable engaging in the rough and tumble of ecclesiastical politics than O'Connell, that busy and somewhat cynical Roman gadfly. Keane had also been born in Ireland, was also the son of an artisan — his father had been a successful tailor in Ballyshannon, County Donegal — and had also come to America as a child: he was nine years old when, in 1848, the family settled into their new home in Baltimore. John, the eldest of five Keane children and the only one to survive into adulthood, was a delicate lad, and indeed he was never to be physically strong. He went to a school taught by the Christian Brothers until he was seventeen and proved himself a clever boy, good at his books, so that his parents hoped he would continue his education at Georgetown, "the splendid college kept by the Jesuit fathers." But young John determined to make his fortune in commerce, and between 1856 and 1859 he worked, first for a firm of Catholic booksellers and then for a wholesale drygoods house.

His decision to go to the seminary was, in its suddenness, typical of one who, later, would put so much religious stock in the direct

*John Joseph Keane, Bishop of Richmond
(from Shea, Catholic Hierarchy, 1886)*

intervention of Providence. One Sunday morning, he recalled, "I read [in the Baltimore diocesan weekly] about a good French woman whose son had been a priest, who was martyred in China, and every day she prayed to her martyred son, and it struck me at the moment, 'I will go and become a priest.' "[44] In September 1859 Keane entered St. Charles College, the same institution to be attended later by Denis O'Connell (he was ten years older than O'Connell and a year and a day younger than John Ireland). His record at the college was phenomenal, and when he left, after finishing the course in record time, his Sulpician masters were unanimous in their praise of his industry and intelligence. They had taught him, among other things, to write French in an elegant hand, a skill no doubt fostered by the faculty at St. Mary's Seminary in Baltimore, where he matriculated next and where all the professors were also French Sulpicians. In his work as a theology student at St. Mary's, Keane, if anything, surpassed his earlier scholastic achievements. He won innumerable prizes, graduated summa cum laude, and, at the end of his four-year course, received from his professors a testimonial that was at once laudatory and yet shrewdly prophetic: "[Keane has] a more than ordinary quickness of apprehension with a never failing felicity of expression, and an ever ready memory. His judgment, although sound, is occasionally carried by some precipitancy. A most generous heart, stronger in his affection than sensitive." On July 2, 1866, John Joseph Keane was ordained priest for the Archdiocese of Baltimore.

His assignment as curate to St. Patrick's parish in Washington——and the only assignment he ever had before he became a bishop—was singularly fortunate for a person with Keane's rather vulnerable emotional makeup. The pastor greeted him at the presbytery door and said: "I asked for you, Keane, because I thought you were a man I could get along with. And now understand, we are to be partners and brothers. This is not *my* house; it is *our* house, and your friends are as welcome here as mine." The pastor was as good as his word, and this parochial ideal of shared labor and mutual respect—so often honored only in the breach—sustained Keane for the dozen years he spent at St. Patrick's. He plunged heartily into all the good works associated with the parish, preaching, catechizing, organizing clubs and sodalities for the young people, opening a library of books and periodicals in order to stimulate the intellectual life of his parishioners and of other Catholics in Washington. He was especially zealous in promoting the cause of total abstinence; like John Ireland he boasted of having first taken the pledge as a boy from Father Theobald Mathew himself.[45] Like Ireland, too, Keane took particular pains with the preparation and delivery of his Sunday sermons, so much so that he soon gained a reputation for eloquence in Washington city and beyond.

In 1872 Keane seriously considered joining Isaac Hecker's Paulist community, and went so far as to apply to his archbishop for a release to do so. Hecker, who had measured Keane for a specific responsibility, seconded the young priest's petition. He wrote Archbishop James Roosevelt Bayley, explaining that his health was bad and suggesting that Keane might edit the *Catholic World*, the influential journal Hecker had founded in 1865. "It is one of the mightiest of my responsibilities and most taxing of my cares. F. Keane has a good pen, a literary taste and turn of mind, and many other qualifications which make him suitable for such a position." But Bayley refused permission on the grounds that, though Keane might make a good Paulist and a good editor for the *Catholic World*, "he makes also an excellent priest on the mission, . . . and we have much need of priests especially such as he is." Bayley also observed at the time that Keane was "destined for a bishopric."[46]

He was indeed, but not until after Bayley died. Gibbons, the new archbishop, whom Keane had known since his seminary days, immediately set the wheels in motion. In October 1877 a provincial terna was drawn up for Richmond with Keane's name only in second place, but Gibbons wrote privately to Propaganda and urged that Keane be appointed nonetheless. Denis O'Connell, in Rome to secure Gibbons's pallium, lobbied for the same end. Rumors abounded for some weeks and into the new year, while Keane, "blushing," as one parishioner recalled it, "like a school girl," busily denied that there was any prospect of him leaving St. Patrick's. He knew better, of course, but convention demanded the denials, and the red face that accompanied them did him at least some small credit.

On April 13, 1878, John Joseph Keane was appointed bishop of Richmond and administrator of the Vicariate of North Carolina.[47] At thirty-nine he was a slender, slope-shouldered man with a receding hairline, whose deep-set grey eyes, behind their rimless spectacles, gave him a perpetually serious air. Six years later he had changed little in appearance, except for a bit of weight gained in the interval and for a squint that testified to the impairment of vision he had begun to experience (and would continue to suffer intermittently for the rest of his life). He brought with him to the council the reputation of a hard-working and conscientious bishop, prayerful, studious, gentle, perhaps a little weak.

At the very end of the procession of November 9, 1884, came James Gibbons,[48] ninth archbishop of Baltimore, and, by appointment of the Holy See, apostolic delegate to the Third Plenary Council. In the latter capacity it was Gibbons's duty to preside over the conciliar sessions, to see to it that all the proper formalities were maintained, and to prepare the council's decrees for promulgation. Had Cardinal McCloskey not been ill, this prestigious office would no doubt have fallen to him. Had certain influential members of the Roman curia had their way, the apostolic delegate would have been an Italian bishop. Either eventuality would have involved an injustice, for the Third Plenary Council was uniquely Gibbons's achievement, and he deserved as no one else did formal recognition in it.

He was a small, wiry, smooth-faced man of fifty, neat about his

*James Cardinal Gibbons,
about 1890* (Archdiocesan Archives, Archdiocese of St. Paul and Minneapolis)

personal appearance but never unduly fussy. He smiled often and warmly, and there was about him an aura of deep inner calm. He appeared very much at peace with himself, a quality that lent him a strength and an effectiveness beyond the reach of others more talented than he. For if he lacked the vigor of an Ireland or a McQuaid, the brilliance of a Spalding or a Corrigan, James Gibbons possessed a combination of moral and intellectual gifts that made him indispensable — as none of them could ever have claimed to be — to the young American Catholic church, groping its way out of its adolescence.

Born in this city of Baltimore, christened in this cathedral, Gibbons as a child of three had been taken back to his parents' native County Mayo. He helped bury his father there, beneath the old sod, and returned to the United States with his mother and siblings when he was nearly nineteen, settling this time in New Orleans. He worked as clerk in a grocery store for a while, but his religious interests gradually led him to wonder whether he had a calling to the priesthood. Whatever doubts he entertained in this regard were pretty well resolved by a parish mission[49] he participated in early in 1854. Always a practical person, Gibbons, once he had made his decision, applied to his parish priest for instruction in Latin, and, in the late summer of 1855, he departed New Orleans for Baltimore and St. Charles College.

Why Gibbons chose to apply for admission as a church student with the diocese of his birth rather than that of his current residence remains unclear, but the association with Baltimore proved to be fruitful and, with the exception of his first decade as a bishop, permanent. He sailed through St. Charles and St. Mary's Seminary with flying colors, forming, as he did so, a lifelong attachment to the Sulpicians. He was ordained priest on June 30, 1861 — about three weeks, that is, before Deacon John Ireland boarded the ship at Le Havre that would bring him back to America and his own ordination six months later.

Gibbons's exercise of the pastoral ministry was brief but intense. He served two parishes at the same time, both in the rundown waterfront district of Baltimore but separated by a broad river, so that the pastor had to row a skiff across the water during the dark hours of the morning to take care of one congregation and then return the same way for duty in the other. This exertion was undertaken, of course, in accord with the old fasting laws, and later in life Gibbons blamed it for his chronically troublesome digestion.

Young Father Gibbons won the hearts of the poor people of his parishes who found him a devoted and selfless shepherd. When, in the summer of 1865, they learned he was to be taken from them, they petitioned the ecclesiastical authorities to keep him in their midst. But the high-minded and industrious Gibbons had favorably impressed others also, among them the recently appointed archbishop of Baltimore, Martin John Spalding, who was Lancaster Spalding's uncle. He insisted upon his own larger needs and those of the archdiocese, and accordingly James Gibbons, just before the new year, 1866, moved into the cathedral rectory and assumed his duties as the archbishop's secretary. Spalding was not disappointed in his performance, and indeed within a few months was laying the groundwork for his protégé's promotion to the episcopacy. It came in February 1868, when Gibbons — ordained fewer than seven years earlier — was named the first vicar apostolic of North Carolina.

Considering its worldly prospects, one would be hard put to think of a more dismal "promotion" in the Catholic world of 1868 than that to the Vicariate of North Carolina. Gibbons's new jurisdiction included the whole state of nearly fifty thousand square miles with a population of over a million, of whom scarcely seven hundred, or less than one-tenth of 1 percent, were Catholic. Of the three priests the vicar had to help him, only one, Denis O'Connell's uncle, the pastor at Charlotte, actually belonged to the vicariate; the other two were on loan from Baltimore and Charleston. The economy in North Carolina, as in all the states of the old Confederacy, lay prostrate in the wake of the Civil War. Literacy was low, and political disorder high. The overwhelmingly rural character of the state — Wilmington, with a population of thirteen thousand, was its largest town — rendered the missioner's work all the more daunting. So did the pathetic plight of hundreds of thousands of recently emancipated blacks.

The significance of Gibbons's four-year sojourn in North Carolina lay not in any great statistical triumphs he achieved there. When he left to go to Richmond in 1872, there were a few more priests at work in the vicariate, two Catholic schools where there had been none before, a handful of new church buildings, perhaps a few more people who called themselves Catholics. Only the most interested observer could have detected any measurable difference the presence of the vicar had made. But to Gibbons himself, as well as to his colleagues in the American hierarchy — who might have wondered how Spalding's untried young favorite would fare — his apostolate in North Carolina demonstrated that he could do a difficult job, do it effectively and unostentatiously, do it without complaining, do it in a manner that gained him the affection of his own people and the respect of the rest of the community. (That it took a decade after Gibbons was transferred to Richmond to persuade any priest to accept the vicariate indicated how burdensome an assignment it was considered to be.[55]) He showed steely determination and capacity as he had in the slum-parishes in Baltimore, and as he would again in Virginia, which, though an improvement over North Carolina, was hardly a lively center of Catholicism. Meanwhile, the young bishop scored a remarkable triumph in an unexpected quarter. In 1876 appeared *The Faith of Our Fathers,* a manual of instruction, simply and pleasingly written and designed by its author to serve the kind of people he had encountered so frequently in the southern missions—non-believers who expressed some interest in the Catholic religion, and Catholics who had had virtually no chance to learn about their faith. The spectacular success of his book—there were thirteen reprints within the first three years—brought Gibbons a host of accolades, including a personal commendation from Pope Pius IX. Little wonder that in 1877, when Martin Spalding's ailing successor, James Roosevelt Bayley, asked Rome to give him a coadjutor, the choice fell, to almost universal satisfaction, upon James Gibbons. He had surely paid his dues.

And now, as he walked up the steps of the lovely church in which he had been baptized, he was archbishop of the premier see in the United States and apostolic delegate. Ironically enough, Gibbons in league with the other eastern archbishops—Lancaster Spalding's "old fogies"—had originally opposed the convening of a plenary council. But the almost unanimous desire of the western and midwestern bishops to hold such a meeting, together with ever-increasing pressure from Rome, led Gibbons to change his mind. And here is a key to understanding his remarkable career. Gibbons was a persuadable man, never afraid to change his mind when circumstances dictated it. Once he did, he went forward cheerfully to do the job that, under other circumstances, he would have preferred not to do. If there had to be a plenary council, then Gibbons was determined that it should be as successful a council as human effort could accomplish. To bring that about he applied to the project his best administrative tools: an enormous capacity for work, a sharp eye for detail, a natural amiability.

Gibbons was above all else a realist. He indulged in no visions, he dreamed no dreams. This does not mean that he was without idealism or lofty moral purpose. It does mean, however, that he took the world as he found it, and that he accepted the people he had to deal with as they were, and not as he might have liked them to be. His winning ways with persons of all ranks and all shades of opinion rested upon his willingness to treat everyone in his or her own individuality. For Gibbons the small kindnesses he performed every day amounted to a method of governance. And he learned early—or perhaps he knew intuitively—that in the human equation tact and courtesy win more arguments than bluster. He could hold a point of view strongly, but never with rancor; he never sought a quarrel or searched for bad intentions in his opponents. He was genuinely principled, but not inflexibly so: in the real world one does what one can, even though one cannot do everything.

The criticism most often leveled at Gibbons—that he was not forceful enough, that his very sweetness of demeanor led him to be hesitant and irresolute—had some truth in it. Certainly he prized peace so much that he was prepared at times to blur the lines of an argument in order to bring contending factions into a semblance of harmony. Whether this characteristic was a species of weakness or simply Gibbons's own brand of realism is perhaps debatable. But great rulers have habitually not so much solved problems—for many problems do not admit of solution—as outwaited them. Gibbons frequently followed this course, much to the impatience of more aggressive personalities, like John Ireland.

THE THIRD PLENARY COUNCIL of Baltimore lasted a month, until December 7, 1884. It proceeded smoothly and efficiently, thanks in large measure to the careful preparations overseen by Gibbons. A full year before the council convened the archbishop of Baltimore had led a delegation of American prelates to Rome, where extended discussions with the cardinals of Propaganda resulted in a mutually acceptable agenda for the council. It was the sort of setting in which Gibbons was at his best. Firm, yet always tactful, he stated the prevailing view among his colleagues on such touchy matters as ecclesiastical trials, the membership of Catholics in secret societies like the Masons or the Odd Fellows, alienation of church property, and the establishment of irremovable rectorships among the lower clergy and of diocesan boards of priest-consultors who were to give consent to the bishop before he could act in certain defined areas. These Roman conferences were highly successful, even though the Americans' resistance to the appointment of an Italian apostolic delegate to preside over the council ruffled the feathers of some curial officials. They did not, however, press the point, and Pope Leo XIII named Gibbons to the post.[50] That decision pleased most American observers, among them John Ireland, who concluded a letter to Gibbons early in 1884: "Welcoming you back to America and congratulating you on not having brought over an Italian to preside over the council, I remain very respectfully etc."[51]

Back home Gibbons still had plenty of work left to do before the scheduled opening of the council in November: committees had to be set up, theologians enlisted, preachers appointed, documentation prepared, and even hospitality arranged. Throughout the performance of these various and arduous tasks the archbishop of Baltimore was careful above all to consult with his colleagues, to involve as many of them as possible in the preparatory stage, so that when the council actually met, the participants would be au courant with the issues to be discussed and would feel themselves full sharers in the process. All this he did with a fine diplomatic hand, assuming the responsibility for distributing the proposals that came to him from the bishops and consistently thanking and encouraging those who sent him ideas. Thus in late August he assured John Ireland that the bishop of St. Paul's "excellent suggestions" about Sunday observance, temperance, and Indian affairs would receive the council's careful attention.[52]

The serious business of the council began on Monday, November 10. As a basis for debate, the bishops had in hand a document of about one hundred pages, drawn up by Gibbons's corps of theologians, which incorporated the points made in the Roman conversations of the year before with the material submitted by the bishops themselves over the course of the spring and summer. They met in executive session five days a week at St. Mary's Seminary, with Gibbons in the chair. John Ireland took an active role in many of the discussions,[53] and his recommendations covered a wide spectrum. For example, he wanted the council to legislate against parish picnics on Sundays or at any time when liquor was served. He thought the number of holy days of obligation should be reduced and the one on January 1 eliminated, on the grounds that widespread neglect of this duty on the part of the Catholic people led to a general contempt for law. He lobbied against the condemnation of the Ancient Order of Hibernians as a secret society. He strenuously opposed parish dances and considered the musical training of seminarians an unneeded luxury—neither suggestion surprising from a man for whom all music was a dead letter.[54]

The attitudes of the bishop of St. Paul could be discerned also when the more substantive issues were debated. Thus Ireland insisted that each bishop have ultimate control of all Catholic schools in his diocese, notwithstanding the status of any religious order. He approved in principle of what amounted to state-sponsored competency examinations for teachers in parochial schools, including nuns. In one of the stormiest sessions of the council, Ireland strongly supported Lancaster Spalding's opposition to the establishment of irremovable rectorships. During the debate Ireland suddenly addressed the chair, and asked Gibbons to express his opinion on this much controverted matter. The apostolic delegate, who seldom intervened in the conciliar deliberations, responded in his mild way that if the bishops-in-council failed to set aside 10 percent of the parishes in each diocese for tenured pastors, then Rome would do so anyway, to the inevitable embarrassment of the American hierarchy.[55] The alliance of the young Turks from Peoria and St. Paul had more luck in persuading the council to set limits upon the rights of religious orders to own property without reference to the local bishop.[56]

But the most memorable event for Ireland at the Third Plenary Council occurred on the evening of Monday, November 10. The conciliar schedule called for services in the cathedral five evenings a week—vespers on Sunday and Benediction of the Blessed Sacrament[57] on the week nights—at which one of the bishops delivered a sermon. Ireland was fortunate that his turn came so early, because by the time the council was over the weary participants had been exposed to a veritable orgy of oratory. Gibbons assigned the subjects of the sermons, which ranged from "De Mortuis—our Deceased Prelates" (preached by Corrigan on November 13) to "Catholic Societies" (Keane, November 25) to "The Progress of the Church in the United States" (McQuaid, November 26).[58] Ireland had plenty of time to prepare his contribution: the invitation and assignment of topic had reached him in April.[59]

"The Church—the Support of Just Government"[60] lasted for ninety minutes. It had been memorized, except for the quotations, which the speaker read. Given the occasion and the prestigious audience, it was the most important speech Ireland had delivered up to that time. But it was important, too, because in it he gave formal expression to a theme which he had been developing for many years and which was to dominate his thought and action for many more years to come. He made his major point near the beginning: "I love too deeply the Catholic Church and the American republic not to be ever ready to labor that the relations of the one with the other be not misunderstood. It is true, the choicest field which providence offers in the world to-day to the occupancy of the Church is this republic, and she welcomes with delight the signs of the times that indicate a glorious future for her beneath the starry banner. But it is true, also, the surest safeguards for her own life and prosperity the republic will find in the teachings of the Catholic Church, and the more America acknowledges those teachings, the more durable will her civil institutions be made."

Here was the marriage contracted in heaven, Catholicism and America. Far from being mutually antagonistic or exclusive, the two of them, properly understood, were perfectly mated. The evils of anarchy on the one hand, he went on, and tyranny on the other—"the clamorings and violences of Communists and nihilists" and "the deathly grasp of military Caesarism"—were rooted in a modern social theory, "led by Hobbes and Rousseau," which asserted that "God counts for nothing in society; He gives nothing to society, and social affairs have no reference to Him." The Catholic church, guarantor of divine revelation, refuted in her teachings "absurdities of this kind. . . . God may no more be removed from society than he may be from any part of the cosmos." The church alone could effectively guard against that "forgetfulness of the divine origin of society and of government, [which] leaves no choice for the state between anarchy and despotism."

Moreover, Ireland continued, the church had ever been the advocate of liberty. "I lose all patience when I hear prejudice still surviving to the extent to assert that the Catholic Church is not the friend of free institutions." Then, invoking a dubious reading of medieval and early modern history, he asked rhetorically: "Did not the Middle Ages under [the church's] guidance gradually emerge from Roman despotism and barbarian feudalism into the possession of political liberty, so that we may truly say she started the nations on the road to the highest forms of liberty? . . . Protestantism did nothing for liberty; . . . if it was anything in civil and political matters, it was political anarchy." But the organizational grandeur of Catholicism—a feature of their religion Ireland so often insisted upon to his people back in Minnesota—was starkly different from "Protestantism which is not an organized force, and its contribution of positive power to any cause must necessarily be next to nothing." Contrast such historically manifest impotence, Ireland invited his distinguished congregation, to the "power [of] the [Catholic] Church, [which] by the abolition of slavery and serfdom widened the ranks of freemen and citizens."

Americans would do well, Ireland argued, to accept what the Catholic church has uniquely to offer. "No form of government as much as a republic demands wisdom and virtue in the people. The many control the ship of State; the many, consequently, must be able to control their own passions, else swift shipwreck awaits it. . . . To Americans, then, who love the republic, I fearlessly say, your hope is in the Catholic Church, because she is the mighty power today to resist unbelief and vice." But he had a message also for Catholics, who now and in past ages may not have shared his "love and admiration for the republican form of government. . . . This much . . . I know, that if they prefer other forms they are not compelled in their choice by Catholic principles or Catholic history. This much, too, I know, that I transgress no one iota of Catholic teaching when I speak forth my own judgment this evening, and salute the republic as the government I most cordially cherish. Republic of America," he concluded,

> receive from me the tribute of my love and of my loyalty. I am proud to do thee homage, and I pray from my heart that thy glory may never be dimmed. . . . Thou bearest in thy hands the brightest hopes of the human race. God's mission to thee is to show to nations that man is capable of the highest liberty. Oh! be ever free and prosperous that liberty triumph over the earth from the rising to the setting sun. *Esto perpetua!*[61]

Ireland's address was listened to with enthusiasm by many, though not by all. One of the more sophisticated hearers noted in his diary: "Sermon . . . on the Church and liberty by Bp. Ireland.

An essay good and useful in itself, though entirely lacking in originality. . . . A dreary thing. . . . Hard to hear—Habit of dropping his voice to be more impressive—Want of naturalness—the besetting sin of those who commit to memory."[62] The sermon did not get high marks either in some portions of the secular press, which found it difficult to reconcile Ireland's claims for Catholicism as a defender of liberty with Pius IX's Syllabus of Errors[63] and other popish pretensions that so outraged nineteenth-century liberals.[64] But as a statement of Ireland's personal credo and of his policy goals for the future, the sermon—including its extravagances and its purple prose—could hardly have been improved upon. And it was also an unabashed declaration of his own new status: by the time he left Baltimore early in December 1884, to go back to St. Paul,[65] John Ireland had served notice that he was now a man to be reckoned with.

IX

"In Aspiration I Am a Scholar"

1885–86

T HE THIRD PLENARY COUNCIL had produced plenty of lively debate among the bishops assembled at Baltimore, but its sessions did not reveal the profound differences, professional and personal, that, as events would shortly demonstrate, in fact divided the participants. This was due in large measure to the thoroughness with which Gibbons had prepared for the council and to the smooth and courteously supple manner in which he presided over it. The conciliar legislation was of extreme importance in the life of the American Catholic church — a hallmark, indeed — but its passage signaled an end, rather than a beginning, to an era of good feeling.[1]

John Ireland was scarcely home from the council when a small but significant straw in the wind gave a hint of larger troubles to come. The School Sisters of St. Francis, a religious order founded in 1874, was composed mostly of German immigrants who, at the invitation of Bishop Grace, had determined to establish their mother house within the Diocese of St. Paul. In 1884 the sisters, who already staffed twelve parish schools in southern Minnesota, settled in Winona, a bustling Mississippi River town in the southeast corner of the diocese. There they put up a modest building intended to serve as a girls' school and as the order's headquarters. In January 1885, Ireland, accompanied by his protégé and fellow stalwart in the temperance movement, Joseph Cotter,[2] arrived at the new St. Mary's Convent and Academy to preside over the dedication ceremonies. Cotter celebrated the festive mass, and afterwards the bishop uttered a few conventional pieties to the small congregation. "Inside [this convent]," he said, "shall reign the peace, the pure joys of the celestial harbor. . . . The world needs more than wealth for its life and its happiness. If it had but millionaires, railroads, and stock exchanges, it would indeed be miserable. It needs the refreshing dew of divine grace; it needs the high ideal of moral perfection; and these blessings the religious orders in the Catholic Church give to it in a supereminent degree."[3]

Dinner followed the mass, and after that a tense interview between Ireland and the mother-founder of the order, Alexia Hoell. Were there, the bishop asked, any postulants[4] in the order from Minnesota? A few, Mother Alexia answered. Any from Germany? More than a few. Where were the sisters presently teaching? Mostly in predominantly German parishes in Wisconsin and Minnesota. Did not Mother Alexia realize, Ireland said, how important it was that the church in America shed its foreign image? Mother Alexia, herself German born, remained noncommittal. Ireland then tersely laid down three conditions to be fulfilled before he would grant permission for the School Sisters to set up their mother house in his diocese: they must accept no more postulants from Europe; no sister could be assigned to teach in a parish without having first attended an American normal school; and finally the order had to be canonically established as a diocesan community, subject to the authority of the bishop.

Mother Alexia, a woman of intelligence and spirit, professed herself ready to compromise — she would accept, for example, the teacher-training requirement, which (though she probably did not know it) had been discussed at the Third Plenary Council and was a good idea in any event — but to acquiesce to the bishop's other demands, she said, would be tantamount to an unacceptably radical alteration of the order she had founded. Ireland replied with a shrug that in that case he would permit the School Sisters to operate an academy in Winona but not to locate their mother house there. Three years later the sisters had departed Winona for the more friendly environment of Milwaukee. Ireland bought the property they left behind for thirty thousand dollars (they had asked thirty-five thousand) and turned it over to the Sisters of St. Joseph, now governed locally by his sister Ellen, Mother Seraphine, for use as a hospital. This project did not thrive, and in 1894 a different branch of Franciscan sisters purchased the site and began upon it a successful women's college.

The small drama played out in a nuns' parlor in Winona gave expression to two of John Ireland's strongest convictions: that the autonomy of the religious orders had to be curbed as much as possible by the local bishop; and that the image of "foreignism," inevitably linked to a church largely composed of immigrants, had to be eliminated as soon as possible. Moreover, the confrontation with Mother Alexia showed that the two issues had merged for Ireland into one: it was precisely the independence and the international character of the religious orders, particularly those dominated by tough-minded Germans, that promoted the continuation among Catholics in the United States of what he considered an unhealthy cultural and linguistic separatism. These ideas were not new to him, but now that he enjoyed the authority of an ordinary in his own right, he could implement them as policy, even though to do so meant repudiating, at least in the case of the School Sisters of St. Francis, an explicit commitment made by his venerated predecessor.

A further linkage, to Ireland's most sacred cause, revealed itself at roughly the same time. Northwest of St. Paul about ninety miles, near the town of St. Cloud, lay the flourishing Benedictine Abbey of St. John's, also heavily German in its personnel. The monks had settled there originally in 1856 at the invitation of Bishop Cretin. They had done yeoman work as missionaries to the German settlers in central Minnesota, and their relations with the bishops of St. Paul had been relatively placid. Indeed, Bishop Grace had sent many of his seminarians, including Joseph Cotter, to study in the excellent monastic school there. After 1875, with the creation of the Vicariate of Northern Minnesota—the first vicar of which, Rupert Seidenbusch, had been abbot of St. John's—the monastery was no longer within the boundaries of the Diocese of St. Paul, and so the likelihood of conflict with the bishop was rendered remote. But Ireland was intensely irritated when a monk of St. John's, with the splendidly German name of Othmar Erren, published during the winter of 1885 several articles in which he poked fun at what he called temperance zealots. Here was a reminder for the new bishop of St. Paul that German-speaking Catholics often spearheaded the opposition to the total abstinence movement, dismissing it as needful only for shiftless Irishmen who could not control their appetites. It was not a long step for him to place German and religious order and anti-temperance into one disreputable category, and he took some satisfaction in denying Father Othmar—who had also quarreled with his abbot and left the monastery—faculties to function as a priest in the Diocese of St. Paul.[5]

Of course a large foundation like St. John's, representing the most ancient and revered order in the Latin church, was a far more formidable opponent than a little group of nuns struggling to start their congregation. And, besides, Ireland was not without sympathy for the Benedictine ideal, at least in the abstract. "Better far, in my opinion," he wrote in 1885, "for Religious Orders and for the Church, if the Benedictine Rule had remained more than it has, the type of religious life." The Benedictines, he added, had been content to see themselves as an "element of activity, of strength in the Church," and had not aimed, as the Jesuits had, "consciously or unconsciously to be the whole Church."[6] Even so, he looked with stern disfavor upon the monks' missionary activities, which he described as "their incursions over Northern Minnesota." And when the abbot of St. John's asked, as a "personal favor," that Benedictine nuns be allowed to staff the school maintained by the Assumption German parish in St. Paul, Ireland stonily refused: "The matter," he said without elaborating, "is too important for religion in St. Paul" to accede to the abbot's request.[7]

This suspicion of the religious orders helped spur Ireland on to tackle another project, one that he had long thought about and his predecessors had tried in vain to initiate. If the diocese had its own seminary, it would not be necessary to send aspirants to the priesthood to be trained by monks and other strangers. At the beginning of 1885, the time seemed ripe. For one thing, the economic and human growth of Minnesota had continued at an extraordinary rate. The population of St. Paul now approached 120,000, ten times what it had been when Ireland had come home from the war. But Minneapolis had grown even faster, and for the first time had outdistanced in numbers its sister city. Water systems were installed during the 1880s, sewers laid, streets paved, thousands of homes constructed. James J. Hill built himself a massive mansion on top of a hill, one sign of the money to be earned in the railroad business in St. Paul, where twelve separate lines intertwined to make the city one of the major transportation hubs in the nation. By 1890 the state's farmers were shipping thirty-five million bushels of wheat over the new rails, while its sawmills turned out 650 million feet of timber. The miners of iron ore incorporated, between 1885 and 1890, no fewer than 284 companies.[8]

Catholic growth continued apace. During the same half-decade Ireland founded thirty-eight new parishes in the diocese, including ten in St. Paul and four in Minneapolis. In addition a school for deaf children was opened, as well as a boys' orphanage, three homes for "friendless and unprotected" girls, two hospitals, and perhaps fifteen grammar and secondary schools.[9] Such signs of overall prosperity and confessional vigor were prefaced, so to speak, by Ireland's announcement, published on December 4, 1884: "Taking into account the wondrous development of religion in the diocese of St. Paul, . . . we propose with God's help to open in September, 1885, in St. Paul, a seminary in which the youth of the diocese whom God may inspire with a vocation to the priesthood, will be enabled to pursue at least their classical studies. . . . The diocesan seminary will be the principal work of our episcopate, and from it we expect the most fruitful result."[10]

What Ireland clearly had in mind was an American Meximieux, a petit séminaire staffed by diocesan priests and governed by himself. One obstacle to the plan had been removed by Grace's retirement, for the old bishop, though he had tried manfully for many years to found just such an institution, had grown weary of the struggle and, in 1879, had even invited the German Jesuits, headquartered at Buffalo, to come to St. Paul and assume responsibility for training the future priests of the diocese. It was just as well that nothing came of this initiative; the prospect of Coadjutor Ireland inheriting a regiment of German Jesuits entrenched within his jurisdiction leaves the imagination reeling.[11]

A suitable locale for the new seminary was at hand. In 1874 Bishop Grace had purchased at a bargain price a farm of 452 acres, located west of St. Paul and just across the Mississippi from Minneapolis. Three years later he realized a long-cherished goal when the Catholic Industrial School of Minnesota began operations on the site, with a staff of three religious brothers and a clientele of twenty boys, all housed in a three-storied frame building. Aside from the intrinsic worth of such a facility, both the bishop and Father Ireland urged its necessity because of the notorious proselytizing carried on routinely by Protestant clergymen in the state reform school. The intention was that the Industrial School would provide a haven and a place of vocational training for orphans and the mentally retarded as well as for youngsters in trouble.[12] But it never aroused much interest or support in the Catholic community, and in 1879, the venture clearly a failure, the school was transferred to an uncertain future in Ireland's colony at Clontarf.[13]

Ireland himself, however, with the generous aid of the original owner of the farm, purchased the building and 280 contiguous acres. Late in 1880 an announcement appeared in the diocesan weekly that a seminary would open on the site the following autumn. But this notice was apparently a trial balloon; 1881 came and went, and no action was taken. The difficulty proved to be the familiar one, a shortage of money. The annual seminary collection taken up in all the parishes of the diocese hovered around three thousand dollars, and part of this amount had to support the thirty or so seminarians studying at various institutions in the United States and Europe. The yearly deficit in the seminary account gave Grace pause; despite Ireland's importuning, he was reluctant to proceed with any elaborate plans for a facility within the diocese until he had some cash in hand. His caution earned him at least a limited reward: through the early 1880s the diocesan collections gradually increased to the point that, by the time the old bishop retired, a modest reserve fund of $1,474 had accumulated.[14]

That was enough for John Ireland. His administrative style was always to press a project forward with what resources were available at the moment, to keep up always a bold public front, and then to deal later with problems as they emerged. He was inspired not so much by rashness as by a sublime confidence in himself, in his mission, and in the limitless possibilities he discerned in a rapidly expanding America. To seize an opportunity seemed more important to him than any risk of failure. "Enthusiasm begets enthusiasm," he was to write later. "It fits a man to be a leader; it secures a following." And he brushed aside those pusillanimous souls who accused him of temerity: "Who ever tries to do something out-

side routine lines against whom hands are not raised and whose motives and acts are not misconstrued?"[15]

During the spring and summer of 1885 Ireland did not need to
worry that his motives were being "misconstrued," but the task of
getting the seminary ready to open its doors in September was
demanding enough. The bishop wasted no time. Carpenters and
masons went promptly to work adding a new wing to the Industrial
School building, and then the whole structure was covered with a
red brick exterior. The construction and renovation proceeded on
schedule and were finished by mid–August, when the priests of the
diocese assembled there for their annual retreat. Bringing the clergy
together at what Ireland had decided to call St. Thomas Aquinas
Seminary[16] was a significant and calculated act on Ireland's part; he
was determined that the new institution should forge from the beginning close links with the diocesan priests who, he hoped, would
come to identify with it and over the long term serve as recruiters
for it in their parishes and offer it moral and pecuniary support. The
retreat of 1885 may have been memorable for another reason: conducting it was the eloquent bishop of Richmond, Ireland's good
friend, John J. Keane.[17]

The morning of September 8 — the feast of the Nativity of the
Virgin Mary — dawned cool and cloudy. The grounds were wet after a thunderstorm the night before. In the seminary's little chapel
the rector celebrated mass in the presence of his five faculty colleagues and sixty-two students. The rest of the day was taken up
with the chores of registration. Classes opened the next afternoon,
but the sessions were brief. "There being no books, no desks," the
rector noted in his diary, "very little was possible." The rector was
Thomas O'Gorman.

O'Gorman had followed a pilgrim's track since his return from
France in 1865.[18] He spent the first twelve years of his priesthood
as pastor of Rochester, Minnesota, ministering to the Catholics in
that thriving community as well as to those in four mission stations
in the nearby countryside. It was an arduous life, but the stocky,
good-natured, bookish O'Gorman took it all in stride and performed the multitude of duties of the frontier missionary with pa-
nache. Besides building churches and schools, he founded literary
and benevolent societies, and, predictably, devoted special efforts to

St. Thomas Aquinas Seminary, about 1893, with Lake Mennith in the fore-ground (MHS)

the cause of total abstinence. He soon enjoyed the reputation of a gifted pulpit and platform orator who, if he did not possess the riveting rhetorical skills of his former schoolmate, nevertheless spoke clearly, interestingly, and sometimes eloquently. Testimony that he stood high among the local intelligentsia came from no less a personage than Dr. William Worrall Mayo, who, though not a Catholic, took pains to consult O'Gorman before deciding upon the educational program for his sons Charlie and Will.[19]

Like so many priests of his generation — like Ireland, Keane, and even the young Michael Corrigan — O'Gorman was immensely impressed by the work of Isaac Hecker and the Paulists. At the end of 1877 he asked and received Bishop Grace's permission to resign his pastorate and to join the Paulist community in New York. For the next four years O'Gorman labored as a member of the Paulist mission band all over the northeastern United States. It was said that during this time he became Cardinal McCloskey's favorite preacher. He indulged his literary interests too, and contributed several articles to Hecker's *Catholic World*. He returned to Minnesota in 1882, perhaps with the prospect of serving in the new seminary, but, with the delay in launching that project, he was assigned meanwhile as parish priest to Faribault — another lively southern Minnesota town, where John Ireland's famous school plan was to be inaugurated a few years later.

Though it may have appeared natural for Ireland to entrust the supervision of his new seminary to someone he had known since they were boys together, the choice did not prove a particularly happy one. The bishop, indeed, had foreseen the difficulty and had tried to secure a rector from outside the diocese.[20] Only when this attempt failed had he turned to his old friend. O'Gorman, to be sure, had had a varied career; he was intelligent, adaptable, and something of a clerical man of the world. But as an educator he was essentially an amateur. He had no scholastic training beyond what he had received at Montbel more than twenty years earlier. He had no experience either as an administrator or as a teacher. He discovered during his brief tenure that operating an institution of higher learning was a far cry from managing a parish. As for Ireland, he came to doubt that O'Gorman even had the proper instincts for the job. "I say to you *confidentially*," he wrote to a prospective replacement during O'Gorman's second year at the helm, "that Father O'Gorman has not the educational experience, nor the educational mind, to secure success." And he added a week or so later: "My trouble is not from my professors; they are pleased, doing well — as far as the general direction allows. The trouble is simply that I have not the proper man at the head of the Seminary, and it is this trouble that I am seeking to remedy. F. O'Gorman has formally resigned."[21]

Ireland's assertion that he had no "trouble" from his faculty members — among whom O'Gorman, after resigning the rectorship, took his place as professor of theology and history — may have been strictly true, but the enormous turnover in staff underscored the basic problems any American bishop faced in trying to create, virtually out of nothing, a viable collegiate or seminary program. During the first three years of its existence Ireland assigned two dozen different priests to St. Thomas's six or seven faculty positions. They were all willing enough, and a few of them were able, but, like O'Gorman, they lacked any formal education beyond that attained during their own seminary days and any classroom experience. The occasional lay instructor, who might teach subjects like chemistry or mathematics, was so miserably paid that he rarely tarried at St. Thomas very long.[22]

If a faculty so unsettled led to an absence of stability and of long-range planning, even the stated purpose of the school and the composition of its student body suggested ambiguity. The word "seminary," it turned out, admitted many shades of meaning. "The studies to be pursued," read a statement issued six weeks before the first class was taught at St. Thomas, "will make the young man a scholar, in the true and full sense of the word, ready for the theological seminary, or for the schools of law and medicine, or qualified for any social position he may covet."[23] The result was an educational hodge-podge that included—in the terminology of a later, more bureaucratic time—a theologate, a preparatory seminary, a junior college, a high school, and a junior high school. Roughly one-quarter of the students in the seminary were seminarians in the strict sense of that word; Ireland ordained sixty-three of them before 1894, when a separate grand séminaire was built across the street.[24] Meanwhile, a thirteen-year-old lad, just beginning to learn to parse a Latin sentence, was the schoolfellow of a graduate student in his mid-twenties.

Yet St. Thomas, despite these unpromising circumstances, not only survived but ultimately flourished. And in the many crises of its first years it survived because John Ireland would not have it otherwise. There was no clearer demonstration of the man's iron will, nor of his deep and abiding love for the place. He had his own Meximieux now, and something more, and he gave the institution the full measure of his devotion. Even after the departure of the major seminarians, when St. Thomas evolved into a military academy and a junior college, it remained the apple of his eye. Nothing pleased him more than to arrive unannounced at a classroom and to lead the students through a reading of his beloved Virgil or Horace. He enjoyed dining with the faculty and engaging in the donnish conversation that he imagined to be his forte. "In aspiration I am a scholar," he liked to say. "My dream is to study, but I have no time." Men of action commonly express such sentiments, which must be taken with a grain of salt. But Ireland was a man of genuine, if narrow, intellectual interests, who knew and appreciated the classics, who read omnivorously in three languages, who understood the value of a liberal education. And if in the foundation of St. Thomas he demanded sacrifices from O'Gorman and many others, he did not hesitate to give of his own substance as well. The land upon which St. Thomas stood had been his personal gift. And of the $72,000 the first buildings had cost, he had paid $46,000 out of his own pocket.[25]

Neither the daily burdens of the bishop of St. Paul nor all the work and worry that went into the founding of St. Thomas Aquinas Seminary were enough to monopolize John Ireland's attention during his first years as an ordinary. Indeed, another educational enterprise — also concerned with Ireland's missionary and clericalist ideal of a well-trained corps of priests — preoccupied him almost as much as the St. Thomas venture did.

The notion of a national university under Catholic auspices was hardly novel to Ireland, who had for years shared a house with one of its most fervent sponsors. Bishop Grace urged the project upon anyone who would listen. Among those who did was John Lancaster Spalding of Peoria, one of the few American bishops who had himself attended a university — Louvain, in the early 1860s. "Bishop Grace of St. Paul," Spalding observed during the late summer of 1880, "has begged me to undertake" the promotion of a national university, "at least to make the attempt; and as he is a holy man I have thought it might be the will of God."[26] This was the very time when Ireland was most in Spalding's company, when the two of them were out together on the hustings, seeking support for the colonization movement.[27] Whether at home or on the road, Ireland was sure to hear about the merits of an American Catholic university, and there is no reason to suppose he listened without sympathy.

During the years just prior to Baltimore III the proposal became for Spalding a kind of crusade. He energetically lobbied his fellow bishops, even to the point of confessing to Cardinal McCloskey: "I should be willing to devote my whole life to such a work, for I am persuaded that in no other way shall we be able to meet the demands which the near future will make upon us."[28] The response was at best mixed, but Spalding was not deterred, even though he had not yet sorted out in his own mind exactly what kind of institution he wanted to see founded. "I am not speaking of a university," he declared in a speech in Milwaukee in June 1881, "but of something far simpler, less expensive, and, in my opinion, better fitted to supply the most pressing want of American Catholics. The institution of which I am thinking might be called a High School of Philosophy and Theology. . . . Such a college would not be [geared] to make profound theologians, learned exegetes, or skillful metaphysicians, or specialists of whatever kind, but rather it would teach theology as a subject of contemplation. It would seek to impart not professional skill but cultivation of mind."[29] When he went to Rome in the winter of 1882 he brought the matter to the attention of the highest curial officials, who all, he reported to Ireland, "have received with great favor [the notion of] a university college of Philosophy and Theology."[30]

As he gradually refined his own thinking, Spalding found at least qualified support in some quarters. Even Bishop McQuaid of Rochester did not reject out of hand the idea of "a Theological School of higher studies" as he did a larger Catholic university, for which latter, he insisted, there was neither money nor interest. Spalding was gratified, too, that the subject was receiving wide attention in the Catholic press. During the discussions held in Rome at the end of 1883, preliminary to the plenary council, the university proposal did not come up, but the following spring, when the American bishops were themselves suggesting items for the council's agenda, at least one voice—Bishop Grace's—was raised in its behalf. Archbishop Heiss informed Gibbons of the deliberations within the Province of Milwaukee: "The proposition for a 'Catholic University' or rather for a higher 'Seminary for Philosophy and Theology' has been made by Rt. Rev. Grace, without having much support from the majority of the Bishops; the most of them are of the opinion, all [that] can be done now, would be to improve the studies of our larger or Provincial seminaries." Gibbons himself, who held no strong views on the subject, may nevertheless have signaled which way he was leaning when he assigned Spalding his sermon topic at the council: "The Higher Education of the Priesthood."[31]

But what a cynic has labeled the mother's milk of politics is an indispensable nutritive too for ecclesiastical projects. Two weeks before the first solemn session of the council the archbishop of Baltimore received a note from the bishop of Peoria. "Miss Mary Caldwell," Spalding wrote, "has informed me that she intends to be present at the opening of the Council and as she is disposed to be very generous in aid of the project of founding *Unum Seminarium Principale,* I am very anxious she should have a good seat. She will I suppose be accompanied by one or two friends. May I ask your assistance in this matter?" Spalding knew whereof he spoke. On November 13, 1884, Mary Gwendoline Caldwell, aged twenty-one, heiress together with her younger sister, Mary Elizabeth, to a large fortune, set down in writing her intention to donate three hundred thousand dollars for the establishment of "a National Catholic School of Philosophy and Theology" to be governed by a committee of American bishops, and "never to be under the control of any religious order" or affiliated with any other institution, and finally under the proviso that other faculties might be later added "with a view to form a Catholic University."[32] Three evenings later, on Sunday, November 16, Spalding delivered his powerful address from the pulpit of the Baltimore cathedral. "Let there be . . . an American Catholic university, where our young men, in the atmosphere of faith and purity, of high thinking and plain living, shall become more intimately conscious of the truth of their religion and of the genius of their country."[33] Spalding's eloquence and Caldwell's money carried the day. The inevitable committee was then appointed, and on December 2 it recommended acceptance of Miss Caldwell's gift and her conditions, which recommendation the council duly agreed to.[34]

Up to this point John Ireland had been more or less a benevolent bystander. But on December 5 Mary Caldwell — familiarly known as "Mamie" — replied to Gibbons's request that she inform the council whom she wanted to serve on the governing committee of the university of which she was now officially designated foundress. Besides several prominent laymen and one priest, she named the archbishops of Baltimore, Boston, Philadelphia, and Milwaukee, the coadjutor of New York, and the bishops of Peoria and St. Paul. There is no doubt that Spalding drew up this list, nor any doubt either that Ireland was included on it because Spalding considered him a reliable ally. The council accepted the list, with the qualification that other names might be added in due course, so long as the bishops on the committee continued to outnumber the laymen and priests combined.[35]

With the coming of the new year Gibbons, chairman of the committee but by no means yet a zealot for the cause, attempted to persuade Mamie Caldwell to hand over the three hundred thousand dollars she had promised. Her refusal — on the sensible grounds that her money was intended to pay for the implementation of definite plans and, until then, she would continue to enjoy the interest on it herself — led the archbishop of Baltimore to indulge in a rare show of impatience, more perhaps at her adviser, Bishop Spalding, than at the saucy young woman herself. At the end of January 1885, several members of the committee (Gibbons not among them) took advantage of their presence in New York to meet informally at Cardinal McCloskey's residence.[36] There was some discussion about endowment of professorial salaries. Ireland received unanimous agreement to his suggestion that the institution be called the Catholic University of America. But most of the conversation turned upon the question of an appropriate site; one proposal seriously advanced was the purchase of the Newark diocesan college, Seton Hall, in South Orange.

Early in February, however, Spalding and Caldwell, in separate communications to Gibbons, urged that the university be located in Washington. Resistance to that idea was felt almost immediately. The archbishop of Cincinnati and the bishop of Cleveland, both men of influence, objected strenuously. The Jesuits inquired, not without reason, what would happen to their venerable Georgetown College if another Catholic institution of higher learning were to be established in the same city. Some objectors thought Washington too distracting for ecclesiastical students, others thought it too "southern." Most ominous was the reaction in the New York area, the center of wealth and population and therefore logically the place to locate a national university. Seton Hall, in nearby New Jersey, could serve the purpose admirably, in the opinion of Bernard McQuaid and Michael Corrigan, both of whom — if sentiment were to play a part — were also past presidents of that school.[37]

All this was a source of embarrassment for Gibbons, because

Washington lay within the boundaries of his diocese, and so it could be argued that the benefit of the university's presence in the nation's capital—if benefit it were—would accrue to him. He was besides anxious to avoid any hint of rivalry between Baltimore and New York. Yet if Miss Caldwell, directed by Spalding, insisted upon Washington, then Washington it would have to be. Faced by this conflict of opinion Gibbons, not for the last time, hesitated. And John Ireland, not for the last time either, pressed him to act. "You will please bear with me," he wrote on March 26,

> if I ask what is being done with our university project? I am afraid that with our delay the interest felt in it through the country will be lost. Already two of those whom we expected to be chief benefactors have died; others may pass away. I may not understand things in my remote quarter of the country; but it does seem to me that it were better if we were showing some signs of life. It was very unfortunate that you were not able to attend the New York meeting. In your absence we would decide nothing. Is it not advisable, then, to have a meeting soon, at which there will be a full attendance? Early in May Bp. Spalding and myself will be in Chicago for a colonization meeting, and we could without much trouble continue our journey to Baltimore or New York.

Ireland concluded this appeal with a succinct and highly significant expression of one of his guiding principles: "I feel a deep interest in the University, both for the merits of the project itself, and for the sake of the [Third Plenary] Council, whose honor is staked upon the realization of all its measures."[38]

Gibbons responded promptly and scheduled a meeting for Baltimore on May 7. Ireland assured him of his own and Spalding's presence, and then added a veiled warning passed on to him by the bishop of Peoria: "Miss Caldwell professes herself ready to pay over the money at any moment we need it to pay for ground, or for a building. She will not give it, she says, merely to have it lie in a bank. All this makes it the more necessary for us to go to work, as we are near allowing her too much time within which she may change her mind."[39] The meeting went smoothly enough. Spalding, vigorously seconded by Ireland, moved for the adoption of a site in Washington, and the committe approved; if Corrigan had any objections, he said nothing about them. Heiss of Milwaukee, another potential opponent of the whole university idea, was absent, which may have explained why German-speaking Martin Marty, vicar apostolic of Dakota, was added to the committee. Far more important in the long run was the addition to the governing body of another bishop, Gibbons's close collaborator, John J. Keane.[40]

While these organizational arrangements were proceeding, the archbishop of Baltimore was busily engaged in placing another of his protégés in a high and sensitive position. The rectorship of the North American College in Rome had been vacant since early in 1884. Propaganda had the right of final appointment to the post, after the usual submission of a terna by a panel of American bishops. Gibbons abided by the standard procedure and submitted three names, but he made strong private representations to the Roman officials on behalf of Denis J. O'Connell who, a month after the university committee meeting in Baltimore, was duly appointed.[41] Gibbons in this initiative cared less about the administration of the college than he did about having in Rome an agent who could deal effectively with the curia in the name of the American hierarchy. O'Connell, already a practiced veteran of the Roman system, fitted the bill perfectly. Nor was the attractiveness of his candidacy diminished in Gibbons's eyes by the fact that O'Connell realized the rectorship to be only the latest in a series of personal favors done him by the archbishop of Baltimore. Mild-mannered and somewhat hesitant Gibbons may have been; naïve he was not.

For the sake of the infant university the timing of O'Connell's appointment was opportune. The new Roman agent was able to forewarn Gibbons and to advise him about pitfalls the project might encounter within the toils of the curia. For example, the university, approved indeed by the council, had not been a subject included in the preconciliar discussions with Propaganda, and therefore Propaganda, always extremely fussy about its prerogatives, required that the review of the council's decrees on the university be a separate negotiation. But this was a procedural, rather than a substantive, obstacle, especially since the pope himself had told Gibbons, in a private letter, of his pleasure at the prospect of a Catholic University in the United States. Meanwhile, back home, practical matters went forward: land was purchased in Washington, potential donors contacted, a public relations campaign mounted.[42] Ireland, with characteristic bravura, played his part in the last-named activity. In a newspaper interview given in October—scarcely a month after his own St. Thomas Seminary had held its first classes—he claimed that six hundred thousand dollars had already been raised for the university, and then added: "Ours will be a University of a grade above anything that has yet been attempted in this country."[43]

A month later, when the expanded committee met again in Baltimore, the chief topic of discussion was the immediate need for money. It would seem that Ireland's figure of six hundred thousand dollars in hand was, to say the least, overblown. The committee determined at any rate to authorize four of its members—Spalding, Keane, Marty, and Ireland—to solicit funds across the country, while Gibbons agreed to write a letter to all the bishops pleading for their cooperation in the campaign. To the annoyance of the collectors Gibbons did not fulfill his part of the arrangement for nearly three months. But the really chilling news came from New York. Keane was stunned to discover that Michael Corrigan—now archbishop in his own right since McCloskey had died, October 10, 1885—no longer supported the university "in its present shape," and that he believed a Jesuit university should be located in New York City. He therefore declined to endorse collections for the Washington project in his diocese.[44] Reduced therefore to appealing to individuals, Keane, joined by Spalding in February 1886, moved his canvass to Brooklyn and then to Albany, Boston, and Philadelphia, but in none of these important places did he find a much warmer welcome.

From the Midwest the tidings were somewhat better, though even the ever-sanguine bishop of St. Paul adopted a rather more muted tone than usual. "I have lately seen Bishop Marty," Ireland told Gibbons at the end of March, "who is working earnestly among the Germans for the university." He went on to ask Gibbons to postpone the next meeting of the university committee, originally to be held during Easter week, because the long distance the Vicar of Dakota would have to travel might prevent him from arriving in time. "As he represents the Germans, it will be rather unfortunate if we have the meeting without him." If Ireland already knew that the most influential German-born prelate, Heiss of Milwaukee, was about to resign from the committee, he did not say so. Instead he accentuated the positive. "Moreover a few days work after Easter by Bp. Spalding and myself in collecting would have good results. Lent brought us all to our homes; after Easter we will be again free."[45]

Gibbons accordingly rescheduled the committee meeting for May 12 in Baltimore, but for some reason Ireland did not attend. The collectors who were present reported the fruits of their labors: Keane a disappointing $24,000 total from the relatively affluent Northeast; Spalding $91,000, which included $50,000 from Mamie Caldwell's sister; and Marty a vague confidence that a letter he had circulated would bring in eventually $100,000 — so much for the "earnestness" of the vicar's efforts among the Germans as compensation for the loss of Heiss. A tense moment in the meeting came when, during a discussion of the progress report to be sent to the Holy See, Keane demanded that there be joined to it a formal request that Rome sanction no other Catholic university in the United States for the next twenty-five years. Corrigan, against whose plans this intervention was directed, suggested amending the motion to the effect that Roman approval be denied until the next plenary council, but he said nothing else. Keane accepted the amendment, and the motion passed. The exchange puzzled the other committee members, including Gibbons, to whom Keane explained the matter when the meeting was over.[46]

But for sheer drama nothing at the meeting of May 12 compared to the *gran rifuto* of John Lancaster Spalding. For the purpose of selecting a rector for the university, the four archbishops present — Gibbons, Corrigan, Ryan of Philadelphia, and Williams of Boston—were constituted a subcommittee. They met separately at midday, and, almost as a matter of course, offered the position to the bishop of Peoria. For months it had been taken for granted by all sectors of the Catholic public that Spalding, who almost singlehandedly had brought the university into being, would be its first rector. Ireland, had he been present at the meeting, would surely have endorsed the archbishops' choice—he had often observed in his candid way that Spalding was the only bishop in America who knew anything about universities—and in later years, even when the two had fallen out, Spalding took special pains to deny rumors that Ireland had opposed his nomination.[47] Nevertheless, to the amazement of all, Spalding flatly refused to accept the appointment. The subcommittee then unanimously recommended John J. Keane, who was no less surprised than anyone else. "I was utterly astonished," he wrote, "for I had always considered it a matter of course that, as the establishment of the University was mainly owing to the eloquent appeal of Bishop Spalding and to the generousity [*sic*] of his protégée Miss Caldwell, it would naturally be that he would have charge of it." Only when assured that Spalding emphatically seconded the archbishops' recommendation did Keane agree to accept it.[48]

Whether the Catholic University of America would have fared differently, especially in its tumultuous early years, under Spalding's strong hand than it did under Keane's rather more tentative one, it is of course impossible to say. Many shared the opinion of Denis O'Connell who told Gibbons a year before the rector was named: "It may be objected that [Spalding] is to[o] ardent for the office of presidency, but it will be some time yet before the place will be ready for the services of . . . calm presiding officers, and the ardor of Peoria is required to build it."[49] "The ardor of Peoria" was placed at the disposal of the university in a variety of supportive ways through succeeding years, but not in its "presidency." And Spalding, who always played the lone hand and always abided by the dictum that one should explain nothing and apologize for nothing, remained in Peoria for the rest of his life. He had declined preferment several times before 1886,[50] and in 1894, with an intellectual's unique brand of hauteur, he let the world know his personal estimate of the ordinary methods of ecclesiastical promotion: "It is not and never has been in the power of any man or body of men to keep me from a coveted position or office, for I have coveted or covet none."[51] This resolve weakened, however, some years afterward, and only then were the few individuals privy to the course of events reminded of Archbishop Ryan's uneasiness in 1885: if Spalding were appointed rector of the university and lived in Washington, Ryan told Corrigan, "I fear Miss C[aldwell] will be constantly there and attract much comment."[52]

It had always been intended that the university would be a "pontifical" institution, that the degrees it granted would be recognized by the Vatican as equivalent to those of its own Roman universities. The appointment of a rector, therefore, was about as far as the university committee could go without formally submitting its plans for scrutiny and confirmation to Propaganda. Even the new rector's identity could not be made public until this step was taken. Keane accordingly was commissioned to go to Rome in the fall of 1886, and John Ireland, who would at the same time make his *ad limina* visit,[53] was to accompany him. In the interval Keane attempted quietly to raise some money for the project, and he also visited several university campuses in order to get some clear idea of the kind of administrative structure his institution ought to have.[54]

Ireland spent the summer preparing his ad limina report and seeing to routine matters before he embarked upon a protracted absence from the diocese. In late May he participated, along with Archbishop Heiss's other suffragans, in the first Provincial Council of Milwaukee, at which he listened with equanimity to one of his colleagues denounce the practice of teaching catechism in German which, asserted Marty of Dakota, had led to "thousands and thousands" of German defections from the church. The predominance of German prelates at the council further led the bishop of St. Paul to ponder the feasibility of a new, western province of his own. The speculation had nothing to do with Michael Heiss personally, who was, as always, courteous and accommodating.[55] In July Ireland presided at the "impressive ceremonies attending the laying of the corner-stone of the Catholic Orphan Asylum" in Minneapolis, on which occasion he gave a stirring appeal for support of Catholic charitable institutions, and also, in testimony that he had an opinion on everything, laid down the principle that only childless couples were appropriate foster-parents: "When there are other children, the orphan is looked upon as the slave of the other children."[56] In September he explored with Henry M. Rice, one of Minnesota's senior statesmen, the possibility of persuading either the national Democratic or Republican party to put a temperance plank in its platform.[57]

And on October 30, 1886, John Ireland sailed for Liverpool aboard the *Aurania,* a voyage that carried him into a time of struggle and peril and fame.

~ X ~
# All Things Do Converge
1886–87

W HEN JAMES GIBBONS bid Keane and Ireland adieu at the
end of October 1886, he did so in his new capacity as
cardinal-elect.[1] Rumors about this honor to be conferred upon the
archbishop of Baltimore had reached Minnesota by the preceding
March, when Ireland had written to him: "I need not say how elated
the Catholics of the West are at your elevation to the cardinalate.
The honor was due to you for your many labors in the cause of religion, and for your monumental work in the Third Plenary Council of Baltimore."[2] By mid-May the rumors had been confirmed by
official notification from the Holy See, and on June 30 the first of
the several required ceremonial acts — the bestowal upon Gibbons
of the red biretta brought by a special Roman emissary — took place
in the Cathedral of the Assumption in Baltimore.[3] So there was
joined in Gibbons's person the unofficial primacy of the American
church with membership in the sacred college, an international
body of more than ordinary prestige. That the appointment had
been predictable since McCloskey's death the previous autumn did
not make it less popular among Catholics or indeed with the public
at large. Gibbons assumed his princely rank with the same quiet and
affable dignity with which he conducted the whole of his official
life. He was to be the only American cardinal for the next twenty-
five years.

Three days before Keane and Ireland boarded their ship the
university committee gathered in Baltimore to draw up the descriptive documents to be brought to Rome by the two bishops. The
meeting proceeded smoothly, and all the members signed the
lengthy letters addressed to the pope and to Giovanni Cardinal

Simeoni, the prefect of Propaganda. The next day, October 28, the canny Gibbons invited the five other archbishops[4] who were in the city for another meeting to add their signatures, and they did so. Thus the university project had received an unusually powerful mandate of which the Roman officials would necessarily have to take account. Among the signatories, of course, was Archbishop Corrigan of New York.

Keane and Ireland had scarcely landed in England when the time of troubles began. From Liverpool — where Ireland renewed his acquaintance with Monsignor Nugent and was perhaps painfully reminded of the Connemara colonists — they traveled to London, and found disquieting news awaiting them there. An agent representing disgruntled German American Catholics had appeared at Propaganda with a list of complaints against the American hierarchy. Ireland departed immediately for Rome, and arrived there only "just in time to delay action." Keane followed some days later.[5]

THE CRISES seemed to come all at once, descending upon the American church as suddenly as a summer storm, and so melded together that to separate them one from another grew increasingly difficult with every passing day. The bishops who had been all cordiality at the Third Plenary Council, or at least had expressed their disagreements within the accepted parameters of parliamentary debate, now found themselves driven into opposing camps, or, many of them, shifting uneasily between one faction and the other. Yet the potential for this contentiousness had been accumulating for a long time. The university question indeed provided the spark for the conflagration, but the tinder, it soon became clear, was lying all around.

There was, first of all, the smoldering German problem. The German-American Catholics formed a relatively prosperous, close-knit community, strongly devoted to its cultural and linguistic heritage and convinced that the survival of the faith in a new land depended upon maintaining that heritage. They thought themselves discriminated against by a hierarchy of domineering Irishmen who denied them rightful self-determination and imposed unwanted and unneeded temperance programs upon them — programs that were un-Catholic, too, in their judgment: the Germans disdainfully dismissed Sunday closing laws as ushering in a "Protestant Sunday."[6] Worst of all, the Irish threatened the existence of German parochial schools in which their children could learn the habits and devotions of the old country in their own treasured language.

Whatever legitimacy some of their complaints may have had, the opposing view had plenty of persuasive arguments on its side. The Germans had left Germany to try their fortunes in a new country. Why should they hold fast to old customs? Should they not adapt to the circumstances in which Providence had placed them? Did German Catholics in Germany insist upon speaking English or any other foreign tongue? And, anyway, how could the Germany of Bismarck and the Kulturkampf[7] be advanced as an ideal Catholics should want to preserve? If the Germans had their way, why not the Poles and Italians and every other immigrant group, so that the church in America would become a menagerie of competing nationalist ghettoes? What hope would there be then for the conversion of America to Catholicism?

Basic to this pragmatic line of reasoning was a deeper, more ideological one. The Germans should give up their nostalgia for the homeland, simply because the United States — "one nation, indivisible, with liberty and justice for all" — was a better place to live than Germany or indeed all the European countries put together. And better too for the Catholic Church: "The choicest field," as Ireland had put it in his speech at the council, "which providence offers in the world to-day to the occupancy of the Church is this republic."[8] The tired regimes of the Old World showed nothing but hostility toward the Catholicism that had nurtured them: witness the triumph of anti-clericals in almost every nation in western Europe. By contrast the bright, young American republic allowed the church the fullest scope in performing its mission and refused, on principle, to interfere with it in any way. Indeed, might it not be argued therefore that traditionally European Catholicism ought to look to America for its future ecclesial model, rather than the other way around?

This point of view — by no means fully articulated or even thought out by Ireland or anyone else at the end of 1886 — ultimately developed into the fundamental tenet of that faction called the Americanist or liberal party.[9] Meanwhile it colored the debates, increasingly shrill, of the next decade and a half, and, because of the complexity of the issues involved, called into being all sorts of unexpected alliances. Thus the proposal for a Catholic university, and where it should be located, and, more important, what should be its particular genius, merged with the unsettled status of German-American Catholics. So seemingly benign an institution as the little red parochial schoolhouse, mandated in every parish by the Third Plenary Council, could be viewed — and was by some — as a vehicle to perpetuate German nationalism and therefore as an obstacle to the necessary process of immigrant amalgamation. The social question got mixed up with the problem posed by the multiplicity of secret societies in the United States, organizations devoted primarily to fraternity and mutual insurance and yet apparently not dissimilar in their enthusiasm for pseudo-mystical rituals to the European Masonic lodges, hotbeds of anti-clerical and anti-religious agitation; the church, always so jealous of its children's allegiance, faced a severe dilemma in deciding how to react when such societies claimed they had to be "secret" precisely because their activities were designed to ameliorate the lot of laboring people and of the poor, so many of whom were Catholics.[10]

All these subjects left room for honest disagreement, but they took on added intensity when they were exacerbated by the suspicions ambitious men harbored about each other. So the parties gradually formed themselves: Ireland, Keane, O'Connell, a sometimes reluctant Gibbons, the Paulists, the Catholic temperance forces, the more intellectually adventuresome clergy on one side; and Corrigan, McQuaid, the Germans, the Jesuits, and most of the other religious orders on the other. The lines of division, fluid at first, eventually became unyielding. Yet not everyone wore a partisan label; Lancaster Spalding, for example, followed his own lonely course, as perhaps befitted one who traced his lineage back to medieval English kings.[11] It was at any rate a struggle between elites, one that affected little the daily lives of the American Catholic masses. But the stakes for the future were not small.

THE ROME toward which John Ireland hurried during the last days of November 1886 looked much the same as it did when he had first seen it more than sixteen years before. It was still the baroque city of Bernini, all domes and fountains and obelisks, stucco façades of dark yellow fronting the streets and behind them sumptuous gardens and courtyards. The ruins of a half-dozen proud civilizations still lay casually about, the same stone angels stood guard on the Ponte Elio, and, atop the Janiculum, the inevitable umbrella pines were pasted against a gloomy winter sky.

But profound changes had occurred nonetheless. The old papal Rome had given way to the capital of the new Kingdom of Italy, and the pope was seen no more in the streets of what had been his city for a thousand years. Indeed, the pope was seen hardly at all. The grand liturgical ceremonies Ireland remembered were not held now, for the pope, cabined up within the walls of the Vatican, removed himself from Roman public life as a way of protesting the aggression that had deprived him of his temporal power. The great doors of St. Peter's Basilica would remain shut up tight, it was said, so long as the King of Piedmont held court in the Quirinal.[12] The papal bureaucracy, crippled by hostile legislation and by the threat and reality of confiscation of its remaining properties, continued nevertheless to function. The vast palazzo of Propaganda still stood on the edge of the Piazza di Spagna. Yet Roman ecclesiastics, understandably fearful of anti-clerical agitation, trod more warily than they had used to do.[13]

But John Ireland in the interval of years had changed, too. No longer the young tourist, wide eyed at the first sight of the splendors of *la città,* he moved into his quarters at the North American College on the Via dell'Umiltà with the brisk, authoritative air of a man of affairs, a middle-aged bishop with important business to attend to. If he felt ill at ease at the presence of another lodger at the college—whose presence indeed had hastened his trip from London—he gave no sign.

Peter M. Abbelen was a prominent priest of the Archdiocese of Milwaukee who was also well connected in German clerical circles around the country.[14] He had served at the Third Plenary Council as Archbishop Heiss's theological adviser. In October 1886 he applied to Cardinal Gibbons for a letter of recommendation to the officials of Propaganda, a letter stating that he was a reliable man and "sufficiently Americanized not to be a one-sided partisan in this question." The "question," he explained, had to do with the legal relationship between national and territorial parishes. Abbelen assured the cardinal that Heiss had consented to this mission and that the prefect of Propaganda had agreed to see him. Gibbons, under the impression that the business had to do with Milwaukee only (though Abbelen had not said so), complied with the request, and on October 13, Abbelen, armed with Gibbons's letter, sailed from New York.[15]

Once in Rome, Abbelen resided with Denis O'Connell at the American College, and it was no doubt the rector who sent word to Keane and Ireland in London about the Milwaukee priest's arrival and about the memorial he had prepared for Propaganda. By early December, Keane having joined Ireland on the Via dell'Umiltà, they had managed to obtain a copy of Abbelen's memorial—probably through O'Connell's connections—had had it printed, and dispatched it on December 10 with a covering letter to selected members of the American hierarchy. They described Abbelen as "the delegate of German bishops and priests in America," who, besides his written memorial, had made "numerous viva voce statements" to Propaganda and solicited "numberless private letters from parties in America." There was, Keane and Ireland insisted, "a conspiracy wide-spread and well organized against English-speaking bishops and priests," and the best way to combat it was to flood Propaganda with telegrams and follow-up letters as soon as possible. "If you can trust other bishops, give them word, and get them also to send telegrams and letters," without, however, letting the Roman officials know the source of their information. Meanwhile, the bishops of St. Paul and Richmond—which Keane technically still was—assured their colleagues at home that they had submitted a rebuttal in their own names.[16]

The Abbelen Memorial[17] dealt primarily with a legal issue which had long been debated in America and in Rome and which for all practical purposes had been settled. National parishes could indeed co-exist with territorial ones, and children still living under the parental roof were obliged to attend the national parish if their parents did.[18] Abbelen raised in addition the related question as to whether pastors of national parishes should enjoy the same rights to irremovable rectorships as did their territorial brethren. He also asked that bishops be "admonished" (*"moneantur"*) not to suppress "the language, manners, customs, usages and devotions" of German Catholics, and be obliged to appoint German-speaking vicars if they were ignorant of the language themselves.[19] There appeared to be, therefore, nothing terribly new in Abbelen's proposals, and nothing of so grave a nature as to have aroused such a fevered reaction.

Yet John Keane said of them that he had seldom seen "a more villainous tissue of misstatements," and he denounced Abbelen himself as "a secret emissary of a clique of German bishops among us." Perhaps the trouble was rather that Abbelen's mission had not been "secret" enough: he had, after all, secured permission beforehand from Propaganda to make his presentation, had informed Gibbons of it prior to his departure from the United States, and, while in Rome, had resided cheek by jowl with Denis O'Connell.[20] As for the "clique of German bishops," Keane was probably referring to what was indeed an ominous feature of Abbelen's memorial: at the bottom of it was the signature of the most prominent German-American prelate, Michael Heiss, together with the notation, "*Legi et approbavi* [I have read this statement and have approved it]".[21]

But if the substance of the memorial did not amount to much, its truculent and boastful tone was almost bound to have provoked a strong response. The document bore no title, and from its abrupt, teutonic opening, Abbelen laid down a rhetorical challenge that could hardly have been ignored. All American Catholics, he said, aside from a trifling number of old native families, were recent immigrants or the children of immigrants. Yet the so-called Catholici Anglici, who were virtually all Irish immigrants themselves, lorded it over those of other nations and enjoyed "special ecclesiastical privileges." Before the bar of American civil law, Germans stood equal to the Irish; why should it be different with regard to the universal law of the church? "Are then the Irish Catholics so much better than the Germans that special ecclesiastical privileges beyond the law should be granted them? Far be it from me, by the smallest word, to disdain the faith and morals of the Irish." But had they displayed a superior virtue?[22]

Let the statistical record, Abbelen implied, answer that question: the million and a half German Catholics in the United States in

1875, the 2,067 priests in 1881, the flourishing German religious orders, the 117,000 children enrolled in German Catholic schools—almost exactly the same number as those attending all other Catholic schools—the 30,000 German laymen organized into the Central Verein[23] for the defense and promotion of the faith, the five daily German-Catholic newspapers maintained for the same purpose.[24] The Germans resided peacefully in their parishes, unless they were meddled with (*in negotia immiscere*) by neighboring Irish priests. Let the Irish abide by their own customs; they preferred, for example, the simple, humdrum liturgies they learned when they lived under the lash of the penal laws in Ireland. But the Germans, whose sacramental celebrations were splendid and characterized by pomp and elevated by music, should enjoy similar freedom in choosing their modes of worship. The trouble, according to Abbelen, was the hurry on the part of some to "Americanize" the immigrant. "The 'Americanization' of the German immigrants should be a slow and natural process. It should not be hastened to the detriment of the religion of the Germans, least of all by bishops and priests who are not themselves German. Otherwise [the Germans] will kick against the goad."[25]

The reply to Abbelen, filed at Propaganda on December 6, 1886, bore the signatures of both Ireland and Keane, but judging by the flavor of the rhetoric employed, as well as the arguments adduced and the evidence cited, it was clearly written by the bishop of St. Paul—perhaps drafted before Keane arrived in Rome. Spalding had assured Ireland years before that his knowledge of French would serve him well in dealing with the curia,[26] and so indeed it turned out: here was the first of a long series of communications in that language from him who, as a boy, had wrestled with French composition in the schoolrooms of Meximieux.

If Abbelen's memorial had been short on substance, the same could be said about Ireland's and Keane's rejoinder. But Abbelen, by adopting a harsh and provocative tone in what he wrote, invited invective in return, and invective was what he got. Indeed, the real significance of the Abbelen affair lay not in the issues raised but in the heated manner in which they were expressed.

Ireland began by asserting his and Keane's "surprise" that this self-styled representative of German Catholics should have brought forward proposals "entirely new and exceptional" without the knowledge of the American hierarchy at large or even of many German-speaking bishops. If adopted these proposals would bring "disaster" upon the Catholic church in the United States. Their colleagues, Ireland insisted, "would not forgive us" if he and the bishop of Richmond did not take steps — and here was a very serious charge indeed — to expose "the bad faith of this German party."[27]

Father Abbelen, Ireland charged, had distorted the question, which was not rivalry between Irish and German but between those who spoke the English language — "which is the language of the United States" — and those who refused to do so. There were no "Irish" parishes in America, though it might be said that "Irish Catholics, even recent immigrants, . . . adopt American ideas and manners, and they understand, . . . whatever their attachment to the land of their birth, . . . they must, for the general good, put aside their national spirit." This the Germans stubbornly refused to do, or at least the party of Germans for whom Abbelen had spoken. As for the statistics in Abbelen's memorial, Ireland branded them highly misleading. The 2,067 German priests included all priests who spoke German as a first or a second language — "Poles, Slavs, Bohemians, Dutch, even English or Irish." The directory Abbelen used to reach this figure counted anybody who had a German-sounding name. "Described, on this list, as German priests serving in the Diocese of St. Paul were two French priests and a lay saloon-keeper who on Sunday teaches catechism to the children of the parish." Avoca, one of Ireland's colonies in western Minnesota, was called a German parish, because the pastor had a German name, even though its two hundred families were mostly Irish. Moreover, Ireland continued, the boast that as many children were pupils in German Catholic schools as in English-speaking ones could be substantiated only by falsely labeling parishes of mixed nationalities as German. Skewing the numbers was simply a way for Abbelen and his friends to justify "special privileges" for themselves and to further their intention to "Germanize" the church in America. "Religion [for these people] has to be German, and the bishop who advises differently will be treated as though he were an enemy of the Germans, as the Bishop of St. Paul knows from experiences he has had with some of his German priests."[28]

Ireland further claimed to have heard from German religious that the insistence upon teaching children the catechism in German was precisely the reason why they did not learn it and why so many of them defected from the church upon reaching their majority. Far from converting America to Catholicism, such practices would alienate the public from even considering the merits of the church, much as does the German pastor who fatigued his congregation Sunday after Sunday with his "jargon Allemand-Anglais" until gradually the people stopped attending mass altogether. Nor did Ireland hesitate to name prominent names: Heiss of Milwaukee made "the official language of a Catholic bishop in an American city a language foreign to the country"; Dwenger of Fort Wayne "reduced [the English-speaking priests in his diocese] to a dozen."[29]

Ireland did not underestimate German capacity to make trouble, and, in order to persuade the officials of Propaganda of the danger, he invoked a name calculated to send chills down curial spines: "The war to secure [special] rights for the Germans is prosecuted with the obstinacy and aggressiveness characteristic of the countrymen of M. de Bismarck."[30] But the wickedness of the Germans did not stop there: "The socialist movements in the United States have had for the most part Germans for leaders." And in a country that boasted an admirable respect for the sanctity of the sabbath, it was well known, Ireland said, that "the Germans have little regard for Sunday observance." Finally, in addressing Abbelen's demand that bishops speak German or appoint vicars who did, Ireland delivered his unkindest cut of all.

> We must add that the complaints about bishops who do not speak German[31] do not come from the German people as a people; they come rather from the self-appointed popular tribunes, from the [German] journalists, who see in the continuation of their language the life of their enterprises; and from certain priests and prelates who . . . understand that the maintenance of their livelihood and their power depends upon preserving a permanent Germany in America.

Until now, Ireland argued, the bishops of the United States had "had confidence in each other" and had trusted that "the questions affecting the interests of religion" could be discussed among themselves "in peace and fraternal love." Abbelen and his party, with "ces intrigues sinistres," had placed all such amity in jeopardy.[32]

This strong rebuttal to Abbelen's memorial certainly gave Propaganda pause. Meanwhile, back home, Gibbons moved swiftly to repair the damage his friendly letter to Abbelen had occasioned. (Propaganda confessed itself puzzled that the emissary who severely criticized practices in the Archdiocese of Baltimore[33] should have brought with him to Rome a warm recommendation from the ordinary of that see.) In mid-December the archbishops of Boston, New York, Philadelphia, and Baltimore decided to dispatch a joint letter, to be drawn up by Corrigan, protesting Abbelen's initiative and denying his charges. Following Ireland's and Keane's appeal, they urged other bishops, including one or two moderate Germans, to write in a similar vein. By early January 1887, Keane and Ireland were able to assemble a formidable collection of these communiqués and present it to the prefect of Propaganda, with the result that Simeoni agreed to delay the congregation's formal consideration of Abbelen's memorial.[34]

While thus engaged in confronting what they sincerely believed to be the German menace, the bishops of Richmond and St. Paul did not neglect the main business that had brought them to Rome in the first place. On December 6, the same day the answer to Abbelen was finished, they submitted to Propaganda the petition drawn up and signed in October by the members of the university committee as well as by the other five archbishops. To this Keane and Ireland appended an exegesis of their own composition, a seven-page printed document in which they addressed the various objections that had been, or could be, raised to the university project. For example, they described the funding as well advanced, with $500,000 in hand,[35] leaving $150,000 still to be secured to reach a figure adequate for the support of a graduate theology and philosophy faculty; they expressed confidence that once the Holy See had approved the overall plan this latter sum would be quickly realized. Pointing out the new university's uniqueness, they brushed aside any worries that it would lack sufficient feeder institutions, or that it would threaten the well-being of other Catholic colleges or seminaries or even the American College in Rome. They admitted that there had been some difference of opinion about the location of the university, but, after full discussion, a practical unanimity had emerged among the members of the committee to the effect that the American hierarchy's first university ought to be in Washington, "the center of the moral and intellectual forces of the whole Nation." They discreetly explained the committee's request that the Holy See sanction no other American Catholic university until the next plenary council by pointing to the financial difficulties experienced by the French bishops who, in the late 1870s, had founded five universities at once.[36] Finally, they protested against the "insinuation" that members of the university committee had signified their endorsement of the statement to Propaganda without in fact being in favor of it: "We indignantly reject and repudiate this most disgraceful accusation against our honesty and truthfulness."[37]

Where they had heard the "insinuation," Keane and Ireland did not say. Three days later, on December 9, Ireland had his ad limina audience with Leo XIII, and he took the opportunity to present the pope the university committee's letter. He requested that he and Keane be granted a separate audience at a later time to present the proposal formally, and Leo readily agreed. Meanwhile, the unpleasant rumors about dissidence on the university committee persisted. To reassure themselves about one possible source of trouble, Keane and Ireland called upon the Jesuit Cardinal Mazzella, who had resided and taught in the United States for many years; in answer to their direct question, Mazzella told them he foresaw no difficulty in the university coexisting in Washington with Jesuit Georgetown College, since the two institutions would offer entirely different programs of study.[38]

Then, sometime before December 14, Keane and Ireland, thanks to a leak at Propaganda, discovered that the "most disgraceful accusation" was indeed true. So back to the printing press they went.

> Since our arrival in Rome, we have done all that we could in furtherance of the petition concerning our proposed Catholic University, which the representatives of the American Hierarchy signed and commissioned us to lay before the Holy See. But we find that our efforts are paralyzed by an unexpected obstacle of a most painful character. Somebody has whispered that some of the Prelates' signatures do not mean what they say,—in other words, were not given in good faith but deceptively. This is said

in the Propaganda, and by the Holy Father himself; it is even asserted among the laity!

The consequences are obvious. Suspicion is cast upon all the signatures; our mission is turned into a farce; and, worst of all, the most shocking discredit is thrown upon the character of our Prelates for truth and honesty.

We have, as in duty bound, repelled the imputation with the indignation it deserves. But we are powerless to remove the wretched impression produced. This can be done only by the declarations of the Prelates individually. We therefore appeal to each of the Prelates who have signed the petition, to send us, and that immediately, such a declaration on the subject as will enable us to silence this calumny.[39]

The fact was that, when Cardinal Simeoni had privately invited Corrigan to state his views about the university project, the archbishop had written to Propaganda a stinging and wide-ranging denunciation of the whole plan. He had sent that letter to Rome a full two weeks before he signed the university committee's documents at the end of October.[40]

If Keane and Ireland had hoped their circular would force the hand of the archbishop of New York, they were disappointed. No word came from Corrigan in response to their appeal, a circumstance which especially outraged John Ireland, for whom plain speech was one of the highest of virtues. Nevertheless, he and Keane, like all supporters of the university, realized that New York's opposition could be severely damaging, perhaps fatal, to their aspirations. What they did not know at this stage was that Corrigan's letter to Simeoni enjoyed the hearty endorsement of leading American Jesuits,[41] and that an increasingly waspish McQuaid, for whom the university had become "this failure," "this abortion," this captive of "Southern bishops, priests and laymen," was egging his metropolitan on, as well as bombarding fellow bishops and even Propaganda itself with objections of his own. "[I can] say things in a stronger and less dignified way," the bishop of Rochester told Corrigan, "than it would become one in your position to say the same."[42] Thus it was that this imbroglio hastened the gradual development of party lines more directly than did, as yet, the German question.

So did another matter connected with Keane's and Ireland's mission to Rome, one that brought about even more conflict with the prelates from New York. The 1880s was a decade of much labor unrest in the United States. Unions were in their infancy and were often held suspect as havens for anarchists and socialists. Powerful monied interests were allied against combinations of working men, and public opinion generally frowned upon the strikes and secondary boycotts that were the unions' ultimate weapons. The Haymarket riot of May 1886, in Chicago, in which several policemen were killed, underscored public fears that labor agitation—in this case for the eight-hour day—led to disorder and possibly to revolution. The economic and social status of most Catholics, however, was such that many of them were drawn to unionism, despite its unsavory reputation among the more privileged classes. The American bishops therefore had to proceed with care lest they appear to condone allegations of socialism or of violence on the one hand or alienate a large proportion of their people on the other.

The problem was complicated by the fact that the leading organization of working men at the time was the Noble and Holy Order of the Knights of Labor of America, whose very name suggested its character as a secret society.[43] The order did indeed employ certain rituals and verbal formulae known only to the initiated and reminiscent of that Masonry which the Catholic church had traditionally, and not unreasonably with regard to its European variety, considered a mortal enemy. On this latter point no disagreement existed between the Roman authorities and the American hierarchy. The question remained, however, whether the Knights of Labor really was a species of European Masonry, whether, that is, membership in the organization involved adherence to principles hostile to Catholicism.

The bishops could not decide. At the Third Plenary Council they discussed the larger problem of the proliferation of secret societies in the United States during the last quarter of the nineteenth century—not only the Knights of Labor but the Odd Fellows, the Ancient Order of Hibernians, the Grand Army of the Republic, the Knights of Pythias—without reaching any conclusions. Rome demanded that they take a determined stand against any organization they judged to be genuinely Masonic (in the pejorative sense of the word), nor were the bishops loath to do so; but Rome added the sensible qualification that forbade blanket indictments and necessitated close scrutiny of each group before any condemnation was recommended. The upshot was that out of the council emerged a committee composed of all the metropolitans whose mandate was to investigate, as occasion dictated, individual secret societies. But this committee proved even more useless than most, because it was stipulated that unless the members arrived at a unanimous decision, the fate of the secret society under examination had to be referred to Rome.[44]

This is what happened in the case of the Knights of Labor. The archbishops indeed met on the subject in Baltimore on October 28, 1886, the day after the meeting of the university committee, but, to the surprise of no one, they expressed varying opinions. Gibbons strongly held the view that a condemnation of the Knights would be disastrous for the church. He pointed to a membership roll that had grown by the mid-1880s to over seven hundred thousand Knights, two-thirds of whom, it was said, were Catholics. He was convinced that the ritualistic aspects of the order were basically harmless, and he offered to his colleagues the guarantee of the Master Workman, as the head of the order was called, that features objectionable to the prelates would be excised from the Knights' constitution. Practical observers agreed that the American labor movement would soon cast off the trappings of a secret society. But in the meantime, the cardinal added, it was not unreasonable to suppose that the secrecy imposed upon the Knights had nothing to do with cult but a great deal to do with employers' antagonisms toward any labor organization.

The archbishops of St. Louis and Santa Fe remained, however, unconvinced, and called for an unequivocal edict forbidding Catholics to associate with the order. They cited as precedent the Roman condemnation of the Canadian branch of the Knights of Labor — of whom the archbishop of Quebec was a fanatical foe — and called for the extension of that ban to the United States. Corrigan, as was his wont, took no such definite stand, but his basic hostility to the Order was clear enough, as was that of Williams of Boston. The other archbishops, more or less enthusiastically, supported Gibbons, and so the whole question automatically reverted to the Roman curia for final adjudication. Gibbons surely expected this result, and he was prepared to take the next step. He put the minutes of the Baltimore meeting in the mail to Rome, and when Keane and Ireland sailed for Europe a few days later, they took with them a copy (and a translation) of the constitution of the Knights of Labor and other relevant documents. By early December these were under study within the walls of Propaganda, and there, for the time being, the matter rested.[45]

In the Archdiocese of New York, however, the status of the Knights of Labor, and indeed the social question generally, had another dimension, added by the meteoric pastor of St. Stephen's parish in lower Manhattan, Edward McGlynn.[46] Familiarly known as "the Doctor," McGlynn was a brilliantly gifted man, possessed of immense charm and magnetism. He had hardly an equal in the art of extemporaneous oratory, and many a massive crowd was moved to the extremities of emotion by his stirring words. But he had difficulty harnessing his own emotions. Extravagant and ill-disciplined, erratic in his personal habits, and oblivious to any obligations that he did not choose for himself, McGlynn took up social causes the way other men fell in love—totally, unreservedly, and with a large measure of ruthlessness.

Long an advocate of the most extreme elements of anti-British agitation in Ireland, McGlynn was converted, in the early 1880s, to the theories of Henry George, a self-styled social reformer, who argued for what he called "the single tax," that is, a tax upon the increase of the value of land.[47] The revenue accruing to the government from such an excise would be so plenteous, said George, that all other taxes could be eliminated and, at the same time, a massive welfare program could be supported. McGlynn saw in this idea, applicable to the United States, Ireland, and everywhere else in the world, the end of poverty, and he espoused it with even more enthusiasm than George did himself. No one could quarrel with his admirable objective, but many did quarrel with what appeared to be a crackpot scheme and, moreover, one that seemed at variance with the Catholic church's traditional insistence on the sacredness of private property.

Ecclesiastical authorities, both in Rome and in various parts of the United States—the Doctor lectured widely outside New

York—grew exceedingly troubled at McGlynn's ever more inflammatory rhetoric. "A landlord is a thief," he said on more than one occasion. Then, in the fateful year 1886, Henry George declared himself third-party candidate for mayor of New York City, and McGlynn prepared to take to the stump in his behalf. Corrigan forbade him to do so, and when McGlynn disobeyed, the archbishop suspended him for a fortnight. So began the long personal duel between the two men, so markedly different in temperament, whose mutual animosity went back nearly thirty years, to the time when they had been students together in Rome—the flamboyant, careless, brazenly virile McGlynn and the fastidious, almost feline Corrigan—a duel into which John Ireland in his turn would be drawn. On November 2, when the tally was counted, the Democratic candidate won the mayor's race, but George came in a close enough second to suggest that McGlynn had siphoned off a significant proportion of the Irish Catholic vote upon which Tammany Hall could usually depend. (Third in the poll stood the Republican candidate, a young nabob named Theodore Roosevelt.)

So here was the context within which Archbishop Corrigan viewed the ecclesiastical debate over the Knights of Labor: with his mind's eye he could see, probably for the rest of his life, the vision of Henry George, Edward McGlynn, and Terrence Powderly—the Master Worker of the Noble and Holy Order—arm-in-arm touring the polling places on election day, 1886. A month later Propaganda ordered McGlynn to come to Rome and explain himself. The Doctor refused. At this point Ireland and Keane, much to Corrigan's annoyance when he learned of it, sent McGlynn a cable: "Have seen Cardinal [Simeoni], his feelings toward you are truly fatherly. We assure you all will be well [if you come to Rome]." But the Doctor still refused, despite Ireland's confident assertion to the contrary in a private conversation with Simeoni.[48] Corrigan therefore extended his suspension to the end of the year, and on January 14, 1887, removed him from St. Stephen's. In March McGlynn founded the Anti-Poverty Society, and before huge crowds on Sunday nights at the Academy of Music, he lashed out at "the ecclesiastical machine" and its "blunders and mistakes and . . . crimes." He compared himself to Galileo, and Henry George compared him admiringly to

Luther. When he ignored a second summons to Rome, he was ex-communicated, effective July 1, 1887.[49]

But Edward McGlynn did not go away. He was to cast a disproportionately long shadow over the American church for many years to come. And if Michael Corrigan preferred simply to categorize him as a disobedient priest with dubious ideas and disreputable supporters—like the Knights of Labor—the Doctor's continuing public support, though diminished, rendered that solution unlikely. It is understandable that for Corrigan, the McGlynn affair signaled the need to condemn the Knights of Labor and the theories of Henry George.[50] But not everyone interpreted the events that way. As Gibbons wrote candidly to Propaganda in February 1887: "If consequences have been so deplorable for the peace of the Church from the condemnation of only one priest, because he was regarded as a friend of the people, what will not be the consequences to be feared from a condemnation which would fall directly upon the people themselves in the exercise of what they consider their legitimate right?"[51] Thus McGlynn's case converged with Abbelen's, and the fate of the Knights of Labor with that of the Catholic University, to stir up a tempest, the first winds of which blew over the bishops of St. Paul and Richmond in their lodgings on the Via dell'Umiltà.

They spent upwards of five months there as Denis O'Connell's guests and were joined in the late winter of 1887 by Cardinal Gibbons. During that time, it seems safe to say, the personal bonds of the Americanist party were firmly established and perhaps some of its agenda as well. The setting was appropriate if for no other reason than O'Connell's lively and demonstrative patriotism. The rector saw to it that the American College proudly displayed its nationality—it was O'Connell who made July 4 a great feast day at the college, with flags and bunting, patriotic songs, and a fine dinner. On a deeper level, he was determined that its students should cultivate those virtues of manliness and self-reliance that he thought peculiarly American. Sometimes his passionate devotion to his adopted land led to oddities of behavior; on one notorious occasion, for example, he declined, when a guest at a diplomatic reception, to stand for the playing of "God Save the Queen"; and he habitually refused to admit he had been born in Ireland.[52]

Whatever his eccentricities, O'Connell was an able administrator, and he governed the institution, particularly its often troubled finances, perhaps more effectively than any of his predecessors. Not that the job was all that taxing: O'Connell employed several aides to assist him in watching over the spiritual, intellectual, and physical needs of fifty or sixty relatively docile and serious students. He had plenty of time and energy left over for other, even more congenial tasks, like acting as host for American dignitaries visiting Rome and, most important, as unoffical agent of the American bishops to the curia. This latter capacity presumed a certain objectivity on his part, which with the passing years O'Connell found increasingly difficult to fulfill. Aside from his personal loyalty to Gibbons, perhaps his partisan commitment began with the long evenings of conversation he shared with Keane and Ireland through the damp Roman winter of 1886–87.[53]

On December 21, 1886, Ireland observed the silver jubilee of his priesthood and the eleventh anniversary of his episcopal consecration by celebrating pontifical mass in the college chapel. He delivered several conferences to the seminarians during his residence, stressing the natural virtues, particularly (of course) temperance. Most of the students admired Ireland's eloquence and vigor, though at least one of them found his oratorical style "almost grotesque." "You cannot imagine," O'Connell told him, "what an influence you gained over the students. Several of them are resolved on Total Abstinence after they leave here."[54] Yet popular as the bishop of St. Paul undoubtedly was at the college, affection for him did not match that won by the sometimes grumpy anti-Americanist, McQuaid of Rochester, who, whatever their ideological differences, kept on good terms with O'Connell and resided with him at the college on several occasions. McQuaid despised the so-called continental breakfast, and it was he who insisted that the students begin the day with genuine American fare of beefsteak and eggs; it was McQuaid also who persuaded O'Connell to abandon the absurdity of requiring the seminarians to wear their cassocks when they played baseball.[55]

During the early weeks of 1887 Ireland learned at first hand the leisurely pace at which business was conducted in Rome. He learned, too, that rank enjoyed distinct privileges. After the hectic activity of the preceding December, all the initiatives embarked upon by him and Keane seemed to languish in the murmur of the curial officials, "We must wait until the cardinal comes." The reference was to Gibbons, scheduled to arrive the second week of February and to receive his red hat at a consistory a month later. One such occasion prompted an outburst of the famous Ireland temper. When he and Keane approached Archbishop Jacobini to discuss the university question, the secretary of Propaganda replied smoothly that that matter was to be held over until Gibbons came, and after that it would be postponed indefinitely. The two bishops, indignant at this bureaucratic arrogance, went directly from the Piazza di Spagna across the Tiber to the Vatican, where they demanded an immediate audience with the pope. Leo XIII saw them the next day, listened to them attentively, and calmed them by saying that, despite Jacobini's assertion, he had not yet made up his mind about the university. He asked them to remain in Rome "until the cardinal comes." The pontiff's general demeanor was extremely friendly, and Keane and Ireland were heartened when he shook his head with stern disapproval at the news of Corrigan's plan for a Jesuit university in New York.[56]

The cardinal came on February 13. By that time Ireland had left Rome for a brief visit to the treasured scenes of his youth. He went first to Montluel and preached at Clemence Cretin's parish church, and then up the Lyon–Geneva post road a few miles to Meximieux, where twenty of his former schoolmates joined him in a reunion. On February 19 he was in Belley, where, as the bishop's guest, he dined with the cathedral chapter, went to the seminary, and gave a speech which, the diocesan weekly reported rather breathlessly, "was so full of ardor that it went straight to the hearts of the students." In an interview he described the remarkable growth of the church in the United States, as well as the prosperity of the Catholic temperance movement, and in so doing rattled the reporter into a confusion of ecclesiastical titles: "[Bishop Ireland] has earned the name of founder of this marvelous movement, the glorious name of the Brother Mathew of America!"[57]

When he returned to the Via dell'Umiltà some days later, he found his friends in a bleak mood. Gibbons, in a conversation with Simeoni, had learned that Corrigan had indeed entered a protest against the proposed university in Washington. The cardinal, as Keane remembered it,

> was so disheartened by this opposition that he proposed to me that we should abandon the undertaking and leave the responsibility of the failure where it belonged. To this I agreed very willingly, only too glad to escape from such contention. But when Bp. Ireland, who then was absent for a few days, returned to Rome, he protested bitterly against, as he expressed it, so cowardly a surrender to so unworthy an opposition, and insisted that we must at least win the approval asked for by the [university committee], and then give up the project if we thought it best to do so. His advice prevailed.[58]

Prevailed, however, with a conciliatory gesture toward the "unworthy opposition." In the letter he addressed to the pope on March 9, Gibbons formally asked for approval of the university but with the proviso that the question of its location be reopened for further discussion among the American bishops.[59] Leo XIII replied positively in a flowery Latin brief, dated April 10,[60] but the news of his endorsement had leaked some time earlier, so that Gibbons was speedily able to assure Corrigan that "my request is granted that the question of site be reconsidered."[61]

Gibbons, a relative latecomer to advocacy of the university, needed less persuasion about another issue much discussed by him and his three friends in the House on Humility Street. A week after his arrival in Rome he put his name to what he himself called "an elaborate paper showing the injustice, the danger and the folly of denouncing [the Knights of Labor]."[62] Of all the services rendered to his church by the cardinal of Baltimore over a long and illustrious career, this memorandum to Propaganda may well have been the greatest. The French document, fifteen pages of print, naturally divided into two parts. In the first Gibbons rehearsed the arguments he had advanced at the meeting of the archbishops the previous October: that the Knights were not in fact a secret society in the masonic sense; that a large majority of the membership and most of the officers were Catholics; that labor violence could not be fairly attributed to the Order; that an often ruthless economic structure and the emergence of monopolies — "l'avarice sans coeur" — had aroused "not only the complaints of workers, but also the opposition of public men and legislators" and had necessitated labor to organize itself. American Catholic workers had refrained from joining any genuinely subversive group—"l'organisation Masonnique"—out of loyalty to the Holy See; that loyalty, Gibbons argued, deserved accommodation to what they judged to be their sacred right of self-protection.

But it was in the second part of his memorandum that Gibbons, with the straightforward eloquence of a firm believer, laid down some general principles that showed how well in tune he was with the imperatives of his position and of his age.

> The social condition of our country leaves me deeply convinced that we touch here upon a question which concerns not only the rights of the working classes, who ought to be especially dear to the Church established by our divine Lord to preach to the poor, but also a question in which is included the most fundamental interests of the Church and of human society for the future. . . . Assuredly, in our democratic nation, it is the title Friend of the People . . . which has gained for the Catholic Church not only the enthusiastic devotion of millions of its own children but the respect and admiration as well of all our citizens, whatever be their religious belief.

The condemnation of the Knights, Gibbons warned, would lead to alienation and rebellion, and—it was a practical man talking to other practical men—to an "immense" reduction in the church's revenues, including financial support for the Holy See. Let Propaganda take note of the upheaval caused by the censure of McGlynn. As for the archbishop of Quebec and his colleagues who had fulminated against the Canadian Knights, we, Gibbons concluded with a trace of sarcasm, have nothing to say. "We would consider it an impertinence to involve ourselves in the ecclesiastical matters of another country, which has its own hierarchy and about the needs and social conditions of which we do not pretend to have any understanding."[63]

That John Ireland supported this intervention goes without saying. How much he had to do with preparing it is rather more difficult to determine. In his reminiscences Cardinal Gibbons "gratefully acknowledge[d] the valuable aid of the venerable Archbishop Ireland," but he did not elaborate.[64] Keane intimated later

that Gibbons signed what the other three had prepared for him beforehand.[65] It has been said that Gibbons needed Ireland to put the
statement on paper, because Gibbons's own knowledge of French
was so limited[66]; but if this were the case, Keane could have done
the job, for his written French was equal to Ireland's. Ireland certainly accepted defense of the Knights as part of a program which
also included issues, like the German question and the university
project, about which he felt more strongly; over his lifetime, however, he exhibited less enthusiasm for organized labor than did
many of his colleagues. As far as Gibbons's memorandum of 1887
is concerned, the simple fact is that Ireland was not present in Rome
the day it was signed or for several days before that. The document
bears the date February 20; Ireland was in France on February 19
and could not possibly have returned to Italy before February 22 or
23.[67]

   That did not mean that he failed to join in the rejoicing that was
prompted by the immediate and startling success Gibbons's letter
enjoyed at Propaganda and the Holy Office.[68] On February 28
Keane reported to Manning "most gratifying results."[69] By March
3 part of the document had been leaked to the American press, but
Ireland assured Gilmour of Cleveland a few days later that even that
indiscretion would not alter the happy conclusion. "The Knights
will not be condemned in Rome. The point is as good as settled."[70]
At the end of the month, *Le Moniteur de Rome,* a paper with which
O'Connell had close connections, published the full text of the
statement, except, significantly, the short paragraph that referred
directly to Edward McGlynn.[71]

   The Americanists had reason to feel satisfied about the progress
they had achieved in promoting the tangle of causes they had come
to Rome to espouse. The pope and his curia were never swift in
promulgating official decisions, but all signs and informed gossip
pointed to favorable responses on the Abbelen petition, the university, and the Knights of Labor. On March 17 Gibbons formally
received his red hat, and the following week he took possession of
his titular church, the Basilica of Santa Maria in Trastevere. There,
amid the pomp of the Latin liturgy performed in one of the most
ancient of Roman churches, the cardinal declared his faith in the old
religion and in the new world. "I proclaim, with a deep sense of

pride and gratitude, and in this great capital of Christendom, that I belong to a country where the civil government holds over us the aegis of its protection without interfering in the legitimate exercise of our sublime mission as ministers of the Gospel of Jesus Christ. . . . Our nation is strong, and her strength lies, under Providence, in the majesty and supremacy of the law, in the loyalty of her citizens to that law, and in the affection of our people for their free institutions."[72]

John Ireland, nearby, beamed and nodded. For a man of his character no delight exceeds that which comes with victory, and in this convergence of crises his side had won hands down. Nor was it in his nature to mask his feelings. "You cannot imagine," his friend Denis O'Connell observed a little later, "how much pleasure it affords me to see the joy you experience over the result of your hard work in Rome. I do not know if you ever spent any months of your life that will have such far-reaching and lasting effects."[73]

~ XI ~
"Ireland Would Do Well Anywhere"
1887–89

THE ROMAN SPRING of 1887 found Denis O'Connell's three guests on the Via dell'Umiltà preparing for the journey home. They had reason to be satisfied. Most of the proposals they had brought to the curia had been accepted, and they had also managed to head off, for the time being, the appointment of a permanent papal representative to the United States, something the American hierarchy had long resisted. Since they believed that one of their German opponents, Bishop Dwenger of Fort Wayne, was conniving to secure the position for himself,[1] their success in this regard was all the sweeter. But the victory proved short lived, for Leo XIII, a pope who played the game of diplomacy with more than ordinary skill and zest, was determined to have a nuncio, or at least an apostolic delegate, in Washington[2]; nor was it without irony that the contentiousness among the American bishops, revealed or perhaps stirred up by the other negotiations carried on by Gibbons, Ireland, Keane, and O'Connell, would in the slightly longer run provide the Holy See with all the excuse it needed to insist upon sending a resident ambassador. Gibbons was whistling in the dark when he said, shortly after his return to the United States, that "as far as can be ascertained, the Holy See does not entertain . . . a desire" to appoint a nuncio.[3]

But the danger had been avoided for the moment, and the four friends could be excused their euphoria. For John Ireland, however, this happy interval was tinged with personal sadness: on March 18 he received the news of the death of his father. Mindful of the Irish proclivity to observe rites of passage with liquid refreshment, the bishop is said to have sent off a two-word cable to St. Paul: "No wake."[4] On the very day Richard Ireland died, his son had his farewell audience with Leo XIII. They spoke briefly about Ireland's temperance work, and the pope promised to issue a public statement in support of it.[5]

It is unlikely that on this largely ceremonial occasion the bishop of St. Paul said anything to the pontiff about his desire to be archbishop of St. Paul, but the campaign to bring about such a change was already well under way. Even before Ireland left for Europe the previous autumn, both he and Bishop Marty had written Cardinal Simeoni asking that a new ecclesiastical province to include Minnesota and Dakota Territory be erected. Milwaukee, they complained, was too far away and too uncongenial, and prelates east of the Mississippi, they added with some hyperbole, had little in common with their western colleagues.[6] Archbishop Heiss opposed the division, but Ireland in conversations at Propaganda followed up the original request and made some progress. When he departed Rome, early in April, he left the matter in the capable hands of Denis O'Connell.

Ireland went from Rome to Paris where he met Gibbons, and the two of them toured a model factory nearby, operated under the auspices of several leading French Catholic intellectuals. The workers, Ireland reported, roundly cheered the cardinal of Baltimore, defender of the Knights of Labor.[7] From there the bishop of St. Paul crossed over to Ireland, lectured in Dublin, Limerick, and Cork, and visited the national seminary at Maynooth, where he was delighted to learn that a large majority of the students claimed to be total abstainers.[8] "Your triumphant course through Ireland" was widely publicized, O'Connell told him, and back at the American College in Rome—"the house was lonesome after you left"—the students read about it "with shouts of joy."[9]

John Ireland sailed from Queenstown on Sunday, May 1. He spent a few days in New York, during which time he called on Archbishop Corrigan for a tense ninety minutes. Ireland complained bitterly that Corrigan's Roman agent, Ella Edes,[10] was working against the university; Corrigan—giving evidence of the subject most on his mind—retorted that ignorant people were interfering in the McGlynn case.[11] He felt no need to elaborate. On July 14 Ireland stepped off the train at the St. Paul Union Depot, greeted there by Bishop Grace and a delegation of clergy and laymen. When he arrived at his residence he was presented with a new carriage and team of horses, a "trifling testimonial," said a spokesman, of the high regard of his many friends. Next day, from the cathedral pulpit, he assured the congregation that of all the grand sights he had seen on his journey none was grander than his beloved home city standing proudly on the banks of the majestic Mississippi. That afternoon he drove to St. Thomas Seminary in the company of Augustin Ravoux—now Monsignor Ravoux, for Ireland had brought back from Rome a domestic prelacy for the old missioner[12]—and, after dinner, told the enthusiastic students that he had not forgotten them during his trip abroad and had purchased "many thousand valuable books" for their library.[13]

As he settled back into his administrative routine, Ireland continued to keep a close watch on the course of events that had begun to unfold during his Roman sojourn. On June 8 Simeoni sent Gibbons Propaganda's formal decision on the Abbelen Memorial with the request that he forward it to the other archbishops who, in turn, were to inform their suffragans. Due to a clerical error and the resultant confusion,[14] Ireland did not receive official notification from Heiss until the following October, but he was fully cognizant of the decree's content long before that.[15] In effect the status quo ante prevailed: national and territorial parishes could co-exist; rectors of national parishes could be irremovable, in accord with the general provisions of the Third Plenary Council; and children still living at home ordinarily belonged to the parish of their parents, so long as their freedom to attend any Catholic school was guaranteed. The other items petitioned for by Abbelen were rejected.[16]

Ireland, meanwhile, turned over a copy of the Abbelen Memorial to the editor of the *Northwestern Chronicle* who proceeded to publish parts of it and to attack Abbelen himself, whom he dubbed sarcastically "the delegate." And later in the summer there appeared from a most unexpected source a harsh denunciation of the Germans by a priest named John Gmeiner, a professor in the Milwaukee seminary and editor of a German-language newspaper. "The Catholic Church," wrote Gmeiner, "is no literary club to foster peculiar linguistic tastes, nor any ethnological society to advance any particular national cause, but a divinely instituted organization to bring men of 'all nations, and tribes, and peoples, and tongues,' to eternal salvation."[17] Here were sentiments, out of the very camp of the enemy, calculated to warm John Ireland's heart, and it probably came as no surprise, to friend and foe alike, that Gmeiner soon transferred from the Archdiocese of Milwaukee to the Diocese of St. Paul and assumed a teaching position at St. Thomas Aquinas Seminary.[18]

Abbelen for his part received notice of Propaganda's decision on July 18, and, he wrote on September 1, he had resolved at that time to consider the matter closed and not to enter into controversy about his memorial, though many of his friends had urged him to do so. But when Bishop Ireland released the text and promoted attacks upon him in the *Northwestern Chronicle,* he decided to respond in the pages of one publication that had been friendly to him. He addressed his thanks to its editor "for having come so graciously to the assistance of that 'Delegate' who was so harshly treated in the Northwestern Chronicle . . . [by] mouthings which seem to attack my personal honor and love of the truth." He went on to cover much of the same old ground and to insist that his petition had asked only for fair treatment, not for special privileges.[19] Abbelen's rhetoric in this communication was much less heated than that in his original memorial, but the same could hardly be said of the series of bitter diatribes published in the wake of Gmeiner's pamphlet.[20] Neither Propaganda nor John Ireland had heard the last of the German question.

As for the university project, it appeared to proceed apace during the summer of 1887. Its supporters might have been depressed had they known that Archbishop Corrigan was contemplating resignation from the governing committee. In Rome O'Connell considered the cause lost: "I never expect that university to survive the dark attacks of its enemies here and in America."[21] But Keane kept soldiering on; after touring some of the famous universities on the continent and in England, he returned home in June, and took up the dreary task of raising money. Ireland and Spalding helped him prepare a begging letter to be sent to all the priests in the United States.[22] On September 7 the governing committee—now the board of trustees—met and formally named Keane rector of the Catholic University of America. Before they came face to face in Baltimore, however, Ireland, hoping to keep the lines of communication open, wrote to Corrigan and assured the archbishop of New York that he fully approved of the condemnation of McGlynn.[23] Perhaps Corrigan appreciated this gesture of reconciliation, but he could not have been pleased at Gibbons's announcement at the meeting that a poll of the American hierarchy showed overwhelming preference for Washington as the site of the university.[24]

Three weeks later the bishop of St. Paul welcomed to Minnesota the cardinal of Baltimore. Gibbons, on his way to the West Coast, passed through Chicago and Milwaukee, where he was warmly greeted—indeed, his trip became early on a kind of triumphal tour. The "good little man," as McQuaid contemptuously called him, visibly enjoyed the attention he was receiving; as for the people he met, nobody in the Midwest had ever seen a cardinal before, and Gibbons, ever courteous and affable, possessed exactly the right chemistry to elicit a positive response from the friendly and curious crowds.[25]

John Ireland was determined not to be outdone by the cardinal's other hosts, and from the moment, on Thursday, September 29, when Gibbons detrained at the Union Depot—a massive pile of turreted Victorian gingerbread, which had cost $125,000 a few years before and of which the citizens of St. Paul were intensely proud[26]—he was plunged into a round of ceremonies and receptions that lasted through the following Sunday. The social high point of the cardinal's visit was reached the first evening when Ireland presided at a banquet at the Ryan Hotel, St. Paul's finest. In attendance were the civic and business leaders of city and state. The speeches—or rather the preassigned replies on various edifying subjects to "toasts" drunk in non-alcoholic beverages—went on into the night, and included a verbal tribute to "America" by United States Senator Cushman K. Davis and another to "Education" by the recently deposed rector of St. Thomas Aquinas Seminary, Father O'Gorman. It was well that the "good little man," along with the rest of the festive company, had been fortified beforehand by a dinner of oysters, turtle soup, roast tenderloin of beef, pheasant with bread sauce, chicken salad, shrimp salad, a variety of vegetables, puddings, cakes, grapes, pears, peaches, nuts, vanilla ice cream, Rocquefort cheese, and coffee.[27]

This pleasant interlude did not long distract Ireland from his major preoccupation of that summer and autumn. Both at home and abroad he pressed ahead with his plan to create a new ecclesiastical province with himself at its head. The idea, leaving aside the question of Irish-German hostility and the imperatives of personal ambition, was sensible from a purely quantitative point of view: a thousand miles lay between Milwaukee and the western reaches of Dakota, and if the division did occur Archbishop Heiss's province would still include the state of Wisconsin and the Upper Peninsula of Michigan. His suffragans unanimously approved the division, though Heiss himself agreed to it only grudgingly and, in his report to Propaganda, showed that not only Ireland could invoke the specter of excessive nationalism: "I could not persuade myself that a division of this Province is necessary now or useful, but I gave my consent, in order that the peace might not be disturbed and that nationalism, from which beyond doubt this motion has arisen, might not be more exacerbated."[28] Ireland meanwhile bombarded O'Connell with instructions to carry the scheme forward in Rome, to which the rector responded with constancy: "You may rest assured (D[eo] V[olente]) I shall do my part."[29]

To expedite the business O'Connell recruited the services of a Propaganda functionary named Donato Sbarretti, who proved willing enough and even zealous in the cause, especially after Ireland agreed to supply him with mass stipends.[30] O'Connell gave Sbarretti ten dollars to tide him over, "not to keep him waiting," he told Ireland, "until I hear from you, and to have [the masses] said for your poor [deceased] soul."[31] Propaganda, however, would not be hurried, and even though Ireland's check for Sbarretti reached him in mid-September,[32] O'Connell had to advise patience until the "compromise" with Heiss could be worked out — the archbishop insisted that the decrees of the council held in Milwaukee in 1886[33] be promulgated prior to the dismemberment of his province, and Propaganda agreed. It was not till early in the new year that O'Connell was able to inform Ireland that the deed was as good as done, with only the pope's final endorsement of Propaganda's decision — a formality — still to be obtained. "I put [in] a good many papers on the matter," O'Connell reminded his friend in St. Paul, and then added a cynical afterthought: "Sbarretti pushed your matters ahead of many others—such is the power of 'prayer.' "[34] By March 15, 1888, the basic arrangement had been settled: St. Paul was to be elevated to metropolitan status, with John Ireland as archbishop and with two suffragan sees in Minnesota and two more in Dakota. The decision would remain confidential, however, until the decrees of Heiss's council had been formally approved, and, wrote O'Connell, "I beg you for pity sake not to let this out to anyone."[35]

While these negotiations were proceeding toward their inevitable conclusion, the relations between the Americanists and the archbishop of New York were deteriorating further. Early in November 1887, Cardinal Gibbons circulated a form letter to the American bishops in which he pleaded for support for Keane and his fellow-collectors—prominent among whom was John Ireland—as they toured the country seeking funds for the university. Corrigan, citing the financial burdens of his archdiocese, declined to allow, much less to welcome, such solicitation in New York. He also tendered his resignation from the board of trustees. The blow could hardly have been unexpected, but Gibbons, hoping to ward it off, begged Corrigan to reconsider. The archbishop of New York frostily refused: "I have calmly considered the question of remaining in the University Board, and regret, for your sake particularly, that I cannot withdraw my resignation."[36] Ireland wrote Corrigan too, a little later, and adopted an uncharacteristically gentle tone. He granted that the archbishop of New York might have legitimate complaints about some decisions taken by the university committee, and that the resources of the archdiocese were no doubt under serious strain. "But," he added, "an open rupture with us will do no good, and I trust it may be prevented." Corrigan replied promptly: "I have studiously avoided a rupture and simply and quietly withdrawn, so much so that if any one learn of my resignation, the knowledge will come first from others."[37]

This exchange occurred in January 1888, while Ireland and Keane were collecting funds for the university in Baltimore, Washington, and Philadelphia. Their efforts netted more than one hundred thousand dollars in the Archdiocese of Baltimore alone. Ireland returned to Philadelphia later in the spring for another round of appeals to prospective contributors. In between these visits to the East he sent an encouraging word to Gibbons from St. Paul: "The West remains enthusiastic for the University. The withdrawal of Abp. Corrigan has not done a particle of harm. The Chicago Tribune said editorially that this withdrawal surprises no one, as Abp. Corrigan is a small man, foolishing [*sic*] jealous of the towering position occupied by Card. Gibbons."[38] He had the modesty not to mention that the same editorial had suggested that Corrigan was similarly jealous of Ireland and Keane. Gibbons, at any rate, might have been more consoled by this sturdy statement of support had St. Paul been capable of marshalling financial resources to the same measure as New York. Plans went ahead anyway for the laying of the cornerstone of the university's first building, Caldwell Hall, on May 24, 1888.

There was confirmation of Ireland's optimism from Rome, though, once again, it did nothing to relieve the fiscal danger to the university involved in Corrigan's antipathy toward it. O'Connell reported that while the top officials of Propaganda, Simeoni and Jacobini, continued to grumble about the university and to try to find obstacles to put in its path, the pope himself remained enthusiastic about the project.[39] "You stand well in Rome," the rector assured Ireland, "and so does Bp. Keane. Time proved the wisdom of all you did here." By contrast, Corrigan's "condition seems truly pitiable. It was unfortunate for him to have been guided by that woman [Ella Edes]."[40]

Pitiable or not, the archbishop of New York's standing in Rome did not prevent him and his allies from carrying the battle to other fronts. On March 19, Gibbons wrote Ireland in alarm that another attempt had been mounted to place the works of Henry George on the Index of Forbidden Books. The cardinal asked the bishop of St. Paul to write "a stirring letter" to O'Connell, which the rector would at his discretion place in the appropriate hands, a letter saying "that H. George is politically dead, that a condemnation would only resuscitate a book now almost forgotten, that a condemnation would be unnecessary and unwise. It was McGlynn's association with George that gave prominence to [*Progress and Poverty*], and now they are separated." Gibbons urged Ireland to persuade Marty,

Spalding, Heiss, and Feehan of Chicago to address Rome in a similar sense.[41]

Ireland of course complied, and even did the cardinal one better. He wrote not only to O'Connell but also to *Le Moniteur de Rome,* and, "telling of various matters, and by way of news, [brought] out strongly the fact that George's doctrines are dead and buried, and that nothing can revive them except the imprudent notices given to them by men well-meaning, but not observant of the march of ideas. You may be sure that Rome will keep quiet." Ireland also followed the cardinal's suggestion and approached Marty and Spalding. "I did not write to Abps. Heiss and Feehan; they would do nothing."[42]

The tactic of employing a friendly newspaper to help bring pressure to bear in high places was not a new device to Ireland and his friends, and they were to use it often in the future.[43] This particular intervention, however, was on Ireland's part as much an act of friendship as of principle. He understood that Gibbons, temperamentally a peace-loving man, harbored a fierce sense of obligation toward the masses of working-class American Catholics, and that therefore of all the controversial issues in which the cardinal was inevitably (and often reluctantly) involved, he felt strongest about maintaining the reality and the perception of the church as the "Friend of the People." Indeed, as Ireland observed to O'Connell, "If [George] is put on [the Index], there will be a vacancy in Baltimore from a broken heart."[44] The *Moniteur* did its part, and Ireland continued to do his. "I presume," he wrote Gibbons in early May,

> you have seen in the "Moniteur" our American letter on the social question in the United States. . . . Mgr. O'Connell writes that the books are actually before the Congr. of the Index "at the request of an American bishop." How provoking! We must do all we can to prevent a condemnation. Having noticed that our friend Card. Schiaffino has been named prefect of the Congr. of the Index, I wrote him a congratulatory letter and took occasion to emphasize my conviction that the good of religion demands absolutely that George be left in oblivion. I have confidence in Card. Schiaffino.[45]

During these various threats and alarums John Ireland did not neglect his oldest and dearest cause. Indeed, aboard the steamer in

May 1887, on his way back from Europe, he spent his spare time administering the pledge to any of the passengers in steerage he could convince to take it.[46] But his combativeness on other issues led at least once to a rebuff of his nationwide efforts to spread the gospel of total abstinence. In the letter to Corrigan of January 1888, in which he chided the archbishop for resigning from the university board of trustees, he also asked permission to address a temperance rally in New York. Corrigan refused, and Ireland meekly acquiesced,[47] though one may be permitted to imagine that he muttered to himself a further imprecation upon the son of a rumseller.[48] A few weeks later, however, a group of civic leaders in Chicago asked Ireland to come to their city and speak on the same subject that had prompted the invitation from New York: the technique of restricting the number of liquor retailers by means of a legally imposed "high license."[49]

On the evening of April 6, 1888, John Ireland strode onto the rostrum of the Central Music Hall in Chicago, and looked down over a huge, standing-room-only crowd. The speech he delivered, titled simply "The Saloon," was arguably the most powerful and persuasive of his career. It also marked a significant shift in the overall strategy of his temperance endeavors. In the beginning Ireland had stoutly resisted any government intrusion into the battle against strong drink. He had even declined to support Sunday-closing legislation in Minnesota, maintaining that moral suasion and religious preachment were the proper weapons in a struggle that aimed to convert the drinker to better habits or, to put it another way, to curtail the demand for liquor. By the mid-1880s he had changed his mind, as had indeed most of his colleagues in the national Catholic Total Abstinence Union and those non-sectarian reformers who, like the sponsors of the Chicago rally, were in alliance with it. The liquor interests had grown to such monstrous size and exerted such pervasive political influence that the time had come to invoke the power of the state in order to "attack the supply."[50] This new conviction was not unrelated to Ireland's evolving thought on other questions, all of which, it increasingly seemed to him, admitted of answers within the uniquely benign framework of the American political system. Let the state close down the saloons, he said today; let the state educate Catholic children, he would say tomorrow.

There was abroad in the land, Ireland cried, "an organized conspiracy for the promotion of intemperance." Brewers, distillers, publicans had banded together to feed upon broken homes and broken lives. "The principle governing their trade? To make money. Little they reck the misery drink causes, if they are thereby enriched. They deal it out to the tottering inebriate; to the youth surely entering on a life of sin and shame; to the workingman whose family are enduring famine; to the woman whose virtue dies as she lifts the poisoned cup to her lips."[51]

Not least among the sins of the liquor trade, to Ireland's mind, was political corruption on a colossal scale. "It means our national disgrace, that America be ruled by the liquor power." The time had come to attack the supply: to drive from office the politicians who cowered in the face of the saloonkeepers. Of course he allowed a part in the crusade for moral and religious exhortation, but to fight so widespread an evil required also "wise laws and the enforcement of laws." The state had "a positive duty" to intervene. It was often said that that government governs best which governs least. "But when there is a need, the best government is that which is coextensive with the need." Ireland was not ready to recommend prohibition, at least not yet. If he did so, it would be because the situation had so deteriorated that "public expediency" demanded "extreme legislation — a sort of martial law. . . . I have not said that we have as yet come to this pass. I do not say we may not."

What then? "Some form of restrictive legislation," an example of which had recently enjoyed much success. "I take pleasure," he said, "in mentioning high license," in which the pioneering efforts of Illinois had been profitably imitated in Minnesota and elsewhere. Ireland refused to accept the proposition that if you closed a hundred saloons, another hundred would simply double their business. "You do not know human nature. Half of our virtues, says an old adage, are from the absence of temptations." In St. Paul a few weeks earlier, a brewer told a reporter that high license had ruined his business. "A Minnesota liquor man, incautiously invited to contribute to the building of a church, in language stern if not polite, offered an order upon Bishop Ireland for a part of the damage done

to his business by high license." Ireland knew of a town where the
brewery wagon used to deliver daily; now, he said, it came twice
a week and soon but once. "I know of another town" of eight hundred families that used to support ten or twelve taverns; now there
was none, "and the bankers of the place have told me" how "amaz-
ingly large" the deposits of the suddenly thrifty people have become
every Saturday night. One county in Minnesota was so impressed
with the results of its five hundred dollar license that it had since
raised the levy to fifteen hundred dollars.

His summing up was to the point: "Whenever public opinion is
so civilized and Christianized in a place that citizens of their own
free will demand [high license] and are prepared to enforce it in this
free land, they are entitled to the privilege." He smiled and waved
and paid his tribute to the "Queen City of the Lakes" and her virtuous citizenry. "I am inspired with magnificent hopes. . . . I thank
you with all the warmth of my soul."

IF THE OVATION his new-style temperance appeal had gained him in
Chicago was balm to John Ireland's spirit, no less so was the news
he received from Rome shortly afterward. Messages of congratulation began to pour in upon the new archbishop of St. Paul. "I beg
leave to thank you very sincerely," he wrote to Gibbons, "for your
telegram. . . . I assure you from no one else among the members
of the hierarchy could come a [congratulatory message] in whose
truthfulness I would put more confidence, and upon which I would
set more value. The resolution of Propaganda, as approved by the
Holy Father, . . . [was] just as I had desired—Mgr. O'Connell
seconding, of course, my wishes with his usual diplomatic skill."
The formal papal brief, establishing the Archdiocese of St. Paul, was
dated May 15, 1888.[52]

The "resolution," however—"St. Paul . . . a metropolitan
See . . . [with] two new episcopal Sees, one in southern Minnesota and another in Northern Dakota"—was in fact not quite all
Ireland desired. He wanted the Vicariate of Northern Minnesota,
presided over since its foundation in 1875 by the Benedictine
Rupert Seidenbusch, to be divided into two distinct dioceses, one
in St. Cloud and the other in Duluth. "Duluth is growing very
rapidly, and," he prophesied, "[it] will be an important city."[53] And

since "candidates for those [new] dioceses [were] to be submitted to Rome by the bishops of the new province"—Ireland himself, Marty of Dakota, and Seidenbusch—he wanted, above all, to be rid of Seidenbusch.

The vicar apostolic of northern Minnesota, Bavarian born and educated, was a fifty-seven-year-old monk who had come to the United States in 1850. In 1866 he had been elected the first abbot of St. John's, the Benedictine monastery eleven miles from St. Cloud. Father Rupert was a good-natured man, conventionally pious, hard working, compassionate, and not particularly forceful. When Thomas Grace petitioned Rome for a division of his diocese in 1875, he urged the appointment of Seidenbusch, on the grounds that most Catholics in northern Minnesota were German immigrants and that most of the missioners working there were German monks who belonged to St. John's Abbey. After he became a bishop he continued to enjoy the simple pleasures of monastic conversation or of a card game with a glass of beer or wine. He was of medium height, wore an impressively thick beard and tiny spectacles, and, in his later years, had grown very fat, so much so that his health and general activity were seriously impaired.[54]

Seidenbusch never proved an effective administrator, even after the Dakota section of the vicariate was detached from his jurisdiction in 1879. He got along well enough with his fellow Germans and Benedictines, but the handful of secular priests—especially several truculent French Canadians whom he ill-advisedly incardinated into the vicariate—caused him untold trouble. In 1885 he suffered a severe heart attack from which he never completely recovered, and which necessitated his absence for long periods from north-central Minnesota and its often harsh climate. He refused, even so, to consider resignation, and instead appointed Abbot Alexius Edelbrock, his successor at St. John's, as administrator of the vicariate. Abbot Alexius—the tough, hard-driving antithesis to Seidenbusch—was under no illusions. "[The] vicariate is in deplorable condition," he wrote, "and if the good Bishop will live many years he will see hard times ahead. . . . He has only a few [secular] priests, but one is worse than the other and he is in fights with nearly all. I have settled some troubles for him, yet there are enough yet on hand."[55]

It need hardly be said that Rupert Seidenbusch—a religious, a German, a beer drinker, a semi-invalid who was seldom on the job—did not measure up to expectations of the new metropolitan of St. Paul for a suffragan bishop. Marty of Dakota was also a monk, to be sure, and an inept executive, but he was Swiss, not German, and he belonged to a different branch of the Benedictines from that of the monks of St. John's, so he had no power base within the province. Since his appointment to the Vicariate of Dakota in 1879 he had shown himself consistently ready to follow John Ireland's lead, and so no objection was raised to his appointment as one of the new ordinaries in Dakota Territory.

The case with Seidenbusch was far different. From the beginning of the negotiations with Propaganda Ireland pressed for his removal prior to the designation of the new dioceses.[56] Ireland charged that the vicar's negligence had left the jurisdiction in tatters; the secular priests serving there, Ireland told Jacobini, were nothing but the refuse of other dioceses, while the Benedictines quarreled so among themselves that their ministry was paralyzed. The situation had reached the disaster point.[57] O'Connell, once again, counseled patience; Seidenbusch's resignation, he said, "is contemplated" and "has already been gently suggested" by the congregation, but the Roman officials were loath to force the issue.[58] The ailing vicar traveled to Rome at the beginning of 1888, but his conversations with Propaganda went at cross purposes. Even after the new province was formally established, in the late spring of that year, Bishop Seidenbusch still held out. Ireland wrote him a scolding letter, and Seidenbusch, in the high summer, sent a pathetically stubborn one in return. "It is true," he began, "I should have written to His Eminence [Cardinal Simeoni] some time ago, but when I came home I was so busy with writing letters." It was also true that he had told Simeoni that he was "willing and ready to resign, but I thought at the time that everything was settled and in peace"—that is, he had assumed that the priests of the vicariate with whom he was quarreling would have been silenced by Roman intervention. That had not happened, and so "a good and learned friend" had advised him

> not to resign, for such resignation would appear a great triumph of those bad priests, and they certainly would make it appear so. I have come to the conclusion to try and observe the residence.

If it should kill me, I may as well die on the battlefield as in a retired position. If I resign, where shall I go and how I shall [*sic*]
live? It would put me in an altogether new position, and I am
affraid [*sic*] it would affect my health worse than remaining and
working where I am at present.

If Simeoni demanded his resignation, Seidenbusch would accede,
"though I do not think I deserve such treatment which I believe
simply proceeds from the accusations of those poor and bad French
priests."[59]

A week or so later he visited Ireland in St. Paul, but, to the archbishop's intense exasperation, still refused to commit himself to
resignation. Ireland's strong complaint to his friend and agent in
Rome brought a warning to go slowly and to take care of more permanent concerns. To press at Propaganda for Seidenbusch's ouster,
O'Connell said, might well arouse "the Brotherhood," and "it is the
Brotherhood that is principally opposed to the Vicar's resignation. . . . If you cannot gain the resignation at once without
strong and risky pressure, why not use the matter as a means of carrying through your other plans of putting the right men in Dakota
and the new dioceses of St. Paul [*sic*], and then you can command
the future as long as you live. The Vic. Ap. of Northern Minnesota
would yield to you on those points."[60] The advice was sound, and
Ireland wisely abided by it.

Bishop Seidenbusch's reluctance to step aside was an irritant to
Ireland, but it did not keep him from enjoying the ceremonial fruits
of his new status. O'Connell had wanted, and certainly deserved,
to share in the festivities. "You must let me bring your pallium
over," he had written at a time when the negotiations were far from
complete.[61] But when, after a papal consistory in mid-June, 1888,
the pallium was entrusted to him for delivery to the new archbishop, the rector did not feel up to the journey—he complained often that summer of uncertain health and physical "prostration" from
overwork. He assigned the task to one of the newly ordained students of the American College who was returning home to New
York and who would either bring the vestment to St. Paul or deposit it for safe-keeping with his own archbishop.[62]

The wonderfully ironic prospect of Ireland receiving his pallium
from the hands of Michael Corrigan never materialized. Bishop

Keane brought it with him from New York to the University of Notre Dame, where he was residing during August while he put the finishing touches to the statutes he was preparing for his own university.[63] On August 15 the venerable Father Edward Sorin, founder of Notre Dame, observed the golden jubilee of his ordination. Gibbons came to Indiana for the celebration, as did Ireland, who preached at the pontifical mass.[64] In the evening, after dinner, Keane presented the pallium to his friend, and Gibbons spoke briefly. The occasion therefore was something of a partisan affair, but such at the moment was the fluidity of the relationships among the antagonists within the American hierarchy that the enigmatic Corrigan might in fact have been welcome at it. Ireland, in New York two weeks or so later, "called on Abp. Corrigan, and found him in every respect a changed man. He is determined, he says, to show himself in harmony with his brother bishops on all important questions, and will be present as a director at the next meeting of the University Board."[65] Gibbons was consoled by this news—the university had had "up-hill work" in the face of "the opposition of a great diocese reinforced by unfriendly and intangible agencies in Rome"[66]—but, a more subtle man than Ireland, he must also have been puzzled by Corrigan's abrupt about-face.

The solemn conferral of Ireland's pallium took place in the Cathedral of St. Paul on September 27, when, appropriately, Thomas Langdon Grace, in the presence of a dozen bishops, hundreds of priests, and an "immense throng" of the people Ireland knew and loved best, draped the piece of symbolic sheepskin over the shoulders of his successor.[67] The preacher for the occasion, John J. Keane, conformed to the fashion of the day and spoke at mind-numbing length, but few in the friendly congregation thought he exaggerated when he said: "The voice of honest truth will declare that . . . [for much] that is good and noble of the period we live in, the credit is largely due to the Bishop of St. Paul."[68]

One among his hearers who might not have subscribed to Keane's sentiments was the vicar apostolic of northern Minnesota. But Rupert Seidenbusch's days were numbered. A statement he had submitted to Propaganda explaining why he ought to retain his post was summarily rejected, and on September 30 Cardinal Simeoni formally requested his resignation from the vicariate.[69] Seidenbusch, having exhausted all means of evasion, reluctantly complied, though six more weeks passed before the formalities had been completed. A major obstacle to Ireland's designs for his province had thus been removed, and the archbishop, appointed interim administrator of the vicariate, could now proceed to implement his plans for the new suffragan sees.

Nevertheless, the difficulties with the Benedictines of northern Minnesota continued. Alexius Edelbrock, Seidenbusch's strong-minded successor as abbot of St. John's, vigorously supported his confrere throughout the resignation crisis. But Edelbrock had concurrent problems of his own.[70] Never popular among his own monks, he adopted policies that alienated many of them, and at the time his friend Seidenbusch was being forced into retirement a suit had been entered at Propaganda against Edelbrock himself. The complainant, allegedly spokesman for a large number of his brethren, was none other than the St. John's monk, Othmar Erren, whose published lampoons of the temperance movement had earned him Ireland's displeasure a few years before. This turn of events put the archbishop of St. Paul in a quandary. "I am keeping out of the trouble," he told O'Connell, "and refused to give Erren a letter to Cardinal Simeoni." A complicating factor was that, though his own relations with Edelbrock had been more or less cordial over the years, Bishop Marty, himself a Benedictine, sternly disapproved of the abbot and had made himself a sponsor of Erren's cause. "The fact of the case is," Ireland said, "that this Benedictine Order in Minnesota is all torn up. The majority are dreadfully opposed to the Abbot, whom they accuse of fearful things. Some fathers have run off in disgust. Religion suffers more than writing can tell." The best he could recommend to O'Connell was, "without implicating yourself in his business," to "show [Erren] some kindness and, if occasion offers, and prudence permits, give him some advice."[71]

Erren remained in Rome pressing his case until November 22, O'Connell all the while acting as his discreet mentor. The rector did not think the monk lived up to his reputation as a rebel and troublemaker: "He is just like a child, nothing wicked or bad in him. As far as I could see, [he] talks out just as he thinks, open and brave, and meaning well."[72] Erren's appeal at any rate impressed Propaganda to the extent that Jacobini early on told O'Connell that, whatever happened, no Benedictine would wear a miter in northern Minnesota: "We will have to put a secular in there," he said.[73] In the end sufficient weight was found in Erren's charges—especially those that accused Abbot Edelbrock of playing fast and loose with abbey finances—to open a formal investigation. O'Connell informed Ireland that the archbishop could expect to be named apostolic visitor to the Benedictines of northern Minnesota; he would be instructed especially to "take a good peep at their books," to find out, for example, how much Benedictine money had gone into the building of mission churches and schools and how much had been collected from the faithful, and thus determine with whom the ownership of such property should lie.[74] Simeoni made the appointment as predicted on December 20.

Always just beneath the surface of these broils lay the German question, or, for a German like Edelbrock, the Irish question. Indeed the abbot of St. John's ultimately came to see the attack upon him as at root an instance of Irish malevolence.[75] And John Ireland never forgot, nor did he let any one else forget, that the deteriorating situation in the vicariate was a German product. But he was not thinking specifically of northern Minnesota when he told Denis O'Connell in the summer of 1888: "The German question is reviving, in view of the approaching convention in Cincinnati, but reviving with the cough of death in its throat." He referred rather to the meeting of German-speaking priests—the Deutsche-Amerikanischer Priester-Verein—scheduled for the Ohio city in early September.[76]

There had been a similar meeting—the first of its kind—the year before in Chicago, at which a papal blessing had been dispensed to the three hundred participants. This was a fairly routine act of benignity on the part of the pope who regularly dispatched blessings-by-cable upon various Catholic gatherings in various parts of the world. But the priest who had secured the blessing for the Chicago convention was a subject of the Belgian-born Camillus P. Maes, bishop of Covington, Kentucky, who looked askance at "a clique of German priests [whose] prevailing spirit is dangerous [and whose] purpose is to counteract the wise efforts of the bishops to create gradually a single homogeneous Catholic people in the United States."[77] Maes was determined that no blessing should be sent from Rome to the Cincinnati convention. In that tense atmosphere, even so seemingly inoffensive a gesture as the pope's blessing could become a bone of contention.

Maes sent Ireland a copy of the protest he had drawn up for Simeoni, and the archbishop of St. Paul jumped with alacrity into the fray. "It is vital," he told O'Connell, that "the Powers that be in Propaganda" permit "no blessings [to] be sent to the coming Cincinnati convention. Rome sheds around blessings rather profusely. In America they are looked upon as positive 'approvals;' and a blessing sent to Cincinnati will be taken as the approving seal of infallibility upon German tricks. I view this as a very vital matter, and beg that you attend to it."[78]

O'Connell duly approached Simeoni in Ireland's name, only to discover that the blessing had already been dispatched to the organizers of the convention. Then Maes's letter had arrived in Rome, and then Ireland's protest, and the prefect of Propaganda was reduced to the ludicrous expedient of "recalling" the blessing after the convention was over. Ireland meanwhile fired off salvos in the pages of the *Northwestern Chronicle* and insisted on the importance of the Roman reversal. "The meaning is that Rome will not tolerate any movement among Catholics in America that breaks up among them unity, and that separates from the general body sections or divisions of Catholics, resulting from distinctions of foreign nationalism. The revocation of that blessing is an act most significant that all Catholics will do well to note."[79]

Ireland sent the article from the *Chronicle* to Gibbons and observed in a covering letter: "I consider this revocation a great triumph for our American policy. Next year the German convention will meet in Cleveland and receive its coup de grace from gentle Richard."[80] "Richard" was the notoriously ungentle Bishop Gilmour of Cleveland, to whom Ireland also wrote: "Our vigorous American policy is in the ascendancy. I trust I shall be able to keep you in the front ranks. Providence wills that you meet the foe on your own ground. . . . I have thanked God for this. Of all the places in America, where I would wish them to meet, Cleveland is my choice."[81] Gibbons responded warmly that the "setback" Ireland had inflicted on the Germans would contribute to the general welfare by making them "less aggressive and more modest and submissive in the future."[82] Perhaps more important—particularly in the light of later criticism of Ireland for interfering in other people's jurisdictions — was the approval his intervention received from the cautious Archbishop Elder of Cincinnati.[83] O'Connell indeed had taken special pains to assure the Roman officials that Elder agreed with Ireland about the revocation of the papal blessing. But the rector also warned Ireland that he had stirred up again the enmity of the German faction at Propaganda: "In that quarter, you are pretty well written off, but you have your Pallium now."[84]

It was not, however, only in faraway places that the archbishop of St. Paul contended with his teutonic foe. At the very moment the Cincinnati affair was heating up, the German Catholics of his own diocese were making final arrangements for a modest convention of their own. As a matter of course they invited their archbishop to attend the Katholikentag and asked him also to secure for their meeting a papal blessing. Ireland curtly refused on the grounds, he said, that the projected assembly manifested "a spirit of ultra-nationalism, hardly consistent with the fullness of Catholic unity which should characterize the life of the Church in America."[85] The Germans protested mildly that they had organized their Tag under the auspices of the Central Verein, whose social and fraternal activities the archbishop had always supported, and that they had no intention of sponsoring an exclusively clerical session of the sort contemplated in Cincinnati. These reassurances apparently satisfied Ireland, because when the Katholikentag was held in mid-October 1888, he presided at the mass that opened the day's observances, and afterward addressed the delegates. The speech was vintage Ireland, beginning with faint praise for the Germans for the probity of their lives and for the beauty of their language, warning nevertheless against "an exaggerated love of old habits," insisting that "the children of the Church in America . . . [must be] to the core Americans in love and loyalty," and concluding with the testimonial, repeated a thousand times over the years, of his own double loyalty.

> To me, all Catholics, whencesoever they have come, are Catholics and nothing else. I know, in my ministrations, no race. The motto of the Diocese, chosen by its first bishop, is "All to All," and I pray that my tongue be stilled, and my arm fall nerveless, if ever I am not true to it. Catholic I shall be in faith, and

American in nationality, and thus I shall be one with all, who, whatever their origins, are Catholics and Americans.[86]

The congregation, which had listened to a sermon preached in German during the mass, seemed to receive the archbishop's message with a properly docile spirit, and Ireland, always ready to look on the bright side, reported serenely a little later: "The German question in the West is, for the time being at least, in perfect repose."[87]

By contrast, "affairs in Northern Minnesota"—where the conflict of nationalities had its own relevance—"are as bad as they well can be," and with the new year of 1889 Ireland, in his dual capacity as administrator of the vicariate and apostolic visitor to the monks of St. John's Abbey, prepared to settle matters there once and for all. He moved, however, with care and deliberation. The formal visitation lasted off and on from February to May, during which interval Ireland visited the main Benedictine centers in northern Minnesota, including selected Indian missions, and interviewed all the monks and nuns. The procedure he followed and the questions he asked hewed carefully to the line of inquiry laid down in the instructions sent him by Propaganda. The most crucial portion of the visitation was carried out at St. John's itself, upon which Ireland descended on May 3 and 4. Edelbrock bitterly summarized the questions:

> How is the order or Rule kept? Does the Abbot—Alexius Edelbrock—attend choir? Does the Abbot run around much? Is the Abbot cruel and tyrannical? Is the Chapter free? How many fathers were expelled? How many ran off? Is the Abbot after money? Why have you so many missions? Have the clerics time to study? Do they teach classes? [Ireland] placed great stress on the time allowed the clerics for studying; he thought the clerics ought not to teach, they ought to have *five* years in the clericate and should not be Prefects, should stand under strict obedience. The *intellectual* and *spiritual* training at St. John's Abbey and University was by him considered too low.[88]

The visitation was by no means a witch-hunt, but Edelbrock and his allies fretted at the leisurely pace at which Ireland conducted it, understandably fearful that the longer the investigation dragged on the more the visitator's notorious lack of sympathy for Germans and religious would assert itself. Ireland, though not normally given to dawdling, adamantly insisted that the visitation proceed with no appearance of haste or of crisis, lest the newspapers should get wind of it; he added that Cardinal Simeoni had recommended prolonging the process in hopes that tempers might cool on both sides. Whatever defects may have been discerned in Ireland's methods by those who had to endure them, the archbishop's stock in Rome did not suffer thereby. When O'Connell remarked to Jacobini how well Ireland was doing in northern Minnesota, the secretary of Propaganda replied, "Ireland would do well anywhere."[89]

Abbot Edelbrock was particularly irritated at what seemed Ireland's determination to avoid a face-to-face meeting with him. They did finally come together at Ireland's residence in St. Paul on June 14, and Edelbrock left the meeting convinced that the archbishop, despite assurances that he was "friendly disposed," would press Propaganda to force his resignation. His impression was correct.

By that time Abbot Alexius had decided to take his case in person to Rome. He arrived there on July 6, and two days later he had his first interview with Simeoni. The cardinal-prefect appeared cordial, listened to him attentively, and then asked whether the visitation had been satisfactory. The abbot later described his own response: "Here Abbot Edelbrock arose like a lion and dissected the whole *Modus agendi* of Msgr. Ireland; he imitated even the gestures of Msgr. Ireland to perfection and told His Eminence of the wrong done me and our Order."[90] These histrionics proved to be the high point of the abbot's mission to Rome; if he had thought Ireland's progress in the spring had been too slow, he now discovered how little speed counted for in the deliberations of the Roman curia. "There must be a great deal of silliness about the man," O'Connell reported to Ireland, "or unacquaintance with the ways of Rome, because he looked for a decision on [his case] from the congregation of yesterday."[91] The decision did not come in July, nor for months afterward, until Edelbrock was gradually worn down by conflicting counsels and by O'Connell's insinuations, inspired by Ireland, that his resignation was the only acceptable "compromise." "Really I don't know what is best," one of Edelbrock's fellow abbots wrote him from the United States. "Mgr. O'Connell says Ireland assures him your case is much against you, and now that Ireland has gone into the business I fear he will fight to the end. . . . I am glad your monastery is not in his diocese; the documents which he put in against you are crushing; he does not mean well with you." On November 27, 1889, Father Alexius Edelbrock, second abbot of St. John's, formally resigned his office. "The Irish will regret this," he said.[92]

That was dubious consolation, and in any case a debatable proposition. As early as April 25 Ireland and Marty had met in St. Paul to draw up a list of candidates for the new bishoprics in the province. For the most part agreement between them was guaranteed from the start. There still lingered in some quarters at Propaganda reluctance to implement Ireland's scheme to divide the northern vicariate into two dioceses, for fear neither would be economically viable, but Jacobini brushed aside this objection as "not of much account."[93]

So by a papal brief signed on September 16, 1889, Martin Marty became bishop of Sioux Falls with the entire state of South Dakota (admitted to the Union November 2, 1889) for his jurisdiction. Three of Ireland's most devoted disciples were promoted to the episcopate: John Shanley, who as a student had traveled to Rome with Ireland in 1869, was sent to Jamestown, North Dakota, and made responsible for the whole of that new state; James McGolrick, Ireland's theological consultant at the Third Plenary Council, was named bishop of Duluth; and Joseph Cotter, sometime president of the Catholic Total Abstinence Union of America,[94] was assigned the southernmost tier of Minnesota counties, with Winona as his see city.

Nevertheless, the new province was not created totally in John Ireland's image and likeness. To the Diocese of St. Cloud went Otto J. Zardetti,[95] a peripatetic Swiss priest who had served since 1885 as Marty's vicar general. Zardetti was multilingual, relatively well-educated, and an ecclesiastical intriguer worthy of the steel of Denis O'Connell, whom he assiduously cultivated during the months the appointments to the new sees were pending. And not without success: "I believe [Zardetti] expects one [of the new sees]," O'Connell told Ireland in February, "and I suppose Marty would urge him. My opinion is this: that tho' he may not be absolutely the best man, he is the best compromise you can find. [He] may be the solution of

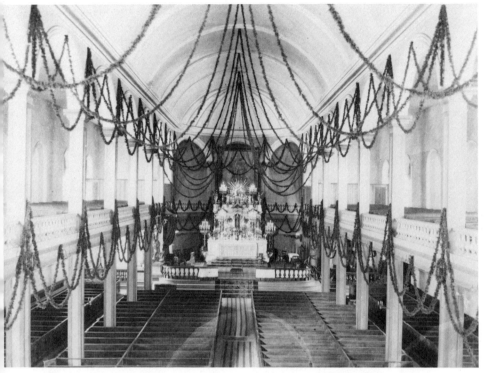

The second Cathedral of St. Paul, decorated for the consecration of Bishops John Shanley, Joseph Cotter, and James McGolrick on December 27, 1889 (MHS)

many problems, and many inconveniences for you might follow his setting aside."[96] Over the long term this prophecy missed its mark, but it made sense at the time and meshed nicely with two of Ireland's specific concerns: that Marty be rewarded for his loyalty, and that the new bishop located only eleven miles from St. John's Abbey not be an Irishman.

Two days after Christmas 1889, Shanley, McGolrick, and Cotter were consecrated bishops by John Ireland, aided by Grace and Marty, in a four-and-a-half-hour-long ceremony in the Cathedral of St. Paul. The event was unique in the annals of the American church up to that time: never before had three men from the same diocese been elevated to the episcopate for service in the same province.[97] The preacher of the day was the Paulist, Walter Elliott, just then finishing his biography of Isaac Hecker. In attendance was Monsignor Denis J. O'Connell, who, at the banquet following the mass, delivered a short but graceful address. It was, all in all, a most satisfactory occasion for the archbishop of St. Paul, who could reflect with pride on the accolade from his friend in Baltimore: "Never perhaps in the history of the Church has a province bloomed as rapidly as St. Paul's. Its growth is typical of the American Church."[98]

"The Consecrated Blizzard"

1889

A T THE END OF 1889 Cardinal Gibbons received an inquiry from the prefect of Propaganda about the prospects for the conversion to Catholicism of Swedish immigrants living in Chicago, St. Louis, and other "western" American cities. The reason for the Roman interest was significant: converted Swedes might return to Europe and "be a good leaven to their countrymen etc."[1] Simeoni and his colleagues, one should remember, were specifically charged with the task of promoting the spread and sustenance of Catholicism in mission lands; but even they remained thoroughly Old World in their point of view and tended to judge the value of a policy in terms of its impact upon the European scene. And if the officers of Propaganda displayed such a mind-set, the rest of the Roman bureaucracy could hardly be expected to do otherwise. Indeed, the curial officials often displayed an even narrower attitude toward the emigration question, seeming to be concerned almost exclusively with the status of Italians settled in the United States. This proclivity was a source of particular annoyance to the American bishops, who found the Italians, of all the immigrant groups, the least likely to practice their religion or to contribute to its support.[2] The Roman sense of priorities was not necessarily malevolent; but it was certainly out of tune with the aspirations of those American churchmen who believed that the United States was "the choicest field which providence offers [Catholicism] in the world today."[3]

No collision occurred on this occasion, however. Gibbons merely passed Simeoni's request on to the archbishop of St. Paul who, he presumed, would know something about the subject. "I am quite familiar with all the bearings of the question," John Ireland replied, "and have for years given to it serious consideration." He went on at length to speak, not of Swedes only, but of Scandinavians — "the general name we give in the West to Swedes, Norwegians and Danes. The three populations are so nearly similar, that one can scarcely be considered without the other." The states of the Upper Midwest, he reported, "are largely overrun with them," but their influence was greatest in Minnesota where they number three hundred thousand. "They are intelligent, industrious, aggressive. . . . They learn English rapidly. . . . They are always largely represented in the legislature and in various state and municipal offices." A decade ago "they were addicted to drunkenness, but their ministers have worked hard, . . . and they are now the most temperate element of our general population, next to the Irish-American. I have not seldom spoken in their temperance gatherings." "Chastity," he added primly, "is not their dominating virtue."[4]

Most Scandinavians "are Lutherans of the old school — though Methodism has made since their arrival in America some progress among them." To effect conversions within their community "we need priests . . . with peculiar gifts of soul. The Scandinavians are intelligent, and they will have to be reasoned into belief." But accepting "as they do nearly all our dogmas, claiming the same sacramental system, and freed in America from social pressure and local conditions under which they suffer at home, I have always believed that the Church rightly presented to them would gain among them many adherents." Ireland himself had made "serious efforts" for fifteen years to find the kind of priests appropriately equipped to work among the Scandinavians, without, however, much success. "I have now studying for this diocese three young Norwegians in the Jesuit College of Copenhagen selected purposely for me by the Vicar Apostolic of Norway. . . . You see, I have not been forgetting the Scandinavians. . . . I have myself in the course of my ministry received a score of them into the Church." Yet, though "we have in Minnesota some few Scandinavian converts in almost every mission," without trained personnel it remained "so difficult to do anything."

"The Church rightly presented" — here was Ireland's watchword, consistently invoked, however difficult the apostolate may have been. His efforts to Americanize Catholic immigrants should not obscure the other broad aim of his policy, to win acceptance for Catholicism among groups, like the Scandinavians, who were hostile or indifferent to it. Indeed the two objectives were closely intertwined. When the American people came to realize that Catholicism stood guard over their own civic ideals, and that a commitment to it involved no essentially foreign entanglement, Ireland was convinced that conversions would abound. A temperate, law-abiding, hard-working, thrifty, English-speaking Catholic community, unfettered by outmoded European customs, offered the republic its surest moral support. And *moral* is a word that in this context needs special stress. Doctrinal differences appeared to Ireland largely irrelevant, not because he had any sympathy for syncretism but because he thought Protestantism as a system incapable of maintaining the traditional Christian dogmas and practices that most people still prized, and therefore he judged "Lutherans of the old school" to be fruit ripe for Catholic picking.[5]

Ireland possessed no sense of an ecumenism as a later time would understand that term. His relationships with non-Catholics were cordial without being close, and he never lost the sense he had had as a young man that his was the obligation to rebut any criticism leveled against his communion. The foundation in the late 1880s — and its rapid growth in succeeding years — of the American Protective Association (APA),[6] with its odious echoes of the know-nothingism of thirty years earlier, heightened his vigilance. In January 1889, for example, when a local divine delivered three "lectures on Romanism" that attracted large crowds in Minneapolis, Ireland mounted his pulpit in the cathedral and preached a withering attack upon "Protestant bigotry"; he had the text published on the front page of the *Northwestern Chronicle* under the headline, "A Valiant Champion of the Church." The sarcasm of his opening lines he maintained throughout: "Mr. Mabie, a Baptist minister, preached for some two years in St. Paul. He did not, however, waste his anti-Catholic eloquence on the desert air of Eighth and Canada streets. This rare gift he reserved — why I will not attempt to say — for Minneapolis."[7] But so long as he was unprovoked, Ireland usually abided by the principle he enunciated in his Civil War reminiscence: "The American people are fair to the Catholic Church[;] . . .

prejudices exist where Catholics give cause for them, and seldom elsewhere."[8]

Such was not the case, however, with regard to blacks of whatever religion, and on the race question John Ireland consistently adopted a stand that was as courageous as it was unpopular. "All the black men want is fair play," he said in the summer of 1889. "That given, they will care for themselves. The equality of man is an American principle; it is also religious teaching. . . . We are all brothers in Christ, and brothers do not look at color or race."[9] Had this kind of bland statement exhausted Ireland's views on the subject—and were it then combined with his rather off-hand treatment of the American Indians under his charge, whom he seemed content to regard as simply wards of the state[10]—there would be little reason to remark about the archbishop's campaign against racial intolerance. What was extraordinary was the specificity he brought to his pronouncements.

> There is but one solution of the problem, and it is to obliterate all color line. . . . In many states the law forbids marriage between black and white—in this manner fomenting immorality and putting injury no less upon the white, whom it pretends to elevate, than upon the black, for whose degradation it has no care. Let the negro be our equal in the enjoyment of all political rights of the citizen. The constitution grants him those rights; let us be loyal to the constitution. I would open to the negro all industrial and professional avenues—the test for his advance being his ability, but never his color. I would in all public gatherings and in all public resorts . . . and hotels treat the black man as I treat the white. I might shun the [rude] man, whatever his color; but the gentleman, whatever his color, I would never push away from me.[11]

Ireland did not have a large black Catholic constituency in his archdiocese; there was but one black parish in St. Paul in his time, which he called a "temporary expedient" for the convenience of the blacks themselves. As early as 1888 a black student was enrolled in his seminary, a phenomenon practically unheard of at the time.[12] To be sure, even among those most favorably disposed, the unsavory stereotypes died hard. When Ireland, in the spring of 1890, delivered a sermon in Washington, which was a stinging indictment of Catholic segregationists, Denis O'Connell, then a guest of Cardinal

Gibbons, wrote to congratulate him: "Your sermon in Washington has stirred the Negro question to its depths. You made many converts to your views, the 'Mirror' among them. A gentleman from Washington told me the negroes were strutting through the departments with their heads in the air saying, 'He is the first man that ever put the nigger in his right place.' The Cardinal enjoyed it."[13] But Ireland remained admirably true to his principles when he espoused the cause of a hapless people downtrodden in the North no less than in the South, by Catholics no less than by Protestants: "I rejoiced in my soul when slavery ceased. I will rejoice in my soul when this social prejudice shall cease, and in the meantime I will work in the name of humanity, of religion and [of] patriotism to kill it out."[14]

Ireland's treatment of another minority group, however, led directly to disastrous consequences for the Catholic church in the United States. Two weeks after writing the long report to Cardinal Gibbons about the Scandinavians, on December 19, 1889, the archbishop of St. Paul gave an interview in his office to Father Alexis Georgievich Toth, recently arrived in the United States from his birthplace and the scene of his early priestly ministry in the Austro-Hungarian Empire. Toth, a learned man of thirty-six, was a Uniate — that is, he belonged to one of the non–Latin rites in union with the Roman See but distinctive in their liturgical languages and ecclesiastical customs.[15] A group of Ruthenian Uniates had established their own parish earlier in the year in Northeast Minneapolis — where a good many eastern European immigrants had settled — and had called Father Toth to be their pastor.

The priest presented the archbishop his credentials, and, as Toth recalled it,[16] Ireland's hands trembled as he read them. Then he looked up, and said abruptly in Latin: "Have you a wife?"

"No," Toth answered in the same language.

"But you had one?"

"Yes, I am a widower."

Ireland tossed the documents on the desk in front of him. "I have already written to Rome protesting against this kind of priest being sent to me!"

"What kind of priest do you mean?"

"Your kind."

"I am a Catholic priest of the Greek rite," Toth protested. "I am a Uniate and was ordained by a regular Catholic bishop."

"I do not consider that either you or this bishop of yours are Catholic; besides I do not need any Greek Catholic priests here; a Polish priest in Minneapolis is quite sufficient; the Greeks can also have him for their priest."

This rude and testy reaction on Ireland's part was only the beginning of his vendetta against the Uniates. He immediately instructed the clergy in Northeast Minneapolis to have no association with Toth and, furthermore, to state publicly from their pulpits that not even the Ruthenian Catholics were permitted to approach the Uniate priest for the sacraments. Nor was the archbishop content to manifest his dislike within the limits of his own jurisdiction. In every national forum during succeeding years he pressed for a general prohibition of Uniate activity, and he carried his case directly to Propaganda. Father Toth, meantime, was not one to be intimidated; he carried on his ministry in the face of Ireland's hostility until 1891, when he and 365 of his parishioners, refusing in effect to be either Americanized or Latinized, were formally received into the Russian Orthodox church. What started as a trickle in Minnesota soon swelled into a vast wave of schism all around the country, costing the Roman church, by conservative estimates, a quarter of a million communicants.[17]

Ireland's bias against the Uniates was by no means unique; his episcopal colleagues, Americanist and anti-Americanist alike, shared it, or at least condoned it and thereby participated in causing the massive exodus. Their conduct, if tragically shortsighted, was perfectly predictable. One principal reason for it can be seen in the very first part of the exchange between Ireland and Toth: celibacy for the parochial clergy was not a requirement in the Eastern tradition, whether Uniate or Orthodox. Some bishops feared — though Ireland himself did not stress this point — that their Latin-rite priests would demand wives if the married Uniates established parishes nearby. For Ireland, however, the problem was not so much one of sexual expression as of status and conformity. In the United States a Catholic priest was, in the popular mind, defined as an unmarried man, and indeed enjoyed a certain position within his community as a result. Would it do to try to explain to the average Catholic parishioner that Father Toth was as much a priest as, say, Monsignor Ravoux? But of course he was, as the Catholic church had taught consistently for unnumbered centuries, and Ireland knew it. His attitude therefore is hard to forgive, but not hard to explain. And even leaving aside the celibacy issue, his obsession with the process of Americanization would have led him to strike hard at the Uniates, who were notoriously attached to their Old-World customs. Bad enough the Germans, who at least worshiped in the Latin tongue and maintained an unmarried clergy like other Catholics.

Finally, the conflict boiled down, as did so many conflicts in John Ireland's career, to the issue of governance. Toth's credentials came from his bishop back in Slovakia. They stated clearly that Toth and those like him were subject to the local Latin ordinary, until such time as a Uniate jurisdiction were established in the United States. This was a perfectly reasonable and canonically acceptable position to take. But Ireland and the rest of the hierarchy stubbornly resisted any such intrusion into their authority. Propaganda, so often annoyed at the American bishops' claims to independence of Rome, supinely surrendered to their demands vis-à-vis the Uniates,[18] and so shared responsibility for the catastrophe that followed. When on one occasion Ireland wrote Simeoni to thank him for his support against the "Greeks," he put succinctly the principle of policy that meant more to him than any other: "The difficulties encountered by the Church in America due to diverse populations coming to our shores are immense. The only remedy, I am convinced, is to strengthen the authority of the bishops [*les bras episcopals*]. It is the only way to bind the different elements together and prevent chaos and schism."[19] These words have a hollow sound in the light of events then going on before Ireland's eyes.

If Ireland's advocacy of the blacks displayed him at his best, his belligerence toward the Uniates showed him at his bull-headed worst. Meanwhile, the American dream still awaited fulfillment for all that multitude of diverse peoples who had settled the new land, but Ireland never doubted that his own mixture of religion and patriotism could bring that happy day ever closer. An occasion for Catholics to celebrate that prospect occurred at the end of 1889 with the observance of the hundredth anniversary of the establishment of the hierarchy in the United States. In an era that loved pomp and parades and long public speeches a centenary was not a milestone to be lightly passed over, especially for so self-conscious and so insecure a group, in many ways, as the American Catholics. The main burden for arranging the celebration inevitably fell upon Cardinal Gibbons, but he had no more reliable a helper than John Ireland. An added inducement for both of them was the coincidental opening of the Catholic University of America, of which they could legitimately claim to be two of the three founders.

The third founder of that institution—if one leaves aside the contribution of the precursor, Spalding of Peoria—had not been idle in its behalf. John J. Keane had begun the year 1889 in Rome negotiating with Propaganda the university's governing statutes and curriculum. He stayed again with O'Connell. "Here I am in your old room," he told Ireland, "Bp. McQuaid having the one I occupied last time. What an aroma of pleasant memories you have left in the room, and, for that matter, in all Rome!" And not unaware that his friend in St. Paul could always put up with a little extra flattery, he added: "Every one here smiles and looks happy when Bishop Ireland (as we naturally still call you) is spoken of. And the old city and its way-back-yonder officials, stand as much as ever in need of the good hard shaking up which you alone can give them."[20]

As usual the Roman process consumed a good deal of time, but the university, as Keane put it, "seems pretty safe." He had submitted the proposed statutes for review. "How I missed *your* name from the documents to Pope and Propaganda." His confidant on the scene was Archbishop Riordan of San Francisco,[21] a staunch supporter of the university, who was advising Keane on another major endeavor, the recruitment of faculty. Riordan argued against recruiting members of any religious orders. "I would prefer a corps of seculars," said Keane, "but will it do to exclude all Religious? Riordan says *yes*. What say you?" If a certain candidate did not meet Ireland's specifications, "Do me the favor to *telegraph* me your final advice— . . . just the word *choose* or *don't choose*." And concluding with a sample of the sort of exaggeration for which Ireland had a peculiar weakness, he wrote: "Congratulations on your *triumph*. The German question is killed here, and you are Dictator!"

By mid-April 1889, an "exhausted" Keane was at Louvain

University, in Belgium, and nearing the end of his European tour. The Roman phase of his mission, he reported to Ireland, "turned out to our entire satisfaction—though, as you might expect, after months of anxious effort and often deep discouragement and disgust." But all requests had been granted and statutes approved: "*This* required skillful management and will save us from endless trouble in the future." Keane had assured the officials at Propaganda that "we would never confer degrees for lower requirements than those of Rome, and that they could therefore safely give us the faculties [to grant degrees] in perpetuity. But I trust that our conditions for degrees will be far above those of Rome, as near to Germany and Louvain as possible."[22]

As for faculty, Keane had enlisted a half-dozen "first class" European scholars, among whom the most notable—for the tempest he would cause later on, if for no other reason—was a German moral theologian named Joseph Schroeder. But when Keane proposed a Roman candidate for the chair of canon law, O'Connell, giving vent to his budding Americanism, "opposed it bitterly, as bringing into our midst an enemy, a spy, a meddler of the most dangerous character—for such, he said, would *surely* be any man in Rome in *that* line of study especially." O'Connell urged instead the appointment of a priest of the Diocese of Newark named Sebastian Messmer, "a prodigy of industry and of learning, . . . and heartily an American." Keane acquiesced, and, since O'Connell proved no better a prophet than Keane himself, thus was added to the faculty of the university one who would be, in the future, a stern adversary of them both.

At home the university project proceeded so placidly that Ireland skipped the board meeting of November 1888, since he did not "perceive any special need that I be there."[23] Corrigan attended that meeting, however, and, to Gibbons's relief, "seemed to take an active interest in the discussions, and even participated in them."[24] Perhaps the archbishop of New York had heard the same Roman whispers Denis O'Connell had, that if Corrigan's signature did not appear on the documents prepared by the board at its November meeting, the pope would be "very much" offended.[25] Ireland at any rate took quite understandable satisfaction at this turn of events. "I trust you now pardon me," he told Gibbons, "for having when in

Rome with you insisted that you should not abandon the project."[26] But Corrigan's more outspoken ally, the bishop of Rochester, served notice that he, at least, continued in opposition. "Bp. McQuaid was a constant torture the whole time I was in Rome," the sensitive Keane complained. "He is *malignant* towards the University and all connected with it." He might have been more malignant still had he known that Ireland and O'Connell were exercising veto power over the selection of the university's faculty. It was not at any rate a soothing moment in McQuaid's life. He lost the legal wrangle that had brought him to Rome and had kept him there for eight tedious months, and, though the Holy Office did indeed condemn the works of Henry George, it stipulated that its decree need not be published. "What's the use of it, when you can't publish it," exclaimed the bishop of Rochester in disgust.[27]

But McQuaid's "puerile" antagonism, as Ireland termed it, could not cloud the archbishop's horizon: "Nothing now remains, but to prepare magnificent celebrations in Baltimore and Washington for November, 1889."[28] His personal participation was soon settled when Gibbons invited him to preach one of the featured sermons for the centenary on the life of Archbishop John Carroll,[29] or on the history of the church in the United States, or even on "our hopes and needs, or any appropriate subject."[30] "With your permission," Ireland replied, "I will in my discourse look rather toward the future than the past. Let my subject be something of this kind: 'Our hopes and duties.' "[31]

Ireland soon found himself directly involved in another phase of the preparations for the centenary. For some years leading Catholic laymen had been discussing the feasibility of organizing a lay congress in the United States as their co-religionists had been doing in Europe for a generation and more. In the late winter of 1889, William J. Onahan of Chicago, Ireland's old comrade from colonization days, and Henry F. Brownson, a lawyer from Detroit and the son of the great convert-journalist, Orestes Brownson, raised the question among themselves and like-minded friends. Given his earlier associations, it was natural for Onahan to contact Ireland and Spalding, among other bishops, and ask their advice.[32] Ireland liked the idea and agreed to broach it to Gibbons. "I have been asked to give my approval to a congress of Catholic laymen to be held in

Baltimore next November. Messers. Brownson and Onahan, the promoters of the project, have no doubt corresponded with you. I have been unwilling to say a word until I would have heard from you. . . . I am inclined to think that good would come from the project. Our centenary is, certainly, a capital occasion for the holding of the congress. Indeed, the congress would bring the centenary new éclat. . . . Please tell me briefly your views."[33]

The cardinal's views were, as so often the case, marked by caution and hesitancy, but, as he genially observed later, pressure had been exerted upon him from the "western part of the country. . . . And you know that the people of the west are not very easily suppressed."[34] Gibbons had alleged as his original objection a fear that not enough time would be available to prepare, to present, and to debate papers of substance, the delivery of which would be the main work of the proposed congress. The indifferent quality of the papers actually given in Baltimore in November 1889 tended to confirm the cardinal's premonition, if indeed he had had one. It is much more likely, however, that his reluctance stemmed from a danger that such a congress might give rise to controversy at home and displeasure in Rome if its participants were not rigidly controlled and if it presumed to deal with one especially hot issue which, at that moment, was acutely on the mind of the pope and his aides, that of the dealings between the Holy See and the Kingdom of Italy.

The relations between the two had been bad since 1870. In the summer of 1887, with the formation of a new, more radically anticlerical Italian ministry, they grew rapidly much worse. A prolonged crisis ensued, which lasted for the rest of the decade.[35] A symbolic high point in the tension was reached in June 1889 with the formal unveiling of a statue of the sixteenth- century heresiarch, Giordano Bruno, in the Campo dei Fiori, an event that unleashed a level of anti-papal activity in Rome scarcely experienced before.[36] By that time Gibbons and the other American archbishops, responding to overtures from the Vatican, had dispatched a long public letter of sympathy to Leo XIII, while declining privately to organize "spontaneous" demonstrations among their people to protest the Italian government's aggresssive policy.[37] Ireland fully endorsed this step. "The letter to the Holy Father . . . satisfies me," he wrote, "and I have signed it very willingly. Bp. Keane writes me [from Rome] that something more is expected of us than a mere letter. I certainly do not see what more we can do with safety to our own interests at home and in consistency with [the] political convictions of Americans."[38]

The matter was extremely sensitive, as a man with James Gibbons's finely tuned antennae realized better than most—certainly better than Ireland. On the one hand, the cardinal deplored the hostile actions of the Italian anti-clericals, and he sympathized from the heart, both personally and professionally, with the plight of Leo XIII. But, at the same time, he recognized, as did Ireland, how little enthusiasm existed among American Catholics for the temporal power, a political issue which, to most of them, was largely irrelevant. As far as any of them could see—and most of them, of course, never gave it a thought—the papacy had exercised its worldwide responsibilities with as much freedom after 1870 as before that date. And if the concept of *il Papa-Re*—the pope-king of Rome—aroused no sympathy in Catholics, to many non-Catholics, egged on by the propaganda of the American Protective Association, it had the same effect as a red flag waved in the face of a bull.

The issue was moreover not without ambiguity even within Vatican circles. Certainly there were members of the curia who held out for a full restoration of papal civil sovereignty as it had existed for a thousand years before 1870; they would hardly have been human had they not argued that the events of only two decades, an infinitesimal span of time when measured against the long and tumultuous history of the papacy, could be successfully reversed. But, as Keane told Ireland, this position was not necessarily in accord with the pope's own mind. Sbarretti assured him, Keane, that what Leo wanted was "*religious independence* (nothing said of the temporal power)." Monsignor Boeglin, editor of the *Moniteur de Rome,* confirmed that the pope had "no desire for such kingship as existed before 1870, but for independence, secured by an international administration of Rome." Keane himself remained unconvinced,[39] but no one knew for sure what the artful pontiff was really thinking.

When therefore the organizers of the lay congress met in Detroit early in June 1889, they determined to follow a prudential course and omit the subject of the independence of the Holy See from the proposed list of papers to be read.[40] The fine hand of John Ireland can be discerned at work behind this decision, not least because his suffragan, Bishop Marty, presided at the meeting. But less to the liking of the archbishop of St. Paul was the exclusion of temperance, another potentially controversial topic. A month later the laymen discovered that their original decisions would not be allowed to stand. Gibbons had learned from O'Connell that Rome very much approved of the idea of a congress, but insisted that it treat of the pope's independence and, incidentally, of the scandal of the Bruno monument. Gibbons instructed Ireland to enlist "without delay" the services of Thomas O'Gorman—whose scholarly hobby was the study of the history of the church—"to prepare a first class paper on the subject—strong and vigorous, calm and judicious, having in view the wishes of the Holy See and the temper of our own country, which should not be antagonized. Your Grace will be kind enough to supervise the paper."[41]

So when the organizing committee of the congress met again, this time in St. Louis, temperance and papal independence were added to the list at the advice, Onahan said, of Archbishop Ireland. Ireland also promised Gibbons that "Father O'Gorman will write the paper on the Independence of the Holy See and the Giordano monument, and I am sure his paper will be entirely satisfactory to you." Nor should the cardinal misconstrue any of Ireland's earlier correspondence to mean that he recommended a free hand to the laymen. Rather, "I intended to convey the idea that those gentlemen, who are foremost in organizing the Congress, could be controlled, and that the Congress would be so conducted as to suit you." Of the organizers, Brownson, "who is naturally cantankerous, has been objecting to certain decisions. . . . I have written to Bp. Foley [of Detroit], asking him to quiet Brownson, and I am certain he will succeed in the task."[42] Foley, Gibbons's former secretary, was of a mind with Ireland on keeping a firm rein on the laymen. It was he who had insisted that all papers be submitted beforehand to an episcopal oversight committee, so that, he said, "they might be classified and prepared for printing and for immediate distribution." "That was the reason I assigned [in public]," he told Gibbons, "but in my own mind was the idea that we should get hold of all the papers and have a committee of bishops to . . . pass upon the character of the papers."[43] Foley's notion of lay initiative was perfectly in accord with Ireland's: "Mr. Onahan," he informed the cardinal, "will write to you in the name of [his] committee asking you to appoint an episcopal commission, to which all papers etc. will be submitted. I thought it would be better to have the laymen ask for this commission than to have it apparently imposed upon them."[44]

But even with all the care they took to maintain episcopal control of the centenary celebration, Gibbons and Ireland did not find the sailing altogether smooth. McQuaid refused to attend. The aged and notoriously ill-tempered Archbishop Kenrick of St. Louis[45] refused also, on the grounds that the lay congress introduced a "mixed character" into the occasion. The Catholic press generally criticized the program of the congress, because no one had thought to include a paper on the Catholic press. The omission was duly corrected, but not before, as Ireland expressed it, "the opposition of some Catholic papers — foolish and groundless — [had] done some harm. The German Catholic papers," he added, "are nearly all against us. We must work, as our honor is at stake, and with work I am sure we will overcome all difficulties."[46]

Another point of honor, strongly felt by John Ireland, was the manner in which the Roman authorities were to participate in the centenary. He had two major concerns about which he belabored the ever-patient cardinal of Baltimore. Ireland had heard from O'Connell[47] that Corrigan had already invited Archbishop Jacobini. "Now whoever is to come should come on your invitation. This is a most important point. Mgr. Corrigan is not to be allowed to appear as the leader of the hierarchy." Secondly, "if 'Romans' come as your guests, and not as the immediate delegates of the Holy See, they will know their 'place' and keep it, and will not undertake to eclipse all America." Ireland was less concerned about who was to be invited, but he was not without an opinion: "For myself, in view of the fact that Jacobini already half expects to come, and inasmuch as it is an occasion to impress Propaganda with our importance, I would like to see Jacobini your guest, with Sbarretti as his secretary. Sbarretti has written to me his ardent wish to come."[48] In the end neither the secretary nor the minutante appeared at the centenary. Gibbons diplomatically invited the pope to send a representative without indicating any preference, and the pontiff chose a particular favorite of his own, the recently consecrated Archbishop Francesco Satolli.[49]

The cardinal of Baltimore proved himself, once again, the master of ecclesiastical revels. Thanks in great measure to Gibbons's careful preparations and his mastery in dealing with the various personalities involved, the celebration of the centennial of the founding of the American hierarchy was an unqualified success, earning plaudits both at home and abroad. A pontifical mass opened the festivities on the morning of Sunday, November 10; that evening, at half-past seven, Archbishop Heiss of Milwaukee celebrated vespers and — the coupling perhaps a sign of Gibbons's never-ending desire for harmony among his colleagues — John Ireland preached.[50] In substance the message he imparted was not new, and even some of the phraseology he employed strongly suggested the speech he had given at the Third Plenary Council five years before. Yet this time the tone was firmer, the manner more confident, the rhetoric somewhat more controlled.

"I bid you," he began, "turn to the future. The past our fathers wrought; the future will be wrought by us." To see that future, "no prophet's eye is needed. As we will it, so shall the story be. . . . The duty of the moment is to . . . do the full work that Heaven has allotted to us. . . . With us it will be done; without us it will not be done." Then he confronted head-on the charge that had already been leveled at him countless times and would haunt him to the end of his days: that he spurned the cultivation of supernatural for the sake of natural virtue. "Do not imagine that I am losing sight of the necessity of the divine. The lesson of faith is not forgotten: 'Unless the Lord build the house, they labor in vain who build it.' But it is no less the teaching of faith that in producing results the human blends with the divine, and the absence of the one renders the other sterile. Too often we refuse to do our part; we seem to wish that God would do all. God will not alter the rulings of His providence to make up for our inaction."

"As we will it, so shall the story be." This centenary sermon, probably the most frequently quoted of all Ireland's pulpit performances, gave expression, in its buoyant optimism about the capacities of the human spirit, to a long tradition that stretched back at least into the sixteenth century. This version of the triumph of the will represented to a spectacular degree a flowering of the tridentine and post-Reformation Roman Catholicism that had taken cultural root three hundred years earlier as an alternative to Protestantism.[51] Whether or not Ireland read history correctly matters little; here is how he read it: "The inevitable reaction from the teachings of the [Protestant] reformers, as to the total depravity of the fallen [human] race, quickened in man the spirit of self-assertion. Then came the wondrous feats and discoveries of the past hundred years to embolden the intellect, and nature at last proclaimed its self-sufficiency and its independence." Sectarian strife had worked its way to its final hour, and Ireland offered the erstwhile Protestant competitor neither honor nor hostility, but only a brusque dismissal: "As a religious system, Protestantism is in process of dissolution; it is without value as a doctrinal or a moral power, and it is no longer a foe with which we need reckon."

There was an irony at work here, because Ireland's major criticism of his own communion was what he perceived to be its timidity and its reluctance to venture into the struggles necessary to achieve a Christian victory. More than that, and worse than that, was the large element of fatalism or even fideism he discerned in contemporary Catholicism — as though Catholics, rather than Protestants, had rejected the value of works and relied upon salvation by faith alone. "There are countries," he said in Baltimore, "where faithful Catholics pray, administer, or receive sacraments, but fear to go further. I cannot name a country where they are fully alive to their opportunities and duties. . . . As Catholics too often are and too often do, failure in religion is inevitable." Ireland's was a fighting religion, and the battlefield imagery he habitually employed called to mind the quasi-military structure that that old soldier, Ignatius of Loyola, had put together for the original Society of Jesus. Yet the Jesuits of the nineteenth century, with only a few significant exceptions, stood foremost among Ireland's bêtes noires, because, in his judgment, they had exchanged their founder's vigor for a mess of the status quo, for that "conservatism which, wish[ing] to be ever safe, is dry-rot."

Ireland gloried in being a man of his time. "I love my age," he cried. "I love its aspirations and its resolves. I revel in its feats of valor, its industries, and its discoveries. . . . I seek no backward voyage across the sea of time; I will ever press forward. I believe that God intends the present to be better than the past, and the future to be better than the present." Yet — the irony thickens — he was also in many ways a throwback to the early, vital days of the Counter Reformation, to the age of the English martyrs, of Borromeo and Teresa of Avila, of the Jesuit missioners in Asia and North America, and especially to the Catholic culture of France in the seventeenth century, when Vincent de Paul ministered to the poor in the slums of Paris and Bossuet (Ireland's intellectual hero since his school days) thundered from the pulpit of the cathedral of Meaux. Not that Ireland recommended a mimicry of other times and places. "Seek out men," he pleaded. "Speak to them not in stilted phrase or seventeenth-century sermon style, but in burning words that go to their hearts, as well as to their minds, and in accents that are familiar to their ears." But the spirit of the age called for the same energy, the same confidence in one's self and in the efficacy of one's deeds that inspired the de Pauls and the Bossuets of an earlier day. "The Church is the same to-day as when she overthrew pagan Rome, or won to grace ferocious Northmen. . . . God's arm is not shortened. What, then, is wanting? Our own resolute will to put to profit God's graces and God's opportunities. . . . These are days of action, of warfare. It is not the age of the timid and fugitive virtue."

Of all the criticism John Ireland had to endure — and he doubtless merited his share of criticism — none was more unfair or farther from the mark than that he stood outside the genuine Catholic tradition which, after all, is a house of many mansions. The accusation raised most often against him by his co-religionists was that he sacrificed the supernatural order for the natural. But what he said in Baltimore in 1889, and in a host of other places over his career, did not differ in essence or even in nuance from the decrees of the Council of Trent. "We know that the Church is the sole owner of the truths and graces of salvation. Would we not that she pour upon the souls of friends and fellow-citizens the gifts of the Incarnate God? The touch of her sacred hand will strengthen and sublimate the rich heritage of nature's virtues, which is the portion of America and of America's children."

These were not platitudes to John Ireland. No locale appeared to fit his religious sentiments as well as America in the late nineteenth century, a perception his personal experience tended to confirm. Youthful, optimistic, confident, vigorous: here was the land of unbounded opportunity where everyone could succeed if only he had the will to do so. John Ireland preached, vulgarly at times, a get-up-and-go variety of religion to a society that avidly read the works of Horatio Alger. Moreover, "in America we have no princes, no hereditary classes." In America even an immigrant boy from County Kilkenny, with not a farthing in his pocket, could grow into a man who walked into the White House by the front door and sat down to confer with the president of the United States himself.[52] So, in Baltimore, he invoked his favorite double theme. "The Catholic Church will preserve as no human power, no human church can preserve, the liberties of the Republic." "We cannot but believe that a singular mission is assigned to America, glorious for itself and beneficent to the whole race, the mission of bringing about a new social and political order, based more than any other upon the common brotherhood of man, and more than any other securing to the multitude of the people social happiness and equality of rights."

It may be that Ireland habitually romanticized the American Gilded Age and chose to overlook its ugliness and venality. But in his enormously long centenary sermon he did not neglect to instruct his hearers to "seek out social evils, and lead in movements that tend to rectify them. Speak of vested rights, for this is necessary; but speak, too, of vested wrongs, and strive, by word and example, by the enactment and enforcement of good laws, to correct them. Glance mercifully into factories at etiolated youths and infancy. Pour fresh air into the crowded tenement quarters of the poor. Follow upon the streets the crowds of vagrant children."

He touched, of course, upon the need for temperance and upon the "danger" of "large accessions" of immigrants: "I will not intrude on their personal affections and tastes; but these, if foreign, shall not encrust themselves upon the Church. Americans have no longing for a Church with a foreign aspect." At these words Michael Heiss may well have stirred uneasily upon his throne in the cathedral sanctuary. And toward the end, down in the pews, William Onahan and Henry Brownson, so recently manipulated by the preacher in the organization of the lay congress, may have been startled to hear him say: "Let there be individual action. Layman need not wait for priest, nor priest for bishop, nor bishop for pope. The timid move in crowds, the brave in single file." But they understood shortly afterward when he added in true clericalist style: "What I have said applies to all—to priests, who, as leaders, must be the first to act, as well as to command; and, in great measure, to laymen. . . . Priests are officers, laymen are soldiers." Here was a basic truth for John Ireland, and here—in the thesis sentence of his sermon—was another: "In all truth, the greatest epoch of human history, if we except that which witnessed the coming of God upon earth, is upon us; and of this epoch our wisdom and our energy will make the Church supreme mistress."

The next morning, Monday, November 12, the lay congress got underway. There was another pontifical mass—this one celebrated by Corrigan—and another long sermon, before the delegates, about two thousand of them, repaired to the Concordia Opera House and began their formal sessions. Ireland offered the opening prayer, after which the usual organizational matters were attended to. Toward noon Gibbons appeared and delivered the kind of short and graceful speech Ireland had recommended.[53] The reading of the approved papers occupied the next day and a half; notable among the generally undistinguished presentations was that of the historian John Gilmary Shea, who overcame his initial reluctance and agreed finally to attend.[54] The cautiously pro-papal paper on "The Independence of the Holy See," apparently written by O'Gorman, was read by a prominent Baltimorean named Bonaparte, a grandnephew of the great Napoleon[55]; no one on the scene commented on how droll it was to have that subject expounded on by a member of that family. On Tuesday afternoon, just before the congress adjourned, Ireland congratulated the participants and confessed himself "overjoyed to listen to such magnificent discourses and such grand papers, and to have realized that there is among our Catholics in America so much talent, so much strong faith."[56]

Next day, under leaden skies and through a cold drizzle, the cavalcade of prelates moved from Baltimore to Washington for the formal opening of the Catholic University and the dedication of its single building, Caldwell Hall. The pope's representative, Archbishop Satolli, himself a professor at the Urban College of Propaganda, sang the mass. Afterward 250 special guests assembled for a festive banquet at which President Benjamin Harrison and his entourage were in attendance. The usual speeches in response to "toasts" were given — Satolli, for example, responded to "The Pope" and Secretary of State Blaine to "Our Country and Her President."

Archbishop Ryan of Philadelphia, a last-minute substitute for Gibbons, had for his subject, "The Hierarchy of the United States." Ryan, reputedly a wit, played a word-game with the mottoes or nicknames or even recent misadventures of some of his more prominent colleagues, leaving his audience the not too difficult task of guessing whom he had in mind. Each bishop was different, Ryan said. One possessed gentleness as a "Christian Heritage" and a constituent of "the Faith of Our Fathers," the titles of Gibbons's two books. Another was solid as a rock (*petra*), an allusion to Peter Kenrick of St. Louis. Still another was a brave soldier in the battles of the church who was in the end triumphant even when he had met his Waterloo. Here Ryan showed himself too clever by half: the reference was to the absent McQuaid who had recently lost a suit in Rome to one of his priests, the pastor at Waterloo, New York. The bishop of Rochester, when he learned of the joke at his expense, was not amused.[57]

Ryan also alluded to bishops who had to struggle for the church in pioneer settings and whose zeal had more force in it than "consecrated blizzards" or the consumption of "new wine" might stir up. Ireland no doubt chuckled with the rest of the company, since he must have known that some wag had dubbed him "the Consecrated Blizzard of the Northwest." The archbishop of Philadelphia's imagery may have been appropriate for the light patter of an after-dinner talk, but, for all its humorous and good-natured intent, it seems in retrospect strikingly unsuitable. Minnesota was indeed famous for its harsh winter storms, but another natural phenomenon, also unhappily common in the Upper Midwest, might have provided a better metaphor. The raging prairie fire that consumed all in its path, its heat and energy and volatility driving it ever forward, sometimes uncontrollable and unpredictable but always purgative of the ground it passed over — or that fire which, it has been said, purified the sons of Levi—surely would have suggested the warm and passionate temperament of John Ireland better than did the bitter cold of a Minnesota blizzard. And so did that stark assertion of the usually gentle Carpenter of Nazareth whom Ireland professed to serve: "I have come to cast fire upon the earth, and what would I but that it be kindled?"[58]

~ XIII ~

"We Are in War"

1890-91

D ENIS J. O'CONNELL spent nearly a year in the United States
between the autumn of 1889 and the late summer of 1890.
He attended the centennial celebrations in Baltimore and Washington and traveled to St. Paul to be present at the consecration of
Ireland's three new suffragans. Much of the rest of the time he
toured the country seeking funds for the support of the American
College in Rome. His absence from the Eternal City meant that
Ireland's ordinary source of information about Roman affairs was
cut off. O'Connell's secretary, a young priest of the Diocese of
Nashville named John P. Farrelly, remained on duty at the college,
and, though he was no substitute for his superior, he did send an
occasional gossipy letter. It was Farrelly, for instance, who told Ireland, early in the new year 1890, that Archbishop Jacobini, the
secretary of Propaganda, wanted a copy of Ireland's centenary sermon, which he intended to study in the course of the English lessons he was taking.[1]

Ireland gave no indication that he thought Jacobini's request was
in any way odd. He promptly sent off to Rome the souvenir volume
containing the text of his sermon as well as other documents connected with the centenary. By the time the book arrived, however,
any suspicions Ireland may have had were irrelevant, because
Jacobini, a diabetic, had fallen severely ill with pneumonia. "I shall
make the presentation [of the book] to Sbarretti today," Farrelly
wrote, and the minutante would pass it along to the archbishop
when the latter felt better.[2] But, Farrelly added, Jacobini was "not
in the highest favor" at the moment, and the rumor was that his illness might be used as a pretext to get rid of him from Propaganda.[3]

Among the other bits of gossip Farrelly shared, the archbishop of St. Paul took special notice of the doings of his colleague from New York. Corrigan had arrived in Rome at the end of January and had stayed less than a week. He had presented the Peter's Pence[4] to the pope in person and had taken the occasion to show the pontiff pictures of recent embellishments of St. Patrick's Cathedral as well as plans for a proposed seminary in Yonkers. Corrigan, Farrelly reported, "seemed listless and indifferent about his trip[;] didn't know what route, how long he would be gone. . . . He doesn't look very strong." Ireland no doubt was interested in the further news that the archbishop of New York planned to return to Rome in April for an extended stay.

The idea that Jacobini had ulterior motives for asking to see Ireland's sermon does not square with the secretary's ordinary demeanor toward the archbishop of St. Paul, which, on the whole, was friendly. But some reaction to the Baltimore speech, particularly that from England, suggested that it might not have won approval in certain Roman circles. J. E. C. Bodley, for example, a friend of Cardinal Manning and a prominent Catholic layman with Roman connections of his own, congratulated Ireland for the speech, which clearly suggested to him parallels between the American and English situations. Bodley especially liked Ireland's phrase "hot house debility," because, he said, it "precisely describes the mental condition of some of our best-born English Catholic families. . . . Unfortunately since Cardinal Manning's great age has prevented his visits to Rome, that small clique has obtained a momentary importance at the Vatican quite out of proportion to its real influence."[5] The old cardinal himself wrote somewhat later in a similar vein. He wished he could talk to Ireland "about your grand sermon at the Centenary. Either you and I are right, or we ought to be burnt." Each time a curial official journeys to "the new world, like Mgr. Satolli, he comes back repeating our words. Will he stand out in Rome?"[6]

The time was not far off when Satolli would "stand out" in places other than Rome. Meanwhile, the winter and spring of 1890 passed in relative serenity for John Ireland — a veritable lull before the storm. He remained at home for the most part, catching up on administrative tasks and attempting to fulfill some literary commit-

ments. Among the latter the most notable was the introduction he
agreed to write for Walter Elliott's official biography of Isaac
Hecker. Father Hecker, who had died in 1888, had possessed many
of the qualities John Ireland most admired. In particular the founder
of the Paulists was as devoted as the archbishop of St. Paul to the
double mission of converting America to Catholicism and, at the
same time, incorporating into Catholic life the best features of the
American ethos.

The preparation of Ireland's tribute to Hecker did not, however,
proceed altogether smoothly. Elliott, Hecker's confrere and intimate for many years, planned to publish his work first serially in
the Paulist organ, the *Catholic World.* The first chapter of the *Life*
duly appeared in the April 1890 issue of the *World,* with a demure
footnote stating that the manuscript of the introduction had arrived
"too late" for inclusion. The fact was that Elliott refused to publish
the introduction in the form in which he received it. "I have
snatched your article from the jaws of the press," he told Ireland
early in May, "and have done my best to set everything right." But
the language Ireland used about the traditional religious orders—
Hecker had first joined and then been expelled from the Redemptorists before he founded his own congregation—was too forceful.
Not that Ireland's and Hecker's views on the subject were different.
"I only mitigate the language," Elliott protested. "Bear in mind that
you do not stand alone in the responsibility for the words used; it
is in an Introduction to the Life of Father Hecker that the old orders
are arraigned for sterility, for rustiness of weapons, and for Chinese
[*sic*] methods." Everything Ireland said about the old orders—not
the new ones, like the Paulists, "subject to the immediate authority
of the Bishops"—Hecker would have agreed with, "but it was never
his *method* to say such things in public."[7]

The result, which appeared in the June issue of the *Catholic World,*
was a brief and relatively bland piece from Ireland's pen, not without, however, the sentiments by now familiar to any who had heard
him or read him before. He owed his personal debt to Hecker, "the
ornament, the flower of the American priesthood." He argued that
"each century calls for its type of Christian perfection. At one time
it was martyrdom; at another it was the humility of the cloister. Today we need the Christian gentleman and the Christian citizen. An

honest ballot and social decorum among Catholics will do more for God's glory and the salvation of souls than midnight flagellations and Compostellan pilgrimages." And he restrained himself enough to praise the Paulists without castigating the "Chinese methods" of the Redemptorists.[8] Elliott offered a word of consolation and of reassurance that Ireland's zest for battle need not be suppressed: "If your article were not an Introduction to the Life, I shouldn't touch a syllable of it, 'pon [my] honor. As it is, you are not made to say a word that will hinder your saying hereafter all you want to say — and may the Lord gather the remnants of your foes and give them decent burial."[9] A year later, when the *Life* appeared in book form, with Michael Corrigan's imprimatur, it aroused only moderate interest.[10]

While Ireland was writing his essay on Hecker, he was also undertaking a dramatic alteration in his domestic arrangements. After living for nearly thirty years with Bishop Grace in the cathedral presbytery, he purchased a large house about two miles away, at the corner of Portland and Chatsworth, in a fashionable residential district.[11] The move, which signaled the archbishop's growing involvement in activities outside his immediate jurisdiction, was prompted by the need to provide space for official entertaining and adequate quarters for a modest-sized staff and an ever-increasing number of important visitors. The change of residence was also probably related to Ireland's plans to build a new cathedral, plans that did not in fact materialize until much later.[12] The chancery, such as it was, remained in the basement of the presbytery, and Grace — who was ill much of the winter[13] — settled into full retirement at St. Thomas Seminary.

The archbishop's new house was a peaceful haven, far away from the noise and bustle of downtown St. Paul. But things never remained quiet in John Ireland's life for long. Rumbles of a new controversy were soon heard from nearby Wisconsin. On March 13, 1890, a statement signed by Archbishop Heiss of Milwaukee and his two suffragans, Kilian Flasch of LaCrosse and Frederick X. Katzer of Green Bay, was released to the press. The three bishops, purporting to speak for the 350,000 Catholics living in Wisconsin — and in effect aligning themselves with many Lutheran congregations that had already spoken out on the subject — raised a formal objection to a piece of legislation popularly called the Bennett Law, which had gone into the Wisconsin statute book the previous year. "After calm and careful study of the Bennett Law," the bishops wrote, "we hold that it interferes with the rights of the church and of parents. We, moreover, conscientiously believe that the real object of this law is not so much to secure a greater amount of instruction in and knowledge of the English language as rather to bring our parochial and private schools under the control of the state. And in this attempt, we cannot but apprehend the ultimate intention—gradually to destroy the parochial school system altogether."[14]

The Bennett Law had indeed mandated compulsory school attendance for children between the ages of eight and fourteen as well as classes to be taught in English. Its strong penal provisions—a law "fairly bristling with threats of prosecutions and fines," as the bishops put it—apparently aimed at hastening the process of the Americanization of immigrant groups by guaranteeing that the next generation of Germans or Poles would be fluent in the English language. It need hardly be said that John Ireland would have looked benignly upon legislation of that kind. But the Wisconsin bishops—all three of them German born—insisted that the Bennett Law was not only unjust and offensive to Catholics; it was also, they said, unnecessary, because in Wisconsin's three hundred or so Catholic schools, instruction in English more than satisfied the requirements of the Bennett Law. Moreover, they shifted the local argument to a different, more ideological ground: the right to educate lay, not with the state, but with parents who might, or might not, delegate that right to the state. If not, "all the state can demand of such parents for the common good, is that they do not allow their children to grow up in such ignorance or to acquire such knowledge as would make useless or dangerous citizens of their children."

This Wisconsin imbroglio was only the latest in a long series of sectarian disputes about American education, and indeed it was but one of several confrontations of a similar kind going on in various states at the same time.[15] Catholics had long considered themselves an embattled minority on this issue, systematically discriminated against, they charged, in tax-supported schools that, with their mandatory readings from the King James Version of the Bible and with the predominant part played in their administration by Protestant clergymen, were in fact centers of proselytization.[16] Thanks at least in part to these objections, and thanks also to the changing character of American Protestantism, the public schools by 1890 displayed a far less distinctly denominational bias than they had a generation earlier, but certainly most Americans would have agreed that the schools still cultivated, and ought to have cultivated, those civic values that were at once an American and a Protestant heritage.

For Catholics, however, with their claims to a monopoly upon the fullness of Christian revelation, this solution was no solution. There could be no genuine education without true—that is to say, without their—religion as an integral part of it. Nor, in their judgment, could a watered-down, lowest-common-denominator form of Protestantism in the classroom successfully resist what Catholics of all ideological stripes were beginning to fear as the real danger of the times, the materialism, formal unbelief, and "secularism" that had already ravaged large portions of traditionally Christian Europe.[17] So American Catholics, poor as they were, turned increasingly to building and maintaining schools of their own. On the eve of the Third Plenary Council of Baltimore there were twenty-five hundred of these institutions across the country, with an enrollment of half a million pupils. The fathers of the council, with little disagreement as to the substance of the matter, accelerated this process by forsaking the hortatory language of earlier legislation and commanding that every Catholic parish in the United States erect a school within two years.[18]

Yet the ideal of every Catholic child in a Catholic school remained beyond attainment. Even in the most prosperous dioceses less than half the potential clientele could be serviced in Catholic institutions. Had it not been for the self-sacrifice of the religious sisters, who staffed the Catholic schools for less than a pittance, the idea could not even have been contemplated. Even so, the Catholic populace groaned under what they called the unfair double burden of supporting their own schools and paying taxes for the schools of others. They argued, as John Ireland had argued when a young pastor in the 1860s, that tax monies should be expended to pay for the nonreligious instruction carried on in the parochial schools. The

more or less strident reply of the majority to this complaint was that
the public schools were available to every one and, if the Catholics
(and to a lesser extent the ethnic Lutherans) did not choose to attend
them, the state had no obligation to subsidize their eccentricities.
The argument very often descended to the level of name calling: we
will not send our children to godless schools, cried the minority;
anyone who impugns the integrity of the republic's greatest
boast—free, universal, compulsory public education—must be at
heart un-American or the victim of Roman priestcraft, retorted the
majority. Adding fuel to the flames were the bigots of the American
Protective Association, who predicted that if the hordes of popish
foreigners had their way, chalk and blackboard would ultimately
give way to the thumbscrew and the rack.[19]

A problem already complicated and potentially explosive was
greatly exacerbated by strains placed upon American society by the
continuation into the 1890s of massive immigration. And in this
connection, John Ireland, as he watched the controversy in Wisconsin unfold, found himself in a quandary. He could not but sym-
pathize with the intent of the Bennett Law to hasten the Americanization of immigrants by forcing them to accept English-language
training for their children. Nor did he quarrel with the state's right
to impose upon all schools, public and parochial, a minimum attendance requirement. At the same time he was as committed as any
other Catholic prelate to the decrees of Baltimore III, with their insistence upon the need for a rapid expansion of the parochial education system. As for the proposed religiously "neutral" classroom,
even the ever-optimistic Ireland professed dismay at "the devastating blast of unbelief" beating against the little red schoolhouse,
"scorning the salvation which is offered in the teachings and graces
of Christ Jesus, sneering at the Biblical page. . . . We [must not]
play into the hands of unbelievers and secularists. We have given
over to them the school, the nursery of thought. Are we not securing to them the mastery of the future?"[20] The secularized public
school, founded solely upon the cultivation of civic virtue, would
never satisfy even the most broad-minded American Catholics.

But Ireland was anxious to avoid the kind of theoretical discussion embarked upon by the bishops of Wisconsin. To argue that
parents by divine law possessed the right to ignore state require-

ments with regard to mandatory attendance or teacher certification appeared feckless to one with John Ireland's pragmatic temperament. And, as an administrator facing the enormous costs involved in supporting a separate system of schools, his day-to-day preoccupations confirmed the natural inclination to find some way of accommodating Catholic aspirations with cultural and political realities. Yet he kept a close eye on the situation in Wisconsin, where the bishops' manifesto had loosed a storm of controversy. The ink was scarcely dry on that document when another complication arose: Michael Heiss suddenly died, and Bishop Katzer of Green Bay, already in the forefront of the assault upon the Bennett Law, automatically became a leading candidate for the archbishopric of Milwaukee.[21]

This development filled Ireland with foreboding, for Katzer was, in Ireland's view, a much more belligerent and dangerous German obstructionist than the mild-mannered Heiss. He shared his alarm with Gibbons:

> The contest in Milwaukee is growing warm. You have, no doubt, received a letter from the English-speaking consultors. They have similarly addressed most of the archbishops. The bishops [suffragan to Milwaukee] have not yet sent me their list. If you have received it, please inform me by telegram, as I am leaving home Friday evening, and would like to have some information before I do go. I have written to the archbishops, asking them to delay writing to Rome until I will have the leisure to write to them in full. I incline to believe that the Wisconsin bishops will not notify me until very late in the proceedings with a view of preventing me from acting. The German consultors chose Bp. Katzer pro primo loco [in first place on their terna] — a man thoroughly German and thoroughly unfit to be an archbishop. This Milwaukee question is a most important one for the American Church, and I will rely on your enlightened cooperation in solving it.

Some weeks later he stated his goal explicitly to Denis O'Connell: "John Lancaster Spalding is the only man for Milwaukee. We may as well decide that at once and work up to it."[22]

For the time being the archbishop of St. Paul had to let "the contest in Milwaukee" follow its own course. But the nagging problem posed by the status of the parochial schools did not go away, and

Ireland remained determined to find a solution which was at once American and Catholic. With this goal in mind, and in the spirit of a good legal researcher, Ireland sought a precedent. He found one easily enough. Since 1873 St. Peter's parish in Poughkeepsie, New York, had maintained an agreement with the local school board whereby the board rented the parish school buildings for a nominal fee, operated in them every day a legally recognized public school, appointed and certified the teachers, and paid all ordinary expenses. Control of the facilities reverted to the parish after regular school hours, during which time religious instruction could be given.[23] This Poughkeepsie arrangement was only the most famous among many similar plans prevailing in various isolated places around the country, and not unlike what Ireland had proposed to the St. Paul school board more than twenty years before. In the early summer of 1890, while the controversy in Wisconsin waxed hotter—the Bennett Law was the work of a Republican administration, and the Democrats, in an election year, scented an issue in the widespread discontent with it[24]—John Ireland sent a private inquiry about the details of the system to the pastor of St. Peter's in Poughkeepsie, Father James Nilan.

Nilan belonged to a coterie of New York archdiocesan priests whose chief luminary was Edward McGlynn and whose outstanding characteristic was an unflagging and bitter animosity toward the policies and person of Michael Corrigan.[25] Indeed, Nilan's upstate assignment, far from the lights of the big city, was itself a species of exile imposed upon him by his archbishop. Ireland, though not unwilling to meddle in the still lively McGlynn affair both before and after this date, was careful not do so on this occasion, nor did Nilan attempt to draw him into it. He simply offered his "contribution towards an intelligent comprehension" of the workings of the school system he had inherited from his predecessor.[26]

The town in effect operated two schools in the parish, staffed by five Sisters of Charity and several "Catholic young ladies, mostly graduates of the high school." The nuns were "much respected" in the community, and one of them served as principal for both schools. "There is no Catholic on the Board. There is simply an understanding to employ Catholic teachers. It is hardly in conformity with law to make or expect a contract to this end." The board, Nilan added, was apolitical, balanced equally between Democrats and Republicans. All of Poughkeepsie formed one school district, "so that Catholic children may come [to St. Peter's] from every part." Nilan was convinced that the overwhelming majority of the Protestants in the community supported the program, and that a referendum on it, if held, would prove that contention. For evidence he enclosed for Ireland's perusal testimonials from three prominent citizens.[27]

Ireland could console himself that he did not stand alone among the Americanists in his hopes to resolve the school question in a manner that did not open a breach between Catholics and the larger American society. On May 10 Denis O'Connell, speaking at Gibbons's behest, expressed in a press interview his confidence that a mutually agreeable solution could be worked out.[28] And the previous summer, at the convention of the National Education Association (NEA) in Nashville, both Keane and Gibbons had read papers far more conciliatory in substance and in rhetoric than Bishop Katzer could have approved of.[29] Ireland had thought "the Nashville Teachers' convention a grand thing for the Church,"[30] and now, a year later, he was about to address the same gathering himself.

This occasion had provided his immediate purpose in requesting detailed information from Nilan. The annual teachers' convention was to meet in St. Paul that summer of 1890, and the archbishop had been invited to address it. Or rather, the local organizing committee had invited him to speak, only to have the president of the national association cancel the invitation. This executive intrusion may have seemed prudent to the president—a bureaucrat from Lawrence, Kansas, named James H. Canfield—and it testified at any rate to how intensely controversial the parochial school issue had become. But it caused only anger and consternation among the group in St. Paul charged with arranging for the comfort and well-being of the twenty thousand delegates scheduled to arrive from all over the country. Canfield was informed in no uncertain terms that John Ireland was the most popular public figure in the Twin Cities and probably in the state of Minnesota, and that an insult to him guaranteed a sour local welcome to the convention. Canfield hurried off to St. Paul to repair the damage he had done, and in person abjectly offered Ireland a second invitation, which the archbishop, with no show of irritation, accepted.[31]

The session of the convention at which Ireland delivered his address, "The State School and the Parish School—Is Union between Them Impossible?",[32] met in the People's Church on Thursday, July 10, 1890, at nine o'clock in the morning. He shared the platform with five professional educators, one of whom also read a prepared paper while the others made up a discussion panel.[33] He spoke for about twenty or twenty-five minutes—far more briefly than was his custom. The relative brevity served him well; the speech, while it displayed its share of rhetorical flourishes, was more tightly drawn and less repetitious than many of Ireland's other famous discourses. It also proved that he could speak effectively before a potentially hostile audience, and not just before docile congregations in a cathedral or adoring throngs at temperance rallies.

"I beg leave to make at once my profession of faith," he began. "I declare unbounded loyalty to the constitution of my country. I desire no favors; I claim no rights that are not in consonance with its letter and spirit." Then he moved quickly to reassure his listeners, but also to stake out the basic grounds of his argument: "I am a friend and an advocate of the state school. In the circumstances of the present time I uphold the parish school. I sincerely wish that the need for it did not exist. I would have all schools for the children of the people to be state schools." There could be no question, he went on, about the need for publicly sponsored education. "The child must have instruction, and in no mean degree, if the man is to earn for himself an honest competence, and acquit himself of the duties which, for its own life and prosperity, society exacts from its members." And such instruction must be gratuitous: "Free schools! Blest indeed is the nation whose vales and hillsides they adorn. . . . No tax is more legitimate than that which is levied in order to dispel mental darkness." The general welfare also demands, he said, that attendance at school be compulsory: "Instruction is so much needed by the citizen for his own sake and for that of society that the parent who neglects to provide for the education of the child sins against the child and against society, and should be punished by the State." Then, lifting his fist high above his head, John Ireland spoke the line more often quoted perhaps than any he uttered during his long life: "The free school of America! Withered be the hand raised in sign of its destruction!"

Why then, he asked rhetorically, the parish school? Why specifically have American Catholics placed 750,000 of their children outside the common school system? "The state school . . . as it is at present organized . . . tends to eliminate religion from the minds and hearts of the youth of the country." Nor should the problem be viewed merely as the grievance of a single religious communion. "I am Catholic, of course, to the tiniest fibre of my heart, unflinching and uncompromising in my faith." But "believe me, my Protestant fellow-citizens, I am absolutely sincere, when I declare that I speak for the weal of Protestantism as well as for that of Catholicism. . . . Let me be your ally in warding off from the country irreligion, the destroyer of Christian life and of Christian civilization. What we have to fear is the materialism that does not see beyond the universe a living personal God, and the agnosticism that reduces Him to an unknown perhaps." The state schools, Ireland charged, have been left in the hands of the secularists who, at best, reduce the great truths of Christianity to sentimentality and inculcate "vague and weak" moral standards "which passion is not slow to scorn."

> Secularists and unbelievers will demand their rights. I concede their rights. I will not impose upon them my religion, which is Christianity. But let them not impose upon me and my fellow-Christians their religion, which is secularism. Secularism is a religion of its [own] kind, and usually a very loud-spoken and intolerant religion. Non-sectarianism is not secularism, and, when non-sectarianism is intended, the secularist sect must not claim for itself the field which it refuses to others.

That distinction, he argued, must form the basis of a solution to the school question. Since the Christians in the United States were so adamantly divided among themselves, "a compromise becomes necessary. Is it not a thousand times better to make a compromise than to allow secularism to triumph and own the country?" In the name of "the spirit of American liberty and American institutions," Ireland offered two concrete alternatives as means of putting "an end to the constant murmurings and bitter recriminations with which our school war fills the land." One possibility, in imitation of the English model, was to "permeate the regular state school with the religion of the majority of the children of the land, be this religion as Protestant as Protestantism can be." A corollary would follow that the state "pay for the secular instruction given in denominational schools according to results; that is, every pupil passing the examination before state officials, and in full accordance with the state program, would secure to his school the cost of the tuition of a pupil in the state school."

In Ireland's judgment, this arrangement did not amount to "paying for religious instruction." Neither, he maintained, did his second suggestion. "I would do as Protestants and Catholics in Poughkeepsie and other places . . . have agreed to do, to the entire satisfaction of all citizens and the great advancement of educational interests." He then briefly reviewed the Poughkeepsie plan as Nilan had explained it to him. "Do not," he concluded, "tell me of difficulties of detail in the working out of either of my schemes. There are difficulties; but will not the result be ample compensation for the struggle to overcome them?" If other, better proposals were put forward, by all means let them be implemented instead. But until something be done, the basic challenge would remain: "Do the schools of America fear contact with religion? Catholics demand the Christian state school. In so doing, they prove themselves truest friends of the school and of the state."

The audience's reaction to Ireland's blunt speech was mixed. Strong rebuttal to it came almost immediately. Among the panelists scheduled to comment on the session's papers was Jesse B. Thayer, superintendent of education for the state of Wisconsin and therefore the officer in charge of enforcing the Bennett Law. He made it clear from the start that he was in no mood to compromise. His speech was a bitter attack upon the "sectarians" who questioned "that education which relates primarily to the rights, duties and needs of sovereignty of citizens" belonged exclusively to the state. "[Ireland's] paper," he said, "has complicated somewhat though it has revealed the practical inherent difficulties involved." When his time ran out, Thayer pleaded he was not "half-finished," and the chairman, President Canfield, smilingly allowed him to continue—a small measure of revenge perhaps for his recent embarrassment. Thayer plunged ahead, increasingly biting and sarcastic. Opposition to the Bennett

Law, he said, confirmed the suspicion that the "ultramontane jesuit-ical element of the Roman Catholics in America" was ready to defy the state. If so, Thayer hurled at them an unequivocal warning: "Unless the question that is now up for discussion is settled in har-mony with the principles of this government there will be conflict between the jesuitical hierarchy of the vatican, armed with the sylla-bus [of errors], and the American people."[34]

So John Ireland learned firsthand the kind of reaction to his school plan he could expect from at least one element of the non-Catholic community. The secular press around the country, though generally not so acerbic as Thayer, nevertheless emphasized that in the last analysis this Catholic archbishop was demanding tax sup-port for sectarian schools. What his co-religionists thought of it all took a bit more time to discover. His intimate friends and protégés quickly rallied to him: Bishop McGolrick of Duluth gave an inter-view to a Minneapolis newspaper in which he echoed the senti-ments of his chief. Catholic papers were mostly guarded in their comments, except of course the *Northwestern Chronicle,* which en-dorsed Ireland's position totally and printed his address on its front page. Nilan's predecessor in Poughkeepsie, the priest who had in-itiated the agreement with the school board there, wrote to con-gratulate him.[35] Only a day or two after his speech Ireland opened another letter from New York state, perhaps with some trepidation. But Bernard McQuaid, an exceedingly outspoken advocate of in-dependent parochial schools, made only oblique reference to educa-tion and did not mention Ireland's proposed "compromise" with the state, about which he may not yet have heard. After answering a routine inquiry about a priest's incardination, the bishop of Roches-ter wrote: "You will be always welcome to visit the little diocese of Rochester and see what we are trying to do in the educational line." And then, with that trenchant candor laced with wit that made it difficult even for his enemies to dislike him personally, McQuaid twitted his brother of St. Paul: "I have another institution in which I take considerable pride, but which cannot, of course, in-terest you. This is my vineyard and wine cellars." Since he hoped eventually to use profits from the sale of wine to pay for his semi-nary, and since meanwhile most of the wine was consumed in the celebration of the Eucharist, "I may hope for condonation of this piece of wickedness, even at your hands."[36]

So when Ireland traveled east, later in the month, he had yet to discover what degree of Catholic support, or opposition, his school plan might encounter. Meanwhile, he had another, though not un-related, objective in mind: to secure the appointment of John Lan-caster Spalding as archbishop of Milwaukee or at worst to prevent the appointment of Frederick Katzer. The place was Boston, the date July 23, 1890, and the occasion the first annual meeting of the American archbishops. The Third Plenary Council had constituted these twelve prelates a committee to review church policy toward the secret societies, and out of this experience had evolved the deci-sion for them to come together regularly in order to discuss matters of mutual concern and, when appropriate, to recommend joint ac-tion.[37] This body had no canonical status, but it promised to be a useful administrative structure and Propaganda did not object to it. The theory was that the metropolitans in their meetings could speak for their suffragans as well as for themselves, though Michael Cor-rigan and some bishops, notably McQuaid and Ireland's suffragan at St. Cloud, Zardetti, remained suspicious of the arrangement as lending itself too easily to domination by a clique or by a strong-willed individual.[38]

John Ireland—whom these bishops may have had in mind, as Corrigan certainly did—became the thirteenth member of this committee upon his promotion to archiepiscopal rank in 1888. And at Boston his junior standing did not inhibit him from strongly ad-vocating Spalding to fill the vacancy in Milwaukee. Gibbons, who as unofficial primate presided at the meeting, was Ireland's ally in this endeavor, and they persuaded a majority of their colleagues to reject the ternae received from Milwaukee and to draw up a new one, with Spalding in first place, Marty of Sioux Falls in second— surely Ireland's stalking-horse—and the German-born Bishop Richter of Grand Rapids in third.[39] The total elimination of Katzer rejoiced Ireland's heart, and neither he nor the other archbishops ap-pear to have realized that in submitting a list of their own, they had exceeded their rather informal and ill-defined authority.

Roman authorities, always sensitive to *their* authority, would testily inform the Americans of the fact in due course. But for the

moment Ireland's attention was brought back to the school question, because, when explicitly negative reaction to his NEA address
began to roll in, the tidings came from a very disturbing source. In
mid-August, O'Connell, finally back in Rome, warned Ireland that
"you have a little case yourself before the Prop[agan]da. Don't
laugh, a little case of doctrine, your last speech. It was sent from
America to the Congregation of the Council,[40] and thence to the
Propda." Sbarretti, who had been put to work translating the speech
into Italian for his superiors at Propaganda, "didn't seem to take the
matter very gravely," though O'Connell quoted another Roman in-
sider who thought Ireland a "lunatic" for having taken the line he
did at the NEA convention. More alarming than that was the demeanor of the cardinal prefect, who "spoke to me of it with a very
long face." O'Connell in his rejoinder stressed that Ireland never
proposed a policy without a firm grasp on the facts of the case, and
that his care in avoiding the inflammatory language indulged in by
many American clerics — who habitually described the public
schools as godless and as " 'hotbeds of vice' " — was one measure of
the archbishop of St. Paul's credibility on the issue.[41]

Two weeks later Simeoni told O'Connell "that protests continue
to come in against [Ireland's] last address. Some Bishop or Bishops
have submitted it" for censure. The rector, by his own account at
least, responded to the cardinal sharply, arguing that Ireland "understood better than many other Bps. in the country, that the burden of our parochial school[s] was crushing our pastors, that [male]
teachers could not be found for the boys, that our people were
growing tired of pressure and that our public schools were far better than the schools frequented by the children in Italy and France."
Later O'Connell asked Sbarretti "what this thing was going to
amount to." The minutante, who liked to describe Ireland as "amico
mio," replied: " 'I understand; but remain tranquil.' "[42]

Tranquility, however, eluded Denis O'Connell that summer,
and for a goodly time afterward. His frequent letters to Ireland revealed a troubled spirit, a growing bitterness, and even on occasion
a serious lack of balance. He took to writing long screeds in which
he did not so much dispense information and gossip, as he had used
to do, as complain endlessly about the stupid and malevolent men
with whom he had to deal. He repeated over and over his disgust

at everything Italian: "The public tone here is one of despair." He adopted the curious practice, when he recounted his conversations with curial officials, of enclosing his own words in quotation marks, as though punctuation would enhance their credibility; needless to say, these direct quotations always represented the rector as a model of candor and disinterested integrity. His favorite preachment was a furious denunciation of the canon law, "the embodiment, more or less complete, of the principles and traditions that brought down Europe to what it is!" He may have been right, of course, as anyone expressing an opinion may be right; but mere assertion did not make him so, and O'Connell, clever to be sure, was nevertheless too indolent and badly educated to contribute much beyond assertion to a speculative question of this kind. Perhaps he sensed a measure of inadequacy within himself, because much of his communication, at least to Ireland, now became so many pages of tedious self-justification, boastful descriptions of how he had set straight the duplicitous Simeoni, the venal Jacobini, the craven Sbarretti, the silly old pope. ("Poor old soul," O'Connell called him. "Active measures are in operation looking to the election of the next Pope. All other hope is gone, and a feeling of utter despair prevails.")[43]

Leo XIII was indeed a very old man in 1890, but he was destined to reign another thirteen years, and some of his more remarkable initiatives still lay ahead of him. For an agent *en scène* thus to have misread the single most important factor at work on his mission raises questions about his reliability as a source of information. And, in fact, the news O'Connell sent to Ireland during these months was more often wrong than right.[44] A rush of communiqués alternated with unexplained silences, leading one to wonder whether the "despair" to which O'Connell so frequently alluded lodged in his Roman surroundings or within himself. The rector constantly protested his loyalty to his friend in St. Paul: "You may rest assured that in everything appertaining to you I will show more attention than if it appertained to myself."[45] There is no reason to dispute the sincerity of this declaration and of the many others like it. But then O'Connell might out of moodiness or habitual carelessness leave Ireland in the dark for crucial weeks on end, and excuse himself for his silence, as he did once, by declaring his "unwillingness to bother you with the attacks [in Rome] on yourself."⁴⁶ One doubts that Ireland would have thought such intelligence a "bother." The rector seemed constitutionally incapable of assuming responsibility for these strange lapses. He indulged instead in elaborate evasions that invariably portrayed himself as hero or long-suffering friend.

An almost embarrassing instance occurred in the summer of 1890, when O'Connell returned to Europe with the assignment of helping recruit professors for Ireland's seminary. Among other vacancies the archbishop of St. Paul needed to fill was that left by Thomas O'Gorman, whose ideological credentials, if not his academic ones, had won him the chair in ecclesiastical history at the Catholic University in Washington. "I am afraid I made you suffer some pain of suspense concerning the professors," O'Connell wrote from Grottaferrata on August 30, "but I assure you it could have been nothing to the continued suspense and fear of defeat that everywhere faced me." He went on to recite an extraordinary litany of the troubles he had experienced from the time he landed at Le Havre at the end of June, forced to travel all over Belgium as well as to Paris, Lille, Munich, Cologne, and Switzerland.

> I was continually on the go, visiting, writing, writing, telegraphing, persuing [*sic*] phantoms and half-successes. . . . Thank God, I have finally succeeded, with a trial of patience and suspense with slow-moving people that you can form no idea of. I promised you to get you professors, and I determined to dare anything rather than fail. But I knew all the time how my silence made you suffer. But better that than make you share my pain of suspense and irritation. Anyhow, thank God, it is now all over, and you have *two first-class* young men, doctors of widespre[a]d reputation. . . . So now, dear Archbishop, I congratulate myself that I have succeeded at last.⁴⁷

O'Connell indulged in all this verbal subterfuge because he had been too lazy to write a letter earlier. But that was not the worst part of the story. Of the "two first-class young men" he had recruited, one shortly proved to be a spy, a veritable viper in Ireland's bosom. D. H. A. Minkenberg, a native of Luxembourg, had distinguished himself at the Urban College of Propaganda, so much so that Satolli called him "the best [student] he ever had." Once in St. Paul, however, Minkenberg busied himself less with teaching than with scribbling down every derogatory rumor he heard about Ireland. The result was a long denunciation sent to Propaganda within months of Minkenberg's arrival in the United States. Ireland, said the young priest, was an adamant foe of the temporal power, a trimmer in doctrinal matters, an advocate of the theory of evolution, and an enemy of all those—Germans, Jesuits, Archbishop Corrigan, and Bishop Zardetti of St. Cloud—who professed loyalty to the Holy See. The archbishop of St. Paul, he continued, was also lax in matters of discipline, an example of which laxity was the scandalously opulent life-style he encouraged among the professors of his seminary. The pope's recent statement on the social question Ireland dismissed as the work of a "foreigner," while the whole system of scholastic theology he described as "scarcely credible." As for the temperance crusade, it was nothing more, according to Minkenberg, than a hypocritical exercise that gave Ireland an excuse to mingle with Protestants.[48] Here was shabby recompense indeed for the professorship Minkenberg had received from Ireland's hand. But it was also a signal about Denis O'Connell's judgment. It would become clear to Ireland only much later that such a man, for all his warm heart and good intentions, could be a dangerous friend.

By early September O'Connell believed that the likelihood of a censure against Ireland's speech before the NEA had largely receded: "I think you are free from the Inquisition for some time more. . . . So let it blow over." Three weeks later he was even more certain: "Now, thank God, I think it is all over."[49] Gibbons had rushed to Ireland's defense in a strong letter to O'Connell: "Archbishop Ireland has been severely handled by some of the Catholic papers on account of his address on the school question. I hope it will not hurt him in Rome. He is really a power here and has more public influence than half a dozen of his neighbors. Such a man should not be under a cloud. . . . The representations against [him] were, doubtless, made by parties who are narrow and do not understand the country in which they live. . . . Had he been a dumb dog, no whelp would have barked at him here. . . . There is no prelate, in the United States, who has done more to elevate and advance the Catholic religion here than Archbishop Ireland."[50] O'Connell learned soon after that the "representations" had come not from predictable sources, like Corrigan or McQuaid, but from "some German[s] and some priests."[51]

Whatever the source, Ireland professed himself to Gibbons "exceedingly glad that my discourse on the school question was reported in Rome," because "it elicited from you such a deep interest in me. I thank you most cordially for the many evidences . . . of your valued friendship, and of your promptness to extend over me, at the first sign of danger, the shield of your powerful influence. I would be willing in the hope of similar rewards to see myself frequently torn to shreds in the Piazza d'Espagna [*sic*]." But besides his personal gratitude, the archbishop of St. Paul also expressed his growing impatience with what he perceived to be the caprice with which the church in America was governed.

> Somehow I had never felt much alarmed as to the outcome, not believing it possible that Propaganda could have taken such a rash step as to censure me. Yet, I do not, I suppose, realize what Rome is, or may do, and certainly, as you indicate, a whisper that Rome had taken adverse action on my words, would have done me immense harm. My enemies would have rejoiced, and utterances of mine in the future would be without power. But sad it is that right among us . . . are our own men, watching eagerly for occasions to slay us. Bishops are in fearful straits; their whole power is their influence; and word from Rome destroys this influence, and efforts will be made, whenever there is a chance to obtain that word. Our one hope is to be united, work together and hold by [one] another. It is well that we have another motive in our labors than to please men, whether these men be in America or in Rome.[52]

Throughout the autumn the rumors swirled back and forth about the status of Ireland's ideas on education and about the appointment to Milwaukee. One of the stories O'Connell heard — that the school question would be submitted for judgment to the committee of American archbishops — indicated that the two issues had become closely linked. The reported fortunes of the various candidates for Milwaukee shifted wildly. At first it was said that Spalding had no chance: "You know [the officials at Propaganda] don't trust Spalding. Sbarretti said he rec'd very few votes." Katzer remained out of the question, because he was too visibly the head of a faction.

"Marty, no, they do not want him." The lackluster Richter of Grand Rapids, third on the list sent by the archbishops in July, enjoyed the advantage of widespread if unenthusiastic support. Then Spalding's stock went up: though Simeoni was "down on him," Jacobini "wheeled around a little in [his] favor." Indeed, O'Connell said, if Ireland did not want Richter as his neighbor to the east, he, Ireland, would have to supply "the sinews of war. . . . Agitation in Milwaukee against Richter will help greatly. . . . It is simply Richter or Spalding. You might as well come out bravely[;] they can't hate you more[;] only a few more names [on letters of support from within the Milwaukee province], and you have Spalding."[53]

Ireland did write to Simeoni and told the prefect that Spalding's appointment would be received with "universal jubilation."[54] He also wrote privately to Jacobini, recommending O'Connell for a somewhat less significant vacancy, the bishopric of Omaha, and "enclosing at the same time a good donation for Mgr. Jacobini's societies."[55] But by then, mid-November, discussion of the school question was heating up within the curia again. One report had it that Ireland was to be summoned to Rome to defend himself. O'Connell went to the pope and showed him Gibbons's letter of the preceding September, and Leo replied that he would seek a formal statement from the cardinal of Baltimore. Ireland himself remained remarkably unperturbed. He spent some days in Washington at this time, interviewing President Harrison about one of his favorite projects, the provision of Catholic chaplains for the American armed forces.[56]

Just before Christmas the bombshell exploded: Frederick Katzer, the first name on the local ternae, was named archbishop of Milwaukee. Ireland's fury was almost boundless, but at Gibbons's urging he agreed to write a pro forma letter of congratulation, "a difficult task, one, certainly, I would not have done had you not made the request."[57] He could not resist, however, including in it his protest against Katzer's "Germainizing," particularly at the convention of the Deutsch-Amerikanischer Priester-Verein the preceding September. Katzer replied mildly. "Many thanks for your kind congratulations but also for your frank and brotherly letter. . . . But as regards the objections, which you mention in your letter, I beg leave to say that you judge me wrongly." Before September of 1890, Katzer declared, "I had *nothing whatsoever* to do with the Priester-Verein." He did attend the convention then, but as "scarcely more than a looker-on." He had always tried, he said, to be a Catholic bishop "in the full sense of the word. . . . I am glad you have been so frank, and I will always endeavor to deserve the fraternal affection of yours [*sic*] and the other Archbishops."[58] The likes of Katzer could always expect frankness from the archbishop of St. Paul, but "fraternal affection" was another matter. On this occasion, anyway, the major villain was not Katzer: "What is most galling in the whole affair," Ireland growled to Gibbons, "is the slight put upon the archbishops by Rome." Nor did Propaganda's retort, as O'Connell informed him of it, mollify him: " 'The archbishops have a right if they wish to send us their views on the candidates; they have no right to send another list.' "[59] But for the combative John Ireland one battle lost did not end the war: "The English-speaking priests and laymen demand an English-speaking bishop in Green Bay [to succeed Katzer]. If they succeed, the German 'Wisconsin Union' is broken."[60]

The papal secretary of state, Cardinal Rampolla, had meanwhile forwarded to Gibbons the pope's request for a statement on the school question. Gibbons in turn asked Ireland to prepare a kind of commentary on the speech before the NEA which the cardinal could use as a guideline for his own letter. Sometime during the fortnight before Christmas Ireland complied. The result was a long document, eloquent and for the most part measured, in which the archbishop of St. Paul carefully went over all the ground covered in the original address and took account of the criticisms that had since appeared. Among the critics was that old antagonist, Peter Abbelen of Milwaukee, who had "raised a dreadful clamor in Milwaukee papers, German and English." Indeed, most of the hostile reaction to the speech emanated from German sources: "Why, said one priest in a German paper, Abp. Ireland has lost his faith." Abbelen even advanced the argument that the gospel injunction "teach all nations" implied "teaching all that children have to learn — quod est absurdum [which is absurd]. . . . The church is not established to teach writing and ciphering, but to teach morals and faith; and she teaches writing and ciphering only when otherwise morals and faith could not be taught." But in the final analysis Ireland demanded, quite properly, that his text — which he was translating into French — be judged for what it said and not for what others said it said. "I cannot bring myself to believe that those in Rome, finding fault with me, could have had my whole discourse before their eyes; garbled extracts were sent to them, and from these their judgment is formed. My best defense is a perusal of the whole discourse. . . . If fault were to be found . . . let the precise point . . . be quietly pointed out to me, and I will give explanation, and if necessary quietly withdraw it." But he did not conclude without a threat: "A public condemnation from Rome of the address would set America in fury, as it would be a direct attack on principles which America will not give up."[61]

Along with this elaborate exegesis Ireland also sent Gibbons more prosaic information, including statistics about the state of Catholic education in the Archdiocese of St. Paul: "As a plain matter of fact, I have been so zealous in the matter of Catholic schools, that in not a few instances I have laid upon parishes rather unbearable burdens, in order to give them schools." But he could not forebear reiterating his warning: "Leaving self out — I may say that any re-proof from Rome for the 'address' — direct or indirect, would create in the minds of Americans in the West intense irritation against Rome. The reproof would be taken as a censure of my 'American-ism,' and as a proof of the hopeless foreignism of the Church. This, too, is what my German friends are hoping for. They hate America, and they hate me for being an American."[62]

In his letter to the pope, dated December 30, 1890, Gibbons refrained from shaking a metaphorical fist, but his support for Ire-land was as sturdy and unequivocal as the latter could possibly have wanted. If "the ardor of his temperament and the enthusiastic character of his mind" sometimes led Ireland to excessively strong speech, Gibbons maintained, the fact remained that "it would be a disaster for religion and the Church in the United States if the de-signs of Mgr. Ireland's enemies were crowned with success and if Rome by its action reduced to impotency its most energetic, faithful and devoted champion."[63] Ireland himself, aware of the "outlines" of Gibbons's letter before it was sent, professed himself delighted at "the predicament into which I have got. . . . I will seem a great man in the eyes of our Roman friends. The 'address' which brings out from your Eminence such an elaborate defence of me may well be called 'Felix Sermo.' "[64]

There the matter rested for the time being, except for hints from the pope that the combination of Gibbons's support and Ireland's willingness to modify, if need be, what he had said was satisfactory. But O'Connell still sensed an undercurrent of hostility, and at one point he urged Ireland to come to Rome to make his case in person.[65] And the rector continued to hear alarming rumors too, the most outrageous (and erroneous) of which was that Ireland and Katzer were to be called to Rome to debate their respective positions on education before the cardinals of Propaganda.[66] This bit of gossip drew from Ireland a retort rich in unintended irony: "Imagine the insult to myself and to the Republic, to be brought to argue with Katzer, a man who knows as little of America as a Huron."[67]

But O'Connell's tales of Roman intrigue plunged Ireland for a time into a rare mood of despondency. "I am amused but no longer rally to my old hopefulness," he confided wearily to Keane. "The rose color has for my eyes vanished from the horizon. The Church—humanly speaking—is stuck fast in old grooves; and he loses his time who strives to move her out. Bp. Spalding is about right: each one to his own shanty, and write poetry, or save his soul." And he added a curt word of censure to his friend: "I do not scold; I will do that no more. But your University has been captured by the Teutons, and Americans will shun it."[68] Later in the spring his depression deepened with the death of Bishop Gilmour of Cleveland, the forthright old Scot with whom Ireland had grown "intimate" in recent years. "We have buried poor dear Richard. How I gazed intently on his silent features, each trait of which bore the indelible mark of his noble soul." The night before the funeral Ireland slept in Gilmour's room and paged through the late bishop's scrapbooks—"the history of his fights and ideas and proposals"— and pondered how Gilmour, stoutly anti-German, had nevertheless made clerical appointments in the diocese, which virtually assured that a heavily German terna would go to Rome.[69]

Ennui, however, could not hold John Ireland in its grip for long, especially when a new crisis involving "the Teutons" erupted, or rather a new stage in an old one. Peter Paul Cahensly,[70] a distinguished fifty-two-year-old German Catholic layman and politician, had long taken an interest in the material and spiritual welfare of those who emigrated from his country to the New World. With a germanic flair for organization, he had been instrumental in founding the St. Raphaelsverein[71] the purpose of which was to provide succor to Catholic emigrants in the ports of embarkation, on shipboard, and, finally, at their places of destination. Nor did Cahensly restrict his concerns merely to his fellow countrymen: by 1890 branches of the St. Raphaelsverein were active in Italy, Belgium, and Austria-Hungary, as well as in Germany. A branch was also founded in New York, with the cooperation of Archbishop Corrigan. Cahensly himself visited the United States on several occasions and traveled there extensively, though he established few contacts outside German-immigrant circles; he cultivated Rupert Seidenbusch, for example, but he ignored John Ireland. Cahensly firmly held the opinion that huge numbers of Catholic immigrants had given up their faith, because, once settled in rough-hewn and egalitarian America, they had been set adrift from their linguistic and cultural moorings.[72]

On December 9, 1890, a small group of delegates representing the European St. Raphaelsverein met in Lucerne, Switzerland. Leading lights at this gathering were Cahensly and the Italian Marchese Giovanni Battista Volpe-Landi. On the second day of the conference Volpe-Landi presented a series of resolutions that suggested concrete steps to diminish the alleged leakage from the church among Catholics who had settled in the United States. The delegates accepted his proposals, and further deputed Volpe-Landi and Cahensly to present them formally to the Holy See. The resolutions were drawn up into a document signed ultimately by fifty-one persons from seven nations, including French, Swiss, and French-Canadian observers. Circulating the document took time, however, and not until April 1891 did Volpe-Landi and Cahensly arrive in Rome. By sheer coincidence Volpe-Landi was called away before a papal audience could be arranged, and so, on April 16, Cahensly went by himself to see Leo XIII. The pontiff received him kindly and diplomatically — Cahensly had many friends in Rome, especially at Propaganda, and he was an important member of the Center (Catholic) party in Germany—and promised to examine carefully the document Cahensly presented him.

The eight recommendations of the Lucerne Memorial, as it came to be called, echoed much of what Peter Abbelen had petitioned Rome for in 1886. There was a familiar call for national parishes, equal canonical rights for clergy serving such parishes, and preservation of the immigrants' linguistic heritage in parochial schools. But the most provocative recommendation by far was the seventh one.

> It seems very desirable that the Catholics of each nationality, wherever it is deemed possible, have in the episcopate of the country where they immigrate, several bishops who are of the same origin. It seems that in this way the organization of the Church would be perfect, for in the assemblies of the bishops, every immigrant race would be represented, and its interests and needs would be protected.[73]

The memorial became public knowledge the first week of May. On May 8 O'Connell's friend, Monsignor Eugène Boeglin, published the text in his *Moniteur de Rome,* and the same day the first of three Associated Press dispatches on the subject was released in Rome; the other two, from Brussels and Berlin respectively, were issued on May 27 and 28. These cables, which provided the American press with its reports of the memorial, were filled with innuendo and misstatement, including charges that Cahensly alone was responsible for the memorial, that he worked hand in glove with the German minister to the Vatican, that Katzer's appointment to Milwaukee reflected the influence of Berlin with the Vatican, that the active agent in the United States of this foreign conspiracy was that very association of German priests—the Priester-Verein—which had been John Ireland's bugaboo for several years.

In St. Paul Ireland granted an interview to the Associated Press, and on May 31 his words were read in newspapers all over the country:

> What is the most strange feature in this whole Lucerne movement is the impudence of the men undertaking to meddle under any pretext in the Catholic affairs of America. This is simply unpardonable and all American Catholics will treasure up the af-

front for future action. We acknowledge the Pope of Rome as our chieftain in spiritual matters and we are glad to receive directions from him, but men in Germany or Switzerland or Ireland must mind their own business and be still as to ours. Nor is this the most irritating fact in this movement. The inspiration of the work in Europe comes, the dispatch tells us, from a clique in America.[74]

But where did the dispatch come from? Ten days earlier Ireland had written O'Connell: "Well, God bless Boeglin and the Associated Press, and the friends associated with him in the writing of the dispatches. They are so cleverly put, and always hit the nail on the head. . . . They are creating a tremendous sensation, and affecting more than aught else could have done. . . . Of course to me the guiding hand is clear."[75] That guiding hand belonged to Denis O'Connell, who had seized upon the opportunity offered by the insensitivity and obtuseness of the St. Raphaelsverein to fabricate a crisis. Whether he actually wrote the dispatches or not, he surely arranged for their publication and he surely knew that much of what they contained was false. Ireland could not get enough of them. "Send more," he cabled in early June. "Send all. Miracles of good done."[76] "I exercise a modest direction," O'Connell replied in mock self-deprecation, and a few days later he explained how the end in this case justified his means: "I know [the shock produced by the dispatches] will shatter this [German] movement for at least ten years to come, but I was afraid it would excite public opinion too much. Anyhow, . . . I deemed a conflict of some kind inevitable, and a more favorable moment than the present I cannot imagine."[77] His moral standards did not trouble the archbishop of St. Paul. "The last message of the Associated Press . . . was a daisy. It has made a sensation." To Ireland, with his fondness for military metaphor, the old adage no doubt occurred: all's fair in love and war, and, he told O'Connell, "We are in war, and we must use all our powder."[78]

The effect produced within the United States by O'Connell's manipulation of the press was exactly what he and Ireland desired. The non-German bishops rose up as one to denounce foreign interference in American affairs. Even Corrigan, one of only a few bishops who knew Cahensly personally, chided the German statesman. Politicians and editors across the land applauded Ireland's interview of May 31. President Harrison discussed the matter with

Gibbons and expressed grave concern about the propriety of any intrusion of a foreign power upon an American institution. The average Catholic man and woman, to the extent that they paid attention to such broils, read in the newspapers, as Ireland hoped they would, of a conspiracy based in Berlin, and of the admirable determination of the archbishop of St. Paul and his friends to resist it. The Germans, for their part, were overwhelmed by embarrassment. The executive secretary of the Priester-Verein denied, truthfully, that his organization had had anything to do with the Lucerne Memorial, but, though confirmed by Cahensly, the denial had little effect. Poor Katzer, preparing his departure from Green Bay for Milwaukee, found himself a figure of international disrepute.

Then, as though they had not occasioned trouble enough already, Volpe-Landi and Cahensly submitted a second memorandum to the Vatican. This one came in response to an invitation from Rampolla, the cardinal secretary of state, who received it some time early in June. Its two authors—speaking, they insisted, for themselves only and not for the St. Raphaelsverein—asserted, on the flimsiest evidence, that "Catholicism in [the] great American republic up to the present has suffered a loss of sixteen million souls." They cited the by-now hackneyed reasons for this enormous loss, and, casually tossing gasoline upon the fire, added to them "the frequently exorbitant financial sacrifices . . . asked from the faithful" and "the public schools."[79]

By June 13 O'Connell had obtained a copy of this second memorial—"it is the whole cancer in a nutshell"—and had sent it to Ireland. "Considering the excited condition of public opinion and the provoking character of the second document of the Cahensly party," he wrote, "I deemed it wiser to have the paper first submitted to you, and not to permit the blind risk of a jump into the 'Herald.' "[80] Ireland in turn prepared the memorial for publication by the Associated Press, and appended to it a biting introduction "which, I think, was good." He toyed next with the idea of addressing the pope directly. But his largest objective at this juncture was to stir Gibbons into action. "I am still at work on the Cardinal to have him call a meeting of the archbishops, so as to send out a fierce protest. This I deem most important."[81] Off went the missives from St. Paul to Baltimore, bearing a tone more peremptory than ever before.

Is there no protest to be made by us as regards what has been so
aptly called the 'Lucerne Conspiracy'? . . . The American
Church has been deeply insulted. We look to you as our leader
to invite the archbishops to meet with you. The time picked for
our November meeting is too distant. By that date the whole
value will be lost to our protest. I know your delicacy of sentiment, which might tempt you not to act, lest jealous minds complain. I honor this delicacy. Yet, it must, at times, yield before
stern duty. . . . You will say I am hasty, and need to be re-
pressed. Not so this time, I think. We are American bishops; an
effort is made to dethrone us and to foreignize our country.[82]

As the summer wore on, and the dispatches from abroad and
editorials at home multiplied, Ireland hammered away at the same
theme. On July 2 he sent a copy of the second memorial to Baltimore.

Note the calumnies against the whole Church of America; note
the insults to the Republic, promising influence over her affairs to
foreign powers. . . . I ask—Have we no duty toward our
fellow-citizens in the way of assuring them officially and formally
that we are Americans? Are we satisfied to let base calumnies go
out to Rome against us, our priests and people without refuting
them? Ought we not take this opportunity to assert ourselves before Rome, and compel her to have in the future some regard for
us! . . . I will abide by your decision, cheerfully; but it is my
own decided conviction that you ought to call the archbps together. . . . At home we are surrounded by spies and traitors.
We should put them down, or at least frighten them.[83]

But this appeal fell on deaf ears. It did not jibe with the cardinal's
naturally cautious temperament nor with his responsibility, as he
saw it, to promote calm and harmony within the American church.
Joint action by the archbishops had not prevented Katzer's appointment to Milwaukee, and Gibbons was not about to try that tactic
again so soon, especially since the great see of Cleveland had fallen
vacant with Richard Gilmour's death in April, and Green Bay also
had to be filled. Besides, though he agreed in substance with his
fiery collaborators, he entertained a more reverential attitude toward Rome than they did. When he learned that the pope himself
would within a few weeks respond negatively to the Lucerne

Memorials, he decided to bide his time, avoid precipitate action, and let tempers cool. How much he knew about the dubious methods O'Connell and Ireland had employed to instigate the crisis remains obscure; Ireland had alluded to them at the end of May: "Mgr. O'Connell and Dr. Boeglin are serving us well. . . . You have noticed, no doubt, how shrewdly they send some dispatches from Berlin and Brussels?"[84] But at about the same time the cardinal received a categorical denial from the embattled Katzer—who, Ireland chortled, "is fearfully annoyed. Everyone in Wisconsin looks upon him as von Schlözer's prelate"[85]—that he had had any prior knowledge of "this deplorable Cahensly affair."[86]

So the archbishops' meeting was not rescheduled, and at the end of June Rampolla forwarded to Gibbons the pope's rejection of the Lucerne recommendations as "neither opportune nor necessary."[87] This decision apparently confirmed the prudent course the cardinal had adopted, and even President Harrison declared himself satisfied by the news. The furor gradually died down, and when Gibbons traveled to Milwaukee in mid-August to confer the pallium upon Katzer—the invitation to do so had been itself a gesture of reconciliation—he hoped to put a final quietus to the controversy. With wounds so deep, and mutual recriminations so widespread, that hope was in vain. But the sermon Gibbons preached, in that stronghold of German nationalism, was testimony that the "little man," famous for his prudence, was not without his share of intestinal fortitude as well.

> Woe to him, my brethren, who would destroy or impair [the] blessed harmony that reigns among us! . . . Brothers we are, whatever be our nationality, and brothers we shall remain. We will prove to our countrymen that the ties formed by grace and faith are stronger than flesh and blood. God and our country—this our watchword. Loyalty to God's Church and to our country—this our religious and political faith.[88]

Ireland, who of course was present in Milwaukee for the occasion, listened appreciatively to these forthright words. He even managed a grudging compliment to his and Gibbons's hosts: "I presume you have been edified and captivated with the culture and refined manners of the German priests and dignitaries of the West. It is but justice to say that they were at their best." But vigilance, he insisted, must not slacken, because the enemy still lurked, ever ready to pounce. The Diocese of La Crosse as well as Green Bay was vacant — the bishop of the former place had recently died — and it was imperative that the new appointees be English speaking. "If there is failure [in this regard]," Ireland said, "the fault will lie entirely with Abp. Katzer."[89]

Ireland and Katzer met again a little more than a month later, this time on neutral ground, in Dubuque, whose bishop was celebrating the silver jubilee of his consecration. On this occasion Katzer learned firsthand, as did many of his episcopal colleagues also in attendance, how strong and even frenzied a following Ireland had created. Religious ceremonies occupied the morning of September 30, 1891, and in the mid-afternoon the clergy in attendance, about 250 strong, assembled for a festive dinner. There followed the inevitable round of speeches, and Ireland, when his turn came, responded to the toast, "Our Church and Our Country," which performance provoked a tumultuous scene.

> The speech of Archbishop Ireland aroused his auditors to the highest pitch of enthusiasm. Joined with a peculiar intensity of voice and manner, the burning words of the great Bishop of St. Paul went home to every heart, and made each aglow with love of Church and Country, patriotism and virtue. The hall resounded again and again with cheers and applause at the end of each rounded period. When the Archbishop sat down a perfect storm of cheering rent the air, amid which a young Priest jumped on a chair and screamed at the top of his voice: "God bless the mother that bore you and the breast that gave you suck."[90]

The reaction of the archbishop of Milwaukee was not recorded.

"Tolerari Potest"

1891–92

Pope Leo XIII had intervened personally in the Cahensly crisis of 1891 and had decided that the recommendations of the Lucerne Memorials were "neither opportune nor necessary." It was a minimalist decision, so to speak, because it addressed only the concrete proposals advanced by Cahensly and his colleagues without attempting to deal with the ideological basis of those proposals. It was also standard administrative procedure. An able ruler, however absolute his power in theory, seldom contradicts his subordinates or upsets the governmental machinery in place for the sake of an abstract principle. The application of legal precedent or plain expediency to the particular case at hand commits an administrator far less than does a sweeping speculative endorsement, which always involves the risk of prying open the lid of Pandora's box. Pope Leo, an able ruler indeed, abided by the maxim that it is far preferable to say too little than too much. He did not challenge Cahensly's assumptions or rebut his arguments; he merely declared authoritatively that the solutions Cahensly suggested were impractical. It is therefore legitimate to wonder whether the pope ever really grasped why the Americanists were so hurt and angry at the charges of the Cahensly party and why two of them at least—Ireland and O'Connell—felt justified in combating those charges by dishonorable means. The victory of the Americanists over Cahensly was therefore a qualified one, because it stemmed from administrative convenience rather than from a commonly held principle. Note the last sentence of the seventh recommendation of the first Lucerne Memorial: "The organization of the Church [in the United States] would be perfect [if nationalist quotas determined the selection of bishops], for in the assemblies of the bishops, every immigrant race would be represented, and its interests and needs would be protected." At first glance this proposal might have appeared unexceptionable, and especially so when brought forward by persons as reputable as the members of the St. Raphaelsverein: every group of immigrants deserved its own episcopal guardian who would oversee its spiritual well-being and defend its cultural and linguistic heritage. And Roman officialdom saw nothing theoretically amiss in such a proposition. As one curial cardinal put it in O'Connell's hearing: "When these men come to us and request us to look after the interests of their *Connazionali* that they say are losing their faith in America, we are bound to hear them."[1]

But the cardinal's very use of the Italian word meaning "fellow countrymen" revealed an assumption as crass as it was presumptuous: the United States, the memorial was saying, was no more than a collection of displaced Europeans, discrete colonies of Germans and Poles and Italians, with no national character of its own. Furthermore, there could be nothing peculiarly American about the church in America, because America itself was nothing more than a locale—unhappily overflowing with heretics and Masons—where Catholic settlers went when circumstances forced them to go. Naturally such people preferred to maintain the customs and language of the country of their origin. And naturally "the organization of the Church in the United States would be perfect" when it reflected this aspiration.

The arrogance of Cahensly and his friends was compounded by their failure even to pretend that the opinion of Americans on this subject might be relevant. That they did not poll the American bishops or at least the German members of the hierarchy was muddle-headed, if possibly understandable from a tactical point of view. But not even the one chapter of the St. Raphaelsverein located in the United States was invited to send delegates to Lucerne. The memorial was drawn up in Europe by Europeans and then submitted for approval to other Europeans at the Roman curia. American Catholics, it seemed, were children, incapable of sensibly arranging their own affairs. So proud and patriotic a man as John Ireland found this implication intolerable.

And the larger question, at least for ecclesiastics, remained open.

The pope had indeed turned aside the pretensions of Cahensly. But did he, in so doing, admit the *distinctive character* of the American people and the *maturity* of the American church? The very fact that Catholics in the United States remained under the immediate jurisdiction of Propaganda suggested a negative answer. Propaganda, after all, was concerned with mission lands, with Siam and the Solomon Islands and other such exotic places. Did the pope put the great republic of the west into such a category? If he did, then he must think that the United States of America was still occupied, as Ireland might have put it, by wandering bands of Hurons. So the debate perforce continued, and the issue of it depended ultimately upon the judgment of one man.

Pope Leo XIII, born Gioacchino Pecci, was descended from the petty nobility of the old States of the Church. He had worked as a young man on the civil side of the papal bureaucracy, looking after such duties as criminal law enforcement, road building, and tax collection while he served as governor of the enclave of Benevento and later of Perugia. In 1843, when he was thirty-three, he was assigned nuncio to Belgium, and three years after that bishop of Perugia.[2] There, far up the waters of the Tiber from the ecclesiastical hub in Rome, he languished for thirty-two years — if one can be said to languish amid the rolling hills and purple landscapes of Umbria. But in 1878, when the conclave met to elect a successor to Pius IX, Pecci's long exile from the curia proved an inestimable advantage to him, because, unidentified with the preceding regime, he remained unencumbered by its specific policies. The disasters of Pius IX's pontificate could not be laid at Pecci's door.[3] So the cardinal-electors, as they have so often in the history of the papacy, turned to a candidate strikingly different from the incumbent who had just died.

One must not, however, read too much into their decision. Papal continuity was (and is) a lodestar for whoever sat upon the throne of St. Peter, and though a pope might quietly set aside this or that initiative undertaken by a predecessor, he never explicitly repudiated it. But style was something else, as were personality, emphasis, and method. In these respects the papal election of 1878 produced startling contrasts. Gone was Pius IX, a florid, warm-hearted man, ruled often by his emotions and his simple piety, handsome and eloquent and stubborn, who confronted the challenges of modernity with blunt incomprehension. In his place was Leo XIII, a scholar of sorts, an accomplished writer of Italian and Latin prose, above all a diplomat who prided himself on possessing the diplomat's gift for patient negotiation, as stern an opponent as his predecessor of the modern liberal temper but better equipped to discern its nuances and readier to accommodate its slogans and lesser shibboleths. Even in physical appearance and manner the two were markedly different. Leo was a tiny man, increasingly wizened as the years took their toll, with a large head and a hooked nose and puffs of white hair over protruding ears. Though he was invariably courteous and attentive in private conversation, he disliked crowds, and his status as the remote "prisoner of the Vatican" suited him temperamentally far better than it had Pius IX who, august *Papa-Re* of Rome as he may have been, had nevertheless always possessed a genuinely populist flair.[4]

The genial Pius had seen Mazzini lurking behind every liberal statesman. The thoughtful, reserved Leo was far too intelligent to commit that mistake. He presided over a more efficient administration, too, and, though like all modern autocrats since the time of Elizabeth I, he routinely played off one subordinate against another, he never let slip from his hands, as Pius often had, the reins of ultimate decision making. No disreputable Antonelli haunted Leo XIII's retinue; his secretary of state (from 1887) was the relatively young Mariano Rampolla del Tindaro, scion of a wealthy and noble Sicilian family, a stocky, beetle-browed man of ferocious work habits and generous impulses, who understood the intentions of his master as though they were his own.[5] The atmosphere of the Leonine Vatican was less truculent, more subtle than it had been before. Typical of it were the encyclicals[6] Leo XIII issued, artistic compositions and instruments of teaching rather than the outraged denunciations that had been Pius IX's stock in trade.

Yet it had been Pecci of Perugia who had first proposed a compilation of nineteenth-century political, social, and intellectual aberrations, which eventually evolved into the Syllabus of Errors (1864) with its defiance of "modern civilization."[7] Nor should it be supposed that Leo was less interested than Pius had been in furthering the process of Roman centralization within the Catholic church; he too moved firmly against particularist tendencies wherever he found them, and anyone who hoped for office or honor from him had better be prepared to demonstrate wholehearted loyalty to the Holy See. And, in the directly political sphere, if Pius IX had lost the temporal power, Leo XIII was determined to get it back—not the old sovereignty from Gaeta to Bologna—he was too much a realist to expect that—but something, some small part of it, *la città* itself perhaps, some international guarantee of his independent monarchical status at the very least.[8] He could put no divisions into the field to achieve this reversal of events, but he had the tools of diplomacy and the weight of hundreds of millions of religious adherents around the world who looked upon him as their spiritual father.

Leo XIII was a sophisticated man, genuinely cosmopolitan when compared to his immediate predecessors, but the grooves of his mind rendered it difficult for him to see anything outside a European context. What was true of him was true also of the less talented men who worked for him. This was not a surprising circumstance; the nineteenth, after all, was the century of Europe, the temporal culmination of a long process whereby the littlest continent imposed its hegemony upon the rest of the world culturally, economically, and politically. That many of its achievements appeared antipathetic to Catholicism tended to heighten rather than diminish the pope's Europeanist preoccupations. Leo XIII might not have maintained, as Belloc did later, that the Catholic faith was Europe and Europe was the faith. But to understand the United States as meaning something more than an extension of Europe was probably beyond him. It is significant in the history of John Ireland's professional and personal life that only years later, when "Americanism" came dressed in French clothing, did the pope think it worthy of censure.[9]

Perhaps the single most difficult American institution for this supple diplomat to appreciate was the absolute separation of church and state. "A free church in a free state" sounded an alarm in papal ears, because it had been a slogan employed by European anticlericals to justify acts of spoliation and sometimes persecution.[10] But, more to the point here, Leo XIII, with his exclusively European orientation, had little experience with a government that on principle refrained from interfering in ecclesiastical affairs. Indeed, the pope thought habitually in terms of relations between sovereigns, and he was sincerely puzzled when told that he could not treat with the president of the United States as he did with the mikado of Japan.[11] Denis O'Connell believed that this explained why the Vatican treated the American hierarchy so lightly. In the midst of the fuss over Cahenslyism the rector recounted for Ireland an interview he had had with Rampolla: "When I spoke . . . of the indignation the Amer. Bps. would feel, if the Cahensly plan were approved, it made no impression on him. They were Irish, they were interested and their opposition and indignation were only a matter of course. But when I said that the American government would settle the matter for itself without Cahensly, the Cardinal changed his manner. It was an idea they never contemplated, and I said a Culturkamp [sic] was as possible in America as in Germany."[12] Ireland felt the same as his friend, and was perfectly prepared to use his connections in the Republican party to exert political pressure upon the Vatican. "Americans are most angry—and I am sure that in the next congress Cahensly will get an airing. If I were not afraid to injure Blaine's presidential campaign, I would secure at once from him an expression." He did enlist, closer to home, another politician, Senator Cushman Davis of Minnesota, who promised to raise the issue of foreignism on the floor of the United States Senate.[13]

If the pope and his advisers preferred to negotiate with the secular rather than the clerical estate, Ireland appeared ready to dare them to do so. Meanwhile, he moved forward to get them to accommodate themselves to another prized American institution, the public school. Long before Senator Davis fired his verbal shots at Cahenslyism, the Roman officials were mulling over the events in two suddenly prominent little towns in Minnesota of which they had never heard before.[14]

FARIBAULT, about fifty miles south of Minneapolis and St. Paul, lies in the midst of a fertile agricultural district. In 1890 its population stood at sixty-five hundred, reflecting a rich ethnic and religious mix. Approximately one-third of the town's inhabitants were

Catholic. The first parish, that of the Immaculate Conception, had been formed in 1858 and for some years after that had been the sole place for Catholic worship in Rice County. More recently, however, two national parishes had been established in the town, one to serve the Germans and another the French. These departures had naturally meant a smaller congregation at the mother-territorial parish and a narrower financial base. Indeed, by the summer of 1891 Immaculate Conception was desperately short of money, a situation that had been chronic since the pastorate of the free-spending Thomas O'Gorman (1882–85). The parish maintained a grammar school with about 150 pupils staffed by Dominican sisters, who also operated a boarding high school for girls.

Stillwater, a picturesque river town, is located on the other side of the Twin Cities, a little more than twenty miles northeast of St. Paul on the St. Croix River. Twice as populous as Faribault, it too supported a territorial parish, St. Michael's, as well as separate parishes for French- and German-speaking Catholics. Its economy, almost exclusively based upon logging and the timber industry, tended to give Stillwater's local politics an oligarchic flavor, with much local power wielded by the owners of the sawmills. The Catholics, though numerous, were by and large poorer and less influential than their co-religionists in Faribault.

On August 22, 1891, the Faribault school board held its regularly scheduled meeting. In attendance was James J. Conry, pastor of Immaculate Conception parish. Father Conry informed the board that due to financial difficulties his parochial school would not open for the fall term. This news was received with some consternation by most members of the board, since upon them would fall the obligation of providing within two weeks staff and facilities for an additional 150 to 200 pupils. One of them, however, a Catholic lawyer named M. H. Keeley, was not surprised, because he and Conry, under the unpublicized direction of John Ireland, were about to propose bringing Poughkeepsie to Minnesota.

Conry went on to say that if thrusting a large number of children into the public system would work a hardship on the community, he was willing to entertain the idea of placing his school "under the control of the city board of education," so long as its "integrity" was preserved. When asked to explain this rather obscure proposition, Conry offered to rent the Immaculate Conception school for a nominal fee to the board, to provide faculty for it, and to guarantee that no religious instruction would take place in it during mandated school hours. The encounter apparently was cordial. The board met again on August 26, and the debate raged hotly for several hours, after which by a vote of three to two Conry's proposal was tentatively accepted and the priest was asked to submit a statement in writing. This he did, in a letter filled with patriotic sentiments and fixing the yearly rental at one dollar, and when the board met for a third time the next day, the vote to accept the arrangement was unanimous.[15]

The archbishop of St. Paul was not mentioned in the course of these negotiations, nor was allusion made to his speech delivered the summer before to the National Education Association. Ireland's directive role was played entirely from behind the scenes. To shun publicity did not accord with his ordinary mode of action, but it was in character for him to give practical implementation, if he could, to an idea he approved of. The Poughkeepsie plan worked in New York, and so it should work in Minnesota as well. Though he later found fault with Conry's handling of the affair — "the priest at Faribault bungled things somewhat and in his desire to avert Protestant bigotry used some expressions which Catholics can well criticize"[16] — the experiment in Faribault began promisingly and with widespread support in the community. That Ireland intended it as the first step in a larger program seems clear from a remark made to him by Keeley: "[The board's vote was] a great victory for us, and if we are discreet and judicious in its enjoyment, it may go far towards working out satisfactorily to all citizens the problem of the education of the masses at public expense."[17]

Careful planning had led to an initial success in Faribault. The situation in Stillwater developed very differently. On August 25, three days after Conry had made his original proposal to the Faribault board, the lay trustees of St. Michael's parish[18] met with Archbishop Ireland at the latter's residence in St. Paul. The state of St. Michael's was parlous in the extreme, particularly since the pastor, a priest named M. E. Murphy, had departed without explanation the previous spring.[19] Ireland promised the trustees to replace Murphy — though to avoid scandal he insisted publicly that Murphy was merely on leave of absence—and on August 28 Father Charles Corcoran took up his new duties in Stillwater. Corcoran, ordained two years earlier after theological studies at the University of Louvain, was a highly gifted young man, but it took no great intellect to grasp how straitened were the finances of St. Michael's.

Sometime in the middle of September Corcoran sought Ireland's permission to propose the Faribault plan to the Stillwater school board. Because of an epidemic of diphtheria the opening of the fall term had been put off there till October 5. Thus, when Corcoran, with Ireland's consent, made his presentation, the members of the board were confronted with a situation not dissimilar to that which had prevailed in Faribault. The public schools, due to open in a few weeks, faced the prospect of needing to provide staff, space, and facilities for upwards of 350 more pupils. A local newspaper estimated that to refuse Corcoran's offer would mean an immediate outlay of fifteen thousand dollars of public funds, to say nothing of a substantial and permanent addition to the educational budget for ordinary expenses. Besides, if the Catholic children were absorbed into Stillwater's common schools, the town would receive a proportionate increase of support from the state of Minnesota. These fiscal realities proved decisive to the board, which, on October 13, voted unanimously to approve the plan.

Before that, however, Ireland was urging Corcoran "to be very careful in wording any document you may place before the board. Mistakes have elsewhere been made, that are injuring us, and that must not be repeated. I would wish to revise, or to see, any draft you may be preparing. We must say nothing that might alarm either Catholics or Protestants. The gist of the whole matter is that you lease the building 'during school hours.'"[20] The "mistakes" to which Ireland referred were undoubtedly those of Conry and Keeley, who in their enthusiasm had neglected to specify that the Faribault board would control Immaculate Conception only during regular school hours.[21] Conry's ebullience moreover had led him so to praise "the benefits that result from American training" that he appeared to imply that parochial schools did not offer "American training."[22] Despite these lapses—or perhaps because of them—the euphoria over the school arrangement continued in Faribault through the autumn and into the winter.

Not so in Stillwater. There opposition from non-Catholic groups was in evidence almost from the beginning. The local ministerial association demanded that the contract between St. Michael's and the city be abrogated. In early November two of the three school board members standing for reelection were defeated, and the third survived at the polls only by announcing his willingness to terminate the agreement. The opposition spread and intensified quickly. Various Protestant groups in Minnesota and elsewhere adopted resolutions condemning the Faribault-Stillwater plan as a "subtle encroachment of the Roman Catholic Church on the integrity of our public schools." They pointed to the religious symbols—crucifixes, statues, and the like—that decorated the parochial school classrooms, to the religious garb of the nuns who taught there, and to the sectarian instruction that went on in them every day. Ireland was prepared to meet one of these objections. "Adhere to your plan," he directed Corcoran, "to have no prayers in school hours, and take down *all* religious pictures. Pictures are in no manner necessary, and let us do without them. Please act on this at once."[23] Compromise on the other two objections, however, remained beyond his reach.

For the archbishop of St. Paul had to heed the danger of a cross fire. "I have found myself," he told Gibbons, "in a singular predicament on this whole Faribault matter. I am between two enemies—one Catholic, and one Protestant. I placate one, I arouse the other. The concessions to our school, and its continued identity as a Catholic school, are so important that I dare not fully state them—lest I bring down the wrath of anti-Catholic bigots. If I defend the plan against Protestants, Catholic extremists are alarmed. I am, then, condemned to be silent." And he did indeed for the most part hold his tongue and console himself with an optimism that proved to be quite ill-founded: "With a little prudence, we will in a brief time have the whole school question settled in Minnesota. Public opinion favors us."[24]

Ireland always looked on the bright side. In this instance his sanguine hopes rested upon the personal relationships he imagined he had with the principals involved. "The Members of the School Board[s] in [Faribault and Stillwater] are personal friends of mine," he protested. This claim was unlikely at best, but Ireland topped it

Sister Dominica Borgerding with the students of Room 2, "Stillwater School," 1890 (MHS)

when he brushed aside as legal niceties certain admonitions delivered by Minnesota State Superintendent of Schools D. L. Kiehle[25]: "Mr. Kiehle is a friend of mine, and many things are done and permitted practically in our favor, through one kind of influence or another, that cannot be elevated into the strictness of a law, and that at the same time to all appearances must be within the letter of the law."[26] "Appearances" indeed figured largely in so delicate an arrangement. "Be sure to fix up the yard properly," Ireland told Corcoran. "Get some maps, too, for the rooms. Make things look somewhat respectable — even if some money has to be expended. Your school will be visited. Let it not seem to be a 'rat-trap.' "[27]

Yet Ireland's confidence in a network of "friendships" revealed the fatal flaw in the Faribault-Stillwater plan, and, for that matter, in its precursor at Poughkeepsie as well. The success of the plan depended upon a gentlemen's agreement, which presumed a willingness to wink at "the strictness of the law." Even leaving aside the contentious issue of the teaching-sisters' clothing — which for many non-Catholics summed up all that they disliked about the Roman church—there remained other unstated but crucial particulars about which gentlemen might well disagree. For example, the plan could not work unless the Catholic children were assigned exclusively to the former parochial school instead of to the public schools in their respective neighborhoods. Nor could it work if the board were to send non-Catholic teachers to serve the Catholic clientele assembled in the former parochial school. But were not such administrative restrictions—to say nothing of their inconvenience—equivalent to a religious test? So it seemed to many citizens of Faribault and Stillwater who were by no means all "anti-Catholic bigots."

Ireland for his part had to have these concessions if he were to rebut the charges of "Catholic extremists" that he was merely secularizing the parochial schools. His consistent argument was that a critical mass of Catholic teachers and pupils gathered together for the learning experience would itself guarantee the properly religious ambience, even though explicitly Catholic symbols were banished from the classroom and neither prayer nor catechetical instruction occurred there between nine in the morning and half-past three in the afternoon. And concessions of the kind had been made elsewhere. The agreement had held in Poughkeepsie for nearly a generation, but it may have been that gentlemen were relatively plentiful in upstate New York. At any rate Ireland complained, justifiably, that not until *he* espoused the plan did it come under attack from his co-religionists.[28] Such perhaps was the fate of this strong-willed man who confided wistfully to the young pastor of Stillwater: "So much depends on the success of the present experiment."[29]

While John Ireland watched closely the progress of his two parochial-public schools—each called, by odd coincidence, the Hill School, since each was perched atop the highest ground in its respective town—the education question was shifted suddenly from a pragmatic to a speculative plane by the publication in mid-November of a thirty-one page tract, titled *Education: To Whom Does It Belong?*[30] Its author was Thomas Bouquillon, a fifty-one-year-old professor of theology at the Catholic University of America. Bouquillon, a Belgian-born priest whom Keane had recruited for the university faculty, had come to the United States with an established academic reputation. His scholarly interests were varied, but he had concentrated them recently upon a study of contemporary social questions.

Education: To Whom Does It Belong? had been submitted many months before to the editor of the *American Catholic Quarterly Review,* a journal published in Philadelphia. But the editor, supported by the cautious Archbishop Ryan, had refused to publish it, because, as Ryan put it, Bouquillon's argument "would be at once applied to our circumstances and be regarded as an invitation to compulsory education."[31] Gibbons had then suggested that Bouquillon rework his material into a piece to be published independently, and the theologian had followed this advice. It was widely rumored — on the basis of the timing of the pamphlet's appearance — that Ireland had inspired or perhaps subsidized its publication in order to gain support for his initiative at Faribault and Stillwater, a subject sure to come up at the meeting of the archbishops scheduled for late November. But the archbishop of St. Paul vigorously denied the allegation. "I neither wrote it, nor inspired it, nor knew anything of its existence, until I saw it in print, and it had no influence upon my action, for the arrangement at Faribault and Stillwater had been completed many months before the pamphlet appeared."[32]

Bouquillon argued that "the State has been endowed with the right of founding the schools that contribute to its welfare." Secular governments, he went on, share this right with the family and the church, and, though philosophers may designate the right as accidental when compared to that of a parent, it does not follow that the state lacks *real* "authority over education, . . . the right of watching over, controlling and directing education." Nor can this power be reduced to something "vague and general": every "legitimate association" must be granted the capacity to preserve itself, and in the field of education, therefore, the state, a genuinely legitimate association, enjoys the right of "establishing schools, appointing teachers, prescribing methods and programmes of study in the same way as it governs and judges, viz., through delegates fitted for such functions." To whom does education belong? "It belongs to the individual, . . . to the family, to the State, to the Church, to none of these solely and exclusively, but to all four combined in harmonious working for the reason that man is not an isolated but a social being."[33]

John Ireland had in no way prompted Bouquillon's pamphlet, but he heartily subscribed to its thesis. Nor had he been totally unaware of the general direction of the author's thought on the matter: when he learned that Ryan had vetoed its publication as an article in the *Quarterly,* Ireland had retorted, "Well, I am not surprised—oh, the servile timidity of some men!"[34] Basic to the Faribault plan, as well as to the argument put forward in Ireland's speech before the NEA in 1890, were the tenets about states' educational rights spelled out by Bouquillon. But if those assumptions were straightforward and, from the vantage point of a hundred years later, entirely unexceptionable, they did not necessarily seem so at the time. On the contrary, Bouquillon advanced a view that certainly sounded novel and, in the judgment of many Catholics, posed a threat to the parochial school system they had sacrificed so much to create. Bouquillon himself protested that his argument was a speculative exercise and that he intended no specific practical application of it. In the heated atmosphere of the time this distinction was bound to go unheeded.

Within days the first of many rejoinders to Bouquillon came off the press. A Jesuit ethician named René Holaind pleaded in his preface to *The Parent First*[35] that shortage of time detracted from his ability to present an orderly refutation of Dr. Bouquillon's arguments, but, since the latter clearly aimed, he said, toward influencing the imminent archbishops' meeting, even a hurried answer to them was better than none. Holaind's pamphlet did indeed compare unfavorably in tone and substance to Bouquillon's, but it made the salient point that Bouquillon (and, by implication, John Ireland) erred in granting the state an *intrinsic* right to educate; any power the state enjoyed in this regard was *delegated* by parents who, if they chose, could withhold it. On this difference of opinion turned the controversy that followed, in a veritable storm of articles, brochures, editorials, and reviews, of varying length and quality, which lasted into the following summer.[36]

At the meeting of the archbishops, however, neither Bouquillon nor Holaind was mentioned. At two o'clock in the afternoon of Sunday, November 29, all thirteen American metropolitans gathered in the residence of Archbishop Kenrick of St. Louis, who that same day celebrated the fiftieth anniversary of his episcopal consecration. Ireland, the junior member, kept the minutes.[37] Discussion ranged over the status of certain secret societies, touched upon Catholic participation in the Chicago world's fair scheduled for 1893, noted the need for continued apostolic endeavors among Negroes and American Indians, and dismissed as unfounded allegations that convent chaplains threatened the virtue of the nuns entrusted to their spiritual care. All the archbishops, including Katzer, joined in condemning the recommendations of Peter Paul Cahensly. Ireland, reporting on his negotiations with the service secretaries, spoke passionately about the shortage of Catholic chaplains in the armed forces.

Before the session adjourned Cardinal Gibbons asked Ireland to brief his colleagues on the status of the Faribault-Stillwater plan. Ireland did so, and apparently he received several positive reactions — particularly so from Williams of Boston — and no negative ones. But for some reason he did not record this part of the meeting in the minutes, an omission which a few months later opened the door to much contention and misunderstanding.[38] For the time being, however, the archbishop of St. Paul had no reason to suppose that his school experiment had excited any undue opposition among his fellow prelates.

Indeed, he seems to have emerged from the meeting in an especially feisty mood. The next evening at the banquet in honor of Kenrick's jubilee, he fired a parting salvo at the Cahenslyites. One of the featured after-dinner orators was a distinguished German priest, a close of friend of Kenrick — St. Louis had long had a sturdy German-Catholic community — whom the speaker praised for having "discovered in Catholic immigration, not a danger, . . . but a priceless acquisition." "We have a country," the priest added, "but we are not as yet a nation. . . . A hundred, perhaps more, years must roll on ere the typical American will be produced." The applause which greeted these remarks was mingled with calls for Archbishop Ireland, who rose in his place and delivered a scornful rebuttal, along with an insinuation that such sentiments as the audience had just heard smacked of disloyalty: "We recognize in civil matters no other power than the authorities at Washington, and in religious matters no other power than the Pontiff of the Vatican."[39]

Ireland's cheerful bellicosity did not abate over the succeeding weeks. From St. Louis he went to Washington, and then to New York, where he gave a long interview to a reporter from the *Herald*. In it the archbishop — "the picture of perfect health, cordial in manner and perfectly free and frank in expressing his convictions" — ranged over the whole education question, explained and defended the Faribault plan, and reiterated the principles of his NEA speech. He strongly defended Bouquillon's pamphlet and witheringly dismissed Holaind's: "The world moves. Father Holaind remains stationary. That's the whole question as between the Jesuit Father and the Professor of the Catholic University. . . . I beg the American people to take his words as those of Father Holaind and not as those of the Catholic Church."[40] This last remark was aimed at a specific target, and one not far away from the Fifth Avenue Hotel where he uttered it, for Ireland was already convinced that Holaind had written his pamphlet at the direction of Michael Corrigan.[41]

Ireland was back home in time for Christmas, mulling over the episcopal appointments announced in Rome the same day as his interview with the *Herald*. They did not contribute to his enjoyment of the season. To succeed Gilmour at Cleveland had gone Ignatius Horstmann of Philadelphia, the very editor of the *American Catholic Quarterly* who had first rejected Bouquillon's article. James Schwebach had been given La Crosse and Sebastian Messmer, O'Connell's favorite canon lawyer, Green Bay.[42] Still, in Ireland's judgment, it could have been worse: Horstmann was at least of American birth, though of German parentage, while Schwebach was a Luxembourger and Messmer was Swiss. More bothersome to him at the moment was the arbitrary decision of the Stillwater school board to forbid the teaching of catechism in the Hill School at any hours whatsoever. "On what ground do they claim to control the use of the buildings outside school hours?" he irritably asked Father Corcoran.[43]

But the archbishop of St. Paul did receive a compensating gift, even if it did not reach him till after the holiday. An Associated Press dispatch, datelined Berlin and published in a Baltimore newspaper on December 23, described the educational arrangements arrived at by church and state in various European countries. The cable concluded:

> First, . . . the Catholic church does not practically contest the right of the state over primary schools, and . . . this implied recognition is especially admitted in German-speaking countries; second, . . . the Church everwhere strives to have religious instructions given in the public schools by adapting itself to existing laws; third, . . . the church never condemns to deprivation of the sacraments those who send their children to public schools in which there is no immediate and certain danger to faith and morals; fourth, . . . the State schools in which religious instruction is given seem to be the practical ideal of the Catholic parties on the continent.[44]

The cable was the fruit of a promise given Ireland by O'Connell two months earlier: "You will soon see in the 'Press' an article on schools in Europe that will give your enemies something to think about."[45] Following the pragmatic rule that what had worked before might well work again, O'Connell and Boeglin had once more moved to manage the news. Three days after Christmas Ireland wrote Gibbons: "I thank you for sending me the extract from the Baltimore Sun containing the Berlin cablegram on Schools in Europe. This cablegram somehow did not appear in our Western papers. I was looking for it. Our friends Dr. O'Connell and Boeglin prepared it at much trouble to themselves and sent it forward from Berlin. This is, of course, a great secret."[46]

By that time he was "quite busy, getting ready for the trip," the trip to Rome that he had contemplated and then set aside the winter before. Now, with the implementation of the Faribault plan and the fevered debate stirred up by Bouquillon's pamphlet, the school controversy had assumed a sensitive new dimension, and Ireland was determined to secure Roman sanction for his policy. O'Connell urged him along in the name of the pope. "The Holy Father is most anxious to see you," the rector wrote. Leo XIII was studying Ireland's speech before the NEA. "I said you would be here soon to give light if necessary, and it pleased and relieved him to hear it. You can do more in Rome in one week now tha[n] you can do in a year in America. Come on then, and roll back this reactionism forever into its grave. . . . The Propda. will be delighted to see you."[47]

Early in January 1892, Ireland made a hurried trip to Chicago for preliminary and informal conversations with lay and clerical notables charged with planning Catholic participation in the world's fair scheduled for 1893. "Our meeting," he told Gibbons, "was very satisfactory," and, in the manipulative spirit exhibited during the organization of the lay congress three years earlier, he added: "We will have no trouble in shaping matters to our entire satisfaction."[48] Then, having appointed Louis Caillet administrator of the archdiocese in his absence, he sailed for Europe aboard the *Burgoyne* on January 16.[49] After landing at Le Havre, he went first to Liege, Belgium, where he had promised to attend a conference of European Catholics interested in "social questions." "It was a most agreeable and instructive gathering." By January 28 he was in Paris, and a few days later he left for Rome, stopping at Lyon along the way.[50] O'Connell welcomed him to the Via dell'Umiltà during the first week in February.

Before he arrived John Ireland knew that a significant changing of the guard had occurred at Propaganda. The preceding summer the secretary, Jacobini, had received the diplomatic post he coveted in Lisbon, and had been replaced by Archbishop Ignazio Persico.[51] And in the stead of Simeoni, who died of the "grippe" in January, the new prefect was Miecislaus Cardinal Ledochowski, formerly an archbishop in Prussian Poland and, though an opponent of Bismarck during the Kulturkampf, reputedly a friend of Kaiser Wilhelm II and of Cahensly. Such connections understandably worried Ireland, but, having met Ledochowski in 1887, he had "conceived a rather high opinion of him. I trust I may have reason to continue in the same opinion."[52] The first meetings between the prefect and the archbishop of St. Paul allayed the latter's fears; Ireland immediately liked Ledochowski, who was "not at all German in his feelings. He is a man of superior mind, keen perception. I prefer him much to Card. Simeoni."[53]

As he passed from one curial office to another, Ireland quickly perceived that the battle lines had already been drawn up. His chief opponents were the Jesuits and the German faction among the cardinals of Propaganda. These powerful people were abetted by certain influential American Catholic laymen, who took exception to the "liberalism" expressed most recently in Ireland's interview with the *New York Herald*,[54] and by Corrigan's agent, Miss Edes, who "watches and whenever she finds a number [of a journal] steeped in gall, she puts it into Propaganda." Public hostility, Ireland said, was most manifest in "all the papers owned and controlled by Jesuits in Italy, [which] are writing fierce articles against Dr. Bouquillon and myself." Prominent among them was *La Civiltà Cattolica,* published in Rome and often described as a semi-official organ of the Vatican. One of its editors, Salvatore Brandi, formerly a professor in a Jesuit theologate in Maryland, equated "liberals" with "revolutionary men," and confided to his confrere, René Holaind, that "Archbishop Ireland is now well known in Rome as a liberal and revolutionary bishop."[55] Brandi was reinforced in this opinion by Cardinal Mazzella, another Jesuit who also had lived for a time in America. Members of the Society of Jesus, victimized all over Europe by the secularization of their schools,[56] could have been expected to try to attach the label "revolutionary" to anyone advocating something like the Faribault plan.

Ireland chafed under the fire of criticism. "My advisers here will not allow me to come out in the papers, or to answer the Civiltà. I do not agree with them in my heart; but I yield."[57] Meanwhile he plunged into a round of meetings: "I am busy from morning till night, talking, writing, visiting, etc., etc." The results were mixed. One cardinal, "an old doctrinaire, wants us to war constantly against the State"; the rector of a prestigious Roman seminary, on the other hand, "endorses all Dr. Bouquillon's ideas, cordially and fully." Archbishop Satolli had offered strong support and had praised Ireland for his loyalty in having brought his case directly to the Holy See. But, in the end, only one person had to be convinced: "The Holy Father is my friend; he understands better than ten cardinals would, and I am keeping as much as possible to him." But the pope insisted that he confer with the responsible curial officials, "and I must go from one to another."

During the third week of February Ireland had his first audience with the pope. It lasted an hour. "He was most affectionate, most eulogistic, most familiar. He talked of social questions — fortunately I knew the encyclical [*Rerum novarum*] almost by heart — of his general democratic policy, of French affairs. Toward the end he mentioned Bouquillon. He evidently had been spoken to by an enemy. I argued mildly, and asked permission to write for him some memoranda. He said he would gladly read them, and then talk to me of the contents."[58]

The pope's eagerness to converse with Ireland "of French affairs" and "of democratic policy" suggested that the old diplomat—as Leo XIII liked to consider himself—had on his mind something besides the means of educating Catholic children in far-off Minnesota. His first political concern remained the reassertion of papal sovereignty over, or at least independence within, the city of Rome. To achieve that goal intervention by one or another of the European powers was, to him, an obvious necessity. Early in his pontificate he had reposed some hope for aid in Austria or Germany, especially after the settlement of the Kulturkampf with Bismarck. But the Italians checkmated him in 1882 by entering into the Triple Alliance with the two German-speaking empires, one important provision of which committed the signatories to maintaining secular control of Rome. When the Triple Alliance was renewed in 1887—accompanied by another bitter wave of anti-clericalism in Italy—the pope began to contemplate a rapprochement with France, the natural rival of Italy and Germany. Indeed, it was widely believed that the appointment that year of Rampolla as secretary of state signaled the shift in papal policy.[59]

But Rampolla's notoriously pro-French sentiments could not by themselves ameliorate a situation that bristled with difficulties. The French Third Republic had carved out a strong anti-clerical program of its own, though the more virulent features of it had subsided somewhat by the late 1880s. Significantly, the struggle between church and state in France had centered upon the secularization of education and had included the expulsion of the Jesuit order from the country. French Catholics remained by and large monarchists who despised the republican regime and longed for the return of the king. The pope was wise enough and realisitic enough to know that that aspiration could never be realized, and that so long as it was entertained the church in France condemned itself to futility and isolation from the public life of the nation. Therefore, with Rampolla his strong right arm, Leo XIII initiated the policy known as the *ralliement,* the "rallying" of French Catholic allegiance to the Third Republic.[60]

Here was where the archbishop of St. Paul came in. Ireland had already witnessed firsthand how stubbornly his French co-religionists clung to their monarchist illusions. "Intense confusion," he wrote Caillet from Paris, "prevails in France among Catholics — the Pope pressing upon them the Republic, they in large numbers resisting, respectfully but firmly."[61] But could not Ireland himself — a Francophile from his youth, fluent in the language, and, above all, the most visible exponent of harmony between the church and republicanism — could not Ireland play a role in rallying French Catholics to an endorsement of the pope's policy? O'Connell had probably told Leo how popular Ireland was in at least some Catholic circles in Paris, how certain notables had urged the rector to persuade the archbishop of St. Paul to come to France and speak out his message in person.[62] Little wonder that the pope welcomed Ireland warmly and listened with sympathy to a description of the Faribault plan — lilting French name! — or that the secretary of state nodded approvingly as the archbishop fulminated against the Germans. "Rampolla is all right. . . . He is the dead enemy of the 'Triplici aleanza' [*sic*] — the dark advance of which over America I pictured to him in Cahenslyism and its allies. I am all right with him, and he inspires the Pope."[63]

In these circumstances the enmity of the Jesuits and the Germans did Ireland's mission little harm: they "keep up the fight," he reported, "but to no purpose." Not surprisingly given his temperament he read more ideological commitment into the pope's benignity — "He is most kind and paternal to me"[64] — than was really there. But the battle in any event still had to be fought out on its own ground, and one disturbing element in it was the continuing bad news from Stillwater. Shortly after Ireland's departure for Europe the board transferred teachers and pupils from the Hill School as a step toward integrating them more fully into the public system.[65] Ireland put the best face he could upon this development and explained to Propaganda that "every morning Sister Hyacinth[e] goes over [to a public school] with her beads and her habit and her children and teaches class."[66] Privately he expressed great alarm, less however with the clear breakdown of the plan in Stillwater than

with the possible repercussions in Rome. Administrator Caillet had
done right, he said, in directing that "Sr. Hyacinthe yield to circumstances. After we have recognized the right of the Board, we will
more easily obtain favors. . . . Our enemies—the Germans and
the Jesuits—watch all details and send word at once to the Roman
authorities, so as to prejudice them against us. The plea is—have
nothing to do with the state. It is Protestant, it is infidel. Indeed the
cry practically is, have nothing to do with the American people."[67]

More trouble was brewing than that connected with Sister Hyacinthe and her beads. On March 4 *Le Moniteur de Rome*—Boeglin's
paper—published a strong endorsement of Ireland's educational arrangements.[68] The article, cabled to the United States, "caused a
genuine sensation" there, with the German-Jesuit faction gleefully
confusing the *Moniteur* with *Le Journal de Rome,* whose editor for
some reason had fallen "under the displeasure of the pope." Thomas
O'Gorman rushed into print to correct the error and still the
critics.[69] But that proved to be a triviality compared to the next
journalistic adventure. On March 6, apparently yielding no longer
to his advisers, Ireland addressed the director of the *Civiltà Cattolica*
and demanded that he insert in his pages a private letter written by
Gibbons to O'Connell the preceding December.[70] Brandi complied
in the issue of the *Civiltà* dated March 19, and printed as well
Ireland's letter along with some hostile editorial comments. Gibbons's letter was an account of the discussion of the Faribault plan
at the archbishops' meeting in St. Louis, and it contained this
provocative paragraph:

> [Archbishop Ireland] expressed a willingness to discontinue this
> system, if his colleagues advised him. But he got no such advice,
> for the advantage is all on his side. The Archbishop answered
> several questions, put by his colleagues, and the result was a tri-
> umphant vindication of his course.

At least Michael Corrigan though it provocative. On March 28
the archbishop of New York addressed a frigid remonstrance to the
cardinal of Baltimore.

> Your Eminence has probably seen in the last number of the *Civiltà*
> a document addressed to Msgr. O'Connell, from which, at least
> on the principle that 'silence gives consent' one might infer that

all the Archbishops of the United States sanctioned the Faribault affair.

No reference to such approval is found, as far as I know, in the official record of the meeting drawn up by Msgr. Ireland himself. Personally I have no recollection of it, and my memory is strengthened by another prelate present at the conference who writes that an "Explanation of the plan was given, but no opinion of its merits was asked at St. Louis."

Gibbons was acutely embarrassed by this turn of events, for O'Connell and Ireland had published his letter without his knowledge or consent, overstepping in this attempt to use the press to their own advantage the bounds of good taste and even of friendship. But the cardinal, angry rather at New York's challenge to his veracity, stuck to his guns, and replied to Corrigan that, since "none of the prelates advised [Ireland] to give up his plan, though [St. Louis] seemed to be the time and place to do so, if that plan had been considered . . . truly objectionable," he retracted nothing of what he had written to O'Connell. Indeed, his response to New York was simply a shorter, testier version of the message of support for Ireland he had sent directly to the pope on March 1.[71]

Once again the ever-faithful Gibbons had come to the help of his friend. But Corrigan, sensing a weakness in Ireland's position, struck as hard as he could and in a manner characteristic of him. He had already privately informed Simeoni of his disapproval of the Faribault scheme, which he designated "a certain new and foreign theory: that state schools best suited the needs of our times." Early in April he was quoted in a New York newspaper to the effect that articles in the *Civiltà* were pre-censored at the Vatican and therefore enjoyed special authority. Next he quietly circularized his fellow archbishops — all except Ireland and Gibbons — and invited them to correct the assertion that Ireland had been "triumphantly vindicated" in St. Louis. Six of the eleven agreed, and so a statement with seven signatures went in mid-April to Brandi, with a copy to Ledochowski, thanking the *Civiltà* "for having so ably defended that which we undoubtedly believe to be the right of the family and of the Church," and asserting that Ireland's school plan had arisen only "incidentally" at St. Louis with no judgment asked from or given by the assembled archbishops, much less "an approval of the secularization of the [Faribault and Stillwater] schools."[72]

But Ireland, bursting with energy — "I am, thank God, in excellent health and, on the whole, quite busy"[73] — assumed the offensive on the Roman front. First he wrote directly to the pope: "I wish to extend to your Holiness my absolute assurances that I permit not the slightest interference by the State in the teaching of doctrine or morals" in the Faribault and Stillwater schools, despite what "our enemies — some Germans and Jesuits and certain [American] Catholics reluctant . . . to see any reconciliation between the church and the Republic" — might have said.[74] Late in March, even before Corrigan had rounded up his six allies, the archbishop of St. Paul submitted his own memorial to the committee of five cardinals charged by Propaganda to hear the case. It was a long document — sixteen pages of print[75] — somewhat rambling, and, despite the work that went into its preparation,[76] rather carelessly crafted. But it stated the issues clearly, and at the beginning of it Ireland declared his intention to eschew abstract argumentation (he had already deposited at Propaganda a formal letter in support of Bouquillon[77]): "I simply wish to treat [here] of an Act of Administration in my diocese whereby, following the dictates of my judgment and of my conscience, I did what I believe to have been best for the cause of Catholic education in the two little towns of Faribault and Stillwater." He reviewed once again the thesis of his NEA address and denied the charge that he had publicly deplored "the existence of the parochial school. . . . I deplored the necessity of the Catholics being obliged after paying in tax for the Support of State schools to maintain again by voluntary contributions schools of their own."

He then reproduced in detail the budgets of the two parishes in question — $4,040 total for Faribault, $6,300 for Stillwater — taking care to address what had long been a sore point in Roman circles.

> It might seem to Your Eminence [Ledochowski] that the salaries paid to the priests [$800 per annum] and to the Sisters [$250] seem rather large, and certainly they would constitute rather large salaries in Italy. Expenses of living must be taken into consideration. It is true that in some parts of the United States priests receive a great deal of money, maybe more than they actually need, but such is far from being the case in the diocese of St. Paul. It

is all that the poor sisters and priests can do to support themselves decently.

As for the agreement reached with the state, Ireland stressed that his model, St. Peter's in Poughkeepsie, came from Corrigan's jurisdiction, that Katzer of Milwaukee tolerated at least eight such arrangements, and that even the Jesuits, in a parish they operated in Pennsylvania, did the like. He then added an assertion which, later on in the controversy, might have been labeled disingenuous: "The Faribault transaction is no part of any system whatever but simply an honest effort on my part to secure by the aid of the State Catholic education for our children in two villages where without such aid that education was impossible."

No one, Ireland continued, could honestly accuse him of being behindhand in providing parochial schools for his people: "St. Paul, though a new diocese, surpasses in that respect even the older and wealthier dioceses of Boston and New York," with St. Paul directly educating one in fourteen of its population, while Boston's rate was one in nineteen and New York's one in twenty.[78] But the fact remained that two-thirds of the Catholic children nationwide attended public schools and that that proportion, despite the best efforts of the American hierarchy, could only change adversely. Loyalty to the mandates of Baltimore III — and Ireland claimed absolute loyalty to them, no matter "the combined attacks of the German and Jesuit press throughout the world" — did not rule out special arrangements to meet special circumstances, of which Faribault and Stillwater supplied an example.

Finally, Ireland warned the cardinals not to be beguiled by the siren song that Catholic electoral power in the United States would soon force the government to grant outright support for denominational schools. Indeed, agitation against public education, the most cherished American institution, could lead to dire political consequences for Catholics.

> Unfortunately today the question has been so much ventilated that public opinion regards me as the representative of the party of the Church in America in favour of the Government of the United States, and regards my opponents as those who would combine the foreigners in the United States into a danger for the republic. For myself personally, what the consequences are, I care

very little; for the country at large in case of mistake I have reasons for alarm. We are only one to eight in the United States without wealth or influence and a larger proportion than that of wealth and population did not prevent a Kulturkampf in Germany.

Once his memorial had been delivered to Propaganda, Ireland could do nothing except wait. So he went off for a two-week holiday in Sicily, an indulgence he granted himself, as he put it to Keane, "only after my guns had been fully loaded."[79] But in New York the ever-watchful Michael Corrigan received surreptitiously a copy of the memorial—"My report to Prop., in spite of all efforts to keep it secret, has . . . reached Corrigan. Miss Eads [sic], I knew, was searching for it. She must have bought up the printer of Propaganda."[80] Fastening upon Ireland's reference to the Kulturkampf, Corrigan on April 25 persuaded his suffragans to join him in still another protest, this one an appeal to the pope pleading with the pontiff not to endanger the parochial school system because of a cynical and fraudulent threat of impending persecution.

By then, however, the battle was over. Four days earlier the cardinals had reached their verdict: "The arrangement entered into by Archbishop Ireland concerning the schools at Faribault and Stillwater, taking into consideration all the circumstances, can be tolerated [tolerari potest]."[81] The pope endorsed their decision the same day. Ireland was duly told of it, and instructed to keep the information confidential until the formal announcement on April 30. Once his triumph became public knowledge in Rome, the archbishop departed the city for a nostalgic trip to Meximieux. He confessed to a deep fatigue, but, he reported, "my spirits have been all right, thank God."[82]

Meanwhile rumors and claims and counter-claims swirled through the press. The first reports published in the United States had it that the Faribault plan had been condemned, but these were promptly contradicted. Then, on May 5, at a gathering of bishops and clergy in Albany—one more in the seemingly endless round of clerical banquets—Corrigan rose in his place, waved a cablegram over his head, and announced, "Faribault system condemned. Special case tolerated." Ireland's friend, Archbishop Riordan of San Francisco, reacted to the scene: "The saddest sight that the American Church has yet witnessed was that when the Archbishop of its greatest see stood up amidst the merriment of a banquet, the clinking of glasses, and read with an air of triumph amidst the vociferous cheers of hundreds of priests a telegram from what he called a most trustworthy informant (one of Eads [*sic*] [illegible word], I suppose), announcing the condemnation of the Faribault plan."[83]

But Corrigan's exultation proved short lived, and by May 11, with the publication of a letter of Ireland to one of his priests back in Minnesota, all the world knew to whom the victory belonged.

> I believe the papers have been speaking sufficiently about me to render it unnecessary for me to give details to my friends at home. Apart from the annoyance of being away from Minnesota, my stay in Rome could scarcely have been more pleasant and instructive. I have been made to feel perfectly at home, indeed loaded down with kindness. The Pope, Cardinals, . . . etc. seemed not to be able to do too much for me. The good Pope, particularly, is most loving toward me.
>
> The so-called Faribault plan is now formally allowed in spite of Germans and Jesuits. The decision is "tolerari potest," which means canonically "is fully allowed." A letter addressed to me in the name of the Propaganda brings out the full practical meaning of the words. The plan is, of course, a departure from the ideal, and in case of a departure the canonical language is "tolerari potest." But they imply for practice a full approval.

The *Faribault Democrat,* quoting from this letter, crowed, "It is a great victory for the future of America that John Ireland has won."[84]

There followed inevitably some skirmishing and some recriminations. By early May Riordan had told Gibbons of the cabal of the seven, though the cardinal had to wait a couple of weeks to learn their precise number and identity. "Archbishop Riordan is an honest and straightforward man," one of Gibbons's friends told Ireland, "but his brother prelate of N. Y. does not seem to be very remarkable in that regard." The cardinal had suspected as much, but now he had "certainty of it. How far [Corrigan] succeeded in bringing the Abps to sign that document, the import of which was to impeach the Cardinal's truthfulness, we do not know, but you may learn in Rome, and, if necessary, defeat his purpose."[85] Gibbons was deeply hurt by the rebuff given him by his episcopal colleagues, but, following his conception of his duty and echoing the appeals voiced in the Vatican documents, he called for moderation and for a restoration of harmony. "Be sure," he advised Ireland, "that no public expression will come from you which might be used by your enemies against you. Do nothing to wound or irritate. Your victory is a sufficient ground for the humiliation of others."[86]

But John Ireland was temperamentally incapable of repressing himself in the wake of his triumph. Back in Rome, he released two letters to the press, one from Ledochowski in which the prefect of Propaganda confirmed Ireland's broad interpretation of the decree, and one from Rampolla in which the secretary of state flatly denied Corrigan's contention that *La Civiltà Cattolica* possessed semiofficial standing.[87] The letter from Rampolla, Ireland exulted, "was my crowning victory. . . . The prestige of the Civiltà is gone; the Jesuits never in the century received such a blow." "If favor in the Vatican and Propaganda were any satisfaction to a bishop," he added, "I surely have it."[88] His cup truly overflowed: while he savored the discomfiture of his enemies, the post brought him a letter from Senator Cushman Davis and a copy of the *Congressional Record* in which there appeared the fulfillment of Davis's promise, an attack against Cahenslyism on the floor of the United States Senate. On April 22, Davis had blasted "the attempts of Herr Cahensly . . . to denationalize American institutions," and then had paid tribute to Leo XIII, "the greatest statesman since Ganganelli [*sic*] who has sat in the Chair of St. Peter." Ireland might have written that part of the speech (and probably did): Giovanni Gangannelli, Clement XIV (d. 1774), seldom listed among the great popes of history, had suppressed the Jesuit order in the eighteenth century, a bit of ecclesiastical lore unlikely to have been familiar to the Protestant senator from Minnesota.[89]

Corrigan and his allies for their part seemed unable to leave things well enough alone. On May 12 the archbishop of New York told the *Herald* that "tolerari potest" clearly meant that each Faribault-like arrangement would need a separate decision from Propaganda. On May 18 the *Civiltà* described the Faribault plan as "evil" and offered seven interpretations of the Latin verb "tolerare." And on May 23 Corrigan gave public and sarcastic vent to his anger and frustration: "No one can have a higher appreciation than I of the zeal, energy and courage of the Archbishop of St. Paul. His friends and admirers would be only too thankful if he possessed in an equal degree the grace of courtesy, the virtue of prudence and attention to the value of words."[90]

But no verbal barb could spoil what Ireland called "victory over the Dreibund,"[91] not even the evidence that one claim made in his memorial — "I have the approval of nearly all the archbishops" — was not in fact the case. In his euphoria he offered his adversaries only a pen full of scorn. "Corrigan's two protests fell flat," he wrote Gibbons.

> One signed by himself and four others on the occasion of the consecration of the Bp of Brooklyn was sent to the Pope himself, who told me all about it. Corrigan said that I was bent upon destroying the parish-school, that no doubt I would declare I had the Country with me. To undermine this supposed argument of mine he insinuated that my condemnation would not create a ripple of excitement. The Pope read to me his reply — which was a lesson to Corrigan and a justification of myself.
>
> The protest in the name of the seven archbps came to Propaganda. Ledochowski said to me, that he understood it at once. For him, it was the protest of one, who beguiled others into it — and, he added, were it the protest of seven he would prefer to them Cardinal Gibbons and the Abp of St. Paul. He emphatically impressed on me the duty of assuring you of his utter confidence in the veracity of your report. So far as Rome is concerned, you are the fidelis servus in quo non est dolus [the faithful servant in whom there is no guile]; the Seven are men not having the courage of their convictions when they should speak [at St. Louis] — and intriguers when they think they are not to be found out.[92]

His business thus brought to a successful conclusion, John Ireland left Rome on June 1. He went first to Genoa, and thence to Paris[93] where he fulfilled part of the bargain he had reached with Leo XIII. On the evening of June 18, in the Hall of the Geographical Society, he addressed an overflow crowd of twelve hundred distinguished persons, the elite, he said later, of Parisian society, on *"La situation du catholicisme aux États-Unis."*[94] He spoke in French and nostalgically recalled the time "when I spoke it by day, and dreamed in it by night." The speech was a paean of praise for America, a loving montage of history and of political and religious commentary, which only toward the end made its real point, an explicit if muted recommendation of the pope's call for a ralliement: "Arriving in Rome a few months ago, I heard from the summit of the Vatican Hill: 'Of all the forms of civil government which the Church has recognized, and of which she has made trial, she cannot say from which she has received more harm or more good.' Just now she is resolved to make trial in France of the Republic; and I, as a citizen of a republic, say to the Church: 'In this experiment thou shalt succeed.' "

On June 30, just before he sailed from Queenstown, Ireland scribbled a note to O'Connell. "My last message is for Rome, for you, my only friend — but one that is worth thousands. Ho detto basta — come Io dichiaro. Io credo. Addio. [I've said enough — as I declare. So I believe. Farewell.]"[95] The ship belonged to the White Star Line, whose officials were most solicitous for the archbishop's comfort. He had "the best stateroom" (for only eighty dollars), and "one of the deck parlors was put at my disposal." There he studied Italian and, inevitably, wrote letters. For John Keane's benefit he alluded darkly to the struggles he had just undergone: "I forgive the Germans — they are blinded by a false patriotism. But the Jesuits and Corrigan and [the] other bishops of America! Sad the revelations made to me!"[96] As the ship approached landfall, his mood reflected a new sense of loneliness and isolation. "I am resolved not to go near Corrigan. . . . I will be polite to all my episcopal brethren, but, otherwise, I will act entirely for myself and by myself. . . . I have lost confidence in my American friends. I touch American soil, feeling I am alone. Well," he cried to O'Connell, "help me."[97]

Once in New York Ireland's spirits revived. He checked into the Fifth Avenue Hotel, and though he declined all requests for interviews with the press, he did meet privately with Charles Dana, editor of the *New York Sun,* a paper generally favorable to Archbishop Corrigan. The meeting, held at Dana's request, led Ireland to conclude that Dana was "more with us than with Corrigan."[98] Ireland, true to his resolution, avoided any contacts with the archbishop of New York. On July 9, however, he received a visit from Edward McGlynn, and spent some time closeted with the Doctor, still Corrigan's bitterest enemy.[99] The next day Ireland boarded the train for

Baltimore, where he stayed as the guest of Cardinal Gibbons. From there, accompanied by Professors Bouquillon and O'Gorman, he set out on the last stage of the journey which had begun six months before. He paused long enough in Chicago to tell a reporter that "assuredly" the solution arrived at in Faribault was applicable wherever similar circumstances prevailed.[100]

On July 15 the archbishop arrived in St. Paul for a deeply ironic homecoming. He had crossed the sea to do battle in behalf of his school plan and had won a smashing victory, only to have its local manifestation collapse in his absence. The civil authorities in Stillwater had already dismantled the arrangement, and those in Faribault were in the process of doing the same.[101] Nor could Ireland's presence have saved the situation; the Faribault school plan was doomed by its own incoherence and by the publicity that turned it into a cause célèbre. Still, it was bitter medicine for a proud man to swallow, and Ireland, when he looked back, preferred to remember, not the shabby little schoolrooms in Faribault and Stillwater, but the refectory of the North American College in Rome, on that lovely spring day when the "tolerari potest" decree was made public and Denis O'Connell's students cheered him to the rafters.[102]

~ XV ~

The Fourteen Propositions
1892–93

JOHN IRELAND'S Roman victory in the spring of 1892, though it bore no fruit in Faribault or Stillwater, left him "a big man" at the Vatican[1] — so big indeed that rumors about his imminent promotion began to be heard. He heard them himself, and they were to beguile him for most of the rest of his life. "A great many hints," he told Gibbons early in June,

> — rather strong — were thrown out to me by Rampolla and Ledochowski that a great honor is coming to me. This, and nothing more, about the cardinalate. Rampolla, bidding me farewell, said with a big smile and a bow — you know, it is only until next year. Ledochowski repeated that nothing short of the great act which the Pope was preparing in my favor would conclusively stop the opposition. For myself I am not much concerned. Certainly New York is *gone up!* Actually, he is ruined in Rome.[2]

The demurral was not meant seriously: Corrigan's discomfiture was always welcome, but a cardinal's rank for himself — both as a personal honor and a confirmation of his policies — would have been even better. And though a red hat was not something for which he could campaign directly, steps had already been taken in Ireland's behalf. While he was still in Rome he learned that two of his many admirers among the Catholic laity, Richard C. Kerens, a Republican politician from Missouri, and Austin Ford, editor of the *Freeman's Journal* of New York, had sent to the Vatican informal statements given by President Harrison and Secretary of State Blaine to the effect that Ireland's promotion to the sacred college would be gratifying to the national administration.[3] Kerens asked Gibbons to support this effort and the cardinal did so, but only after

348

much hesitation—which led Ireland, when he heard of it, to comment: "Gibbons is exactly the weak man we have imagined him but good at heart."[4] Gibbons actually would have preferred, at least at this point, to have seen a red hat go to an even more unlikely candidate, Denis O'Connell.[5] The rector himself, meanwhile, kept his friend in St. Paul informed and reassured, though aside from projecting a general euphoria he had little enough to tell: "Nothing new yet about the new cardinals," he wrote in mid-July, "nothing new or unfavorable, on the contrary," with regard to Ireland's chances at the next consistory, to be held, O'Connell surmised, probably in November.[6]

The low level to which the fortunes of the archbishop of New York had fallen was certainly a fact. "Ruined in Rome" proved too strong a phrase—exaggeration of course was Ireland's habitual mode of expression—but Corrigan, who since his student days had prided himself and indeed had built his career upon his dedication to romanità, now looked in vain for friends at Propaganda or at the Vatican. Leo XIII had rebuked him for his allegation that Ireland and Gibbons had lied in their brief for the Faribault school plan by falsely invoking a threat of persecution in America if it were not approved.[7] When Corrigan persisted by pointing to Ireland's use of the word "Kulturkampf" in his memorial,[8] the pope reacted angrily, spoke of Corrigan's small-mindedness, and wondered aloud at an archbishop who would call into question the veracity of the pontiff himself. To his chagrin, Corrigan read about his troubles daily in the secular and Catholic press.[9]

Not that the archbishop of New York, even at this dark time, was entirely without allies. In Rome, that tireless intriguer, Otto Zardetti, Ireland's suffragan and neighbor at St. Cloud—and, now that he had his miter, his metropolitan's bitter opponent—tried to persuade Ledochowski of the correctness of Corrigan's charges, but the prefect of Propaganda impatiently brushed such protestations aside. Zardetti had come to Rome to pursue a quarrel over church property he was embroiled in with the Benedictines of northern Minnesota, and Ireland, who routinely challenged the right of religious orders to own anything, lent him strong support.[10] But the bishop of St. Cloud did not allow this favor to divert him from an all-round assault upon his archbishop, though he did it in fear and trembling. "The matter is the most difficult and delicate one for me," he had written shortly before. "Archbishop Ireland is a violent, powerful man. . . . Should he find out that I was denouncing him in Rome he would take vengeance and could make life very bitter, nay, unbearable for me." Ireland, he went on, was "extremely dangerous. He is first American, then Archbp. . . . [His] agitation against Cahensly is criminal. It is he who kindled the whole flame. It is he who will, and you will hear it, provoque [*sic*] agitation in the [U.S.] Senate simply to terrify Rome. 'Rome needs a lesson,' he told me, and he will be down on Rome unless it does what he wants." Given his own way, Ireland would destroy the parochial schools. "Unless Rome will act and proclaim who is right, we are loosing [*sic*] ground."[11] Ireland for his part knew Zardetti was up to no good, but he remained in the dark as to the bishop's precise course: "I wonder what Zardetti said to the Pope," he mused early in May.[12]

Contributing to Zardetti's alarm was his conviction that Ireland would indeed soon be promoted to the cardinalate. Another who expressed the same opinion around Rome, but with a notably different humor, was Francesco Satolli, titular archbishop of Lepanto and professor at the Urban College of Propaganda, who had been the papal representative to the centennial celebrations in Baltimore in 1889.[13] Satolli, who was fifty-three, enjoyed the special favor of the pope, whom he had accompanied to Rome from Perugia in 1878. He was reputed to be an expert in Thomistic philosophy and theology, the cultivation of which disciplines Leo XIII considered fundamental to the overall intellectual revival he hoped to stimulate within the church.[14] But Satolli, a garrulous, fickle, and shallow man, was a frail reed against which to lean so ambitious an enterprise, and his career at the Urban College was living proof of how superficial the study of St. Thomas Aquinas remained in the Roman universities, despite the pope's good intentions.[15]

His pedagogical days were in any event numbered. "Satolli is preparing to go to America," O'Connell wrote Ireland in July, 1892. "He will start in the late fall."[16] The rector's tone did not suggest that this news would surprise the archbishop of St. Paul, and it did not, for Ireland had learned in conversations with the pope that the latter intended to dispatch an emissary to the United States

who would settle the school question once and for all and then remain as resident apostolic delegate. Before he left Europe for home
a few weeks earlier Ireland had remarked to Gibbons: "The
Pope . . . has taken occasion from our controversies to revive the
talk of a delegate. Of this more, when I meet you."[17] They met in
Baltimore on July 11, and Ireland tried to persuade the cardinal that
the long and deep aversion felt by the American bishops toward the
presence in the country of a papal representative was, under present
circumstances, misplaced. "I spoke of the delegate," he wrote
O'Connell, "telling [Gibbons] that the delegate would be confided
to him, that Leo was determined, that we must stand by Leo."[18]
Flushed with his recent triumphs and constantly reassured about his
standing at the Vatican—"Your work in Paris was a success, and has
strengthened your position very much"; "With the Pope your position is stronger than ever"[19]—Ireland proposed to employ papal
power and prestige to put down his enemies. If that meant he had
to reverse himself as to the desirability of an apostolic delegate, and
in doing so to alienate a large majority of his peers and colleagues,
he was prepared to assume the risk. It was a fateful throw of the
dice, determined upon during a "night's deliberation" at the college
on the Via dell'Umlità.[20]

O'Connell skillfully did his part. "Well, my dear Friend," he
wrote Ireland on August 3,

> I have just had a long talk with the Pope, and it is all ar-
> ranged. . . . Satolli and I are to leave here about the middle of
> September to assist at the dedication services [at] Chi-
> cago. . . . Then after a little tour, he returns to Washington to
> remain in the University at least the first year. . . . [Satolli's] in-
> structions must be made out just now under the influence of the
> favorable sentiments that are dominant at present. Then . . . the
> mission of . . . New York and Zardetti will end in smoke. . . .
> I have an invitation to the dedication services. You must secure
> one for Satolli. Now I count on you to carry these plans out
> firmly, and have us met down the Bay [of New York harbor]. I
> shall write the Cardinal to send a [railway] car to meet us at
> N. Y. I told the Pope you would meet us at Balto. and take us to
> Chicago. Then I saw Satolli. He puts himself entirely in my hands.
> "In manu tua, he said, vita mea" [*sic;* "In your hands, I place my

life"]. And in everything he will be guided by me. That means the perpetuation of your victory.[21]

The "dedication services" at Chicago to which O'Connell referred were the ceremonies connected with the opening of the buildings to be used at the world's fair — or the World Columbian Exposition — scheduled for the following year. Ireland was already involved as Catholic representative in the planning for the fair, and, when he learned its managers were anxious to exhibit maps and charts of an age with Christopher Columbus — the most serviceable of which were preserved in the Vatican museums — he suggested that the pope be invited to display such materials at the exposition and to entrust their delivery to a special emissary. This bit of subterfuge proceeded satisfactorily, until the president of the planning board objected that such an invitation would outrage the anti-Catholic portion of the American public and so imperil the success of the fair. Gibbons was then called to the rescue, and the cardinal, negotiating directly with Secretary of State Foster, arranged that the invitation be extended in the name of the United States government. Both the pope and Rampolla were delighted by this turn of events, and, after some quibbling over protocol and over the wording of the letter sent from Washington to Rome, Satolli was duly commissioned "ablegate" or temporary representative of the Holy See to the exposition.[22]

Part of the ritual of John Ireland's homecoming, the rousing sermon he delivered from the pulpit of his cathedral on the third Sunday in July, was calculated to give public expression to his new papalist enthusiasm. His subject was the virtues of Leo XIII. "Pontiff of the age!" he cried. "Leo surely lives in his age and for his age. All its aspirations possess his mind; all its energies consume his heart; all its ambitions find in him sympathy and counsel. . . . The age has not one thought true, or good, or noble, that Leo does not interpret and approve."[23] With these intoxicating sentiments whirling through his mind, the archbishop passed August and September in St. Paul, preparing for Satolli's arrival and nursing an illusion. So confident was he of his elevation to the cardinalate that he instructed O'Connell to delay the ablegate's mission if a consistory were suddenly called in the interval, so that the rector could "be the bearer of the hat. . . . You cannot come over twice in [a] short time."[24] He even found encouragement in Rampolla's smoothly non-committal reply to Gibbons's hesitant nomination of the spring: the pope, Rampolla had explained, could not speak to a hat for Ireland, " 'parce que le consistoire a été differé [because the consistory has been put off].' The letter is diplomatic," Ireland explained, "yet it reads well. It looks as if he meant to say that the postponement of the consistory is the only cause why no pronouncement has been made."[25]

At the same time Ireland almost succeeded in abiding by the unanimous advice of his friends to remain silent on all controversial issues.[26] The sole exception was to alude in an interview to the allegedly underhanded manner in which Corrigan had obtained a copy of the memorial on the Faribault plan. O'Connell did not mind this exception: "You must make hay while it is time, but don't fight everybody at once. Work the Memorial treason well."[27] Nor did Ireland need a reminder to press this point at headquarters; Corrigan, McQuaid, and Ella Edes, he charged to Ledochowski, first secured a copy of the memorial by dishonorable means, and then proceeded to distort its meaning.[28]

Corrigan for his part confided to Austin Ford that he bore the archbishop of St. Paul no "personal" animosity but that he wondered at Ireland's discourtesy at not calling on him when he landed in New York and at his brazenness in receiving McGlynn. But these were luckless days for Corrigan. Even as Ford was purporting to act as an intermediary between the two archbishops—he claimed in public to be "a friend to both of you"—the highly strung editor of the *Freeman's Journal* privately urged Ireland to beware of the machinations of Corrigan whose real intent, he warned, was to "call you before the Pope on personal charges."[29] Indeed, if Ireland had chosen at that particular moment to "fight everybody at once," he would not have had to look far for adversaries. Katzer wrote him a blistering denunciation of an article, written by John Conway, one of Ireland's priests, which contained "unfounded, false and most malicious charges . . . against me, accusing me of conspiracy against our country" and collusion with the German government. Appealing "to your Grace's sense of justice," he demanded a published retraction, and, if he did not get one, he threatened to carry his complaint to Rome.[30] "I replied that I would join him [in a Roman appeal], so as to know what can be done with Catholic writers who attack bishops—as I had suffered immensely from Katzer's official German paper." But this time Ireland was not to be drawn into a quarrel with his brother of Milwaukee; instead he decided to dismiss Conway from the editorship of the *Northwestern Chronicle,* a post the Kilkenny-born priest had held for some years. "He is reckless, erratic," the archbishop observed irritably, "and I am put down as inspiring what he writes in spite of me."[31]

Ireland would not in any event allow himself to be distracted by this small tempest from his major strategic objective during those warm summer days: the capture of Satolli and, if possible, the further embarrassment of Corrigan. "If the Pope would, . . . as he said to me he would, remit Mgr. Satolli formally into Card. Gibbons' hands and mine, all is well. I would then do much which I cannot otherwise do. . . . If you can at all," he told O'Connell, "obtain from the Vatican a few lines for me telling me to look after the 'delegate,' and aid him for [the] first few weeks."[32] The rector complied—"[Satolli] is commended especially to your care"—and obtained for himself appointment as the delegate's secretary and companion during the trip to America. "I saw the Pope yesterday. He said: 'Satolli metterà Corrigan al muro [Satolli will put Corrigan in an untenable position].' "[33] The pieces in the little plot were all in place, and the very boldness of it gave even John Ireland pause: "My! You take the breath from me. Surely things move rapidly. Now that all comes before me in sternest reality, I am almost affrighted, and almost wish I were to be left quiet and undisturbed on my prairies. But, I suppose, we must go ahead."[34]

Satolli and O'Connell departed Rome in the middle of September, traveled at a leisurely pace across France—in Paris the talkative ablegate revealed to a virtual stranger that among his missions in America was the reconciliation of McGlynn and the sounding out of public opinion about a red hat for Ireland[35]—and sailed from Liverpool on October 5 aboard the *Majestic*. The timing had been carefully planned. Just before sailing O'Connell sent notice to Corrigan—by letter, not by cable[36]—of the ablegate's imminent arrival in New York. Meantime Ireland dispatched Thomas O'Gorman to Baltimore as his emissary: "He will give you all my ideas."[37] Gibbons readily fell in with those ideas, though he had less confidence than Ireland did in O'Gorman's ability to carry them out. The cardinal commissioned Richard Kerens to call upon the secretary of the treasury — as did O'Gorman — and ask to have a "revenue cutter or tug . . . meet Mgr. Satolli down the bay," take him off the larger ship, deposit him at an unspecified wharf, and, as a courtesy to a guest of the United States government, waive all customs regulations. "By arranging matters with the Secy of the Treasury," Gibbons observed disingenuously, "no reasonable offense can be taken by the ecclesiastical authority in N. Y."[38]

But the whole point of the Americanists' arrangements was to exclude the archbishop of New York from sharing in the formal welcome to the delegate. Another part of their scenario was to manage the press. "The coming of the delegate suits me thoroughly," Ireland told Austin Ford. "I have been long aware of the Pope's intentions in this regard, and have thoroughly acquiesced. . . . Dr. O'Gorman will be in N. York to welcome the delegate in my name," and through him Editor Ford should seek an interview with O'Connell. "The policy to be followed out by the delegate," Ireland predicted, "will be fully along the lines of Americanism."[39] On October 11, twenty-four hours before the *Majestic*'s scheduled arrival, Ford informed Corrigan that the government had agreed to convey Satolli to shore in a special vessel, and the archbishop of New York spent the rest of the day fruitlessly trying to discover where exactly the federal collector of the port would land the delegate's party. The next afternoon the cutter *General Grant,* with O'Gorman and Gibbons's representative, Alphonse Magnien,[40] on board, duly met the *Majestic* "down the bay," removed Satolli and O'Connell and their luggage, and brought them ashore. They proceeded by carriage to Corrigan's residence on Madison Avenue where they dined and spent the night, with Satolli visibly offended — as it was intended that he should be — by the failure of the archdiocese of New York to have participated in welcoming him. Corrigan saw the affair as "a bold attempt . . . to capture [Satolli] for the Republican party by Mgr. Ireland's henchman, Dr. O'Gorman."[41]

On October 13 the campaign to impress the delegate began in earnest. He, together with his Americanist companions, traveled in a special railway car to Baltimore where Gibbons greeted him warmly. Two days later, the whole party went to Washington, and

Satolli, accompanied by Gibbons and Keane, met with Secretary of State John W. Foster, who assured the delegate that had Mrs. Harrison not been gravely ill, the president himself would have greeted the representative of the Holy See. On October 18 John Ireland joined the group in Washington, and almost immediately they all boarded still another special railway carriage for the trip to Chicago. There, at the ceremonies preliminary to the World Columbian Exposition, Ireland gave a speech and Gibbons an invocation, and Satolli had the opportunity to witness the high regard these prelates appeared to enjoy among influential segments of the American public. By way of confirmation was the cordial reception Satolli received from Vice President Levi P. Morton, who even attended a banquet held in the delegate's honor.[42] Never before had the professor from Perugia been so lionized, and he would have needed more virtue than most people possess not to have had his head turned. When the celebrations in Chicago were finished, he and O'Connell went off to St. Paul to spend the next several weeks as the guests of John Ireland.

The annual archbishops' meeting had been scheduled for New York in mid-October, but the date had been pushed back to November 16 in order to accommodate the arrival of the pope's ablegate. During the interval Satolli lodged in Ireland's house on Portland Avenue and was treated to tours of the flourishing institutions of the archdiocese of St. Paul. He was cheerfully at the disposal of his host and, since he spoke only Italian (and, probably, classroom Latin), even more at that of his traveling companion, Denis O'Connell. The pleasant holiday in Minnesota was marred only by the appearance of a particularly virulent pamphlet on the school question, written in Italian: "a vile and contemptible thing," in Ireland's words, seconded by Satolli who denounced it for its "abuse and calumny against a venerable prelate of the American Church."[43] Ireland remained convinced that Corrigan was behind its publication, and he had not changed his opinion when he, Satolli, and O'Connell went to New York for the fateful gathering of the American metropolitans. One sign of Satolli's frame of mind was his chilly refusal to accept the hospitality of Archbishop Corrigan: he preferred, he said, to stay in a hotel, where anyone who chose might have private access to him.

Visitors at John Ireland's house, 1892. From left: Thomas O'Gorman, Ireland, Patrick Riordan, Francesco Satolli, Denis O'Connell, Joseph Cotter, and Alexander Cestelli, who taught at St. Thomas Seminary. The figure at right is not identified. (Archdiocesan Archives, Archdiocese of St. Paul and Minneapolis)

The major item on the archbishops' agenda, in accord with the directive of Propaganda, was the provision of catechetical instruction for the large numbers of children not enrolled in Catholic schools. Before any discussion of this subject could begin, however, Gibbons introduced Satolli to the assembly. The delegate, with O'Connell close by his side, told the archbishops that it was the will of the Holy Father that they join with him in settling the school question for good and all. To accomplish this much-desired objective he proposed, not for their consideration, but for their acceptance, fourteen propositions that, he said, represented the mind of the pope. As Satolli read his prepared statement, the archbishops listened for the most part with equanimity, but they bristled at points five and eleven.

[5] We strictly forbid any one, whether bishop or priest—and this is the express prohibition of the Sovereign Pontiff through the Sacred Congregation—either by act or by threat, to exclude from the sacraments, as unworthy, parents who choose to send their children to the public schools. As regards the children themselves, this enactment applies with still greater force. . . .

[11] It is greatly to be desired and will be a most happy arrangement, if the bishop agree with the civil authorities, or with members of the school board, to conduct the school with mutual attention and due consideration for their respective rights.[44]

Satolli's "express prohibition" of spiritual punishments for those who declined to support or patronize the parochial schools was in harmony with the generally softer line Rome had recently taken on this question when compared to that of the American bishops. At Baltimore III the fathers had threatened parishes that refused to build a school with interdict,[45] only to have Propaganda water down the final decree to the level of episcopal persuasion "by the most efficacious and prudent means possible." And though the council had defeated the motion to refuse absolution[46] to parents who chose public over parochial schools for their children, the vote had been extremely close.[47] As for Satolli's proposition eleven, it clearly stated a generalized endorsement of the Faribault plan, the fruit, many of the archbishops must have thought, of the weeks just spent by the ablegate in St. Paul.[48]

Many of them at any rate were astonished and alarmed at what seemed to them a direct assault upon the viability of the parochial school system and upon the decrees of Baltimore III. But Satolli was not finished. "He went on further to say that he had . . . been charged by Leo XIII to inform the Metropolitans that according to the traditional policy of the Holy See to appoint Delegates to reside permanently in countries wherein the Hierarchy is well established and religion is flourishing, . . . it was the Pope's heartfelt desire that now a permanent Apostolic Delegation should be established in the United States with the kind concurrance [*sic*] of the Most Reverend Metropolitans."[49] With that Satolli and O'Connell retired to another room in Corrigan's house.

The rest of the morning session was taken up with a desultory discussion of matters on the original agenda. In the afternoon, the archbishops turned their attention to Satolli's propositions, which all of them (except Ireland) agreed, tended to subvert the well-being of the Catholic schools and granted too much theoretical power to the state. Satolli then returned to the meeting, and the blunt question as to the authority of his statement on education was laid on the table before him. He replied that while the principles upon which his propositions were based issued directly from the pope and therefore admitted of no alteration, he would entertain changes in wording or the addition of statements of fact that would contribute to the strength and coherence of the document. The meeting then adjourned, and, back at his hotel, Satolli received a note from Corrigan, pleading that the delegate not permit John Ireland "to impose his fantasies upon the entire American episcopacy. It is a question on which millions of souls hang." Little did the archbishop of New York know that that very afternoon, in that very hotel, Satolli had met with an advocate of Edward McGlynn and had thus begun the process of reconciling the maverick priest with the church.[50]

The next morning, November 17, the archbishops reconvened their meeting. Over Ireland's objections they returned to a discussion of the religious instruction to be given public school children. Inevitably, however, the fourteen propositions came up, and most of the commentary, again with the exception of Ireland's, was negative. Corrigan wondered aloud whether the delegate in fact spoke the mind of the pope, and Gibbons assured him that he did. Satolli attended the afternoon session, granted a few minor concessions on the wording of his propositions, and then demanded that the archbishops demonstrate their acceptance of them by signing the document. Before he departed he reiterated the pope's desire to establish a permanent delegation, and to this matter, once he was gone, the archbishops directed their discussion. With Ireland alone dissenting, they decided that they could not respond to such an important proposal without careful consultation with their suffragans.

The meeting dragged on through the next day, and at the end of it the archbishops, at the instance of Ryan of Philadelphia, formally determined "to promote the erection of Catholic schools so that there may be accom[m]odation in them for more, and, if possible, for all our Catholic children"; to provide "Sunday schools" and classes on other days of the week to serve public school children; and to subscribe once more to the educational decrees of Baltimore III: "The decision of the Holy See as to the Faribault plan does not affect these decrees accept to strengthen them. Parochial schools are the rule. Plans of various kinds are tolerated exceptions, where this [ideal] cannot be carried out." Satolli attended the final session of the meeting on November 19, but when Corrigan asked him some pointed questions about the fourteen propositions, he stormed out of the room and refused to return, even when Ireland hurried after him and asked him to do so. He did agree, however, to substitute for the metropolitans' signatures an ambiguous formula at the end of the propositions—"All the above was read and considered in the meeting of the Archbishops, the difficulties answered, and the requisite alterations made"—and not to publish them until the hierarchy's opinion could be made known at Rome.[51]

The day before he lost his temper Satolli reported to Rampolla that all had gone well with his presentation to the archbishops on the school question and that they had unanimously agreed to his propositions—a conclusion he may have reached due to Ireland's misguided persuasion.[52] The delegate read more accurately the archbishops' attitude toward a permanent apostolic delegation, but he did not think their reluctance to accept the idea would translate into resistance once the delegation was established, and in this prophecy he proved to be correct. As for a red hat for John Ireland, Satolli counseled delay, and in so doing may have demonstrated more independence of mind than the archbishop of St. Paul had given him credit for. Ireland was indeed "a prelate exceptional in the goodness of his heart and the nobililty of his actions [*per la rettitudine del suo cruore e delle sue azioni*]." He enjoyed high regard among American civil authorities, and he clearly governed his diocese well. But "in ecclesiastical circles," whether among the lower clergy outside St. Paul or among the bishops and archbishops, Ireland inspired "neither trust nor sincere affection, which perhaps in this world is the lot of those whose gifts elevate them above the crowd [*sopra gli altri*]." To promote Ireland to the sacred college now, Satolli concluded, would be "inexpedient," would "cause too many difficulties."[53]

Denis O'Connell wrote out this report at Satolli's dictation. Whether or not the rector confided the negative recommendation to his friend who was no doubt in a room nearby—it seems unlikely—Ireland had already heard an account that, because of their quarrel, neither he nor Corrigan would be promoted to the cardinalate: "I would not be astonished if there were much truth in it."[54] Even so, the campaign to keep the papal representative firmly in the Americanist camp continued. Satolli, scarcely mollified by the archbishops' unanimous resolution "that the Most Em[inent] Chairman should convey to the Most Reverend Apostolic Delegate their grateful acknowledgement, deep sense of respect and best wishes for his person and sacred character,"[55] left New York for Washington, where he went into residence at the Catholic University and so became the guest of John J. Keane. O'Connell, who all the while had been vigorously lobbying Rampolla,[56] stayed close to the delegate until he returned to Rome in mid-December, when Thomas O'Gorman took over the watch. As one hostile observer put it, Keane became the jailer, O'Gorman the sub-jailer.[57]

Satolli next turned his attention to the McGlynn case. Quarrels between American bishops and their priests had long given dissatisfaction in Rome, and McGlynn provided the most spectacular instance of the problem. The Doctor had been blessed in his friends—especially Bishop Moore of St. Augustine—who continued to work for his restoration, even when the subject of their concern persisted in his bizarre behavior and even after his mass appeal had pretty much withered away. Moore and Nilan of Poughkeepsie had asked Ireland to intervene in McGlynn's behalf with the curia,[58] and by the time he left Rome in June 1892, the archbishop of St. Paul had learned that "the McGlynn case will be reopened with splendid chances for the poor man." But Ireland's major interest was the effect such a development would have on McGlynn's embattled ordinary: "This will break Corrigan's head and heart."[59]

On November 18 Satolli asked Rampolla for faculties to absolve and restore McGlynn. The delegate proposed to demand the fulfillment of two conditions: that McGlynn retract any of his teachings on "public economy" at variance with Catholic doctrine; and that McGlynn, once all censures against him were lifted, go to Rome at his earliest convenience and explain his conduct to the pope in person. Rampolla replied affirmatively, and by the beginning of December Satolli was in contact with McGlynn. The Doctor responded to these overtures by giving a speech in which he praised the delegate's fourteen propositions and by preparing, at Satolli's request, a statement of his controverted opinions. This document[60] Satolli submitted to a committee of Catholic University professors — O'Gorman, Bouquillon, and two others similarly disposed — who found nothing in it to conflict with Catholic orthodoxy. Two days before Christmas McGlynn addressed to Satolli a formal letter of submission, which, however, was by no means craven: "Let me assure you that I have never consciously said, nor will I say, anything contrary to the teachings of the Church and of the Apostolic See, to whose teachings, and especially those in the encyclical *Rerum Novarum,* I give, and have always given, adherence." Satolli then juridically removed from the Doctor the penalties of excommunication and suspension.[61]

Corrigan read about McGlynn's reconciliation in the newspaper on Christmas Eve. He had been working over the previous weeks to rally his brother bishops in opposition to Satolli's fourteen propositions. His correspondence with Katzer, Zardetti, Ryan, his own suffragans, and Elder of Cincinnati — who was particularly distressed by what he discerned as a dire threat to the parochial school system — led Corrigan to believe that his cause was not yet lost. He had no difficulty in working the bishop of Rochester into a state of high dudgeon. "We are all in a nice pickle thanks to Leo XIII and his delegate," McQuaid wrote angrily. "It is only a question of time, when [the propositions have] wrought incalculable mischief, that we, schoolchildren of the hierarchy, will again receive a lesson in our Catechism from another Italian sent out to enlighten us."[62] On December 16 the archbishop of New York addressed a long and involved screed to Rampolla, in which he took aim at the publication of the fourteen propositions — contrary to Satolli's pledge — and added a pledge of his own: "We will not turn over our Catholic people to the unbelieving teacher [*maestro ateo*] or the non-denominational school."[63]

Satolli's restoration of McGlynn to official good odor may not have broken Corrigan's "head and heart," as Ireland had hoped, but it did heighten the New Yorker's native caution and intensify his fears that Rome might take action against him. Yet in fact the manner in which the reconciliation was effected won Corrigan a good deal of support among his fellow bishops, because Satolli (and his Roman superiors) foolishly did not impose upon McGlynn any obligation to retract the often savage attacks he had mounted against Corrigan over the years. It was not difficult in this case for the archbishop of New York to assume the stance of the injured party. He got no sympathy, however, from certain quarters. "Corrigan and his crew are in extremis," O'Gorman told Austin Ford[64]; "Corrigan is a taboed [*sic*] man," he told Ireland.

It was chiefly O'Gorman who kept Ireland, back in St. Paul, au courant with these events, and if anything the servant was more feisty and jaunty than the master. O'Gorman cheerfully confessed that it was he who had leaked the minutes of the archbishops' meeting to the newspapers: he was, he said, working "hand-in-hand" with the agent of the United Press. He had scant regard for putative allies. "The Card. has got his back straightened and strengthened," the professor of history reported. "He is very brave now, though he was downcast a few days ago. They are a pack of cowards, Gibbons, Keane et al."[65] If more restrained in his criticism to other correspondents, O'Gorman nevertheless gave apt expression to the Americanist strategy: "The fight is no longer between the Corriganites and Ireland, but between the Holy See and the Corriganites."[66]

This was Ireland's line as well: to oppose the fourteen propositions on the school question, submitted by the pope's own representative, was to oppose the pope himself. Once set upon this track, there was no turning back, and, as Ireland strode down it, he found himself in many a strange new locale. Less than two years before, in his fury at the appointment of Katzer to Milwaukee, he had exclaimed to Gibbons: "What they want in Rome is, that we be ever on our knees before them—before Cardinal and monk and clerk. The one who does all that is a hero. Well, principle and conscience will stand to us."[67] Now principle dictated a different course, to "act entirely for myself and by myself," with the conviction that "now my danger is my friends in America, who are reckless fools."[68] This conclusion committed Ireland to a novel definition of recklessness and even, perhaps, of friendship. O'Gorman at any rate egged him on: "[I am] glad you [leave] Gibbons and Keane out of the count and stand as the defender of no one but yourself and the legate (which means Leo XIII)."[69]

The mode of expression, however—positive, confident, hyperbolic—was still the old Ireland. "Most Eminent Lord," he addressed Rampolla in mid-December, "despite some noisy objections, the result of wounded pride and, very likely, of a vain hope of aborting or at least limiting his mission, the fact is that Monsignor Satolli has scored an unqualified success." And if the notion of a permanent delegation had not won favor among certain prelates, "simply because they fear a diminishment of episcopal power," even they would bow to the "lofty wisdom [*haute sagesse*]" of the pope in this regard, while most of the priests would be "enchanted" and the lay faithful would "see in the delegate a new sign of union with the Holy see and a new mark of the Pontiff's love for America."

> The country at large shows itself day-by-day ever more favorable to Mgr Satolli: his discourse [the fourteen propositions] has imprinted upon the minds of the nation the best possible impression. I do not hesitate to say that the American people desire that he prolong here his sojourn and that he should not be without a specified successor when it is necessary for him to leave us. Mgr. Satolli has done immense good among us. . . . The results of his presence so far demonstrate the need for an apostolic delegation in the United States, and when he is recalled to Rome the Holy See will be able to send another in his place and receive the plaudits of the whole world.

Ireland recommended there be no delay in granting Satolli "full powers," because a disgruntled faction within "certain ecclesiastical circles," one "not without energy and resources," has mounted "a bold and devilish plot [*conjuration Satanique et audacieuse*]" to undermine the delegate's authority as spokesman for the pope on the school question. "The words of Mgr Satolli have brought a message of harmony through our whole country as well as relief to troubled spirits; to a degree they are for America what the words of the Holy Father have been for France."[70]

Ireland's voice, saying what the pope and Rampolla wanted to hear, was loud but lonely. He made sure his views attained a measure of publicity by inserting them into an editorial in the *North-*

western Chronicle. Most of the bishops said nothing. Gibbons, who had to say something and who dreaded to be out of harmony with either his colleagues or the Holy See, sent two letters to O'Connell at Rome, one deprecating and the other endorsing a permanent delegation, and left it to the rector to present the right one.[71] No such equivocation, however, for the fiery bishop of Peoria. In a press interview during the third week of December Spalding contemptuously brushed aside the arguments advanced in the *Northwestern Chronicle.* "There is," he said, "and has been for years" among American Catholics "a deep feeling of opposition to the appointment of a permanent Delegate for this country. This opposition arises in part from the fixed and strongly-rooted desire . . . to manage as far as possible one's own affairs. . . . [American Catholics] are devoted to the Church; they recognize in the Pope Christ's Vicar, and gladly receive from him the doctrines of faith and morals; but for the rest, they ask him to interfere as little as may be." As for Satolli's statement of his propositions, "if it means anything other than what the Baltimore Council teaches, . . . the harm it will do would not be compensated for [by] the settlement of whatever number of quarrels between Bishops and priests."[72]

By coincidence Propaganda was in the process just at this time of appointing a coadjutor to the aged Archbishop Kenrick of St. Louis. The terna of the bishops of the province placed Spalding in the first position, but the Americanist party could not countenance the promotion to such a prestigious position anyone who opposed the delegation. "Evidently Spalding is crazy," O'Gorman reported from Washington, "and Satolli is on to him[;] his interview [in] today's papers is in Satolli's drawer, and when I told Sat. that Spalding was in the S. Louis terna, he smiled broadly and shook his head."[73]

John Ireland, as an archbishop, had the right to comment on the St. Louis list, and he did so with a vengeance. Though he had urged Spalding's appointment to Milwaukee two years previously, "certain traits of character," Ireland wrote Ledochowski, "have since become so accentuated that I cannot speak of him as I did before." Spalding's public repudiation of the delegation had been a "scandal," and, though the bishop of Peoria had the right to form his own opinion, he did not have the right to speak as he did "before the whole country, and in terms so little respectful. . . . Mgr Spalding is an orator and a writer of high merit, and he has occupied a place of great distinction in the Church in the United States. His weakness [*malheur*] is that he speaks without reflection, sometimes denying today what he affirmed yesterday." Spalding was unstable. "He fails in constancy of thought," swinging violently from moods of exhilaration to deep depression. Nor was Spalding's piety, by Ireland's current canons, up to the mark. Finally, "[Spalding] exhibits from time to time a levity [*légèreté*] which is quite unedifying, as well as a scorn for public opinion which an ecclesiastic ought not to permit himself."[74] For good measure Ireland also wrote Rampolla, and argued that public opposition to the delegation should be warrant enough for leaving the bishop of Peoria where he was: "Should Mgr. Spalding become coadjutor of St. Louis, one of our principal archiepiscopal sees, the authority of the Pope would suffer unimaginably."[75]

Much had transpired since the days of comradeship in the colonization movement and the evenings of banter at William Onahan's house in Chicago.

Leo XIII had intended that Satolli's mission would not only settle the school question but also restore a measure of harmony among the warring American prelates. Instead the hostilities, fought out every day in the pages of the nation's newspapers, raged unabated into the new year 1893, and indeed assumed a higher level of stridency than ever before. During the first week of January, John Ireland rushed off to Chicago in response to information that another Corrigan-inspired plot had been uncovered. A former New York newspaperman, whom Corrigan had occasionally used to leak stories to the press in that city and who had since moved to the Midwest, told Ireland that the archbishop of New York and several of his priests had orchestrated the attacks upon him and Satolli that had poured from the printing presses ever since the archbishops' meeting of the previous November. In proof the reporter gave Ireland a letter in Corrigan's hand as well as other relevant documents. Among the latter were copies of a circular addressed by the rector of St. Patrick's Cathedral in New York to several prominent midwestern Catholic laymen, urging them to speak out against Ireland's "unfortunate influence" in Rome and Satolli's "offensive and annoying" interference in American Catholic affairs.[76] One who received this communication was the noted literateur, Maurice Francis Egan, at that time a professor at Notre Dame and an ardent admirer of the archbishop of St. Paul.[77] While in Chicago Ireland interviewed Egan, and, after hearing his account, turned all the material he had received over to the editors of the *Chicago Post*.[78] He gave his own version of the story while the details of it were still hot on his mind.

> I saw the autograph letters of Mgr. Corrigan and of Father Lavelle [rector of St. Patrick's]. The letter of the former was addressed to a reporter, now in Chicago, formerly when living in New York accustomed to do dirty literary work for Madison Avenue. Lavelle wrote to no less a person than Maurice F. Egan. For the present this name is not to be made public. But if need be Mr. Egan will give us the letter. Egan is ashamed that he was asked to be party to a vile conspiracy. He knows Corrigan.[79]

The *Post* article, which appeared Sunday, January 8, caused a sensation. Rumors spread nationwide that Corrigan was about to be summoned to Rome and, once there, summarily deposed. In Washington O'Gorman crowed over the prospect of impending "revolution" among the priests of New York "once Corrigan is on the ocean and Satolli with his [delegate's] powers gets to work."[80] In St. Paul Ireland's anger was clearly mixed with his sense that an opportunity was at hand to destroy Corrigan. "Now what is to be done?" he exclaimed to Gibbons. "Are we to allow this liar and hypocrite and plotter to traduce our good name thro' America and Europe? I am at the end of my patience, and I am going to do something to rid the Church of him, or of his influence."[81]

What he did was to send to Rampolla a long and bitter bill of indictment. He recounted first the rising incidence of attacks upon himself and Satolli in newspapers and pamphlets both in the United States and abroad, and then he said: "The author of this disastrous [*néfaste*] propaganda against the Archbishop of St. Paul, Mgr Satolli, and the Holy Father himself, the chief who directs these warlike operations, is Monsignor Corrigan of New York." Ireland went on to describe in detail the revelations contained in the *Post* of January 8, a copy of which he enclosed, and to specify some of the more spectacular instances of Corrigan's malevolence.[82] "Thus you discern a conspiracy; thus you see its primary author and supreme commander, Mgr. Corrigan."

> Your Eminence can now easily understand that the opposition to Mgr. Satolli emanates from New York and from those influenced by New York. What is to be done to check this conspiracy and to suppress its authors and agents? The Holy See must be the judge. For myself I pray the Holy See to do something to stop this infamous war, of which I am one of the victims. I am beginning to grow weary. Not that I have been injured; no one can injure me in the United States, thanks to the spirit of justice and the good will in my regard which prevail among the American people. But it is a torment to me to know that a fellow archbishop seeks in every way to injure me, and if I lift a hand to defend myself I simply compound the scandal.

Particularly damaging, Ireland pointedly added, were the tracts hostile to him written in French—the responsibility for which he also laid at Corrigan's door: "In my visit to Paris [in June, 1892, on behalf of the ralliement] I tried loyally to serve the H. See, and now I am accused of sinning against the Syllabus [of Errors] and of injuring the H. See." Given the real state of affairs, he concluded, only one solution was possible: Satolli had to be "strongly supported in everything," even to the point of naming him permanent delegate as soon as possible.[83]

The latter step had already been taken, on January 3, and Satolli's lofty new status became public knowledge on January 14. "Well, my dear Friend," O'Connell commented from Rome, "it is accomplished. . . . Under the circumstances, I do not see what better could be done. . . . Some inconveniences may be involved for the future, but it seems they have to be accepted under the present stress. . . . 'Après nous le deluge [After us the flood].' "[84] The announcement must have seemed to Ireland the sweet confirmation of his hegemony, but in fact—though no one, least of all Ireland himself, could have predicted so at the time—it was his high tide, which began inexorably to recede. The first small sign of reversal appeared almost simultaneously, when Satolli circularized the American bishops to the effect that the pope wanted each of them to submit in writing an opinion of the fourteen propositions, and furthermore that this communication be sent not through the delegate nor through any curial congregation but directly to Leo XIII himself. O'Connell thought the pope's directive merely a sop to the hierarchy's self-esteem, a formality that, once gone through, could be safely forgotten. O'Gorman, on the other hand, recommended a belligerent counterstroke: since we know, he told Ireland, the bishops will react unfavorably, we should stir up the lower clergy and, "if necessary," the laity.[85]

The reaction of the bishops was indeed overwhelmingly unfavorable.[86] Of eighty-four possible responses, fifty-three bishops signified opposition to Satolli's propositions to one degree or another, while only eleven gave them unqualified approval and six approved them with reservations.[87] Among the archbishops only Baltimore, Santa Fe, and Boston joined forces with St. Paul. Gibbons maintained that "the doctrine contained in these propositions is so just, so opportune, and is so greatly appreciated by unprejudiced people."[88] He was seconded eloquently by Keane,[89] and not so eloquently by several other bishops who argued simply that supporting an entirely independent parochial school system was beyond their fiscal capacity.

In his own letter Ireland took the speculative high road, toned down his rhetoric, and attacked nobody by name. There was nothing new for him to say, but he could and did endorse Satolli's propositions "in toto," because they were "true in principle and wise in view of the practical applications which can follow upon [them]." All in all Ireland made a persuasive, if familiar, case, and at the end he played the card upon which he had come to stake so much: "The opposition to [Satolli] on the school question is, at root, an opposition to to his mission and to his presence. . . . I beg your Holiness to sustain the Delegate in all things; to abandon him on the smallest point would be for him a fatal check."[90]

But by sheer weight of numbers the bishops who disagreed with Satolli and Ireland — who thought they discerned in a wide application of the Faribault plan an assault on the parochial schools and a virtual repudiation of the decrees of the Third Plenary Council of Baltimore — dominated the field. Besides stating their objections to the propositions, many of them took the occasion to tell the pope that the imbroglio resulted from the intrigues of Ireland and the "credulity" of Satolli.[91] Not surprisingly, Katzer was particularly severe with Ireland, whom he accused of "unworthy tactics" like falsifying cablegrams, planting vicious articles in newspapers, and creating the impression that "to dissent from the innovations of the Archbishop of St. Paul is the same as opposition to the Holy See."[92] Corrigan himself, whom Katzer praised lavishly in his letter, wrote in the embarrassingly servile style that he habitually adopted when addressing Roman officials, but he did not back down from his basic position: since any "treaty" between public and private schools was unconstitutional and therefore unacceptable to the American people, "the schema of our venerable brother Satolli seems to suggest that sooner or later our Catholic children will attend public schools."[93] He did not mention Ireland, nor did McQuaid, who stressed in his letter the practical danger that implementation of the Faribault plan would inevitably sap the energy and resolve of the American Catholic community to maintain its own schools.[94] Patrick Riordan of San Francisco, a friend of Ireland and on most issues an ally, subjected each of the propositions to minute analysis and found them, as a whole, wanting and inconsistent with the decrees of Baltimore III.[95]

In sharp contrast to Riordan's analytical approach was the white heat with which John Lancaster Spalding addressed the pontiff. The words tumbled from him, chasing each other across the page, with no paragraph divisions and scarcely any punctuation. For him, Satolli's propositions, which he dismissed out of hand, were only an incidental target: "The schema, to speak of it first, has already done irreparable harm to the Catholic schools which are almost the only hope of the Church in this country. . . . I have no doubt that . . . the pronunciamento of Mgr Satolli . . . has been edited in accord with the interests of Mgr Ireland and his coterie." It was no more than an "apologia" for the public schools, which were "fatal to all positive religion. . . . The agitation of Mgr Ireland and his Faribault school plan—which is genuinely absurd, a compromise without any sense, which neither Protestants nor Catholics can accept—has done immense harm to the Church." And added to "this scandalous and extremely dangerous procedure," John Ireland, Spalding charged, had loosed upon the American church the dogs of war.

It is impossible to understand the course of the St. Paul prelate. He has tried to excite hatred against the German Catholics in the United States; he has labeled the Jesuits as universal enemies; he has attempted a coup d'état in our religious education; and now he proclaims that one of his confrères [Corrigan] is a conspirator against the authority of the pope. He has made the Catholic University a center of agitation for these ideas to the extent that the total ruin of that poor institution is a distinct possibility. And in all that he has done, he has represented himself as the special friend and authorized agent of your Holiness.

Ireland had also represented himself as the uniquely qualified spokesman of those Catholics who prized their ties to America, a claim which made Spalding's distinguished blood boil: "I am American, and he is Irish, and I am convinced that I know the American character as well as he [*aussi bien que lui*], and I do not hesitate to say to your Holiness, what I would say were I standing in the presence of God, that his manner of action threatens us with a vast ruin."

As for the delegation and poor Satolli, the bishop of Peoria hardly tried to disguise his contempt. The presence of a delegate, he said, simply encouraged those who subscribed to the tenets of the American Protective Association, that the Catholic church is a foreign intruder. Criticism of the delegation in the press was bound to come, and little by little "the authority of the Holy See will be weakened and destroyed. Mgr Satolli made a terrible blunder [*faux pas*] in setting himself up as the protector of McGlynn and O'Flaherty. Not even Luther spoke of the papacy more ignobly or tastelessly than McGlynn."[96] Satolli's inability to speak English or German or French, together with his ignorance of the country and its customs, had left him "simply an instrument in the hands of an unworthy clique, which has used him to outrage Mgr Corrigan and Mgr McQuaid. I have no intimacy with these gentlemen [*messieurs*], and I regard the affair in an impersonal manner." Clearly he no longer enjoyed "intimacy" with John Ireland either, as he blamed the archbishop of St. Paul for "the extremely serious" crisis into which the American church had fallen. Still, he concluded with a disclaimer, which hinted perhaps at sadness over a wrecked friendship: "In conclusion, Holy Father, I wish to say that I would not have written to your Holiness had the request not been made, and what I have written I have written in the presence of God."[97]

This outpouring of passion had little, if any, effect upon the pope and the curial officials, who had long since dismissed Spalding as a crank. But the dissent of the large majority of the American bishops from Satolli's propositions did pose a serious problem for Rome. Clearly it would have been imprudent to try to override the strong objections of nearly 80 percent of a local hierarchy. Yet Satolli, now the fully accredited apostolic delegate, had to be sustained. The continuing conflict between the parties headed by Ireland and Corrigan, aside from being administratively messy and disagreeable, was a source of public scandal as well as a threat to the very harmony with and docility to Rome which the pope, in dispatching a personal representative to the United States, wanted to bring about.

There was at work, however, a complicating factor: the papal bureaucracy was at odds within itself as to how to proceed, because of a growing rift between the Piazza di Spagna and the Vatican. German influence continued to be strong at Propaganda, and Corrigan—who among other favors supervised the congregation's investment portfolio in the United States[98]—still had friends there. Satolli, on the other hand, was peculiarly the pope's and Rampolla's man, a living symbol, as it were, of their pro-French and therefore pro-republican policy. Cardinal Ledochowski, a vigorous supporter of Ireland in 1892, had gradually drawn away from the Americanist faction, partly out of irritation that he and Propaganda had been scarcely consulted in the process leading up to Satolli's appointment.[99] His relations with Rampolla grew so strained, O'Connell reported at the end of January, that he had "returned to his first love, i.e. to Prussia." And some months later the rector observed: "Ledochowski is now the open friend of the Kaiser."[100]

One result of this bureaucratic wrangling seems to have been that, contrary to the fervent hopes of O'Connell and Ireland, the pope decided to leave the American church under the jurisdiction of Propaganda, to which Delegate Satolli would report and from which he would receive his ordinary instructions. At Propaganda therefore the episcopal letters to the pope on the school question were examined and recommendations to the pope pondered.[101] Meanwhile, as they waited, the American parties hardened and, to a slight degree, shifted. Ireland continued to fulminate against his enemies — "We live in fearful times; malice and fraud abound. . . . Nothing cunning from [Corrigan and his allies] will astonish me; they are capable of any badness." Assuming Bishop Kain left Wheeling, West Virginia, for St. Louis, Ireland urged Gibbons to "get a very good man to take his place. There are so few in the episcopate."[102] But the other side had not conceded St. Louis, not yet. "New York is working hard for Spalding," O'Connell wrote from Rome.[103] And from Washington O'Gorman reported: "Spalding has been for some time at the 5. Ave [Hotel], and Corrigan has made calls on him and her [Mamie Caldwell?]; in their presence she has pitched into Satolli. They are all working together."[104]

On May 31, 1893, Leo XIII addressed to Gibbons a formal letter in which he tried to put the school question to rest. It was an ingenious piece of administrative prose. Satolli, the pope said, "this illustrious man, not less preeminent by his learning than by his virtues," had been sent to the United States as a "manifest" sign of papal affection and solicitude. "Above all," the delegate had been commissioned "to use all his endeavors and all the skill of his fraternal charity for the extirpation of all the germs of dissension developed in the too well-known controversies concerning the proper instruction of Catholic youth." This mission he had accomplished brilliantly. "After carefully weighing the matter" — after examining the propositions, the minutes of the archbishops' meeting, and the bishops' written responses to him personally — the pope solemnly decided in effect that the problem had, like magic, disappeared. Anybody who thought the propositions conflicted with the decrees of Baltimore III was simply mistaken. But at the same time there remained in effect the mandate *tolerari potest:* "Whatever else has been prescribed by the Roman Pontiffs, whether directly or through the Sacred Congregations, concerning the same matter are [*sic*] to be steadfastly observed."[105] The fight over American Catholic education was officially declared a draw.

Controversy by no means ceased after Leo XIII's ambiguous tour de force, though, except for some inevitable aftershocks, the scholastic portion of it did. The course of events might have been very different had Ireland's school plan proved practicable. But Corrigan and Spalding were right at least on that score; Faribault-

XVI

"Down in the Borderland of Pessimism"

1893–94

SOME CYNIC has observed that it is not money, but the shortage of money, that is the root of all evil. John Ireland, by the summer of 1893, had reason to ponder the aphorism in either of its forms. The downward turn in his financial fortunes was sudden and traumatic, and, coinciding as it did with an increasing professional isolation—most of his episcopal colleagues remained bruised and resentful from the quarrels over the Faribault plan and the establishment of the apostolic delegation—it ushered in for him a season of discontent, when even chimeric victories came few and far between. For a man who put as much stock as Ireland did in the possibilities of the American dream, and who took understandable pride in pointing to his own career as an instance of the fulfillment of that dream, the panic of 1893—the worst and most prolonged depression the United States had experienced up to that time—had a sobering and depressing effect.

Ireland had begun to speculate in real estate during the late 1870s. His activities as a colonizer in western Minnesota provided the occasion; though he was restrained by covenants with the railroads from purchasing their right-of-way properties, nothing prevented him from acquiring in his own name much cheap land nearby, which, thanks to the success of his colonies, rapidly appreciated in value. A decade later he had accumulated sufficient capital to shift the bulk of his investments from rural to suburban areas, specifically to that part of the present city of St. Paul appropriately called the Midway District, that is, roughly midway between

downtown St. Paul and downtown Minneapolis. Here, just to the
east of the Mississippi, where he had established St. Thomas Aquinas Seminary, he dreamed, in the grandiose fashion characteristic
of him, that in due time would emerge the political, cultural, and
commercial center of a single great city, "Paulopolis," an urban
showplace and a rational alternative to two medium-sized "twin"
towns in perpetual and puerile competition with each other. "Tread
reverently upon this ground," Ireland advised in 1890. "It is the
Midway, the very heart of the coming great city. Look at it! Admire
it! Has not providence been generous to it. It is the precious gift by
which St. Paul will woo and win fair Minneapolis."[1]

Ireland, along with many other civic leaders, lobbied hard for a
new state capitol building to be located in the Midway, a first step,
they hoped, in the merging of the Twin Cities into one. Part of the
archbishop's commitment involved construction of a magnificent
new cathedral nearby, a project Ireland had been contemplating for
some years. But the legislature dashed these expectations in 1893,
when it determined that the Capitol remain near its original site in
the old downtown area. Even so, the dream of Paulopolis did not
need to come true in order to justify real estate investment in the
Midway. The city of St. Paul was growing inexorably in all directions, including westward, toward the looping Mississippi, and
soon it would swallow up the rolling, wooded countryside known
as Groveland Park, Desnoyer Park, and Merriam Park. Property
values were bound to go up there, and go up they did. Not a small
contribution to this process was another plan fostered by Archbishop Ireland, the provision of modern transport into the area. On
February 22, 1890, St. Paul's first electric streetcar line began operation along Grand Avenue, linking Groveland Park with the downtown four miles away. Ireland joined other speculators in forming
the company that financed the line and, unfortunately for him, in
assuming liability for it.[2]

It has been said that in their heyday the Medici of Florence so
mingled their domestic finances with those of the Republic that it
was impossible to tell the difference. So it often appeared in John
Ireland's case. Some of the property he bought in the Midway belonged to the archdiocese, some to himself, and he never bothered
to advertise the distinction. But, however sketchy his bookkeeping

*St. Paul's first electric streetcar line on Grand Avenue, February 22, 1890;
Thomas Lowry and Archbishop John Ireland sit in the front seat. (MHS)*

methods, he always kept track of his various transactions, knew
which parcel of land was his own and which was not, and observed
all the legal requirements involved. As long as the times remained
prosperous, he had no trouble fending off criticisms of his wheeling
and dealing.

In 1892, for instance, a fifty-cent pamphlet, beguilingly titled
The Great Archbishop, Whose Kingdom Is of This World, appeared on
the newsstands in St. Paul. The author, one S. J. Ahern, who had
for a time served on the staff of the *Northwestern Chronicle,* charged
that Ireland had cheated him in a land deal and had moreover secured vast tracts of property in the Midway by dishonest means.
But Ahern's accusations possessed more vitriol than evidence—
"The carpenter's son of St. Paul, picked up from under the lee of
wash tubs in [this] city, turns up a bigger man, and a more pompous
man, than the carpenter's Son of Nazareth"—and nothing came of
them, except a craven apology in writing which Ireland extracted
from Ahern a few months after the pamphlet's publication.[3] Inevitably a copy of it made its way to Rome, but Denis O'Connell
assured Ireland that it would do him no harm there.[4]

Nor should it have, even though curial officials habitually complained about the allegedly opulent life-style adopted by American
clergymen. Ireland's various promotions, with all their flavor of the

Gilded Age, were not out of harmony with the very old tradition that a bishop must be a man of his city, dedicated to its well-being in material as well as in spiritual ways. John Ireland plunged with zest into the civic life of St. Paul and of the region. No good cause escaped his endorsement, nor a bad one—like the staging of prizefights[5]—his condemnation. Even his land transactions had much more to do with Ireland's public than with his private persona. He did not intend to heap up riches for himself. Whatever profit accrued to his investments went for the most part into diocesan projects, as had been the case with St. Thomas Aquinas Seminary. There was no question, moreover, that the steady expansion of facilities for the large fraction of the population that was Catholic served to stimulate the local economy.

That is not to say that John Ireland equated piety with penury; on the contrary, he quite purposely made of himself a bourgeois gentleman. He lived in simple comfort, traveled extensively, maintained a decent carriage and stable, bought the books he wanted to read, and, in short, enjoyed the benefits that accompany financial independence. But while he made no fetish of deprivation ("Material comfort—there is abundant room for it beneath the broad mantle of Christian love"[6]) neither did he display any hankering after self-indulgence. An archbishop, after all, was not an anchorite who swore a vow of poverty. An archbishop was by definition a leading citizen, and the trappings of leadership were particularly important among the immigrant Catholic constituency that adhered to John Ireland. Had he, in that time and place, been other than a model of middle-class propriety and success, it is doubtful that that constituency would have paid him much heed. The popularity he enjoyed among his own—even when outsiders were most opposed to him and his works—seems to bear out that contention.

Ireland's heady aspirations for the Midway had received an enormous boost in the late summer of 1890, when James J. Hill offered a gift of five hundred thousand dollars to build and endow a major seminary on a site to be selected by the archbishop. "I was delighted to . . . learn your immense good news," O'Connell wrote. " 'Westward the Star of Empire, etc.,' and St. Paul must lead. . . . Now . . . you are a millionaire."[7] Ireland promptly set aside an attractive piece of land on a bluff above the Mississippi, a short distance from St. Thomas and part of the large farm he had originally purchased in 1880. He announced that the St. Paul Seminary would open its doors within twenty-four months,[8] but Hill, who, as things turned out, kept strictly in his own hands the construction as well as the funding of the institution, proceeded at a more leisurely pace,[9] and not until the fall of 1894 did sixty-five seminarians move from St. Thomas to their new and relatively sumptuous accommodations.

There appear to have been several reasons why Hill, a non-Catholic, pledged himself to such a generous benefaction. One was touchingly personal: "For nearly thirty years I have lived in a Roman Catholic household, and daily have had the earnest devotion, watchful care and Christian example of a Roman Catholic wife, of whom it may be said, 'Blessed are the pure in heart, for they shall see God,' and on whose behalf I desire to present the seminary and its endowment." Related to this tribute to Mary Theresa Mehegan was Hill's regard for her mentor, Louis Caillet: "I may say truthfully that had it not been for my intimate knowledge of and admiration for his character as a Christian pastor and a personal friend, it is very probable that I would never have thought of assuming the responsibility for [this] work."[10] (Ireland saw to it that Father Caillet quickly became Monsignor Caillet, and he prudently appointed him the seminary's first rector.[11]) It may have been also that the "Empire Builder's" gift was a measure of compensation for the favor unconsciously done in the 1870s for James J. Hill, the struggling entrepreneur, by John Ireland, the colonizer.[12]

Yet Hill did not leave out of account larger public concerns when he decided to provide the Archdiocese of St. Paul with a grand séminaire. Like most men in his position he believed that the masses could stand a good bit of the right kind of religion. But the American Catholic community, "with its large number of working men and women," lacked the financial resources of other denominations, and its people had "little else than their faith in God and those devoted men who have been placed in charge of their spiritual welfare."[13] It was crucial for social peace and prosperity that these "devoted men" be trained not in clerical obscurantism but along the lines of what Hill perceived to be Ireland's progressive ecclesiastical views and patriotic commitment. "An American character," Ireland assured him, "is impressed today as never before upon the Church in the United States. I know your convictions in this regard, and I am sure that you will hear this news with pleasure."[14]

Approval of Ireland's ideology, so far as he understood it, may have led to Hill's cordial agreement to specify in his seminary's charter that "at no time" was the institution to be "under the control or management of any particular society or [religious] order." But it did not extend to allowing the archbishop carte blanche with a half-million dollars. Ireland indeed was hardly more than a by-stander, as Hill himself oversaw every detail of the construction project, and kept track of every penny of the $240,000 it cost. Nothing was too trivial for his personal attention, and every decision — about plumbing or grading or fire insurance premiums or the quality of brick used or how the students' rooms were to be furnished — was exclusively his own. When the six buildings were completed, Hill determined how the balance of the money was to be invested and how the endowment income was to be spent through a trusteeship to last through the lifetime of his three sons and for twenty-one years thereafter.[15] Relentless attention to detail and total direction were not notable departures from Hill's ordinary way of doing business, but in this instance he had another excuse to keep control of expenditures in his own hands: he did not trust John Ireland's financial judgment. And with good reason.

On December 1, 1892, when the seminary construction was well started, Ireland wrote a hurried note to Hill's secretary: "Permit me to ask whether you have had a message from Mr. J. J. Hill in my regard? If so, please send me by bearer the check which I am expecting." But there was no check that day, and on December 3 Ireland wired Hill, who was in New York: "Please send to Stevens for Monday forenoon the promised message."[16] Apparently the telegram got results, for on December 5 there was entered into Hill's meticulously kept books notice of a twenty-five-thousand-dollar loan to Archbishop Ireland. A little more than a month later another entry recorded another loan of the same amount.[17]

Unhappily for Ireland, that was only the beginning of a thrall-dom that was to last for fifteen years. Nor did the first fifty thousand dollars, it would seem, sustain him for long. "I have letters from Messers. Cudahy and Onahan of Chicago," he wrote Hill on April

9, 1893, "telling me of an interview they had with you last Friday. . . . You promised them a letter, which they are anxious to have." Then, slipping into the imperative mode that was habitual with him, he added: "My purpose in now writing to you is to remind you of this in case it has not been already sent. Please, attend to this matter without delay. . . . In the letter, speak well of the land."[18] But two weeks later the tone he employed was entirely different, perhaps because of a rebuff from Hill or simply because of a heightened recognition of the peril in which he stood. John Ireland in either case had put on the unwonted garb of a suppliant.

> My dear Sir, . . . you have given me such unbounded proofs of favor and friendship, that while I am overpowered by my sense of gratitude, and my wonder that you have done so much for me, I am emboldened to talk to you as "my friend"—one to whom I can afford to talk unreservedly.
>
> I am simply crushed down with this load of debt. My power for work is impaired. The responsibilities of my position, in view of a loss of public credit, take from me all peace of mind. Moreover, I have come to the point, when something must occur—for weal or woe. . . . There is no other way out of this dreadful crisis into which I have got, but your friendship, and in that I put fullest confidence. Send me soon word that all is right, and I shall be a happy man.[19]

Specifically Ireland asked Hill to use his influence to help sell some of Ireland's personal property. "Put it to your friends that by taking this property, at the figures named, they will do me an immeasurable service, *please you,* and, withal, get back in a few years their money with reasonable profit. . . . Please furthermore make no delay. I must have money by the *middle of May.*"

At the moment Ireland penned this appeal—and thus placed himself "unreservedly" in the hands of one of the great "Robber Barons" of the era—the depression had already achieved doleful results: thousands of American firms had gone into bankruptcy, hundreds of banks had closed their doors, one railroad in six was in receivership, nearly three million industrial workers were unemployed, the bottom had fallen out of farm prices. And the value of Ireland's real estate, all of it mortgaged to the hilt, had plummeted. The archbishop was land-rich and cash-poor. The solution he proposed was to sell some of his holdings at far above their market value, and in that way meet the notes on the property he retained. In the midst of an economic crisis only very wealthy men, only tycoons like James J. Hill, could afford such a transaction, and so save him from complete ruin. Like the desperate penitent he was John Ireland fervently promised never to do it again: "The relief which the proposed sale will bring, will amply suffice to put me beyond all possible difficulties, and with the experience gained, all future risks are out of the question."

Ireland secured and forwarded to Hill appraisals stating that his property in the Midway totaled about 225 acres, scattered in blocks and lots along the river near St. Thomas and the new seminary, and worth between one and three thousand dollars an acre.[20] A rather more thorough analysis undertaken two years later revealed that the archbishop possessed assets of $593,532 against liabilities of $464,600. The trouble was, however, that the assets could not be converted into cash: "Not that there is any market for this class of property at present," in the laconic language of the appraisers.[21]

From the spring of 1893 onward Ireland was caught in this credit squeeze, and it drove him to the verge of distraction. At first he hoped that disposal of one thirty-acre parcel of land could save him. On May 9 he telegraphed Hill's Wall Street office: "I entreat you, do something. Matters nearing an end. I can do nothing without you. Please send me hopeful message."[22] But James J. Hill had become a philanthropist because he was rich, not the other way around. He bought and sold according to the realities of the market, and so did his powerful associates with whom Ireland begged him to intercede. None of them was prepared to buy real estate at the price it would have brought two or three years before the depression struck or might bring two or three years afterward. "I am in receipt of your telegram," Ireland wrote the next day,

> telling me that present conditions in New York prevent you from making a sale of real estate for me. I have only to throw myself on your mercy. You have done so much for me already that I do not believe you will abandon me. I see nothing before me, but to beg that you take yourself the thirty acre piece. I realize fully the boldness of my request, and the difficulties which compliance with it brings to you. I have confidence in your friendship for me,

and I hope you will save me. . . . You are the only one to whom I have the courage to talk frankly, and from whom I could expect a supreme act of friendship. . . . Now my dear Mr. Hill, send me a telegram, saying that you will take care of me. How much relief that telegram will bring me. I need not tell you how great my gratitude will be.[23]

But the president of the Great Northern was not buying. He recommended instead that Ireland place his property in trust or form a holding syndicate. Such suggestions, which in time bore fruit, could not quiet Ireland's hysteria of the moment. "Excuse appeal," he wired on May 17. "I absolutely need aid at once, whatever arrangements afterwards. Please act immediately, either ordering direct aid or securing credit for me." And a day later: "Anxiously awaiting favor. Tomorrow comes pressing need. Please don't disappoint."[24]

John Ireland was unused to begging, and the psychic cost to him of these financial troubles, as they dragged out over the years, must have been immense. It may well have been compounded by his naturally sanguine temperament, which led him repeatedly to see a final solution just around the corner. "I feel that this visit of yours to Chicago," he told Hill late in 1895, "will be decisive."[25] In fact not till eleven more years had elapsed was a final quietus written to the crisis: in January 1907, Hill gave Ireland a last recorded gift of fifteen thousand dollars.[26] During that long period Hill was consistently helpful, but on his own terms and in his own way. Ireland received from Hill at least $110,000 in cash over the five years after December 1892, not enough to deliver the archbishop from the threat of bankruptcy, but enough to keep the wolves from the door.[27] Hill moreover enlisted the aid of his fellow financiers and magnates, and the list of those who contributed money to Archbishop Ireland or who later joined his property syndicate—which essentially amounted to the same thing—sounded like a roll call of the gods of the Gilded Age: Henry O. Havemeyer, Jacob Henry Schiff, Michael Cudahy, Marshall Field, Philip D. Armour, Marcus Daly, Henry E. Huntington, William K. Vanderbilt, John D. Rockefeller. Only Pierpont Morgan eluded the net, and not for a lack of fervor on Ireland's part. At one point, when Hill told him Morgan declined to subscribe, Ireland pleaded by telegraph: "[Though] what you say is very true . . . could you not put down Morgan for at least fifteen [thousand], because two or three others we have reason to believe will follow his example." Hill responded with a brusque rebuke: "Message received. I have no authority to act for him. This is final."[28]

Twice Ireland, with Hill's help, appealed for relief to these eastern money-men, almost all of whom were also powers in the Republican party. Though the figure cannot be determined with certainty, it would seem that the efforts of 1894 and 1897–98 netted him about $500,000.[29] His property meanwhile had been placed in a trust under the supervision of Hill's son-in-law.[30] But there was never quite enough to stop the hemorrhaging. Ireland always needed another $100,000 "to finish the matter," or he sought a "proper distribution" of the real estate still in his possession "and the use of $200,000 [to] discharge all . . . indebtedness."[31] And all the while the pathetic chant went on. "You will, I trust, be patient with me if I ask you to remember your kind promise to come to my aid." "Please don't forget me while you are in New York. . . . I have imposed so much already upon you that I am ashamed of the trouble I am now asking you to take upon yourself. But it is very much like in the Scripture: To whom else can I go—in this fearful ordeal of mine." "As I am finding out every day, I am now in a position as never before—both in Rome and in America—to do much for religion and country; but this load of debt not only prevents me from using my influence, but threatens every day to destroy altogether this influence."[32]

But what a man must sometimes admit in private does not necessarily extend to his public pronouncements. Thus no contrast could have been sharper than that between Ireland's plaintive cries for help to James J. Hill and the bold front he adopted when, in response to discreet inquiries, he explained his finances to the pope's delegate. "Busy friends have been calculating how much I lost by depreciation of real estate," he wired Satolli's secretary. "No doubt values reduced, but enough left and no trouble."[33] He followed up the telegram with a long letter calculated "to quiet the anxiety of the . . . delegate."

> The reports spread around through the press have surprised and annoyed myself as much as they did [Satolli]. The whole thing

originated in New York. . . . A special reporter of the N. Y. Journal [came to] St. Paul with orders to investigate thoroughly my affairs. . . . He left no stone unturned to find out all he could against me. He discovered—what any child could do—that real estate had declined considerably in the West and in St. Paul as in any other city; that being the holder of a good deal of property I am not today as rich as I thought myself to be some years ago. He discovered, also, that some pieces of my property being encumbered with purchase-money mortgages, and the value shrinking nearly down to the mortgage border, I had concluded to transfer them to the mortgagees rather than continue to carry them, and expose myself to any possible future trouble. . . . From these discoveries a story was written—that my fortune had shrunk by a million and a half, that I am today a poor man. Well, my fortune with all allowances for depression did not shrink a tithe of that sum, and I am not such a poor man.

Much property remains. There is no possibility of trouble. I have property—and lots of friends—and if good times return property will rise to its old selling value. What has happened to me has happened to every man in the West.

The property which I hold in my own name is entirely personal—churches, colleges, institutions, etc. forming special corporations.[34]

The straitened circumstances of the archbishop of St. Paul could not be kept entirely from public knowledge. But Ireland himself consistently maintained that he had suffered only a minor and a temporary setback. Nor did he reveal the extent of his difficulties to his closest ecclesiastical friends and allies. Indeed, aside from a few oblique references, he never alluded to the problem, not even to Denis O'Connell. When, for instance, the rector and Cardinal Gibbons pressed him to contribute to the support of the *Moniteur de Rome*—their favorite journalist, Monsignor Boeglin, had fallen into a financial crisis of his own—Ireland promised to send mass stipends but not the five thousand dollars requested. "Times are hard this year: property does not sell . . . in these times of financial stringency."[35]

More indicative perhaps of his distracted state of mind were the gloom and waspishness he displayed in his comments about the situation of the American church. "Brandi is a devil," he said flatly of the editor of the *Civiltà Cattolica*, in which an article hostile to the Catholic University had appeared, "[and] Corrigan equals Brandi. . . . Who can put faith in any Jesuit writing? I cannot." "Spalding is bitter against [O'Connell] and me. . . . It is comical to hear him *pose* in the name of Catholic schools." "I am thoroughly disgusted with Abps Corrigan and Ryan, and while I shall always, I trust, know how to act toward them as a gentleman and a christian, I shall never forget their cunning and deceit." The archbishops' meeting of October 1893 brought him no solace: "Are we to be forever at war? If so, is life worth living?" Yet when Corrigan, at one point during the discussion, seemed to go out of his way to side with Ireland rather than with Ryan—"the biggest fool of them all"—the archbishop of St. Paul was not appeased: "I was dignified and made, I assure you, no compromising advances." Even the glittering prize that he had recently thought within his grasp had now turned into a handful of dust:

> The last cable of [the New York] Herald was that the Jesuits were opposing my being a cardinal. Confound that cardinal business. I am ashamed before the country. Get all correspondents to drop me, to forget that I live. . . . How I wish I had remained in my obscurity. The devil is loos[e] in the Church, and anybody who does anything is persecuted. It is best to let him have his way. My soul is decidedly down in the borderland of pessimism, there to stay. When I come before the public, my old-time ardor gets the better of me; but only for the moment.[36]

Those moments continued to be frequent, however. In June 1893 Ireland spoke on temperance and on "Social Purity" to one of the innumerable congresses held in conjunction with the World Columbian Exposition. The former speech was standard fare, while the latter, a stern Victorian lecture on the evils of pornography, was a reminder that for all his patriotism Ireland was by no means an entirely uncritical observer of the American scene. "See the wiles and activity and open warfare of impurity," he cried. "The popular literature of the day is largely subservient to it. Novels exhaling its stygian stench burden news stands and book agents' markets. Papers teeming with salaciousness obtain readers by the hundreds of thousands, and drive out of the market self-respecting and decent publications." Painting and sculpture, "whose mission it should be to elevate and ennoble the mind by the representations of humanity's best deeds and dreams, reveal [instead] the human form in hideous suggestiveness." He protested "theatrical posters, [which give] . . . our young people unmistakable object lessons in lasciviousness," as well as "immodest fashions in dances and in female dress." He called for laws against pimps and male seducers, and for sensible welfare legislation, too, since the sexual degradation of women was so closely linked to their poverty.[37]

In September John Ireland returned to Chicago — convinced that Archbishop Feehan of that city was "desperately jealous of my influence . . . and mad that I am invited and not he"[38] — for still another brace of speeches before the Exposition. One was a statement of the Catholic Church's role in labor relations, with special emphasis on Leo XIII's encyclical *Rerum novarum*. The other was his contribution to the Parliament of Religions, an interdenominational "assemblage of intelligent and conscientious men, presenting their religious convictions without minimizing, without acrimony, without controversy, with love and truth and humanity."[39] For this grandiose, two-week-long religious extravaganza, John J. Keane, at Ireland's urging, orchestrated the Catholic participation, which, though vaguely blessed by the body of archbishops, bore a strongly Americanist stamp.[40]

Denis O'Connell, sensing perhaps Ireland's mood of despondency, reacted to the latter's Chicago performances with a warmth unusual even for him. "My heart went out to you when I read your grand orations at Chicago. You are back in your element, doing good away from intrigues, and mean little dishonesties. What a man you would be if you were untrammeled, and what benefits your great big heart could pour out on humanity. That's your field, and every seed you sow there grows. I told all to Rampolla, and he says the Pope will be delighted." Delighted especially, the rector added, by "the Workingmen's speech," because Leo XIII was partial to anyone who spoke out boldly in support of *Rerum novarum*.[41]

The most spectacular of Ireland's appearances "before the public" occurred at Baltimore in mid-October, at the celebration of Gibbons's twenty-fifth anniversary as a bishop. Corrigan preached at the morning service, Ireland at the evening. "The cardinal desires to show there is peace. Well, let appearances go for what they are worth."[42] Before a huge throng gathered in the cathedral, Ireland sounded again his favorite theme, "The Church and the Age." A graceful tribute to Gibbons—"Often have I thanked God that in the latter quarter of the nineteenth century Cardinal Gibbons has been given to us"—followed a glowing one to the pope—"May Leo's spirit long dominate in the Vatican! All then will be well." But the heart of his message was the familiar summons—delivered here perhaps more eloquently than ever—to "the most glorious crusade. Church and Age! Unite them in the name of humanity, in the name of God. . . . We desire to win the age. Let us not, then, stand isolated from it. Our place is in the world as well as in the sanctuary; in the world, wherever we can prove our love for it or render it a service."[43]

"The Church and the Age" was enthusiastically received—"My Baltimore sermon is making an immense sensation. I am having it printed in pamphlet form. I hope it has not frightened the Vatican. Satolli approves it highly."[44] Ireland's sagging spirits were further buoyed up by Gibbons's warm appreciation, an objective the kindhearted cardinal may have intended to effect when he wrote: "Your sermon is still 'the talk of the town.' " There was "suppressed applause" in the pews "at the close of some sentences. . . . I feel like sending you a heavy bill for being the occasion of lifting you up so high on the pinnacle of fame." Satolli was preparing a translation to send to Rome, and, Gibbons added, "making a few verbal changes to save you from misconception."[45]

It is not likely that Ireland saw anything ominous in the delegate's introduction of "a few verbal changes" into his sermon. But in fact a subtle alteration in the relationship between the two men had already begun. One cause of it had been the Parliament of Religions in Chicago, which the delegate had attended in Ireland's company. Nothing Francesco Satolli had experienced in Perugia or Rome had prepared him for the spectacle of Catholic prelates mingling on professionally equal terms with all conceivable varieties of heathen. He could not have failed to notice that while his friends Ireland and Keane were engaged in this exercise, his alleged enemies—Corrigan, McQuaid, and the Germans—were as unsympathetic to the venture as he was himself. Thus the education of

Satolli had proceeded a small but—for John Ireland—an inauspicious step.

Before that, during the summer of 1893, Satolli had been a guest once more in St. Paul, whence he had traveled in style to the Pacific Coast, thanks to the private railroad car provided by James J. Hill.[46] Ireland's influence appeared as paramount as before. Upon his return to Washington the delegate found himself still beset by the conflicting signals coming to him from Propaganda and the secretariate of state, departments of the curia that continued at odds in their judgments about the ecclesiastical situation in the United States. But overriding Ledochowski's and Rampolla's competing policy objectives was the pope's own weariness at the persisting controversy among the American bishops. Having settled the school question, as he thought, by the artful compromise of May 31, 1893, Leo now wanted a rapprochement between Corrigan and Satolli. Gibbons, always an apostle of harmony, was readily recruited to carry forward this good cause. On August 15 the delegate celebrated pontifical mass in a crowded St. Patrick's Cathedral, and the archbishop of New York preached a carefully crafted sermon of reconciliation: "Whatever has been said in public or in private against the undoubted rights or sacred character of our honored guest, we reject and put aside as something not to be countenanced for an instant." Satolli professed himself satisfied, ready to forgive Corrigan his transgressions, had there been any, and in any case to forget the unpleasantnesses of the past.[47]

Ireland could not but be alarmed at this turn of events. "I presume your good offices have brought around the New York meeting," he told Gibbons. "I am glad of it for the sake of public edification. But," he added darkly, "be assured [that] many a poisoned shaft will be aimed at the Delegate's ear. I think Satolli will not waver, however, in his opinion of men and things."[48] Here surely the wish was father to the thought. Ireland had staked everything on maintaining an ascendancy over Satolli, and he clung to the delegate like a drowning man. "Satolli," he assured O'Connell in the autumn, "remains firm," reporting to Rome often "and always along our lines." "Satolli is holding out magnificently, improving every day. He goes away beyond us on all questions, in grand liberal ideas. He loses no opportunity to show his friendship for me—all of which is most annoying to our confreres." Many of those confreres gathered together shortly afterward to celebrate the silver jubilee of the bishop of Buffalo. "I never saw Satolli in better humor, more friendly to me, more determined in all our views than I did at Buffalo. 'I move into new house, he shouted when first seeing me, on the 16th [of November], l'anniversario.' What anniversary! I asked. 'When all, uno excepto, decided to defeat me.' "[49]

A year had indeed passed since the archbishops' meeting in New York at which Ireland alone had supported the fourteen propositions and the establishment of the delegation. Now Satolli had a house of his own, at Second and I Streets, N.W., in Washington, and two Italian secretaries instead of his Americanist warders, Keane and O'Gorman. "Some weeks" before he departed his rooms at the university O'Gorman "felt impelled to tell him of the 'bastardy' rumor. He was most thankful and is going to investigate." The story making the rounds was that Satolli was the natural son of Leo XIII, a libel on both men, to be sure, but one that persisted for many years. Given the delegate's allegiances to date, there was no reason for him to think the scurrilous rumor emanated from Americanist sources; perhaps that was why O'Gorman "felt impelled" to tell him about it. O'Gorman at any rate saw no sign that changing residences would weaken the delegate's devotion to John Ireland. Quite the contrary, in fact: "Satolli . . . told me he is confident that his last letter, the one he spoke of to you, will bring about your promotion [to the cardinalate]."[50]

Yet the delegate's removal to his new quarters coincided with still another negative sign. The two German-speaking professors on the faculty of the Catholic University, Schroeder and Joseph Pohle, who were notoriously at odds with Keane and with the whole Americanist program, were "most graciously" received by Satolli, who listened patiently and, Schroeder thought, with sympathy to their complaints. Keane did manage to force Pohle's resignation in the spring of 1894, but Schroeder hung on—despite the fact that several of his colleagues would not speak to him—and continued to cultivate the support of Corrigan and Bishop Horstmann of Cleveland, an increasingly powerful and articulate anti-Americanist figure.[51]

Ireland began the new year 1894 in a mood of isolated melancholy: "It is easy for you and Boeglin in Rome," he wrote crossly to O'Connell on January 7, "to say what America should do. But the America you talk of is reduced to mighty few individuals—so few that my 'solitude'—so far as bishops go—is almost Robinson Crusoean."[52] He perked up a few months later, however, when a new series of "revelations" about Corrigan's opposition to the delegation and to the Vatican policy behind it were published by a sometime editor of the *New York Catholic Herald* named Michael Walsh. Ireland stayed in close communication with Walsh, who also corresponded about Corrigan's villainy with Rampolla.[53] Ireland exulted that Corrigan was at last about to receive his just deserts: "I am told all around that C[orrigan] is just now quite frightened: he begins to believe that he is found out. . . . He knows that W[alsh] holds the key to the situation."[54] But Ireland had once more underestimated the supple Corrigan, who had no doubt conspired with Walsh but who had not left the unambiguous evidence of links to the journalist that Ireland had hoped for. Walsh, as it turned out, was more venal than virtuous, more interested in extracting money from Corrigan—he did not succeed—than in fighting the Americanist cause. So when Ireland came to New York in early April to give a speech, and paid a courtesy call at Madison Avenue, he found the chilly, smiling, non-commital Corrigan still very much in charge.[55] By far the most significant reaction to this latest flurry of publicity was Satolli's. Instead of the anger at Corrigan he had manifested over the *Chicago Post* stories of a year earlier, the delegate this time was all magnanimity toward New York, assuring Corrigan of his personal confidence and of his sorrow that "such malicious insinuations" were not indictable.[56]

As the excitement momentarily died away, O'Connell sent Ireland some personal advice. "Now, take some repose if you can and save yourself. You have too much for any one man to do. When [the Walsh affair] is settled, . . . break away for awhile and rest your feverish soul. It will add years to your existence and give some happiness to your life."[57] Whether or not he was following this counsel, the summer of 1894 was relatively quiet for John Ireland. He stayed at home for the most part, and while his money problems persisted, at least they grew no worse.

He enjoyed the leisure as well to meditate upon another of

O'Connell's predictions: "When the fight has died out and there is only one party, and that party is yours, I suppose you must be made Cardinal. . . . You have suffered much, and now you triumph."[58] As though to hasten the realization of that end Ireland dispatched to Rome one of the stalwarts of his party, Thomas O'Gorman, and, ahead of him, a strong letter of recommendation to Rampolla. This "very worthy ecclesiastic," he wrote, "has consistently shown himself most devoted to Mgr Satolli and has been able to render important services to the apostolic delegation, thanks to his influence with the press and with the administration in Washington. Dr. O'Gorman is well informed on the situation of the Church in the United States and is au courant, as few others are, with our difficulties and controversies, no less than with our hopes for the future."[59] This summer emissary, according to O'Connell, did his job superlatively: "[The pope] likes O'Gorman, respects his opinions, and speaks of him in the most favorable manner." Leo XIII, who was preparing an encyclical specifically directed to the United States, said that he had received many good ideas from O'Gorman.[60] This was welcome news to the archbishop of St. Paul, who was by now grooming his old schoolfellow for a miter.

An episcopal opening had occurred in the Province of St. Paul earlier in the year when Otto Zardetti had been transferred by Propaganda to, of all places, Bucharest, Romania. In his request for a change Zardetti cited as a reason only his delicate health, adversely affected by the severe Minnesota climate, and he said nothing about any problems with his metropolitan. His departure delighted Ireland, because it removed from his immediate sphere of influence an inveterate if somewhat timid enemy, and because it opened the way for him to rearrange his suffragans more to his liking. He proposed to shift Martin Marty from Sioux Falls to St. Cloud and to administer the South Dakota see himself until a suitable candidate could be named. O'Gorman was the candidate he had in mind, and he foresaw no difficulty in getting Marty to agree to a transfer.

Yet these days nothing, it seemed, went smoothly for John Ireland. He explained to Ledochowski that Bishop Marty's vast, thinly populated diocese, staffed by an unruly clergy he could not control, was too much for him. "Religion visibly languishes [in South Dakota], and only a strong and vigorous hand of a bishop chosen with the needs in mind will be able to rehabilitate it." Marty was an old missionary, and Ireland always kept a soft spot in his heart for old missionaries: "Mgr Marty . . . can conduct with honor to himself and to the Church the spiritual and temporal affairs [of St. Cloud], enjoying all the while the tranquility which his great works during long years of priesthood and episcopate have earned for him." But reverence for the past did not include putting up with any opposition to well-laid plans. When Marty at first acquiesced, and then, displaying an unwonted spark of independence, changed his mind and announced that he wanted to stay in Sioux Falls after all, he brought the full force of Ireland's wrath down upon himself. He was summoned to St. Paul and forced to write to Ledochowski "that he will go to St. Cloud if your Eminence decides this for him." The archbishop did not intend to put up with "these vacillations of Mgr Marty, which proceed in my opinion from mental and physical weakness." So bad was the ecclesiastical situation in South Dakota, wrote Ireland, that without the proposed transfer "I shall be obliged in conscience to request a formal inquiry by [Propaganda] with the purpose of securing the dismissal of Mgr Marty as bishop of Sioux Falls." Marty went to St. Cloud.[61]

And O'Gorman went to Sioux Falls, though not immediately. In the interval the good impression he created in Rome during the summer sojourn of 1894 ultimately played its part in his promotion. Certainly O'Gorman favorably impressed Denis O'Connell. These two most feisty and outspoken of the Americanists, only casual acquaintances before, traveled to southern France together and then shared some curiously intimate correspondence. "On leaving you at Avignon," O'Gorman wrote from Brussels, "loneliness took seat by my side. . . . Of all the memories of this summer — and some of them make me vain — the sweetest is now and ever shall be the trip with you to Avignon and Laura's grave."[62] O'Connell sent in reply one of his gossipy letters, which had in it a reference to Satolli's doubtful parentage and which concluded on a somewhat unconventional note: "Poor dear little lamb that you are, lamenting your lost innocent [*sic*] because you came to Rome. What a sweet dear little fox you became in a few days and just as natural as if you had been born one."[63]

Their mutual friend back in Minnesota meanwhile waited hopefully for the appointment of "a special commission of cardinals in Rome . . . [to examine] Mgr. Corrigan's conduct, and from all accounts," he told Gibbons, "things are likely to go hard with your venerable confrère and neighbor of New York."[64] But not all Ireland's attention was focused upon the rumors—so often ill-founded—of Roman intrigue. He was that summer absorbed, like most of his fellow citizens, in the violent progress of the Pullman strike in Chicago. When President Grover Cleveland intervened and dispatched federal troops to quell the disturbances, he received the hearty endorsement of John Ireland. "Pressed by both Catholics and Protestants to speak" on the issue, he did so, while on a day's excursion to Detroit. "The fatal mistake which has been made in connection with this strike," he said in a widely published interview, "is that property has been destroyed, the liberty of citizens interfered with, human lives endangered, social order menaced. . . . Labor must learn that, however sacred its rights be, there is something above them, one absolutely supreme social order and the laws of public justice."[65] These sentiments made better reading in board rooms than in union halls, but Ireland did not apologize for them.

> The Church must be kept before the American people as the great prop of social order and law—all the more so that Catholics are numerous in strikes and riots. Socialistic ideas have gone into our people, and into many of our priests. We have been siding with labor in its grievances: the unthinking ones transgress the golden mean, and rush into war against property.[66]

Yet a few weeks later, when talking to a correspondent of the Parisian daily, *Le Figaro,* Ireland smilingly said that he did not mind being called "the socialist bishop," as he had been in some French circles, if the word merely designated one who sought to eliminate social evils, even to the point of allowing reasonable powers of intervention to the civil power.[67]

A real socialist would have scoffed at the label. A more useful key to an understanding of John Ireland's politics—which were about to assume center stage—may have been his willingness to grant the right of the state to intervene in the affairs of its citizens. Certainly the activist and nationalist character of the Republican party appealed to him. The Democrats, by contrast, were the party of states' rights, with the philosophy that that government ruled best that ruled least. For them national initiatives were abhorrent. Ireland approved Cleveland's actions in Chicago, because they smacked more of Republican than of Democratic ideology. Something of a moral imperialist himself, supremely confident in his own program of social improvement for his particular constituency, the Catholic immigrants, he was much more at home in the ranks of the Republicans, the more "progressive" of whom seemed as ready to pursue universalist ideals as he was himself. The sectionalism of the Democrats was analogous, in Ireland's mind, to the parochialism of Catholic leaders like Michael Corrigan.

Two moral issues close to Ireland's heart led him in the same political direction. Though Republican practice never lived up to Republican rhetoric on the race question, it would have been inconceivable for a person with Ireland's enlightened views on the rights of blacks to have supported the national Democratic party of the 1890s. More compelling still, the cause of total abstinence from alcohol loomed so large in his mind that Ireland was bound to be set on a collision course with the "wet" Democratic party. In this regard, too, the Republicans displayed more timidity than the archbishop of St. Paul liked. But, at least in the northern states, they were the politicians who expressed sympathy for the cause, and it was on the platforms of temperance rallies that Ireland first met William McKinley and Theodore Roosevelt, both of whom heaped praise upon him for his efforts to promote sobriety among the immigrant masses. Ireland for his part gradually came to believe that the Americanization of the immigrants to which he was so dedicated involved, among other things, the kind of middle-class probity which the Republicans seemed to stand for and in which sober behavior played an essential part. Among his friends Keane and especially O'Gorman urged him on in his partisanship.[68] But then so did the eastern financiers to whom he turned for deliverance from his financial troubles.[69]

On October 10, 1894, Ireland, fresh from brow-beating Martin Marty, attended the annual meeting of the archbishops in Philadelphia. From there he went to New York, and he remained in that city or its environs for the better part of the next month. In light of the bitter public wrangle that followed upon his activities there, Ireland's own detailed explanation of them deserves attention.[70] His purpose, he said, in going to "the commercial and financial center of the United States" was "a very important transaction" he needed to complete, "the sale of land of quite considerable value." That municipal elections should have been held while he was in New York was, he said, "a coincidence" and "entirely accidental."

The week before those elections a rally was held in "a great hall" of the city, the principal speaker at which was the former Republican president, Benjamin Harrison, who "in all likelihood," Ireland contended, would be president again after 1896. The archbishop went to the rally as a sign of respect for Harrison, who while in office had done Ireland and the church many favors "and had bestowed the honors of the nation upon Mgr. Satolli" when the latter had come to the United States representing the pope in 1892. Upon his arrival at the rally Ireland had sought an unobtrusive spot from which to watch the proceedings (*"dans la salle une place obscure"*), but against his will (*"malgré moi"*) he had been seated next to the former president, "who was flattered by my presence. As I saw for myself, in attending the rally I had done a deed with happy results for the Church."

Also, during the course of his stay in New York, Ireland gave an interview to the newspapers in which he attacked Tammany Hall—"a political association [that] . . . for twenty years has dominated New York's civil administration and which has been guilty of the worst kind of corruption." Tammany was indeed an arm of the Democratic party, but on its sorry record it had been repudiated, Ireland maintained, by respectable Democrats and Republicans alike. But his larger intention had been to rebut the claim of the Democratic party, "whether in the city or state of New York or in the country at large," that "it alone is the partisan of religious liberty, while it accuses the republicans of harboring intentions of persecuting Catholics." In order to make that case, the Democrats had pointed to an alleged "secret alliance" between the Republican party and the American Protective Association. The latter group, Ireland admitted, was genuinely anti-Catholic, but he denied it any importance: "This association presents no danger; it cannot prosper in the United States." The Democrats had set up a straw man in the APA as a way of seducing Catholic voters. In New York City such a tactic resulted in Catholics being urged to support the gangsters of Tammany Hall, and in fact many priests, in press and pulpit, had done exactly that.

> Under these circumstances I believed it my duty to speak out, and I would have done so had I been in St. Paul. I spoke in New York because I happened to be in that city. I hold it as certain that the republican party has no connection with the A. P. A. and that the assertion that it does is nothing more than a political ruse. Why then . . . should I allow the republican party, including as it does among its adherents an immense number of Americans, among whom are the most eminent and influential men in the country, to be falsely accused? And why should I allow my co-religionists to be duped by politicians? It was perfectly clear to me that the republicans were on the eve of a great victory and that they would hold power for years to come. What a disaster for the Church it would be if these victors . . . should believe that Catholics are their enemies! . . . And specifically what a disaster for the Church in New York if at the last moment she should attach herself to the ignominious Tammany, so that, in the eyes of the whole country, Tammany's defeat would be the defeat also of the Catholic Church!

The Republicans did in fact win the New York elections in 1894, and Ireland's strong conviction (*"doctrine cardinale"*) that Catholics "in the interests of their religion" should be represented in both political parties and not be a captive to one appeared to receive thereby a measure of justification.

It did not seem so to the fiery old bishop of Rochester. On Sunday, November 25, Bernard McQuaid ascended the pulpit in his cathedral and delivered a blast at John Ireland heard round the world.[71] "Now that the election, with its excitement, turmoil, and passion has passed away," he began,

> I judge it my duty to refer, in this public manner, to some incidents and scandals connected therewith. I contend that this coming to New York of the Archbishop of St. Paul, to take part in a political contest, was undignified, disgraceful to his episcopal office, and a scandal in the eyes of all right-minded Catholics of both par-

ties. . . . If Archbishop Ireland had made himself as conspicuous in favor of the Democratic party, he would be just as blameworthy in my estimation. . . . The legislature of Minnesota is itself sadly in need of purification, and his Grace might have found full scope for his political scheming and skill right at home, if politician he would be. But it is well known . . . that it was no love for good government that kept Archbishop Ireland so many weeks in New York City and so far from his diocese, where the law of residence obliged him to be. It was to pay a debt to the Republican party that his services were rendered.

Ideological antagonism, building up for nearly a decade, drove McQuaid's attack, and personal passion did, too. In the spring of the year the candidacy of the bishop of Rochester for the single seat reserved for a Catholic on the Board of University Regents—which controlled all levels of education throughout New York state—had been defeated, thanks to Ireland's direct lobbying with his Republican friends in Albany, in favor of one Sylvester Malone, a priest of the Diocese of Brooklyn and a friend of Edward McGlynn. "It was none of the Archbishop's business," McQuaid cried, "to meddle with what did not legitimately concern him." Malone, he charged, was a notorious enemy of parochial education, and so, by implication, was the propounder of the infamous Faribault school plan.

Finally, McQuaid fired his salvo as a way of defending his one-time protégé, Michael Augustine Corrigan.

> The Holy See has no truer son, no more devoted servant, no Bishop sounder in the faith . . . than the Archbishop of New York. His loyalty is of the heart and on principle; yet, strange to say, this clerical clique [headed by Ireland, Keane, Malone, and McGlynn] has contrived to make many believe, by the help of manufactured cable dispatches and newspaper articles, that the Archbishop of New York is antagonizing the Apostolic Delegate, in the first place, and, in the second place, is in alliance with Tammany Hall. The two calumnies are persistently repeated until Catholics are annoyed and grieved, and non-Catholics believe the charges, emanating from Catholics, must have some foundation in fact. . . . This scandal deserved rebuke as public as the offense committed. I sincerely hope that the Church will be spared its repetition.

This stunning broadside, at once principled and spiteful, brought completely into the open all the resentments, misunderstandings, rash judgments, and genuine differences of opinion that combined to divide the Americanists from the anti-Americanists. The reaction followed predictable party lines, but it was also decidedly muted on both sides, as though the antagonists were suddenly startled and alarmed by the level of violence to which their long quarrel had risen. Satolli reported to Propaganda that McQuaid's attack was intelligible only within the context of "a longstanding rancor"; he thought McQuaid deserved a reprimand, but he did not rally as forcefully to Ireland's side as he might have done two years earlier.[72] Gibbons wrote to Rampolla of the "profound sadness" he felt and of the widespread scandal for which he blamed McQuaid; but significantly the cardinal did not try to defend Ireland's conduct: "I do not know the reasons for his trip to and sojourn in New York."[73] Corrigan admitted that his friend in Rochester had shown himself "not very prudent [*non troppo prudente*]," but he insisted that McQuaid had been provoked. "I do not approve of the method adopted by the Bishop of Rochester, but neither do I approve of the activities of the Archbishop of St. Paul, . . . [who consorts] with priests notable for their rebelliousness toward ecclesiastical authority."[74]

As for the two principals, so much alike in the vigor and frequent heedlessness of their personalities, they both remained stoutly at their guns, without however firing at one another publicly. Instead each of them defended himself at length to the Roman curia, though it is not without significance that McQuaid did so in a much more leisurely fashion: he wrote a full report of the affair only at the end February 1895.[75] No American bishop was more trenchantly anti-Italian, in private, than McQuaid, but of course that did not mean he was anti-papal. An old war horse, long used to the rough-and-tumble of ecclesiastical politics, he knew full well that in the real world of the 1890s he had opened himself to rebuke or worse at the hands of the pope. Yet in the long term he had risked less than Ireland, because he had had less to lose. Now well past seventy, and with no further ambitions other than to continue to govern his diocese in the firm—some called it tyrannical—fashion he had in the past, he could afford to look toward a Roman decision, however it went, with a certain serenity. He could afford, too, to beat the foreign-born archbishop of St. Paul with the same stick Spalding had used eleven months earlier: "We are Americans, and we fervently love the land of our birth."[76]

John Ireland, on the other hand, had forged a universalist policy and was struggling to implement a program to sustain it. But to achieve his Americanist ends—which were no less personal for him than professional—he had hitched his wagon to the Roman star even to the point of alienating the majority of his American colleagues. "You know," he told Gibbons, "how few there are in the hierarchy . . . whose opinions weigh with me."[77] The antipathy had clearly become mutual, and Ireland's incursion into New York had done nothing to soften it. But there was no drawing back on his part, as he demonstrated in his rejoinder to one of McQuaid's complaints.

> Mgr. McQuaid is particularly angry because I helped Father Malone obtain the position of "regent" of the University of the State of New York, and he invokes the principle that a bishop ought rigorously to refrain from using his influence in civil or political affairs outside his own diocese. As for the principle, I reject it, because it is unAmerican. I am a citizen of the nation. I do not meddle in things ecclesiastical outside my diocese. But in civil concerns I am my own master [*chez moi*] anywhere in the United States. . . . My letters [in behalf of Malone], coming from a distance, had, unhappily for Mgr. McQuaid, more effect than all the efforts he and his friends made in their own state. He was defeated, and he will not forgive me for that.[78]

For a brief moment the policy makers in the Vatican appeared ready to award Ireland a victory in the one place it mattered most. On December 16 Rampolla wrote a draft of a letter to Gibbons, in which he described the anger and determination of the pope to force McQuaid to make "proper reparation" for his deed. "If the Bishop of Rochester does not accept this verdict with docility, the august pontiff will consider the necessary measures he ought to take in the exercise of his apostolic ministry." But the secretary of state never sent this message, and the threat just quoted was crossed out of the draft, perhaps by the hand of the "august pontiff" himself.[79] Instead Rampolla communicated to McQuaid the pope's "pain" at his outburst, and McQuaid replied that he regretted the necessity of having to inflict pain upon the Holy Father.

In the public forum an archbishop had been labeled by one of his colleagues a liar, a meddler, and a tool of dark political interests, and the colleague had received a tap on the wrist. That archbishop had been moreover the lonely chevalier who had heretofore successfully bearded Germans and Jesuits, and had in the teeth of almost universal opposition brought about the establishment of the apostolic delegation. The archbishop had to wonder if the wheel of fortune had now turned against him.

XVII

The Travails
of "Asperity Ipswich"
1895–97

DURING THE 1890s John Ireland became so familiar a cor-respondent in the offices of the Great Northern Railway at Seattle and New York and St. Paul that he acquired a code name: James J. Hill's employees dubbed him "Asperity Ipswich."[1] How they arrived at this designation remains a mystery. They may have been led to "Asperity" after having experienced the rough edge of Ireland's temper, or they may have noted the often gravelly quality of his speaking voice. "Ipswich" defies even a guess. However it happened, the money troubles that had brought Ireland into fre-quent contact with Hill and his associates continued apace through-out the decade, and, as other troubles followed in swift succession, the times proved harsh enough for the archbishop of St. Paul to make at least the first part of the epithet appropriate.

As the rumbles of the McQuaid affair reverberated around him, he adopted a sober but unrepentant demeanor, insisting that victory imposed a coherence of its own on the recent events in New York.

> I can say, before God, that I had in view only the interests of the Church, which I desired to put above all political parties, the queen of all, the servant of none. Had nothing been said, the vic-tors of today [in the New York elections] would have reason to hold the Church as their enemy. I admit that it would have been better to let some one else speak, but no one else was at hand. . . . However, I am coming fast to the conclusion that for peace['s] sake it is best, so far as I am concerned, to let the Church jog her way, whatever the way be. I think I have definitely en-tered into winter quarters.[2]

It was not of course in Ireland's nature to withdraw for long from the hurly-burly; opposition indeed tended to stoke his combative fires. And, besides McQuaid's frontal attack, there was plenty of opposition in evidence, including Satolli's gradual retirement into the camp of the enemy and Keane's continuing difficulties at the Catholic University. These latter two problems appeared increasingly under one aspect, because the driving anti-Americanist force at the university, Monsignor Schroeder, had become Satolli's intimate. O'Gorman, Schroeder's colleague on the faculty, longed to find something incriminating with which to force the old Cahenslyite out of his professorship, but in vain.[3] In the spring of 1895 Schroeder accompanied Satolli to a small town in Pennsylvania where the latter presided at the laying of the cornerstone of a German parochial school. After the ceremony the delegate went out of his way to praise German-American Catholics who, he said, employed the customs and language "inherited from their fathers . . . as an important and effective means of maintaining intact religious and domestic virtues."[4]

Such sentiments from his putative ally might have been easier for Ireland to stomach had he been able to point to a group of thriving schools conducted along the lines of the Faribault-Stillwater model, but, despite his claims to the contrary,[5] he could not. In Rome it was being said that Leo XIII was highly irritated with Ireland, who had unleashed such turmoil over the school question and then in effect had deceived the pope by persuading him that the Faribault plan was a genuinely viable alternative to parochial education.[6] Ireland did discern the hint of a silver lining among these thunderheads. Archbishop Corrigan of New York, as the final step in the long, tortured process of reconciliation, had restored Edward McGlynn to a pastorate, outside the city indeed but an assignment in good standing nonetheless. The Doctor promptly received a warm telegram of congratulation from St. Paul.[7]

But the appearance at the beginning of 1895 of the papal encyclical addressed to the American Catholic community — about which O'Gorman had been consulted the previous summer — did little to relieve the overall gloom. In Longinqua oceani, as the document was titled, the pope praised the progress of the church in the United States, and much more lavishly praised himself, for having founded

the Catholic University and for having crowned the accomplishments of Baltimore III by establishing the apostolic delegation—the
chief functions of which, Ireland and McQuaid must have noted,
included promoting among the bishops "mutual charity" and
guaranteeing that "one [bishop] shall not impede another in matters
of government" and that "one shall not pry into the . . . conduct
of another." The pope said not a word about delivering the American church from the jurisdiction of Propaganda, and, though paying tribute "to the equity of the laws which obtain in America and
to the customs of the well-ordered Republic," he added pointedly:
"It would be very erroneous to draw the conclusion that in America
is to be sought the type of the most desirable status of the Church,
or that it would be universally lawful or expedient for State and
Church to be, as in America, dissevered and divorced."[8] Ireland was
bitterly disappointed: "The Encyclical has not made a ripple on the
surface of American thought. So much was expected, and so little
came. I was engaged by the North American [Review] for an article
in March on the Encyclical, but now I do not want to write it. That
unfortunate allusion to Church and State cannot be explained to
Americans."[9]

The pope also alluded in *Longinqua oceani* to another matter
difficult for Americans to understand: "Let this conclusion remain
firm—to shun not only those associations which have been openly
condemned by the judgment of the Church, but those also which,
in the opinion . . . especially of the bishops, are regarded as suspicious and dangerous." Neither Baltimore III nor the mechanism of
the archbishops' committee set up by the council had succeeded in
settling the question of Catholic membership in "secret societies."
Gibbons's heroic defense of the Knights of Labor in 1887 still
prevailed—*Longinqua oceani* explicitly excepted from its monitum
"associations for the promotion of . . . the working classes'
interests"—but the proliferation of other fraternal and mutual-
benefit organizations in the United States, all with a pseudo-
masonic aura, continued to perplex and divide ecclesiastical
authorities. The "opinion of the bishops," which the pope invoked
as a guide, was hardly to the point, since the status of the societies
had become just one among many partisan issues within the Ameri-

can church. Ireland warned that a Roman condemnation of the societies "would be a great triumph for Corrigan and Katzer."[10]

A condemnation nevertheless came, and no event since Archbishop Katzer's appointment to Milwaukee angered John Ireland more. "I am amazed and saddened beyond expression," he wrote Gibbons at the end of 1894, "by the letter of Mgr. Satolli telling us that the Pope wishes to have the condemnation of the Societies — Sons of Temperance, Odd Fellows and Knights of Pythias — promulgated . . . and communicated at once to the Suffragans." The condemnation actually had been issued the previous August, with instructions to Satolli that he communicate the decision to the archbishops' meeting in October. He did so, with the surprising result that the archbishops unanimously agreed "that it was inopportune under the present circumstances to publish said condemnation." That Katzer, Corrigan, and several other prelates known to be hostile to the societies should have taken this stance was probably due to their anxiety over the then rising tide of anti-Catholic feeling, promoted by the American Protective Association.[11] But Rome was adamant, and insisted that the decree — a terse statement from the Holy Office, unqualified and unexplained — be given full publicity. "In what a ridiculous position bishops will be placed," Ireland protested, "when they, the teachers of Israel, know not why those societies, which they must condemn, are worthy of censure! . . . The Lord save us from the Inquisition and its Sallvos [*sic*]!"[12]

More clearly perhaps on this issue than on any other did the exclusively European mind-set of the Roman curia display itself. Because the lodges in Italy, France, and elsewhere in Latin Europe were demonstrably anti-Catholic and even anti-theistic, the same had to be true of American benevolent societies that indulged in secret handshakes and encouraged their initiates to wear funny costumes. And the cavalier fashion in which the curia ignored the unanimous recommendation of the archbishops put Ireland back into the frame of mind he had had before his victories of 1892. "Few things occurring within the last decade of years have annoyed me so much as this condemnation, and the setting aside included therein of all regard for the episcopate of America, or at least the larger portion of it."[13]

Confusion dominated the first months of 1895. Some dioceses, among them New York and Brooklyn, promulgated the condemnation, while others did not. Denis O'Connell's intelligence—he reported early on that the decree had been shelved—proved unreliable. Gibbons was uncharacteristically stubborn in resisting the Holy Office's directive and appeared at one point to have won concessions from the vacillating Satolli. The cardinal, with the same pastoral sense that had led him to champion so strenuously the Knights of Labor, stressed the financial loss low- and middle-income Catholics would needlessly suffer if they were forced to withdraw from the societies in question.[14] John Ireland concurred with him in this argument, but he registered in addition a stronger ideological objection in the protest he filed in Rome, at Gibbons's urging. "I am persuaded," he told Rampolla,

> that the promulgation of the decree will cause the gravest embarrassment and great damage to souls and to the Church itself. . . . Americans are passionately devoted to clubs and societies, and particularly to those which include an element of mutual benevolence. The extreme political individualism upon which they base their institutions seems to lead them to cherish all the more voluntary organizations for their social and commercial lives. . . . The members of these three [condemned] societies—Catholics and Protestants alike—see them as nothing more than benevolent associations; they do not find in the constitutions or customs of the societies anything in opposition to the divine, natural or ecclesiastical law. This is the universal conviction, most Eminent Lord, . . . and I am myself of the same opinion. I have examined with care the charters and official books of these societies and interviewed their leaders. . . . There is much about them offensive to my taste, much I consider useless and even childish, but there is nothing about them contrary to a Christian or Catholic conscience.

A decree of this kind only played into the hands of those "who harbor absurd prejudices" against Catholicism. It posed new obstacles to conversion, Ireland contended, for the church would have "to demand from a prospective neophyte that he leave an association from which he derives important temporal advantages and in which he sees nothing wrong or injurious." Good Catholics would be needlessly penalized, while those weak in the faith would simply leave the church. He saved his clinching argument for the end and advanced it, he said, "from the bottom of my heart."

> The general population of the United States will be offended [by the condemnation]. It will be seen as an act intrinsically opposed to American principles and ideas. It will invite defiance of the Holy See, and create a fear of the uses of the pontifical power . . . . We are marching forward today in America; each year we record new victories; the Holy See grows perceptibly in influence. Alas [*Eh bien*]! This decree, I am sure, will change all that, and will put us back at least a half-century.[15]

Rampolla did not answer this letter, and by late February, when reports appeared in French newspapers to the effect that the archbishop of St. Paul had publicly repudiated the Vatican's policy on secret societies, Ireland wrote the secretary of state again, this time with some alarm. "Your Eminence can imagine with what painful dismay I read the pages of those journals. I, in defiance of the Holy See! I, for whom all thoughts of respect and all affections of the heart breathe devotion to the Holy See!" Rampolla replied soothingly that Ireland's loyalty had not been questioned, but he offered no comment on the substantive issue.[16] Gibbons meanwhile had determined to go to Rome in person to seek a reversal of the condemnation, and Ireland urged him on: "Please go to Rome. . . . You are needed there. Go to conquer, and return to us having conquered."[17]

Ireland's apprehensions mounted during the spring. He wrote repeatedly to Frederick Z. Rooker, Satolli's newly appointed secretary and a protégé of O'Connell, but received no reassurance. "The documents [hostile to the societies] prepared by the other side," Rooker replied, "were masterpieces and dovetailed so nicely together that there was no doubt of the care and concern with which they had been prepared." Ireland and his friends — "you will not think me bold if I suggest" — had by contrast proceeded too casually and too tardily. Their presentation had been "evidently prepared in a great hurry, at the last moment and without research or collection of proofs. I read all six papers more than a year ago in Rome and at that time said that if the Holy See had to decide the case on those documents there could be but one decision expected, and that an unqualified condemnation."[18] O'Gorman, who was still in close contact with Satolli, had no better news.[19]

Ireland consoled himself as best he could with overseeing the first year's operation of the new seminary and in planning that institution's festive dedication, scheduled for the following September. He had assembled what he called "a brilliant staff" of teachers, and the buildings, almost complete, looked "magnificent."[20] A trip to Chicago and a speech before the Union League Club on "American Citizenship" also cheered him up considerably.

> I had a wonderful time in Chicago. . . . The so-called élite of the city, five or six thousand, were my hearers. The applause lasted several minutes when I said: The American refusing to vote merits disfranchisement or exile! People were wicked enough to see in those words an allusion to his Lordship of Rochester. . . . The discourse had a wondrous effect in Chicago; it wrought up the people to fever-heat. I trust it will have thro' the whole country the effect of linking the Catholic Church in the minds of the American people with high American patriotism.[21]

Before returning home Ireland traveled the short distance to Notre Dame, a place he frequently visited and where he always found a warm welcome. On this occasion he delivered a rousing address to the student body, which responded, to his evident satisfaction, with tumultuous enthusiasm.[22]

In mid-May Gibbons sailed for Rome in hopes of securing a reversal of the condemnation of the three secret societies. But he did not succeed in repeating the victory he had had with regard to the Knights of Labor eight years earlier. On the contrary, he learned that the pope was personally annoyed that the decree had not been promulgated in Baltimore or in St. Paul. The "triumph" Ireland had wished for him never came to pass. Far worse than that, and far more ominous, was the news that the pope had demanded Denis O'Connell's resignation from his position at the North American College. Indisputably, the rector had made himself vulnerable as he was irritatingly visible to the anti-Americanists in Rome and in the United States. In theory the agent of all the American bishops, his strong partisan stands on the controverted issues of the day had alienated those opposed to the Gibbons-Ireland group, but it had also alarmed those prelates, like Archbishop Williams of Boston, who did their best to steer clear of both parties. It was widely said that O'Connell's relations with Cardinal Ledochowski had grown so strained that the two men did not speak — an intolerable situation so long as the American hierarchy had to deal routinely with the prefect of Propaganda.

O'Connell compounded the problem for himself by his frequent and lengthy absences from the college and by the rather cavalier attitude he assumed toward its administration. There was not, to be sure, all that much at the North American to occupy a clever man's attention. O'Connell maintained a competent staff, and even his enemies admitted that he handled its finances extremely well. Nevertheless, he created the impression that the college was for him a mere sinecure that hardly deserved his day-to-day ministrations. His friends tried to admonish him on this score, but to little effect. He continued to absent himself regularly from his post, and on occasion he displayed less than a prudent regard for the proprieties. "I am afraid that the war may now turn on you," Ireland had warned him late in 1893. "I hear mutterings. . . . The Cardinal [Gibbons] says he will stick to you . . . and I am sure he will. But take an advice. Don't be away from the college; give up this trip to [the] Holy Land of which Virginia spoke to me. Keep some of our friends at a little greater distance."[23]

"Virginia" was Virginia Mactavish, a pious spinster of an old Maryland Catholic family with which O'Connell had a close connection. There is no evidence that his relationship with her was anything but platonic, but his travels in her company set tongues wagging, and her reception by the queen of Italy, just after O'Connell had arranged a papal audience for her, outraged Vatican protocol.[24] This was the sort of misstep noted carefully by the watchful archbishop of New York and his Roman agents. "I am certain," Ireland said, "that our foes track us at every step, spy [on] us. All this makes life a burthen: but then, for the time being, we must be careful." He knew whereof he spoke. In the spring of 1892, while he awaited the decision of Propaganda on the Faribault school plan, he had gone on holiday in Sicily with the count and countess of Tarravicino di Revel. "Corrigan told Austin Ford of the Contessa, and of her trip with me to Sicily. In fact, he has put out that I had my own 'Miss Eades' [*sic*] — only with huge ostentation."

But O'Connell ignored his friend's advice and went off with Miss Mactavish the following spring for a tour of the Middle East that lasted a couple of months. Upon his return in June 1894, he waxed lyrical: "I have just done what you ought to do," he told Ireland. "You cannot imagine what heavenly bliss it is to get away for a while from all care and bother and to find yourself again as a child amidst the lovely and refreshing surroundings of sweet simple nature. It is worth more than years of life spent in the weary disappointment of dishonest and endless struggle."[25] Obviously the rector sensed no threat to his position, nor was his self-confidence as yet misplaced. O'Connell's Roman standing remained secure as long as Leo XIII continued to hold him in special regard, to treat him, almost, like a pet. Then, in the spring of 1895, the pope heard — perhaps from Corrigan — that O'Connell was spreading the canard about Satolli's illegitimacy. He summoned the rector to his presence, and after a stormy private interview — nobody, not even Rampolla, admitted knowing exactly what was said — O'Connell submitted his resignation.[26]

The harsh judgment of O'Connell rendered some years later — "a clever, accomplished intriguer — but an imprudent and unsafe confidant; vainglorious of his own influence and authority"[27] — possessed enough truth to lend a certain poetic justice to his fall, caused, it would seem, by his weakness for the gossip of the salons. But O'Connell, whatever his faults, was more than a mere trifler; he did in fact stand for something, and his removal from office was therefore a severe blow to the Americanist party, both substantively and symbolically. The automatic entrée the Americanists had enjoyed along the corridors of power at the Vatican and the Piazza di Spagna was now gone. The new rector — also coincidentally named O'Connell[28] — had his own agenda, which did not include risking his ambitions for the sake of controversial causes. And the favor in high places that Denis O'Connell's position had heretofore signified was gone, too. During the summer the press in the United States and abroad declared that the sacking of the rector demonstrated that Ireland's star was clearly setting and Corrigan's rising, that Ireland's influence in Rome had become "almost nil."[29]

O'Connell himself, always a moody man, now suffered from an extended period of depression. He unreasonably blamed Gibbons for his dismissal, and he withdrew for some months from any contact with his erstwhile allies. Ireland, who had experienced before O'Connell's petulant and inexplicable swings from verbosity to utter silence,[30] appeared less sensitive than Gibbons to their friend's psychic state or to the larger significance of his fall from favor. "I sorry to have to say," he told the cardinal, "that I have received no reply to my letter to Mgr O'Connell—written at your instigation. Before I wrote that letter, I was used frequently to hear from him; since then, there is absolute silence. Why and wherefore—I cannot imagine."[31] In the autumn O'Connell departed Rome for another trip to the Middle East, and remained for all practical purposes incommunicado. Gibbons hoped he would return to the United States, at least for a time, but O'Connell had become too much imbued with romanità to find that prospect attractive. By the spring of 1896, somewhat recovered in spirits, he had come back to *la città* and moved into an apartment on the fashionable Via del Tritone. The ever-generous Gibbons provided for his support by naming him vicar of the cardinal's titular church, Santa Maria in Trastevere.[32]

In the interval Ireland presided at the dedication of his new grand séminaire. Satolli traveled to St. Paul for the occasion and testified to the splendor of the ceremonies—which celebrated particularly the merits of the donor, James J. Hill, and his family—and to the excellence of the seminary's physical plant and its faculty.[33] The delegate appeared to be on the same friendly terms with the archbishop of St. Paul as ever, and, for the time being at least, the unhappy fate of Denis O'Connell cast no great shadow.[34]

For John Ireland, the opening of the seminary was a red-letter day. During the rest of his life he found the keenest personal pleasure in visiting the seminary, chatting with and lecturing to the students, and holding learned conversations with the faculty, much as he had done at St. Thomas in previous years. While he never lost his affection for the latter institution, which continued to keep vivid his nostalgia for Meximieux, the seminary offered a more direct route to the fulfillment of his deepest ambitions as an ecclesiastical statesman. The Americanization of the church was not only a goal to be pursued within the national arena; it possessed a local dimension, too. And to Ireland that meant primarily the provision for his own diocese of a native-born clergy well trained in the sacred sciences, disciplined, devoted to the best American ideals (as he conceived them), and loyal to himself and his successors. In the seminary he had in his hands what he conceived to be the most suitable instrument to mold a high-minded American Catholicism for the present and future generations.[35]

Experience had taught the archbishop, as it had other ordinaries with less authoritarian instincts than his, the necessity to impose control over the lower clergy, a control which a major seminary could allow him to inculcate from an aspirant's young and impressionable years. For among the travails endured by "Asperity Ipswich" during the mid-1890s none tried his patience more than the shenanigans of some of the priests subject to his jurisdiction. The number of these clerical culprits was relatively small, and much of the difficulty they caused could hardly have been avoided, since the frontier church, with its rapidly expanding Catholic population, had had to gamble on accepting the services of priests who carried with them to their parochial assignments the baggage of failure, eccentricity, or worse. Probably the real shame was that they often brought undeserved disrepute upon their brethren, that large majority who labored with a genuine missionary spirit reminiscent of Ireland's model, Joseph Cretin. The archbishop at any rate noted grimly that most of the trouble-makers were foreign-born and educated outside diocesan supervision.

Take the case of Patrick K. Ryan, which distracted Ireland for nearly twenty-five years.[36] Ordained in 1870 by Bishop Grace, Ryan displayed early in his ministry a weakness for drink. Late in 1885, when he was pastor in the flourishing Minnesota River town of Mankato, Ryan was suspended by Bishop Ireland for public intoxication. There was no canonical process; it sufficed for the bishop that Father Ryan had been "often sent to jail" for drunkenness. But that did not suffice for Rome, to which Ryan, after wandering for a while in an ecclesiastical limbo, ultimately appealed. Here was an instance, though perhaps not a very edifying one, of the tension within the American church produced by the absence of ordinary legal procedures to settle disputes between bishops and their clergy. A major reason for the establishment of the apostolic delegation was to stanch the flood of appeals sent by American priests to the Roman congregations, which, before Satolli came, were their only defense against arbitrary bishops.

P. K. Ryan was apparently a man who believed in going straight to the top. The apostolic delegation did not yet exist in 1892, and so he wrote to the pope, whom he asked to direct Ireland to reinstate him. Ireland refused and insisted that Ryan, who was still drinking, take up residence in a monastery. He offered to grant Ryan an annual stipend of 1,725 francs. Propaganda instructed him to raise the amount to 2,500 francs, or about five hundred dollars. Ryan accordingly took up residence in a religious house in the English midlands, but before long he had repaired to his native Dublin and moved in with "a respectable family." Ireland promptly cut off his subsidy, and Ryan appealed this time to Satolli. "I have suffered much being almost ten years without any work or position. I am unable now to be sent from place to place."

The case was now entangled in the Roman bureaucracy, and Ireland had to explain himself to Propaganda. "I promised [Ryan] six years ago," he told Ledochowski in 1896, "to maintain him in a monastery or a retreat house, either in America or Europe. He chose to go to Europe, and to this day he has cost me three thousand dollars." The archbishop added wryly that he would be grateful for the cardinal's advice on this "insoluble problem." Ryan meanwhile had returned to England and had arrived drunk at a religious house near Manchester. Ireland agreed to send a pound a week to pay for his keep. "The Archbishop has done all he could do for him," the superior reported, "even was willing to pay Dr. and for medicine if wanted[;] also wee [sic] have done all we could do for him, but I am sorrow to say that F. Ryan is a ungrateful man, I think his wish was to have some money in hand to spent it for drink, and he would certain spent it for drink only." The pitiful Ryan somehow made his way back to the United States and was taken in by religious brothers who operated a mental hospital in Wisconsin. "I am here with the Alexian Brothers 2 years," he wrote Sebastiano Martinelli, Satolli's successor, in 1899, "no fit place for a Priest to be among Lunatics, feeble-minded and Epileptics." He pleaded with the delegate to force Ireland to send him money "to procure clothing which I need badly, . . . so that I can live as a Priest, not as a pauper."

Not all the clerical problems in which Ireland was embroiled were so long-lived as that of Patrick Ryan, but each of them took its own toll in time and energy. For example, at the end of 1895 Satolli inquired about a complaint registered with him from a couple named Nichols, who had contracted to work as janitor and housekeeper for the pastor at Hutchinson, Minnesota, at a wage of twenty dollars a month. After seven months employment they had collected only ten dollars, and the priest "was sent away." They complained to Ireland, but to no avail. "I think it is getting very bad," Mr. Nichols told the delegate, "when a priest will cheat poor people out of their wages. We staid with him when no one else would and for him not to pay us I think is awful and here it is winter and we haven't anything to live on." Ireland's response was succinct.

> I beg leave to say that the matter referred to in the enclosed letter is very plain and simple. As the complainant alleges, the Rev. T. McMahon owes him money. Unfortunately, the Rev. McMahon owes money to several people. I have removed him from his parish and made him assistant to another priest and I am using all prudent means to compel him to pay his debts as fast as possible. In due time he will reach the complainant, Mr. Nichols. Meanwhile, neither the bishop nor the parish is obliged to pay the said Mr. Nicholls [sic].[37]

It must have occurred to Ireland occasionally that his success in promoting the apostolic delegation had paid him scant dividends, for it was the delegate more than once who forced upon his attention parochial problems he would have preferred to forget. Such was the hilarious affair of Schneider versus Stultz, which Martinelli repeatedly asked the archbishop of St. Paul to attend to.[38] "The controversy between Rev. W. M. Stultz and Peter Schneider of Shakopee, Minn., is in itself a trivial affair," Ireland finally replied, "but it takes more than an archbishop's power to settle, and I shall be very glad if the apostolic delegate's power suffices. Father Stultz and Mr. Schneider are both hard-headed Germans, and neither will give in; each one is bound to conquer." Their quarrel began over a contested will, after which Schneider removed himself from the German- to the English-speaking parish. Mrs. Schneider, an invalid, could speak only German, and her husband demanded that Stultz come to hear her confession. "The wife does not care what priest comes, but the old man declares that it must be Stultz, just because Stultz will not come."

Ireland arranged that a German-speaking priest some five miles distant come regularly to the Schneider home to administer to Mrs. Schneider the sacrament of penance, and that the English-speaking priest in Shakopee bring her Holy Communion.

> But no. Schneider wants Stultz. I requested Father Stultz to go; I commanded; I threatened; he went once or twice, and then invoking canon law and theology he said he could not absolve Mrs. Schneider for reasons known only to himself. I have had this case of Stultz vs. Schneider on my hands for three years. I give up. One thing remains — it is to suspend Fr. Stultz. If you wish, it can be done. . . . But what Schneider wants is victory over Stultz. He has tried me; he is now trying the Delegate; he next intends to try the pope. If I am permitted to make a suggestion to your Excellency, it is that you pay no attention to the matter. . . . In my opinion, both Stultz and Schneider are fools, and must be treated somewhat as such — i.e., let alone.

More bizarre were the transgressions of Father Wenn, of the little hamlet of Loretto, who, according to the notarized statements of several witnesses, urinated from the back steps of the church into the cemetery — among the graves of "our beloved dead" — and who also "made his water" into the mass vessels in the sacristy. Incensed when an aged parishioner complained at having been overcharged for his daughter's funeral, Wenn, alleged to have been a habitual drunkard, ordered his sexton to kick and beat the old man. "I was able to walk off," the latter recalled, "and walkt home and get ready for the evening train to see Most Rev. Archbishop Ireland and saw his Grace. And he said when he heard this complain, that is shame, that is a shame, it is very rough, it is very rough, he said I will write him about it. I told him if it would not be settled I would take him by Law, but his Grace said you can not take the Pastor by Law, only the hire man. . . . We ar here in a wery bad circomstances."[39]

George Pax, the pastor at Sleepy Eye, combined in his person two constituents that automatically aroused the suspicions of the archbishop of St. Paul: he was an extern, having been ordained originally for the Diocese of Buffalo, and he had for a time been a Carthusian monk in France. Ireland thought Pax too harsh in dealing with parishioners who belonged to the Odd Fellows or the Knights of Pythias, and decided to transfer him to New Trier, a distinct demotion. But the pastor of New Trier refused to move, even though Ireland accused him of wasting parish funds and of discouraging mass attendance among the young people of the parish because he was "too protracted in the services," and he and Pax both appealed to the delegate. In the end, after a lengthy game of ecclesiastical musical chairs, W. M. Stultz became pastor of Sleepy Eye, delivered at last from the clutches of Peter Schneider.[40]

Then there was William J. Keul, who "ruined three young women" in three years. "The man is radically bad," Ireland asserted. "He brought one woman into the sanctuary, put on his stole and 'married' himself to her." He borrowed money under false pretenses, fled the diocese, married, fathered a child, and operated a cigar store in Chicago and later in Philadelphia. In 1896, five years after he had begun these merry pranks, Keul applied for readmission to the active ministry in St. Paul.[41] Another problem was Peter Rosen, originally a priest of Sioux Falls whom Bishop Marty could not handle. "I took him," Ireland admitted ruefully to Satolli, "thinking that I could manage him." Rosen, an unusually articulate man, used the funds of his parish in Fairfax to pay his personal debts, and when Ireland disciplined him he initiated a literary campaign against the archbishop that included a printed pamphlet and continued well past the year 1900.[42]

Sometimes the archbishop confronted not just an individual priest but a whole parish. When a quarrel broke out within the Polish settlement at Wilno, in far western Minnesota, Ireland — persuaded by "a wicked man of no religion," in the words of a group of petitioners who approached Martinelli — removed the pastor. A month later a delegation went to St. Paul, and later reported that Ireland told them they were "unworthy, vagabo[n]ds, rebel[l]ious; we do not posses[s] our own churches, that our country is divided up between three european powers, and all other things; and without any reason, saying that he will not give us a priest at all."[43] Whatever the justice of their accusation, it demonstrated that the nationality issue was by no means dead. Nor the temperance issue, either, at least in John Ireland's mind. In the autumn of 1898 he placed the Catholic parish at Ghent — one of his colonies — under interdict. When the delegate asked for an explanation, Ireland sent him an angry rejoinder.

> The writers of the [complaining] letter omit to state that Sunday after Sunday the people of Ghent, all Belgian Flemings, were wont to adjourn from church to saloon, and engage in fights which culminated at last in a brutal murder—the newspaper accounts of which brought disgrace upon the Catholic Church. I forbade the celebration of Mass in Ghent—the people being told to go to another church five miles distant, until I received a promise signed by a large majority of the people that people would not visit saloons on Sunday. I received that promise a week ago, and allowed Mass to be again said in Ghent. In your reply please tell the people of Ghent to refrain from getting drunk and murdering people on Sundays.[44]

This recital of petty clerical abuses in the outlands of Minnesota serves as a reminder that not all John Ireland's joustings were with Corrigan and McQuaid and sophisticated Italian Jesuits, and that the glamorous issues of national significance in which he was involved did not relieve him from the humdrum tasks, some of them distasteful, incumbent upon the administrator of any large organization. It also underscores the importance Ireland placed upon the foundation of his own major seminary; he was confident that his control over recruitment and training of prospective priests would eliminate much of the difficulty personified by Fathers Ryan and Keul, and he was surely correct in that assumption. At the same time it must be stressed that the very documentation of these cases indicates that they were by no means typical. Ordinary people performing their ordinary duties leave few traces in the archives. For the most part the priests of Ireland's jurisdiction, both before and after the opening of the St. Paul Seminary, functioned more than adequately and responded positively to the often charismatic leadership he offered them, with the result that the Catholic people of the Archdiocese of St. Paul were by and large well served. This generalization was doubtless truer of the urban areas than of the countryside, for Ireland made it a policy to assign his clerical problem-children to rural parishes.[45] But then the Catholic church has never claimed to be a communion of the elect, and any segment of it at any time—including Minnesota during the 1890s—reveals moral sluggishness aplenty. John Ireland, who was not without warts and blemishes of his own, struggled manfully to be a worthy spiritual leader to his own people, and the sometimes uneasy combination of a choleric disposition and lofty ideals helped him, on balance, to succeed admirably. Even so, he must often have turned with relief from the feud between Stultz and Schneider to concerns of rather greater moment.

One of these, at the beginning of 1896, was the promotion of Thomas O'Gorman. Ever since the translation of Bishop Marty to St. Cloud, Ireland had been working to secure for O'Gorman the bishopric of Sioux Falls. Given the changing dynamics within the Roman curia — symbolized eloquently by the fall of Denis O'Connell — together with O'Gorman's reputation as an outspoken Americanist and a "henchman" (Corrigan's word) of the archbishop of St. Paul, the task was bristling with difficulties.[46] Cardinal Gibbons supported the candidacy, but he warned Ireland that all opposition to it had to be defeated beforehand: "Otherwise it would be a blow to you and to the University."[47] O'Gorman, aware from the first of what was afoot, had to content himself with fulfilling his usual obligations at the Catholic University and prodding his chief with an occasional reminder: "I suppose the Sioux Falls nomination will not be made before May or June [of 1895]."[48]

In fact Ireland initiated the formal process sooner than that. By March he had secured the ternae from the priests of Sioux Falls and the bishops of the Province of St. Paul, on both of which — hardly a surprise — O'Gorman's name stood in first place. Satolli endorsed the choice and forwarded the papers to Rome on March 22. A few days earlier Ireland wrote his statement for Ledochowski. "I take the liberty of recommending [O'Gorman] to you in a special manner," he wrote. For years American public opinion had marked out the brilliant O'Gorman for a miter, and now, "as your Eminence knows," the deplorable condition of the Diocese of Sioux Falls had need of a man of such prestige and stature. The only conceivable objection, Ireland contended, was O'Gorman's work at the Catholic University, "where in fact he does fill an honorable role." However, there was a second ecclesiastical historian at the university: "It is the modern part, and consequently the less important part [of the course], which is confided to Dr. O'Gorman. He can be replaced without difficulty." Whether he intended a small irony in that assertion it is impossible to say. Ireland went on at any rate to laud O'Gorman's prudence, judgment, maturity, fluency in languages, and, of course, the all-important "devotion to the Holy See." He made no reference to their shared experience as schoolboys, nor to O'Gorman's years in the Paulists, but he may have had in mind some specific events of bygone days when he observed: "As a young man he gave evidence of a certain temperamental inconstancy and capriciousness; with the passage of years this fault has been entirely eliminated."[49]

Then, to Ireland's intense irritation, nothing happened. In the late summer he asked Satolli to inquire at the Vatican, and the delegate, still personally friendly toward Ireland and O'Gorman despite his ideological drift away from them, readily obliged.[50] In October Ireland wrote Propaganda again. Sioux Falls should be filled without delay, he said. Eight months of vacancy there had led to "a great detriment to souls and a great confusion of all religious interests." Since O'Gorman had been first choice on both ternae, Ireland professed bewilderment that he had not been duly appointed. "It is said that certain ecclesiastics have presented you with objections about his candidacy." What grounds could be advanced, he wondered, to support opposition to so talented a nominee? "I am profoundly convinced that Monsieur O'Gorman is more than any other person who could be named the man for Sioux Falls. I would have strong regrets if due to malcontented and unjust critics he were set aside."[51] By mid-December Ireland learned that his appeal had been successful, affording him "one crumb of comfort," as he described it to Gibbons, in an otherwise hungry time. "It appears that ferocious attacks were made on our whole list [the two ternae] as liberal, semi-heretical, etc. Especially was O'Gorman torn to pieces. But he is all right now."[52]

Thomas O'Gorman chose St. Patrick's Church in Washington as the site of his consecration as second bishop of Sioux Falls. On Sunday, April 19, 1896, Satolli, just recently named a cardinal, acted as the consecrating prelate, assisted by Martin Marty and John J. Keane. John Ireland, returning the favor O'Gorman had done him twenty-one years earlier, preached the festive sermon. It was not remarkable for its general tone or substance, nor for its brief personal allusions, but it did contain a passage that helps explain why Ireland, despite his occasional troubles with them, was popular among the secular clergy, who liked to consider themselves "the order of St. Peter" and to hear public pronouncements about "the dignity of the ministry of saving souls."

> The priesthood which I commend with all my earnestness . . . is the diocesan priesthood. There is room and work in the Church for the religious orders of priests. . . . But their organization and purpose . . . takes them to a large degree from the Bishop's jurisdiction; so when we speak of the Bishop's priests in his diocese they fall outside this enumeration. He cannot depend upon them. . . . The members of the diocesan clergy depend upon the Bishop; upon them he counts. They are the sons of the diocese. . . . The diocesan clergy have been underestimated and neglected. The rough and ready work fell largely to their lot, and leisure for study was not afforded them. . . . It must never be forgotten that the normal clergy for a diocese are its own incardinated priests; as they grow and work, so will the diocese expand and prosper.[53]

Ireland spent the rest of the week in the Washington–Baltimore area, and on April 26 he delivered an informal address to the students of St. Mary's Seminary. The subject of his sermon for O'Gorman was apparently still on his mind, for he spoke to the seminarians on "the divine origins of the secular priesthood." Some of his hearers, however, interpreted his remarks as a direct attack upon the Jesuits. "In fact, in the heat of the moment and on the dizzy height of a [rhetorical] climax, he mentioned the order by name, and, . . . with a vigorous thrust of his hand, he took us by storm when he uttered the words, 'Drive them out!' " Ireland denied having used the offensive phrase. "My purpose was to give the young [men] a high idea of their own priesthood. . . . I am unfortunate," he told Satolli, to whom a complaint had been sent, "in being misunderstood and misquoted."[54]

That the apostolic delegate should have been moved to inquire into so trivial a matter was worrisome. Much more so was the fact that Satolli had taken the occasion of O'Gorman's consecration to confide to Ireland his strong displeasure with the rector of the Catholic University. Ireland alerted Keane and urged him to set things right with the delegate. The rector responded by writing Satolli a haughty letter that simply exacerbated the situation.[55] But it is unlikely that Satolli, with Keane's enemy, Schroeder, ever at his elbow, could have been pacified by anything Keane might have said. Not that personal dislike or ideological opposition sufficed by themselves to explain Keane's predicament: the state of the university was so parlous that only a perpetually sanguine chief administrator could have expected to escape severe criticism. Keane, like O'Connell in Rome, had neither tried nor aspired to stay above the Americanist–anti-Americanist struggle, and the institution from its inception had been a battleground between the likes of O'Gorman and Bouquillon on the one side and Schroeder and his various foreign-born allies on the other. Nor did this conflict-torn faculty possess any striking academic distinction: O'Gorman's "doctorate," for instance, was merely a courtesy title given him by the pope.[56] Add to these unpromising circumstances the enduring hostility of the Jesuits and of powerful prelates like Corrigan and McQuaid, the chronic financial difficulties, and the reluctance of the bishops to send students to Washington—only twenty-six matriculated in 1894—and one gets a sense of the rector's vulnerability. Yet even his closest associates failed to appreciate the danger and the consequent need to lend him aid in strengthening the institution. Thus in 1895, when Keane requested Ireland to assign one of the latter's brightest young priests as a science professor at the university, the archbishop brusquely refused, on the grounds that James J. Hill insisted on a strong program in science at the St. Paul Seminary: "I am sure that [Hill] would not forgive me if I were to part with Fr. Shields."[57]

Keane, like the whole Americanist party, had risked all upon the friendship of Satolli. "Your Eminence will not be surprised to hear," the rector wrote Rampolla in 1893, "that the university regards the cause of the Apostolic Delegate as its own cause. . . . Those who attack the delegation are the same who range themselves against the University."[58] And Satolli gave the university good marks in his reports to Rome through most of 1894. But by the summer of 1896, which Keane spent on holiday in France, the atmosphere had changed drastically, and Satolli, who apparently never liked Keane—or Gibbons, for that matter—as much as he did Ireland, determined to bring the rector down. In a series of letters to Rampolla the delegate condemned Keane, not, it should be noted, for his ideology or doctrine, but for his alleged inability to administer the university properly. The students, few as they were, lacked all discipline; they frequented taverns and theaters instead of tending to their spiritual exercises. Keane, habitually given to "talking nonsense," wanted to expand the institution instead of concentrating on its original purpose, the formation of young priests in the ecclesiastical sciences. The finances of the university were in tatters, and the rector wasted his and the institution's resources on promoting athletic contests. Non-Catholic professors had been hired, Satolli complained, and the rumor was abroad that the rector even contemplated the admission of women to the student body! The only solution, in Satolli's judgment, was the immediate dismissal of Keane, an act which indubitably would stir up a momentary furor among the American hierarchy, but the delegate assured the secretary of state that the fuss would quickly subside: "I know these chickens [questi polli], good people at heart, although often childish."[59]

There seems little reason to doubt that by this time Satolli, under the tutelage of Schroeder and others of his ilk, suspected Keane and indeed all the Americanists of holding unsafe doctrinal positions.[60] But he chose to accuse the rector instead of administrative failure, a charge for which the argument, if not conclusive, was at least persuasive in some circles. This tactic of the delegate helps to explain Keane's twofold reaction to the shocking news of his dismissal when it was transmitted to him by an almost tearful Gibbons at the end of September 1896. At first Keane refused to accept the face-saving device the pope offered—a titular archbishopric joined to a post in the Roman curia or, if he preferred, a metropolitan see in the United States—and announced his retirement from public life. By early October, after conferring with a "gloomy" Ireland in Chicago, he had fled to California in the company of his friend, Archbishop Riordan, and had taken up residence in a facility operated by the Sisters of Charity in San Jose. "I have lots of health and peace," he wrote on November 1, "and lots of good work mapped out. I only pray that I may be left in quiet to enjoy it all."[61] Far away, the bishop of Rochester could not but crow over the prostration of his enemies.

"The news from Rome is astounding. . . . What collapses on every side! Gibbons, Ireland, and Keane!!! They were cock of the walk for a while and dictated to the country and thought to run our dioceses for us. They may change their policy and repent. They can never repair the harm done in the past."[62] Perhaps the strongest indication of how the atmosphere had changed in four short years was Satolli's departure for Rome in mid-October; he had arrived almost furtively in New York in 1892, and now, a cardinal going home to assume a position in the curia, he was bade a fond farewell from the same port by Corrigan and the bishops of the province, a hundred priests, a thousand lay persons, and two bands.[63]

But Bernard McQuaid's thinking was premature if he expected the Americanists to give up the fight and don sackcloth and ashes. True enough, there was some panic in their ranks, displayed notably by Father Bouquillon, who, fearful that he might lose his own job, wrote almost hysterically to Rampolla: "Eminence, it is true I have always tried to help [Keane]; he was my superior, appointed by the pope, and I owed him my loyalty [*dévouement*]. But if Mgr Keane has committed errors, I affirm before God that it was not I who led him to make them."[64] Others were more stalwart, however, and, as Satolli had predicted, Keane's ouster produced a strong reaction, particularly among certain segments of the press.[65] Keane himself, once convinced that his orthodoxy had not been formally called into question, regained his confidence, returned to the East during the last week in November, and declared himself ready to accept the pope's offer of a curial post. "I should have preferred," he went so far as to tell one reporter, "to remain always at rest and in retirement, but . . . the Holy Father in his wisdom saw fit to call me to a much higher post of honor and responsibility in the Church."[66] This remarkable statement elicited from the maverick bishop of Peoria a savage comment, which may well have expressed the views of others growing weary of the seemingly endless controversy.

The impression in Rome is that the Pope, in slapping Bp. Keane in the face, has given a death blow to the University. With Bp. Keane himself I have lost patience. If the Pope had him down on all fours kicking him, each time he lifted his foot the enthusiastic bishop would shout—See how the Holy Father honors me. A more disgusting state of things than our ecclesiastical situation is hardly conceivable. The only important question, it seems, is whether Abp. Ireland is falling or rising in favor with Rome. If we could only hear nothing more of him, it matters little whether he fall or rise.[67]

Far from hearing nothing more of John Ireland, Spalding, along with the rest of the country, was just then hearing more of him than ever before. Not with reference to the Keane case, however, for the archbishop of St. Paul said relatively little about that, and what he said was not without ambiguity. "Bp Keane . . . goes to Rome . . . to fight Satolli and Satolli's allies," he remarked approvingly to Alphonse Magnien, while with Satolli himself he adopted a hopeful and conciliatory tone and lauded the former delegate for helping to arrange Keane's "Roman honors."[68] The fact was that in the midst of the rumpus over Keane's dismissal Ireland's mind was on another subject altogether. A hint of his preoccupation appeared in a newspaper interview published at the end of October. Ireland, in Washington for a meeting of the Catholic University Board, observed casually that "the change in the rectorship" would not diminish his enthusiasm for that institution. The reporter, however, was much more interested in the call Ireland had made at the White House. "It is understood that the President praised in the highest terms the stand taken by the Archbishop on the issues of the present campaign."[69]

"The present campaign" referred to the contest for the presidency, just then approaching its conclusion, between the Republican, McKinley, and the Democrat, William Jennings Bryan. Outgoing President Cleveland, though a Democrat, had no sympathy for Bryan and his Populist views, and indeed one of the reasons Bryan had been perceived to have no chance of winning the race was the shattered state of the party he led. Another disaffected Democrat was James J. Hill. But Bryan, "the Boy Orator of the Platte," had confounded the experts by appealing to the electorate in a manner that smacked more of a crusade than of a political campaign. In the early days of October he came to Minnesota and scored a stunning personal triumph. Crowds unprecedented in size and enthusiasm greeted him everywhere. In Minneapolis cheers punctuated almost every sentence of his speeches. In St. Paul the labor unions presented him with a gold pen in a silver holder, an apt gift for one who had gained immortality by a single sentence, uttered at the Democratic National Convention the previous July: "You shall not crucify mankind upon a cross of gold." Bryan at thirty-six — tall, handsome, bursting with energy and good health, bubbling over with optimism and affability, tireless, single-minded, his rich sonorous voice reaching to the farthest edge of the largest crowd — Bryan had seized upon the Populist issue of free silver versus the gold standard, and virtually by himself had so stirred the country that a Democratic victory, unthinkable a few months before, had become a distinct possibility.[70]

Bryan had moved on by October 11. On that day the Associated Press put on the wire a statement by Archbishop Ireland of St. Paul, a statement purportedly in response to inquiries made by "twenty representative men." "I am not unwilling," Ireland wrote, "in this crisis through which the country is now passing, to speak for the integrity of the nation, for social order, for the prosperity of the people, for the honor of America, and the permanency of free institutions." He did not argue in behalf of McKinley, and he never mentioned Bryan by name; he directed all his fire at the Democratic platform. To those who objected to a churchman mixing into politics, he responded: "There are occasions when a political platform means disaster to the country, when politics is closely connected with morals and religion, and on those occasions the churchman must be the patriot . . . and must take in hand the moral or religious issue, even if it be vested in the garment of politics." Indeed, every citizen should speak out against the "delusion" of free silver, which, if enacted, would destroy the American economy. But the monetary question, he contended, was of secondary importance. What the Democratic platform really recommended was a renewal of secession — "the secession of 1861 which our soldiers believed they had consigned to death at Appomattox. . . . There is the annulment of the Union. [And even] worse to my mind . . . is the spirit of socialism and anarchy . . . which has issued from the [Democratic] convention. . . . It is the 'International' of Europe now taking body in America. They are lighting torches, which, borne in the hands of reckless men, may light up in the country the lurid fires of a 'Commune.' The war of class upon class is upon us."[71]

The statement ran to four columns in the newspapers in which it was published locally and all over the country. The Republican national organization printed it in pamphlet form and distributed 250,000 copies.[72] Despite the characteristic exaggerations (or perhaps because of them), it clearly expressed Ireland's genuine views. But, though he never admitted the fact, he had not, in issuing the statement, acted as an independent agent; it had been exacted from "Asperity Ipswich" as a partial payment for favors rendered and favors hoped for.

When by late September it had become clear that Bryan was rapidly closing the gap between himself and McKinley, thus making the electoral votes in the Upper Midwest crucial to Republican success, the president of the Great Northern Railway swung into action.[73] "In the two Dakotas and Minnesota," Hill informed Marcus Hanna, McKinley's campaign manager, "I have already paid out over $60,000, and will have to pay twenty-five or thirty thousand more, in addition to my own subscription of $15,000 to the State fund." To carry Montana for McKinley "will at least require $10,000," which Hill was willing to spend. "Bryan is expected here in the first days of October, and we will have to overcome any of his efforts." Hill doubted that 20 percent of union members in Minnesota would vote for McKinley "as things stand today," but he had at hand a weapon that might cut into Bryan's working-class, heavily Catholic constituency: "We are giving Archbishop Ireland, through a non-partisan letter signed by twenty representative men, an opportunity to state his views fully, which he is prepared to do, and I am sure he will cover the ground, stripping the [Democratic] platform to the bone."[74]

Whether Ireland's intervention contributed to the outcome of the watershed election of 1896, it is of course impossible to say. But McKinley did carry Minnesota by sixty thousand votes (out of 340,000 cast), and of the forty-two electoral votes at stake in the Upper Midwest Bryan won only four. The Democrats were understandably furious. William Randolph Hearst, publisher of the *New York Journal,* cabled Rampolla and demanded to know whether Ireland represented the official view of the Catholic church. The secretary of state did not reply, but he hastily sought information from the new apostolic delegate. Martinelli reported that Ireland claimed to speak as a private citizen, not as archbishop, and certainly not in a way to compromise the Holy See. No doubt Ireland had employed hyperbole in his accusations against the Democratic party, but such, Martinelli observed with a shrug, was the nature of American politics. Ireland himself wrote Rampolla in mid-November and pointed out that he now held the president-elect in his debt: "Never has an American Catholic bishop enjoyed the influence which is now mine. And that influence will be entirely and always at the disposal of the Church and its Head." This was music to a papal diplomat's ears, and Rampolla hastened to assure Ireland of the pope's "continued esteem and benevolence."[75]

It was probably more than coincidence that there appeared in Hearst's *Journal* a report to the effect that Satolli from Rome had denounced Ireland as "an apostle of heresy." A reinvigorated Denis O'Connell urged Ireland to initiate a civil action against the *Journal* and thus to flush out Corrigan and perhaps Ryan of Philadelphia with whom O'Connell thought Satolli had been conniving.[76] The other ex-rector, Keane, also now in Rome as the new titular archbishop of Damascus and consultor to Propaganda, had recovered his habitual optimism; though not so belligerent as O'Connell, he pressed upon the archbishop of St. Paul the need to follow up his success. The election of McKinley had impressed the Roman officials, Keane said, "in favor of the good cause which we represent. They appreciate also what your power now is in America, and how important is your plan in regard to the ministers to Paris and the Quirinal. Your getting those matters into good shape will be of immense weight in the Vatican. So your stock never was higher, or as high."[77]

Certainly Ireland had gained a measure of influence over the incoming administration. In December he was among those invited to McKinley's home in Canton, and there he made his case for the appointment of a Catholic to the cabinet.[78] In negotiating with McKinley he worked closely with Senator Stephen B. Elkins of West Virginia in behalf of the Republican committeeman from Missouri, Richard Kerens, who had lobbied Rome to bestow a red hat on Ireland a few years before.[79] Kerens still had this project much at heart, and he wrote to Rampolla, seconded by Elkins, to point out that contrary to rumor it was Ireland, not Corrigan, who wielded influence over the incoming administration.[80]

For whatever reason the president-elect refused to elevate Kerens to the cabinet, but he did agree eventually to appoint another Catholic, Joseph McKenna of California, attorney general.[81] McKinley also smoothly assured Ireland that he had no sympathy with the American Protective Association, and that he would appoint envoys to France and Italy who, though necessarily Protestants, would not be unfriendly to Catholic interests. In defiance of this condition Ireland recommended for the embassy in Paris a former congressman and McKinley's fellow-Ohioan, Bellamy Storer, who, with his wife, Maria Longworth, was a convert to Catholicism and a fervent disciple of Ireland and Keane. The Storers were also close friends of Theodore Roosevelt, who lobbied in their behalf with the president-elect as they did in his.[82] Maria Storer, a much more formidable personality than her husband, was not slow to remind McKinley that she had contributed heavily to his campaign (as she had to John Ireland's real estate "syndicate"[83]), and that she wanted as reward for Bellamy either Paris or the post of assistant secretary of state. She got neither; in the end the Storers had to accept the second-rank embassy at Brussels, which they did with little grace.[84]

More crucial to Ireland's own designs was the appointment as minister to Italy of a Minnesota Republican whom he knew well and whom presumably he could direct. His first choice was the distinguished former governor, William R. Merriam, but when that gentleman declined to be considered Ireland turned to his old Civil War commander, Lucius Hubbard, also a former governor. Hubbard was willing enough to accept the post, but neither he nor Ireland reckoned with the man who at that moment was the real political kingmaker in the Upper Midwest. "It is of the greatest consequence," James J. Hill telegraphed Marcus Hanna on March 6, 1897, "that no foreign appointment is promised from this State until you receive my letter." The letter, dated the same day, dashed any hopes Hubbard may have had of hobnobbing with the diplomatic community at the Quirinal.

> Archbishop Ireland, who, you know, has taken a very active interest in the Presidential election, . . . [is] in a 'peck of troubles,'

having urged the appointment of Governor Hubbard and afterwards [having] found out that he was totally unfit for the place.
Hubbard was a good soldier during the war, but while Governor
of Minnesota got into some business difficulties which were of
such a character as to destroy all confidence in his business integrity. He was in partnership with a man named Lawrence, in
the grain business. They issued grain receipts and borrowed
money in the East on the security of . . . grain supposed to be
stored in their own elevators. An investigation showed there had
never been a bushel of grain in the elevators. The Archbishop
knew nothing of this, and consequently feels dreadfully mor-
tified. He will undoubtedly write the President on the subject.[85]

So Hubbard's candidacy went whistling down the wind, and Ireland had to be satisfied with the appointment of William Draper, a
millionaire textile manufacturer from Massachusetts, as minister to
Italy. O'Connell passed along a word of reassurance: "It was a triumph and an evidence of power to send Draper here. Everybody
knows that Ireland did it, and on their arrival here, Mrs. Draper said
so plainly. . . . The impression at the Vatican was surprising."[86]
Yet when Ireland transmitted to Rampolla McKinley's vague wish
that Draper be of service to the Holy See and requested a papal audience for his wife, the secretary of state frostily replied that neither
Draper nor any other representative to the Quirinal could have direct relations with the Vatican.[87]

It was therefore a time of mixed signals for Ireland, as well as
an exceedingly busy time. At the very moment Keane was telling
him how high his stock stood in Rome, he heard of "the terrible
prospect of [Gibbons] having Lavelle or Schroeder for coadjutor."
This rumor proved, like so many others, a false alarm, but meanwhile, Ireland told the cardinal, "I was determined to stand by you,
and whatever else was to happen, I should not [have] allowed a
coadjutor to be imposed upon you."[88] Besides worries like this one
of cosmic proportions, the archbishop had a host of lesser obligations clamoring for his attention. Among them was seeing through
the press the collection of his sermons and addresses which became
the first volume of *The Church and Modern Society*. He left the reading
of the proofs to two of his more talented young priests, to one of
whom he confided: "I have never been so busy as I am these days."[89]

As if ordinary administrative duties, literary pursuits, national politics, the crisis at Catholic University ("The University is dead," Ireland wrote Gibbons; "nothing can revive it. The Jesuits have triumphed there for good"[90]) and the shifting sands of Vatican policy were not enough to occupy his mind, Ireland found himself caught up once more in the tangled ecclesiastical affairs of northern Minnesota. Bishop Marty of St. Cloud died in September 1896. By mid-November Ireland forwarded the two ternae to Propaganda. First on the list of the bishops of the province was J. M. Solnce and third was James Trobec, both pastors in St. Paul. Neither of these names appeared on the list of the consultors of the Diocese of St. Cloud. Indeed, the only candidate common to both ternae was a priest of St. Cloud who suffered from heart disease and who for that reason was quickly eliminated from consideration. In his covering letter Ireland dismissed the St. Cloud list as "merit[ing] no attention at all." Father Solnce, he argued, was "altogether worthy of the episcopate; and if he is chosen by the Holy See, he will bring honor to the Church from his private virtues, his zeal, his eloquence, his ability to manage activities whether spiritual or temporal."[91]

But because the ternae were so much at variance, the apostolic delegate, Martinelli, initiated some private inquiries of his own within the province. He discovered that the opposition to Solnce was strong, and not only in St. Cloud but also among Solnce's priestly colleagues in St. Paul and Minneapolis. Charges ranged from alleged hostility to Germans and the members of religious orders to a weakness for drink and an over-familiarity with women. So Ireland wrote to Ledochowski again, because "according to our information" opposition, as yet unspecified, to the bishops' choice had been mounted, "astonishing to me," he protested, "for I have always known [Solnce] as an exemplary priest, beyond all reproach." The opposition has no doubt arisen "from a spirit of immoderate nationalism" and "from the desire of the good Benedictine fathers [at St. John's Abbey] to have the Bishop of St. Cloud under their power, as they have been accustomed up to the present." As for Martinelli's investigation, Ireland clearly did not like it. "The right of the Apostolic Delegation so to act encounters in practice some serious difficulties. . . . I do not know what [the opponents of

Solnce] have written to the Delegate, but they are boasting at having defeated the will of the bishops."

Ireland's advocacy, strongly seconded by Archbishop Keane in his capacity as consultor to Propaganda, was to no avail. At the end of March 1897, Ledochowski suggested that the bishops submit a new terna. A month later Ireland did so, with Solnce once more occupying the first place: "The accusations which have been made against him are devoid of foundation and born of envy and hatred. . . . I commit myself to a position beyond racial antagonism of any kind. . . . [I have] bound myself always, in accord with my principles, to nominate only priests who possess all the qualities required of an American bishop, loving the land of their adoption and knowing well its language." The rest of the list contained three rather than the customary two names, because the bishops could not agree on the third position. In Ireland's judgment James Trobec's merit had diminished by one slot since the previous autumn, and his name had fallen to fourth place among the four. Keane tried to force the issue by complaining to Ledochowski of the "vicious assaults" against Ireland in German newspapers. "They have attacked Father Solnce precisely because Mgr Ireland and his suffragans have indicated that he, Solnce, would be the best bishop for St. Cloud." To ignore the will of the bishops, warned Keane — sounding a very old theme indeed — would leave the church in America ungovernable, would "result not in peace but in disorder." In the high summer of 1897 the pope named James Trobec third bishop of St. Cloud.

The defeat was a severe one for John Ireland; if he could not prevail within his own province, what must be his standing within the larger ecclesiastical power structure? According to the fevered imaginations of certain journalists, the contest for St. Cloud revealed the depths to which Ireland's prestige had fallen: an especially preposterous report had it that at the beginning of the selection process the archbishop of St. Paul had felt it prudent to promote the cause of Monsignor Joseph Schroeder of the Catholic University for St. Cloud.[92] Perhaps things were bad, but they were not that bad, and in fact the Americanists were poised to take out their accumulated frustrations upon that same Schroeder, a particular bête noire of theirs.

Ireland called it the "War of 1897," and it was war to the knife.[93] Cardinal Gibbons hoped that a direct confrontation with Schroeder could be avoided, but Ireland insisted the time had come to get rid of the offensive professor, the ally of Cahensly and Corrigan, the bloated intriguer who had corrupted Satolli and had engineered the disgrace of Keane: "All America is laughing at us, deriding us for being kept in awe by a Dutch beer-guzzler."[94] But Schroeder, indeed a fat, ungainly, and less than attractive man, had adherents of his own, including the several powerful cardinals-in-curia who identified his cause with their own. The moment of truth — or of reckoning — arrived on October 20, when the university's governing board convened its annual meeting. Fourteen bishops, including Keane who had traveled from Rome for the purpose, one priest, and one layman answered the roll call, with Gibbons in the chair. The first item on the agenda was financial business, and after the discussion the lay trustee withdrew. The priest, pastor of a parish in Washington, remained.

Thomas Conaty, Keane's successor in the rectorship, then presented a three-fold bill of indictment against Schroeder.[95] He was, first, a "continual source of quarrels both in the University itself and in the country at large"; he showed little aptitude for university teaching; and finally "he was guilty of having frequented very often saloons [*cabarets*] — even saloons of the lowest kind — and from time to time of being drunk, to the great scandal of the students and the people of Washington." Before any motion could be entertained, however, Gibbons read a cable from Rampolla "giving counsel," as Ireland expressed it, "not to demand the dismissal of Mr. Schroeder. The situation was very difficult for the Directors [members of the board]." While they desired to respect the wishes of the Holy See, they could not close their eyes to such serious charges. So they determined to render a decision in the form of a recommendation to the pope.

Conaty still held the floor. He proceeded to present a series of statements, given "under oath" (in Keane's words) and notarized, in which twelve witnesses attested to Schroeder's public drunkenness. Only one of them claimed actually to have stood at a bar with Schroeder and seen him consume "six or eight glasses of Münich [*sic*] beer," but another, a streetcar conductor, maintained that he had once seen the professor drunk, "the evidence of such intoxication being the odor from his breath and the fact that the saliva was drooling down from his mouth over his clothing, and from the further fact of his unsteadiness on his feet." This aspect of the case against Schroeder had been carefully prepared and had involved shadowing him since at least the previous spring. The most damning account was that which associated him with the "low bar" operated by one Lena Beuchert on Eighth and H Streets.

> I have heard that Mrs. Beuchert is a widow, and I myself have seen whites and negroes enter this saloon promiscuously, and I have seen them drinking there. This I have seen several times. A saloon in which whites and negroes drink together is considered in our City of Washington as being very low and common.
>
> On one occasion, April 27th of this year, I saw Monsignore Schroeder come out of this place (Beuchert's Saloon) about 8:30 p.m., accompanied by a woman and a young priest. The three entered a carriage and drove around the city (inside and outside the city), and returned to the saloon about 10:00 p.m. The young priest came out about 11:30 p.m. At 12:00 o'clock (midnight) the doors of the saloon were closed to the public, but the Professor was still inside. It is my opinion that he remained there all night.

The debate which followed waxed warm. At the end of it the motion to demand Schroeder's resignation from the faculty passed by ten votes to four, Gibbons abstaining ("as is the custom in our country for one who presides at a meeting"), and the minority being composed of Corrigan, Ryan of Philadelphia, Horstmann of Cleveland, and the priest, Father Lee.

That evening Horstmann approached Schroeder and suggested he write a letter of resignation, in return for which the board would agree "that the reasons to be laid before the Sovereign Pontiff for the resignation of Mgr. Schroeder be restricted exclusively to those affecting his professional duties and those showing that the peace and harmony of the University required his departure." In other words, the professor's alcoholic escapades would be kept out of the record. Schroeder accepted the bargain, with the face-saving proviso that his letter contain the phrase "subject to the approval of the pope," and that he be free to submit it at his discretion during the course of the academic year. This arrangement was formalized at the board's meeting the next day, October 21.

Schroeder soon regretted his acceptance of Horstmann's offer (as Horstmann probably did himself), because, though Gibbons's official report to Leo XIII honored the agreement and omitted any reference to Schroeder's personal misdeeds, neither Ireland nor Keane felt so bound. Indeed, they spent the days immediately after the board meeting notarizing the documents that testified to Schroeder's excessive drinking.[96] Then Ireland wrote directly to Rampolla and told him that Schroeder's drunkenness was "a notorious fact in Washington," and Keane, upon his return to Rome in early November, handed the notarized statements over to the secretary of state. "They have my long memoir and [the] corroborative documents in their archives," Keane reported to Ireland on November 17. "Now you must see that the Cardinal [Gibbons] will not attempt any conciliating measures as to Schroeder, but simply stand to the situation as it is."[97]

Even before Schroeder submitted his letter of resignation from the faculty of the Catholic University of America, the Prussian government assigned him to a professorship at the Catholic Academy of Münster. John Ireland saw that act as evidence that Schroeder had been a German agent all along: "You see, Germany is grateful to him; he was doing her work in America."[98] Schroeder shortly afterward prepared a memorandum for Rampolla in hopes of regaining respectability in the eyes of the Roman authorities. It was a whining litany of self-pity and bogus piety; it told of the "torment" and pressure he had lived under in Washington, and of how his agreement to resign, that "tactical error," had been wrung from him by devious means.

> Why am I then an "element of discord," and why do I continue so to this very day? Because I have not shared certain doctrines or ideas with these gentlemen; because I did not support Mgr Ireland on the school question, as Bouquillon did; . . . because I did not favor the "parliament of religions" which was in the eyes of Mgr Keane "an inspiration from on high"; because, in a word, I have not given in to their "American," "progressive," "liberal" ideas.

And so, with a final insinuating whimper, Joseph Schroeder departed the scene.

From Rome Denis O'Connell offered Ireland his congratulations: "The Schroeder case is ended, . . . and yours is now the only party worth counting in the American Church."[99] Ireland, needless to say, agreed: "The downfall of Schroeder is the end of anti-liberalism and Cahenslyism, and a great defeat for Corrigan. . . . [Schroeder] was a Cahenslyite—but the last of the Mohicans. The greatest and last battle of the war has been fought and won."[100] This boast, like so many similar ones voiced over the preceding dozen years, proved wildly overstated, and it suggested besides how the long and uninterrupted controversy had distorted the participants' sense of values. Significant ideological issues remained at stake, but they had grown obscured by both sides indulging in too many moral compromises, too much readiness to let the end justify the means, too much exaggeration, innuendo, half-truth, outright mendacity. Far from having been the greatest battle, "l'affaire Schroeder," as Gibbons called it, was a wretched little business, surely the nadir in the contest for control of the Catholic church in the United States. Over against the mean, duplicitous, faintly comic figure of Joseph Schroeder, who called anyone who disagreed with him a heretic, stood his prelatial opponents who brought him down by counting the number of glasses of beer he drank, by monitoring his comings and goings at Mrs. Beuchert's tavern, and by zestfully describing the spit dripping down his chin. It was a process that cheapened and coarsened all who partook of it. Perhaps the worst travail through which "Asperity Ipswich" had to pass during his whole life was the need he felt to descend to Joseph Schroeder's level in order to win the war. Shabby is as shabby does.

XVIII

The Fortunes of War
1898–1900

"WITH GERMANS AS GERMANS, you have no contention whatever." Denis O'Connell instructed Ireland on this point many months before the fall of Schroeder. "You never failed in all your life to express yr. repulsion for war of race on race. . . . Your contention is for an *idea*. That *idea* is progress, and that's yr. battle cry. . . . Your only opponents are the reactionaries, wherever they be. . . . The little clique of Germans that attacked you in America do not represent the Germans. Germany is a most progressive country and the reactionaries are in the minority." And there were "progressives" in other European Catholic communities, in France certainly and even in Italy. O'Connell's nimble wits, fully recovered from their malaise of eighteen months previously, had seized upon the idea of internationalizing Americanism, of forging a "combination" of like-minded activists of whatever nation who would "demoralize yr. enemies and multiply tenfold your friends." Americanism had moved to a higher stage, from a pragmatic concern to mesh immigrant Catholics in the United States with the dominant culture, much of it admirable, to an ideological crusade for the application of American political and cultural ideals across the whole spectrum of ecclesiastical life. And O'Connell had assigned Ireland his role in carrying forward this heady design: "On a suitable occasion, and that very near, you must seek an opportunity of publishing your real program to the world, i.e., not war of race on race, but idea on idea, of progress on stagnation. Do it, . . . and you will lead the world."[1]

Here was a siren song indeed, and John Ireland had not been slow to whistle the tune. On March 28, 1897, he had preached a widely publicized sermon titled "The New Age," in which he took up the theme O'Connell had given him: "We are to have no name at all, we are the same old thing all the time. We are no party at all. We are the Church. All the other fellows[,] the opposition[,] are a party . . . in the Church, and they are the '*Refractaires.*' "[2] Ireland's use of O'Connell's very word was not inappropriate, since réfractaire was the term Leo XIII had used to designate the resistance in France to his policy of ralliement, the policy with which the archbishop of St. Paul had long been identified.

> "Refractaires," rebels against Leo, are found outside of France. . . . Those in America who resist the direction given by Leo are rebels and refractaires, however much they dare push themselves as the only true and trustworthy Catholics. . . . It is thought sometimes that Catholics in America are divided . . . on lines of race and religion. It is not so. . . . The line of division is that the great majority follow Leo's direction, and some hold themselves aloof from him. The loyal Catholics and the refractaires are confined to no one language. . . . There is for me no race, no language, no color. I rise above all such accidentals. . . . When I move away from Catholics, I move away from refractaires, and from none other. When the French Catholics, . . . the German Catholics are with the Pope, I am with them; when they are against the Pope, I am against them.[3]

O'Connell had maintained that this speech "cleared the atmosphere for us here, and rendered all explanations about opposition to Germans superfluous." What he meant exactly by that claim is difficult to judge. Certainly Catholics of German heritage living in the United States remained as suspicious as ever of John Ireland and his allies, although the simple passage of time and the ennui produced by more than a decade of unrelieved controversy had taken much of the steam out of that issue. Indeed, the weary and strife-torn body of American Catholics was less prone to quarrel now than before, and "Americanism" was too abstract a notion to stir up the passions as Cahensly had or the school question had. What the former rector may have meant therefore was that "The New Age" eased his own overtures to certain "advanced" Catholic intellectuals in Germany itself, whom, however, he warned Ireland to steer clear of on the grounds that they were suspect in Rome.[4]

John Ireland, 1898 (Photo by C. A. Zimmerman; Archives of the College of St. Thomas)

Nor did O'Connell share with his friend in St. Paul all the details of his negotiations, so that it seemed as though the Americanist right hand did not know what the left hand was up to. In fact the Europeans whom O'Connell was assiduously cultivating not only used the anti-Jesuit rhetoric that Ireland appreciated, but they also opposed on principle the sort of absolute papal monarchy that most of the Jesuits propounded and Ireland himself had endorsed, once again, in "The New Age." Thus did the radical incoherence, or perhaps the simple thoughtlessness, of the Americanist strategy at this point reveal itself, a circumstance to which Ireland gave rueful witness at the end of 1897: "You are the 'Diplomat,'" he told O'Connell, "even if a little of Machiavelli gets in occasionally; between ourselves, Machiavelli was no fool, and I am thinking of reading carefully 'Il Principe.' "[5]

That year at any rate had witnessed a spectacular flowering of internationalist Americanism. The command post for the movement was established at O'Connell's apartment at 61 Via del Tritone, nicknamed "Liberty Hall," where every Tuesday evening gathered members of the "Lodge," permanent residents in Rome like Keane and John Zahm and the historian, Louis Duchesne, and occasional right-thinking visitors from England, France, or Germany. Even a maverick Italian cardinal—a "conciliationist," one who favored an end to the conflict between the Holy See and the Kingdom of Italy—might turn up now and then.[6] More important than the clever conversation that doubtless enlivened these soirées was the preparation of a translation of Ireland's speeches into Italian, a task taken on at O'Connell's behest by his and Ireland's friend, the Countess Sabina Parravicino di Revel.[7] And more important still was the publication of a French translation of Walter Elliott's Life of Father Hecker, the same book for which Ireland had written a spirited introduction when it first appeared in 1891.

The editor of this French version had been one Félix Klein,[8] a professor of literature at the Institut catholique in Paris. Abbé Klein had long admired John Ireland and had translated some of the latter's sermons into French.[9] Mild, courteous, somewhat timid, he nevertheless boldly asserted the view that Catholicism in France could do no better than to emulate its sister church in the United States, and he was prepared to give his all to secure that objective. The Life of Hecker seemed to him to provide a literary model of all that was best in the priesthood, and a model too, if its lessons were learned, of the prodigies the Catholic church might achieve as the nineteenth century gave way to the twentieth. So he oversaw a translation of Elliott's work (and Ireland's introduction), and he added an argumentative preface of his own. Hecker, he proclaimed, had pioneered a spirituality appropriate to an age of scientific discovery and growing personal independence, a spirituality more supple, more interior — though by no means inactive in addressing the needs of the modern world — and more sensitive to the promptings of the Holy Spirit in a manner and degree that promised to enrich the traditional structures of the church.[10] O'Connell was ecstatic. "You seem really," he wrote to Klein, "to have been raised up by Providence . . . to give to [Hecker's] work that potency which he always desired for it and for which in his last days he hardly dared any longer to hope."[11]

Le père Hecker had exploded like a bombshell within the French church, already riven by the controversies occasioned by Leo XIII's call to "rally" to the republic and, since 1895, deeply disturbed by the dark tragedy of the Dreyfus case.[12] Catholic press and pulpit rapidly chose sides on the Americanist issue, and the vigor, not to mention the invective, of attack and support turned Klein for a while into a minor celebrity.[13] Many French Catholics of both persuasions, including Klein himself, had been present at an international conference held in Fribourg, Switzerland, in August 1897, when Denis O'Connell had made a rare foray into the public arena. In a short speech, later printed as a pamphlet called *A New Idea in the Life of Father Hecker,* he had argued forcefully in defense of "political" Americanism — by which he meant the moral superiority of Anglo-American common law over Roman and hence traditional canon law, a conviction of O'Connell's of long standing[14] — and of "ecclesiastical" Americanism, or the harmonious relationship that existed between church and state in the United States. O'Connell's strong implication was that Americanism in either of these senses deserved the cordial endorsement of the Roman church, and he asserted that "the idea expressed by [both senses] shines like a golden thread from beginning to end of [Elliott's *Life*], and gives to the work its character and meaning."[15] How O'Connell knew this, since he had never bothered to read the book — it was too long, he complained — he did not explain. But he was proud of what he called "my little brochure," and he took credit for the fact that "the whole atmosphere of Europe is now redolent of Americanism. . . . There is more Americanism here than in the Church in America."[16]

There were of course plenty of European antagonists determined that O'Connell's assertion remain an empty boast. The printing presses rattled away. Even before Klein's version of the biography of Hecker had appeared, the French Catholic public had been treated to a series of articles denouncing Americanism, however it was defined, written by Georges Périès, a canon lawyer whom Keane had recruited for and then, in 1896, discharged from the faculty of the Catholic University.[17] His fulminations, however, and those of other anti-Americanist pundits and preachers, were child's play compared to the assaults mounted through March and into April 1898 in the pages of the Parisian daily *La vérité*. Their author, who signed himself "Martel," the Hammer, was a priest named Charles Maignen, who pronounced Hecker a fraud, Ireland, Keane, and O'Connell virtually schismatics, and Americanism itself a dark conspiracy, tending toward, if not inextricably tangled in, doctrinal heterodoxy.[18] Americanism had indeed become an international phenomenon, and the war over it had, too.

But meantime another war intervened.

ON MARCH 27, 1898, the editors of *La vérité* announced that Maignen's essays would be published as a book, under the title *Le père Hecker, est-il un saint?* That afternoon — it was Passion Sunday, which ushered in the last two weeks of the penitential season of Lent — John Joseph Keane, titular archbishop of Damascus, left his lodgings in the Canadian College on the Via delle Quattro Fontane and walked the short distance to the church of San Silvestro, where he presided and preached at a vesper service. When he returned afterward to the sacristy, he found waiting for him a messenger who handed him an envelope emblazoned with the papal coat of arms.

> The danger of war breaking out between the United States and Spain has profoundly stirred the heart of the Supreme Pontiff, the Common Father of the Faithful. Knowing well that Archbishop Ireland of St. Paul . . . might for various reasons be listened to favorably by the President of the United States, [the pope] has expressed his keen desire that the worthy Archbishop take whatever measures might contribute to a peaceful solution to the current

crisis. I take the liberty of communicating this wish of his Holiness to your Grace, a close friend of Archbishop Ireland, and, uniting my own warm wishes to this request, I take advantage of the opportunity to offer you the sincerest regards of your devoted servant, M[ariano] Cardinal Rampolla.[19]

Keane left San Silvestro immediately, went to the cable office nearby, and sent a message. A tense forty-eight hours followed, and then on Tuesday afternoon he received a reply: John Ireland, en route from St. Paul to Washington, asked that instructions be forwarded to him in care of the Honorable Bellamy Storer of Ohio, at whose residence he proposed to spend the night of March 30.[20] The next morning Keane, after conferring with Rampolla, sent a terse Latin cable to Cincinnati: "The pope will act with impartiality toward Spain and America. But he can promise nothing until he hears from you. Meanwhile prevent a declaration of war." On the evening of Thursday, March 31, the archbishop of St. Paul, accompanied by Storer, home on a brief leave from the legation in Brussels, unobtrusively departed the train station in central Washington and took a carriage to the apostolic delegation on Second and I streets.[21]

The tension between Spain and the United States resulted directly from the chronic troubles in Cuba.[22] For at least a generation American public opinion had been outraged by the misrule of that island by a succession of brutal and inefficient colonial administrations. In 1895 a new wave of anti-Spanish violence brought down upon the unhappy Cubans even more severe repression — including the establishment of concentration camps in which thousands died — without, however, quelling the insurgency. At the end of November 1897, the ministry in Madrid offered to grant Cuba virtual home rule within the rag-tag Spanish Empire, and as a token of good faith dispatched a new governor to Havana, who promptly rescinded the draconian measures of his predecessor. But the leaders of the revolution correctly judged this overture to be an admission of weakness, and, counting upon eventual military support from the United States, they determined to carry on their struggle until they attained complete independence for Cuba.

The Cleveland administration had declined to recognize the insurgents, and President McKinley had followed suit. The pressures upon him to intervene in their behalf, however, grew ever more intense, particularly after the battleship *Maine* mysteriously blew up in Havana harbor on the night of February 15, 1898, with a loss of 258 American lives. The belligerent mood of the American people, sustained and even stimulated by the press, was reflected in an unruly Congress, which clamored for the president to adopt an aggressively anti-Spanish policy, even if that led to war. Many who recommended this course were moved not only by revulsion at the Spaniards' sorry record of exploitation and atrocity and by a more or less idealistic sympathy for a people striving for self-determination, but also by strategic considerations in the Caribbean and larger geopolitical ambitions that were proper, they argued, to America as a newly emerged world power. These convictions — loudly expressed within the administration by the assistant secretary of the navy, Theodore Roosevelt — received support from those who thought patriotism itself needed an infusion of blood now and then, a view not infrequently advanced by John Ireland. "It is fortunate," he said in 1894, "for a people that from time to time supreme emergencies arise testing its patriotism to the highest pitch. If patriotism remains dormant for a long period it may lessen in strength, while the reflection and self-consciousness which resolute action awakens result in a fuller estimate of the value of the country and institutions which it is the duty of patriotism to defend."[23]

McKinley himself sincerely opposed war, but as the tumultuous weeks passed he found it increasingly difficult to swim against the rising tide. The conduct of foreign affairs was not in any event a task for which he was well equipped, nor did he possess the strength of character that would have enabled him to tame the congressional barons in his own party. On March 29 — the day John Ireland boarded the train for Cincinnati — the president sent an ultimatum to Madrid, demanding an immediate six-month armistice in Cuba, during which time negotiations between Spain and the insurgents would be held under the friendly auspices of the United States. Two days later the Spanish ministry declared this proposal entirely unacceptable.

At the Vatican Rampolla had long watched with foreboding the American involvement in the Cuban revolution. As early as June 15, 1895, he had written Satolli: "The Spanish government believes that the Irish associations of Jacksonville and New York are supporting the insurrection in Cuba." The pope wanted such activities stopped: "Catholics should not contribute to the difficulties of a Catholic government like Spain." The illusion that the unstable regimes of Latin Europe, given to periodic bouts of violent anti-clericalism, were somehow still "Catholic" died hard with papal policy-makers, not least with Rampolla himself who, before his appointment as secretary of state, had served as nuncio to Madrid. His bias probably lent urgency to his efforts to preserve the peace between Spain and the United States. By December 1897, at any rate, he had decided, in addressing the "delicate" Cuban problem, to enlist the services of the archbishop of St. Paul, because of the latter's "cordial" and "intimate" relations with President McKinley.[24] Rampolla no doubt recalled one of John Ireland's more extravagant claims, passed on to him by Satolli: when Ireland had met McKinley in Chicago in 1894 and hailed him as future president, McKinley had allegedly replied, "Within two years you and I will be governing the United States."[25]

That McKinley, who was cautious to an almost pathological degree, ever said anything of the kind is most unlikely. Nevertheless, Rampolla was not mistaken in thinking that Ireland's standing within the Republican party could gain him entrée to the highest levels of the national administration. Indeed, only a few weeks before his peace mission began, the archbishop was in New York, still seeking money to rescue his real estate ventures. "J. D. Rockefeller, W. K. Vanderbilt, and Thompson of the Penn. Ry.," he reported cheerfully, "have promised at least $10,000 each." More significant was the identity of the chief collector on the scene: "Hanna is working like a Trojan, . . . doing so well, . . . at it the whole day."[26] Senator Marcus Hanna, mastermind of McKinley's 1896 electoral victory and *capo* of the national party, was a man who paid his political debts.

It was no surprise therefore that the president agreed to see Ireland about the Cuban crisis. The meeting took place at the White House, under the utmost secrecy, on Friday, April 1. In attendance were McKinley, Ireland, Storer, and Undersecretary of State William R. Day.[27] Afterward Ireland was able to assure Rampolla of McKinley's ardent desire for peace, but the president needed "assistance to attain it [*aiuto attenerla*]," Ireland said in the first of the many cables sent to Rome over the next twenty days, because of the bellicose passions gripping the Congress and the people at large. The armistice, which he had demanded on March 29 and which Madrid had rejected, remained for McKinley an absolute minimum requirement for a peaceful solution.[28]

The following day, Saturday, Ireland called on his old friend from Minnesota, Senator Cushman Davis, a key player in the drama as chairman of the Senate Foreign Relations Committee. The archbishop, however, found little sympathy for his mission in this quarter: Davis, like most politicians on Capitol Hill, was as fervent a hawk as McKinley was a dove. He and other leaders in both houses said plainly that they awaited with impatience the president's message on the Cuban situation, scheduled to be delivered to them on April 6, and that if the message did not invite them to declare war upon Spain they would very likely do so without an invitation.[29] "The war party in congress," Ireland warned Rampolla, "is very strong. The peace party needs a concession from Spain," at the very least "an armistice in the sense in which the president has proposed it. The situation here is extremely grave; each day brings the crisis closer, a fact Spain seems not to appreciate. If the Holy Father is willing, you should insist that Spain offer such an armistice." That evening Ireland repaired to the home of another political friend, Stephen B. Elkins, in order to plot strategy. Elkins of West Virginia was one of the few senators who supported McKinley's refusal to recognize the Cuban insurgents and his efforts to end the crisis without armed conflict.[30]

Palm Sunday morning, at eleven o'clock, Ireland returned to Elkins's residence for a prearranged meeting with the Spanish minister to the United States, Polo de Bernabé. Once the customary verbal courtesies had been exchanged, Ireland launched into a "vigorous and emphatic" homily on the obligation of the Spaniards to accept McKinley's proposal for an armistice and negotiations, while Polo listened politely and caused some embarrassment by calling Ireland, whom he assumed to be a cardinal, "Eminence." After lengthy discussion the reluctant minister agreed to raise the question of an armistice with his government, but he stated flatly that Spain could never *request* an armistice. Here was the sticking point. The Spaniards were willing, even eager, for a cessation of hostilities in Cuba, so long as the rebels asked for it. But the rebels, confident that continuing armed resistance would sooner or later bring decisive American intervention to bear in their favor, had no incentive to accept an armistice, much less to request one.

So McKinley showed little interest when Elkins came to the White House in the middle of Sunday afternoon and recapitulated the conversation between Ireland and Polo. Ireland himself, after an encouraging visit to the cordial and supportive French ambassador, returned to the apostolic delegation to find a cablegram from Rome with the news that the pope had dispatched an urgent message to the Spanish queen-regent, imploring her to accept McKinley's demand for an armistice, "in order to avoid bloodshed and other disastrous consequences." At nine in the evening Ireland brought the cable to Elkins's house, and fifteen minutes later three newspapermen in search of a story found one when they caught sight of him coming out again, Elkins by his side, and setting off toward Pennsylvania Avenue. "The senator and the churchman walked slowly, and the latter, as is characteristic with him, would nearly halt about every ten feet, and his conversation was earnest."[31] Once in sight of the presidential mansion, the two men parted, the archbishop walking east for several blocks, while Elkins went directly to the White House. He showed the cable to the president who appeared more cheerful than he had earlier in the day. Outside again, where the senator encountered a swarm of reporters who asked him to explain Ireland's presence in Washington, he denied knowing anything about it.[32]

At half-past twelve Elkins was roused from sleep and summoned to return immediately to the White House. There he found McKinley, Day, and several lesser functionaries in a state of angry consternation over a message just received from the American minister to Madrid, Stewart L. Woodford. On Sunday afternoon—it was now early Monday morning, April 4—the Spanish foreign minister had called at the American embassy and told a startled Woodford that, "gladly yielding to the request of the Holy Father, who was acting on the earnest petition of the President of the United States," his government had decided to publish an armistice. Woodford had the Spaniard repeat the statement twice, then asked him to write it down, then brought in an interpreter to verify the meaning of the text. Only after these precautions had been taken did he forward it to Washington.[33]

A public assertion that he had "petitioned" the pope to intervene in behalf of an objective of United States foreign policy placed McKinley in an impossible position politically. The image of an American president groveling at the feet of the pontiff would not only have provided grist for the propaganda mills of the American Protective Association but also would have outraged the vast majority of the populace which, though by no means explicitly bigoted against Catholics, nevertheless harbored deep, hereditary suspicions of the Church of Rome. The sleepy Elkins could not but agree upon the necessity for an instant and unequivocal denial.

This crisis within a crisis had arisen out of a misinterpretation of John Ireland's dispatch to Rampolla of April 1, in which he had spoken of McKinley's need for "assistance" in maintaining the peace. Ireland had meant that the Spanish government had to lend assistance to the process by acceding to the president's demand for an armistice in Cuba. Rampolla, ever eager to enhance the diplomatic prestige of the papacy, had seized upon the word "aiuto" and had chosen to understand it as a request for the pope to "assist" American diplomacy by urging Spain to declare an armistice— which indeed the pope had done. The embattled Spanish ministry for its part rejoiced at what appeared to be a solution to its dilemma: it could initiate a cease-fire and yet save face by explaining that it did so out of respect for Leo XIII rather than because of Yankee pressure. It was no doubt an honest mistake all round—the words in the April 1 cable admitted of both interpretations—but there can be no doubt either that this turn of events severely hampered John Ireland's mission. McKinley, who understandably suspected that a careless and potentially dangerous use had been made of the prestige of his office, kept his distance from Ireland throughout the balance of the negotiations.

But that unfortunate circumstance did not for a moment inhibit the archbishop of St. Paul's vigor or deter him from pursuing his goal with admirable dedication. He spent part of Monday, April 4—the same day Woodford in Madrid was instructed to repudiate the pope's "assistance"—pressing Polo with his arguments for an armistice, and the rest of the time, in tandem with Rampolla's efforts at the Vatican, urging the French and Austrian ministers to recommend that their governments declare a willingness to act as honest brokers between Spain and the United States. Just before he retired for the night, he was handed a dispatch from Rome. "Spain encounters grave difficulties," Rampolla said, "in accepting proposal made by you, on account of the excited state of minds, especially in the army. Nevertheless, at the instance of the Holy Father, she is disposed to grant suspension of arms. She desires, however, that the President should also do something to facilitate a peaceful solution by withdrawing all the [American] fleet or a part of it from Cuban waters; for there is really the difficulty."

Ireland sent a translation of this cable by messenger to Elkins the next morning, and asked him to show it to the president. Elkins instead prudently consulted Undersecretary Day, who told him that McKinley would entertain no such concession. This curt refusal, which the senator conveyed to Ireland at the apostolic delegation, left the archbishop "very much discouraged." But while the two men were still conversing, another cable was delivered, this one stating that while Leo XIII "hoped" the fleet would be withdrawn, he did not believe the armistice depended upon fulfillment of that condition. After lunch, Ireland, at Senator Elkins's suggestion, took this latest communiqué to the Department of State and read it to Day, who listened attentively but without substantive comment. From there Ireland again made the round of the foreign embassies, and late in the afternoon he sent Rampolla a strongly worded note that emphasized the dangerous pitch war fever in the United States had reached. By nine in the evening he was sitting in Elkins's study, exhausted but relatively optimistic. There was only silence from Madrid, Ireland said, but the major European powers—even Russia, thanks to Rampolla's strenuous initiatives—had agreed to act in concert in requesting the United States to refrain for the time being from military action in the Caribbean; France and Austria moreover had offered to guarantee the integrity of the Spanish monarchy should the army or any dissident elements threaten it because of concessions offered to the Cubans. The archbishop departed about midnight, "feeling hopeful that the armistice would be proposed tomorrow, Wednesday."

That was the day, April 6, on which the president's message on the crisis was to be delivered to Congress. On his way to the Capitol Elkins stopped off to see Ireland, who, however, had no news and said he expected none before early afternoon. Actually he received no information until seven o'clock, and then only that the pope had renewed his plea with Spain to suspend hostilities. In the interval President McKinley had disappointed most of the Congress and the large crowds which jammed the Capitol corridors and galleries by sending up to the Hill not the promised message but only a terse announcement that he had decided to put off any statement for five days in order to facilitate the evacuation of American citizens from Cuba. This surely was one reason for the postponement, and the president's doubts about the state of readiness of his military forces may well have been another.[34] But it was in some measure a tribute as well to the courage of McKinley in the face of almost universal opposition, and to the remarkable exertions of John Ireland.

The morning of Holy Thursday passed with still no word from Madrid. In the afternoon McKinley received in the Blue Room the representatives of Britain, France, Germany, Italy, Russia, and Austria-Hungary. This meeting, the product largely of Rampolla's and Ireland's endeavors, was a bland affair, with the ambassadors saying that they hoped war could be avoided and McKinley replying that he hoped so, too. More lively was an exchange going on at about the same time inside the Spanish embassy. Ireland, his nerves beginning to show the strain of recent days, laid down the law to Polo. If war should come, he shouted at the minister, the United States would seize Cuba, Puerto Rico, and the Philippines, and "would surely bombard Barcelona." The burden remained squarely on Spanish shoulders, because failure to reach a solution meant "farewell to Spain as a nation."

But threats seemed unable to hurry the Spaniards, accustomed, in Bellamy Storer's words, to "the usual world-old [*sic*] Spanish delay and sinuosity."[35] Good Friday was entirely uneventful, and, in his by now routine evening conversation with Elkins, "No news is good news" was about the only comment John Ireland could muster. The breakthrough came the following evening. Shortly before seven o'clock, Frederick Rooker, Martinelli's American secretary and Ireland's aide throughout the negotiations, opened a cablegram from Rampolla that announced the Spanish offer of an armistice to the Cuban insurgents. Since Ireland was for the moment absent from the delegation, Rooker hurried to Elkins's house, and Ireland arrived there a few minutes later. They joyously discussed this apparently decisive development over dinner, after which Elkins went to the White House to tell McKinley of what Rampolla had happily described "as an Easter offering." The president heard the news with relief and offered his thanks and congratulations. But Elkins felt a hint of fatalism in the air: Spain had indeed capitulated, but, given the temper of American public opinion, had the capitulation come in time?

Easter Sunday, April 10, witnessed some inevitable but mostly inconsequential snags. The Spanish governor of Cuba professed not to understand the terms of the armistice. A testy minister Polo, reacting perhaps to the verbal scourging Ireland had given him earlier, complained bitterly about Americans who demanded everything and gave nothing. McKinley, calm in the eye of the hurricane, met twice with his cabinet, preparing the message he would deliver to Congress the next day, and in between greeted a stream of visitors, including Elkins and Storer, who, echoing Ireland, pleaded with him to keep the message moderate in substance and tone. Ireland himself received, through Rampolla, an appeal from the queen-regent, who hoped McKinley could be persuaded to "say some word pleasing to Spain, and thus do something to quiet the susceptibilities of the Army and People of Spain."

The message, read to the members of Congress on the afternoon of Easter Monday, lacked the soothing phraseology the queen-regent wanted, but she and her government could scarcely have expected a more favorable recommendation: the president asked Congress to approve a policy of neutral intervention at his own discretion, or, in effect, to endorse his supervision of the Cuban armistice, the basis of his official conduct all along. He said not a word about recognizing the independence of Cuba. John Ireland had reason to give vent to his natural optimism, but the wire of jubilation mixed with flattery he sent the Vatican, even before McKinley's message had reached Capitol Hill, displayed a serious misunderstanding of the situation as it really was.

I offer my felicitations to the Holy Father. The armistice has produced an excellent impression; without doubt there will now be peace. There will be bellicose speeches in congress, but without effect. The President in his message will recognize the benevolent action of Spain. The influence of the Holy Father in securing the armistice is gratefully recognized by the American people. The armistice is a triumph whose excellence will be celebrated in history as an imperishable monument.

But all was sour anti-climax after that. Ireland had spoken too soon as well as too extravagantly. The Cuban rebels predictably refused to accept the armistice, and the Congress refused to accept McKinley's recommendation. War was what the American people and the people's representatives wanted, and war they were bound to have. On Tuesday, April 12, Ireland once more testified to Rampolla his belief that peace was "certain," but he couched his confidence this time in sobering second thoughts. Over the succeeding tumultuous seven days, he watched with dismay as the rhetorical violence intensified on Capitol Hill, with his friend Cushman Davis among those leading the charge. When the Vatican published his triumphant announcement of success in the *Osservatore Romano*, he cabled Keane to warn Rampolla of the danger such publicity posed for the prospects of peace.[36] Congressmen, when they were not denouncing the cowardice of the McKinley administration, must have grumbled about the popish interference in American politics by the archbishop of St. Paul.

At the end of the week he departed Washington for New York, probably to attend once again to his tangled financial affairs. On April 17 he instructed Rooker by telegraph to inform Rampolla that a straw of hope still fluttered in the wind, because the Senate and the House of Representatives remained "at cross purposes." Rooker had his doubts about the wisdom of sending such a communication. "From what I gather," he wrote to Senator Elkins, "there is no probability of any serious or protracted disagreement between the two houses."[37] The cable went anyway, over Ireland's name, but three days later the archbishop, returned to Washington, had to follow it up with a doleful message which began, "Tutto finito." McKinley had bowed at last to the immense pressures, and had called for 125,000 volunteers. "All is finished. An ultimatum demanding the evacuation of Cuba will be sent to Madrid this evening. Time limit set next Saturday at noon [April 23]." "I regret that every effort to secure peace has been in vain," he added the following day. "I feel honored to have been chosen to have a small part in the historic struggle for peace. I am now going home."[38]

Back home in Minnesota Ireland inevitably felt a sense of depression and disappointment, which he expressed in a sad little note to the editor of a popular magazine: "I am in receipt of your letter asking that I write you something under the title 'The Inspiration of the Flag.' I beg leave to say that just for the moment the flag does not inspire me much, and I must be silent until this war is over."[39] Not that that mood affected his basic loyalties. To O'Connell, who commended him for having "done [his] duty as a priest" and advised him to put the failure firmly behind him, Ireland replied, "Of course now I am for war — for the Stars and Stripes — I am all right as an American. . . . America is whipping poor Spain. I confess, my sympathies are largely with Spain, but the fact is, she is beaten. Now Americanism will triumph."[40] A week after his return to St. Paul he tried to sum up for Rampolla what had happened. "I had hoped until the last moment that war could have been avoided, and I was not alone: the ambassadors of the great powers, President McKinley himself and his cabinet, a great number of the more serious and thoughtful people in the country shared my hopes." But the forces of jingoism, fomented by the press and exploited for partisan advantage — "Mr. Bryan declared himself in favor of war, because, he said, this was what the country wanted" — had in the end been too strong, even though "the 'pars sanior [saner part]' of the nation regrets it." The archbishop remained convinced that had he had two months at his disposal, or even one, the outcome of the negotiations could have been different.[41]

A ripple of resentment against Ireland's allegedly too-sanguine reports from Washington manifested itself in some curial circles. One story, told widely by an American resident in Rome who mingled socially with many high ecclesiastics, had it that Rampolla, basing his words upon information received from Ireland, assured the Spanish minister only twenty-four hours before the declaration of war that the negotiations had succeeded. "Archbishop Ireland's credit at the Vatican sank below zero. I think Leo XIII never forgave him for so misleading him."[42] Keane and O'Connell heard similar complaints: one curial cardinal, in "a monstrous misrepresentation," depicted Ireland as "a child, piping peace all the time."[43] Ireland was irritated, and justifiably so; the cable he had ordered sent on April 17 — offering a faint hope due to the "discord" between the Senate and the House — was a venial transgression at worst, hardly to be compared to the imprudence of Rampolla, a seasoned diplomat, in misunderstanding McKinley's desire for "assistance" or in publishing Ireland's "peace is certain" cable of April 11. Indeed, after the euphoria of April 11, Ireland's communiqués consistently testified to the increasing gravity of the situation. "I always knew that Rome is too anxious to obtain prestige for political intervention," he observed with some bitterness. "This put me on my guard, it should have put me more so. . . . What those people want is success, and when success does not come they make no allowance. . . . I risked everything to serve the Vatican."[44]

But Ireland did not intend to accept blame for the failure of a process that all along had been beyond his control. He gathered testimonials from involved parties and saw to it that they found their way to Rome. The Austrian minister to the United States said "that he had never in his life been called on to admire a man for indefatigable zeal and heroic struggle against odds as he had admired [Ireland] all through [the negotiations]."[45] The French ambassador echoed the same sentiments[46] and exclaimed in Bellamy Storer's hearing: "Monseigneur Ireland, what a great man!" "In the estimation of the most intelligent people in the United States," Storer maintained, "never has the Vatican, its policies and proposals, as represented by Leo XIII and Mgr. Ireland, been held in such high regard as today. . . . [Thanks to] the action and influence of Mgr. Ireland, all people of good will and intelligence applaud the intervention of the Vatican."[47] Woodford, the American minister in Madrid, saw nothing amiss about the goals or the methods of the Vatican diplomatic effort, and even Senator Cushman Davis, whose opinion on the issues had differed sharply from Ireland's, paid tribute to his fellow-Minnesotan: "I was frequently in conference with Archbishop Ireland during these proceedings. His labors for peace were most arduous and incessant. . . . But what was done [Spain's offer of an armistice] was done too late."[48] Frederick

Rooker, an old Roman hand, advised Ireland not to take too seriously the criticism he heard, especially from a certain source: "We
must take [Denis O'Connell's] character into consideration. I do
not care to say he is an alarmist, but at times he gets excited."
Rooker doubted that O'Connell's contacts within the ecclesiastical
bureaucracy, where he was still a persona non grata, were in a position to reflect the genuine views of the pope or the secretary of
state.[49]

So, thus reassured, John Ireland was calmer and more reflective
when, at the end of May, he again wrote Rampolla at length. He
went over some familiar ground, defended his dispatch of April
11 — "the President and his advisers were similarly convinced that
peace had been achieved" — and protested once more that failure
"was due solely to a lack of time." He played the prophet, too, with
mixed results, predicting that, unless the war ended quickly, the
United States would annex the Philippines, the Caroline Islands,
Puerto Rico, and also, after a decent interval, Cuba. The United
States was reluctant to take on colonies "far from its shores," but the
nation had to assume its responsibilities as "one of the great powers
in the world." The church, he said, had nothing to fear from an
American presence in these territories, "so long as the clergy accepts
with good grace, at least externally, the new order of things." Clerical privilege and church-state union would of course disappear, but
McKinley had already shown his good will by appointing as governor in Manila General Wesley Merritt, "a moderate man and
favorably disposed toward Catholics." As for the military situation
itself, the veteran of the Battle of Corinth described it with a certain
zest, and he praised the "gallantry of the Spanish sailors" fighting in
the Caribbean — "a courage . . . worthy of the chivalrous spirit of
their traditions" — much as he had praised, long ago, Colonel
Rogers and his comrades who had hurled themselves at the guns of
Battery Robinett. Now as then, however, heroism alone did not
suffice: "About the final result there is no doubt. We have the men
and the money."[50]

THE SPANISH-AMERICAN WAR did indeed end by the middle of August 1898, but the ecclesiastical war raged on, and the two were not
unrelated. On that much, it seemed, Americanist and anti-

Americanist in Europe could agree. "For me," O'Connell wrote to Ireland at the end of May,

> this is not simply a question of Cuba. If it were, it were no question or a poor question. Then let the "greasers" eat one another up and save the lives of our dear boys. But for me it is a question of much more moment — it is the question of two civilizations. It is the question of all that is old and vile and mean and rotten and cruel and false in Europe against all [that] is free and noble and open and true and humane in America. When Spain is swept of [f] the seas much of the meanness and narrowness of old Europe goes with it to be replaced by the freedom and openness of America. This is God's way of developing the world. And all continental Europe feels the war is against itself, and that is why they are all against us, Rome more than all. . . . I am a partisan of the Anglo-American alliance [for the good of mankind]; together they are invincible and they will impose a new civilization. Now is your opportunity — and at the end of the war as the Vatican always goes after a strong man you will likewise become her intermediary. . . . Only one word more: all doubts and hesitations to the wind and on with the banner of Americanism which is the banner of God and humanity. Now realize all the dreams you ever dreamed, and force upon the Curia by the great triumph of Americanism that recognition of English speaking peoples that you know is needed.[51]

But the war served the polemical turn of the anti-Americanists as well. Charles Maignen added some new essays to his studies on Americanism in which he deplored what he labeled unjust United States aggression against Spain, an aggression not merely political, but commercial, racial, and religious as well. America was a money-mad place, full of Protestants and Masons and Jews, all of whom conspired to snatch Cuba and the Philippines out of Catholic hands. The war demonstrated the malevolence of the Americans toward the Catholic faith, and, no less, the absurdity of proposing that the church substitute an Americanist for a European model in its polity and spirituality. These and other similarly harsh sentiments were ordinary reading fare in Rome during the early summer, because Maignen's articles, as his editors had promised, were now in book form and, more than that, the book had stamped upon it a Vatican imprimatur.[52]

The cardinal of Paris, who disapproved of Maignen's attacks upon his brother bishops in the United States, declined to grant the book a permit for publication within his diocese. The editors of *La vérité*, taking advantage of their right to publish the book and to seek an imprimatur elsewhere, brought Maignen's pot-boiler to Rome and approached the relevant curial officer, the master of the sacred palace. In 1898 Dominican friar Alberto Lepidi bore this elegant title, which meant he was the pope's chief theological adviser. When in mid-May he granted the imprimatur, the Americanists reacted with a curious mixture of anger and lassitude. Keane protested in writing twice to the cardinal secretary of state, engaging in what he called "a fierce skirmish" with Rampolla and Lepidi: "They see they are in a hornets' nest, are apologetic, but don't make amends." Convinced that "the enemy is implacable," the archbishop of Damascus nevertheless saw no need to modify his plans for a lengthy absence from the scene of the battle; on June 25 he departed for a month's holiday in France, then a stay of "a week or more" with the Storers in Brussels, after which, in early August, he sailed for the United States. He did not get back to Rome until November, contending meanwhile, as the news from there grew more ominous, that an earlier return by him "w'd be only a ridiculous fiasco. You are the only man," he assured Ireland, "who now can speak so as to be heard and heeded. I wish that you would just run to Rome."[53]

But O'Connell did not believe Ireland "could do much by coming."[54] Early in July the former rector had spoken to Lepidi, who told him blandly, as he had told Keane, that his function as censor was to protect faith and morals but not to stifle legitimate controversy. O'Connell's reply was in effect that Maignen's vicious misrepresentations and personal attacks hardly conformed to the rules of civilized debate, and that an imprimatur granted by the Vatican was widely interpreted as pontifical approval for Maignen's distortions. He shared with his confidants his suspicion that, despite Rampolla's denials, Lepidi had acted under orders, but he failed to tell them that he himself had given Lepidi a signed repudiation of something he termed "religious Americanism, . . . a peculiar kind of religious subjectivism" associated by some with Father Hecker[55] —very different, to be sure, from the varieties of Americanism O'Connell had put forward in his speech at Fribourg, but not so different from the description of Heckerism O'Connell had lauded in Klein's preface to the *Le père Hecker*. Much to O'Connell's embarrassment, this written statement was turned over to Maignen, who gleefully published it in the middle of August, about the time O'Connell set off from Rome to visit his new German friends. "A dirty piece of bad faith Lepidi played on me," O'Connell complained about a maneuver that appeared to show that Lepidi was just as self-serving as Denis O'Connell himself.[56]

So by mid-summer all the Americanist chieftains were gone from Rome—Zahm had returned to Notre Dame as superior of the Congregation of Holy Cross in the United States[57]—and John Ireland had to get his curial gossip second and third hand. Most of it had a somberly reactionary ring: the frail old pope was completely in the hands of the Jesuits, some said, or of Satolli, others said; disciplinary steps would soon be taken against Catholics who advocated evolution or the higher biblical criticism; the *Life of Hecker* would shortly be placed on the index of forbidden books; a special commission of cardinals had been set up to examine Americanism; the Vatican's French policy lay in tatters, and Rampolla therefore stood in danger of dismissal; the pope had reserved a final decision on Americanism to himself. Each of these snippets of rumor possessed a certain plausibility—Zahm's book on evolution, for instance, was destined for condemnation, though its author, thanks partly to Ireland's intercession, escaped any public obloquy[58]—but only the last one was entirely correct. Leo XIII, no doubt as puzzled at this stage as everyone else about the exact meaning of the word "Americanism,"[59] had determined to try to rescue the subject from the incessant quarreling by rendering a decision on it himself.

This development did not seem to disturb the archbishop of St. Paul. He stirred himself sufficiently to register proper indignation at Lepidi's imprimatur. "I am the terrible Bishop," he wrote Rampolla,

> who is on the point of provoking schism. That is what I and others are accused of. That is what is involved in "Americanism," a terrible menace to the Church and to the Supreme Pontiff. . . . We are accused of invading Rome and conquering the government of the Church with our ideas. Only a diseased brain could have reached such a conclusion. . . . Sinister motives are [even]

attributed to the steps taken in accord with the directives of your Eminence in the interest of promoting peace between Spain and the United States. . . . The prelates who are being thus attacked have only one system, that of the Holy See.[60]

But somehow the protest sounded like a lesson learned by rote, forcefully expressed indeed—" 'Americanism' is being defined in accord with the statements of French apostates, . . . which leaves a false and preposterous impression of our opinions"—and yet hardly more than a wearisome repetition of the same old arguments garbed in the same old rhetoric. It was as though the fires, ablaze so long, had at last been banked. Ireland could not be aroused even by the insinuation of the Austrian minister to the United States that Archbishop Corrigan had been behind Rome's dissatisfaction with the conduct of the peace negotiations.[61] And Corrigan, when asked to endorse Maignen's book, refused to do so; he and his anti-Americanist allies kept silent, perhaps because they sensed a victory, or perhaps because they too had grown tired.[62] "I have received a very full letter from Card. Rampolla," Ireland reported to Gibbons two days after his sixtieth birthday, "in which . . . he reiterates his assurances that I may very safely leave the 'Maignen' book to the Pope, who will in his good time speak and act."[63]

John Ireland's uncharacteristic calm persisted, despite the evidence that his Roman enemies—Cardinal Satolli, the pro-German elements at Propaganda, the Jesuits Mazzella and Brandi, even Ledochowki—were circling round him, and that the pope himself, far from endorsing the intrinsic value of the Catholic experience in the United States, had grown disillusioned about republican virtue as he watched the ralliement in France collapse beneath the weight of the Dreyfus affair. Insult in fact was added to injury when, in early August, an English version of Maignen's book was published in Rome, with a commendatory preface by Satolli. But the archbishop of St. Paul waited, went about his ordinary tasks, and took his consolations as they came to him. Not least among them was an invitation from the bishop of Orléans to preach the following May at the annual fête in that city in honor of Joan of Arc.[64] Hardly less gratifying was a letter from a princess of Spain, who thanked him for the compassion he had shown for her countrymen and who signed herself, "Your obedient child."[65] About the same time he received the author's copies of *La Chiesa et la Società moderna,* translated by the Countess Sabina: "Well, that little woman has made you famous in Italy," O'Connell wrote, "and she [has] made Milan run mad about you. In every paper, in every Review, etc., Ireland, Ireland."[66] Particularly sweet to the sometime chaplain of the Fifth Minnesota Volunteers was the greeting of Theodore Roosevelt, to whom Ireland had wired congratulations once the fighting in Cuba was over: "My dear Archbishop," wrote the hero of San Juan Hill, "I feel tempted to begin my letter, 'My dear Comrade!' "[67] Indeed, the past was much on Ireland's mind that summer, a nostalgia proper enough for a man entering the seventh decade of his life: he was busy gathering materials for a projected biography of his first patron, Bishop Cretin, and reading proofs of his article in praise of Cretin's missionary comrade, Loras of Dubuque.[68]

O'Connell and Keane had urged their friend to use the annual meeting of the archbishops as a forum to discuss the Lepidi imprimatur and, if possible, to secure from that group a joint protest to the Vatican.[69] Ireland agreed to this tactic, but, when the meeting took place in Washington on October 12, he unaccountably absented himself,[70] and so did not hear Archbishop Corrigan read the restrained statement of the Paulist Fathers of New York, objecting to the widespread attacks upon their revered founder.[71] "What a pity you were not here last week!" Keane said to Ireland in a remark as close as he ever came to a rebuke. "Archbishop Corrigan presented with much depreciation and trepidation a protest from the Paulists. He argued that [the archbishops] had better keep out of the controversy[;] so did Feehan [of Chicago], so did Ryan, so did Katzer, *so did Williams* [of Boston]. And so it was dropped, just as [Corrigan] anticipated. No strong voice there for truth and justice."[72] Ireland, who chose neither to apologize nor to explain, wrote to Paulist Walter Elliott: "I regretted [my absence] very much, . . . as I was anxious to break a lance against all comers in defense of Heckerism. . . . It is as well; I like to fight — and to conquer with few allies. You owe nothing, or but little, when the victory is won. We are going to win. . . . I shall soon invade Africa, and either Lepidi or Ireland will go into winter quarters." This blustery assertion must have been a hard saying for Elliott and the other Paulists, who had been warned by Corrigan that the suspicion in which they were held by the curia originated not from Hecker's doctrine but from their association with Ireland and Keane.[73]

The archbishop of St. Paul had in any event determined to go to Rome, a trip he had contemplated and put off for many months. Meanwhile the rumors continued to swirl back and forth. When Rampolla informed Gibbons of Leo XIII's intention to issue a formal decision on the subject of Americanism, Ireland commented: "I do not see what else the Pope could have done, if letters from Cardinal Gibbons and myself have weight any longer."[74] The question then became, what would the pope say, and here again reliable information was exceedingly hard to come by. One bad sign for Ireland and his allies was the cool reception John Keane received when he returned to Rome in November. The rector of the Canadian College, where he had resided for nearly two years, informed the archbishop of Damascus that the spiteful Satolli had told him, the rector, that his institution was compromised by Keane's presence there. "His Eminence," Keane wrote directly to the pope, "thus carries forward the work he began in obtaining from your Holiness my dismissal [*deposition*] from the rectorship of the Catholic University of America. . . . This petty act of persecution, a trifle in itself, . . . is closely connected with a whole system of aggression, a genuine war . . . against what is termed 'Americanism' and against certain American prelates, specifically Cardinal Gibbons, Mgr. Ireland, Mgr. O'Connell and me."[75] Keane did not seek new lodgings, but his days in the Eternal City were in any case numbered.

As the Americanist struggle approached its climax, John Ireland too was the victim of small-minded complaints and vexations, his every word and gesture scrutinized, his basic loyalties subjected to examination. On December 13, for instance, he preached at a memorial service in Washington for one of the leading Cuban insurgents, General Garcia, and was alleged to have spoken disparagingly of Spain and to have contrasted "the Catholicity of the Spanish friars with the free and virile Catholicity of the United States." Rampolla, still rankled over the humiliating defeat of Spain in the recent war, instructed Martinelli to find out the truth of this charge "con certezza." The "certainty" to emerge from the delegate's investigation was that at the funeral the Protestant hymn "Nearer My

God to Thee" had been sung and that Ireland had said no more than Ireland always said on such occasions: "This is the pride of America, that nothing keeps a man down but himself. . . . Beneath the American flag is absolute religious liberty, and the very fact that that flag has once touched Cuba is a guaranty given the island she is free in her religion." The sensible Martinelli found "nothing incriminating in the form or substance of the sermon."[76]

Then, a few weeks later, trouble flared up closer to home, in the venerable German parish of the Assumption which, next to the cathedral, was the oldest in St. Paul. The pastor of the Assumption, a Benedictine monk named Alfred Mayer, had long been a thorn in Ireland's side, having publicly opposed the archbishop on matters like the Faribault school plan and the status of secret societies. After efforts lasting several years, Ireland finally prevailed upon the abbot of St. John's, whose subject Mayer was, to remove him from the pastorate of the Assumption. The disgruntled monk organized resistance within the parish, six members of which petitioned the apostolic delegate to reverse the abbot's directive. Mayer's removal, the parishioners argued, was "unjust and tyrannical," "without cause," due to "mere envy, jealousy, and prejudice," and was Ireland's way of "making room for the religious liberalism or so-called Americanism which your most eminent predecessor himself [Satolli] has condemned as pernicious and a danger to Catholicism." The abbot, by no means anxious to renew the warfare of earlier days between his order and the archbishop of St. Paul, refused to sanction the petition, and Martinelli rejected it out of hand. Nevertheless, the dispute was still pending when Ireland departed on his fateful journey to Rome in mid-January 1899, and it was a nagging reminder that resistance to his most cherished goals continued even within a few blocks of his home.[77]

Rumor proclaimed — and this time the rumor proved correct — that the pope's letter on Americanism had already been printed. Ireland met with Rampolla on January 27 and with the pope four days later. But the die had been cast: on January 31 *Testem Benevolentiae,* as the document was called, was dispatched to Gibbons, to whom it was formally addressed, and the next day — perhaps at the very time Ireland was conversing with Leo XIII — a bundle of one hundred copies was forwarded to Martinelli for distribution among the

American hierarchy.[78] "All that giant will could do," Ireland insisted,

> was done by me to prevent the publication. But the forces against
> us were enormous—Jesuits, Dominicans and Redemptorists
> fought for very life—and again and again Abp. Corrigan's letter
> to Lepidi [which supposedly congratulated him for granting the
> imprimatur] was flung in my face. . . . Read [*Testem Benevolen-
> tiae*] carefully—and you will see that the Americanism con-
> demned is Maignen's Nightmare, v[erbi] g[ratia], who ever "pre-
> ferred" natural to supernatural virtues? Who ever taught that the
> practice of natural virtues was not to be vitalized and super-
> naturalized by divine grace? Who ever taught that in hearkening
> to the H. Ghost the Christian was not to be constantly guided by
> the visible magisterium of the Church? etc. Fanatics conjured up
> an "Americanism"—and put such before the Pope. Lepidi and
> Mazzella wrote the body of the letter—I cannot pray that God
> forgive them.[79]

These rhetorical questions were perfectly appropriate, since the
strictures of *Testem Benevolentiae*[80] seemed to have little to do with
any program Ireland had ever advanced. The pope indeed went out
of his way to praise American Catholics for "the works . . . done
so wisely and well in furthering and protecting the interests of
Catholicity," and to distinguish the "Americanism" he condemned
from "the characteristic qualities which reflect honor on the people
of America." He also stressed that if Elliott's *Life of Hecker* had occasioned the controversy, the need for papal intervention arose
"chiefly through the action of those who have undertaken to publish and interpret [that book] in a foreign language." Félix Klein's
French version of the biography therefore was the target, and more
particularly the preface Klein had written for it—the preface which,
as an English Catholic editor observed, "rather out-Heckers Hecker
precisely in those points on which it were possible for a critic bent
on fault-finding to attach to his words a meaning of doubtful orthodoxy."[81]

Whatever the validity of that judgment, Leo XIII did concentrate his fire upon what he termed "certain opinions . . . concerning the manner of living a Christian life." Leaning heavily, it
would seem, upon a draft prepared by Lepidi,[82] the pope declared

it wrong to assert that the Holy Spirit bestows more charisms in the present day than in earlier ages; that direct inspiration obviates the need for spiritual direction; that natural virtues are preferable to supernatural, because the former prepare the Christian better for action in the world; that therefore active virtues are to be preferred to passive ones like humility, meekness, and obedience; that the vows taken by members of religious orders inhibit liberty and hence are out of step with the imperatives of the present age; that new methods, more in harmony with contemporary reality, should be employed to convert non-Catholic Christians.[83] Such views, the pope maintained, constituted a great danger "to Catholic doctrine and discipline, inasmuch as the followers of these novelties judge that a certain liberty ought to be introduced into the Church," in imitation of "that liberty which, though quite recently introduced, is now the law and foundation of almost every civil community." But "the Church . . . is of divine right, while all other associations . . . subsist by the free will of men." And therefore "the Bishops of America [should] be the first to repudiate" these "opinions," which some people label "Americanism," for otherwise they might fall under suspicion of "desir[ing] a church in America different from that which is in the rest of the world," which enjoyed a church "one in the unity of doctrine as in the unity of government," with "its center and foundation in the Chair of Peter."[84]

John Ireland was quick to offer the repudiation asked for, but not without drawing a sharp and, to him, obvious distinction. On February 22, 1899, the text of *Testem Benevolentiae* was published in *Osservatore Romano,* and two days later a letter of the archbishop of St. Paul to the pope appeared in the same journal. "I repudiate and condemn," he wrote, "all the opinions which the Apostolic Letter repudiates and condemns, . . . [but I] cannot but be indignant that such a wrong should have been done us—our Bishops, our faithful people, and our whole nature—as to designate, as some have come to do, by the word 'Americanism' errors and extravagances of this sort." Gibbons replied similarly, employing, if anything, stronger language than his brother of St. Paul: "This doctrine, which [is] . . . extravagant and absurd, this Americanism as it has been called, has nothing in common with the views, aspirations, doctrine and conduct of Americans. I do not think that there

can be found in the entire country a bishop, a priest, or even a layman with a knowledge of his religion who has ever uttered such
enormities."[85] Keane submitted immediately in the same vein, as did
Klein, who withdrew *Le père Hecker,* by then in its seventh printing,
from circulation. O'Connell remained silent, apparently confident
that his written statements to Lepidi of the previous July would
satisfy the authorities.[86]

Ireland spent the rest of that gloomy spring in Italy, consoling
himself that the publication of his letter in the *Osservatore* amounted
to an acceptance by the pope of his distinction between genuine
Americanism and a few bizarre ideas "set afloat in France." He even
rebuked the Paulists for their gratuitous offer to "correct" Elliott's
biography of Hecker. "The [benign] beginning and . . . end of
[*Testem Benevolentiae*] were dictated by the Pope," he added, "and let
us all out."[87] But that conclusion was not shared by all Ireland's
episcopal colleagues, many of whom remained non-committal
while others, reflecting rivalries now more than a decade old, seized
the occasion to strike one more blow. Horstmann of Cleveland rejoiced that *Testem Benevolentiae* revealed the "errors" contained in the
Life of Hecker and the general tendency to minimize Catholic principles in order to cater to the Protestant American public.[88] Corrigan
and his suffragans, early in March, formally thanked the pope, in the
most servile tone, for having delivered Catholics in the United
States from the "snare" of Americanism, which otherwise "would
have taken tranquil possession in our midst, ever increasing its conquests," while, a little later, the province of Milwaukee expressed
"just indignation" that "not a few" American churchmen "affirmed
that they reprobated [the] errors, but did not hesitate to proclaim, . . . in Jansenistic fashion, that there was hardly an American who had held them."[89]

John Ireland was in and out of Rome over the succeeding weeks.
In public he kept up a bold and optimistic front, but his private
mood was darker, perhaps because of insinuations from curial
officials that Americanism disguised behind its simplistic patriotism
the heterodoxies they thought they saw emerging among certain
French and German intellectuals. "Life has become too serious," he
wrote O'Connell from Naples. "I have made up my mind to say
nothing in defence until after Orléans. Then I will . . . denounce

my calumniators." And, later, from Turin: "I am rested — resigned
to my lot — working. Only you and Abp Keane know and will
know my inmost thoughts. C'est la triplice [This is the triple alliance] — and I swear to it eternal allegiance."[90]

Despite such assurances, however, the alliance was in fact breaking up. O'Connell was playing a different game now, one which
linked him closely to Franz Xaver Kraus and other dissaffected German Catholic thinkers and which included grandiose and totally
unrealistic aspirations to "democratize" the papacy and to elect as
pope a "progressive" Italian conciliationist at the next conclave.[91]
During February O'Connell had introduced Ireland to Kraus, who
was also in Rome, and in April the former rector accompanied the
archbishop to Milan. Here Ireland planned to prepare his sermon
for the Joan of Arc festival in Orléans, and here, it would seem,
O'Connell attempted to persuade him to use that occasion to raise
the banner of internationalist Americanism.[92] Ireland, who had already accepted an official invitation, arranged by Kraus, to visit
Germany later in the spring, now grew wary, and O'Connell
departed Milan without having achieved his goal. Kraus and his
colleagues were bitterly anti-Jesuit — and Ireland had no quarrel
with that — but, as Germans, they were also anti-French, which
went strongly against Ireland's life-long predilictions. Indeed, the
situation for the Americanists in France in the wake of *Testem
Benevolentiae* was complicated enough without adding a hostile
German element.[93] As for capturing the papacy itself, Ireland entertained no such pipe dreams. "My heart is in [conciliationist Serafino
Cardinal] Vannutelli's election," he told O'Connell a little later,
"[but] not my expectation. You need not give him up, but don't anger Rampolla."[94] For Rampolla represented the real world in
Ireland's mind, the set of real power relationships with which he
had worked throughout his career. Americanism for him meant at
root home rule and cultural adaptation of the masses, not the establishment of an ecclesiastical democracy designed to protect the
speculations of European savants.

So at Orléans on May 8 John Ireland preached a conventional
paean of praise for the French people and nation, sprinkled over
with adequate doses of traditional Americanism, to be sure, but
with none of the more adventuresome variety O'Connell had es-

poused.[95] The archbishop went on to Paris, Belgium, England, and Ireland, and the adulation that greeted him everywhere gradually buoyed his spirits and convinced him that no new strategy was needed. He renigged on his promise to go to Germany. "All France would depict me as a hypocrite," he informed O'Connell. "I cannot carry the two countries."[96] He proposed to send in his stead Bishop O'Gorman, who had joined him in Paris, but in the end the German initiative was simply cancelled—which led O'Connell to blurt out his current appraisal of the archbishop of St. Paul to a confidante of Kraus: "Ireland is no Thinker. He is our Drummer. From now on he is to be accepted as nothing more than that."[97] He remained more than that, however, to Thomas O'Gorman, who, no longer beguiled by memories of Avignon[98] and demonstrating perhaps that the truest disciple is an old disciple, addressed to Rampolla at about the same time a fierce and moving appeal in behalf of the chief he had first encountered nearly a half-century earlier on the road from Chicago to Galena. "Use this man, Eminence," O'Gorman pleaded. "He is an army."[99]

At the end of July 1899, John Ireland returned to the United States ready and eager to carry on the battle along the familiar lines. Aboard ship he wrote O'Connell a stern admonition, which indicated that he knew an estrangement had begun without realizing exactly how or why it had happened. He insisted that O'Connell practice "prudence," that he disband Liberty Hall, that he avoid the company of "the suspect," that he even spend the bulk of his time away from Rome. "I will not give up the fight. I cannot abandon my friends. But on that account I must take the measures that lead to victory," one of which surely was to expect more circumspection from O'Connell. "I will write often and fully, but on condition that you promise to burn all my letters, past, present and future. I will do the same with yours. . . . Write me your solemn promise."[100] But the fact was that this parting of friends had roots deeper than O'Connell's garrulousness and weakness for manipulation and intrigue, or Ireland's indubitable vanity—that "winning, magnetic personality," which, with its "caprice, momentary impulse, and . . . great receptivity for flattery," was, according to one of Kraus's intimates, "*absolutely* Celtic!"[101] The fact was that the two men no longer agreed on the principles that had held them together over so many years. For Ireland the old Americanism, linked, not dishonorably, to his own ambitions, still sufficed. For the mercurial O'Connell, natively intelligent but always unstudious and superficial, a modern church in a modern world demanded something more, what precisely he was in the long run too inconstant to decide.[102]

The first chance Ireland had to renew the struggle came at the archbishops' meeting in October. There he hoped to confront Katzer and Corrigan, who with their suffragans had maintained that the "Americanism" of *Testem Benevolentiae* had indeed penetrated the church in the United States. With Riordan of San Francisco and Kain of St. Louis in support, Ireland moved that the bishops be polled to discover whether these "errors do exist" in their dioceses or elsewhere, and, if so, "then to specify *where* they exist and by *whom* they are held." Corrigan opposed the motion—Katzer was absent—on the grounds that such an inquiry "would be disrespectful to the Holy Father." After some parliamentary maneuvering, the motion failed to pass, the deciding negative vote cast by Gibbons.[103] "Baltimore cried 'peace, peace—death for the sake of peace' " Ireland reported bitterly, "and nothing was effected." Then, as the tense meeting continued, the archbishops of St. Paul and New York exchanged hot words. "The chasm between him and me is most wide."[104]

Perhaps it was, but the issues that divided them had ceased to be compelling for most people, and Ireland admitted as much: "Americanism! The country never thinks of it. . . . Nothing is heard here of [it]. No one seems to know that the Pope ever wrote—outside of Corrigan and the Jesuits—who gloat over their supposed triumph."[105] And the cardinal of Baltimore, as usual, gauged the mood of nearly all concerned with uncanny accuracy: the time had come to still the drums and the tumult. The Americanist crisis sputtered out quickly, leaving only a handful of sparks behind. Not without some parting shots, to be sure. Périès took up his bitter pen once more, and the ineffable Joseph Schroeder followed suit. Ireland himself, under a pseudonym, certainly wrote one article for the press and possibly another. But there was little left for him to say except to pronounce an epitaph: "In Europe,

Americanism was cradled as well as entombed; in America it was unknown until it was condemned."[106]

The only intervention of significance after the appearance of *Testem Benevolentiae* was that of the eccentric bishop of Peoria. Lancaster Spalding, never one to despise a cause simply because it was lost, had for the most part kept himself clear of the controversies of the preceding years. When the pope's condemnation of Americanism was published, he expressed sympathy for the Paulists and added a barb for his erstwhile friend, John Ireland, who, rumor was saying again, might be made a cardinal: "I should be glad to see him made anything that would keep him silent."[107] On October 13, 1899, the day after the rancorous archbishops' meeting, Spalding gave a formal address on his favorite subject, the moral value of higher education, which included these lines: "What sacredness is there in Europe more than in America? . . . Why should Europe be an object of awe or admiration for Catholics? Half its population has revolted from the church, and in the so-called Catholic nations, which are largely governed by atheists, what vital manifestation of religious life and power can we behold?" Of the potentates present for the speech, Martinelli and Corrigan looked uneasy and annoyed and Ireland visibly pleased.[108]

After the new year Spalding traveled to Europe, and in early February he had an audience with Leo XIII. By his own account he told the pope that the errors described in *Testem Benevolentiae* did not exist in the United States, and, when the pope offered a derogatory comment about Hecker, the bishop replied, "Holy Father, did you know Hecker? Well, . . . I did and a better Catholic we never had."[109] Six weeks later, from, of all places, the pulpit of the Gesù, the principal Jesuit church in Rome, Spalding delivered a rousing sermon about the need for the universal church to take account of the hegemony rapidly being imposed upon the world by the English-speaking peoples, with their devotion to individual liberty and enterprise, lest Catholics "more and more drift away from the vital movements of the age" and find themselves "immured in a spiritual ghetto."[110] "My how Spalding has sounded the bugle," exclaimed a delighted Denis O'Connell,[111] who promptly put the bishop of Peoria into contact with his German allies. Spalding, accompanied by Mamie Caldwell (now the Marchise Monstiers-

Merinville[112]), spent three days with Kraus in Florence, then went on to Milan and a meeting with the Countess Sabina — who thought Spalding potentially "a great man" but "an icicle" compared to the "volcano" Ireland — and finally, at the end of April, to Paris, where Félix Klein warmly greeted him.[113] Indeed, as Benedetto Lorenzelli, the highly biased nuncio to Paris, remembered it, Spalding became overnight the toast "of the liberal school of Kraus," with Klein and the other agents of the "false Anglo-German intellectualism" raising "a continual hymn" to the bishop of Peoria, even as they maintained a "calculated silence" toward the archbishop of St. Paul, their former hero. This "purposeful disparagement of Mgr. Ireland," Lorenzelli assured Rampolla, arose "precisely because Ireland, when he was in Paris in July 1900 (and a little later in Italy), showed such honesty and docility with regard to the great socio-religious truths of Catholicism. He and I conversed about this many times."[114] Abbé Klein was in any event impressed enough to translate and publish the Gesù sermon, and to arrange for the publication in France of a collection of Spalding's lectures and essays.[115] But if Klein or Kraus or their associates imagined they had found the spokesman of their movement and of Lorenzelli's nightmare, the misconception stemmed from a failure to realize that temperamentally the bishop of Peoria could not belong to any party, much less lead one.

Spalding had been back in Illinois for some weeks when John Ireland returned to Paris, this time as an official emissary of the United States. The occasion was the dedication of a statue of Lafayette, a gift from American schoolchildren to the people of France, and McKinley expressed his satisfaction that so "eminent [a] representative of American patriotism and eloquence" had been chosen to deliver the main address.[116] On July 5, 1900, in the Place du Carrousel, enfolded within the long stone arms of the Louvre, a distinguished audience, including the president of the Republic and his cabinet — bitter anti-clericals to a man — listened for nearly an hour to the archbishop of St. Paul laud the glories of the eldest daughter of the church, of the *gesta Dei per Francos,* of "a land above all other lands the land of chivalry, of noble impulse, of generous sacrifice."[117]

After a round of social events and a few more public appearances, Ireland set out for Italy. He carried with him not only the echoes of Parisian applause, a sound he particularly savored, but also the impressions of recent conversations at the Paris nunciature with Archbishop Lorenzelli, to whom he had confided his worries that he had lost the confidence of the Holy See and that the misuses of the term "Americanism" would harm the interests of the church in the United States. The nuncio, who, contrary to his expectations, had found the archbishop of St. Paul suitably docile, had reassured him as best he could, while warning him to keep at arm's length the "heterodox tendencies and aberrations" of certain "pseudo-intellectuals."[118] In Rome, on August 16, Ireland got an opportunity to heed that advice, at least to a degree, when he, along with several other visiting prelates, was invited to attend the festive consistory held in honor of the pope's name day.[119] Several routinely complimentary speeches were made, and then Leo XIII invited Ireland to the rostrum and asked him to comment to the assembled cardinals on the present political situation of the Holy See. Ireland responded with a twenty-minute address to the effect that "the only solution of the Roman Question is the Pope's civil princedom; and until the civil princedom is recovered the Pope's protest will continue against the existing condition of things."[120]

The pope, then and later, professed himself extremely pleased at Ireland's *orazione in circolo:* the archbishop of St. Paul had passed the basic litmus test of filial loyalty.[121] But in doing so he sacrificed whatever small chance remained of exercising leadership over O'Connell's movement of "internationalized" Americanism. The members of that group could scarcely find adjectives pejorative enough to describe the heinousness of St. Paul's treason; they ascribed it simply to his ungovernable lust for the red hat, and, reflecting their German prejudices, to his involvement in Rampolla's failed policy of ralliement in France.[122] Unquestionably they were right about Ireland's desire for promotion to the sacred college, and they had company in assuming that his speech at the consistory had been far from a spontaneous outburst of devotion.[123] Yet it may be reasonably asked whether one can betray a cause to which one has never subscribed. Ireland did not share the views held by Kraus and, for a brief interlude, by O'Connell, and so less convincing was their allegation that he lacked sincerity in proposing a distinction between a "civil princedom" and the old "temporal power," between a necessary political independence of the pope on the one hand and a restoration of the papal states on the other. A similar position had been outlined for Ireland by Keane more than a decade before,[124] and, though he never displayed any enthusiasm for the temporal power,[125] the archbishop of St. Paul consistently maintained the need for the pope to enjoy an independent political status.[126]

From Rome John Ireland made his leisurely way to Switzerland and then to the cherished valley of the Rhone. At Belley he joined a reunion of his old schoolfellows from Meximieux, and noted with sadness how the nearby churches, so full and flourishing when he had been a student more than forty years before, now often stood deserted. In Paris, at a special ceremony held on September 6, 1900, he received the prized ribbon of a Commander of the Legion of Honor.[127] It was a fitting accolade for a lover of France and for an old soldier, most of whose battles were now over.

~ XIX ~

The Lady and the Hat
1900-07

J OHN IRELAND, who paid tribute to his time and place by the ripeness of his rhetoric, by his childlike trust in the value of real estate investment, and by his dedication to the Manifest Destiny of the United States in the world, also displayed himself as a quintessential man of the American Gilded Age by the manner in which he dealt with the press. He recognized and respected its power, and in his many controversies, he never hesitated to use it to his advantage—even, if possible, to manipulate it.[1] He learned early how important the accommodation of newspapermen was to the creation of a favorable public persona.[2] Besides, he liked most members of the fourth estate, and they him. When the ship bringing him back from Europe landed in New York on a mid-October day of 1900,[3] Ireland found a group of reporters waiting for him, among them the celebrated Carl Hovey. As one journalist remembered,

> The wise old prelate would not tell his news—"not a word," he said to the reporters, "not a single word." They were all balked but Hovey, who told [his readers] how the archbishop refused to talk. He reported how he looked, how he waved his long, canny finger, smiling, as he warned the reporters not to make up a fake; and how he came upon a crowd [of them] lying on the deck, their heads together, trying to fake up something—the fine old priest came up, cast his shadow over them, and startled them with his "Now, now, now, what are you all up to?" [The] readers *saw* that happen, and they saw the archbishop and the kind of dignified, humorous, fine human being he was; and that was half the news of that day.[4]

The prelate Hovey described was, at sixty-two, a portly figure who carried his weight with a youthful, springy step. His hair had turned to silver and begun to thin in the front, but his brows were still blue-black and the eyes beneath them as bright and piercing as ever. His ruddy complexion proclaimed his good health, and neither age nor flesh had diminished a whit the jutting line of his jaw. And if he declined to share any news with Hovey and his confreres at the New York docks, the archbishop soon put himself right with the press by recounting for publication the somewhat dubious story that the pope and all the potentates of Europe had confided to him their urgent wish that President McKinley be reelected.[5]

If, as is likely, Ireland called at 452 Madison Avenue before boarding his train for St. Paul, he probably found the archbishop of New York surprisingly friendly. Michael Corrigan too had been in Paris during the summer of 1900, and he too had spent some hours of conversation with the nuncio there. Lorenzelli dutifully reported to Rampolla—as an old Roman hand like Corrigan knew he would—how glowingly New York spoke of St. Paul, "paying tribute to his rectitude, sincerity, talent and overall good influence," and to his unique role as "mediator" between Catholic and Protestant Americans.[6] It was a wispy olive branch perhaps, but a significant one, and even more significant was the relative silence maintained by crusty old Bernard McQuaid since his outburst at the end of 1894; only in the immediate wake of *Testem Benevolentiae* had the bishop of Rochester taken a public stand critical of the Americanists, and then with no direct allusions to John Ireland.[7] A story was told, however, by an American layman of independent means named Francis MacNutt, who lived in Rome and performed some minor ceremonial functions in the papal court, that he had learned by chance of the pope's intention to create Ireland a cardinal. MacNutt shared this information with McQuaid just before the latter was ushered into a private audience with Leo XIII. "When [the bishop] came out, half an hour later, he looked very satisfied and . . . he thanked me, saying that Archbishop Ireland's name had been scratched off the Pope's list in his presence."[8]

Little credence need be given to MacNutt's anecdote, but surely, as Ireland rolled westward toward home, he was pondering his chances for the cardinalate, a goal that by then had become almost an obsession with him. At that very moment, indeed, Thomas O'Gorman was busy lobbying for the cause in European centers of influence. The bishop of Sioux Falls stopped first in Paris, where he urged Ireland's French friends to exert pressure upon the ministry to inform the Vatican that a red hat for the archbishop of St. Paul would be most agreeable to the Quai d'Orsay. Once in Rome, "I caused a wire to be sent to Rooker, signed by O'C[onnell], to the effect that if McK[inley] could be got to signify to Martinelli his wish in the matter, and if M[artinelli] so wired the Vatican, we would be sure of the coup. . . . Now I have great hopes even for this consistory."[9]

On October 19 O'Gorman spent thirty minutes in private conversation with Leo XIII. The pope praised Ireland extravagantly, and spoke with special appreciation of the speech *in circolo* of the previous summer. O'Gorman then said that some concrete manifestation of the Holy Father's good opinion might well be forthcoming. "Ah!" Leo replied "laughingly" in French, "there is opposition to him in your country and here, there are difficulties." O'Gorman could only argue the point that the former ideological controversies that had divided the American hierarchy, like the school question, had passed, and only personal animosities remained. Corrigan, he insisted, was isolated, while Ireland enjoyed the confidence of his colleagues. A day or two after this inconclusive exchange, the bishop of Sioux Falls discovered what he judged to be the single greatest obstacle to Ireland's ambition, his association with Denis O'Connell. One of O'Gorman's sources asserted that Ireland had committed the ultimate imprudence by traveling with O'Connell to Milan in the spring of 1899. "Ledoch[owski] said O'C was constantly boasting he carried the American Church in his pocket, especially Gibbons, Ireland, etc. I have no confidence in O'C; I believe he does you harm, though he may not mean to do so." Before he left Rome, O'Gorman received an indication that the ecclesiastical wars indeed were over when the American and English assistants to the general of the Jesuits paid him a courtesy call. "They are anxious for peace, I know," he observed, and then, construing the visit as a sign of Ireland's impending honor, he added: "Or is it that they see the inevitable coming? . . . Don't forget to preach and circulate the sermon in sense of circolo [*sic*]. It is expected by Pope and Ramp[olla]."[10]

But the consistory came and went, and there was no hat for John Ireland. Roman gossip had it that as the cardinals discussed the various candidates his cause proceeded satisfactorily, until Corrigan's partisans complained "gently" of the "humiliation" to the great see of New York if it were passed over in favor of a jurisdiction only a fraction its size. There were, moreover, many other American dioceses besides New York with larger Catholic populations than St. Paul. And, since all the participants agreed that three American cardinals were one too many, there the matter rested. "France did nothing for you," O'Connell maintained.[11] Meanwhile, Ireland, back in Minnesota again after an absence of four months, pondered one other troubling bit of information O'Gorman had forwarded to him, the talk around the Vatican to the effect that the incessant travels of the archbishop of St. Paul had led to neglect of his diocese.[12] This allegation was hardly novel—McQuaid had expressed it forcefully enough years before—but its source and timing lent urgency to the preparation of the decennial report Ireland submitted to Propaganda at about this time. He was anxious to still any such criticism.

The picture he drew was indeed an impressive one, and if the statistics of growth were modest when compared to those of New York, they nevertheless demonstrated the remarkable development that had occurred in the forty years during which John Ireland had been directly involved in the apostolate in the Upper Midwest. There were, he reported, 220,000 Catholics in the Archdiocese of St. Paul, out of a total population of about one million. The people were served in 214 parishes, of which only ten (he was no doubt happy to testify) were staffed by religious clergy—five Benedictine parishes, three Franciscan, one Dominican, one Marist. The 230 secular priests carried on the rest of the parochial ministry and also staffed the College of St. Thomas and the St. Paul Seminary. He lavished the greatest praise on, and allotted the most space in the report for, the latter institution, with its splendid setting, its fine buildings, which housed scientific laboratories as well as conventional classrooms and living accommodations, its 140 students, its endowment of three hundred thousand dollars, administered by a board composed of the archbishop, priests, and laymen. The archbishop's own income amounted to about twenty thousand dollars per annum, out of which sum he "was able to carry on charitable and educational good works, and live sufficiently." The archdiocese maintained eighty-three parochial schools, with an enrollment of eleven thousand pupils. The faith of the people was strong and vibrant, he said, but—not even ambition could budge John Ireland from some of his convictions—the papal condemnation of the Odd Fellows and the Knights of Pythias had caused considerable and unnecessary trials to consciences. Participatory democracy, however, was not Ireland's style: "There has been no provincial or diocesan synod, because there has been no opportunity or need for one. The Archbishop has conferred yearly with appropriate people in order to determine the means to achieve the spiritual well-being of the archdiocese, and this has seemed sufficient." And finally he gave a hint of a great project yet to come: "The cathedral church in the city of St. Paul is sound and ample, but, to keep pace with civic development, a new and more magnificent edifice will soon be erected."[13]

Progress was therefore notable, whatever the ordinary's peregrinations, and John Ireland could hardly be blamed if he found mingling with popes and presidents beguiling when compared to the daily grind of the local chancery. One of his friends, no mean traveler himself, unintentionally put the matter in its true light. "You must surely be home by this time," John J. Keane wrote at the end of October 1900. "A thousand welcomes back home from your wonderful triumphal march. How prosy the details of diocesan administration must seem in contrast."[14]

The letter came from nearby Dubuque, to which archiepiscopal dignity Keane had been appointed a few months earlier. He had departed Rome in the late spring of 1899 and returned to the United States to help raise funds for his beloved university. He was still engaged in this endeavor—with little success—by the time he learned, in March 1900, of the death of the archbishop of Dubuque. Immediately the rumor mills had begun to grind out speculation about Keane's chances, and he himself nervously sought hard information from O'Connell in Rome.

His friends had rallied to his support. Gibbons wrote directly to the pope and, for good measure, to Rampolla, reminding them both of the promise, made at the time of Keane's dismissal from the university, of a metropolitan see if he wanted one.[15] And Ireland had followed suit. "Your Eminence will permit me," he told Ledochowski, "to remind you of a conversation I had the honor of having with you the last time I was in Rome about Monseigneur Keane," whose lot since 1896 had been "most sad." In the eyes of the American public he had stood under the shadow of pontifical censure. "He was condemned to live as an exile in Rome an existence of idleness [*oisiveté*] which was absolutely insupportable to him. . . . You know Mgr. Keane; I need not recount to you his merits." So now Ireland took the occasion to recall Ledochowski's commitment that, if Keane were nominated by the bishops of a province, the prefect of Propaganda would use his "high influence to have such episcopal action endorsed by the Holy See."[16]

Keane had indeed been placed first on the terna of the bishops of the province, second on that of the priests of the archdiocese. At Propaganda opposition to him appeared confined mostly to Satolli, whose antagonism stemmed more from personal dislike than from any substantive reasons. Among the American archbishops only Katzer took violent exception to the proposed appointment, because, he said, it would mean the domination of the Midwest by members of the "American-liberal" school and by the "intimate adherents" of the archbishop of St. Paul. Corrigan, by contrast, expressed no objection.[17] The process, even so, had dragged on for months, and not until late summer, when he was taking the waters at a German health spa, had Keane been formally invited to exchange his titular archbishopric for a real one. He had hastened off at once to Paris for a gala banquet of celebration attended by, among others, Bellamy and Maria Storer and John Ireland.[18]

So one more weary combatant withdrew from the field. But the good-hearted and always high-minded John Keane was not allowed to do so without a last cruel wound being inflicted upon him. Accompanying the bull of appointment to Dubuque was a personal letter from the pope, dated August 18, 1900, which sternly admonished the archbishop to avoid in his new ministry the errors set out in *Testem Benevolentiae*. "And this," Keane cried out to Ireland, "at the very time he was virtually apologizing to you for [*Testem*], and saying it was needed only in France. It made me sick — and it was a painful blow to the Cardinal [Gibbons] too—I have not told a living soul of it besides him."[19] Thus the supple ambivalence of Leo XIII manifested itself again, as it had when *Testem Benevolentiae,* whose text and context declared that it addressed certain French aberrations, was dispatched, not to the cardinal of Paris, but to the cardinal of Baltimore.[20] It was with a certain relief therefore that John Keane turned to his new and relatively uncomplicated duties, and before long his persistent good humor revived. "Things go well here. The welcome has been all that [the] heart could wish." In mid-April 1901, Gibbons came to Dubuque to confer the pallium upon his old friend and disciple, and John Ireland, preaching a sermon with some passages as wistful as the sounding of taps, hailed the "friend of my priestly and episcopal years, my fellow-soldier and my leader in all causes we believed to be serviceable to church and to country." But Gibbons, as was fitting, had the last word. At the festive banquet he raised a glass of water in his hand and said, "I confess that the elevation of Archbishop Keane has lengthened my life for many years. It has cheered my heart, has brought sunshine to me, and to me has been the happiest incident of my life in the last ten or fifteen years, and I propose the health of the Archbishop of Dubuque, in his most cherished beverage."[21]

By that time the events had begun to unfold that would thrust John Ireland, for the last time, into the international arena. A world away, in Manila, William Howard Taft, president of the five-member Philippine Commission—which worked in tandem with the military governor in exercising American jurisdiction in the newly acquired islands—replied to a letter sent him by the wife of the United States minister to Spain, Maria Longworth Storer. Judge Taft agreed with his fellow Cincinnatian that the failure to promote the archbishop of St. Paul to the college of cardinals at the recent consistory was deplorable (though a few months before he had refused to request President McKinley to solicit that promotion from the pope). What he really would have liked, the judge added wearily, was to have Ireland named apostolic delegate to the Philippines.[22]

Taft had never met Ireland, so this aspiration did not spring from personal motives. He knew of course that the archbishop was a good Republican, like himself, and an even more ardent imperialist. They had mutual friends, like the Storers and Vice-president Theodore Roosevelt, who assured him that Ireland was a man of enlightened views. The need he felt to have a sympathetic Catholic prelate stand with him in the Philippines resulted from the religio-political quagmire he—a respectable, white, Anglo-Saxon Protestant—had found himself in, dealing, as he had to do, with "little brown men" who professed the Romish religion and who nevertheless routinely assaulted and even killed their priests. Neither his Yale degree nor his position on the federal circuit court of appeals had prepared him for such an eventuality. Taft's mother was wryly amused "that you should . . . identify yourself with religious contests, . . . not being theological in your tastes, or fitted for it by education."[23]

The apostolic delegate in place was Placide L. Chapelle, archbishop of New Orleans, with whom Taft was at odds from the moment he arrived in the Philippines.[24] The bone of contention between them was the tortured question of what to do about the Spanish friars whose presence, the American conquerors quickly discovered, added another source of disruption to a situation already unstable on other accounts. Taft recognized from the start that the Filipino people remained attached to their religion, but the antipathy toward the friars was so widespread and so intense that he was at a loss to see how they could continue to function in the islands.[25] Indeed, during the disorder that followed in the wake of the war and of a series of armed insurrections against the American occupation, at least fifty friars had been murdered. The problem appeared no less acute to the Vatican, which viewed with apprehension a change in sovereignty that might endanger the only Catholic community of consequence in all of Asia. And to serve a population of about six million, scattered over 140,000 square miles and more than seven thousand islands, there were only about sixteen hundred priests, two-thirds of whom were Spanish friars and the rest ill-trained native seculars. Chapelle, for whom John Ireland had scant regard,[26] had his work cut out for him.

The christianization of the Philippine archipelago had been the achievement of the four great orders of friars—Dominican, Franciscan, Augustinian, and Recollect[27]—who had first arrived in the islands in the sixteenth and early seventeenth centuries. Unquestionably they had performed much good over these hundreds of years, but by the time the Spanish-American War broke out they had become so closely identified with the colonial regime, and their religious functions had been so melded into their administrative ones—the friars formed what civil service there was in the Philippines—that they had gained the enmity of a large proportion of the native population. Moreover, they displayed that weakness all too common among missionaries, a patronizing attitude toward those of an allegedly inferior culture and race, and an inability to grasp that their own accomplishments—especially in the field of education—created after a time a small but articulate middle class to whom such patronization was as hateful as it was anachronistic. Animosity toward the friars reached a fever pitch in the wake of the abortive Filipino rebellion of 1896, the failure of which was laid by many at their door. It was then that the gross stories of their lechery and personal cruelty began to circulate in earnest.[28]

But a cause of much more resentment over the long term was the friars' possession of nearly a half-million acres of the best land in Luzon and Mindanao, not to mention the hundreds of buildings that belonged to them and the "pious trusts"—invested capital in support of hospitals, schools, and other institutions—they executed.[29] Now if the friars had been as wicked as their most vociferous opponents charged, they might have been safely swept out of the islands and their property confiscated and distributed to their tenants and other poor peasants. The reality, however, was much more complicated, and Taft was shrewd enough to realize that much of the exaggeration in the charges against the friars was bound up with the Filipino independence movement, which the McKinley administration, strongly supported by American public opinion, did not countenance. The "little brown men," of whom Taft eventually grew very fond, were nevertheless not ready, in his universally shared opinion, to govern themselves. Besides, the friars' legal title to their lands was above dispute, and no American president, of either party, would have dreamed of challenging the sacred right of private ownership, which had been guaranteed in the Philippines by the Treaty of Paris, signed on December 10, 1898, ending the Spanish-American War.

John Ireland, even while the war still raged, had received assurances from McKinley himself that ecclesiastical persons and property in the territories to be annexed would be protected by the American government. At the same time he had warned Cardinal Rampolla that the Catholic church's status in the Philippines would depend upon the willingness of the clergy there to accept "the new order of things."[30] But since then Filipino rebels and schismatics had seized large parcels of the friars' lands, while in the United States certain organs of the Catholic press responded to the charges against the friars by accusing the administration of inventing scapegoats to mask its own American Protective Association–style bigotry. Rumbles of this sort made the politicians in Washington uneasy. Meanwhile, in Manila, Taft tried conscientiously to unravel what was to a man of his class and mind-set a virtually unintelligible riddle. After a careful investigation, which left him still puzzled about many aspects of the situation, his practical conclusion was that the friars had to go, and that Chapelle, the friars' undeviating ally, had to go, too.[31]

Archbishop Ireland's involvement in these seemingly intractable problems remained passive until a few weeks after Keane's celebration in Dubuque. In early May 1901, he went to Washington to attend a banquet in honor of the apostolic delegate, Martinelli, who had received the red hat Ireland himself so sorely wanted. While there he held informal conversations about the situation in the Philippines with Martinelli and with the Honorable Elihu Root of New York. The courtly Root was, as McKinley's secretary of war, responsible for Filipino policy. These discussions bore fruit at the beginning of June. The Holy See, Rampolla wrote Ireland from the Vatican, was concerned with the situation in the Philippines and wished to settle the issues concerning the Catholics there.

> The chief interest of the Holy See is of course religious, but that interest can be served only when the new circumstances that have arisen are taken into account. . . . To do that I need direct contact with some one who can tell me the wishes and intentions of the American government. The absence of diplomatic relations is a detriment to both parties, but it is not for me to insist upon that to American statesmen. What I can do is mention the problem to you who know several of them. If you can make understood in

your country what I have just indicated to you, you will do a great service both for the Church and for your country.[32]

Armed with this general mandate, Ireland began to move the wheels of diplomacy gently forward. Though formal relations between the Vatican and the United States remained unfeasible, he assured Rampolla that the initiative already taken by Secretary Root indicated the American government's eagerness to settle the imbroglio in the Philippines. It was, moreover, a psychologically advantageous moment, because the administration could not realistically hope to do so without the cooperation of the Holy See.[33] All the pope wanted, the secretary of state replied, was the appointment of someone who enjoyed McKinley's confidence to come to Rome and discuss the Filipino situation.[34] Ireland in turn saw to it that the Vatican understood that Chapelle had become a persona non grata with Taft and the rest of the administration,[35] and Rampolla responded by sending the archbishop of New Orleans back to his diocese and replacing him as delegate to Manila with Donato Sbarretti—the same Sbarretti to whom, when he was a poor clerk at Propaganda years before, Ireland had sent mass stipends.

The dismissal of Chapelle gave a clear signal that the Vatican wished to accommodate the McKinley administration, and Ireland spent much of the summer carefully cultivating his contacts with Root. A pleasant distraction for him occurred on July 2, at a sumptuous celebration held on the grounds of his prized grand séminaire in observance of the golden jubilee of Joseph Cretin's arrival as first bishop of St. Paul.[36] But Cretin's protégé of a half-century earlier was soon back at work again, following up the initial diplomatic steps with "a formal request [from Rampolla] thro' me to our government to have some representative from Washington go to Rome to treat with the Vatican about property and other questions." Such a mission would be limited to "temporary and restricted negotiations on special matters [relevant to the Philippines]."[37] Root liked this idea, and so did Taft, with whom Ireland opened direct correspondence on September 19.[38]

Five days before that McKinley died at the hands of an assassin, and for the moment all activity ceased. It was to be expected, however, that once the period of national mourning was over and Theodore Roosevelt had moved into the White House, the plan for a special representative would be pursued with, if anything, more vigor. In the meantime Ireland pursued the goal by quiet persuasion whenever an occasion presented itself. In October, for example, when he went to New Haven to receive an honorary doctorate of laws from Yale—a recognition he accepted only "after much reflection: . . . I am not at all sure that many of my friends will think I have done the proper thing"[39]—he informally discussed the proposal with Roosevelt, who was present to receive an honorary degree of his own, and took the opportunity to solicit the support of Jacob G. Schurman, president of Cornell University and the leading American academic expert on Philippine affairs. Schurman readily agreed to write Roosevelt his approval of the plan, and, at the appropriate moment, to express himself to that effect publicly.[40] Ireland otherwise allowed little fanfare to accompany his brief fling at Yale, probably recalling how Bishop Keane had got into hot water years before by lecturing in the Appleton Chapel at Harvard; but a picture of the new doctor in his ceremonial garb did appear, and, O'Connell assured him, "you looked in your Robes . . . as if you had worn them all your lifetime."[41]

November and most of December Ireland spent in Washington and its environs. He met frequently with Secretary Root, Secretary of State John Hay, and the president himself. He also enlisted Gibbons's prestige and persuasive powers.[42] Roosevelt, ever the political animal, naturally weighed the proposal of a mission to Rome in electoral terms, and, while he was confident that it would gain Catholic votes for the Republicans, he did not thereby want to sacrifice any non-Catholic ones. He therefore assigned the archbishop to go to New York and urge the editors of the influential establishment journals *The Outlook* and *The Independent* to support the administration in this endeavor, "and they have written to the President strongly endorsing the project."[43] In the midst of these heady conferences and negotiations, the annual meeting of the archbishops at the Catholic University on November 21 and 22 must have seemed to Ireland a dull affair, but he could not have been displeased to hear Archbishop Corrigan, in delivering a committee report, go out of his way to praise the caliber and content of the instruction given at the St. Paul Seminary.[44] When he went home for

Christmas, he could tell Gibbons that events had proceeded to his "utter satisfaction."[45]

One matter discussed at the White House and the War Department had been prospective candidates to chair the delegation to be sent to the Vatican. "Theodore and I hold out for you," Ireland told Bellamy Storer, "but it is objected [by Root] that it is undiplomatic to send one minister into the territory of another," and that the person selected needed to have had direct acquaintance with the situation in the Philippines. Storer, by then minister to Spain, nevertheless cabled his readiness — indeed, his eager desire — to be given the appointment, but Root's views prevailed. "It is as well for you," Ireland wrote consolingly. "You could not have gone to Rome, I believe, while still minister to Madrid; and to resign your present position, as you proposed in your cablegram, would, in my opinion, be rather parlous. The work in Rome may be of very short duration."[46]

It is likely that Storer himself had less to do with pressing his claims upon the new president and the archbishop than did his strong-willed wife, whose ambitions had become entangled with those of Theodore Roosevelt and John Ireland, and had launched them all on a path destined to end in a poignant mixture of comedy and tragedy. Maria Longworth, a woman of inherited wealth and high social standing, had left Cincinnati for Washington in 1891 when her husband took his seat in Congress. He served two lackluster terms, after which the local political boss refused to slate him a third time. Storer impressed everyone he met with his high moral and intellectual qualities — "Noble-hearted," McKinley called him, "the most unselfish man I ever knew"[47] — but he had in him also something of the dilettante, who lacked the vigor and force of character so much admired by his generation. Perhaps he was simply too decent a man to survive in the jungle that was Republican politics in Ohio.[48]

His wife, by contrast, was a dynamo of energy. She was also ambitious in a world that allowed little scope for women to achieve recognition except vicariously through the men in their lives. Because she was rich, Maria Storer enjoyed more freedom than most of her sisters, but sexist barriers hemmed her in, too, and, like many females of her class, she had perforce to concentrate her exertions upon cultural and charitable good works. She possessed a quite admirable sense of noblesse oblige, and the deprived of the Cincinnati area had many reasons to be grateful to her. She was also well educated — she spoke and wrote French like a native — and, in an age of talented letter-writers, her pen-pictures, often caustic, bear comparison with the best. Thus she dismissed the statesman John Hay as "a little man of literary talent but small caliber, ruined by opulence." And, describing an audience with Leo XIII shortly after the issuance of *Testem Benevolentiae,* she evoked the scene of the ancient, tiny, shriveled-up pontiff waving his hands in alarm at the bejeweled matron from the Midwest who loomed over him and assuring her that he had intended to condemn nobody, "only some tendencies [*c'etait une tendance etc.*]."[49]

During their sojourn in Washington the Storers became intimate friends of the Roosevelts. The winning and impulsive Theodore, civil service commissioner during the Harrison administration, even then seemed to Maria Storer, ten years his senior (as John Ireland was ten years *her* senior), to possess "the peculiar attraction and fascination" of a child, "with a child's spontaneous outbursts of affection, of fun, and of anger, and with the busy brain and fancy of a child."[50] She assumed an almost maternal attitude toward him, hectoring him and shaking a metaphorical finger at him when he displeased her. But her love for him was genuine, and his rejection of her, when it occurred, filled her with the keenest pain.

Also during her time in Washington Maria Storer joined the Catholic church, and immediately displayed all the fervor of a new convert. The agent of her conversion was John J. Keane, then rector of the Catholic University, and through Keane she met John Ireland.[51] These two men epitomized for her their own grand vision of a universal Catholicism that incorporated the unique values of the American experience and was to be ruled by an aristocracy of talent. And when Keane was dismissed from the university, she dispatched the first in a long series of distressful communiqués to high Roman officials. She pleaded with Rampolla in behalf of "our two great American prelates. . . . Your Eminence, in the name of the small number of American converts . . . of wealth and education . . . who have come into the Church through the influence of . . . Monseigneur Keane and Monseigneur Ireland, . . . I beg the Holy Father with all my heart and soul not to leave us in the darkness. I have found the path—and my daughter and my husband—by the light of our American prelates."[52]

Bellamy had indeed followed her into the church, as had her daughter, married to a titled Frenchman. The conviction then grew upon Maria that her husband's failure to secure the preferment she thought he deserved—despite her financial largesse to McKinley and to Roosevelt[53]—stemmed from antagonism toward his religion. It was only a step from that idea to the notion that promoting the Catholicism which Ireland embodied for her was also a way to advance Bellamy's career. She had been bitterly disappointed when McKinley relegated her husband to the second-rate embassy at Brussels in 1896. The posting to Madrid, coming as it did at the sensitive moment just after the war, thrilled her at first, but soon she was as bored and restless as ever, and she wandered from one swank European resort to another, her minister-husband padding along obediently in her wake.[54] By the time McKinley died, Maria Storer had formulated two concrete goals: to secure for Bellamy a cabinet office or a first-class ambassadorship—Paris, London, or, at the very least, Berlin—and to secure for John Ireland a red hat. So, as was her wont, she put pen to paper. She wrote to Rampolla and directly to Leo XIII, told them of the high esteem the archbishop of St. Paul enjoyed with the new president of the United States, and quoted verbatim some of Roosevelt's earlier indiscreet communications to her and her husband in which he had said that he indeed wanted Ireland promoted to the sacred college and that he was willing "to do anything I can" to achieve that end.[55] Then she addressed "Dear Theodore," and demanded for her husband "either the Navy or War. . . . I pray that Bellamy, who so richly deserves it, shall have a chance for honorable service at home to his country." When Roosevelt answered "My dear Maria" that he could not simply discharge the secretaries of the navy or war—particularly the latter, Root, "the very strongest man in our whole party"—she wrote again, demanding London or Paris and asserting that the present incumbents there "were not proper persons to be ambassadors."[56] Her appeals, however, had no immediate effect, and once, when Ireland was at the White House discussing the Philippine delegation, the president said to him: "Mrs. Storer has written me an awful letter; she allows me no time; try, I beg of you, to calm her."[57]

Whether the principals in those discussions liked it or not, Maria Storer was determined to play a role in them.[58] Ireland returned to Washington in January 1902 and again in late February. By that time Governor-General Taft—as he now was—had taken leave from his post in Manila and arrived in the United States for medical treatment. By March, when the Storers had also come home on leave, the president decided that Taft himself should head the commission to negotiate the frairs' lands question with the Vatican, and that Thomas O'Gorman should accompany him, or rather precede him to Rome and lay the groundwork with the pope and Rampolla. But suddenly Roosevelt, annoyed by criticism of the project voiced not only by Protestant leaders but by some Catholics as well, had a characteristically sudden change of heart. "I think I ought to tell you," Maria Storer informed Ireland, "exactly what seems *just now* to be the condition of Theodore's mind." At a dinner party on March 23 a "very excitable and high-strung" president lashed out at the Vatican for its attempts to use the Philippine negotiations as a means of securing diplomatic recognition from the United States.

> "The more I see of the higher ecclesiastics of your Church the more clearly I can see that our country comes *second;* that they are all anxious simply to propitiate the Vatican—and that the Vatican *comes first!*" I said: "You can't mean Archbishop Ireland, Theodore." And he answered: "I do. I do." I said: "But you know very well that the only reason he or we can wish that he should be a Cardinal is for the welfare of our own country." He only rejoined: "The country comes second with them all. . . . I saw it the last time I saw [Ireland]. He does all these things to help the *Vatican.* This country comes *second!!*"

Roosevelt then added for good measure that, though he wanted to appoint Bellamy to the embassy in Berlin, he could do so only if he were "*sure* that the Emperor will not object to a *Catholic* ambassador." So Maria Storer saw both of her cherished goals threatened in one burst of the president's temper. She urged Ireland to take action, specifically to persuade certain leading German-American newspapers to state editorially that Bellamy would be an acceptable representative in Berlin: "To show the President that *you* got [such endorsements] would do no harm either to you or us."[59]

The archbishop of St. Paul offhandedly complied with this request, but he reserved most of his worries for the fate of the Philippines initiative. "In the presence of Messers. Taft and Root," he exclaimed, "both of these fully acquiescing, after a conference of more than two hours duration, the President said: 'We shall send a mission to the Vatican on Philippine affairs;' and then told me explicitly and clearly that I was authorized to communicate his decision to Cardinal Rampolla."[60] Ireland had also climbed out on a limb by promising Root that he would prevent Rome from allowing Sbarretti—whom Root disliked but who was "the pet of the Curia"[61]—from ever taking up his post as delegate in Manila. A flurry of correspondence followed, but the crisis proved a momentary tempest, reflective of the president's volatile moods and perhaps of irritation at Mrs. Storer's badgering. Taft, who had gone to Cincinnati for minor surgery, exuded the gargantuan serenity worthy of a very fat man when she visited him in the hospital and told him of Roosevelt's tantrum: "You know Theodore," he said. "He has been stampeded by a lot of adverse criticism from some of his advisers. He will come round all right. Of course it is all settled. I am sailing in May, and Bishop O'Gorman goes with me."[62]

So calm was restored, and a relieved Ireland could invoke the cliché, "All is well, that ends well." The president was "in the best humor with me," he wrote Bellamy from Washington in mid-April. "Bishop O'Gorman sails after tomorrow, . . . and I shall return here early in May, when Mr. Taft and Mr. Root will be here."[63] He did return to the capital and bid adieu to Taft, but not without traveling first to New York for another farewell and an event symbolic of the ending of an era in his own life. Michael Augustine Corrigan suddenly died of pneumonia on May 5, 1902, and three days later, his inveterate enemy present among the thousands of mourners, he was buried in the splendor of St. Patrick's Cathedral.[64]

From Rome O'Gorman sent word that a consistory, scheduled for June, would not include appointments to the sacred college. "However, [curial] Card. Ferrata this very day remarked to me that the death of Corrigan (R. I. P.) might possibly make a change in plans. . . . Satolli is very friendly, speaks well of you, is certain the reward will be given."[65] On May 14 O'Gorman had a brief audience with Leo XIII, who was extremely pleased at the prospect of Taft's arrival and who, unlike Rampolla, saw no difficulty in setting aside Sbarretti if that was the wish of the American government. The pope also said that "Mgr. Ireland had done great work and service which were not to be forgotten and deserved reward." "It is a universal feeling," O'Gorman added a few days later, "that [the cardinalate] is a sure thing, especially as now the opposition has no one now to set up against you and rally around." He emphasized that these positive accounts did not originate with Denis O'Connell.[66]

Besides testing the Roman waters for his chief, O'Gorman also lobbied persistently in behalf of the promotion to the episcopate of two of Ireland's priests. In this endeavor Satolli, in his capacity as a consultor of Propaganda, was again a strong ally, fiercely resisting this "senseless opposition to a priest because he was of the diocese of St. Paul. He carried the day."[67] Some of the gossip the bishop of Sioux Falls sent home was, however, less heartening. Ireland's notion of pushing Frederick Rooker for the vacancy in New York appeared fanciful to most of O'Gorman's contacts. Moreover, "Rampolla is losing ground. The French policy is a failure," and the Italian policy, too. "True, this American commission is to Rampolla's credit," but no one could predict its ultimate outcome, and, with the death of Ledochowski expected momentarily, it was commonly whispered that a deeply depressed Rampolla contemplated moving to Propaganda. And as the secretary of state's prospects at the next conclave went down, according to O'Gorman, those of Giuseppe Sarto, the patriarch of Venice, went up.[68] That was not good news to the archbishop of St. Paul, so long identified with the policies of Rampolla.

Taft and his party arrived in Rome on May 31. The governor spent the next day in bed, with a nagging case of tonsilitis. He was sufficiently recovered on June 2 to attend a meeting with Rampolla, and there showed himself "a masterful man." The interview was all warmth and cordiality, as was the audience with Leo XIII three days later. "The Pope was very gracious, quite delighted with the letter of the President and his gift. Taft made a nice address."[69] For his part Taft found "the old boy . . . quite bubbling with humor. He was lively as a cricket. . . . He surprised me very much by his vigor and the resonance of his voice. . . . He said that he had heard of my illness but that my appearance didn't justify any such inference." There followed fifteen minutes of light conversation, after which the pope "asked me to give him the pleasure of shaking hands with him, and then escorted us to the door."[70] Twice during the audience, O'Gorman reported, the pontiff had referred to Ireland's beneficial influence in Washington as an instance of "the attitude of America to the church, also my presence on the commission. Taft is delighted and full of hope."[71]

The bargaining between the American delegation and the committee of five cardinals appointed for the purpose lasted into the early days of July. There were some social distractions, but the Americans tried to keep them to a minimum and to exclude certain undesirables: "O'Connell hangs around us a good deal, but Taft is on his guard as to him and M[a]cNutt who has been trying, but in vain, to give us a reception." As the negotiations proceeded, O'Gorman, who thought "our demands . . . rather exacting," wilted a little under the tension: "I wish it were all over. I am beginning to feel a trifle nervous."[72] In essence, Taft, following Root's instructions, offered to waive all litigation and purchase the friars' lands, for a price to be determined by outside arbitrators, in exchange for the expulsion of the Spanish religious from the islands, or for "driving out the Friars," in Root's remorseless words. The cardinatial committee — three of whose members were themselves friars — replied negatively on the sticking point, much to Taft's exasperation. Rampolla spoke for the committee.

> The Holy See cannot accept the proposition. . . . Such a measure . . . would be contrary to the positive rights guaranteed by the Treaty of Paris, and would put . . . the Holy See in conflict with Spain. . . . Much more, such a measure would be, in the eyes of the Filipinos and of the entire Catholic world, the explicit confirmation of all the accusations brought against the said religious by their enemies, accusations of which the falsity, or at least the evident exaggeration, cannot be disputed.[73]

The negotiation seemed therefore to have failed, but Taft, sensing that sometimes a wink is as good as a nod, did not break it off. He agreed to continue discussions on the purchase of the friars' property between himself and the newly appointed delegate to Manila — Sbarretti was shunted off to an Italian diocese.[74] Rampolla too emphasized the positive, assuring the governor that whatever monies were realized from the sale would not go to the orders but would be devoted to ecclesiastical projects in the Philippines, that the five Spanish-born bishops would be replaced by Americans, and that natural attrition, which was already well under way, would soon reduce the problem of the friars' presence in the islands to an anachronism.[75] So the farewell audience on July 21, if not a love feast, was nevertheless extremely cordial on both sides, with the pope, as Taft put it, "full of honeyed expressions." A month and a day later, when his ship sailed into Manila harbor, the tumultuous welcome the governor received convinced him that his diplomacy had indeed succeeded. "I do not state it too strongly," he told Roosevelt, "when I say that the visit to Rome has done us a great deal of good in this country."[76]

John Ireland was no more than a highly interested observer of these events, but when renewed criticism of the administration's policy and specifically of Taft's mission to Rome began to be heard among Catholics, he entered the fray with his old-time ardor. President Roosevelt, with an eye on the upcoming congressional elections, let the archbishop know that he was "indignant" at the negative reaction, "inasmuch as what we did was done at your suggestion and with the hearty approval of Cardinal Gibbons. I am inclined to think, however, that most of these attacks have really been aimed at you."[77] Taft had derived a similar impression from certain curial officials in Rome, and Ireland himself realized that his reputation as a foe of the religious orders rendered him suspect in the eyes of many: "If I am designated as the leader of the movement against the friars," he observed ruefully to O'Connell, "it is because I obeyed the Vatican in securing the Taft Commission."[78] But in press interviews and speeches — including one at the end of July before a large and hostile audience in Chicago — Ireland unhesitatingly sustained the whole of the administration's position. He even rejected the most serious complaint raised by Catholics against it: that the public school system introduced into the Philippines had been accompanied by systematic Protestant proselytizing.[79] Never, he declared, had there been "in the White House a man more fair-minded and impartial in religious matters than Theodore Roosevelt."[80] And he dismissed the charge of anti-Catholicism within the Filipino schools as an aberration of individuals, unsanctioned by Roosevelt and Taft. There was justice in this rejoinder, and certainly the scarcity of American Catholic teachers and educational administrators available for assignment in the Philippines was not the administration's fault; even so, a more or less explicit Protestant bias continued to show itself within the Filipino public schools for many years.[81]

Gradually a consensus developed among American Catholics, and Americans generally, that the church-state affairs in the Philippines had been adequately handled. Much of the steam went out of in-house controversy in January 1903, when Leo XIII issued a public letter in which he expressed his own satisfaction. His appointment of a new hierarchy composed of Americans, including Frederick Rooker who went to Jaro rather than to New York, contributed to overall reassurance within the United States. The old pope died that summer, and negotiations over the friars' lands slowed for a time. But his successor, Giuseppe Sarto — who styled himself Pius X — pressed for a quick final settlement, and by the end of the year, when the Vatican and Washington agreed to $7,239,000 as compensation for 410,000 acres of land, all but a handful of the Spanish friars were gone from the Philippines.[82] Many individual cases involving church property, either damaged by American military operations or illegally seized by Filipino schismatics, still had to pass through litigation which was expensive and irritating, but Roosevelt did his best to accommodate the new bishops in this regard, as he informed Ireland in mid-1904: "Taft is going to arrange for a special court to try those church property cases which will remove the last vestige of pretext for complaint."[83]

The successful part he played in helping to resolve the problems in the Philippines came too late to secure Ireland the reward he coveted most. The death of Leo XIII in July 1903, and the subsequent dramatic conclave, in which Rampolla's candidacy was vetoed by the Austrian emperor, spelled the end of any real chance the archbishop of St. Paul had to win a red hat. But Ireland, so long an aspirant, could not easily let go of his dream, even though the new regime at the Vatican, with the Anglo-Spaniard, Merry del Val, as secretary of state, was not one calculated to encourage him. Maria Longworth Storer was disappointed, too, because her husband had been posted not to the German but to the Austro-Hungarian Empire. "So long as it could not be London or Paris," Ireland wrote her soothingly, "Vienna suits me. You will be, I believe, happier there than you could have been in Berlin. *Et puis — Londres et Paris restent dans la perspective de l'avenir* [and later — London and Paris remain a strong future possibility]."[84]

The Storers, still apparently on good terms with the Roosevelts, were guests at Oyster Bay during the summer of 1903, about the time Pius X was elected. Out of conversations he had with the president, Bellamy prepared a memorandum that he submitted to the new pope in December. The president of the United States, he told Pius X, would be delighted if Archbishop Ireland were made a cardinal. Ireland was duly grateful and complimentary: "Your visit to the Vatican was a master-piece of diplomatic art. Everything done and said that should, or properly could, have been done and said."[85] But when an enterprising newspaperman sent a dispatch recounting the memorandum back to the United States, Roosevelt's response to Storer was angry and impatient: "As President it is none of my business to interfere for or against the advancement of any man in any church; and as it is impossible to differentiate what I say in my individual capacity from what I say as President — at least in the popular mind and apparently also in the Roman mind — I must request you not to quote me in any way or shape hereafter." Storer, protesting that his campaign for Ireland was really a means of benefiting the Republican party vis-à-vis the Catholic vote, haughtily offered to resign the Austrian embassy. But Roosevelt, confident — too confident indeed — that the minister and his wife had learned their lesson, replied: "Nothing would persuade me to accept your resignation, old fellow."[86]

The leak to the press, which embarrassed both Storer and Roosevelt, issued from another actor who strode onto the stage like a ghost from the past. During the final months of Leo XIII's life Denis O'Connell had been busy mending his Roman fences. He had long since disbanded "Liberty Hall," and his flirtation with Kraus and the "progressive" German school had been as brief as it was insubstantial. O'Connell's way back to favor was eased somewhat by the impartial hand of death: "It really seems," he observed to Ireland, "as if, with the vanishing of Corrigan and Ledochowski, the clouds begin to break."[87] He carefully cultivated the fickle Satolli, and even was reconciled to Ella Edes. But, most important, he had regained to some degree the affection of the old pope, and on January 5, 1903, John Ireland received the astonishing news that O'Connell had been appointed rector of the Catholic University of America. "It is a revolution," cried Ireland, who had led the effort to get O'Connell's name on the terna for the rectorship. "I sit and muse—laugh from very joy. . . . Viva l'americanismo! Viva sempre!"[88]

During the summer of 1903 O'Connell went back to Rome in his new capacity, to seek permission from the Holy See for a yearly collection to be taken up in all the dioceses in the United States in behalf of the financially strapped university. Ireland asked him while there to do what he could to further the campaign for the hat. But Leo XIII died before O'Connell could talk to him, and the rector then made his indiscreet revelation about Storer's memorandum to the newsman.[89] The incident seemed to put the final quietus upon the former intimacy between the two men. "As to O'Connell," Ireland confided to Mrs. Storer,

> I am not, as we say in the States, "particularly stuck" on him—not over confidential with him. But he is there—and he gets into situations, where I must appear; and I have to be in relations with him—say "diplomatic relations." Perhaps the only difference between you and me is that I am a little more *"pratique"*—smothering up occasionally my likes and dislikes, my *"confiances"* and my *"réservations."* You say well—O'Connell . . . has [no] padlock on his mouth.[90]

In candid moments Ireland was prepared to admit that with the fall of Rampolla his chances for the cardinalate were remote. Indeed, the shadow of the old secretary of state fell darkly over him. "Never for a moment did I waver in my loyalty to Rampolla. No one esteemed him more highly than I did. At this moment I am convinced that had I been in the Conclave [of 1903], he would be now Pope." Mrs. Storer, however, had a more naive trust in the merits of the personal approach. In the spring of 1904 she asked a friend of hers, a noblewoman who had known Pius X in Venice, to mention at a private audience the widespread desire among the best people, like herself, that Ireland receive a red hat. The pope was said to have replied, "I have considered the matter. It will be done. [*Ho studiato la causa. Sarà fatto.*]" Maria was overjoyed, and Ireland himself seemed ready to put stock in what was hardly more than a scrap of gossip: "Of course I am glad for my own sake that the matter is concluded favorably. . . . May I now hope that in the future I may prove that your interest in me was somewhat deserved."[91]

But there was no consistory in 1904, none indeed until the last days of 1905. By then rumor had already determined that no Americans were among the four candidates to be elevated. Rumor also brought to the ears of Mrs. Storer the report that Roosevelt had recommended for promotion the new archbishop of New York, John Farley, and that Merry del Val had remarked that since the president favored both Farley and Ireland he must not have cared very deeply about either. In a panic Maria dispatched a battalion of letters: to Taft, to Merry del Val, to Keane, to Rampolla, and, incredibly, to Theodore Roosevelt. Reminding the president of his former endorsements of Ireland's candidacy — the very ones he either regretted having made or denied having made — she demanded that he send her immediately a cable of recommendation which she could take personally to the pope. "You can trust me, really," she pleaded. Roosevelt exploded at this latest extravagance of the woman called mockingly by the Washington diplomatic corps "the United States Ambassadress to Rome." On December 11, 1905, he enclosed in the same envelope two letters to the Storers, one of which instructed Bellamy to read the other to his wife. The language the president used was harsh in the extreme, and he concluded with an ultimatum: "Dear Maria, if you cannot make up your mind absolutely to alter your conduct in this regard while your husband is in the diplomatic service, . . . then Bellamy cannot with propriety continue to remain ambassador of the United States." The Storers did not reply. In March 1906, when they still had not answered him, Roosevelt demanded, and received, Bellamy Storer's resignation.[92]

This sad little drama played itself out over the next year. Officially the resignation was treated simply as routine, though some editorialists wondered in print whether Mrs. Storer's intrusiveness had brought about the demise of her husband's career. At first Bellamy and Maria maintained a tight-lipped silence, the latter satisfied to insert a communication in the *New York Herald* pointing out that the president had stated *in writing* only once, in April 1900, his willingness "to do anything" to secure a red hat for the archbishop of St. Paul.[93] Ireland, so often in the past rightly accused of impulsiveness, now tried to restore calm to the situation. But, showing himself at his very best, he also served notice that he would not be intimidated. When Maria suggested that in the light of what had happened he might not want to see them socially again, the archbishop replied: "I beg leave to assure you, my dear Mrs. Storer—that, President or no President, my affectionate regard for you and Bellamy will never be kept out of sight. A strange thing it were—of which I shall forever be incapable—if to please President Roosevelt . . . or any one else—I feared to meet you, and to be cordial with you in the most open and public manner possible."[94]

But after some months the smoldering anger became too much for Maria to suppress. Early in December 1906, the Storers printed their side of the story in a pamphlet, which included an account of what Roosevelt over the years had said, as well as what he had written, on the subject of Ireland's candidacy. This they circulated among certain senators and other officials of the government. Inevitably a copy fell into the hands of a reporter, and soon the story was splashed upon the front pages of the nation's newspapers. President Roosevelt felt constrained to reply, and he did so with his usual overstatement. Bellamy Storer, he said, was guilty of "not only an untruth but an absurd untruth," of "peculiar perfidy," was "simply dishonorable" and "peculiarly ungentlemanly." "I explained [to the Storers] repeatedly," the president said, "that my friendship and admiration for Archbishop Ireland (which is like my friendship and admiration . . . for many clergymen of many denominations . . .) would make me pleased to see any good fortune attend him, or any churchman like him, of any creed; but that I could not interfere for his promotion, or, indeed, in any way in the ecclesiastical affairs of any church."[95]

The president won hands down the contest in the press for the sympathy of public opinion. Editors gleefully chastized Mrs. Storer as "a gushing intriguer," and one of them treated the episode as an argument in favor of clerical celibacy: "The rulers of the [Roman] church are far-sighted; they know human nature; they have, no doubt, in the flown centuries, considered the awful possibility of a Mrs. Bellamy Storer." These cruel imputations, and many others like them, drove Maria to the verge of hysteria. Theodore Roosevelt, she told Ireland at the beginning of 1907, was "a liar and a coward" and "an unscrupulous demagogue." She felt dirtied by the man, betrayed, "for I loved him as though he had been a younger brother. . . . I hope to heaven for your own sake that you have done with him." When Ireland pleaded with her to moderate her judgment and to consider the matter closed, as in fact it was, she turned her wrath on him. Her pen flew over page after page, quoting Roosevelt yet again, quoting Ireland to himself, implying that he lacked gratitude and compassion, eating relentlessly at her own vitals. Her cold peroration marked the end of their friendship: "Pardon my writing so much. It is the last time I ever shall trouble you again on this subject, and I want to omit nothing. Please keep these copies of your letters — so as not to forget just what has occurred, nor shut your eyes to the cowardice and treachery of Theodore Roosevelt."[96]

Nothing in the long and sometimes dreary story of John Ireland's attempts to secure the cardinalate for himself did him as much honor as the manner in which he endured in silence and without complaint the acute embarrassment caused him by what the newspapers called the " 'Dear Maria' incident." The quest for personal recognition he had carried on for fifteen years was now laid out for a curious public to speculate on and to ridicule. But he had accepted and even encouraged the Storers' aid in attaining his goal, and therefore, though he was not responsible for their indiscretions, naïveté, ill-directed exuberance, and self-service — nor for Roosevelt's, either — his duty clearly was to accept also the consequences. And he did. His stoic demeanor during these months seemed a kind of testimony to his realization that he had to pay for an ambition that the rules of his profession decreed should be entertained only behind a mask of pious subterfuge. It was, and is, a foolish convention, and an invitation to mendacity and intrigue. John Ireland played the game and lost, as much perhaps for his candor

~ XX ~
# *"Evening Is Coming On"*
1907–18

Sunday, June 2, 1907, was one of those late spring days of glorious sunshine and soft, caressing breezes that help Minnesotans forget the harshness of the winter just past. During the morning hours the St. Paul Union Depot bustled with activity as trains bearing the last of an estimated sixty thousand visitors arrived from all parts of the state for what promised to be as great a festival as any of them had ever witnessed. Early in the afternoon, the crowds converged upon St. Anthony Hill, which soared like a watchful sentinel above the busy commercial district of the city and the majestic river beyond. Atop the hill lay a vast construction site of overturned earth and the beginnings of a foundation, with pieces of equipment pulled demurely to the side. Soon the crashing music of massed bands was heard, and a parade of thirty thousand men beneath a jumble of banners came marching jauntily along toward the bend of Summit and Dayton avenues — mounted police, Civil War veterans, old settlers, uniformed cadets from the College of St. Thomas, cadres representative of every Catholic parish in the Twin Cities and of many from outside the metropolitan area — past James J. Hill's sprawling mansion and then, for a full ninety minutes, past the temporary reviewing stand upon which stood the governor, a United States senator, the mayor, thirty-five bishops, and, in the midst of these notable personages, robed in the purple of his office and with a biretta set squarely on his massive head, a beaming John Ireland.

Once the people had formed a huge semi-circle around the stand — not without spilling over into the streets nearby — speeches were duly delivered, wires of congratulation from Pope Pius X and

499

Laying the cornerstone of the new Cathedral of St. Paul, June 2, 1907 (MHS)

President Theodore Roosevelt read, a cannonade fired in salute by a battery of the Minnesota National Guard, and a *Te Deum* sung by a choir of seminarians. But before these rousing performances, all of them displaying a blend of patriotism and religiosity, had occurred the brief and simple ceremony that was the cause for the celebration: the blessing of a cornerstone that bore an inscription, "1841–1907. Succeeding to the lowly chapel — built of old by the river bank — from which our fair city received its glorious name, this noble temple rises; a solemn testimony to the growth of Holy Church, a generous offering of love and gratitude to the Almighty God, of all things Lord and Ruler."[1]

Archbishop Ireland was going to build his cathedral. Indeed, with characteristic bravura, he was going to build two cathedrals at once.

His ideas had taken a long time to bear fruit. As early as 1889 he had confided to his friend John J. Keane his intention to replace soon the commodious but plain building begun in downtown St. Paul by Cretin and completed by Grace. In the beginning, while he still hoped that the Twin Cities would merge into one grand "Paulopolis," he planned to locate the premier church of the archdiocese somewhere in the Midway district, not too distant from his college and seminary or from the location proposed for the state capitol building, and property was acquired with this object in mind. But the dream of a single "federal city" faded away during the 1890s, and this, together with the economic depression and his own far-flung preoccupations, led Ireland to one postponement after another. Not until the spring of 1904 did he decide to proceed with the project, which now, however, involved provision of suitable edifices for both St. Paul and Minneapolis.

The choice of sites for the new churches tells much about the personality and philosophy of John Ireland. In each instance the emphasis was upon *visibility:* in St. Paul the cathedral would stand upon a hilltop and look down magesterially at the business center of the city; in Minneapolis the pro-cathedral—as Ireland incorrectly called it[2]—would bestride an elevated piece of ground just at the edge of the loop and close to the point where Lyndale and Hennepin avenues, the city's two busiest thoroughfares, intersected. Ireland had spent a lifetime arguing the compatibility of Catholicism and the American ideal, urging his immigrant co-religionists to adapt themselves to this new and wondrous land, protesting to his fellow citizens that Catholics deserved as full a participation in national life as any other group. Now he would leave, as his final testament, permanent statements in stone, more eloquent than all his innumerable speeches combined, which proclaimed that the Catholics had indeed arrived, had put down their roots, and had assumed their rightful place in the American secular city.

From a financial point of view the construction of two such buildings at the same time was a mammoth undertaking, even without the usual problems of cost overruns and unforeseen expenditures. Ireland mobilized the resources of the whole archdiocese, with each parish assessed for support of one project or the other. But the Catholic population, though numerous, was not affluent, and shortage of funds was a constant anxiety. A few wealthy donors came forward, to be sure, Catholic and non-Catholic alike; James J. Hill understandably declined to contribute, but his son gave twenty thousand dollars and similar sums were received from a few others.[3] Even so, there were times during the decade it took to build the Cathedral of St. Paul and the Basilica of St. Mary when the workmen nearly had to be called off the job for lack of money to pay them or to pay for the materials they needed.[4]

But the iron will that had driven John Ireland through his career did not fail him now. As each financial crisis arose it was confronted and overcome. The archbishop did not spurn any possible source of support. When he went to a parish to administer confirmation, he urged the children to offer their pennies to help complete a project of which, he promised, they could be proud all their lives. "My dear Child," he wrote one of them in the autumn of 1905,

> I thank you very cordially for your pretty letter of September 19 in which you tell me that you are going to set aside your savings for the benefit of the new Cathedral. This is a splendid idea. I pray God to bless you very richly. Sixty or seventy years from now it will be a great pleasure for you to read your name in the Memorial Volumes. They will contain the names of all the subscribers to the Cathedral. I pray that you may live at least that number of years and that, meantime, you will always be dear to the heart of our blessed Saviour. I shall try to have your example imitated by many of the children of the diocese.[5]

Indeed he did, and the memory of the old archbishop stumping town and countryside for the cathedral became almost a part of Minnesota folklore. "Yeah," one man recalled seventy years later,

> I remember him. He came to [the town of] Savage when we were confirmed. . . . They were building that big cathedral in St. Paul, you know how big that is, and everything—and now he says, ya don't hafta do it, he says, but when you make your First Communion and Confirmation, if ya wanta, each one of you can give a dollar, and he says, when you go to St. Paul, you can look at that and say you put a brick in that building.

He and his friends gave their dollars and were justly proud of the result: "That is quite a building there, you know, way up high and you can see it for miles."[6]

Ireland set up the customary network of committees to oversee the various phases of the construction process, but he remained himself the heart and soul of the endeavor. No detail appeared to him too trivial. Thus, for example, at a dinner party for potential donors, he carefully arranged the seating himself, and was much annoyed when a maid inadvertently changed a few of the place cards.[7] And he was not above practicing a little clerical extortion in behalf of the good cause. When the golden jubilee of his ordination occurred in 1911, Ireland allowed no formal celebration, but, as he put it to Gibbons, "I am tolerating the substantial substratum [of an] offering from the priests of the Diocese of $100,000."[8] Through devices like these, through appeals to friends in New York, through picnics and contests, through benefactions obtained from the wills of the pious deceased, through caustic admonitions to parishes that fell behind in their assessments — "Why, I beg leave to ask, should there be among the parishes of the Diocese of St. Paul those that dispute among themselves the strange honor of being the latest arrivals at the goal of glory?"[9] — the combined costs, which Ireland estimated at just under $3 million, were substantially met.[10]

The archbishop took charge, too, of the aesthetic dimensions of the projects. Originally eleven architectural firms had been invited to submit designs for the cathedral, but only one of them was ever given serious consideration.[11] In 1904 Ireland went to St. Louis for the Louisiana Purchase Exposition and met there the exposition's chief designer, Emmanuel Louis Masqueray. A bearded, forty-three-year-old French bachelor, who affected a cane, yellow gloves, and, occasionally, a cape, Masqueray was an alumnus of the prestigious École des Beaux-Arts in Paris. He had settled in New York in 1887, and, after working for several important architects, opened his own firm in 1901. Ireland apparently liked what he saw in St. Louis, because on the strength of it he offered the position of architect for the cathedral to the relatively young and inexperienced Frenchman. Masqueray promptly accepted the commission. He spent the late summer and fall of 1905 touring cathedrals in France, and then came to St. Paul where he stayed for the rest of his life. The monumental cathedral in St. Paul and basilica in Minneapolis were not Masqueray's only accomplishments; he put the touch of his neo-baroque genius upon many churches across the Midwest, among them a charming small cathedral designed for Thomas O'Gorman in Sioux Falls.[12]

Masqueray and the archbishop worked smoothly together, a circumstance abetted by the latter's francophile tastes. But Ireland could involve himself in no major undertaking, it seemed, without some element of controversy with someone. In this instance the trouble stemmed from Father John T. Harrison, whose parish, St. Joseph's, was to be absorbed by the new cathedral — and who was himself to be assigned elsewhere. At the first meeting Ireland called of the pastors of the city to announce his plans, Harrison's was the sole voice of dissent. This may have been because the other priests present were intimidated by the archbishop, but it is also true that, as Ireland himself said, "Seldom has an act of mine received such universal approval as the selection of [the] site [for the cathedral]." And the employment of that site meant necessarily the suppression of St. Joseph's.[13]

Harrison's initial objection was the frivolous one that nobody would climb the steep St. Anthony's Hill to go to mass. His real motives, however, were not difficult to discern. St. Joseph's was probably the most prosperous and fashionable parish in the archdiocese, which of course was another reason in Ireland's mind to locate the cathedral there. Furthermore, Harrison had already begun the construction of a new church, and his parishioners, with whom he was popular in any case, did not receive kindly the news that this project had to be abandoned in favor of another twenty or thirty times as expensive. When the announcement came that their pastor had been appointed to St. Stephen's parish in Minneapolis, a large number of them, joined by such important non-Catholic neighbors as the governor of the state, signed a petition in Harrison's behalf.

But Harrison committed the fatal error of grasping beyond his reach. He made it plain that his price for relinquishing St. Joseph's — of which he was technically irremovable rector — was a miter, and that if he were not appointed a bishop, he would sue his ordinary in the ecclesiastical courts. Ireland scornfully insisted that he report immediately to St. Stephen's. Harrison refused, citing reasons of health and alleging that the clergy house there was dirty and unhealthy, and he took up residence instead within the confines of his former parish. Drama quickly degenerated into farce. Once it was clear that Harrison was resisting the stated will of the archbishop, his support from the laity practically vanished, so immense was Ireland's prestige among his own people. Indeed, when the priest did appeal his case to the apostolic delegate, several of those who had originally signed the petition in his favor testified against him. Ireland, accustomed to opponents of the stature of Corrigan and McQuaid, had little difficulty brushing aside the likes of John Harrison, who ultimately drifted away to Seattle and was heard from no more.

John Ireland's preoccupation with the building of the cathedral and the basilica helped keep him at home during his last years. He visited the St. Paul site almost every day and frequently went to Minneapolis for the same purpose. The strained relations with Roosevelt meant fewer trips to Washington. After the disappointment in the consistory of December 1905, he traveled to Europe only twice more. In 1906 he visited Milan and Rome, was received courteously by the pope, and held several conversations with Cardinal Merry del Val, who was, he said, "as gracious as could be."[14] A small fuss arose when several cardinals — including that consummate chameleon, Satolli — attended a banquet tendered in Ireland's honor by the American ambassador to the Quirinal and so ignored a principle of diplomatic etiquette about which the Vatican continued to be extremely sensitive. Ireland cheerfully dismissed the matter as a bagatelle fomented by his friends of the fourth estate. On his way home he stopped for several days at his beloved Meximieux.

That visit, however, was his last, because by the time he returned to France in the winter of 1909, the French government had closed the seminary, expelled its students, and confiscated its buildings. It was a bitter blow to an old man to have the treasured scenes of his youth thus snatched from him, and Ireland unhesitatingly gave public expression to his disgust at what he labeled a flagrant act of aggression. He did, however, make a sentimental journey to nearby Montluel in search of souvenirs of Joseph Cretin. At the Vatican, some days later, he joined a party of Minnesotans whom he presented in audience to the very cordial pope. But the Rome of Pius X, shaken by the alleged conspiracy of radical exegetes and philosophers whom the pope called "Modernists," was not a place entirely hospitable to an arch-Americanist: when Ireland preached at a mass held in the Church of San Silvestro, the exceedingly prudent rector of the North American College forbade his students to attend.[15] The archbishop probably had in mind both the anti-clerical atmosphere in Paris and the intense suspiciousness gripping Rome when he wrote his fellow-Americanist, Félix Klein, in 1911:

> The wise mariner sets his sail in accordance with the wind-currents of the moment. This is what you are doing, and in this you show forth your good judgment. It is quite uncertain when I shall again visit the dear land of the "Tricolore." I am very busy with many things—particularly with my new cathedrals, now journeying fast toward completion. And then the wind-currents across the Atlantic are not just now too favorable.[16]

He seemed content to stay at home. Not since the early 1880s had Ireland devoted exclusive attention to his own jurisdiction, and now, as the majestic piles of his two cathedrals rose slowly under his eye, it was as though he had found a second wind. A spate of pastoral letters flowed from his pen. He appeared regularly at the speaker's rostrum in the local observances of religious and civic celebrations. His carriage could be seen at least once or twice a week rolling briskly down Summit Avenue toward St. Thomas and the seminary, and to these outings he added, after 1905, frequent visits to the young women at the new College of St. Catherine, the jewel in the crown of the splendid system of schools the Sisters of St. Joseph had established under the leadership of Ellen Ireland, Mother Seraphine.[17] The archbishop never arrived at these institutions without a bundle of books and magazines under his arm, an old man now perhaps but still anxious to talk to the faculty and students (talk to them, it should be noted, not discuss with them) about literature and history, tell them of his own conversations with Julia Ward Howe and the novelist Marion Crawford,[18] and increasingly reminisce about pioneer days and the Civil War.[19] In 1907 he institutionalized his intense interest in local religious history by founding the St. Paul Catholic Historical Society and launching its learned journal, *Acta et Dicta,* in which the opening chapters of his biography of Joseph Cretin ultimately appeared.[20]

Until 1910, when an auxiliary was assigned him, Ireland performed all the confirmations and parish visitations himself. And in 1916, when the auxiliary was promoted to a see of his own, the archbishop did not ask for a replacement, though Rome quickly offered him one. Indeed, that year a curial cardinal noted wonderingly to Ireland that the archbishop was, in his seventy-eighth year, "more active than ever in preaching in the various parts of your large diocese."[21] He continued to enjoy the keenest pleasure in the grandiose gesture that, like his cathedrals, demonstrated that the church in the Upper Midwest under his tutelage had attained singular distinction. In 1910, for example, he performed an unprecedented liturgical act: "Six bishops, all of one Province, consecrated on the same day by the one metropolitan, . . . a scene rarely witnessed—never heretofore in America—not even," he added slyly to Gibbons, "in Baltimore."[22]

Not that Ireland lost interest in the goings-on in the great world outside Minnesota. He had long employed a clipping service that kept him up to date on the issues in which he himself figured in some way,[23] and he continued to read a variety of newspapers in English and French. Almost to the end of his life he kept up his correspondence with people as various as Lord Bryce, the historian and British ambassador to Washington; Jules Cambon, who had been posted to the French embassy in Berlin; Maurice Francis Egan, the literateur who had become American minister to Denmark; and Shane Leslie, the budding English Catholic literary man whose projected biography of Ireland's hero, Cardinal Manning, was particularly intriguing to the archbishop. These exchanges of compliments and good wishes seldom touched upon substantive matters, but Ireland in his old age took the trouble to keep the contacts lively by spending much of December each year writing New Year's greetings to friends around the world.[24]

Nor did his ambitions wither away with the passage of time. When Pius X died in 1914, and was succeeded by Giachamo della Chiesa—Benedict XV—who had been Rampolla's closest aide in the papal secretariate of state, Ireland's hopes for the cardinalate flickered up once more. "My joy is supreme," he cabled the new

Left: *Ireland reviewing the troops at St. Thomas, 1917 (MHS)* Below: *Mother Seraphine Ireland (MHS)*

pope, and he added a broad hint: "Wonderful memories are re-vived."[25] The ever-faithful O'Gorman was dispatched to Rome yet again, this time crossing the Atlantic during the perilous opening weeks of the First World War. Gibbons, arriving too late for the conclave, nevertheless pressed his friend's suit in a private audience, and, protesting himself not one "to hold out false or vain hopes," thought there was a real chance for success.[26] Even the Storers, now living in Rome, were enlisted into service to the old cause. "Bellamy wrote you about their audience. They are back in your camp, in fact never left it."[27] But though he professed to find enthusiasm every-where for the idea of Ireland's promotion, O'Gorman had difficulty even getting in to see the pope. When he did, Benedict simply said, " 'I am up against a great difficulty, four cardinals in North America,' " and pledged only to give the matter some thought.[28] Ireland let himself be beguiled into the hope of desperation for a while—"Mgr. Della Chiesa . . . was always most gracious to me. . . . Of course he was the friend of Rampolla, his chosen son"[29] — but the connection with Rampolla failed him again. Many people tried to console him by suggesting that once the war was over he would surely have the red hat bestowed on him. If he believed them, it must have been gall and wormwood to have lived long enough to have witnessed, in 1916, the promotion of Donato Sbarretti to the sacred college.

If John Ireland was fascinated by ecclesiastical politics to the end of his life, the same can be said about the secular variety. And he remained steadfastly partisan: his commitment to the Republican party never wavered. Though he did not campaign actively as he had in the past, he still lent his name and prestige to the same candidates and platforms. "I wish," Theodore Roosevelt wrote after the presidential election of 1908, "I could see you so that we might congratulate each other on our victory, for you are one of those who can feel an especial pride in it." The "victory" was that of Roosevelt's protégé, William Howard Taft, who also sent Ireland a warm message of thanks, acknowledging frankly that without the Catholic vote he might very well have lost. The president-elect added: "No one will receive a more cordial welcome in the White House while I am there than the Archbishop of St. Paul."[30]

Even when Taft and Roosevelt quarreled and opposed each other in the 1912 campaign, John Ireland managed to maintain amiable relations with both men. This was of course easier to do with the placid Taft than with the tempestuous Roosevelt.[31] Two years earlier Roosevelt, on holiday in Rome, found himself inadvertently in the midst of a bitter wrangle between the Vatican and the local American Methodist community, which had mounted a strenuous and by all accounts explicitly anti-Catholic program of proselytization within the Eternal City. The upshot was that Merry del Val canceled a papal audience for the former president, and an enraged Roosevelt responded with some intemperate remarks about the opposing forces of "progress" and "reaction" in Italy, leaving no doubt as to where his sympathies lay.[32] Those sympathies, however, were not with the Roman Methodists, and Ireland, who had already chided that group in the public press — "I am not too old to enter a fight when the occasion requires it" — tried to confine the controversy within the narrowest possible limits, asserting that the pope's sensitivity was traceable to the vicious Protestant propaganda of which he, the pontiff, was the primary target.[33] This tactic apparently satisfied Merry del Val and Roosevelt, and the latter assured Ireland in the friendliest fashion that he would offer a full explanation of the spat when next the two met.[34] American Methodists, on the other hand, were understandably less than pleased at Ireland's strictures upon their brethren in Italy, and some verbal gunfire ensued, without permanent damage, it would seem, to either side.

But controversy was not the ordinary coin of Ireland's later years. If he continued to lobby for some pet causes, like the rehabilitation of the Knights of Pythias and other "secret societies," he did so now in a mild and conciliatory tone.[35] Indeed, reconciliation was high on his personal agenda. As early as December 1905 he spent three days in Rochester as Bernard McQuaid's guest.[36] The former close ties with O'Connell remained undone, but as that restless spirit passed through frustrating assignments as rector of the Catholic University and as an unwanted auxiliary in San Francisco until, finally, he became bishop of Richmond — where it had all begun for him so many years before — the two old friends shared some moments of warm nostalgia. In 1910 O'Connell paid a visit to St. Paul from his lonely exile in California: "It seemed like old times," he said, "and I lived again in the past. And truly they were good days, and the fruit of our work still endures." Five years later he sounded a mournfully poignant note as he reported the death of Boeglin, their ally from the Cahenslyite wars: "The sun's going down, and evening is coming on; let us continue the journey together."[37]

Another of their fellow travelers dropped along the wayside. John J. Keane had never enjoyed the sturdy health of his friend in St. Paul, and his active years in Dubuque were cut short by illness, which by 1907 had left him debilitated physically and emotionally. In 1909 and again a year later his condition had worsened so much that he was forced to take up residence at the St. Paul Seminary as Ireland's guest.[38] But these interludes away from his charge, like many similar ones in various parts of the country, proved of only temporary benefit. "I am profoundly grieved," Gibbons told Ireland, "that a luminous mind is clouded, and that a Prelate hardly surpassed for eloquence, zeal and piety is no longer able to exercise his apostolic ministry. He was one of the most beautiful and disin-

terested souls that I ever encountered."[39] The cardinal's use of the
past tense was no doubt unintentional, but it was unhappily appropriate. The Roman authorities curtly refused to provide Keane
with a coadjutor or an auxiliary, and so in January 1911 John Ireland made a sorrowful journey to Dubuque to help his friend prepare a letter of resignation. The kindness and dignity with which his
successor treated him could not arrest the gradual deterioration of
Keane's faculties. His increasing eccentricities, however, exhibited
much of the charm of former, better days. Ireland frequently visited
him, and, on one occasion, Keane, suddenly and without explanation, recited the opening verse of the Canticle of Moses in Greek,
Hebrew, Latin, and Italian. The startled Ireland held out his arms
joyfully and exclaimed: "Waal [*sic*], you are the old Keane again!"
But of course he was not the old Keane, and when he died, in June
1918, John Ireland had already entered upon his last illness.[40]

The archbishop of St. Paul was involved in arranging another
resignation that also must have reminded him of the ravages time
can inflict. After 1900 there had been a reconciliation of sorts between Ireland and John Lancaster Spalding, though each man continued to snipe at the other behind his back.[41] In 1902 Ireland had
reversed his position of a decade earlier and strongly recommended
Spalding for promotion to Chicago. "Though at one time," he observed disingenuously, "[Spalding] spoke a little too openly against
the establishment of the apostolic delegation, he has since reconsidered [*il est revenu*] his old ideas on this subject."[42] But the nomination to Chicago proved Spalding's undoing, because it occasioned
his denunciation in the curia by the Caldwell sisters, now estranged
from him, of sexual improprieties. The smoking gun had been
presented to Spalding's oldest and closest friend in the hierarchy,
Patrick Riordan of San Francisco. "The Baroness [von Zedwitz,
Mary Elizabeth Caldwell] threatens to make it known if [Spalding]
is promoted," Riordan informed the Roman authorities. "If he [is]
left where he is, she can be kept quiet."[43] Needless to say, Chicago
went to someone else.

Ireland knew nothing of the real reason at the time, and perhaps
learned only hints of it later. Meanwhile Spalding experienced the
first of a series of strokes early in 1905 from which he never entirely
recovered. His frequent absences from his diocese thereafter led to

discontent among his clergy, some of whom petitioned Falconio, the apostolic delegate, for a new bishop. Then, as if these troubles were not enough, in the summer of 1908 the Baroness von Zedwitz renewed her threats, and, at the request of Falconio, Ireland traveled to Peoria and asked Spalding to resign. "I must say, I encountered but little opposition," he reported to O'Connell. "He understands that his health is irreparably shattered and that the work to be done in the diocese demands an active bishop."[44] The apostolic delegate was immensely relieved. "I have received [Bishop Spalding's] resignation," he told Ireland, "and truly you deserve the merit of this important step. I shall not forget to mention it in my report to Rome."[45] In retirement Spalding, the most brilliant and most enigmatic prelate in the history of the American church, remained what he had always been: haughty, reserved, and yet somehow appealingly vulnerable. At the end of 1913 Riordan regretted that he had not been able to attend a fête held in Peoria to honor Spalding. "After all," he wrote Ireland, "he did good work, and great work, in his day, and made the Catholic Church known to the non-Catholic public. It was his last celebration."[46] The prediction proved correct, for three years later Spalding was dead, and Riordan was dead, too.

And so one by one the giants passed from the scene until only two of them were left. Ireland and Gibbons, though they saw one another only rarely, grew to be, if anything, closer than before. Ireland's new year's greetings of 1913 — written now in a crabbed and arthritic hand, so different from the confident, sweeping penmanship of earlier days — testified increasingly to Gibbons's unique stature in the Catholic world of his time:

> Wherever else the ravages of time, it has no power to dim the rays, or cool the warmth, of my gratitude for the friendship of many years with which you have honored me, or of the deep-felt and most sincere affection in which I have always held your memory and your name. So let salutes come to you from East and West, from North and South, on the occasion of the Christmas and New Year festivities; none will ring truer and more loving than that wafted today from remote St. Paul to the Cardinal Archbishop of Baltimore. . . . As years flow by, the conviction deepens within me that you were the special gift of Providence

to the Church of America during its momentous life closing the nineteenth and opening the twentieth century.[47]

Gibbons, who wore his dignity with consummate grace, had testimony of his own to deliver to his fiery confrere, so much bolder and more headstrong than himself. "My very dear Friend," he said,

> I have indeed been loyal to you. I have fought your battles and made your cause my own. In doing so I have been impelled by two motives, my sense of the justice of your cause, and, still more, my personal admiration for you. I received many a scar in the conflict, and felt perhaps more keenly than you the sharp stings of the enemy, because I am, I believe, more sensitive. But I never faltered [or] hesitated for a moment, because I believe your cause was right. And now we can rejoice together after the smoke of battle has passed away. . . . I am feeling sad at the departure of old friends. I earnestly hope that you will survive me.[48]

John Ireland's last days were brightened by the thought of his long friendship with the noble James Gibbons. They were marked also by a closer relationship than ever before with the only surviving member of his family, his sister, Ellen. Mother Seraphine of the Sisters of St. Joseph was a person of great talent and accomplishment, sharing much of her brother's strength and forcefulness, but striving in a world where her sex put her at a distinct disadvantage. Their intimacy in his latter years was due in some measure simply to the fact that John Ireland was more in her company than formerly and thus came more readily to appreciate how much Mother Seraphine and her sisters in religion had achieved all across the Upper Midwest. He took great interest in all her endeavors, but especially in the foundation of a college for women. It was he who gave the school its patron and its name, St. Catherine of Alexandria, the symbols of whose martyrdom, the wheel and the palm, had stood for centuries within the church as the signs of learning and holiness. He helped Ellen raise money for the project and even donated the proceeds of a special edition of *The Church and Modern Society* for that purpose. The nuns eventually realized sixty thousand dollars from this latter benefaction, though only at the cost of peddling the volumes all over the Upper Midwest.[49] Not that Ireland readily gave money away, even to his sister: only months before his death he directed an aide to lend Mother Seraphine a certain sum from archdiocesan funds, but only if she were willing to pay 4 percent interest.[50]

There was, however, another aspect of this warm relationship between the old archbishop and Mother Seraphine and her Sisters of St. Joseph. John Ireland was an unabashed patriarch — and, in fact, an opponent of women's suffrage — who, without daughters or granddaughters of his own, found great solace in his last years from his association with the sisters. He liked to fuss over them and have them listen to his stories, or give them little gifts, or intervene for them in some minor squabbles with their superiors. If his attitude toward them was patronizing, it was kindly intended and not out of harmony with the time and place. One sister recalled his visits about 1915 to St. Agatha's Conservatory in St. Paul — a central residence for Josephites teaching in the parochial schools of the city.

> The archbishop must have loved St. Agatha's because he would bring distinguished visitors there. Or he would come himself and we would all go in to meet him. We would sit on the floor in the parlor because we did not have enough chairs for eighty-five Sisters who were in the room. Mother Seraphine . . . would also come. She would sit beside him and prompt him if there was something he forgot. He would do the same with her. He would tell about the early days and so would she. The archbishop would also talk about his journeys, of his trips to Europe.[51]

And so the old man and the old woman, amiably correcting one another like a couple in a nursery rhyme, would try to recreate for their daughters, sitting in a circle at their feet, what it had been like in "the early days."

On Palm Sunday 1915, mass was celebrated for the first time in the new Cathedral of St. Paul, and, in Minneapolis a few months later, in the Basilica of St. Mary — as it came to be called after Ireland's death — was formally dedicated. The interior decoration and permanent furnishing of both buildings were tasks left to the future, but the archbishop took justifiable pride in crowning his career with an achievement doubters had said could not be done. "Ah, your Grace," one Irish priest is reputed to have asserted before a shovelfull of dirt had been turned over, "the socialists will make a hay loft

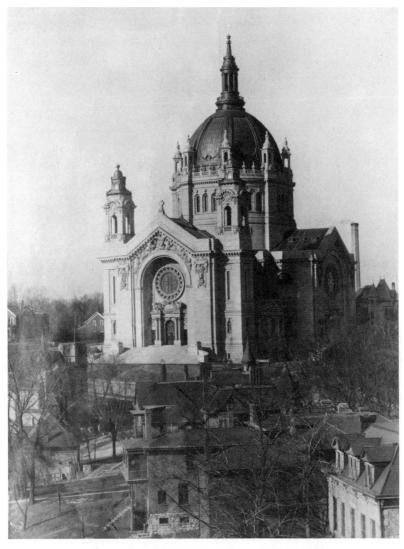

The Cathedral of St. Paul, about 1918 (MHS)

The Basilica of St. Mary, about 1918 (MHS)

out of your fine building." "Who ever tries to do something outside routine lines," Ireland might have retorted, "will always have hands raised against him and have his motives and acts misconstrued."[52] The two monuments in any event stand to his memory.

In 1916 John Ireland, his personal fortune at least partially restored, made out his last will and testament, leaving all his worldly goods — about two hundred thousand dollars in cash, securities, and real estate — to the Archdiocese of St. Paul.[53] His health remained robust for his age, though his powerful physique had shrunk; he walked with a cane now and had lost many of his teeth. Like most thoughtful people he followed the course of the war in Europe, his sympathies for France and Belgium very much to the fore. Henry Ford invited him to sail upon the "peace ship," a dramatic gesture that the archbishop declined to share in.[54] When Congress declared war on Germany in April 1917, Ireland issued his last verbal fanfare: "The United States is at war. The simple announcement tells the duty of the hour, incumbent on each and every citizen of America. The duty is to give support, cordial and plenary, to the nation and to the Government. No reservation of mind, no slackening of earnest act, to be henceforward thought of or allowed."[55] But a week later, in a wonderfully characteristic act, he asserted his right to define for his subjects what "plenary support" meant. When twenty-eight seminarians declared their intention to enlist, Ireland wired their rector: "Tell those twenty-eight students from me that their place is in the seminary. Tell them very decidedly."[56]

Late that summer and through the autumn the archbishop suffered from a series of minor ailments. By November, however, he was seriously ill of arteriosclerosis, and though he rallied, his physicians insisted he avoid the rigors of the Minnesota winter. So in January 1918, he went to Florida and stayed there till April. "I sit out on the porch some time every day," he wrote from St. Augustine, "and am deriving much benefit from the heat and sunshine. I hope before very long to be able to report very notable progress. Progress there is, but more slow than I would like it to be."[57] But there was in fact no progress, and by the end of April he took to his bed again in the large house across from the cathedral to which his belongings had been moved during his sojourn in Florida. He lingered through the summer, growing ever weaker, and by early September all hope was gone. During the last weeks his mind wandered back and forth to the time, more than sixty-five years before, when the Irelands and the O'Gormans had made their trek from Chicago to Galena. In constant attendance at his bedside were the only other survivors of that journey, Ellen Ireland and Thomas O'Gorman. At a few minutes before four o'clock in the morning of Tuesday, September 25, 1918, the great heart stopped beating.[58]

THE NEWS of Ireland's death brought an avalanche of tributes from around the world, as predictable as they were appropriate. Two of them seem worth recording here. One was a note written in a trembling hand to O'Gorman from an old Minnesota pioneer too feeble to attend the funeral.

> The country has lost the help of a great man. Well do I remember some 70 years ago when He and you passed by my store, at the corner of Third and Jackson Street, hanging one on each side of the good Father Ravoux's coat-tail, on your way to take the steamer Nominee, laying at the wharf ready for you to get aboard for France — and eight years later your return home. Such is life.[59]

And a few weeks later, in faraway Baltimore, James Gibbons reflected aloud that with Ireland's death he alone remained of the bishops who had assembled for that landmark event, the Third Plenary Council.

> The last Prelate who has descended below the horizon of the tomb was the Venerable Patriarch of the West, the great Apostle of temperance, the sturdy Patriot who had endeared himself to the American people, without distinction of race or religion, the man who had contributed perhaps more than any other to demonstrate the harmony that exists between the Constitution of the Church and the Constitution of the United States. Needless to say, I am speaking of John Ireland, the Lion of the fold of Juda.[60]

Reference Notes

Abbreviations Used in the Notes

AAB — Archives of the Archdiocese of Baltimore

ACHS — Archives of the Catholic Historical Society of St. Paul.

ACUA — Archives of the Catholic University of America, Washington, D.C.

A&D — *Acta et Dicta,* 7 vols. (St. Paul: 1907–36)

ADR-UND — Archives of the Diocese of Richmond, microfilm, University of Notre Dame, Notre Dame, Ind.

APF-A — Archives of the Sacred Congregation for the Evangelization of Peoples (*Propaganda Fide*), *Acta* (1622–   )

APF-NS — As above, New Series (from 1892)

APF-SCAC — As above, *Scritture Riferite nei Congressi, America Centrale dal Canadà all'Istmo di Panama* (to 1892)

APF-SOCG — As above, *Scritture Originali Riferite nelle Congregazioni Generali* (1622–1892)

ASV-DASU — Secret Vatican Archives, papers of the Apostolic Delegation to the United States

ASV-SdiS — As above, Secretariate of State

AUND — Archives of the University of Notre Dame, Notre Dame, Ind.

HP-MHS — "The John Ireland Collection, 1838-1959," compiled by Helen Angela Hurley, C.S.J., collections of the Minnesota Historical Society

JIP — John Ireland Papers, microfilmed by the Minnesota Historical Society from papers in the collections of the Catholic Historical Society of St. Paul; the Archives of the Archdiocese of St. Paul and Minneapolis; the Archives of the Diocese of Duluth; the Archives of St. John's Abbey, Collegeville, Minn.; the Archives of the College of St. Thomas, St. Paul

JJHP — James J. Hill Papers, Hill Reference Library, St. Paul

JJHP, g.c. — As above, general correspondence

NC — *Northwestern Chronicle* (St. Paul: 1867–1900)

OR — *The War of the Rebellion: Compilation of the Official Records of the Union and Confederate Armies,* 128 vols., Washington, D.C.: Government Printing Office, 1880–1901

Notes to Prologue

1. John Ireland, "Jeanne d'Arc, the Patron Saint of Patriotism," *The Church and Modern Society*, 2 vols. (St. Paul: Pioneer Press, 1904), 2, 58.
2. *La Libre Parole*, quoted in James H. Moynihan, *The Life of Archbishop Ireland* (New York: Harper & Brothers, 1953), 147.
3. Humphrey Moynihan, the secretary, gave this account to Philip Hughes, who told it to me.

Notes to Chapter I, "Beggar's Gabardine"

1. Thomas Carlyle, *Reminiscences of My Irish Journey* (New York: Harper & Brothers, 1882), iii, iv.
2. October 12, 1845. Quoted in J. L. Hammond, *Gladstone and the Irish Nation* (London: Longman, 1938), 51.
3. Based upon the most conservative estimates, the census of 1841 gave the population of Ireland as 8,175,124, a figure almost certainly too low. In 1851 the population stood at 6,552,385, "and the census commissioners calculated that, at a normal rate of increase, the total should have been 9,018,799, so that a loss of at least 2.5 million persons had taken place." Cecil Woodham-Smith, *The Great Hunger: Ireland, 1845–9* (London: Hamish Hamilton, 1962), 411.
4. Carlyle, *Irish Journey*, 75–80.
5. J. N. Brewer, *The Beauties of Ireland*, 2 vols. (London: Sherwood-Jones, 1825), 1:402.
6. Jonathan Binns, *The Miseries and Beauties of Ireland*, 2 vols. (London: Longman, 1837), 2:236.
7. Woodham-Smith, *Great Hunger*, 18.
8. Brewer, *Beauties*, 1:492; Binns, *Miseries*, 2:240.
9. Little is known about the Ireland family in Burnchurch. Snippets of memory, chiefly from John Ireland's sister Ellen and his cousin Ellen Howard have been collected. See Ann Thomasine Sampson, ed., "The Ireland Connection," reminiscences based upon the Oral History Project, Sisters of St. Joseph, St. Paul, 1982, p. 2–4, and Clara Graham, *Works to the King: Reminiscences of Mother Seraphine Ireland* (St. Paul: North Central Publishing Co., 1950), 13–16. More scholarly but highly readable are Patricia Condon Johnston, "Reflected Glory: The Story of Ellen Ireland," *Minnesota History* 48 (Spring 1982): 13–14, and Helen Angela Hurley, *On Good Ground* (Minneapolis: University of Minnesota Press, 1951), 86–88. Hurley also provided a more or less plausible, if somewhat imaginative and diffuse, reconstruction of the Burnchurch years in "John of St. Paul: The Making of Archbishop Ireland," typescript, HP-MHS, 1959, p. 1–18.
10. *The Dictionary of National Biography* 10 (1922): 466–474.
11. Here and below, see Hurley, "John of St. Paul," 1–2.
12. James M. Reardon, *The Catholic Church in the Diocese of St. Paul* (St. Paul: North Central Publishing Co., 1952), 213.
13. See William Makepeace Thackeray, *The Irish Sketch Book of 1842* (New York: Worthington Co., 1887), 288.
14. Woodham-Smith, *Great Hunger*, 20; E. R. R. Green, "Agriculture," in R. Dudley Edwards and T. Desmond Williams, eds., *The Great Famine* (Dublin: Browne and Nolan, 1956), 97.
15. The date assumes the baby was baptized on the day he was born, which would have accorded with custom. The entry in the baptismal register does not give a different date of birth. Ireland's full name was John Richard, but he never used a middle initial.
16. On the availability, variety, and quality of grammar school education in Ireland

in the 1840s, see F. S. L. Lyons, *Ireland Since the Famine* (New York: Scribner's, 1971), 70–77, especially 74. As late as 1861, in a population vastly diminished by the Famine and emigration, only 54 percent of Irish Catholics could read and write. See Emmet Larkin, "The Devotional Revolution in Ireland, 1850–75," *American Historical Review* 77 (1972): 652.

17. Hurley, "John of St. Paul," 7.

18. Larkin, "Devotional Revolution," 637.

19. Alexis de Tocqueville, *Journeys to England and Ireland* (New Haven: Yale University Press, 1958), 141. The bishop of the ancient see of Ossory lived in Kilkenny City, and Tocqueville mistakenly called him "Bishop of Kilkenny."

20. See S. J. Connolly, *Priests and People in Pre-Famine Ireland* (New York: St. Martin's Press, 1982), 87–89, 135–165.

21. "The cause of total abstinence necessarily emerged from [the Famine] weakened and nerveless." John Ireland, "Theobald Mathew," *Catholic World* 52 (October 1890): 4.

22. Here and below, see Woodham-Smith, *Great Hunger*, 73, 195–96.

23. See K. H. Connell, "Land and Population in Ireland, 1780–1845," *Economic History Review*, 2nd series, 2 (1950): 278–289. Ten to twelve pounds of potatoes a day, washed down with a pint of buttermilk, sustained an adult male. This, says Connell (288), is "a conservative estimate."

24. See the account of the debate in the House of Commons (December 1, 1837), *Hansard's Parliamentary Debates,* 3rd series, 39 (1838): 477–502, especially 497.

25. Thomas P. O'Neill, "The Organization and Administration of Relief, 1845–1852," in Edwards and Williams, eds., *Great Famine,* 210.

26. William P. MacArthur, "Medical History of the Famine," in Edwards and Williams, eds., *Great Famine,* 270–280.

27. Quoted by MacArthur, "Medical History," 275.

28. Oliver MacDonagh, "Irish Emigration to the United States of America and the British Colonies during the Famine," in Edwards and Williams, eds., *Great Famine,* 319.

29. Sampson, ed., "Ireland Connection," 3–4.

30. See analysis of the statistical data in MacDonagh, "Irish Emigration," 328–330. The population of Ireland today is less than half what it was in 1840. No other western country, however poor, has experienced a *decrease* in population over the last century and a half.

31. The precise movements of the Ireland family cannot be traced with certainty. See the works cited above, note 7. The best reconstruction, based on second-hand oral testimony, is Hurley, "John of St. Paul," 16 ff., but it too fails to achieve complete coherence.

32. MacDonagh, "Irish Emigration," 365.

33. Ellen Ireland (later Mother Seraphine in religion) recalled late in life the trip to Boston. See Hurley, *On Good Ground,* 87.

Notes to Chapter II, L'Étoile du Nord

1. The Irish-born population of Boston increased from about 2 percent of the total in 1845 to 20 percent in 1855. See William V. Shannon, *The American Irish* (New York: Macmillan, 1963), 28, 41 ff.

2. Carl Wittke, *The Irish in America* (Baton Rouge: Louisiana State University Press, 1956), 62, 71–74; Lawrence J. McCaffrey, *The Irish Diaspora in America* (Bloomington: Indiana University Press, 1976), 6, 58, 63–65, 81–85.

3. Between 1850 and 1853 Chicago's population doubled from 30,000 to 60,000. See J. D. B. De Bow, *Compendium of the Seventh Census* (Washington: A. O. P. Nicholson,

1854), 347. By comparison the population of New York City was 515,000, of Boston 137,000.

4. James P. Gaffey, *Citizen of No Mean City* ([Wilmington]: Consortium Books, 1976), 9. Gaffey says (p. 7) the Irelands were in Chicago as early as 1848.

5. Hurley, "John of St. Paul," 22.

6. Hurley, *On Good Ground,* 88. Hurley calls O'Gorman Richard Ireland's schoolmate. This is unlikely, since O'Gorman was eleven years Ireland's junior.

7. Quoted in Theodore C. Blegen, *Minnesota: A History of the State* (Minneapolis: University of Minnesota Press, 1963), 184.

8. M. Seraphica Marx, "The Life of Thomas O'Gorman, Bishop of Sioux Falls" (master's thesis, University of South Dakota, 1959), 2–5.

9. Quoted in Ann Regan, "The Irish," in June D. Holmquist, ed., *They Chose Minnesota: A Survey of the State's Ethnic Groups* (St. Paul: Minnesota Historical Society Press, 1981), 140. The exact date of arrival is disputed. Reardon, *Diocese of St. Paul,* 214, says May 20, as does Hurley, *On Good Ground,* 88. Moynihan, *Life of Ireland,* 2, says the first week in May.

10. In 1850 there were 6,077 Caucasians living in Minnesota Territory. By 1852 this figure had more than tripled to about 20,000. Of the nine counties Ramsey (which included St. Paul) was the most populous with 2,227. St. Paul itself counted 1,112 inhabitants in 1850, 2,000 in 1853. See De Bow, *Compendium,* 332–333, 380.

11. J. Fletcher Williams, *A History of the City of St. Paul to 1875* (St. Paul: Minnesota Historical Society, 1876; Borealis Book, 1983), 184, 235, 304–308.

12. Sampson, ed., "Ireland Connection," 4, and Johnston, "Reflected Glory," 14–15.

13. Blegen, *Minnesota,* 153, 166–169, 173–174. The Dakota and Ojibway are also known as the Sioux and Chippewa Indians.

14. Virginia B. Kunz, *St. Paul: Saga of an American City* (Woodland Hills, Calif.: Windsor Publications, 1977), 9–22; Williams, *St. Paul,* 208–215; Regan, "The Irish," 145; Blegen, *Minnesota,* 182–185.

15. M. M. Hoffmann, *The Church Founders of the Northwest* (Milwaukee: Bruce, 1937), 292, citing one of Cretin's reports to the Society for the Propagation of the Faith, Lyon (see below, note 40).

16. John Ireland, "Life of Bishop Cretin," *A&D* 5 (1917): 58–59.

17. Ireland, "Life of Bishop Cretin," *A&D* 4 (1916): 187–218, and 5:3–20. See also Hoffmann, *Founders,* 14–19.

18. Ireland, "Life of Cretin," 5:19–41.

19. Louis de Cailly, *Memoirs of Bishop Loras* (New York: Christian Press Association, 1897), 6–8, 40–42, 52–56.

20. John Ireland, "Mathias Loras, the First Bishop of Dubuque" (St. Paul: n.p., 1898), 11. This was the pamphlet form of Ireland's articles in the *Catholic World* 67 (September 1897): 721–731, and 68 (October 1897): 1–12.

21. *Concilia Provincialia, Baltimori Habita ab anno 1829 usque ad annum 1849* (Baltimore: John Murphy, 1851), 9, 131.

22. Hoffmann, *Founders,* 95–98. Notice misprint "August" for "September," 97.

23. Verses 59–60: "Jesus said to another: Follow me. And he said: Lord, suffer me first to go and to bury my father. And Jesus said to him: Let the dead bury their dead, but go thou and preach the kingdom of God."

24. John Ireland, "Introduction," in Samuel Mazzuchelli, *Memoirs of a Missionary Apostolic* (Chicago: W. F. Hull, 1915), viii.

25. Hoffmann, *Founders,* 208, 299–300; Reardon, *Diocese of St. Paul,* 69–72.

26. Hoffmann, *Founders,* 249, 257, 353–357; Ireland, "Loras," 15–21.

27. Civil and ecclesiastical jurisdictions in the Midwest changed rapidly during the 1830s and 1840s. What is now the state of Minnesota *east* of the Mississippi River was

part of the old Northwest Territory ceded by Great Britain to the United States by the Treaty of Paris (1783). Minnesota *west* of the Mississippi was part of the Louisiana Purchase (1803). The area of the present state was included in Missouri, Michigan, Iowa, and Wisconsin territories at various times. As new states were admitted to the Union, the remaining territorial area contracted. In 1849, after Wisconsin gained statehood, Minnesota Territory was formally instituted and included only the present state plus the area of the Dakotas east of the Missouri River (and thus, as above, co-terminous with Bishop Cretin's diocese from 1850). The land east of the Mississippi but west of the St. Croix River was left in Minnesota rather than being incorporated into Wisconsin (see William W. Folwell, *A History of Minnesota,* 4 vols. [St. Paul: Minnesota Historical Society, 1921–1930], 1:231–239).

The Roman Catholic hierarchy grew naturally with the country and organized itself in accord with an age-old model: the chief town of a locality was designated as the seat of a bishop who exercised ecclesiastical jurisdiction over that town and its hinterland (his "diocese" or "see"). During the second quarter of the nineteenth century, as settlement of the Midwest quickened, dioceses tended to be vast territorial units that, like their civil counterparts, were rapidly sub-divided. Thus, for example, until 1837, when Michigan entered the Union, Michigan Territory included the present state of that name, Wisconsin, and Minnesota east of the Mississippi. But until the foundation of the Diocese of Milwaukee (1843), the bishop of Detroit continued to be responsible for Catholics in Prairie du Chien and indeed for all Catholics living to the east of the Mississippi and north of what is now the border between Wisconsin and Illinois. From 1837 the bishop of Dubuque was charged with the area west of the Mississippi and north of the Iowa-Missouri border.

In contemporary terms, therefore, what is now the city of St. Paul (most of it east of the Mississippi) was subject to Detroit until 1843 and to Milwaukee until 1850. What is now the city of Minneapolis (most of it west of the Mississippi), together with Mendota and Fort Snelling, was subject to Dubuque until 1850.

28. Here and below, see Galtier to Grace, Prairie du Chien, January 14, 1864, quoted in John Ireland, "Memoir of Rev. Lucian [*sic*] Galtier, the First Catholic Priest of St. Paul," *Collections of the Minnesota Historical Society* (St. Paul: Minnesota Historical Society, 1880), 3:225. Ireland, who wrote this piece in 1867, freely altered Galtier's very tentative English grammar and syntax. For a printed version of the original text of the letter, see Richard P. Moudry, "The Chapel of St. Paul" (master's thesis, St. Paul Seminary, 1950), 30–31.

29. Ireland, "Galtier," 227; Moudry, "Chapel," 44–46.

30. Reardon, *Diocese of St. Paul,* 44.

31. See especially Moudry, "Chapel," 58–66.

32. Augustin Ravoux, "Labors among the Sioux or Dakota Indians" (St. Paul: n.p., 1897), especially 6–9. This was the pamphlet form of an article in the *St. Paul Pioneer Press,* March 7, 1897.

33. Augustin Ravoux, *Reminiscences, Memoirs and Lectures* (St. Paul: Brown, Treacy and Co., 1890), 72–83. Folwell, *History of Minnesota,* 2:210–211, gives the figure as twenty-four. Ravoux, 73 and 77, explains the discrepancy. (Ravoux's *Reminiscences* appeared in a French version in 1892.)

34. Ravoux, *Reminiscences,* 52.

35. Quoted by Moudry, "Chapel," 124.

36. *Concilia Provincialia* (1851), 273.

37. Roger Aubert, *Le pontificat de Pie IX (1846–1878)* (Paris: Bloud & Gay, 1952), 32–38.

38. That is, under the penalty of mortal sin.

39. The Congregation for the Propagation of the Faith (*Propaganda Fide*), the Vatican

bureau in charge of the administration of the churches in mission lands, endorsed the recommendation of the seventh Provincial Council of Baltimore. "Propongono . . . l'erezione di una nuova Sede nella città o borgo di San Paolo, che è nel nuovo territorio di *Minesota* [*sic*] e che debba comprendere tutto il detto territorio dentro i suoi limiti. *Minesota* è una parte degli Stati Uniti che non è ancora molto populata, ma siccome la populazione va crescendo sembra bene vi sia un Vescovo." In ordinary circumstances such a proposal from the congregation would receive the automatic approval of the pope. See APF-A (1850), 212:444. For Cretin's hesitancy to accept the appointment, see Cretin to Propaganda, Paris, December 10, 1850, APF-SCAC, 15:649, 686–692. For a description of the various files in the Propaganda Archives, see Finbar Kenneally et al., eds., *United States Documents in the Propaganda Fide Archives*, 8 vols. (Washington: Academy of American Franciscan History, 1966–80), 1:xi–xvi.

40. The single greatest source of financial support for Cretin, as it had been for Loras, was the Society for the Propagation of the Faith, headquartered in Lyon—not to be confused with the *Congregation* of the same name (see previous note). Almost as important a source of funding was the Leopoldine Society of Vienna. In 1851 Cretin received 10,000 francs (about $2,000) from Lyon; in 1852 he received 38,000 francs from Lyon and 46,000 francs from Vienna. For a useful summary see Hoffmann, *Founders*, 369–379.

41. Ravoux, *Reminiscences*, 60–62.

42. See Hoffmann, *Founders*, 184–196, 222, 233.

43. See, for example, Augustin Ravoux, "The Labors of A. Ravoux at Mendota, St. Paul and Other Localities from the Spring of 1844 to July, 1851" (St. Paul: n.p., [1897]), especially 14–18.

Notes to Chapter III, *"Ireland, Jean, des États Unis"*

1. Ravoux, *Reminiscences*, 61.

2. Hurley, *On Good Ground*, 19–29.

3. Colman J. Barry, *Worship and Work* (St. Paul: North Central Publishing Co., 1956), 23–38.

4. Johnston, "Reflected Glory," 15–16. Ellen Howard also enrolled at this time. The total annual fee for *both* girls was $1.70. The sisters also educated orphans and destitute children free.

5. Moudry, "Chapel," 139–144.

6. Anatole Oster, "Personal Reminiscences of Bishop Cretin," *A&D* 1 (1907): 74–77; Reardon, *Diocese of St. Paul*, 77.

7. Daniel J. Fisher to Arthur J. Donnelly, St. Paul, [autumn] 1852, in *A&D* 1 (1907): 45–46.

8. See Marx, "O'Gorman," 9–10, and the authorities cited there.

9. Ireland, "Life of Cretin," *A&D* 4:211–212.

10. Oster, "Reminiscences," 81, 76–77.

11. Reardon, *Diocese of St. Paul*, 104–105.

12. Oster, "Reminiscences," 73.

13. James M. Reardon, "The Beginning of the Catholic Total Abstinence Movement in Minnesota," *A&D* 1 (1908), 199–209, and "The Catholic Total Abstinence Movement in Minnesota," *A&D* 2 (1909): 44–93.

14. For examples, see Oster, "Reminiscences," 78, 79, 86.

15. For an example in a different context, see Marvin R. O'Connell, *The Counter Reformation, 1559–1610* (New York: Harper & Row, 1974), 212–214, 226–227, 231–234.

16. See the comment of the historian Peter Guilday, *Catholic Bulletin* (St. Paul), January 9, 1932: "At Cretin's death Minnesota could boast of a perfectly organized church."

17. Oster, "Reminiscences," 85.

18. Reardon, *Diocese of St. Paul*, 215–216, and Marx, "O'Gorman," 11–13.

19. The seminary no longer exists; in 1985 its main building housed the city hall and several blocks of flats.

20. JIP, roll 4, Ireland to Theloz, St. Paul, June, n.d., 1891 (copy).

21. A minor or petit séminaire like Meximieux was a classical collège which offered a program something like that available in an American high school and the first years of college. Its students were aspirants to the priesthood, but since only a minority persevered in that vocation, the curriculum was kept general enough to serve as a preparation for other walks of life as well.

22. Louis and Gabrielle Trenard, *Le diocèse de Belley* (Paris: Éditions Beauchesne, 1978), 154–155. The origins of the diocese went back to the fifth or early sixth century.

23. Reardon, *Diocese of St. Paul*, 99. Marx, "O'Gorman," 10, and Hurley, "John of St. Paul," 31, both suggest that Devie's generosity was compensatory rather than gratuitous. Due to Devie's carelessness, Cretin, after his consecration in 1851, was delayed a month in returning to America and, as a result, incurred considerable expense. When he complained about this to Devie, the bishop of Belley offered to educate two of Cretin's seminarians *gratis*. Hurley cites an aged French priest who, during the 1890s, had been a student of Thomas O'Gorman at the Catholic University of America. Marx cites no source.

24. Henri Daniel-Rops, *The Church in an Age of Revolution* (London: J. M. Dent, 1965), 265–268. Specialized personnel within the Roman Catholic church has traditionally been divided into two broad groups. The "secular" or "diocesan" clergy were ordained priests directly subject to the jurisdiction of a diocesan bishop; they were attached to the diocese itself and served only within its geographical limits. Their normal function was to staff the parishes within the diocese, though they were not infrequently assigned some different work like teaching or diocesan administration. They took no vows, but upon ordination they solemnly promised to obey their bishop and to remain unmarried, thus theoretically retaining scope and freedom to perform their parochial duties in the fullest possible way. There were no restrictions on them as to the ownership of property.

"Religious" belonged to a larger category, which included ordained priests as well as nuns and brothers who had not received the sacrament of order. All religious, ordained or not, took the classic vows of poverty, chastity, and obedience, and theoretically found in the fulfillment thereof the ordinary means of their sanctification. Religious belonged to particular groups or "religious orders"—Redemptorist, Franciscan, Jesuit, Marist, and many more—each with its own garb, its own rules (hence religious were sometimes called "regulars," from *regula,* the Latin word for rule), its own sense of comradeship and community, often with its own specific tasks within the church (like education or care of the sick). Religious owed first allegiance to their order, which might be loosely defined as an ecclesiastical corporation, usually multi-national and so essentially independent of a local bishop. Most religious orders maintained headquarters in Rome, and their superiors dealt directly with Vatican officials.

Religious orders have customarily established their own systems of seminaries distinct from the diocesan. John Ireland, training to be a secular priest, attended a diocesan petit séminaire (Meximieux) and a grand séminaire (Montbel) operated by the Marist order. The distinction is significant, because Ireland's antipathy toward religious orders was one of the grand passions of a passionate life.

25. Aubert, *Pie IX,* 100–123; William E. Echard, *Napoleon III and the Concert of Europe* (Baton Rouge: Louisiana State University Press, 1983), 13–19.

26. See, for example, Jean Maurain, *La politique ecclésiastique du second empire de 1852 à 1869* (Paris: Félix Alcan, 1930), 14–25.

27. JIP, roll 4, Ireland to Theloz, St. Paul, June [n.d.], 1891 (copy).

28. Ireland, "Life of Cretin," *A&D* 4:207.

29. JIP, roll 2, "Vacation Rules," signed "Robelin" (the spiritual director) and dated July 21, 1855. A French copy in longhand, a typed copy in English.

30. *La société de Marie* (Paris: Librairie Letourzey et Ané, 1923), 63–65.

31. See JIP, roll 2, Clemence Cretin to Ireland, Montluel, January 1, 1854, and Marie Cretin to Ireland, Montluel, n.d. (copies).

32. The school had eight forms with about twenty students in each. See JIP, roll 2, Raguin to Ireland, Belley, October 22, 1856 (original and copy).

33. JIP, roll 2, Marie Cretin to Ireland, Montluel, [October 30, 1856] (copy).

34. Whom she called Gorman. See JIP, roll 2, Clemence Cretin to Ireland and "Gorman," Montluel, November 27, 1855 (copy). Throughout his stay in France O'Gorman found that the natives blithely dropped the O-apostrophe from his name. See Hurley, "John of St. Paul," 46.

35. JIP, roll 2, Clemence Cretin to Ireland and O'Gorman, Montluel, February 11, 1854, and April 1, 1854 (copies).

36. JIP, roll 2, Clemence Cretin to Ireland or to Ireland and O'Gorman, Montluel, January 1, 1854, October 29, [1854— erroneously dated 1856 by copyist], February 5, 1856, and November 1, 1856 (copies).

37. JIP, roll 2, Clemence Cretin to Ireland, Montluel, October 29, [1854] (copy).

38. JIP, roll 2, Clemence Cretin to Ireland, Montluel, December 27, 1855, October 29, [1854], April 1, 1854, January 7, 1855 (copies).

39. JIP, roll 2, Clemence Cretin to Ireland, Montluel, October 29, [1854] (copy), and Perrier to Ireland, Trevour, September 22, 1854, and September 29, 1855.

40. JIP, roll 2, Clemence Cretin to Ireland and O'Gorman, January 7, 1855, and June 17, 1857 (copies).

41. JIP, roll 2, Marie Cretin to Ireland, Montluel, February 19, 1857, November 3, 1855, February 5, 1856 (copies).

42. JIP, roll 2, Marie Cretin to Ireland, February 5, 1856 (copy).

43. Only Marie's side of the correspondence has survived (as is the case with Clemence's letters and those of Abbé Perrier and various of Ireland's schoolmates). However, Ireland wrote Marie frequently: more often than not her letters were in reply to his.

44. The curé of the village of Ars was the saintly Jean-Marie Vianney (1786–1859), a priest of the Diocese of Belley. By the mid-1850s, 80,000 pilgrims traveled each year to seek solace from him, usually in the confessional. Ars was about twenty-five miles from Montluel. See Trenard, *Belley*, 178–180, and J. Brugerette, *Le prêtre français et la société contemporaine*, 2 vols. (Paris: P. Lethielleux, 1933), 1:183.

45. JIP, roll 2, Marie Cretin to Ireland, [October 30, 1856] (copy). A more jaded age than hers might find in these sentiments evidence that Marie was infatuated with Ireland, who was probably four or five years her junior. This is possible, but most unlikely. Clemence Cretin certainly would have put a stop to the relationship had she suspected it to have the least sexual overtones. Ireland would not have kept Marie's letters had he thought so. Moreover, intimate language used by religious persons in private correspondence, sometimes startling to our ears, was a commonplace during the nineteenth century. For an example in a different context, see Marvin R. O'Connell, *The Oxford Conspirators* (New York: Macmillan, 1969), 226–232.

46. In the apt phrase of Eugene C. Kennedy, who speaks elsewhere of "the gruff camaraderie of religious life." See *The People Are the Church* (New York: Doubleday, 1969), 87–103, especially 96.

47. See, for example, JIP, roll 2, Perrier to Ireland and O'Gorman, Trevour, September 27, 1856.

48. For a summary, see Christian Dumoulin, *Un Séminaire français au 19ème siècle* (Paris: Téqui, [1977]), 219–223.

49. Thomas E. Wangler, "John Ireland and the Origins of Liberal Catholicism in the United States," *Catholic Historical Review* 56 (1971): 621.

50. Hurley, "John of St. Paul," 45–50.

51. JIP, roll 4, Ireland to Theloz, St. Paul, June, 1891 (copy).

52. Quoted in Reardon, *Diocese of St. Paul,* 217.

53. JIP, roll 2, Maréschal to Ireland, Dompsure, August 26, 1857.

54. Abbé Perrier wrote to Ireland and O'Gorman during the summer holidays in very serviceable (if not always syntactical) English. See JIP, roll 2, letters of September 22, 1854, September 29, 1855, September 27, 1856, August 13, 1857, September 24, 1857.

55. JIP, roll 2, Clemence Cretin to Ireland, Montluel, January 1, 1854, and Marie Cretin to Ireland, Montluel, November 12, [1855] (copies).

56. "In the days of blessed youth I lived within the walls of a cherished seminary in France. There, in prose and poetry, I often read of Jeanne [d'Arc]; often from the lips of revered teachers I heard of her prowess and her holiness. Her deeds were the theme of my boyish essays; with my schoolmates I enacted in playful drama the story of her victories." John Ireland, "Jeanne d'Arc," *Church and Modern Society*, 2:32.

57. O'Gorman did similarly well. See HP-MHS, roll 11, "School records of John Ireland at the Minor Seminary at Meximieux, Ain, France" (preserved in the Biblioteque nationale, Paris).

58. See, for example, Reardon, *Diocese of St. Paul,* 217–218.

59. A hint of this is in JIP, roll 2, Perrier to Ireland and O'Gorman, Trevour, September 22, 1854.

60. JIP, roll 2, "Consécration," July 27, 1857. This two-page document in longhand, dated on Ireland's last day as a student at Meximieux, is a pledge of dedication by the sodality (see below) to the Virgin Mary. Thirteen students besides Ireland signed it.

61. JIP, roll 2, Maréschal to Ireland, Dompsure, August 26, 1857.

62. See JIP, roll 2, Maréschal to Ireland, Dompsure, August 26, 1857. Hurley, "John of St. Paul," 47, says Claude Genis "later followed John Ireland to St. Paul."

63. Ireland, "Life of Cretin," *A&D* 5:53–54. See above, note 44.

64. JIP, roll 4, Ireland to Theloz, St. Paul, June, 1891 (copy) speaks highly of the priest, Joseph Robelin. Theloz had just published a biography of Abbé Robelin.

65. For an extended and somewhat rhapsodic discussion of sodalities, see Hurley, "John of St. Paul," 51–57.

66. JIP, roll 2, Perrier to Ireland and O'Gorman, Trevour, September 27, 1856.

67. JIP, roll 2, Marie Cretin to Ireland, Montluel, [October 30, 1856] (copy).

68. JIP, roll 2, Perrier to Ireland, Trevour, August 13, 1857.

69. JIP, roll 4, Ireland to Theloz, St. Paul, June, 1891 (copy).

70. Ireland, "Life of Cretin," *A&D* 4:207–208.

71. Ireland, "Life of Cretin," *A&D* 4:203. See also Ireland to LaPlace, St. Paul, March 7, 1907, printed in Louis Allong, "Monseigneur Ireland," *Revue d'histoire ecclésiastique et d'archéologie religieuse du diocèse de Belley* 15 (1923): 58–59. Ireland sent LaPlace, the former superior at Meximieux, 2,500 francs. Toward the end of his life it was as though Ireland had blocked out Montbel's existence from his mind. For example, in about 1915, on the information sheet required for filing his official photograph with the Minnesota Historical Society, he wrote down under the education heading, "Cathedral School, St. Paul, and Meximieux, France."

72. JIP, roll 4, Ireland to Theloz, St. Paul, June, 1891 (copy).

73. Not to be confused with another Society of Mary founded in France (Bordeaux)

at almost the same time (1817), the members of which, to distinguish them from the Marists, were known as the Marianists.

74. Allong, "Ireland," 13 (1921): 60.

75. See *Société de Marie*, 29–34, and Trenard, *Belley*, 171–172. For biographical details, see Stanley W. Hosie, *Anonymous Apostle* (New York: Morrow, 1967).

76. This is the technical term designating the full jurisdiction of the pope, temporal and ecclesiastical. Roughly synonymous to it is "the Vatican" (but only after 1870) and, more loosely, "Rome" in the churchly sense.

77. The formal title for a French religious priest was "père"; for a diocesan, "abbé."

78. The first Marist house in the United States was opened in Boston in 1863.

79. See JIP, roll 2, Perrier to Ireland, Trevour, August 13, 1857, in which the Marists at Montbel are described as "her [Mary's] dear society."

80. Colin's original plan, which called for a highly centralized organization with four divisions—priests and lay brothers (auxiliaries to the priests), nuns, professed brothers, and a third order (a pious association of lay persons)—under one headship was rejected by Rome. There emerged instead a Marist "family," in which each division remained canonically distinct from the others.

81. *Société de Marie*, 54.

82. See JIP, roll 2, Perrier to Ireland, Trevour, September 27, 1856: "Poor dear Gros, who instead of going to Belley, as he believed, for his philosophy, is bound to go to our Lady of Montbel near Toulon." Some years later Father Henri Gros was pastor of a French-speaking parish in St. Paul. See Reardon, *Diocese of St. Paul*, 218.

83. There are hints in the correspondence that Ireland resented his role as monitor to the younger boy. See JIP, roll 2, Clemence Cretin to Ireland, Montluel, October 29, [1854] (copy): "Be good, charitable, agreeable, honest, affable with your fellows, but most of all with Thomas whom you should love as a brother. I have told everyone . . . that you love one another as brothers. Do not make me lie." See also Taion to Ireland and O'Gorman, Amberieux, September 5, 1855. O'Gorman himself enrolled at Montbel in 1860.

84. Cretin's agent with the Propagation of the Faith (Lyon) told Ireland that the matriculation of a secular seminarian in a Marist scholasticate was "without precedent." In an order as new as the Marists, however, and with a founder as strong-willed as Père Colin, the breaking of precedents was probably not very significant. See HP-MHS, box 4, Badad to Ireland, Les Chartreux, September 10, 1857 (copy).

85. For a summary of Redwood's relationship with Ireland, see JIP, roll 13, Redwood to O'Gorman, Melbourne, October 5, 1918. See also *NC*, June 29, 1888, and *Catholic Bulletin*, January 12, 1935.

86. For Colin's thoughts on theological education, see Hurley, "John of St. Paul," 80–81.

87. "Ultramontane," literally on the other side of the mountains. The term was applied in the nineteenth century to those Catholics who emphasized the authority of the papacy (which lay on the other side of the Alps from France and Germany) rather than the autonomy of the local or national church. This latter view was designated as "gallican." See Marvin R. O'Connell, "Ultramontanism and Dupanloup: The Compromise of 1865," *Church History* 53 (1984): 200–217.

88. It was asserted by some writers earlier in this century that Ireland was influenced by French Catholic liberalism during his seminary experience. See, for example, Albert Houtin, *L'americanisme* (Paris: Émile Nourry, 1904), 81–82; Claude d'Habloville, *Grandes figures de l'église contemporaine* (Paris: Perrin, 1925), 236–238; and John Foster Carr, *The Outlook* (May 1909), reprinted in *St. Paul Dispatch*, May 1, 1909. Wangler, "Ireland and Liberal Catholicism," 618–619, disposes of this view, though he weakens his own case

unnecessarily by taking too seriously one of Houtin's many unsubstantiated statements. For Colin's view of liberal Catholicism, see Hosie, *Anonymous Apostle,* 229.

89. See JIP, roll 2. Much of the material is illegible.

90. "Number 1" has not survived. One may assume that other notebooks were similarly lost.

91. Compare, for example, the opening sections of Ireland's "De Vera Religione" with Joannes Perrone, *Praelectiones Theologicae,* 9 vols. (Ratisbon: Josephus Manz, 1854), 1:9–37. Thomas E. Wangler, "The Ecclesiology of Archbishop John Ireland" (Ph.D. diss., Marquette University, 1968), 4–6, and "Ireland and Liberal Catholicism," 620–621, assumes these Latin summaries to be class notes. He may well be right about the Latin core texts or at least a great part of them. Shortage of books had led to the practice called *dictates,* whereby the professor read from a manual and the students copied down what he said. For an earlier instance, at Douay in the eighteenth century, see Edwin H. Burton, *The Life and Times of Bishop Challoner, 1691–1781,* 2 vols. (London: Longmans, 1909), 1:35–36.

92. Brownson (1803–75), called by Robert D. Cross "the greatest intellectual convert [to Catholicism]," was a prolific writer on religio-social topics and edited *Brownson's Quarterly Review* (Cross, *The Emergence of Liberal Catholicism in America* [Cambridge, Mass.: Harvard University Press, 1958], 29).

93. Ireland quoted or paraphrased excerpts from *View of the Evidences of Christianity* by Paley (1743–1805), the first edition of which appeared in 1794.

94. Ireland used few dates in the notebooks, but there are enough to show that some material was added after he returned to the United States in the summer of 1861. Therefore one cannot conclude, as Wangler seems to do (see above, note 91) that Ireland was reading the *Pilot* in Montbel.

95. See the reminiscences in John F. Duggan, "The Education of a Priest: Archbishop Ireland's Talks to Seminarians," *American Ecclesiastical Review* 51 (1939): 289–300, 385–398, 494–504.

96. HP-MHS, roll 11, "School Records."

97. At Montbel Ireland received tonsure (formal admittance to the clerical state), the so-called "minor" orders of lector, porter, exorcist, and acolyte, and the "major" orders of subdiaconate (which imposed on him the obligations of celibacy and the daily recitation of the breviary) and diaconate. The ordaining prelate, the bishop of Frèjus, in whose diocese Montbel was located, needed the written permission of Ireland's own bishop, for which see HP-MHS, box 4, Badad to Clemence Cretin, Les Chartreux, February 1, 1861 (copy).

98. It seems likely that Ireland would have stopped at Montluel to bid adieu to Clemence Cretin, but there is no evidence one way or the other. Indeed, it is impossible to say what Ireland's relationship to her was after Bishop Cretin's death and his own transfer to Montbel. There are hints that he continued to spend vacations at her home and that she continued to take care of his domestic needs, but they are not conclusive. See HP-MHS, box 4, Badad to Clemence Cretin, n.p., November 1, 1860, and Grace to Denadit, St. Paul, February 25, 1864 (copies).

Notes to Chapter IV, "You Were with Me at Corinth"

1. Here and three paragraphs below, see Folwell, *History of Minnesota,* 2:22, 64–66; Blegen, *Minnesota,* 195–198; Kunz, *St. Paul,* 23; Williams, *St. Paul,* 388, 393; Reardon, *Diocese of St. Paul,* 654.

2. The Dakota War (also known as the U.S.-Dakota Conflict and the Sioux Uprising),

"one of the worst Indian uprisings in American history" (Blegen, *Minnesota*, 259), lasted for about six weeks during August and September 1862. There were intermittent Indian campaigns launched from the state into Dakota Territory over the next several years. For a thorough description and analysis, see Folwell, *History of Minnesota*, 2:109–301; Kenneth Carley, *The Sioux Uprising* (St. Paul: Minnesota Historical Society, 1976).

3. Sampson, "Ireland Connection," 4.

4. Helen Clapesattle, *The Doctors Mayo* (Minneapolis: University of Minnesota Press, 1941), 32.

5. See Hurley, *Good Ground*, 88–89, and Marx, "O'Gorman," 7. Ireland was defeated in the aldermanic elections of 1854, while O'Gorman, from 1853, held a variety of elective and appointive offices. For Richard Ireland's naturalization papers, dated May 11, 1859, see JIP, roll 2 (copy).

6. As quoted in Albro Martin, *James J. Hill and the Opening of the Northwest* (New York: Oxford University Press, 1976), 27.

7. During the nineteenth century, in the English-speaking world at least, a Catholic bishop was designated "Right Reverend" and an archbishop "Most Reverend." This terminological distinction has since fallen into disuse.

8. For Grace's distinguished lineage, see Reardon, *Diocese of St. Paul*, 137–138.

9. One of the great medieval mendicant orders, which should be differentiated from the orders founded in the nineteenth century, like the Marists whom Ireland had known at Montbel. Distinction between "seculars" and "religious" has become blurred in the late twentieth century. Similarly, on the American frontier the differences did not amount to much; the Dominicans in Ohio and Tennessee did pretty much what seculars like Loras and Cretin did in the Upper Midwest. But once the Catholic church in the United States began to assume a more settled form, it reflected the age-old tensions between seculars and religious as well as the rivalries among the various orders. Religious who became bishops usually lived as secular priests. Even so, when Grace retired as bishop of St. Paul in 1884, he had to secure Rome's approval before he could reside outside a Dominican house. See Reardon, *Diocese of St. Paul*, 200–201.

10. V. F. O'Daniel, *The Right Rev. Edward Dominic Fenwick, O. P.* (New York: Pustet, 1920), 182–229, 374; *History of Saint Agnes Academy, Memphis, Tennessee* (Memphis: John Gasser, 1926), 17–29.

11. Quoted in William Busch, "The Coming of Bishop Grace," *A&D* 7 (1936): 181.

12. APF-SOCG, 18:828–829, Grace to Barnabò, Memphis, March 26, 1859.

13. At least one candidate had already declined the bishopric. See APF-A 222 (1858): 21–28.

14. Busch, "Coming of Grace," 178, 183.

15. Reardon, *Diocese of St. Paul*, 119.

16. Reardon, *Diocese of St. Paul*, 216; Blegen, *Minnesota*, 193. Galtier, as a priest of the Diocese of Milwaukee, was pastor at Prairie du Chien off and on until his death in 1866.

17. The two Ellens were professed in the Congregation of St. Joseph of Carondelet on December 8, 1858. Ellen Ireland was known in religion as Sister (later Mother) Seraphine. She was a great figure in the history of her order and a significant influence in the life of her brother. See Johnston, "Reflected Glory," 16–23.

18. Grace kept a diary on his journey, published as "Journal of Trip to Red River August and September 1861," *A&D* 1 (1908): 166–183.

19. There has been some dispute as to whether the ordination occurred on December 22 or on the day before. See JIP, roll 23, for the formal Latin document, signed by Grace and by Anatole Oster (as witness): "die vigesima secunda Decembris, Dominica quarta Adventus, anno autem millesimo octingesimo sexagesimo primo." Ireland contributed to the confusion by always celebrating the anniversary of his ordination on December

21 and by choosing that date for his episcopal consecration. He may have done this out of deference to Cretin and Grace, both of whom were ordained on December 21. See Reardon, *Diocese of St. Paul*, 253.

20. Williams, *St. Paul*, 390.

21. Grace's engaging manner was noted by the Roman authorities at the time of his appointment. See APF-A 222 (1858): 595, 606–607. "E depinto come un uomo cortese, morigerato, e pio, eloquente e benemerito. . . . Ha saputo conciliarsi la benevolenza di tutti [He is described as a courteous, temperate, and pious man, eloquent and worthy. . . . He is known to have gained the good opinion of all]."

22. Reardon, *Diocese of St. Paul*, 166. The offending pastor, James McGolrick, later became a bishop.

23. For a literary example of these qualities, see Grace's first "Pastoral Letter to the Diocese of St. Paul," dated November 9, 1859 and printed in *A&D* 7 (1936): 196–202.

24. See the copies of Grace's letters, 1860–67, to the presidents of All Hallows, Dublin, for the bishop's efforts to recruit Irish seminarians, HP-MHS, box 1. For example, Grace to Woodlock, St. Paul, August 20, 1860: "The wants of the missions in Minnesota are probably greater than in any part of the United States, [due] to the sudden influx of a very large immigration into a wild region that has scarcely yet been reclaimed from the tribes of roaming savages."

25. Folwell's unforgiving phrase; *History of Minnesota*, 2:76.

26. *St. Paul Pioneer and Democrat*, March 18, 1862. The faded manuscript is in JIP, roll 2.

27. *St. Paul Press*, April 23 and 26, 1861.

28. *OR*, series 3, vol. 3, p. 762–763.

29. See the summary lists in Lucius F. Hubbard, "Narrative of the Fifth Regiment," *Minnesota in the Civil and Indian Wars, 1861–1865*, 2 vols. (St. Paul: Pioneer Press, 1890), 2:ix–xi.

30. Kunz, *St. Paul*, 38.

31. Hubbard, "Narrative," 243–260. The detached companies replaced units of the regular army, which were then free for service on the battlefronts.

32. James P. Shannon, ed., "Archbishop Ireland's Experiences as a Civil War Chaplain," *Catholic Historical Review* 39 (1953): 301. Here is printed the text (301–305) of Ireland's lengthiest reminiscence of his time in the army, written (partly in the third person) entirely from memory in 1892.

33. Reardon, *Diocese of St. Paul*, 158.

34. *OR*, series 3, vol. 1, p. 382.

35. At that date this included all the state units except the First Infantry, which served throughout the war in the eastern (Virginia) theater.

36. Shannon, ed., "Ireland as Chaplain," 302.

37. Hurley, the only writer who treats the question, does not think Ireland accompanied the Fifth, because the St. Paul newspapers "stated specifically that no chaplain had been chosen for the Fifth" at the time of the regiment's embarkation, May 13 ("John of St. Paul," 107). But it is not unlikely that arrangements had already been completed for the appointments of Chaffee and Ireland, though formal announcements were for some reason (perhaps political) delayed. Otherwise it is difficult to explain how Chaffee was mustered in on May 17, when the Fifth was confined to its steamboat in St. Louis (Hubbard, "Narrative," 282). Ireland was certainly wrong in recalling his arrival at the front "shortly after" the Battle of Shiloh (April 6–7, 1862), though of course over the years "shortly after" could have come to encompass a period of six weeks. He was more likely right in saying that he became chaplain of the Fifth "one month" after his arrival (Shannon, ed., "Ireland as Chaplain," 302); he was formally mustered into that position on June 23. Finally, and almost conclusively, Ireland's account written only five months afterward (*St. Paul Press*, November 1, 1862), says this about the Fifth: "Our ranks are some-

what thinner than when *we* sailed down the Mississippi" (emphasis mine). See also note 94, below.

38. Hubbard, "Narrative," 260. For much of what follows I am indebted to my friend and colleague Professor Robert L. Kerby, who knows more about the Civil War than any other living human and who will recognize the oversimplifications perpetrated in the text.

39. *OR,* series 1, vol. 17, part 1, p. 178.

40. Lucius F. Hubbard, "Minnesota in the Battles of Corinth, May to October, 1862," *Minnesota Historical Society Collections* 12 (1908): 536, and "Narrative," 260–261. Colonel Hubbard, commandant and historian of the Fifth, writes vaguely of Farmington where, he says, "the regiment bore itself with the gallantry of veterans." The skirmish was apparently of too little consequence to receive attention in the *Official Records.* Hubbard was himself wounded at Farmington. He was later governor of Minnesota. For a brief notice see *Minnesota Historical Society Collections* 14 (1912): 350.

41. William M. Lamers, *The Edge of Glory: A Biography of General William S. Rosecrans* (New York: Harcourt, Brace, 1961), 90.

42. Beauregard's evacuation was the "first" Battle of Corinth. "Second" Corinth took place on October 3–4, 1862.

43. Hubbard, "Narrative," 261. Lamers, *Edge of Glory,* 92, gives a rather more favorable picture of Camp Clear Creek.

44. Shannon, ed., "Ireland as Chaplain," 302.

45. Hubbard, "Narrative," 282.

46. *Minnesota in the Civil and Indian Wars,* 2:2, 88, 150–156, 203.

47. *OR,* series 3, vol. 1, p. 382, It was not unknown during the Mexican War for Catholic soldiers to be forced to attend Protestant services. See Aidan H. Germain, *Catholic Military and Naval Chaplains, 1776–1917* (Washington: n.p., 1929), 36.

48. Shannon, ed., "Ireland as Chaplain," 302; Germain, *Catholic Chaplains,* 58–59.

49. *OR,* series 3, vol. 4, p. 1207. Comparative figures: a private received $13.00 a month, a captain of cavalry $129.50, a lieutenant colonel of infantry $170.00.

50. Shannon, ed., "Ireland as Chaplain," 304.

51. *OR,* series 3, vol. 1, p. 382, and vol. 4, p. 207.

52. Shannon, ed., "Ireland as Chaplain," 303; Moynihan, *Life of Ireland,* 7.

53. None of Ireland's correspondence for this period survives. The letters to his sister Ellen (Sister Seraphine), including those written during his time in the army, were destroyed by her shortly before her death in 1930. See Reardon, *Diocese of St. Paul,* 219; Hurley, "John of St. Paul," 129.

54. Shannon, ed., "Ireland as Chaplain," 303–305.

55. Kenneth P. Williams, *Lincoln Finds a General,* 5 vols. (New York: Macmillan, 1949–59), 4:1.

56. In Buffalo, September 4, 1897. See Hurley, "John of St. Paul," 120–121.

57. This summary greatly oversimplifies the movement of troops and commanders. For details see Williams, *Lincoln Finds a General,* 4:2–71, and Lamers, *Edge of Glory,* 90–101. For Pope in Minnesota, see Folwell, *History of Minnesota,* 2:187–204.

58. Lamers, *Edge of Glory,* 85.

59. Hubbard, "Narrative," 261.

60. Ireland, *St. Paul Press,* November 1, 1862. This is Ireland's lengthy account, dated October 23, 1862, of the "second" Battle of Corinth.

61. Hubbard succeeded the original colonel of the Fifth, Rudolph von Borgesrode, who resigned his commission during the sojourn in Alabama.

62. Hubbard, "Narrative," 261–262.

63. Contrast Lamers, *Edge of Glory,* 103–130 with Williams, *Lincoln Finds a General,* 4:73–81.

64. Ireland, *St. Paul Press*, November 1, 1862; Shannon, ed., "Ireland as Chaplain," 305.

65. *OR*, series 1, vol. 17, part 2, p. 232–233.

66. Hubbard described the events of October 3–4 on three occasions: in his brief official report written a few days after the battle, *OR*, series 1, vol. 17, part 1, p. 200–201; in the "Narrative" (see above, note 29); and in "Minnesota at Corinth" (see above, note 40), which was an address delivered to the Minnesota Historical Society, January 14, 1907. Ireland was present at the address and responded to it in "Response to Hubbard," *Minnesota Historical Society Collections* 12 (1908): 546–548. Ireland's other account was the piece in the *St. Paul Press* (see above, note 60). In the 1892 memoir, edited by Shannon, there is only one anecdotal reference to Corinth.

67. Hubbard, "Minnesota at Corinth," 540.

68. In 1907 Ireland said flatly, in Hubbard's presence, that the regiment had been forgotten. "Response to Hubbard," 546.

69. Hubbard, "Narrative," 262, and "Minnesota at Corinth," 540; Ireland, *St. Paul Press*, November 1, 1862. Ireland in 1907 remembered the regiment reaching Corinth shortly before midnight.

70. *OR*, series 1, vol. 17, part 1, p. 200.

71. Ireland, "Response to Hubbard," 547.

72. General Napoleon Buford, quoted in Williams, *Lincoln Finds a General*, 4:92.

73. Lamers, *Edge of Glory*, 147 and 149, assumes this to have been appropriate duty, because he entertains the curious notion that the Fifth Minnesota was composed mostly of Indians.

74. Hubbard, "Narrative," 263.

75. The two hour lull after 7:00 A.M. was due to the illness of one of Van Dorn's divisional commanders and the consequent confusion about the timing of the infantry attack.

76. Ireland, "Response to Hubbard," 547.

77. Ireland, *St. Paul Press*, November 1, 1862.

78. *OR*, series 1, vol. 17, part 1, p. 166–170.

79. Hubbard, "Minnesota at Corinth," 541–542.

80. Ireland, "Response to Hubbard," 547.

81. Ireland, *St. Paul Press*, November 1, 1862.

82. *OR*, series 1, vol. 17, part 1, p. 201.

83. Ireland, "Response to Hubbard," 547.

84. Ireland, *St. Paul Press*, November 1, 1862. In both his contemporary account and in his reminiscence of the battle Ireland reversed the order of the Confederate attack, placing the action at Robinett before that at the railroad station. Whether this was due to literary license or to genuine confusion remains unclear.

85. Cyrus Boyd, quoted in Lamers, *Edge of Glory*, 152.

86. Hubbard, "Minnesota at Corinth," 543.

87. Williams, *Lincoln Finds a General*, 4:94–102.

88. Ireland, *St. Paul Press*, November 1, 1862.

89. Shannon, ed., "Ireland as Chaplain," 303.

90. Hubbard, "Narrative," 264–266.

91. Germain, *Catholic Chaplains*, 71–72, prints the text.

92. *OR*, series 1, vol. 24, part 3, p. 151, 159–160, 253.

93. Shannon, ed., "Ireland as Chaplain," 302. Reardon, *Diocese of St. Paul*, 220–221, though aware of Ireland's letter of March 19, ignores it and assigns as the reason for resignation a "fever" Ireland caught "while on duty with the Fifth Minnesota at the siege of Vicksburg." Moynihan, *Life of Ireland*, 8, says simply: "Ireland, broken in health, was forced to return to St. Paul."

94. See JIP, roll 2, William B. McGrorty to his wife, "six miles south of Corinth [Camp Clear Creek]," June 12, 1862: "Father Ireland is with me yet; he is good company for

me but he has seen hard times since he came. I give it as my opinion that if the army of the West is left in the preasent [*sic*] position that on the first of Sept we will not be able to muster ten percent of our present army." Note the date, which indicates, first, that Ireland was with the Fifth weeks before he was mustered in as its chaplain, and, second, that complaints from the men of the Fifth about illness in the army were common from the beginning.

95. See *Minnesota in the Civil and Indian Wars,* 2:280–281, 706–707.

96. Shannon, ed., "Ireland as Chaplain," 305.

97. Ireland, *St. Paul Press,* November 1, 1862.

98. This view is reflected in Reardon, *Diocese of St. Paul,* 219–221, and Moynihan, *Life of Ireland,* 8.

99. *OR,* series 1, vol. 17, part 1, p. 178.

100. Ireland, *St. Paul Press,* November 1, 1862. Ireland changed Stanley's "effective" to "effectual."

101. Hurley, "John of St. Paul," 116–120, lists the publications. As early as 1886 Ireland was known in Minnesota as "the fighting chaplain of the fighting Fifth." See *Minneapolis Tribune,* September 2, 1886.

102. Maurice Francis Egan, "The Most Reverend John Ireland, D. D., Archbishop of St. Paul," *The Pilgrim,* May 1906, p. 6.

103. See the obituaries in *St. Paul Dispatch,* September 25, 1918, and *Minneapolis Tribune,* September 26, 1918. In his otherwise rather pedestrian eulogy of Hubbard, who died early in 1913, Ireland wrote this titillating sentence: "A fortnight before [Hubbard's death] we had sat together, in Minnesota's capitol, in front of a painting recently unfolded on its wall, to commemorate the Battle of Corinth, discoursing together of the happiness of the great day, October the fourth, 1862, and of its important bearings upon the issues of the Civil War." See, for a partial text, JIP, roll 12, February 8, 1913.

104. See, for example, *NC,* August 28, 1884. Speaking at a veterans' reunion, Ireland said: "I belonged to the peaceful and peace-loving wing of the army, the non-combatants. . . . I cheered by soothing words the tired soldier, and in religion's name I pointed towards heaven where he should see the reward of duty loyally performed and of sacrifice patiently suffered." This speech was given, however, before the story of the cartridges began to circulate.

105. *NC,* May 27, 1892.

106. Hubbard's judgment, "Minnesota at Corinth," 545.

107. Rosecrans's brother, Sylvester, became bishop of Columbus. A son became a priest, a daughter a nun; both died young.

108. Shannon, ed., "Ireland as Chaplain," 303.

109. Text in Hubbard, "Narrative," 263–264.

Notes to Chapter V, "Father Mathew of the Northwest"

1. A copy of the text is in HP-MHS, box 1.

2. On the Draft Law of March 1863 and the consequent riots, see Allan Nevins, *The War for the Union,* 4 vols. (New York: Scribner's, 1971), 3:119–124.

3. The bloody riots in New York City (July 13–17, 1863) had a strongly Irish component. Many immigrant Irishmen were very anti-black, because they perceived freedmen as competitors for employment.

4. In JIP, roll 2, there are about thirty sermons and lectures, written in Ireland's hand and delivered between 1862 and 1871. (On roll 1 there is a similar number of sermons, most of them no doubt preached during this period.) A notation on a sermon called "On

the B[lessed] Trinity" indicates that it was preached in St. Paul in May 1863. A venerable Ireland family tradition had it that on his way back to Minnesota John stopped in St. Louis where his sister Ellen (Sister Seraphine) was stationed. He allegedly complained to her superiors about their practice of assigning French nuns to Minnesota and Minnesota-born nuns to St. Louis. See Hurley, *On Good Ground,* 137. The story cannot be sustained, however, because Sister Seraphine did not go to St. Louis until after the fall of Vicksburg (July 1863). John Ireland was in St. Louis in 1866 and may have lodged his protest then. See JIP, roll 2, "De Vita Supernaturali," with the notation that it was preached in St. Vincent's Church, St. Louis, 1866.

5. See *St. Paul Press,* August 1, 1863.

6. Reardon, *Diocese of St. Paul,* 221. Ireland also doubled as Bishop Grace's secretary.

7. See JIP, roll 2, several sermons with notations indicating where they were preached.

8. Mathias Savs, "The Catholic Church in Wright County, Minn.," *A&D* 4 (1916): 222.

9. Reardon, *Diocese of St. Paul,* 582–583; JIP, roll 2, "De Fide Hibernorum" (1869).

10. Estimate published in the *St. Paul Press,* April 15, 1866. The percentage of Germans—many but not all of whom were Catholics—was the same. The American born constituted 27 percent of the city's population. For rather more refined figures, see Regan, "The Irish," 131, 140.

11. Regan, "The Irish," 142.

12. For what follows, see JIP, roll 1, twenty-two pages, in Ireland's hand, of notes and jottings about the "ideal" priest. This document bears no date, but internal evidence places it certainly after 1884 and probably after 1889. It may have been used at priests' retreats and/or at conferences for seminarians. It demonstrates strikingly the ease with which Ireland shifted from English to Latin to French and back again.

13. JIP, roll 2, "De Peccato Originali" (1863).

14. JIP, roll 2, "Union of Church with Christ" (1866).

15. JIP, roll 1, notes on the "ideal" priest (n.d.).

16. For a brief statement, see F. L. Cross, ed., *Dictionary of the Christian Church* (London: Oxford University Press, 1958), 71.

17. JIP, roll 2, "The Divinity of Christ" (1871).

18. For a particularly full statement, see JIP, roll 2, "De Resurrectione" (1864). There is no reason to suppose that Ireland ever altered this position. See also roll 1, "The Divinity of Christ" (n.d.). Toward the end of the century, however, when the Modernist crisis was beginning and Catholic exegetes were questioning the historicity of the New Testament, Ireland's "advanced" views in other areas—see Thomas E. Wangler, "The Ecclesiology of Archbishop John Ireland" (Ph.D. diss., Marquette University, 1968), especially 134 ff.—may have led Roman authorities to suspect his orthodoxy on this point. See above, Prologue.

19. JIP, roll 2, "Extra Ecclesiam nulla Salus" (1864), and roll 1, "The Church" (n.d.) and "The Church: A Historical Fact" (n.d.).

20. JIP, roll 2, "De Spiritu Sancto in Ecclesia" (1872).

21. JIP, roll 2, "Dogmas in Religion of Christ: It Is Not Sufficient to Profess Morality" (1866), and roll 1, "De Regula Fidei" (n.d.), an incomplete series of lectures.

22. See, among others, JIP, roll 2, "De Immutabilitate Ecclesiae" (1865).

23. JIP, roll 1, "[Closing Lecture] On Rule of Faith" (n.d.). See also "Re. D. R. Breed's Defense of Protestantism" (n.d.). Whipple was consecrated Episcopal bishop of Minnesota in 1859. Among his many good works he was especially known for his courageous efforts to bring justice to the Dakota Indians.

24. See, for example, JIP, roll 1, "Cath[olicity] and Protest[antism] in Relation to Wealth and Social Happiness of Nations" (n.d.).

25. JIP, roll 1, "The Church" (n.d.). From internal evidence one can surmise that the

sermon was preached at the dedication of a new church in Minneapolis, most likely that of the Immaculate Conception, in January 1873. See Reardon, *Diocese of St. Paul,* 593.

26. JIP, roll 2, "Sacred Heart" (1866).

27. JIP, roll 1, "Christ, the Saviour [*sic*] of the World" (n.d., but a Christmas sermon).

28. JIP, roll 2, "De Immutabilitate Ecclesiae" (1865). Twenty-eight years later Ireland would proclaim the need for the church to adapt "herself in manner of life and in method of action to the condition of the new order." See John Ireland, *Church and Modern Society,* 1:107.

29. The best example is in JIP, roll 1, "Cath[olicity] and Protest[antism] in Relation to Wealth and Social Happiness of Nations" (n.d.), in which Ireland compared in detail the figures for land ownership in (Protestant) England and (Catholic) France.

30. Wangler, "Ecclesiology of Ireland," 9, implies more references than are actually in the sermons, and therefore concludes more about Ireland's reading habits than the evidence warrants. Among writers cited are H. E. Manning, Frederick Faber, J. A. Moehler, Joseph De Maistre, Martin Spalding, Orestes Brownson, and Isaac Hecker—all prominent nineteenth century Catholic savants. Curiously, John Henry Cardinal Newman is notable by his absence. There is an oblique reference to the Oxford Movement in "De Immutabilitate Ecclesiae" (1865).

31. JIP, roll 1, "Infallibility of Pope; Basis for Union" (n.d., but after 1870). This is a list of authorities and the fragment of a sermon.

32. JIP, roll 2, "Homilia de Ira, Verbis Opprobriosis, et Reconciliatione cum Inimicis" (1864). Matthew 5:22: "I say to you that whoever is angry with his brother shall be in danger of the judgment, and whoever shall say to his brother, Raca, shall be in danger of the council."

33. JIP, roll 2, "De Cultu Interno et Externo" (1865).

34. Pius X (1835–1914). See Cross, ed., *Dictionary of the Christian Church,* 1079–1080.

35. See JIP, roll 2, "The Earnest Christian" (1864).

36. JIP, roll 2, "The Value of a Soul" (1867).

37. JIP, roll 1, "The Spiritual Condition of Man Before Justification through the Merit of Christ" (n.d.).

38. JIP, roll 2, "Deificatio Hominis per Gratiam Sanctificantem" (1865) and "De Vita Supernaturali Filii et Heredes Dei" (1865).

39. See, among others, JIP, roll 2, "De Imitatione Christi" (1865), "J[esus] C[hrist] Triumphs over Sin, Death, and Hell" (1865), "De S[ancto] Nomine Jesu" (1871).

40. JIP, roll 1, "Saints in the Church" (n.d.).

41. JIP, roll 2, "De Peccato Originali, necnon de Immaculata B[eatae] M[ariae] Conceptione" (1863). The doctrine was defined in 1854.

42. JIP, roll 2, "De Rosario Beatae Virginis Mariae" (1863). Ireland's attitude may have been in part a reaction to what he considered excesses in the Marian cult among the Marists, his masters at Montbel. See HP-MHS, box 1, excerpt from "Annales de la société de Marie en Europe et en Angleterre" (n.p., n.d.), 423–453, which recounts various alleged visions and similar phenomena at Montbel during Ireland's residence there.

43. JIP, roll 2, "De S[ancto] Nomine Jesu" (1871).

44. JIP, roll 2, "Persecutions and Triumphs of the Church" (1865).

45. JIP, roll 2, "Sacred Heart" (1866).

46. JIP, roll 1, "Cath[olicity] and Protest[antism] in Relation to Wealth and Social Happiness of Nations" (n.d.). Dickens published *American Notes for General Circulation* in 1842 and *Pictures from Italy* in 1846.

47. JIP, roll 2, "Homilia de Ira, Verbis Opprobriosis, et Reconciliatione cum Inimicis" (1864).

48. JIP, roll 2, "Indestructibility of Pope's Spiritual and Temporal Power" (1867).

49. Six of Ireland's early St. Patrick's Day addresses have survived, three complete and

three incomplete. Internal evidence suggests that five of them were given in the cathedral and the sixth (1871) in the St. Paul Opera House. For an analysis of them see Charles J. Fahey, "Gibbons, Ireland, Keane: The Evolution of a Liberal Catholic Rhetoric in America" (Ph.D. diss., University of Minnesota, 1980), 87–90.

50. JIP, roll 1, "[St. Patrick]" (n.d.).

51. JIP, roll 2, "De Fide Hibernorum" (1869).

52. JIP, roll 2, "De Fide Hibernorum" (1869).

53. JIP, roll 2, "Virtues and Faults of the Irish, at Home and Abroad" (1865).

54. JIP, roll 2, "My Native Land" (1871).

55. Ireland never recommended that Irish-Americans involve themselves directly in the politics of the old country. A year after this sermon was preached he spoke out strongly against the organization of a Fenian "regiment" in St. Paul. He called Fenianism "humbug" and a swindle. In this he followed the lead of Bishop Grace, who was similarly opposed. See Reardon, *Diocese of St. Paul,* 221–222.

56. In the manuscript Ireland originally wrote, "Avoid politics." The words "excess in" were inserted later above the line.

57. JIP, roll 2, "Virtues and Faults of the Irish, at Home and Abroad" (1865). Fifteen hundred people were present to hear this sermon, according to the *St. Paul Pioneer,* March 19, 1865.

58. JIP, roll 1, "[St. Patrick]" (n.d.). On the manuscript Ireland originally wrote "two hundred," then crossed out "two" and inserted "sixteen."

59. A "teetotaler" abstained from malt liquors (beer), wine, and distilled liquors. The term was to distinguish him from one who practiced "temperance" by refraining from distilled liquors but who would indulge in a glass of beer or wine. See Charles J. Carmody, "Rechabites in Purple: A History of the Catholic Temperance Movement in the Northwest" (master's thesis, St. Paul Seminary, 1953), 3, 15. ("Northwest" in Carmody's title means Upper Midwest. For "Rechabites," see Jeremiah 35:2–19.)

60. Blegen, *Minnesota,* 206. See also Reardon, "The Beginning of the Catholic Total Abstinence Movement," 199–209.

61. See Joan Bland, *Hibernian Crusade* (Washington: Catholic University of America Press, 1951), 45–46.

62. Carmody, "Rechabites," 79–83; Bland, *Hibernian Crusade,* 4–20.

63. See JIP, roll 5, "[26th Anniversary of Founding of Father Mathew Total Abstinence Society of St. Paul]," January 10, 1895 (copy). This account appears substantially correct, though there are small variations in other versions of the story. See Hurley, "John of St. Paul," 148–149.

64. Ireland, "Loras," 5.

65. Reminiscences of an old settler, quoted in *NC,* July 3, 1896. After Ireland's death it was asserted widely — though not to my knowledge ever documented — that Richard Ireland's drinking problem was an occasion for his son's interest in the temperance movement.

66. Hurley, "John of St. Paul," 143–144. The St. Vincent de Paul Society was an international association of Catholic laymen who served the poor. It was usually organized on a parochial basis. 67. *NC,* January 13, 1872.

68. At a meeting on January 1, 1871, paraphrased in James M. Reardon, "The Catholic Total Abstinence Movement," 59.

69. The constitution of the society, as quoted in Reardon, "Total Abstinence in Minnesota," 50. The cathedral society was the second formed in the diocese. The first, also named for Father Mathew, was organized in the hamlet of Belle Plaine the preceding November.

70. Reardon, "Total Abstinence in Minnesota," 91–92.

71. Carmody, "Rechabites," 97–99.

72. *NC,* March 20, 1869.
73. Reardon, "Total Abstinence in Minnesota," 49.
74. Carmody, "Rechabites," 103.
75. JIP, roll 6, "The Saloon," Chicago, April 6, 1888 (copy).
76. A partial list is in Reardon, "Total Abstinence in Minnesota," 53–55. For personal reasons I mention one, that of St. Thomas parish, Derrynane Township, Le Sueur County (May 1869). The secretary of this society was Timothy Shea, my great-grandfather.
77. Carmody, "Rechabites," 101–103.
78. Reardon, "Total Abstinence in Minnesota," 55–56.
79. *St. Paul Dispatch,* July 6, 1869.
80. See Thomas D. O'Brien, "Dillon O'Brien," *A&D* 6 (1933): 35–53.
81. Marx, "O'Gorman," 19–24.
82. The priests whom Ireland was later instrumental in promoting to the episcopate all came out of the total abstinence movement: O'Gorman, James McGolrick, Joseph Cotter, John Shanley, James Trobec, Alexander Christie, James J. Keane, John Stahira, and, from a younger generation, James O'Reilly, Patrick Heffron, John Lawler, Timothy Corbett, and Joseph Busch.
83. Isaac Thomas Hecker (1819–88) became a Catholic in 1844. A year later he joined the Redemptorist order. In 1857, after a quarrel with his Redemptorist superiors, Hecker secured the consent of Pius IX to found the Missionary Society of St. Paul the Apostle, or Paulists, to work specifically for Catholic interests in the United States. Bishop Grace had met Hecker at the second Plenary Council of Baltimore (1866) and was favorably impressed by him. For the Paulists in Minnesota, see Reardon, "Total Abstinence in Minnesota," 84.
84. They were both active at the Catholic Total Abstinence Union of America convention in Chicago, October 1874. See Bland, *Hibernian Crusade,* 87–89.
85. *NC,* November 27, 1869. Under the pen name "Juverna" Ireland wrote several articles for the *Chronicle* during his visit to Rome at the time of the first Vatican Council. ("Juverna" was a relatively rare Latin word for Ireland; Juvenal used it rather than the more familiar "Hibernia.") Moynihan, *Life of Ireland,* 11, is incorrect in saying Ireland "left no reminiscences of the Council."
86. Carmody, "Rechabites," 105–109.
87. For example, *NC,* October 22, 1870.
88. Ireland employed this phrase in later speeches. See, for example, JIP, roll 6, "The Saloon," Chicago, April 6, 1888 (copy).
89. *St. Paul Dispatch,* January 21 and 23, 1871.
90. Carmody, "Rechabites," 113–120.
91. Long account in *St. Paul Press,* January 11, 1872.
92. The Minnesota union sent a delegate to the national convention (February 1872). See Reardon, "Total Abstinence in Minnesota," 66.
93. Carmody, "Rechabites," 132–133; Reardon, "Total Abstinence in Minnesota," 71–72.
94. Bland, *Hibernian Crusade,* 81–83.
95. *NC,* February 7, 1874, a report of the C.T.A.U. of Minnesota. The rhetoric is clearly Ireland's.

Notes to Chapter VI, Romanità

1. See JIP, roll 3, Ireland to Markoe, St. Paul, August 18, 1874.
2. JIP, roll 3, "The Church and the Enlightenment" (n.d.).

3. Everybody in the house, for example, was an enthusiastic reader of the works of Orestes Brownson. See UNDA, Brownson papers, Caillet to Brownson, St. Paul, February 4, 1863, and Ireland to Brownson, December 21, 1863.

4. See JIP, roll 2, Clemence Cretin to Ireland, Montluel, October 29, [1854].

5. Here and below, see Martin, *Hill,* 58–64.

6. JIP, roll 2, "Virtues and Faults of the Irish, at Home and Abroad" (1865).

7. *A&D* 7 (1936): 198–199.

8. Reardon, *Diocese of St. Paul,* 172–173.

9. See HP-MHS, box 1, Grace to Donnelly, St. Paul, May 18, 1864 (copy). Congressman Ignatius Donnelly, in exposing graft in the federal Indian Office, found strong support from Grace. See Martin Ridge, *Ignatius Donnelly: The Portrait of a Politician* (Chicago: University of Chicago Press, 1962), 84–85.

10. The so-called Chippewa [Ojibway] Payment. Ireland left on this mission on September 15, 1868, and was gone about four weeks. See *St. Paul Dispatch,* September 8 and October 17, 1868.

11. *St. Paul Press,* November 26, 1873.

12. *St. Paul Press,* March 19, 1872.

13. *St. Paul Dispatch,* June 8, 1869. Clemens Staub, O.S.B., pastor of the Assumption (German) parish, also signed the letter, but he did not participate in the discussions that followed. For attempts in 1867, see *NC,* June 29 and August 10, 1867.

14. Sibley had been favorably impressed by the work of the nuns in Mendota, where he lived. See Hurley, "John of St. Paul," 159. Ireland and Sibley were well acquainted from their association in the Minnesota Historical Society. In 1868 they formed a committee of two and tried unsuccessfully to secure the Joseph N. Nicollet papers for the Society. See *St. Paul Dispatch,* November 10, 1868.

15. *St. Paul Dispatch,* August 3 and 17, 1869.

16. *St. Paul Press,* February 8 and 21 and March 19, 1872.

17. *NC,* April 1, 1871.

18. *St. Paul Dispatch,* January 23, 1871.

19. *St. Paul Dispatch,* September 8, 1869.

20. An instance of this trust was Grace's habit of instructing his young priests to submit their sermons to Ireland's inspection before preaching them. See HP-MHS, box 1, Riordan to Fortune, St. Paul, February 18, 1870 (copy). "Proctor" in the ecclesiastical sense would be roughly equivalent in meaning to "vicar," one who legally substitutes for another.

21. *NC,* October 16, 1869.

22. Ireland was accompanied by John Shanley, who was to enroll in the Urban College (seminary) in Rome. For Shanley, Ireland's long-time disciple, see Helen Angela Hurley, "John Shanley, Bishop of Fargo," *A&D* 7 (1936): 142–164.

23. See James Hennesey, *The First Council of the Vatican: The American Experience* (New York: Herder and Herder, 1963), 53–54.

24. JIP, roll 1, "The Church" (n.d.).

25. "Juverna," *NC,* February 5, 1870. See above, chapter 5, note 85.

26. Of the fifty-five bishops active in the United States in 1869, forty-eight came to the council. See Hennesey, *First Vatican,* 24.

27. A "vicar apostolic" was a bishop whose territory was either so thinly populated or so lacking in resources that he had no established see city and acted as a peripatetic missionary.

28. Hecker was proctor for Bishop Rosecrans of Columbus, brother of Ireland's commandant at the Battle of Corinth.

29. Ireland observed that "this word Oecumenical Council is quite a puzzler to many. One man who thought he had it all right astonished us lately with the Equinotical Coun-

cil. He supposed it took its name from the season of the year, in which all are journeying towards it." "Juverna," *NC,* November 27, 1869.

30. Shanley enrolled at the Urban College on November 19, 1869. See Hurley, "John of St. Paul," 182.

31. Here and below, see "Juverna," *NC,* February 5, 1870.

32. For example, Newman called the infallibilist majority at the council "an insolent, aggressive faction." See Newman to Ullathorne, Birmingham, January 28, 1870, in *Letters and Diaries,* 31 vols. (London: Nelson and Oxford University Press, 1961 ff.), 25:18–19. The most common distinction employed to separate the parties at the council was that between "opportunists," who thought the definition of infallibility was appropriate, and "inopportunists"—that is, only a few fathers denied the doctrine itself, but many thought its conciliar definition imprudent.

33. The others were Hecker and Bartholomew Delorme for the bishop of Nesqually (Oregon). See Hennesey, *First Vatican,* 24.

34. Hennesey, *First Vatican,* 53–54.

35. "Juverna," *NC,* February 13, 1870.

36. "Juverna," *NC,* February 13, 1870.

37. Hurley, "John of St. Paul," 195.

38. JIP, roll 2, "My Native Land" (1871).

39. *NC,* April 3, 1870. The article was signed "Altama" (the Indian?).

40. JIP, roll 2, "My Native Land" (1871). *Minneapolis Tribune,* May 12, 1870, reported that Ireland had called on the U.S. consul in Dublin.

41. *New York World,* June 2, 1879.

42. The winner was a stoneworker named James McCarter (*St. Paul Dispatch,* May 16, 1870) or McCartar (*Minneapolis Tribune,* May 21, 1870) who signed up forty-seven new members.

43. A standard description of the events of July 18, 1870, is Cuthbert Butler, *The Vatican Council, 1869–1870* (London: Longman, Green and Co., 1930; Westminster, Md.: Newman Press, 1962), 412–416.

44. Aubert, *Pie IX,* 359–373.

45. JIP, roll 2, "Indestructibility of Pope's Spiritual and Temporal Power" (1867).

46. *St. Paul Dispatch,* January 23, 1871.

47. See Hennesey, *First Vatican,* 299–327.

48. JIP, roll 1, "Infallibility of Pope; Basis for Union" (n.d., but after 1870).

49. When the *St. Paul Press* praised the integrity of the famous German ecclesiastical historian, Ignaz von Döllinger, who seceded from the Catholic church rather than accept the conciliar definition, Ireland replied with unusual harshness. "How you berate Pius IX for his tyranny! . . . Where the tyranny could be in telling a man to leave a society, who loudly proclaims that it suits him no longer, I cannot see. . . . [Döllinger's] sudden elevation before the world to the pinnacle of scholarship and erudition, your readers may rest assured, is not due to any latent wondrous talent discovered in the man, but to the old source of merit—opposition to Rome." "Catholic," *St. Paul Press,* May 14, 1871. Reprinted under Ireland's name in *NC,* May 20, 1871.

50. *St. Paul Pioneer,* January 13, 1874.

51. *St. Paul Pioneer,* November 10, 1874, and *Minneapolis Tribune,* December 13, 1874.

52. *St. Paul Pioneer,* May 3, 1874. The article was published in the *Collections* of the Minnesota Historical Society in 1880 (see above, chapter 2, note 28). Ireland took a lifelong interest in the work of the Society. As early as 1868 he was elected (along with General Sibley) a vice president of the organization. See *St. Paul Press,* January 21, 1868.

53. *St. Paul Dispatch,* February 16 and 27, 1875.

54. Hurley, "John of St. Paul," 230. Grace left immediately after Easter, which fell that year on March 28. For the St. Patrick's Day address, see JIP, roll 2.

55. The designations in the text were at once territorial and legal. A "province" was a geographical area composed of several "dioceses" or "sees." At the head of it was an "archbishop" who was also a "metropolitan." Usually (though not always) he resided in the region's largest city which, together with its hinterland, made up his "archdiocese." The other bishops in the province were called "suffragans." Archbishop and bishops exercised "ordinary" jurisdiction over their respective dioceses and hence were also called "ordinaries." The important distinction here is between archdiocese and province. The archbishop of St. Louis had direct jurisdiction over his archdiocese, just as the bishop of St. Paul had over his diocese. As metropolitan of the Province of St. Louis, Archbishop Kenrick was a first among equals in that, aside from some appellate jurisdiction, irrelevant here, he had no direct power over Bishop Grace or any other suffragan. But the archbishop, as the ordinary of that see within the province that had (usually) the largest physical and human resources, was automatically a person of influence. For example, it was unlikely that a man would be named a bishop in the province if the metropolitan opposed him. Also, Rome often communicated with the province as a whole through the metropolitan, and specific legislation (as at the Council of Baltimore in 1884) sometimes enhanced the authority of the metropolitan. He presided at the periodic meetings of the bishops of the province—"provincial councils" or "synods"—and province-wide policy was usually established at his initiative.

56. For an English text of the papal brief, dated February 12, 1875, dividing the Province of St. Louis, see Harry H. Heming, *The Church in Wisconsin* (Milwaukee: Catholic Historical Publishing Co., 1898), 245. From this date until 1888, when it too became a metropolitan see, St. Paul was part of the Province of Milwaukee.

57. Now called the Sacred Congregation for the Evangelization of Peoples. "Congregation" in this administrative context is roughly equivalent to a governmental department or ministry.

58. The matter of episcopal appointments was not the only bone of contention. See the highly nuanced treatment in Robert Trisco, "Bishops and Their Priests in the United States," in John Tracy Ellis, ed., *The Catholic Priest in the United States: Historical Investigations* (Collegeville, Minn.: St. John's University Press, 1971), 111–292. See also chapter 13, note 39, below.

59. Propaganda was headed by a prefect who was always a cardinal-in-curia. His chief aide was a secretary, always an archbishop. Important decisions, like episcopal appointments, were made by a board made up of the prefect and other cardinals assigned by the pope who met twice a month in what was called a "general congregation." See *The Catholic Encyclopedia*, 15 vols. (New York: Robert Appleton Company, 1911), 15:458–459. See also Newman's harsh description, to Monsell, January 13, 1863, *Letters and Diaries*, 20:391: "And who is Propaganda? virtually, one sharp man of business, . . . little more than a clerk . . . and two or three clerks under him."

60. APF-A 243 (1875): 283–285. The account in the text should be supplemented by David Francis Sweeney, *The Life of John Lancaster Spalding* (New York: Herder and Herder, 1965), 100–108 and the authorities cited there. Father Sweeney uses other Propaganda documents, but not this one.

61. The clerks of Propaganda, writing in Italian, often had difficulty dealing with anglo names. Thus Wayrich in this document is called "William Weyrich," while Spalding is spelled "Spolding." This latter error is curious since Spalding's late uncle, Martin John Spalding (d. 1872), had been the distinguished archbishop of Baltimore.

62. The document does not specify what the unfavorable reports said or from what sources they came. For Spalding's case, see Sweeney, *Spalding,* 104–106.

63. Hurley declined the appointment, and in 1876 Spalding became first bishop of Peoria.

64. APF-A 243 (1875): 284.

65. Here and below, see APF-A 243 (1875): 283–285, including a copy of Grace to Barnabò, Rome, April 30, 1875.

66. A "coadjutor" bishop acted as an aide to the ordinary. He usually enjoyed the right to succeed the ordinary when the latter died or retired. An "auxiliary" bishop, also an aide to the ordinary, had no rights to succession.

67. Tradition demanded that a bishop who was not an ordinary of a diocese nevertheless have a diocesan title. Therefore sites that had once had a Catholic bishop, but no longer did, were used to provide titles for vicars apostolic, coadjutors, auxiliaries, curial officials, and retired diocesan bishops. North Africa, the Balkans, and the Middle East abounded in such places. Thus Ireland had been appointed titular bishop of Maronea *in partibus infidelium* (often shortened to *in partibus*), that is, bishop of a see in Thrace that no longer had any Catholics living in it. He kept this title until 1884 when he succeeded Grace as bishop of St. Paul.

68. JIP, roll 3, Ireland to Pius IX and Ireland to Grace, St. Paul, April 22, 1875.

69. A diver recovered the mail pouch, and Ireland's packet was returned to him. See Reardon, *Diocese of St. Paul,* 228, and Moynihan, *Life of Ireland,* 13.

70. *St. Paul Dispatch,* May 15, 1875.

71. *St. Paul Dispatch,* June 18, 1875.

72. JIP, roll 3, Pius IX to Ireland, Rome, July 30, 1875. There are several printed copies of the letter of appointment here.

73. "Consecration" was the liturgical act whereby a priest became a bishop and received the fullness of the sacrament of holy orders. The ceremony, integrated into the mass, was filled with symbolism underscoring the bishop's three-fold office of ruling, sanctifying, and teaching. It is now simply called "ordination" of a bishop.

74. NC, December 25, 1875. A "crozier" was the simulated shepherd's crook, symbol of the bishop's authority.

Notes to Chapter VII, "An Invitation to the Land"

1. The proximity that made for smooth administration also meant there was virtually no correspondence between the two men, a severe loss to the historian.

2. ACHS, Grace's account books (2), 1868–97. The bishop's ordinary income came from a modest tax on the parishes called the "cathedraticum."

3. Reardon, *Diocese of St. Paul,* 186, 198, 247; *Sadlier's Catholic Directory* (New York: Sadlier & Co., 1884), 446–456.

4. The definitive study is James P. Shannon, *Catholic Colonization on the Western Frontier* (New Haven: Yale University Press, 1957), an admirably graceful and scholarly work.

5. JIP, roll 2, "Virtues and Faults of the Irish, at Home and Abroad" (1865).

6. Humphrey Moynihan, "Archbishop Ireland's Colonies," *A&D* 6 (1934): 212–231, especially 215. James Moynihan, Humphrey's brother, in the chapter on colonization in his *Life of Ireland,* 20–32, reproduces Humphrey's article, virtually word for word.

7. See, for example, NC, May 11, 1867. O'Brien was for a while an editor of the *Chronicle.*

8. William J. Onahan, "A Chapter of Catholic Colonization," *A&D* 5 (1917): 70.

9. For a summary see Shannon, *Catholic Colonization,* 14–22.

10. Moynihan, "Ireland's Colonies," 213.

11. Henry J. Browne, "Archbishop Hughes and Western Colonization," *Catholic Historical Review* 36 (1950): 257–285, especially 271.

12. Ireland, "Loras," 15.

13. O'Brien, "Dillon O'Brien," 40.

14. *NC*, January 15 and 22, 1876.

15. As quoted in Stewart H. Holbrook, *James J. Hill: A Great Life in Brief* (New York: Alfred A. Knopf, 1955), 160.

16. For what follows see Shannon, *Catholic Colonization*, 8–13, and the authorities cited there.

17. Shannon, *Catholic Colonization*, 47–48.

18. *NC*, January 15, 1876.

19. Shannon, *Catholic Colonization*, 47–49, 87–91.

20. Moynihan, "Ireland's Colonies," 218.

21. [Dillon O'Brien], *Catholic Colonization in Minnesota* (St. Paul: Pioneer Press, 1879), 43.

22. Reardon, *Diocese of St. Paul*, 628, 630.

23. [O'Brien], *Catholic Colonization*, 4.

24. [O'Brien], *Catholic Colonization*, 57.

25. John Sweetman, "The Sweetman Catholic Colony of Currie, Minnesota: A Memoir," *A&D* 3 (1911): 43.

26. Shannon, *Catholic Colonization*, 59.

27. Folwell, *History of Minnesota*, 3:39–57.

28. Joseph G. Pyle, *The Life of James J. Hill*, 2 vols. (New York: Peter Smith, 1936), 1:205–207.

29. [Dillon O'Brien], *Catholic Colonization in Minnesota: Colony of Avoca* (St. Paul: Pioneer Press, 1880), 16–18.

30. See the statistics in John Lancaster Spalding, *The Religious Mission of the Irish People and Catholic Colonization* (New York: Catholic Publication Society, 1880), 110–113. Only one-thirteenth of the Irish immigrants lived on the land.

31. [O'Brien], *Catholic Colonization*, 34–35, and *Avoca*, 16–17; Shannon, *Catholic Colonization*, 88–90, 106. Notice the error in computation on "food and fuel," reproduced verbatim by Shannon, *Catholic Colonization*, 105.

32. Moynihan, "Ireland's Colonies," 217.

33. See the discussion in Shannon, *Catholic Colonization*, 128–131, 147, 150–152.

34. Here and below, see Shannon, *Catholic Colonization*, 108–113.

35. [Dillon O'Brien], *An Invitation to the Land: Reasons and Figures* (St. Paul: Pioneer Press, 1877), 46.

36. On the Connemaras, here and below, see Moynihan, "Ireland's Colonies," 220–222. For Nugent (1822–1905), see *Catholic Encyclopedia*, 11:150–151.

37. Mary Evangela Henthorne, *The Career of the Right Reverend John Lancaster Spalding, Bishop of Peoria, as President of the Irish Catholic Colonization Association of the United States* (Champaign-Urbana: Twin City Printing Company, 1932), 111.

38. Shannon, *Catholic Colonization*, 159.

39. William J. Onahan, quoted in Henthorne, *Colonization Association*, 110.

40. O'Brien, "Dillon O'Brien," 50.

41. *NC*, September 11, 1880.

42. See the analysis in Shannon, *Catholic Colonization*, 161–163.

43. Moynihan, "Ireland's Colonies," 222.

44. Article in the *New York Sun*, quoted by Henthorne, *Colonization Association*, 113.

45. Moynihan, "Ireland's Colonies," 222.

46. Reardon, *Diocese of St. Paul*, 242.

47. Shannon's view is less sanguine. See *Catholic Colonization*, 165–166.

48. Moynihan, "Ireland's Colonies," 222.

49. AAB, Ireland to Gibbons, St. Paul, February 20, 1881.

50. Lyons, *Ireland since the Famine*, 157–161.

51. Sweetman, "Sweetman Colony," 46.

52. Moynihan, "Ireland's Colonies," 229.

53. Shannon, *Catholic Colonization,* 67–70, 167–171.

54. Sweetman, "Sweetman Colony," 64–65. Sweetman visited Currie in 1904 and found it flourishing.

55. See M. Sevina Pahorezki, *The Social and Political Activities of William James Onahan* (Washington: Catholic University Press, 1942), 85–89.

56. Ireland to James O'Connor (Vicar Apostolic of Nebraska), March 29, 1879, quoted by Henthorne, *Colonization Association,* 40.

57. Sweeney, *Life of Spalding,* 120.

58. *St. Paul Globe,* June 15, 1879.

59. Henthorne, *Colonization Association,* 50–51.

60. *New York World,* June 2, 1879. St. Paul's was Hecker's church and the headquarters of the Paulists.

61. Shannon, *Catholic Colonization,* 79–80.

62. Baltimore was mother to all the dioceses in the United States. Rome had declined to name it formally the primatial see, but it was for many practical purposes considered so, not least during the tenure of Archbishop Gibbons (1877–1921, created cardinal, 1886), who enjoyed immense personal esteem and influence. See James Hennesey, *American Catholics: A History of the Roman Catholic Community in the United States* (New York: Oxford University Press, 1981), 110.

63. AAB, Ireland to Gibbons, St. Paul, March 2, 1880. Gibbons's name appeared as a member of the association's governing board.

64. Henthorne, *Colonization Association,* 50–51.

65. *St. Paul Globe,* June 15, 1879. For Purcell's financial troubles, see John H. Lamott, *History of the Archdiocese of Cincinnati* (New York: Pustet, 1921), 189–207.

66. Quoted by Sweeney, *Life of Spalding,* 154.

67. JIP, roll 23, Ireland to "My dear Sir," St. Paul, August 31, 1880. The letter is incomplete (and possibly was never sent). It is a plea for support of the national association. Its argument runs: if Ireland had done so much "single-handed," a nationwide effort "should be capable of doing more than tenfold."

68. The only significant correspondence on the day-to-day business of the colonies to be found are forty-four letters, ACHS-MHS, roll 3, Ireland to Anatole Oster, the pastor in Clontarf. Of these, one is from 1876 and the rest are from 1881 to 1884. Most of them are very brief.

69. JIP, roll 3, Ireland to Oster, St. Paul, February 26, 1881.

70. JIP, roll 3, Ireland to Oster, St. Paul, March 9 and 22, 1881.

71. JIP, roll 3, Ireland to Oster, St. Paul, March 10, 1881.

72. JIP, roll 3, Ireland to Oster, St. Paul, March 29, 1881. And on April 17 he wrote: "You have heard, of course, that Fr. Swift has left De Graff."

73. JIP, roll 3, Ireland to Oster, St. Paul, January 11, 1882.

74. JIP, roll 3, Ireland to Oster, St. Paul, January 22, 1881.

75. JIP, roll 3, Ireland to Oster, St. Paul, December 29, 1883.

76. Reardon, *Diocese of St. Paul,* 657, 674–675. In 1896 the federal government withdrew financial support from all sectarian institutions of this kind.

77. JIP, roll 3, Ireland to Oster, St. Paul, February 26, 1881.

78. JIP, roll 3, Ireland to Oster, St. Paul, March 29 and September 12, 1881.

79. JIP, roll 3, Ireland to Oster, June 2, 1882.

80. Reardon, *Diocese of St. Paul,* 675, says $46,787.89, and adds: "There is no indication of the source of this money."

81. Ireland gave Oster only an obscure hint. See JIP, roll 3, letter of February 23, 1883.

82. The documents on the Keegan case are in JIP, roll 3, in their proper chronological order between 1879 and 1883.

83. JIP, roll 3, "Interesting Case: Bishop Ireland versus the Estate of the Late Michael R. Keegan and the Heirs of His Daughter" (n.p.: n.d.), a seven-page pamphlet which includes the probate judge's decision.

84. See JIP, roll 3, for a typed copy of the decision, dated January 8, 1883.

85. See JIP, roll 3, Onahan to Ireland, Chicago, January 6 and 8, 1883.

86. Shannon, *Catholic Colonization*, 93–94.

87. See the real estate inventory attached to Ireland's "Last Will and Testament" (1916), in JIP, roll 23.

88. JIP, roll 3, Ireland to Oster, St. Paul, February 26, 1881.

89. JIP, roll 3, Ireland to Oster, St. Paul, May 25, 1883.

90. JIP, roll 3, Ireland to Oster, St. Paul, July 20, 1881.

91. JIP, roll 3, Ireland to Oster, St. Paul, April 17, 1881.

92. JJHP, Ireland to Hill, St. Paul, January 8, 1883.

93. O'Brien, "Dillon O'Brien," 51.

Notes to Chapter VIII, A Larger Stage

1. Shannon, *Catholic Colonization*, 91–93, 251. See also Alice E. Smith, "The Sweetman Irish Colony," *Minnesota History* 9 (1928): 339–345.

2. JIP, roll 3, Ireland to Oster, St. Paul, August 15, 1884.

3. See JIP, roll 3, for the texts of two widely circulated speeches: "Intemperance: Our Duty with Regard to the Evil," delivered in Chicago, January 17, 1883, and "Intemperance and Law," Buffalo, March 10, 1884. See also the invitation to Ireland, November [n.d.], 1885, signed by, among others, the mayor of Boston and the governor of Massachusetts, to lecture on temperance in Boston.

4. See JIP, roll 3, Egger to Ireland, St. Gall, September 6, 1880, a formal inquiry from the bishops of Switzerland about immigration to Minnesota.

5. JJHP, Bookseller to Hill, St. Paul, September 14, 1885. A month later Ireland gave a sign that he was shifting his personal real estate investments from the rural areas to the outskirts of St. Paul. Purchase of a twenty-five-acre tract in Ramsey County was completed in December. See JIP, roll 3, Warranty Deed signed by Jacob Bacon et al., December 3, 1885. The price was $20,000, with a ten-year mortgage at 7 percent.

6. See JIP, roll 3, Shea to Ireland, Elizabeth, N.J., May 24, 1879, and February 15, April 27, June 25, and August 13, 1880. The correspondence dealt with Hennepin's arrival in Minnesota in the seventeenth century. See Ireland's remarks, *Minnesota Historical Society Collections* 6 (1894): 65–73, his contribution to the Hennepin bicentennial celebration held in Minneapolis July 3, 1880. That same year Shea published his translation of Hennepin's *A Description of Louisiana*, which he dedicated to Ireland and to J. Fletcher Williams, president of the Minnesota Historical Society: "This work [is] due to their friendly compulsion."

7. JIP, roll 23, Hubbard to Ireland, St. Paul, June 6, 1882.

8. *NC*, July 31, 1884.

9. Until 1888, when Ireland was made an archbishop and Grace was given the titular archbishopric of Siunia.

10. Reardon, *Diocese of St. Paul*, 200–203. St. Thomas was founded the year after Grace's retirement.

11. ASV-DASU, Grace to Martinelli, St. Paul, November 13, 1896. For the office of apostolic delegate, see below. Martinelli replied (November 16) in the kindest tone, but told Grace his faculties allowed only permission to substitute the rosary. For a wider exemption, he said, Grace would have to apply directly to Propaganda.

12. APF-NS, 99:132–134, Ireland to Ledochowski, St. Paul, February 25, 1897.

13. A "plenary" council was a meeting of all the bishops (as well as the superiors of the major male religious orders) in the United States. By reason of its national scope it was therefore distinguished from a "provincial" council, a meeting of a metropolitan (for example, the archbishop of Milwaukee) and his suffragans. The council of 1884 was the third plenary meeting of the American hierarchy; the others were held in 1852 and 1866.

14. JIP, roll 3, Spalding to Ireland, Rome, January 21, 1883. Spalding, at forty-four, was two years Ireland's junior. Of the other major actors in the drama of the next two decades, James Gibbons in 1884 was fifty, Michael Corrigan forty-five, John Keane forty-five, and Denis O'Connell thirty-five. Only Bernard McQuaid of Rochester, who was sixty-one, was arguably from the older generation.

15. Grace chose Spalding as the preacher at his silver jubilee celebration. See Reardon, *Diocese of St. Paul,* 194. Grace was also a long-time supporter of Spalding's most cherished project, a national Catholic university. See Francis P. Cassidy, "Catholic Education in the Third Plenary Council of Baltimore, I," *Catholic Historical Review* 34 (1948): 272. Moreover, in 1878, Grace had tried to secure Spalding's promotion to the coadjutorship of Milwaukee. See AAB, Grace to Gibbons, St. Paul, September 8, 1878.

16. For the official conciliar documents, as approved by the Vatican, see *Acta et Decreta Concilii Plenarii Baltimorensis Tertii; A. D. MDCCCLXXXIV* (Baltimore: John Murphy, 1886). For documents that emerged from the council, including summaries of the debates, see *Acta et Decreta Concilii Plenarii Baltimorensis Tertii in Ecclesia Metropolitana Baltimorensi a die IX. Novembris usque ad diem VII. Decembris A. D. MDCCCLXXXIV* (Baltimore: John Murphy, 1884). For a summary of events, see John Tracy Ellis, *The Life of James Cardinal Gibbons,* 2 vols. (Milwaukee: Bruce, 1952), 1:203–251.

17. Genesis 6:4.

18. Galatians 2:11; Luke 22:33.

19. See Marvin R. O'Connell, "Dupanloup and the Syllabus: The Compromise of 1865," *Church History* 53 (1984): 200–217.

20. A corporate and endowed board of clerics, attached to the cathedral, with certain liturgical obligations and certain constitutional rights, including participation in the election of the local bishop.

21. See Trisco, "Bishops and Their Priests," 150–194. See chapter 10, note 19, below.

22. AAB, Ireland to Gibbons, St. Paul, March 2, 1880 (accepting Mahoney), and February 20, 1881. Mahoney's habits later became notorious also in New York and Rome. See APF-SCAC 39 (1883): 652, Corrigan to Simeoni, New York, May 30, 1883.

23. APF-SCAC 34 (1880): 898–901. I owe this reference, and much other help and kindness, to Father Robert J. Wister, professor of history, Immaculate Conception Seminary, Seton Hall University, South Orange, N.J.

24. See APF-SOCG 1018 (1883): 1170–1180. Wister thinks this unsigned memorandum the work of Cardinal Franzelin, who had for some years expressed reservations about the church in the United States. See, for example, APF-SCAC 29 (1878): 1079, Franzelin to Simeoni, Rome, November 26, 1878.

25. Most of the archbishops, with the notable exception of Heiss of Milwaukee, Ireland's metropolitan, opposed the idea of a plenary council. See, for example, APF-SCAC 36 (1882): 293, Corrigan to Simeoni, New York, January 24, 1882.

26. JIP, roll 3, Spalding to Ireland, Rome, January 21, 1883. Apparently Ireland had planned to accompany Spalding. "I need not tell you," the latter wrote, "how disappointed I was to learn that you would not join me here."

27. For descriptions of the procession, here and below, see John Tracy Ellis, "Episcopal Vision in 1884 and Thereafter," *U.S. Catholic Historian* 4 (1985): 197; Sweeney, *Life of Spalding,* 159 (who quotes a *Chicago Tribune* dispatch with slightly different figures); and Peter Guilday, *A History of the Councils of Baltimore* (New York: Macmillan, 1932), 228.

28. See, for example, Willa Cather, *Death Comes for the Archbishop* (New York: Knopf, 1927).

29. See Florence D. Cohalan, *A Popular History of the Archdiocese of New York* (Yonkers, N.Y.: United States Catholic Historical Society, 1983), 105–108, and Robert Emmett Curran, *Michael Augustine Corrigan and the Shaping of Conservative Catholicism in America, 1878–1902* (New York: Arno Press, 1978), 24–59.

30. The American College — the famous "House on Humility Street" — was, like the other national colleges in Rome, a residence, not a place of instruction. The staff, however, usually included a tutor, as well as a spiritual director. Students took courses in one of the Roman universities. See Robert F. McNamara, *The American College in Rome, 1855–1955* (New York: Christopher Press, 1956), and, for a more nostalgic treatment, Martin W. Doherty, *The House on Humility Street* (New York: Longmans, 1942).

31. Nelson J. Callahan, ed., *The Diary of Richard L. Burtsell, Priest of New York: The Early Years, 1865–1868* (New York: Arno Press, 1978), 77. The entry was dated Monday, June 19, 1865.

32. Frederick J. Zwierlein, *The Life and Letters of Bishop McQuaid*, 3 vols. (Rome: Desclee, 1925), 1:293–354 (quotations p. 297, 319).

33. A view suggested in Curran, *Corrigan*, 36.

34. Unlike Kenrick and almost all the inopportunists, Fitzgerald attended the final session of the council and cast his negative ballot. He is alleged to have said to Pius IX afterward, "Now [after the conciliar vote], Holy Father, I believe it."

35. See the lists in *The Memorial Volume: A History of the Third Plenary Council of Baltimore, November 9–December 7, 1884* (Baltimore: Baltimore Publishing, 1885), 70–79.

36. On O'Connell, here and below, see Gerald P. Fogarty, *The Vatican and the Americanist Crisis: Denis J. O'Connell, American Agent in Rome, 1885–1903* (Roma: Università Gregoriana, 1974), 1–32.

37. To "incardinate" means to adopt into clerical status one who is domiciled in a different jurisdiction — in this case, from the Vicariate of North Carolina into the Diocese of Richmond.

38. O'Connell to Gibbons, Rome, May 3, 1877, quoted in Fogarty, *O'Connell*, 13–14.

39. A "pallium" is a circular band of white wool, with two hanging strips and marked with six purple crosses, worn over the shoulders by the pope as a symbol of his authority. When an archbishop enters upon his office, the pope sends him a pallium as a sign that said archbishop shares in said papal authority. By "faculties" is meant licenses that grant full legal rights to the new incumbent.

40. Conroy, O'Connell told Gibbons, gave him "many useful hints on conduct toward others." See Fogarty, *O'Connell*, 26.

41. For Conroy's report, see APF-SCAC 36 (1882): 194–217.

42. So Fogarty, *O'Connell*, 31, suggests.

43. See Patrick H. Ahern, *The Life of John J. Keane, Educator and Archbishop, 1839–1918* (Milwaukee: Bruce, 1954), 1–61. Keane was pronounced as though it were spelled "Kain." This circumstance led to some confusion, since Keane's seminary classmate, John J. Kain, was bishop of Wheeling and, later, archbishop of St. Louis. To compound the confusion, John Joseph Keane's successor as archbishop of Dubuque was James John Keane.

44. A reminiscence of 1901, quoted in Ahern, *Life of Keane*, 9.

45. If Keane took the pledge from Mathew, he most likely did so when Mathew toured the United States between 1849 and 1851.

46. See the quotations in Ahern, *Life of Keane*, 29–30.

47. Gibbons had been the first vicar apostolic of North Carolina (1868). When he was transferred to Richmond (1872), he continued to administer the vicariate. When Keane

went to Richmond, the vicariate was still vacant and remained so until 1882. It was, to say the least, an uncoveted position.

48. On Gibbons, here and below, see Ellis, *Life of Gibbons,* 1:3–163.

49. "Mission" in this sense means a series of revivalist services, conducted over a period of some days by specially designated priests (often called a "mission band") brought into the parish for this purpose. See Jay P. Dolan, *Catholic Revivalism: The American Experience, 1830–1900* (Notre Dame: University of Notre Dame Press, 1978). Among the priests conducting the mission Gibbons attended were several future Paulists.

50. Ellis, *Life of Gibbons,* 1:207–220.

51. AAB, Ireland to Gibbons, St. Paul, February 28, 1884.

52. JIP, roll 3, Gibbons to Ireland, August 21, 1884.

53. A summary is in Moynihan, *Life of Ireland,* 279–281.

54. That Ireland was tone-deaf I learned in a private interview with Monsignor Lawrence F. Ryan, January 23, 1965. Monsignor Ryan was rector of the St. Paul Cathedral during Ireland's last years.

55. *Acta et Decreta* (1884), xlvii–xlviii.

56. *Acta et Decreta* (1884), xciii, xcvi, xcix. See also Fogarty, *O'Connell,* 47, and Sweeney, *Life of Spalding,* 165–166.

57. A brief worship service directed to the real presence of Christ in the Eucharist.

58. See the list in *Memorial Volume,* 48–49. A similar but shorter series of sermons was preached in German in a nearby church.

59. AAB, Ireland to Foley, St. Paul, April 25, 1884. John Foley was one of Gibbons's secretaries.

60. Printed in *Memorial Volume,* 11–32. (The section of this book devoted to the conciliar sermons has a separate pagination.) Also printed, with a few additional footnotes, in Ireland, *Church and Modern Society,* 1:29–65, under the title "The Church and Civil Society."

61. "Live forever!" For a recent and highly illuminating analysis of the theological context of this sermon, see Dennis J. Dease, "The Theological Influence of Orestes Brownson and Isaac Hecker on John Ireland's Americanist Ecclesiology" (Ph.D. diss., Catholic University of America, 1978), 195–208.

62. Diary of John B. Hogan, November 10, 1884, Sulpician Archives, Baltimore. Hogan was the Sulpician rector of the seminary in Boston. I owe this reference to the kindness of Professor Philip Gleason. For favorable reviews, see Moynihan, *Ireland,* 33–36, and Thomas T. McAvoy, *The Great Crisis in American Catholic History* (Chicago: Henry Regnery, 1957), 99–100.

63. The Syllabus of Errors (1864) was a compilation, under eighty headings, of various positions condemned by Pius IX in his writings from 1846. The celebrated eightieth of these propositions read: "The Roman pontiff can and ought to reconcile and harmonize himself with progress, with liberalism and with modern civilization." For an English text, see Colman J. Barry, ed., *Documents in Church History,* 3 vols. (Westminster, Md.: Newman Press, 1965), 3:70–74. See also note 19, above.

64. See Ellis, "Episcopal Vision," 216–217.

65. Ireland stopped in New York on his way home and participated in the meeting, on December 9, which set up the United States Catholic Historical Society. See Reardon, *Diocese of St. Paul,* 252.

Notes to Chapter IX, "In Aspiration I Am a Scholar"

1. McAvoy, *Great Crisis,* 10, calls the council "the last great manifestation of unity of the Catholic bishops in the nineteenth century."

2. For Cotter as president of the Catholic Total Abstinence Union of America, see Bland, *Hibernian Crusade,* 81, 93–99. Cotter became first bishop of Winona in 1889.

3. Here and in the following two paragraphs, see M. Francis Borgia, *They Sent Two: The Story of the Beginning of the School Sisters of St. Francis* (Milwaukee: Bruce, 1965), 81–84, 92–94. The College of St. Teresa was founded by the Franciscan Sisters headquartered in Rochester, Minnesota, the same group that operated the celebrated St. Mary's Hospital in that city. Ireland was more friendly with the Rochester Franciscans. See Clapesattle, *Doctors Mayo,* 246.

4. From the Latin *postulare,* to request; a postulant was a candidate for admission to a religious order.

5. Barry, *Worship and Work,* 169–170. See also Bland, *Hibernian Crusade,* 136, 138–139.

6. Ireland to the English Benedictine Aidan Gasquet, as quoted in Shane Leslie, *Cardinal Gasquet* (New York: P. J. Kenedy, 1953), 34. Ireland's regard for the Benedictines was not new. Ten years earlier he had congratulated the recently elected abbot of St. John's and had added: "My hearty prayers . . . for your welfare, that under your direction the Benedictine order in Minnesota may be, as it has been in the world for so many centuries, a powerful agency for good in the cause of religion." JIP, roll 22, Ireland to Edelbrock, St. Paul, October 14, 1875.

7. ADR-UND, Ireland to O'Connell, St. Paul, August 4, 1888, and JIP, roll 22, Ireland to Edelbrock, St. Paul, April 10, 1885.

8. See Blegen, *Minnesota,* 326, 340, 343, 364; Kunz, *St. Paul,* 41, 52, 54; *U.S. Census, 1890: Manufacturing Industries,* pt. iii, p. 618.

9. See Reardon, *Diocese of St. Paul,* 585–588, 595–596, 635–640, 658, 665–667, 676.

10. *NC,* December 4, 1884.

11. Joseph B. Connors, *Journey Toward Fulfillment: A History of the College of St. Thomas* (St. Paul: College of St. Thomas, 1986), 27. This study is a model of institutional history.

12. Reardon, *Diocese of St. Paul,* 183–184.

13. See Joseph A. Corrigan, "The Catholic Industrial School," *A&D* 7 (1935): 3–25.

14. *NC,* November 19, 1885. For a summary and analysis of the figures from 1869, see William Busch, "The Diocesan Seminary Project," *A&D* 7 (1935): 70–78.

15. "Introduction" to Walter Elliott, *The Life of Father Hecker* (New York: Columbus Press, 1891), xv.

16. The name was no doubt Ireland's way of acknowledging the emphasis Pope Leo XIII (elected 1878) had recently placed upon the works of Aquinas as central to clerical education and to Catholic education generally. The school became the College of St. Thomas in 1894.

17. Here and below, see Connors, *Fulfillment,* 32–33.

18. See Marx, "O'Gorman," 19–32, and Connors, *Fulfillment,* 40–45.

19. Clapesattle, *Doctors Mayo,* 181. For an example of O'Gorman's pulpit style during his Rochester years, see Archives of the Diocese of Sioux Falls, O'Gorman papers, box 3, "De judicio extremo," October 7, 1867.

20. Archives of Mount St. Mary's College, Emmitsburg, Maryland, Ireland to Allen, St. Paul, June 14, 1885. I owe this reference (and the next one) to my friend Professor Joseph B. Connors.

21. Archives of Mount St. Mary's, Ireland to McSweeny, St. Paul, May 25 and June 2, 1887.

22. Connors, *Fulfillment,* 45.

23. Quoted in Connors, *Fulfillment,* 31.

24. Reardon, *Diocese of St. Paul,* 683–684. For the foundation of the separate theologate, see chapter 16, below.

25. Connors, *Fulfillment,* 44, 90, 106.

26. Spalding to Elder, Peoria, September 16, 1880, quoted in John Tracy Ellis, *The For-*

mative Years of the Catholic University of America (Washington: American Catholic Historical Association, 1946), 71.

27. Spalding had been in Minnesota just prior to the letter to Elder (preceding note); he had accompanied Ireland on the distressful tour of the Connemara colony. See Shannon, *Catholic Colonization,* 160. See also JJHP, Ireland to Hill, St. Paul, September 11, 1880, in which Ireland says he had brought Spalding to Hill's office in hopes of introducing him to the railroad man. Spalding undoubtedly saw Grace on this occasion.

28. Spalding to McCloskey, Peoria, October 23, 1880, quoted in Sweeney, *Life of Spalding,* 132.

29. See J. L. Spalding, "The Catholic Priesthood," *Lectures and Discourses* (New York: Catholic Publishing Society, 1882), 154–156.

30. JIP, roll 3, Spalding to Ireland, Rome, January 21, 1883.

31. Ellis, *Formative Years,* 81–84, 95; *Memorial Volume,* 48–49.

32. Sweeney, *Life of Spalding,* 157–158; Ellis, *Formative Years,* 96–97.

33. *Memorial Volume,* 99–101. Thomas Byrne, theologian at the council to the archbishop of Cincinnati, later himself bishop of Nashville, spoke in favor of the university and recalled many years later: "When I came down from the rostrum the old Archbishop [*sic*] of St. Paul, Abp. Grace, met me at the foot of the steps; took me by the hand, almost embraced me, saying, That's the kind of speech we want—that will make the University" (quoted in Ellis, *Formative Years,* 104–106).

34. For the formal decree of the council as slightly amended in Rome, see *Acta et Decreta* (1886): 93–94.

35. This conclusion seems confirmed by the fact that only the Province of Milwaukee had two members—Heiss and Ireland—on the committee. Heiss was no doubt included in hopes of securing German support for the university. See Ellis, *Formative Years,* 110.

36. For the dedication of the new Paulist church on Fifty-ninth Street.

37. See Ellis, *Life of Gibbons,* 1:389–398, and *Formative Years,* 120–136.

38. AAB, Ireland to Gibbons, St. Paul, March 26, 1885.

39. AAB, Ireland to Gibbons, St. Paul, April 6, 1885.

40. Here and below, see Ellis, *Life of Gibbons,* 1:389–398, and *Formative Years,* 120–136.

41. See Fogarty, *O'Connell,* 63–74, and McNamara, *American College,* 294–309.

42. Ellis, *Formative Years,* 163–170.

43. *Boston Pilot,* October 24, 1885.

44. ACUA, Keane papers, John J. Keane, "Chronicles of the Catholic University of America from 1885," 8. This is a ledger, dated January 9, 1894–October 2, 1896, and containing a sixty-two page narrative in Keane's hand.

45. AAB, Ireland to Gibbons, St. Paul, March 30, 1886.

46. Ellis, *Formative Years,* 177–179.

47. Sweeney, *Life of Spalding,* 181.

48. ACUA, Keane papers, "Chronicles," 8.

49. O'Connell to Gibbons, Rome, May 28, 1885, quoted in Ellis, *Formative Years,* 153.

50. For Milwaukee, Newark, and San Francisco. See Sweeney, *Life of Spalding,* 113–117, 134–135.

51. *Catholic Citizen* (Milwaukee), December 19, 1894, as quoted in Sweeney, *Life of Spalding,* 181.

52. Ryan to Corrigan, Philadelphia, June 4, 1885, quoted in Curran, *Corrigan,* 122. On Spalding's resolve, see chapter 20.

53. The full expression is *ad limina apostolorum,* that is, to the threshold of the apostles, specifically the apostles Peter and Paul who were martyred in Rome, and to the pope as Peter's successor. The ad limina visit was required of European bishops every five years and of those from elsewhere every ten. The bishop was expected to bring with him a detailed report on the spiritual and material state of his diocese.

54. Ahern, *Life of Keane,* 64–65.

55. JIP, roll 3, John Ireland and John J. Keane, "La question allemande dans l'église aux États-Unis," Rome, December 6, 1886, p. 5. This is a printed copy of the memorandum addressed "à son Eminence le cardinal Siméoni, préfet de la S. congrégation de la propagande," in rebuttal of the Abbelen petition (see chapter 10, below). An English translation is in Colman J. Barry, *The Catholic Church and German Americans* (Milwaukee: Bruce, 1953), 296–311. For the text of Ireland's formal speech at the provincial council, see *NC,* May 27, 1886.

56. *The Irish Standard* (Minneapolis), July 10, 1886. I owe this reference to my friend Monsignor J. Jerome Boxleitner.

57. See JIP, roll 3, Rice to Ireland, Georgetown, September 20, 1886.

Notes to Chapter X, All Things Do Converge

1. In the nineteenth century the Sacred College of Cardinals was composed of no more than seventy clerics, the overwhelming majority of whom were Italians assigned to important posts within the Roman curia or bishops of Italian dioceses. The non-Italian cardinals were mostly ordinaries of important sees in their own countries, though occasionally a non-Italian cardinal served as a curial officer. Each cardinal upon appointment was assigned a "titular" church in Rome—that is, he was technically considered the pastor of that parish—because of the tradition that the college had evolved out of the parish priests of Rome, understood as a corporate body. The tradition further was that these priests had enjoyed the franchise in selecting their bishop; hence the single constitutional function of the college, its right to elect the pope, the Bishop of Rome. The office of cardinal, which possessed no sacramental significance, was entirely in the gift of the pope.

2. AAB, Ireland to Gibbons, St. Paul, March 30, 1886.

3. Ellis, *Life of Gibbons,* 1:291–302.

4. St. Louis, Santa Fe, New Orleans, Chicago, and Cincinnati. Adding the four metropolitans on the university committee, this meant nine of twelve American archbishops signed the documents—Milwaukee, San Francisco, and Oregon City alone excepted. See Ellis, *Life of Gibbons,* 401.

5. Ahern, *Life of Keane,* 68. Thomas Wangler, "The Birth of Americanism: 'Westward the Apocalyptic Candlestick,' " *Harvard Theological Review* 65 (1972): 425–431, and elsewhere in his otherwise perceptive analyses of the origins of Americanist thought, makes much of Ireland's and Keane's contact with Cardinal Manning of Westminster on this visit. The depiction of Manning as a kind of proto-Americanist, however, seems to me unconvincing. Nor is there evidence that Keane and especially Ireland (who left London early) did much more than pay a courtesy call on the aged cardinal (he was seventy-eight in 1886). Manning did prove helpful in the Knights of Labor case (see below), and he would have endeared himself to Keane and Ireland as a staunch promoter of the temperance cause. Some months later Manning alluded playfully to Ireland's hasty departure from London: "When you were last here you used me inhospitably, but I forgive you if you will not do it again" (JIP, roll 3, Manning to Ireland, London, October 30, 1887).

6. Bland, *Hibernian Crusade,* 198.

7. Kulturkampf, the battle between cultures, was a repressive political movement in Germany during the 1870s, directed by Bismarck against the Catholic church. Religious orders were expelled from the country, and many prelates imprisoned. The campaign was over by the mid-1880s, thanks to successful resistance by German Catholics and to the changing priorities of Bismarck's policy. In his memorial to Propaganda (see below),

Abbelen spoke of the Kulturkampf as a positive achievement, that is, as a victory that demonstrated the superiority of German Catholicism.

8. *Memorial Volume,* 12.

9. I have purposely chosen not to use the terms "liberal" and "conservative" to describe the basic partisan division within the American hierarchy but rather "Americanist" and (the admittedly awkward) "anti-Americanist." My reason is that through overuse and misuse "liberal" and "conservative" have ceased to be useful categories and are anyhow inappropriate to designate Ireland and his friends on the one hand and their opponents on the other. Of course on those occasions when the participants in the drama themselves employed "liberal" and "conservative" the words will stand in my narrative.

10. For the proliferation of secret societies in the United States during the last quarter of the nineteenth century, see the summary in Ellis, *Life of Gibbons,* 1:439–440.

11. Sweeney, *Life of Spalding,* 160.

12. The palace on the Quirinal had been traditionally the pope's main residence. The House of Savoy, which had become united Italy's ruling dynasty, had originated in that part of northwest Italy called Piedmont, around Turin.

13. See McNamara, *American College,* 195–200.

14. Here and below, for the most recent account of the Abbelen affair, based mostly on documents in the archives of Propaganda, see Gerald P. Fogarty, *The Vatican and the American Hierarchy from 1870 to 1965* (Stuttgart: Anton Hiersemann, 1982), 45–49. See also John J. Meng, "Cahenslyism: The First Stage, 1883–1891," *Catholic Historical Review* 31 (1946): 394–398, and Barry, *German Americans,* 62–69.

15. Ellis, *Life of Gibbons,* 1:348. A "territorial" parish was a legal entity designed to serve the Catholic population within defined geographical limits, a "territory." A "national" parish was one composed of those Catholics of a particular ethnic origin who, of course, also resided within the boundaries of a territorial parish. Among the contentious questions that might arise: could the pastor of a national parish witness marriages only with the permission of the territorial pastor? Could children living with parents belonging to a national parish enroll in the territorial parish?

16. JIP, roll 3, printed letter to "Monseigneur," Rome, December 10, 1886.

17. JIP, roll 3, printed text (Latin), no title, dated September 28, 1886, and endorsed by Michael Heiss, archbishop of Milwaukee, October 3, 1886. (Abbelen's own name does not appear in the document.) For an English translation, with, however, several unexplained omissions and at least one erroneous interpolation (p. 290), see Barry, *German Americans,* 289–296.

18. Fogarty, *Vatican,* 46. On irremovable rectorships, which were established at Baltimore III, see Ellis, *Gibbons,* 1:246.

19. JIP, roll 3, ["Memorial"], 4, 15–17.

20. See Barry, *German Americans,* 64–65.

21. JIP, roll 3, ["Memorial"], 18.

22. JIP, roll 3, ["Memorial"], 6 (missing from Barry's translation).

23. For the founding of Der Deutsche Römisch-Katholische Central-Verein von Nord-Amerika, see Philip Gleason, *The Conservative Reformers: German-American Catholics and the Social Order* (Notre Dame: University of Notre Dame Press, 1968), 23–29.

24. JIP, roll 3, ["Memorial"], 6. Of these statistics the membership in the Verein and the number of newspapers are included in Barry's translation.

25. JIP, roll 3, ["Memorial"], 13–14. " 'Americanizatio' Germanorum sit processus lentus, naturalis; ne acceleretur cum praejudicio religionis Germanorum, minime omnium vero ab episcopis et sacerdotibus non Germanicis. Recalcitrabunt contra stimulum." The clause beginning "least of all" is omitted from Barry's translation.

26. JIP, roll 3, Spalding to Ireland, Rome, January 21, 1883.

27. JIP, roll 3, "La question allemande," 1–2 (see chapter 9, note 55, above).

28. JIP, roll 3, "La question allemande," 5–7, 9. "Il faut que la religion soit Allemande, et l'évêque qui donnerait un conseil différent est traité comme un ennemi des Allemands, ce qui est arrivé à l'évêque de St. Paul parmi certains de ses prêtres Allemands." As late as the 1910s my mother, whose maiden name was Kelly, attended a Minnesota parochial grammar school in which German was a required subject.

29. JIP, roll 3, "La question allemande," 12–13, 18.

30. See note 7, above.

31. The text has the misprint "l'Anglais."

32. JIP, roll 3, "La question allemande," 14, 16, 19, 24.

33. JIP, roll 3, ["Memorial"], 3.

34. Fogarty, *Vatican*, 47.

35. This was one hundred thousand dollars less than Ireland had claimed to be in hand in October.

36. See Marvin R. O'Connell, "Duchesne and Loisy on the Rue de Vaugirard," Nelson H. Minnich et al., eds., *Studies in Catholic History in Honor of John Tracy Ellis* (Wilmington: Michael Glazier, 1985), 591–592.

37. AAB, John Ireland and John J. Keane, "Animadversiones quaedam de Universitate in America fundanda," Rome, December 6, 1886, 1–2, 4, 7.

38. Ellis, *Formative Years*, 206–213.

39. AAB, Keane and Ireland to "Monseigneur," Rome, December 14, 1886.

40. Frederick J. Zwierlein, *Letters of Archbishop Corrigan to Bishop McQuaid and Allied Documents* (Rochester: The Art Print Shop, 1946), 86–87.

41. Curran, *Corrigan*, 58–62.

42. See the correspondence quoted in Ellis, *Formative Years*, 217–221.

43. See Henry J. Browne, *The Catholic Church and the Knights of Labor* (Washington: Catholic University of America Press, 1949), 34–69.

44. *Acta et Decreta* (1886): 143–144.

45. APF-SCAC 45 (1886): 794–797, Gibbons to Simeoni, Baltimore, November 10, 1886; Browne, *Knights*, 215–220, 229.

46. For McGlynn, see Ellis, *Life of Gibbons*, 1:547–570, Cohalan, *New York*, 122–134, and Curran, *Corrigan*, 192–236.

47. Henry George's most important statement of this theory was *Progress and Poverty*, published in 1879. For an analysis, see Charles A. Barker, *Henry George* (New York: Oxford University Press, 1955), 265–304.

48. ADR-UND, Ireland and Keane to McGlynn, Rome, n.d. (copy); APF-SCAC 56 (1891): 15.

49. For Corrigan's negative assessment of McGlynn shortly after, see APF-SCAC 47 (1887): 242, Corrigan to Simeoni, New York, September 9, 1887. The sentence of "excommunication" meant that McGlynn was declared formally outside the community of the church. His earlier "suspension" by Corrigan meant that he was forbidden to perform any of the public offices of the priesthood for the duration of the suspension.

50. APF-SCAC 47 (1887): 1139, Corrigan to Leo XIII, New York, October 31, 1887, requested *Progress and Poverty* be examined by the Congregation of the Index (which censored books). For Gibbons's view — a condemnation "neither opportune nor useful" — see APF-SCAC 46 (1887): 357–358, Gibbons to Simeoni, Rome, February 25, 1887.

51. JIP, roll 3, Gibbons to Simeoni, Rome, February 20, 1887, "La question des 'Chevaliers du Travail' " (printed copy, fifteen pages). For an English translation see Browne, *Knights*, 365–378.

52. Here and below, see McNamara, *American College*, 294–309.

53. Fogarty, *Vatican*, 41, who astutely observes that among Ireland, Keane, and O'Connell "it was difficult, if not impossible at times, to determine who led and who followed."

54. JIP, roll 21, O'Connell to Ireland, Grottaferrata, September 1, 1887 (copy). About half of the eighty or so letters from O'Connell to Ireland preserved in ACHS were lost sometime after Gerald P. Fogarty consulted them for his *O'Connell* (1974). Thanks to the kindness of Father Fogarty, the file has been restored by the insertion of typed copies and photostats of the missing letters in his possession. (Grottaferrata, a village in the Alban Hills, south of Rome, was at this date the site of the American College's summer villa.)

55. McNamara, *American College,* 303, 314–315.

56. ACUA, Keane papers, "Chronicles," 13–14.

57. *Le messager du dimanche* (Belley) 9 (February 26, 1887): 135–138.

58. ACUA, Keane papers, "Chronicles," 19.

59. Summarized in Ellis, *Formative Years,* 224–225.

60. Copy in JIP, roll 3, Leo XIII to Gibbons, the Vatican, April 10, 1887.

61. Gibbons to Corrigan, Rome, March 28, 1887, quoted in Ellis, *Formative Years,* 225–226.

62. Gibbons to Elder, Rome, February 19, 1887, quoted in Browne, *Knights,* 238.

63. JIP, roll 3, "La question des 'Chevaliers du Travail,' " 4–5, 8–9, 10, 12 (see note 54, above, and quotation in text that it covers; McGlynn was not mentioned by name). "Car nous l'estimerions une impertinence que de nous mêler dans les affaires ecclésiastiques d'un autre pays, qui a sa Hiérarchie propre, et dont nous ne prétendons pas comprendre les besoins ni les conditions sociales."

64. James Gibbons, *Retrospect of Fifty Years* (Baltimore: John Murphy, 1916), 1:190.

65. ACUA, Keane papers, "Chronicles," 16.

66. See Browne, *Knights,* 238.

67. ACUA, Keane papers, "Chronicles," 13–14.

68. The Holy Office—formerly called the Roman Inquisition and now the Congregation for the Doctrine of the Faith—was the disciplinary organ of the Vatican bureaucracy, and therefore from it, rather than from Propaganda, a condemnation would have been issued.

69. Keane to Manning, Rome, February 28, 1887, quoted in Ahern, *Life of Keane,* 74.

70. Archives of the Diocese of Cleveland, Ireland to Gilmour, Rome, March 6, 1887, quoted in Browne, *Knights,* 243.

71. *Le moniteur de Rome,* March 26–27, 1887.

72. Quoted in Ellis, *Life of Gibbons,* 1:308–309.

73. JIP, roll 21, O'Connell to Ireland, September 1, 1887 (copy).

Notes to Chapter XI, "Ireland Would Do Well Anywhere"

1. See Fogarty, *O'Connell,* 220–222.

2. A "nuncio" was a papal ambassador with full diplomatic status and accredited to a secular government. If the United States received a nuncio, it would amount to diplomatic recognition of the Holy See, something that Leo XIII, embroiled in controversy with Italy and the other anti-clerical European states, wanted very much indeed but which did not eventuate until the 1980s. An "apostolic delegate" was the permanent representative of the pope to a national hierarchy, and therefore he enjoyed no diplomatic standing.

3. Ellis, *Life of Gibbons,* 1:616.

4. A venerable Ireland anecdote in Minnesota, vouched for by Reardon, *Diocese of St. Paul,* 253. Judith Naughton Ireland lived until 1895.

5. See JIP, roll 3, Leo XIII to Ireland, the Vatican, March 27, 1887 (two printed copies, English).

6. Moynihan, *Life of Ireland,* 14–15.

7. This seems to be the purport of Ireland's account in *NC,* May 19, 1887.

8. See JIP, roll 3, Sheehan et al. to Ireland, Cork, April 29, 1887.

9. JIP, roll 21, O'Connell to Ireland, Rome, June 24, 1887 (copy).

10. Edes was an American newspaperwoman, a convert to Catholicism, and a long-time resident in Rome, with good connections at Propaganda. The Americanists often derisively referred to her as "la Signora" or "la Donna." For a brief notice see Browne, *Knights,* 197.

11. APF-SCAC 46 (1887): 740, Corrigan to Edes, New York, May 11, 1887 (copy).

12. Of the three honorary ranks, all entitling the priest honored to be called "Monsignor," a "domestic prelate" was on the second level, higher than a "papal chamberlain" and lower than a "protonotary apostolic."

13. Reardon, *Diocese of St. Paul,* 254–255.

14. JIP, roll 21, O'Connell to Ireland, Rome, September 1, 1887 (photostat), misplaced in this file under 1889. See also Barry, *German Americans,* 72–76, and Fogarty, *O'Connell,* 125–126.

15. JIP, roll 3, Heiss to Ireland, Milwaukee, October 15, 1887.

16. JIP, roll 3, Simeoni to Gibbons, Rome, June 8, 1887 (printed copy, two pages).

17. John Gmeiner, *The Church and the Various Nationalities in the United States: Are German Catholics Unfairly Treated?* (Milwaukee: H. H. Zahn, 1887), 6–7.

18. For Gmeiner in St. Paul, see Connors, *Fulfillment,* 49–50.

19. JIP, roll 3, Abbelen to Editor of *Columbia,* n.p., September 1, 1887 (copy).

20. Summarized in Barry, *German Americans,* 79–85.

21. JIP, roll 21, O'Connell to Ireland, Rome, August 6, 1887 (copy).

22. Ahern, *Life of Keane,* 81–82.

23. Archives of the Archdiocese of New York, Ireland to Corrigan, St. Paul, July 14, 1887.

24. O'Connell predicted that Gibbons would go to greater lengths than were proper to mollify Corrigan. See JIP, roll 21, O'Connell to Ireland, Grottaferrata, September 1, 1887.

25. Ellis, *Life of Gibbons,* 1:326–328.

26. Kunz, *St. Paul,* 40–42, has a striking photograph of the depot.

27. See JIP, roll 3, for the menu and program.

28. Fogarty, *Vatican,* 44, quotes Heiss to Simeoni, Milwaukee, August 17, 1888 (which must be a misprint for 1887).

29. JIP, roll 21, O'Connell to Ireland, Grottaferrata, August 29, 1887 (photostat). See also APF-SOCG 1025 (1888): Ireland to Simeoni, August 16, 1887.

30. ADR-UND, Ireland to O'Connell, St. Paul, July 11, 1887. Sbarretti was assistant secretary in charge of the American desk at Propaganda. A "mass stipend" was an offering given to a priest for saying mass for the donor's intention, which, more often than not, was the repose of a deceased friend or relative.

31. JIP, roll 21, O'Connell to Ireland, Rome, August 6, 1887 (copy).

32. JIP, roll 21, O'Connell to Ireland, Rome, September 16, 1887 (copy).

33. JIP, roll 21, O'Connell to Ireland, Rome, September 11, 1887 (photostat).

34. JIP, roll 21, O'Connell to Ireland, Rome, February 23, 1888 (copy). See also JIP, roll 4, Sbarretti to Ireland, Rome, n.d. and January 31, 1888.

35. JIP, roll 21, O'Connell to Ireland, Rome, March 15, 1888 (copy).

36. Ellis, *Formative Years,* 258–262.

37. Archives of the Archdiocese of New York, Ireland to Corrigan, Baltimore, January 22, 1888, and Corrigan to Ireland, New York, January 23, 1888 (copy).

38. AAB, Ireland to Gibbons, St. Paul, February 26, 1888.

39. JIP, roll 21, O'Connell to Ireland, Rome, September 16, 1887 (copy).

40. JIP, roll 21, O'Connell to Ireland, Rome, February 23, 1888 (copy).

41. JIP, roll 4, Gibbons to Ireland, Baltimore, March 19, 1888. McGlynn had broken with George over the Cleveland administration's tariff policy.

42. AAB, Ireland to Gibbons, St. Paul, March 26, 1888.

43. The renewed fuss over Henry George had itself been provoked by a leak to the press. See Ellis, *Life of Gibbons*, 1:574–575.

44. ADR-UND, Ireland to O'Connell, St. Paul, April 14, 1888.

45. AAB, Ireland to Gibbons, St. Paul, May 7, 1888.

46. Bland, *Hibernian Crusade*, 141.

47. Archives of the Archdiocese of New York, Ireland to Corrigan, Baltimore, January 22 and 23, 1888, and Corrigan to Ireland, New York, January 23, 1888 (copy).

48. Curran, *Corrigan*, 23.

49. JIP, roll 4, Wright et al. to Ireland, Chicago, February 16, 1888.

50. Bland, *Hibernian Crusade*, 142–174. To see the evolution of Ireland's thought, compare chapter 5, above, with his speech in Buffalo called "Intemperance and the Law" (JIP, roll 3, March 10, 1884) and with "The Saloon" (April 6, 1888).

51. Here and below, see JIP, roll 4, John Ireland, "The Saloon," *C.T.A. News Pamphlets*, Number 1, p. 1–8. On high license in Minnesota, see Blegen, *Minnesota*, 386; Folwell, *History of Minnesota*, 3:171–173.

52. AAB, Ireland to Gibbons, St. Paul, May 7, 1888; JIP, roll 4, Leo XIII to Ireland, the Vatican, May 15, 1888.

53. AAB, Ireland to Gibbons, St. Paul, January 11, 1889.

54. Of the twenty-four monks who participated in the election of Abbot Rupert's successor, nine were Bavarian, seven Westphalian, three Wuertemberger, three Krainer, and two Swiss. Barry, *Worship and Work*, 93–99, 128, 143.

55. Quoted in Barry, *Worship and Work*, 156.

56. See JIP, roll 21, O'Connell to Ireland, Rome, December 31, 1887 (copy).

57. APF-SCAC 49 (1888): 26–29, Ireland to "Monseigneur," St. Paul, July 9, 1888.

58. JIP, roll 21, O'Connell to Ireland, Rome, December 31, 1887 (copy).

59. JIP, roll 4, Seidenbusch to Ireland, St. Cloud, July 19, 1888.

60. JIP, roll 21, O'Connell to Ireland, Rome, August 7, 1888 (copy). Barry says (*Worship and Work*, 176) "the Brotherhood" in this context "obviously" refers to the monks at St. John's. Might it not rather refer to the German faction at Propaganda?

61. JIP, roll 21, O'Connell to Ireland, Rome, September 11, 1887 (photostat).

62. JIP, roll 21, O'Connell to Ireland, Rome, June 15, 1888, and August 7, 1888 (copies).

63. Ellis, *Formative Years*, 309.

64. See Arthur J. Hope, *Notre Dame: A Hundred Years* (Notre Dame: University of Notre Dame Press, 1943), 238–239.

65. AAB, Ireland to Gibbons, St. Paul, September 14, 1888.

66. JIP, roll 4, Gibbons to Ireland, Baltimore, September 17, 1888.

67. *NC*, September 28, 1888. Ireland (AAB, Ireland to Gibbons, St. Paul, September 14, 1888) made a point of excusing the cardinal from undertaking "a long and tiresome journey . . . for such a small affair." Gibbons was grateful. "I thank your Grace," he wrote, "for not obliging me to decline a formal invitation to the Pallium celebration. I could not possibly go. My work is never ending" (JIP, roll 4, Gibbons to Ireland, Baltimore, September 17, 1888).

68. Quoted in Ahern, *Life of Keane*, 89.

69. JIP, roll 21, O'Connell to Ireland, Grottaferrata, September 17, 1888 (copy); Barry, *Worship and Work*, 177.

70. The complicated story is told with admirable clarity and objectivity in Barry, *Worship and Work*, 163–200.

71. ADR-UND, Ireland to O'Connell, St. Paul, August 4, 1888.

72. JIP, roll 21, O'Connell to Ireland, Rome, November 13, 1888 (photostat).

73. JIP, roll 21, O'Connell to Ireland, Grottaferrata, October 8, 1888 (photostat).

74. JIP, roll 21, O'Connell to Ireland, Rome, November 13, 1888 (photostat).

75. Edelbrock to Hofbauer, Rome, October 27 and November 10, 1889, quoted in Barry, *Worship and Work,* 189.

76. ADR-UND, Ireland to O'Connell, St. Paul, July 11, 1888. On the Priester-Verein, see Chapter 13, note 58.

77. JIP, roll 4, Maes to Simeoni, Covington, July 10, 1888 (copies in French and English).

78. ADR-UND, Ireland to O'Connell, St. Paul, August 18, 1888.

79. *NC,* October 12, 1888.

80. AAB, Ireland to Gibbons, St. Paul, October 12, 1888.

81. Archives of the Diocese of Cleveland, Ireland to Gilmour, St. Paul, October 12, 1888, quoted in Barry, *Germans,* 114.

82. JIP, roll 4, Gibbons to Ireland, Baltimore, October 19, 1888.

83. JIP, roll 4, Elder to Ireland, Cincinnati, November 15, 1888.

84. JIP, roll 21, O'Connell to Ireland, Grottaferrata, September 17, 1888 (copy), and October 8, 1888 (photostat).

85. Quoted in Barry, *German Americans,* 116, part of a detailed treatment, 115–120.

86. *NC,* October 26, 1888.

87. AAB, Ireland to Gibbons, St. Paul, January 3, 1889.

88. Quoted in Barry, *Worship and Work,* 181. The "chapter" was the corporate body of professed monks which enjoyed certain rights of advice and consent in the governance of the monastery.

89. JIP, roll 21, O'Connell to Ireland, Rome, February 24, 1889 (photostat).

90. Edelbrock to Hofbauer, Rome, July 9, 1889, quoted in Barry, *Worship and Work,* 185.

91. JIP, roll 21, O'Connell to Ireland, Rome, July 23, 1889 (copy). By "congregation" O'Connell meant the governing board of cardinals, which met each fortnight and made policy decisions in Propaganda.

92. Haid to Edelbrock, Belmont, N.C., October 29 and November 1, 1889, and Edelbrock to Hofbauer, October 27 and November 10, 1889, quoted in Barry, *Worship and Work,* 187–190, 192.

93. JIP, roll 21, O'Connell to Ireland, Rome, July 13 (photostat) and July 23 (copy), 1889.

94. See Bland, *Hibernian Crusade,* 93–99.

95. For a brief notice, see M. Claudia Duratschek, *Builders of God's Kingdom: The History of the Catholic Church in South Dakota* (Sioux Falls: Diocese of Sioux Falls, 1979), 90, 94. See also Benjamin J. Blied, "The Most Rev. Otto Zardetti, D.D.," *The Salesianumn* 12 (1947): 54–62.

96. JIP, roll 21, O'Connell to Ireland, Rome, July 23, 1889 (copy).

97. See Reardon, *Diocese of St. Paul,* 272, and Cohalan, *New York,* 71–72. Zardetti had been consecrated in October in his native Switzerland.

98. JIP, roll 4, Gibbons to Ireland, Baltimore, October 8, 1889.

Notes to Chapter XII, "The Consecrated Blizzard"

1. JIP, roll 4, Gibbons to Ireland, Baltimore, December 2, 1889.

2. Among many possible examples, see APF-SCAC 40 (1884): 501–503, McCloskey to Simeoni, New York, n.d. [1884]. One of the major problems was a lack of Italian-

speaking priests. When Ireland asked O'Connell to find one in Rome for service in St. Paul, the rector replied that such recruitment "must be a work of chance. There is no disposition here in any untainted priest to go to America except as Delegate or Secretary." Eventually, however, O'Connell succeeded. See JIP, roll 21, O'Connell to Ireland, Rome, August 6 and September 16, 1887 (copies).

3. Ireland at the Third Plenary Council, *Memorial Volume,* 12.

4. Here and below, see AAB, Ireland to Gibbons, St. Paul, December 5, 1889.

5. See, for example, *Memorial Volume,* 28–29. Ireland's persistent dismissal of Protestantism as a spent force represented a common attitude among American Catholic spokesmen and was, of course, very offensive to Protestants. See Gleason, "Baltimore III and Education," 277.

6. On the APA, see Donald L. Kinzer, *An Episode in Anti-Catholicism: The American Protective Association* (Seattle: University of Washington Press, 1964).

7. *NC,* January 25, 1889.

8. Shannon, "Ireland as Chaplain," 303.

9. Quoted in Reardon, *Diocese of St. Paul,* 266.

10. Ireland kept a wary eye upon the functioning of the Indian Bureau in Washington. His major preoccupation was that Catholics — especially teachers — receive a proportionate share of employment on the Indian reservations, and he carried his concern to the highest office in the land. See, for example, JIP, roll 4, Harrison to Ireland, Washington, September 7, 1889, and AAB, Ireland to Gibbons, November 20, 1889. See also Francis P. Prucha, *The Churches and the Indian Schools, 1888–1912* (Lincoln: University of Nebraska Press, 1979), 15–16, and chapter 5, above.

11. *NC,* April 11, 1890, and January 9, 1891.

12. Connors, *Fulfillment,* 81–83.

13. JIP, roll 4, O'Connell to Ireland, New York, May 17, 1890. The *Mirror* was the diocesan weekly in Baltimore.

14. Quoted in Reardon, *Diocese of St. Paul,* 268.

15. For the Union of Brest-Litovsk (1596), which formalized the unity of the Ruthenians in the Ukraine with Rome, see O'Connell, *Counter Reformation,* 215–216. In the text I use the word "Uniate" because Toth used it, though it is not a term welcome among many Eastern Rite Catholics. For information on this subject I owe much to conversations with my colleague, Father Robert L. Kerby, and with Father Robert Taft, S.J., and to materials supplied me through the kindness of Metropolitan Archbishop Stephen J. Kocisko of Pittsburgh.

16. The only account of the interview is Toth's own, very often reprinted in full or in part, most recently in Jay P. Dolan, *The American Catholic Experience: A History from Colonial Times to the Present* (New York: Doubleday, 1985), 186–188. The tone is therefore understandably one-sided, but nothing attributed by Toth to Ireland's behavior is incredible or even out of character. The best brief narrative of these events, with adequate quotation and context, is Constance J. Torasar, ed., *Orthodox America, 1794–1976* (Syosset, N.Y.: The Orthodox Church in America, 1975), 50–51.

17. See Gerald P. Fogarty, "The American Catholic Hierarchy and Oriental Rite Catholics, 1890–1907," *Records of the American Catholic Historical Society of Philadelphia* 85 (1974): 1–11 (offprint). Toth carried on the crusade until his death in 1909.

18. See Fogarty, "Oriental Rite Catholics," 4–5, 7–8.

19. APF-SCAC 1041 (1891): 208–209, Ireland to Simeoni, St. Paul, July 13, 1891.

20. Here and below, see JIP, roll 4, Keane to Ireland, Rome, December 22, 1888, and Louvain, April 11, 1889. For the Swiss-born Messmer, see, for example, Fogarty, *Vatican,* 167, and Ahern, *Life of Keane,* 266.

21. Among other matters under discussion was the appointment of Keane's successor in Richmond. O'Connell was the leading candidate, but, Keane said, everybody, includ-

ing the pope and Simeoni, agreed that "O'Connell can't be spared." The rector, Keane added, was content to remain at his post in Rome, though his health remained uncertain. Another candidate for Richmond—and Keane's choice—was Daniel Riordan, brother of the archbishop of San Francisco.

22. See chapter 17, below. Schroeder actually came to the faculty as professor of dogmatic, not moral, theology, when Keane's first choice for the chair in dogma declined his offer. The easy shift of a professor from one theological field to a quite different one says volumes about Keane's own standing as a judge of scholarly talent and about the quality of the university's original faculty. See also Patrick H. Ahern, *The Catholic University of America, 1887–1896: The Rectorship of John J. Keane* (Washington: Catholic University of America Press, 1948), 15–17, 21.

23. AAB, Ireland to Gibbons, St. Paul, October 27, 1888.

24. JIP, roll 4, Gibbons to Ireland, Baltimore, November 14, 1888.

25. JIP, roll 21, O'Connell to Ireland, Grottaferrata, October 8, 1888 (photostat). The documents were the university statutes Keane was to bring with him to Rome.

26. AAB, Ireland to Gibbons, St. Paul, November 23, 1888.

27. JIP, roll 4, Keane to Ireland, Louvain, April 11, 1889, and roll 21, O'Connell to Ireland, Rome, July 23 and July 31, 1889 (copies).

28. AAB, Ireland to Gibbons, St. Paul, October 12 and November 23, 1888.

29. Carroll (1735–1815) was the first (1789) and for a time the only American bishop.

30. JIP, roll 4, Gibbons to Ireland, December 29, 1888.

31. AAB, Ireland to Gibbons, St. Paul, January 3, 1889.

32. A full treatment is in Pahorezki, *Onahan*, 109–136.

33. AAB, Ireland to Gibbons, St. Paul, April 20, 1889.

34. Quoted in Pahorezki, *Onahan*, 122.

35. Roger Aubert, "L'Église catholique de la crise de 1848 à la première guerre mondiale," Roger Aubert et al., eds., *Nouvelle histoire de l'église*, 5 vols. (Paris: Éditions de Seuil, 1975), 5:92–98.

36. Bruno (1548–1600), a Dominican friar, was burned by the Roman Inquisition for his pantheist views on the very spot in the Campo dei Fiori where the heroic bronze statue was erected. In the late nineteenth century Bruno was hailed by anti-clericals as a symbol of resistance to papal obscurantism.

37. See Ellis, *Life of Gibbons*, 2:336–341.

38. AAB, Ireland to Gibbons, St. Paul, January 11, 1889.

39. JIP, roll 4, Keane to Ireland, Rome, December 22, 1888.

40. See Pahorezki, *Onahan*, 112. But also see Ellis, *Life of Gibbons*, 1:413.

41. JIP, roll 4, Gibbons to Ireland, Cape May, July 18, 1889.

42. AAB, Ireland to Gibbons, St. Paul, July 24, 1889.

43. Foley to Gibbons, Detroit, July 11, 1889, quoted in Pahorezki, *Onahan*, 112.

44. AAB, Ireland to Gibbons, St. Paul, July 16, 1889.

45. For Kenrick's lack of "consideration for the feelings of others," see JIP, roll 4, Farrelly to Ireland, Rome, April 29, 1890.

46. AAB, Ireland to Gibbons, August 9, 1889.

47. JIP, roll 21, O'Connell to Ireland, Rome, July 23, 1889 (copy).

48. AAB, Ireland to Gibbons, St. Paul, August 9, 1889.

49. Here and below, see Ellis, *Life of Gibbons*, 1:413–419.

50. Published, with a few notes added, as "The Mission of Catholics in America," *The Church and Modern Society*, 1:71–101, from which the quotations in the text are taken.

51. For a brief discussion of "triumph of the will" as a hallmark of the Counter Reformation, see O'Connell, *Counter Reformation*, 270–276. "Tridentine" refers to the Council of Trent (1545–63), which is usually considered the beginning of modern—that is, Counter Reformation—Catholicism.

52. A few days after the centennial celebrations Ireland, in the company of Secretary of State Blaine and Secretary of the Treasury Windom, called on President Harrison. Their discussion—about the employment practices of the federal Indian Bureau—lasted more than an hour. See AAB, Ireland to Gibbons, Washington, November 20, 1889.

53. AAB, Ireland to Gibbons, St. Paul, October 5, 1889.

54. JIP, roll 4, Shea to Onahan, Elizabeth, N.J., August 14, 1889. Texts of the papers are in the Onahan papers, AUND, and published in *Souvenir Volume Illustrated* (Detroit: W. H. Hughes, 1890[?]).

55. See correspondence between Ireland and Gibbons, cited above, and Ellis, *Life of Gibbons*, 2:343. In the Archives of the Diocese of Sioux Falls, O'Gorman papers, there is, in O'Gorman's hand, an undated draft of a lecture on the history of the papacy, which may have formed part of the paper read by Bonaparte in 1889. The protest against the Bruno statue was quietly dropped: see JIP, roll 4, Gibbons to Ireland, Baltimore, August 2, 1889. Charles J. Bonaparte later served as secretary of the navy and attorney general in Theodore Roosevelt's administration; see Eric F. Goldman, *Charles J. Bonaparte, Patrician Reformer* (Baltimore: Johns Hopkins Press, 1943).

56. Quoted in Pahorezki, *Onahan*, 131.

57. Ellis, *Formative Years*, 383–390. See also note 20, above.

58. Malachi 3:3 and Luke 12:49. On the question of appropriate imagery, see Connors, *Fulfillment*, 26. I have profited enormously from conversations with Professor Connors on this and other matters.

Notes to Chapter XIII, "We Are in War"

1. JIP, roll 4, Farrelly to Ireland, Rome, January 3, 1890.

2. Here and below, see JIP, roll 4, Farrelly to Ireland, Rome, February 15, 1890.

3. So indeed it turned out, though not immediately. Domenico Jacobini was named nuncio to Portugal—a post he coveted—in 1891, was created cardinal in 1896, and made vicar of Rome in 1899.

4. The popular name for the collection taken up in all dioceses annually for the support of the pope.

5. JIP, roll 4, Bodley to Ireland, London, January 4, 1890. For Bodley, see Shane Leslie, *Henry Edward Manning, His Life and Labours* (New York: P. J. Kenedy, 1921), 266, 449, 463.

6. JIP, roll 4, Manning to Ireland, London, June 9, 1890.

7. JIP, roll 4, Elliott to Ireland, New York, May 5, 1890.

8. John Ireland, "Introduction," *Catholic World* 51 (June 1890): 285–293.

9. JIP, roll 4, Elliott to Ireland, New York, May 5, 1890.

10. Walter Elliott, *The Life of Father Hecker* (New York: Columbus Press, 1891).

11. Ireland took up his new residence at 977 Portland (then Leslie) in April 1890, though he did not assume legal ownership until 1892. See Reardon, *Diocese of St. Paul*, 284.

12. JIP, roll 4, Keane to Ireland, Louvain, April 11, 1889. Keane wanted to come to Minnesota in June "and to collect [money for the university] in the Diocese of St. Paul, as you promised we might do this year, before you should have fairly opened the question of your new cathedral."

13. JIP, roll 4, Caillet to Ireland, Milan, February, n.d., 1890.

14. For quotations here and below, see Robert J. Ulrich, "The Bennett Law of 1889: Education and Politics in Wisconsin" (Ph.D. diss., University of Wisconsin, 1965), 214–217.

15. I follow here, in greatly simplified form, the brilliant reconstruction and analysis

of Philip Gleason, "Baltimore III and Education," *U.S. Catholic Historian* 4 (1985): 273–306. In the notes to this article one can also find a reliable guide to the literature on this subject.

16. In most rural public schools in the Midwest during the 1870s and 1880s, prayer exercises with a Protestant flavor were commonplace. See, for example, *The Autobiography of William Allen White* (New York: Macmillan, 1946), 38.

17. Gleason, "Baltimore III and Education," 289–296.

18. Disagreements did arise at the council as to the moral nature of the parental obligation to send children to parochial schools and as to the spiritual penalties to be inflicted upon parents who refused to do so — for example, denial to them of the sacraments. The rigor of the conciliar decrees in this regard was mitigated by the review at Propaganda. See Gleason, "Baltimore III and Education," 299–302.

19. Kinzer, *Episode,* 64–66.

20. John Ireland, "State Schools and Parish Schools," *Church and Modern Society,* 1:221–222. This was the published version of the celebrated speech before the convention of the National Education Association, July 1890. See below.

21. Ulrich, "Bennett Law," 223.

22. AAB, Ireland to Gibbons, St. Paul, April 21, 1890, and ADR-UND, Ireland to O'Connell, St. Paul, May 28, 1890.

23. Described in, among other places, Daniel F. Reilly, *The School Controversy (1891–1893)* (Washington, D.C.: Catholic University of America Press, 1943), 74–76.

24. Ulrich, "Bennett Law," 200–208.

25. The so-called Accademia, for which see Callahan, ed., *Burtsell's Diary, passim,* and Curran, *Corrigan,* 171–172.

26. JIP, roll 4, Nilan to Ireland, Poughkeepsie, June 27, 1890.

27. JIP, roll 4, Nilan to Ireland, Poughkeepsie, June 23, 1890; Wheeler to Nilan, Poughkeepsie, June 18, 1890; Arnold to Nilan, Poughkeepsie, June 22, 1890; Howell to Nilan, New York, June 26, 1890. See in the same file a six-page, longhand (but not Nilan's hand) description of the arrangement, titled "St. Peter's School," n.p., n.d., tentatively dated by an archivist 1888 but perhaps of later composition.

28. Fogarty, *O'Connell,* 188. O'Connell at this date was still in the United States.

29. Their presentations did not alter the essentially hostile atmosphere of the convention. See Gleason, "Baltimore III and Education," 291.

30. AAB, Ireland to Gibbons, St. Paul, August 9, 1889.

31. Ulrich, "Bennett Law," 365–366, citing the *Wisconsin State Journal* (Madison), June 2 and June 11, 1890. Ireland himself, anxious to give the speech, exerted pressure on the local committee. See Timothy H. Morrissey, "Archbishop John Ireland and the Faribault-Stillwater School Plan of the 1890's: A Reappraisal" (Ph.D. diss., University of Notre Dame, 1975), 214.

32. See note 20, above. Quotations in the text are taken from 217 to 232.

33. See JIP, roll 4, "Program" of the convention, July 4–11, 1890.

34. Summarized in Ulrich, "Bennett Law," 374–378.

35. JIP, roll 4, McSweeney to Ireland, New York, July, n.d., 1890.

36. JIP, roll 4, McQuaid to Ireland, Rochester, July 9, 1890.

37. The metropolitan sees at this date were: Baltimore, New York, Philadelphia, Boston, Cincinnati, Chicago, St. Louis, Milwaukee, Santa Fe, New Orleans, San Francisco, and Oregon City.

38. See the treatment and citations in Curran, *Corrigan,* 320–322.

39. APF-SOCG 1037 (1890): 447, Gibbons to Simeoni, Boston, July 25, 1890. After 1884 senior priests within a diocese whose bishop had died or departed gained the formal right to submit nominations to fill the vacancy. There were therefore two ternae: that of such priests and that of the bishops of the province in which the diocese was located.

40. The Congregation of the Council received its name in the sixteenth century when it became that department of the curia charged with implementation of the decrees of the Council of Trent. In the nineteenth century it dealt with, among other matters, administration of ecclesiastical property.

41. JIP, roll 21, O'Connell to Ireland, Grottaferrata, August 18, 1890 (copy, out of chronological order in this file). Among the severest critics of Ireland's speech was the exiled archbishop of Cologne, now a member of Propaganda, who declared that Ireland's views could not be reconciled to "the orthodox faith" nor to the decrees of Baltimore III. See APF-SCAC 53 (1890): 289–290, Melchers to Simeoni, Frascati, August 19, 1890.

42. JIP, roll 21, O'Connell to Ireland, Grottaferrata, August 30, 1890. Both in Rome and among Catholics in the United States, it was thought to be inappropriate for nuns to teach pubescent males. Only a few religious brothers taught in American Catholic schools at this date.

43. See JIP, O'Connell to Ireland, Rome and Grottaferrata, August 18 and 30, September 6, 12, and 21, 1890 (copies and photostats).

44. Fogarty, O'Connell, 131: "From August until November [1890] O'Connell sent numerous letters to Ireland and Gibbons, which in retrospect constitute a masterwork of misinformation."

45. JIP, roll 21, O'Connell to Ireland, Rome, October 1, 1890 (copy).

46. JIP, roll 21, O'Connell to Ireland, Rome, December 31, 1890 (photostat).

47. JIP, roll 21, O'Connell to Ireland, Grottaferrata, August 30, 1890 (photostat).

48. APF-SCAC 56 (1891): 621–624, "Rapporto" of D. H. A. Minkenberg, June 1, 1891. Leo XIII's celebrated encyclical on the social question, Rerum novarum, was published May 15, 1891. Minkenberg had been recommended to O'Connell by Joseph Schroeder as well as by Satolli. Simeoni also had high praise for him. After one year's experience with him, Ireland dismissed Minkenberg as "a crank," who had "no talent" for teaching. The young priest was welcome to remain in the archdiocese, but "I cannot reappoint him as professor." See ADR-UND, Ireland to O'Connell, St. Paul, July 2, 1891, "Private." Minkenberg later served as secretary to Satolli, when the latter was apostolic delegate to the United States. See Curran, Corrigan, 437.

49. JIP, roll 21, O'Connell to Ireland, Grottaferrata, September 6, 1890 (copy, paraphrase, excerpts), and Rome, September 21, 1890 (photostat).

50. Gibbons to O'Connell, Baltimore, September 10, 1890, quoted in Zwierlein, Life of McQuaid, 3:161.

51. JIP, roll 21, O'Connell to Ireland, Rome, November 15, 1890 (photostat).

52. AAB, Ireland to Gibbons, St. Paul, September 23, 1890.

53. JIP, roll 21, O'Connell to Ireland, Rome and Grottaferrata, August 18, August 30, September 21, October 1, and November 15, 1890 (copies and photostats).

54. APF-SOCG 1037 (1890): 486–488, Ireland to Simeoni, St. Paul, November 15, 1890.

55. AAB, Ireland to Gibbons, St. Paul, November 19, 1890. O'Connell had told Ireland earlier: "You must send Jacobini some money for his lottery." See JIP, roll 21, O'Connell to Ireland, Rome, September 21, 1890 (photostat).

56. AAB, Ireland to Gibbons, St. Paul, November 19, 1890.

57. AAB, Ireland to Gibbons, St. Paul, January 2, 1891.

58. JIP, roll 4, Katzer to Ireland, Green Bay, January 5, 1891. The Priester-Verein, an association of German-speaking priests, was formed in February 1887 (see Ellis, Life of Gibbons, 1:361).

59. JIP, roll 21, O'Connell to Ireland, Rome, December 31, 1890 (photostat).

60. AAB, Ireland to Gibbons, St. Paul, January 2, 1891.

61. AAB, Ireland to Gibbons, St. Paul, December 1890. The document does not bear

the day of its composition, but it was certainly written after December 13 and before December 24. For "teach all nations" — "Docete gentes" — see Matthew 28:19.

62. AAB, Ireland to Gibbons, St. Paul, December 22(?), 1890.

63. Text in Reilly, *School Controversy,* 242–247.

64. AAB, Ireland to Gibbons, St. Paul, December 22(?), 1890. "Felix sermo" — "a happy speech" — was perhaps a play upon St. Augustine's description of original sin as "felix culpa," a happy fault, happy because it led to the salvific work of Christ.

65. O'Connell to Ireland, Rome, March 10, 1891, quoted in Fogarty, *O'Connell,* 135. (This letter is missing from the JIP files.)

66. JIP, roll 21, O'Connell to Ireland, Rome, June 11, 1891 (photostat).

67. AAB, Ireland to Gibbons, St. Paul, July 2, 1891.

68. ACUA, Keane papers, Ireland to Keane, St. Paul, March 30, 1891.

69. ADR-UND, Ireland to O'Connell, St. Paul, May 21, 1891.

70. For Cahenslyism, here and below, see the detailed account in Barry, *German Americans,* 131–182. A more recent and more succinct account is Fogarty, *Vatican,* 55–60. See also John J. Meng, "Cahenslyism: The Second Chapter, 1891–1910," *Catholic Historical Review* 32 (1946): 302–340.

71. The Archangel Raphael was the patron of travelers. See the Book of Tobit.

72. Debate raged for many decades over this question of fact. See the standard, but often criticized, work, Gerald Shaughnessy, *Has the Immigrant Kept the Faith?* (New York: Macmillan, 1925).

73. Full text in Barry, *German Americans,* 313–315.

74. *New York Herald,* May 31, 1891.

75. ADR-UND, Ireland to O'Connell, St. Paul, May 21, 1891.

76. ADR-UND, Ireland to O'Connell, St. Paul, June 2, 1891.

77. JIP, roll 21, O'Connell to Ireland, Rome, June 5 and June 11, 1891 (photostats).

78. ADR-UND, Ireland to O'Connell, St. Paul, June 11 and July 2, 1891.

79. Text in Barry, *German Americans,* 316.

80. JIP, roll 21, O'Connell to Ireland, Rome, June 13, 1891 (photostat). At the top of this letter O'Connell wrote: "Read and destroy."

81. ADR-UND, Ireland to O'Connell, St. Paul, July 2, 1891.

82. AAB, Ireland to Gibbons, St. Paul, May 30, 1891.

83. AAB, Ireland to Gibbons, St. Paul, July 2, 1891.

84. AAB, Ireland to Gibbons, St. Paul, May 30, 1891.

85. ADR-UND, Ireland to O'Connell, St. Paul, June 16, 1891. Von Schlözer was the German minister to the Holy See.

86. Katzer to Gibbons, Milwaukee, June 5, 1891, quoted in Meng, "Cahenslyism II," 310.

87. Rampolla to Gibbons, the Vatican, June 28, 1891, quoted in Barry, *German Americans,* 155.

88. Quoted by Ellis, *Life of Gibbons,* 1:376.

89. AAB, Ireland to Gibbons, St. Paul, August 24, 1891.

90. F. J. Sheridan, ed., *Souvenir Volume, Silver Jubilee, Right Rev. John Hennessy, D. D., Bishop of Dubuque* (Dubuque: M. S. Hardie, 1891), 66–68.

Notes to Chapter XIV, "Tolerari Potest"

1. O'Connell to Gibbons, Rome, August 3, 1891, quoted in Fogarty, *O'Connell,* 149. The cardinal was Rampolla, the secretary of state.

2. When he went to Belgium Pecci was consecrated a titular archbishop. He maintained

this personal title afterward, even though Perugia was not a metropolitan see. He was created a cardinal in 1853. On Leo XIII, here and below, see *The Catholic Encyclopedia* 9 (1910): 169–73.

3. For Leo's mixed inheritance, see Roger Aubert, *Le Pontificat de Pie IX (1846–1878)* (Paris: Bloud & Gay, 1951), 497–503.

4. For the contrast see Aubert, "L'église catholique de 1848," 9–18.

5. Giuseppe Mazzini (1805–72), head of the short-lived Roman Republic (1848–49), was in papal eyes the archtype of the nineteenth-century liberal revolutionary. Giacomo Antonelli (1806–76), secretary of state and virtual ruler of the Papal States during Pius IX's pontificate, had an unsavory personal reputation. Rampolla (1843–1913) was the victim of the famous Austrian veto in the conclave of 1903.

6. An "encyclical" is a circular letter sent by the pope to all Catholic dioceses, a message dispensing authoritative but non-infallible teaching. Leo XIII raised the encyclical to an art form.

7. See O'Connell, "Ultramontanism and Dupanloup," 298.

8. JIP, roll 4, Keane to Ireland, Rome, December 22, 1888.

9. See chapter 17, below.

10. See Marvin R. O'Connell, "Montalembert at Mechlin: A Reprise of 1830," *Journal of Church and State* 26 (1984): 516.

11. For example, Gibbons had to dissuade members of the curia from recommending that Leo XIII send a formal message of greeting and good will to President Cleveland as he had to the emperors of China and Japan. See APF-SCAC 43 (1885): 910–914, Gibbons to Simeoni, Baltimore, December 30, 1885.

12. JIP, roll 21, O'Connell to Ireland, Rome, June 11, 1891 (photostat).

13. ADR-UND, Ireland to O'Connell, St. Paul, July 2 and 7, 1891. Blaine, secretary of state in Harrison's cabinet, had Catholics in his family. Ireland had had dealings with him in connection with the Indian Bureau and with the appointment of military chaplains. Ironically this was the same Blaine whose presidential bid in 1884 had suffered from the infamous reference to "rum, Romanism, and rebellion." Harrison was renominated by the Republicans in 1892 and was defeated by Cleveland.

14. For what follows see Morrissey, "Faribault-Stillwater," 168–178, 196–206.

15. JIP, roll 4, Keeley to Ireland, Faribault, August 27, 1891 (two letters of this date).

16. AAB, Ireland to Gibbons, St. Paul, October 17, 1891.

17. JIP, roll 4, Keeley to Ireland, Faribault, August 27, 1891.

18. The corporate structure of parishes in the archdiocese of St. Paul followed the usual pattern to guarantee clerical control before the civil law. The archbishop, his vicar general, and the pastor joined with two lay trustees to form the parish corporation.

19. There is some evidence that Murphy, a strong advocate of parochial education, was in contact with Archbishop Corrigan during 1892. See Morrissey, "Faribault-Stillwater," 201–203, and Curran, *Corrigan,* 356.

20. JIP, roll 4, Ireland to Corcoran, St. Paul, October 4, 1891.

21. See JIP, roll 4, Keeley to Ireland, Faribault, August 27, 1891.

22. See the text of Conry's letter of August 26 in Morrissey, "Faribault-Stillwater," 180–181.

23. JIP, roll 4, Ireland to Corcoran, St. Paul, October 29, 1891.

24. AAB, Ireland to Gibbons, St. Paul, October 17, 1891.

25. Kiehle's office sent out a circular on the Faribault plan on October 21, and on November 7 the superintendent issued a fuller statement. See Reilly, *School Controversy,* 84–86. Kiehle visited Faribault and found nothing amiss. The "experiment," he said, was "wise" and "within the law." He clearly wanted to leave the burden of decision in this controversial area to the local authorities. But his guidelines included several significant warnings, including this one: "If . . . to any class of patrons [the Catholic nuns'] pres-

ence is obnoxious or unacceptable by reason of the significance of their religious garb, the [local] board must either retire them or require them to wear the usual garb of teachers in the school-room."

26. JIP, roll 4, John Ireland, "Memorial" to Ledochowski of Propaganda, Rome, [late March, 1892]. There are in this file a typed copy of the final version; a draft in English, much worked, in a hand other than Ireland's; and a draft in French in Ireland's hand. A final English version is also printed in Reilly, *School Controversy,* 250–266.

27. JIP, roll 4, Ireland to Corcoran, St. Paul, October 30, 1891.

28. JIP, roll 4, "Memorial [March, 1892]."

29. JIP, roll 4, Ireland to Corcoran, St. Paul, October 30, 1891.

30. Baltimore: John Murphy, 1891.

31. Ryan to Gibbons, Philadelphia, June 3, 1891, quoted in Reilly, *School Controversy,* 90.

32. JIP, roll 4, "Memorial [March, 1892]."

33. Summary in Reilly, *School Controversy,* 108–112.

34. AAB, Ireland to Gibbons, St. Paul, May 30, 1891.

35. New York: Benziger, 1891.

36. The intensity and extensiveness of the debate can best be appreciated by an examination of the materials in ACUA, Bouquillon papers, box 2. Bouquillon himself contributed two more pamphlets to the controversy after his original one.

37. JIP, roll 4, "Minutes," typed copy with a brief longhand addition.

38. See Ellis, *Life of Gibbons,* 1:669, and Curran, *Corrigan,* 342–345, and below.

39. Quoted in Barry, *German Americans,* 172–174.

40. *New York Herald,* December 14, 1891.

41. JIP, roll 4, "Memorial [March, 1892]." Holaind was with Corrigan in New York, helping the archbishop prepare for the St. Louis meeting, when Bouquillon's pamphlet appeared. See Curran, *Corrigan,* 341.

42. See Fogarty, *O'Connell,* 141, and Barry, *German Americans,* 164–165.

43. JIP, roll 4, Ireland to Corcoran, St. Paul, December 23, 1891.

44. Quoted in Reilly, *School Controversy,* 103.

45. JIP, roll 21, O'Connell to Ireland, Grottaferrata, October 21, 1891 (photostat).

46. AAB, Ireland to Gibbons, St. Paul, December 28, 1891.

47. JIP, roll 21, O'Connell to Ireland, Rome, November 10, 1891.

48. AAB, Ireland to Gibbons, St. Paul, January 8, 1892.

49. JIP, roll 4, Blaine to diplomatic and consular offices, Washington, January 15, 1892. The secretary of state directed American officials abroad to show Ireland every courtesy.

50. JIP, roll 4, Ireland to Caillet, Paris, January 28, 1892.

51. JIP, roll 4, Persico to Ireland, Rome, July 29, 1891, in which the new secretary thanked Ireland for the latter's letter of congratulation.

52. JIP, roll 4, Ireland to Caillet, Paris, January 28, 1892.

53. JIP, roll 4, Ireland to Caillet, Rome, February 14, 1892.

54. See Reilly, *School Controversy,* 137.

55. Brandi to Gibbons, Rome, January 18, 1892, and to Holaind, Monaco, October 16, 1892, quoted in Fogarty, *O'Connell,* 201.

56. For the troubles experienced by the Jesuits, see Carlton J. H. Hayes, *A Generation of Materialism, 1871–1900* (New York: Harper Bros., 1941), 85–86.

57. AAB, Ireland to Gibbons, Rome, February 21, 1892.

58. JIP, roll 4, Ireland to Caillet, Rome, February 14, 1892, and AAB, Ireland to Gibbons, Rome, February 21, 1892.

59. For the Triple Alliance, see William L. Langer, *European Alliances and Alignments, 1871–1890* (New York: Random House, 1964), 217–247.

60. See Alexander Sedgwick, *The Ralliement in French Politics, 1890–1898* (Cambridge, Mass.: Harvard University Press, 1965).

61. JIP, roll 4, Ireland to Caillet, Paris, January 28, 1892.

62. See, for example, JIP, roll 21, O'Connell to Ireland, Rome, January 12, 1891 (photostat).

63. AAB, Ireland to Gibbons, Rome, February 21, 1892.

64. JIP, roll 4, Ireland to Caillet, Rome, March 14, 1892. Ireland added that the pope had confided to him the change to a pro-French policy.

65. Morrissey, "Faribault-Stillwater," 270–271.

66. JIP, roll 4, "Memorial [March, 1892]."

67. JIP, roll 4, Ireland to Caillet, February 14, 1892. Ireland protested in his memorial that Propaganda learned about Sister Hyacinthe's transfer before he did, thanks "to the vigilant action of the spies by whom I am surrounded."

68. JIP, roll 4. The article was titled "Mgr. Ireland et ses détracteurs."

69. JIP, roll 4, Gibbons to Ireland, Baltimore, March 8, 1892.

70. JIP, Ireland to the Director of the *Civiltà*, Rome, n.d. (copy). For the text of Gibbons's letter, as translated by O'Connell, see APF-SOCG 1042 (1892): 659–661, Gibbons to O'Connell, December 18, 1891.

71. APF-A 262 (1892): 171–173, Gibbons to Leo XIII, Baltimore, March 1, 1892. For a further selection of correspondence, including Corrigan to Gibbons, see Reilly, *School Controversy*, 139–149.

72. See APF-SOCG 1042 (1892): 789–790, Corrigan to Ledochowski, New York, April 22, 1892. Corrigan also cabled Rampolla that the letter was on its way; see APF-SOCG 1042 (1892): 717, Corrigan to Rampolla, New York, April 19, 1892. The signatories of the letter were Corrigan, Katzer, Ryan of Philadelphia, Janssens of New Orleans, Elder of Cincinnati, Feehan of Chicago, and Gross of Oregon City.

73. JIP, roll 4, Ireland to Caillet, Rome, March 14, 1892.

74. APF-SOCG 1042 (1892): 710–712, Ireland to Leo XIII, Rome, March 17, 1892. For an instance of the hostility to the school plan by "some Jesuits," see APF-SOCG 1042 (1892): 791, Campbell [superior of the Maryland Province of the Society of Jesus] to Rampolla, April 22, 1892.

75. JIP, roll 4, "Memorial [March, 1892]."

76. See JIP, roll 4, for the rough drafts of the "Memorial" in English and French.

77. Text in Reilly, *School Controversy*, 267–270.

78. Gibbons made the same point in his letter of March 1 to Leo XIII. See the figures in Morrissey, "Faribault-Stillwater," 341–343.

79. ACUA, Keane papers, Ireland to Keane, Rome, April 26, 1892.

80. AAB, Ireland to Gibbons, Genoa, June 5, 1892.

81. See *Acta Sanctae Sedis* (Roma: S. Congr. de Propaganda Fide, 1891–92), 24:622–624.

82. ADR-UND, Ireland to O'Connell, Meximieux, May 10, 1892. From Meximieux Ireland paid a quick visit (perhaps on business connected with Leo XIII's ralliement policy) to Paris.

83. JIP, roll 4, Riordan to Gibbons, San Francisco, May 29, 1892. Gibbons's confidant, Alphonse Magnien, the Sulpician superior of the seminary in Baltimore, who was present, doubted that many realized what they were cheering about. See Curran, *Corrigan*, 351–352.

84. Ireland to Byrne, Rome, April 27, 1892, in *St. Paul Dispatch*, May 10, 1892; *Faribault Democrat*, May 13, 1892. See also *St. Paul Pioneer Press*, May 12, 1892.

85. JIP, roll 4, Magnien to Ireland, Baltimore, May 3, 1892.

86. JIP, roll 4, Gibbons to Ireland, Baltimore, April 28, 1892.

87. JIP, roll 4, Ledochowski to Ireland, Rome, May 17, 1892, and Rampolla to Ireland, the Vatican, May 23, 1892.

88. AAB, Ireland to Gibbons, Genoa, June 5, 1892, and JIP, roll 4, Ireland to Caillet, Rome, May 15, 1892.

89. JIP, roll 4, Davis to Ireland, Washington, April 22, 1892. For Davis's speech, see *Congressional Record,* 52d Cong. 1st sess., 1892, 23, pt. 4:3532–3533.

90. See Reilly, *School Controversy,* 167, 172–174.

91. ACUA, Keane papers, Ireland to Keane, Rome, April 26, 1892. The *Dreibund* was the Triple Alliance.

92. AAB, Ireland to Gibbons, Genoa, June 5, 1892.

93. See JIP, roll 4, Philippon to Ireland, Paris, June 4, 1892, Villeneueve to Ireland, Paris, June 7, 1892, and Veullot to Ireland, Paris, June 16, 1892.

94. Published as "America in France," *Church and Modern Society,* 1:365–395.

95. ADR-UND, Ireland to O'Connell, the Ocean, [June 30, 1892].

96. ADR-UND, Ireland to Keane, the Ocean, July 3, 1892.

97. ADR-UND, Ireland to O'Connell, the Ocean, July 7, 1892.

98. ADR-UND, Ireland to O'Connell, New York, July 9, 1892.

99. APF-SOCG 1042 (1892): 813–817, Ireland to Ledochowski, St. Paul, August 10, 1892. Ireland had had inquiries made at Propaganda about the terms Rome would demand for McGlynn's submission. See JIP, roll 21, O'Connell to Ireland, Rome, November 15, 1890 (photostat). More recently McGlynn's friends had pressed Ireland to intervene in Rome on McGlynn's behalf. See JIP, roll 4, Nilan to Ireland, Poughkeepsie, March 7, 1891, and Moore to Ireland, St. Augustine, March 31, 1892. Bishop John Moore of St. Augustine, Florida, was McGlynn's stoutest champion.

100. Reilly, *School Controversy,* 194–196.

101. See Morrissey, "Faribault-Stillwater," 270–271, 304–309.

102. McNamara, *American College,* 330.

Notes to Chapter XV, The Fourteen Propositions

1. JIP, roll 21, O'Connell to Ireland, Rome, September 16, 1892 (copy).

2. AAB, Ireland to Gibbons, Genoa, June 5, 1892.

3. ADR-UND, Kerens to Gibbons, Washington, March 28, 1892,and to Rampolla, Washington, April 18, 1892 (copies); Ford to Ireland, New York, April 4, 1892, and to O'Connell, New York, April 18, 1892.

4. ADR-UND, Ireland to O'Connell, St. Paul, August 3, 1892.

5. JIP, roll 4, Gibbons to Ireland, Baltimore, April 28, 1892.

6. JIP, roll 4, O'Connell to Ireland, Rome, July 4 and 19, 1892.

7. APF-SOCG 1042 (1892): 810, Corrigan to Ledochowski, August 5, 1892.

8. APF-SOCG 1042 (1892): 822, Corrigan to Persico, August 19, 1892.

9. See Curran, *Corrigan,* 354–364, a brilliant reconstruction of a complicated series of events.

10. See APF-NS, 50:555–561, Ireland to Ledochowski, Rome, May 28, 1892, and Zardetti to Ireland, Rome, June 13, 1892.

11. APF-NS, 74:336–338, Zardetti to Simeoni, St. Cloud, January 14, 1892, and Zardetti to Ledochowski[?], n.p., n.d. [but prior to Davis's speech in the U.S. Senate, April 22, 1892]. Ireland mentioned in his memorial of March 1892 that Zardetti operated several schools in his diocese along the lines of the Poughkeepsie/Faribault arrangement.

12. ADR-UND, Ireland to O'Connell, Meximieux, May 10, 1892.

13. JIP, roll 21, O'Connell to Ireland, Rome, September 13, 1892 (copy).

14. Leo XIII's third encyclical, *Aeterni Patris* (August 4, 1879), dealt with the revival of Thomism. For the English text see Claudia Carlen, ed., *The Papal Encyclicals, 1878–1903* ([Saginaw, Mich.]: McGrath Publishing Company, 1981), 18–26. Ireland was unenthusiastic about this encyclical: "Dr. I[reland] fails to see the good of Leo XIII['s] letter on Philosophy," the Sulpician Hogan recorded in his diary (November 20, 1884). See chapter 8, note 62, above.

15. O'Connell, reporting to Ireland about the scholastic progress of one of the latter's seminarians at the North American College, inadvertently testified to how little the complexity, subtlety, and profundity of Thomism were comprehended in what passed for university circles in Rome: "Moynahan [*sic*] . . . now knows the Philosophy of St. Thomas" (JIP, roll 21, O'Connell to Ireland, Grottaferrata, August 7, 1888 [copy]). Humphrey Moynihan, who later acted as Ireland's occasional secretary (see Prologue, note 3, above), had enrolled in the Urban College scarcely eight months before this attestation of competence was made.

16. JIP, roll 4, O'Connell to Ireland, Rome, July 19, 1892.

17. AAB, Ireland to Gibbons, Genoa, June 5, 1892.

18. ADR-UND, Ireland to O'Connell, Washington, July 11, 1892.

19. JIP, roll 4, O'Connell to Ireland, Rome, July 14 and 21, 1892.

20. "[Satolli's] coming saved me," Ireland recalled to O'Connell late in 1893. "Our night's deliberation, long ago, on the proposed delegation, was divinely directed." See ADR-UND, Ireland to O'Connell, Chicago, October 9, 1893. Ireland may not have immediately told Gibbons about the permanency of Satolli's delegation, but it is extremely doubtful that he and O'Connell were under any illusions on this point.

21. JIP, roll 21, O'Connell to Ireland, Rome, August 3, 1892 (photostat).

22. See JIP, roll 4, Gibbons to Ireland, Baltimore, August 29, September 21 and 22, 1892; Foster to Rampolla, Washington, September 15, 1892 (copy); and AAB, Ireland to Gibbons, St. Paul, September 14, 1892. John W. Foster had replaced Blaine as secretary of state. Gibbons and Ireland both wrote reassuringly to Rampolla about Satolli's reception. See ASV-SdiS 241, 2a sezione, Missione straordinaria (1892), Gibbons to Rampolla, Baltimore, September 15, 1892, and Ireland to Rampolla, St. Paul, September 27, 1892. I received copies of the correspondence in this important file from my friend, Robert J. Wister.

23. "The Pontiff of the Age," *Church and Modern Society*, 1:394–425.

24. ADR-UND, Ireland to O'Connell, St. Paul, August 3, 1892.

25. ADR-UND, Ireland to O'Connell, Washington, July 11, 1892.

26. For the advice, see, for example, JIP, roll 4, O'Connell to Ireland, Rome, July 19 and 21, 1892.

27. JIP, roll 4, O'Connell to Ireland, Rome, July 23, 1892.

28. APF-SOCG 1042 (1892): 813–817, Ireland to Ledochowski, St. Paul, August 10, 1892.

29. In JIP, roll 4, compare Ford to Ireland, New York, [August 16, 1892], with Ford to Ireland, New York, August 10 and 15, 1892. For Ford's distraught condition, see Ford to Ireland, New York, September 15, 1892.

30. JIP, roll 4, Katzer to Ireland, Milwaukee, August 9, 1892. See John Conway, " 'Cahenslyism' versus Americanism," *Review of Reviews* 6 (1892–93): 43–48, especially p. 46.

31. ADR-UND, Ireland to O'Connell, St. Paul, August 10, 1892.

32. ADR-UND, Ireland to O'Connell, St. Paul, August 20, 1892.

33. JIP, roll 21, O'Connell to Ireland, Rome, September 21, 1892 (copy).

34. ADR-UND, Ireland to O'Connell, St. Paul, August 20, 1892.

35. The listener was John Farley, Corrigan's vicar general, who was, however, no undiscerning admirer of his ordinary; in correspondence with Corrigan, Farley told him nothing of the details of his conversation with Satolli. See Curran, *Corrigan,* 361–365.

36. JIP, roll 21, O'Connell to Ireland, Rome, August 3, 1892 (photostat).

37. AAB, Ireland to Gibbons, St. Paul, September 14, 1892.

38. JIP, roll 4, Gibbons to Ireland, Baltimore, September 2, 1892, "Private." The words "down the bay" were the same ones used by O'Connell to Ireland a month earlier, an indication of the long-term planning involved. For much of what follows, see the most recent and best treatment of Satolli's arrival and subsequent activities: Robert James Wister, *The Establishment of the Apostolic Delegation in the United States of America: The Satolli Mission, 1892–1896* (Roma: Pontificia Universitas Gregoriana, 1981), 56–109. For an introduction to the subject, see the same author, "The Establishment of the Apostolic Delegation in Washington: The Pastoral and Political Motivations," *U.S. Catholic Historian* 3 (1983): 115–128.

39. AUND, Ford papers, Ireland to Ford, St. Paul, September 23, 1892.

40. For Magnien, see chapter 14, note 83.

41. Corrigan to McQuaid, New York, October 13, 1892, quoted in Zwierlein, *Corrigan*, 152.

42. Wister, *Satolli*, 66–68.

43. On the visit to St. Paul, see *St. Paul Dispatch*, October 26, 1892; on the pamphlet, see Reilly, *School Controversy*, 206–207. A friend of Ireland in Rome assured him the pamphlet was the work of one of Corrigan's secretaries, Gherardo Ferrante. See JIP, roll 4, Rooker to Ireland, Rome, December 15, 1892. Curran, *Corrigan*, 398, doubts this atribution. See also below.

44. English text in Reilly, *School Controversy*, 271–276.

45. "Interdict" would amount to the removal of the priest from the penalized parish, thus depriving it of ordinary sacramental ministration.

46. The judicial act of forgiveness given the penitent in the sacrament of penance or confession.

47. The vote was thirty-seven to thirty-two. See Gleason, "Baltimore III and Education," 299–302. An earlier "Instruction" of Propaganda (1875) had mentioned denial of the sacraments for recalcitrant parents, but Ireland, among others of the majority at Baltimore III, argued that the penalty suggested in that document was narrowly limited. See Cassidy, "Catholic Education, II," *Catholic Historical Review* 34 (1948): 416.

48. Fogarty, *O'Connell*, 214–215, thinks O'Connell wrote the fourteen propositions before he and Satolli left Rome. But see Wister, *Satolli*, 75.

49. Here and in the following paragraph, see Wister, *Satolli*, 73–75.

50. See Fogarty, *O'Connell*, 184, and below.

51. Fogarty, *Vatican*, 80–81, Wister, *Satolli*, 76–79; Reilly, *School Controversy*, 207–211, 276.

52. So Wister, *Satolli*, 79, reasonably concludes.

53. ASV–SdiS 241, 2a sezione, Missione straordinaria (1892): Satolli to Rampolla, New York, November 18, 1892.

54. ADR–UND, Ireland to O'Connell, St. Paul, August 10, 1892.

55. "Minutes," quoted in Wister, *Satolli*, 78.

56. See, for example, ASV–SdiS 241, 2a sezione, Missione straordinaria (1892): O'Connell to Rampolla, Baltimore, October 13, 1892, and Chicago, October 22, 1892.

57. Quoted in Curran, *Corrigan*, 397.

58. See chapter 14, note 99.

59. Ireland to Riordan, the Ocean, July 6, 1892, quoted in Wister, *Satolli*, 155.

60. Text in Zwierlein, *Life of McQuaid*, 3:75–79.

61. ASV–SdiS 241, 2a sezione, Missione straordinaria (1892): Satolli to Rampolla, New York, November 18, 1892, Rampolla to Satolli, the Vatican, November 30, 1892 (draft), *Nihil obstat* signed by O'Gorman et al., Washington, December 21, 1892, and McGlynn to Satolli, n.p., December 23, 1892.

62. McQuaid to Corrigan, Rochester, December 13, 1892, quoted in Zwierlein, *Life of McQuaid*, 3:187.

63. ASV-SdiS 280 (1897): fasc. 1, Corrigan to Rampolla, New York, December 16, 1892.

64. AUND, Ford papers, O'Gorman to Ford, n.p., n.d. [December, 1892]. O'Gorman was habitually careless in dating his correspondence, a disconcerting fault in a historian.

65. JIP, roll 4, O'Gorman to Ireland, Washington, December 18, [1892].

66. AUND, Ford papers, O'Gorman to Ford, n.p., n.d. [December, 1892].

67. AAB, Ireland to Gibbons, St. Paul, February 11, 1891.

68. ADR-UND, Ireland to O'Connell, the Ocean, July 7, 1892, and St. Paul, August 10, 1892.

69. JIP, roll 5, O'Gorman to Ireland, Washington, "Wednesday" [January 11, 1893].

70. ASV-SdiS 280 (1897): fasc. 1, Ireland to Rampolla, St. Paul, December 15, 1892.

71. Actually O'Connell out of prudence submitted both letters to the pope, and implied that Gibbons had sent the negative one out of deference to the other archbishops (except of course Ireland). The pope replied: "I am surprised that he allows himself to be impressed by those people." See Fogarty, *O'Connell*, 238–239, and Ellis, *Life of Gibbons*, 1:632–634.

72. See Sweeney, *Life of Spalding*, 212–214.

73. JIP, roll 4, O'Gorman to Ireland, Washington, December 18 [1892].

74. APF-NS, 27:472–475, Ireland to Ledochowski, St. Paul, December 28, 1892. For all his current prominence in Rome, Ireland is listed here (and in previous indices) as "Francesco." Ireland vigorously supported the candidacy of Bishop John J. Kain of Wheeling, second on the terna and a strong advocate of the Faribault school plan (see APF-SOCG 1042 [1892]: 568–581, Kain to Simeoni, Wheeling, December, n.d., 1891). Kain was eventually appointed coadjutor of St. Louis.

75. ASV-SdiS 280 (1897): fasc. 1, Ireland to Rampolla, St. Paul, December 26, 1892. Spalding, consistent with his past practice, apparently declined to be considered for St. Louis. See Sweeney, *Life of Spalding*, 212.

76. See Curran, *Corrigan*, 397–402.

77. Maurice Francis Egan, *Recollections of a Happy Life* (New York: George H. Doran, 1924), 190–191.

78. JIP, roll 5, Macmillan to Ireland, Chicago, January 13 and 26, 1892. Macmillan was an editor of the *Post*.

79. AAB, Ireland to Gibbons, St. Paul, January 8, 1893.

80. JIP, roll 5, O'Gorman to Ireland, Washington, "Wednesday" [January 11, 1893].

81. AAB, Ireland to Gibbons, St. Paul, January 8, 1893.

82. See JIP, roll 4, Murphy to Ireland, Toledo, January 8, 1892 [1893], and January 12, 1893. Murphy, a newspaper reporter, informed Ireland of gossip about the "conspiracy" in Toledo and Philadelphia. Scattered through this part of the collection are copies of letters from Corrigan to "My dear Sir." See, for example, December 1, 1892, suggesting "a judicious inquiry into the 'school conspiracy,' " so long as care is taken in "avoiding personalities."

83. ASV-SdiS 280 (1897): fasc. 1, Ireland to Rampolla, St. Paul, January 10, 1893. The letter is twelve pages long. The quotation begins: "Voici donc une conjuration; voici l'auteur premier et le commandant suprême—Mgr Corrigan."

84. JIP, roll 21, O'Connell to Ireland, Rome, January 25, 1893 (photostat). O'Connell added, "When you have read this, please burn it."

85. JIP, roll 5, O'Gorman to Ireland, Washington, January 18 [1893].

86. For what follows, see APF-NS, 74:90–537, which includes Propaganda's own printed summary of the material (490–507) and the letters themselves, accompanied in

some cases by supporting documents. Almost all of them were written during January 1893.

87. Fourteen prelates failed to answer, including, surprisingly, two of Ireland's protégés, Shanley (Jamestown) and McGolrick (Duluth). However, a few of these *mancanti* (for example, Schwebach of LaCrosse, opposed, 510–511) sent their letters later. For a chart, see Wister, *Satolli,* 100–103.

88. APF-NS, 74:105–106, Baltimore, January 31, 1893. Gibbons began his letter by calling the establishment of the delegation "one of the greatest joys" of his life, for which his sagacious biographer gently chides him: "The Cardinal of Baltimore was, to say the least, taking a liberty with the truth to which he was not ordinarily accustomed" (Ellis, *Life of Gibbons,* 1:636).

89. APF-NS, 74:384–386, Washington, January 23, 1893.

90. APF-NS, 74:318–324, St. Paul, January 18, 1893.

91. For examples, see Matz of Denver, APF-NS, 74:135–137, January 13, 1893, and Goesbriand of Burlington, APF-NS, 74:111–112, January 8, 1893.

92. APF-NS, 74:192–200, Milwaukee, January 30, 1893.

93. APF-NS, 74:246–260, New York, January 16, 1893. The relevant document is at 251–256.

94. APF-NS, 74:299–304, Rochester, January 16, 1893.

95. APF-NS, 74:312–316, San Francisco, n.d.

96. Thomas O'Flaherty was a priest suspended from McQuaid's diocese whom Satolli had also reconciled.

97. APF-NS, 74:278–282, Peoria, January 11, 1893.

98. Curran, *Corrigan,* 310.

99. See Fogarty, *Vatican,* 128.

100. JIP, roll 21, O'Connell to Ireland, Rome, January 25 and August 29, 1893 (photostats).

101. APF-A 263 (1893): 222–240. See the excellent summary in Wister, *Satolli,* 100–109.

102. AAB, Ireland to Gibbons, St. Paul, February 12, 1893.

103. JIP, roll 21, O'Connell to Ireland, Rome, January 25, 1893 (photostat).

104. JIP, roll 5, O'Gorman to Ireland, Washington, February 8 [1893]. The faculty of the Catholic University was already reflecting in microcosm the struggle within the American hierarchy. Two professors of German extraction, Schroeder and Pohle, had supported Cahensly, and Schroeder, by 1893, was in close communication with Corrigan. See ACUA, Keane papers, "Chronicles," 55–57, and Conway, "'Cahenslyism' versus Americanism," 44–45. Ireland had been for some time annoyed at what he thought was Keane's weakness in controlling this situation. See ACUA, Keane papers, Ireland to Keane, Rome, April 26, 1892: "If you cannot freeze out Schroeder, I lose confidence in you."

105. English text in Reilly, *School Controversy,* 226–230.

106. AAB, Ireland to Gibbons, St. Paul, June 13, 1893.

Notes to Chapter XVI, "Down in the Borderland of Pessimism"

1. As quoted in Connors, *Fulfillment,* 54–56.

2. Kunz, *St. Paul,* 66–69. When the Grand Avenue line was absorbed in 1885 into the Twin City Rapid Transit system, there remained an indebtedness of about $50,000 for which Ireland was chiefly liable (see JJHP, g.c., Cochran to Hill, April 17, 1895).

3. JIP, roll 4, Ahern to Ireland, n.p., September 20, 1892.

4. JIP, roll 21, O'Connell to Ireland, Rome, September 16, 1892 (copy).

5. For example, Ireland was for a time president of the Citizens League of St. Paul, which he called "the Law and Order League." See JJHP, g.c., Ireland to Hill, St. Paul, July 22, 1886. In 1891 Ireland was instrumental in preventing the staging of the Hall-Fitzsimmons boxing match in St. Paul. It is said that James J. "Gentleman Jim" Corbett, afterwards heavyweight champion of the world, when he learned the bout had been called off, asked menacingly: "And who is John Ireland?" See Reardon, *Diocese of St. Paul,* 285.

6. From the centenary sermon in Baltimore, 1889, *Church and Modern Society,* 1:85.

7. JIP, roll 21, O'Connell to Ireland, Rome, September 16, 1890 (copy).

8. *NC,* November 5, 1890.

9. In the spring of 1892 Ireland confessed to some impatience: "I hope Mr. Hill will soon approve some plans for our Seminary." See JIP, roll 4, Ireland to Caillet, Rome, March 14, 1892.

10. JJHP, Seminary papers, box 2, Hill's speech at the dedication, September 8, 1895 (typed copy). For their kind help and guidance through the Hill papers I am grateful to W. Thomas White and Kay Gutzmann.

11. JIP, roll 4, Ireland to Caillet, Rome, May 15, 1892.

12. See Pyle, *Life of Hill,* 1:206.

13. JJHP, Seminary papers, box 2, Hill's speech at the dedication.

14. JJHP, g.c., Ireland to Hill, Rome, May 15, 1892.

15. JJHP, Seminary papers, boxes 1 and 2, including Charter.

16. JJHP, g.c., Ireland to "Dear Sir," St. Paul, December 1, 1892, and Ireland to Hill, St. Paul, December 3, 1892 (telegram). "Stevens" was perhaps John F. Stevens, the brilliant engineer who was one of Hill's associates.

17. JJHP, "Notes and Bills Receivable, 1881–1917."

18. JJHP, g.c., Ireland to Hill, St. Paul, April 9, 1893.

19. Here and below, see JJHP, g.c., Ireland to Hill, St. Paul, April 27, 1893 (emphasis Ireland's). The reconstruction of these events is necessarily sketchy, since only Ireland's side of the correspondence survives.

20. JJHP, g.c., Taylor to "Whom it may Concern," and Kavanaugh to "Whom it may Concern," both St. Paul, April 5, 1893.

21. JJHP, g.c., Merriam et al. to Ireland, St. Paul, April 18, 1895. See also Cochran to Hill, St. Paul, April 17, 1895, enclosing a "confidential" summary of assets and liabilities "compiled from [Ireland's] personal records."

22. JJHP, g.c., Ireland to Hill, St. Paul, May 9, 1893 (telegram).

23. JJHP, g.c., Ireland to Hill, St. Paul, May 10, 1893.

24. JJHP, g.c., Ireland to Hill, St. Paul, May 17 and May 18, 1893 (telegrams).

25. JJHP, g.c., Ireland to Hill, St. Paul, November 21, 1893.

26. JJHP, Voucher 26863, receipt marked "Gift" and signed "John Ireland," January 21, 1907.

27. JJHP, "Notes and Bills Receivable, 1881–1917," and "Suspense Records, Journal 7" (1907). The $50,000 in loans mentioned above (December 1892 and January 1893) were written off by Hill's order, December 31, 1907. So were $60,000 advanced to Ireland between 1894 and 1897. Also Ireland intimated in late 1893 that he was receiving unspecified amounts from Hill. These sums do not include the half-million or so secured from other sources through Hill's intercession (see note 29, below) nor the money donated for the seminary, nor the last recorded gift (see preceding note).

28. JJHP, g.c., Ireland to Hill, New York, March 1, 1898 (telegram), and Hill to Ireland, New York, March 1, 1898 (copy of telegram). This exchange took place on the eve of Ireland's efforts to avert the war with Spain. See chapter 18, below. On Ireland's property syndicate, see next note.

29. See the undated list of subscribers and "potential subscribers," JJHP, Seminary papers, box 5.

30. See trust agreement (printed), JJHP, Seminary papers, box 5.

31. JJHP, g.c., Elkins to Hill, Washington, March 11, 1898, and Merriam et al. to Ireland, St. Paul, December 8, 1896.

32. JJHP, g.c., Ireland to Hill, St. Paul, December 26, 1893, December 14, 1896, and June 25, 1897.

33. ASV-DASU, St. Paul, 9, Ireland to Rooker, St. Paul, May 22, 1896 (telegram).

34. ASV-DASU, St. Paul, 9, Ireland to Rooker, St. Paul, May 23, 1896.

35. ADR-UND, Ireland to O'Connell, Chicago, October 9, 1893, and St. Paul, November 14, 1893. See also JIP, roll 5, Gibbons to Ireland, Baltimore, January 1, 1894.

36. ADR-UND, Ireland to O'Connell, Chicago and St. Paul, October 9, November 2, 6, 14, and 24, 1893. O'Gorman assumed that the article in the *Herald*—about the Jesuits opposing Ireland for the cardinalate—was a plant by O'Connell and Boeglin. See JIP, roll 5, O'Gorman to Ireland, Washington, November 18 [1893].

37. For printed versions of both speeches and a copy of "Social Purity" in French, see JIP, roll 5, June 1893; *Church and Modern Society*, 1:349–360.

38. ADR-UND, Ireland to O'Connell, St. Paul, August 10, 1892.

39. John J. Keane, quoted in John H. Barrows, ed., *The World's Parliament of Religions*, 2 vols. (Chicago: Parliament, 1893), 1:16–17.

40. ADR-UND, Keane to O'Connell, Washington, October 10, 1893. For a summary, see Ahern, *Life of Keane*, 144–149.

41. JIP, roll 21, O'Connell to Ireland, Rome, September 25, 1893 (photostat).

42. ADR-UND, Ireland to O'Connell, Chicago, October 9, 1893.

43. "The Church and the Age," printed English and French versions, JIP, roll 5. Also published in *Church and Modern Society*, 1:105–131.

44. ADR-UND, Ireland to O'Connell, St. Paul, November 6, 1893.

45. AAB, Gibbons to Ireland, Baltimore, October 27, 1893.

46. JJHP, g.c., Satolli to Hill, San Francisco, July 11, and St. Paul, July 31, 1893; ASV-SdiS 280 (1897): fasc. 2, Satolli to Rampolla, St. Paul, July 28, 1893.

47. ASV-SdiS 280 (1897): fasc. 2, Satolli to Rampolla, New York, August 15, 1893. See also Wister, *Satolli*, 193–194, and Curran, *Corrigan*, 430–432.

48. AAB, Ireland to Gibbons, St. Paul, August 10, 1893. Gibbons claimed in Rome full credit for ending hostilities between Satolli and Corrigan. See ASV-SdiS 289 (1897): fasc. 2, Gibbons to Rampolla, Baltimore, August 30, 1893.

49. ADR-UND, Ireland to O'Connell, Chicago, October 9, New York, October 23, and St. Paul, November 14, 1893.

50. JIP, roll 5, O'Gorman to Ireland, Washington, November 18 [1893].

51. Ahern, *Life of Keane*, 142–144.

52. ADR-UND, Ireland to O'Connell, St. Paul, January 7, 1894.

53. See JIP, roll 5, Walsh to Rampolla, New York, May 22, 1894, and the accompanying documents. For the beginning of what proved to be a long correspondence, see ASV-SdiS 280 (1897): fasc. 2, Walsh to Rampolla, New York, May 8, May 21 [*sic*], and July 10, 1894. The May 21 letter was accompanied by twelve documents that Walsh thought incriminated Corrigan.

54. ADR-UND, Ireland to O'Connell, n.p., April 29, 1894.

55. On April 4 Ireland spoke on "Patriotism" to the New York Commandery of the Loyal Legion. See JIP, roll 5, for the text. Ireland had also called on Corrigan the preceding autumn and had not found him at home. "The housekeeper, a new one to me, asked at once if I was Archbishop Ireland, and seemed overjoyed when I said yes." ADR-UND, Ireland to O'Connell, St. Paul, November 2, 1893.

56. Curran, *Corrigan*, 440–445.

57. JIP, roll 5, O'Connell to Ireland, Rome, June 24, 1894.

58. JIP, roll 5, O'Connell to Ireland, n.p., n.d. [Rome, August, 1894].

59. ASV-SdiS 280 (1897): fasc. 2, Ireland to Rampolla, St. Paul, June 25, 1894.

60. JIP, roll 5, O'Connell to Ireland, [Rome, August, 1894].

61. For the relevant correspondence see APF-NS, 51:191–242, all letters to Ledochowski: Zardetti, St. Cloud, October 29, 1893, and n.p., July 24, 1894; Marty, Sioux Falls, September 1, 1894, and St. Paul, October 3, 1894; and Ireland, St. Paul, May 19 and October 4, 1894.

62. ADR-UND, O'Gorman to O'Connell, Brussels, September 26 [1894].

63. ACUA, O'Gorman papers, O'Connell to O'Gorman, Rome, September 29 [1894]. There were several words crossed out in the original passage. For "lost," O'Connell had first written "former"; for "because," "since"; for "natural," "foxy."

64. AAB, Ireland to Gibbons, St. Paul, July 21, 1894.

65. Quoted in Moynihan, Life of Ireland, 227.

66. AAB, Ireland to Gibbons, St. Paul, July 21, 1894.

67. Le Figaro, August 29, 1894. See also JIP, roll 5, Zahm to Ireland, Cologne, September 11, 1894. John Zahm, a priest of the Congregation of Holy Cross and a distinguished professor at Notre Dame, claimed that Ireland's interview in Le Figaro had "created a profound sensation from one end of Europe to the other." He also said that the great majority of lower clergy in Europe identified with Ireland's positions. On what he based these conclusions he did not say—but then, hyperbole was the rhetorical coin of the day.

68. See, for example, JIP, roll 5, O'Gorman to Ireland, Washington, November 18 [1893].

69. Hill was a Democrat, but he belonged to the hard-money (Cleveland) wing of the party, and, as in chapter 17, below, supported McKinley in 1896. See Martin, Hill, 305–309.

70. Here and below, see ASV-SdiS 280 (1897): fasc. 3, Ireland to Rampolla, St. Paul, December 13, 1894. The letter was eighteen pages long and was in response to McQuaid's attack (see next note).

71. For quotations, here and in the following two paragraphs, see Zwierlein, Life of McQuaid, 3:207–210.

72. APF-NS, 55:5, Satolli to Ledochowski, Washington, November 20, 1894.

73. ASV-SdiS 280 (1897): fasc. 3, Gibbons to Rampolla, Baltimore, November 29, 1894. Notation at the top: "Pour le S. Père et le Card. Secretaire d'état seulement."

74. APF-NS, 74:598–599, Corrigan to Ledochowski, New York, January 22, 1895.

75. APF-NS, 74:581–588, Ireland to Ledochowski, December 13, 1894, and 600–609, McQuaid to Ledochowski, Rochester, February 15, 1895; ASV-SdiS 280 (1897): fasc. 3, Ireland to Rampolla, St. Paul, December 13, 1894, and McQuaid to Rampolla, Rochester, January 12, 1895. Each wrote at much greater length to the presumably friendlier correspondent: Ireland to Rampolla, McQuaid to Ledochowski.

76. APF-NS, 74:607, McQuaid to Ledochowski, February 15, 1895. "Noi siamo Americani, e con entusiasmo amiamo la nostra patria."

77. AAB, Ireland to Gibbons, St. Paul, July 27, 1894.

78. ASV-SdiS 280 (1897): fasc. 3, Ireland to Rampolla, St. Paul, December 13, 1894.

79. ASV-SdiS 280 (1897): fasc. 3. There are two drafts here of the reply to Gibbons's letter of November 29.

Notes to Chapter XVII, The Travails of "Asperity Ipswich"

1. JJHP, g.c., Samuel Hill to James J. Hill, Seattle, November 6, 1897 (telegram).

2. AAB, Ireland to Gibbons, St. Paul, December 7, 1894.

3. JIP, roll 5, O'Gorman to Ireland, Washington, February 12, 1895.

4. For the text see Barry, *German Americans,* 320–322.

5. See, for example, ADR-UND, Ireland to O'Connell, St. Paul, November 14, 1893, in which the Faribault plan is described as "spreading" all over the country.

6. See Fogarty, *O'Connell,* 243–244.

7. JIP, roll 5, McGlynn to Ireland, Newburgh, January 3, 1895.

8. Text in Carlen, ed., *Encyclicals, 1878–1903,* 363–369.

9. AAB, Ireland to Gibbons, St. Paul, February 6, 1895.

10. ADR-UND, Ireland to O'Connell, St. Paul, November 6, 1893.

11. Such is Ellis's reasonable assumption (*Life of Gibbons,* 1:466–467).

12. AAB, Ireland to Gibbons, St. Paul, December 7, 1894, and March 4, 1895.

13. AAB, Ireland to Gibbons, St. Paul, December 7, 1894.

14. See ASV-SdiS 280 (1897): fasc. 3, Gibbons to Rampolla, Baltimore, December 25, 1894, and JIP, roll 5, Gibbons to Ireland, Baltimore, January 12 and February 17, 1895.

15. ASV-SdiS 280 (1897): fasc. 3, Ireland to Rampolla, St. Paul, December 30, 1894. Ireland's letter was thirteen pages long, Gibbons's (see preceding note) scarcely two. A non-committal acknowlegment of Ireland's letter crossed it.

16. ASV-SdiS 280 (1897): fasc. 3, Ireland to Rampolla, February 1895, and Rampolla to Ireland, Vatican, March 11, 1895. The accounts in French papers were republished in the United States. See *New York Herald,* February 22, 1895, a copy of which is in this file, fasc. 5. It is noteworthy how many copies of or clippings from American newspapers of the time are to be found in the Vatican and Propaganda archives.

17. JIP, roll 5, Gibbons to Ireland, Baltimore, February 9, 1895, and AAB, Ireland to Gibbons, St. Paul, March 14, 1895.

18. JIP, roll 5, Rooker to Ireland, Washington, February 24 and March 4, 1895.

19. JIP, roll 5, O'Gorman to Ireland, Washington, February 12, 1895.

20. ADR-UND, Ireland to O'Connell, Chicago, October 9, 1893. When he first heard of Hill's benefaction, O'Connell had hoped Ireland could recruit for the seminary the young French exegete, Alfred Loisy — "the best Biblical scholar in the Church" (JIP, roll 21, O'Connell to Ireland, Rome, September 21, 1890 [photostat]). Loisy and Ireland corresponded occasionally, but no substantive negotiations were entered into. For the young Loisy, see O'Connell, "Duchesne and Loisy on the Rue de Vaugirard," 589–616.

21. AAB, Ireland to Gibbons, St. Paul, March 4 and March 14, 1895. For a printed version of the text, see JIP, roll 5. In his attack of 1894 upon Ireland McQuaid stated that to avoid involvement in partisan politics he had not voted for more than a quarter of a century.

22. JIP, roll 5, Gibbons to Ireland, Baltimore, March 6, 1895.

23. Here and below, see ADR-UND, Ireland to O'Connell, St. Paul, October 23, 1893. The Countess Sabina, an ardent Americanist, later translated works by both Ireland and Spalding into Italian. See chapter 18, below.

24. After 1870 the popes refused to receive in audience anyone who had been received or was to be received by the usurping — in the papal mind — royal family of Italy.

25. JIP, roll 5, O'Connell to Ireland, Rome, June 24, 1894.

26. See McNamara, *American College,* 325–336, 737–738, and Fogarty, *O'Connell,* 251–255.

27. JIP, roll 9, Bellamy Storer to Ireland, Meran, December 9, 1903.

28. William Henry O'Connell, who died in 1944 as cardinal-archbishop of Boston. Shortly after his appointment as rector Ireland observed, "Dr. O'Connell is from all I hear a good, reliable man" (AAB, Ireland to Gibbons, St. Paul, December 26, 1895). The selection of O'Connell — he was third on the terna — was cited by some as a victory for Corrigan, but the latter claimed to have no acquaintance with him. See APF-NS, 55:155–162, Gibbons and Corrigan to Ledochowski, Washington, October 3, 1895.

29. See, for example, *New York World,* August 14, 1895, and *New York Sun,* September 26, 1895.

30. After one prolonged period of silence due to some unspecified "ordeal" the rector had allegedly been enduring, Ireland "forgave" O'Connell but chided him: "[You] could from time to time have sent me a few lines" (ADR-UND, Ireland to O'Connell, Chicago, October 9, 1893).

31. AAB, Ireland to Gibbons, St. Paul, December 26, 1895.

32. Fogarty, *O'Connell,* 253.

33. ASV-SdiS 280 (1897): fasc. 4, Satolli to Rampolla, Washington, September 17, 1895.

34. Ireland's silence on the dismissal of O'Connell is striking. For example, there is no mention of it in his own papers, and indeed virtually no correspondence to or from him survives from the last half of 1895.

35. See the perceptive treatment in Daniel P. O'Neill, "The Development of an American Priesthood: Archbishop John Ireland and the Saint Paul Diocesan Clergy, 1884–1918," *Journal of American Ethnic History* 4 (1985): 33–52.

36. Here and below, see ASV-DASU, St. Paul, fasc. 7, Ryan to Satolli, Dublin, April 29 and May 14, 1895, and Ryan to Martinelli, Oshkosh, April 27, 1899; APF-NS, 76:594–626, Ryan to Leo XIII, Mount St. Bernard [United Kingdom], September 27, 1892; Ireland to Ledochowski, St. Paul, May 15, 1893, and June 2, 1896; Brother Gerard to Ledochowski, Manchester, June 17, 1896.

37. ASV-DASU, St. Paul, fasc. 8, Nichols to Satolli, Litchfield, December 5, 1895, Satolli to Ireland, Washington, December 9, 1895, and Ireland to Satolli, St. Paul, December 28, 1895.

38. Here and below, see ASV-DASU, St. Paul, fasc. 12, Ireland to Martinelli, St. Paul, January 29, 1897.

39. ASV-DASU, St. Paul, fasc. 14 for the notarized statements, and fasc. 19 for Frik to Martinelli, n.p., January 18, 1897.

40. ASV-DASU, St. Paul, fasc. 16 and 17, Koering to Martinelli, New Trier, December 11, 1897, Pax to Martinelli, Sleepy Eye, September 18, 1897, and Ireland to Koering, St. Paul, December 8, 1897.

41. ASV-DASU, St. Paul, fasc. 1, Ireland to Satolli, St. Paul, September 5, 1896. In 1897 Keul, writing from a Trappist monastery, complained to Martinelli that Ireland would not advance him money for clothing.

42. APF-NS, 111:119, Satolli to Ledochowski, Washington, August 10, 1896, asking authorization to hear Rosen's appeal from the metropolitan court in St. Paul. See also ASV-DASU, St. Paul, fasc. 6, Ireland to Satolli, St. Paul, July 7, 1896, and ASV-SdiS 280 (1898): fasc. 2, Rosen to Rampolla, Madison, Minn., July 3, 1897.

43. ASV-DASU, St. Paul, fasc. 15, six parishioners of Wilno to Martinelli, April 20, 1897.

44. ASV-DASU, St. Paul, fasc. 21, Ireland to Martinelli, St. Paul, October 31, 1898. Two years earlier Ireland had threatened DeGraff, another of his colonies, with interdict because of financial irregularities. See JIP, roll 5, Ireland to O'Connor, St. Paul, December 24, 1896.

45. See the analysis in O'Neill, "American Priesthood," especially p. 47.

46. As quoted in Zwierlein, *Corrigan,* 152.

47. JIP, roll 5, Magnien to Ireland, Baltimore, March 26, 1895.

48. JIP, roll 5, O'Gorman to Ireland, Washington, January 10, 1895.

49. The documents are in APF-NS, 97:613–625, Satolli to Ledochowski, Washington, March 22, 1895, and Ireland to Ledochowski, St. Paul, March 18, 1895.

50. ASV-SdiS 280 (1897): fasc. 4, Satolli to Rampolla, Washington, September 17, 1895.

51. APF-NS, 97:633–641, Ireland to Ledochowski, St. Paul, October 17, 1895, and Ledochowski to O'Gorman, Rome, December 16, 1895 (draft).

52. AAB, Ireland to Gibbons, St. Paul, January 13, 1896. Ireland's information came from his suffragan, Shanley of Jamestown, just back from Rome, where he had gone to defend himself against charges that he supported secret societies. See APF-NS, 79:542–543, Ireland to Ledochowski, St. Paul, December 10, 1895, and 679–681, Satolli to Ledochowski, Washington, August 13, 1895.

53. JIP, roll 5, *Western Watchman* (St. Louis), April 23, 1896, full text. Satolli found the sermon "loyal and sincere" (see ASV-SdiS 280 [1897]: fasc. 4, Satolli to Rampolla, Washington, April 28, 1896).

54. ASV-DASU, St. Paul, fasc. 10, mimeographed narrative of Ireland's remarks, and Ireland to Satolli, St. Paul, June 10, 1896. In this letter Ireland also protested that his financial difficulties had been exaggerated. Satolli reported all this to Rome. APF-NS, 97:948–949, Satolli to Ledochowski, Washington, June 19, 1896.

55. For the text see Ahern, *Life of Keane,* 172.

56. For attempts by John Zahm, C.S.C., to secure a similar doctorate for himself, see APF-NS, 33:422, Zahm to Ledochowski, Notre Dame, June 20, 1893 and May 2, 1894, and 55:198–204, Satolli to Ledochowski, Washington, January 15, 1895.

57. ACUA, Keane papers, Ireland to Keane, St. Paul, July 29, 1895. Thomas E. Shields did join the Catholic University faculty in 1902 and was, at the time of his death in 1921, one of its luminaries.

58. ASV-SdiS 280 (1897): fasc. 2, Keane to Rampolla, Washington, June 23, 1893.

59. ASV-SdiS 43 (1903): fasc. 1, Satolli to Rampolla, Washington, July 10, 1896, n.d., and August 11, 1896. For a close analysis of these and related documents, see the excellent treatment of Wister, *Satolli,* 134–137.

60. See Ahern, *Life of Keane,* 170–178.

61. Keane to Garrigan, San Jose, November 1, 1896, quoted in Ahern, *Life of Keane,* 193.

62. McQuaid to Corrigan, Rochester, October 3, 1896, quoted in Zwierlein, *Life of McQuaid,* 3:241.

63. *Catholic Herald* (New York), October 24, 1896. When Archbishop Sebastiano Martinelli succeeded Satolli, Ireland commented, "I hope Mgr. Martinelli enjoys the success of his predecessor, but he has a difficult task before him . . . to match Cardinal Satolli's prudence and intelligence, and to win as high a place in public esteem" (see ASV-SdiS 280 [1897]: fasc. 4, Ireland to Rampolla, St. Paul, August 23, 1896).

64. ASV-SdiS 43 (1903): fasc. 1, Bouquillon to Rampolla, Washington, November 17, 1896, and Rampolla to Bouquillon, the Vatican, December 3, 1896 (draft), reassuring the agitated professor.

65. See, for example, ASV-SdiS 43 (1903): fasc. 1, Martinelli to Rampolla, Washington, November 17, 1896.

66. See Ahern, *Life of Keane,* 185–197.

67. AUND, Hudson papers, Spalding to Hudson, Peoria, December 6, 1896.

68. ACUA, Bouquillon papers, Ireland to Magnien, St. Paul, November 19, 1896, and ASV-SdiS 43 (1903): fasc. 1, Ireland to Satolli, n.p., n.d. [but before December 5, 1896] (copy).

69. *New York Herald,* October 27, 1896.

70. See Louis W. Koenig, *Bryan* (New York: G. P. Putnam's Sons, 1971), 221–254, especially p. 249.

71. See, for example, *St. Paul Pioneer Press,* October 11, 1896. The "commune" referred to the bloody class conflict in Paris, 1870–71. For "twenty representative men," see note 74, below.

72. Moynihan, *Life of Ireland,* 261.

73. See Martin, *Hill,* 425–428.

74. JJHP, g.c., Hill to Hanna, St. Paul, September 30, 1896 (longhand and typed copies).

75. ASV-SdiS 280 (1898): fasc. 2, Hearst to Rampolla, New York, October 14, 1896 (cable), Rampolla to Martinelli, the Vatican, October 15, 1896 (cable), Martinelli to Rampolla, Washington, October 20, 1896, Ireland to Rampolla, St. Paul, November 16, 1896, and Rampolla to Ireland, the Vatican, December 12, 1896 (cable).

76. JIP, roll 5, O'Connell to Ireland, Rome, December 2, 1896.

77. JIP, roll 5, Keane to Ireland, Rome, December 21, 1896. Despite Satolli's continuing opposition, Keane became consultor to Propaganda and to the Congregation of Studies when he settled in Rome at the end of 1896. See Ahern, *Keane,* 213–243.

78. *New York World,* March 29, 1897.

79. JIP, roll 5, Elkins to Ireland, Washington, December 10, 1896, "confidential."

80. ASV-SdiS 280 (1898): fasc. 2, Kerens to Rampolla, Washington, March 30, 1897, and JIP, roll 6, Elkins to Rampolla, Washington, April 9, 1897 (copy).

81. Margaret Leach, *In the Days of McKinley* (New York: Harper & Brothers, 1959), 106–107, thinks McKinley was ignorant of McKenna's religious affiliation.

82. Edmund Morris, *The Rise of Theodore Roosevelt* (New York: Coward, McCann, & Geoghegan, 1979), 543–545, 559. McKinley appointed Roosevelt assistant secretary of the navy.

83. JJHP, Seminary papers, box 5, "Subscribers." The amount was $10,000.

84. JIP, roll 6, Maria Storer to Ireland, Cincinnati, January 23, 1897.

85. JJHP, g.c., Hill to Hanna, St. Paul, March 6, 1897 (copy). The telegram is quoted in the letter. For Ireland's original preference for Merriam, see *New York World,* March 29, 1897.

86. JIP, roll 6, O'Connell to Ireland, Rome, July 21, 1897.

87. ASV-SdiS 280 (1898): fasc. 2, Ireland to Rampolla, Washington, October 29, 1897, and Rampolla to Ireland, the Vatican, December 1, 1897 (draft).

88. AAB, Ireland to Gibbons, St. Paul, December 2, 1896.

89. JIP, roll 5, Ireland to Moynihan, St. Paul, December 9, 1896. Humphrey Moynihan was aided in this task by James M. Reardon. See Reardon, *Diocese of St. Paul,* 323–324.

90. AAB, Ireland to Gibbons, St. Paul, December 2, 1896.

91. For the whole correspondence, here and below, see APF-NS, 119:643–765, including Ireland to Ledochowski, St. Paul, November 16, 1896, February 10, March 18, and April 29, 1897; Keane to the secretary of Propaganda, Rome, March 5, 1897, and to Ledochowski, Rome, June 11, 1897; Martinelli to Ledochowski, Washington, December 18, 1896; Ledochowski to Ireland, Rome, March 29, 1897, and to Trobec, August 25, 1897.

92. *New York World,* March 26, 1897.

93. Standard accounts in Fogarty, *O'Connell,* 272–274, Barry, *German Americans,* 230–234, Ahern, *Life of Keane,* 237–239, and especially Peter E. Hogan, *The Catholic University of America — 1896–1903: The Rectorship of Thomas J. Conaty* (Washington: Catholic University of America Press, 1949), 132–158, 182–190.

94. ADR-UND, Ireland to O'Connell, St. Paul, September 13, 1897.

95. For what follows see ASV-SdiS 43 (1903): fasc. 2, for four accounts of the meeting: Ireland to Rampolla, Washington, October 28, 1897, Keane to Rampolla, Rome, November 12, 1897, Gibbons to Leo XIII, n.p., n.d., "sur l'affaire Schroeder," and Memorandum to "Eminence," in Schroeder's hand (in French, 15 pages). Also here are the notarized statements attesting to Schroeder's personal habits (and Italian versions of them), as well as Conaty's formal opening statement. The account given here differs from other accounts on the crucial point that Conaty accused Schroeder of drunkenness in his opening statement, as is clear from Ireland's and Keane's letters, but not clear from the

sanitized version printed in Hogan, *Conaty*, 183–188. For confirmation see APF-NS 125 (1898): 637–638, Martinelli to Rampolla, Washington, October 22, 1897 (copy).

96. Eight of the ten statements were notarized between October 22 and October 28 (that is, after the board meeting). Of the other two, one was notarized on October 19 (the day Ireland arrived in Washington) and the other as early as June 30.

97. JIP, roll 6, Keane to Ireland, Rome, November 17, 1897.

98. ADR-UND, Ireland to O'Connell, St. Paul, January 8, 1898.

99. JIP, roll 6, O'Connell to Ireland, Rome, December 2, 1897.

100. ADR-UND, Ireland to O'Connell, St. Paul, December 3, 1897, and January 8, 1898.

Notes to Chapter XVIII, The Fortunes of War

1. JIP, roll 6, O'Connell to Ireland, Rome, January 7, 1897. "Internationalizing Americanism" is Fogarty's happy turn of phrase (*Vatican*, 143–151). About this time O'Connell began to employ some fanciful code names, including "Sparta" for Ireland, "Avignon" for O'Gorman, and "Marathon" for himself.

2. JIP, roll 6, O'Connell to Ireland, Rome, February 1, 1897.

3. Text in *Freeman's Journal* (New York), April 3, 1897.

4. JIP, roll 6, O'Connell to Ireland, Rome, July 24, 1897, and Milan, August 12, 1897.

5. ARD-UND, Ireland to O'Connell, St. Paul, December 3, 1897. O'Connell was in contact with Franz Xaver Kraus, Herman Schell, and their intimates. See the correspondence and analysis in Robert C. Ayers, "The Americanists and Franz Xaver Kraus: An Historical Analysis of an International Liberal Catholic Combination, 1897–1898" (Ph.D. diss., Syracuse University, 1981), 73–93.

6. Fogarty, *O'Connell*, 257.

7. *La Chiesa e la Società moderna. Discorsi di S. E. R. John Ireland* was privately published at Milan the following year.

8. "The most inoffensive of Liberals," Alfred Loisy called him. See Marvin R. O'Connell, "The Bishopric of Monaco, 1902: A Revision," *Catholic Historical Review* 71 (January 1985): 26–27.

9. See the letters from Klein to Ireland in JIP, rolls 5 and 6, beginning June 8, 1894.

10. Summary in McAvoy, *Great Crisis*, 166–168.

11. AUND, Klein papers, O'Connell to Klein, Rome, July 31, 1897. Klein's preface was published separately in *La revue du clergé françcais*.

12. The rigged court martial and conviction of Captain Alfred Dreyfus, a Jew, for passing military secrets to Germany resulted in an orgy of recrimination by Republicans against the army and the army's putative ally, the church. A new wave of anti-clerical legislation followed.

13. See Félix Klein, *Americanism: A Phantom Heresy* (n.p.: Klein, 1951), 25–35, 51–60. As late as 1902 the nuncio to Paris referred to Klein as "il famoso Americanista."

14. See, for example, JIP, roll 21, O'Connell to Ireland, Rome, July 23, 1889 (copy), and September 21, 1890 (photostat). For O'Connell's retrospective view of the same question, not materially different, see JIP, roll 7, O'Connell to Moynahan [*sic*], Rome, January 20, 1900.

15. Full text in Fogarty, *O'Connell*, 319–326.

16. JIP, roll 6, O'Connell to Ireland, Rome, December 2, 1897. For O'Connell's admission to the Countess Sabina that he had not read the *Life of Hecker*, see McAvoy, *Great Crisis*, 174.

17. Ahern, *Life of Keane*, 163–164.

18. Not to be confused with Magnien, Gibbons's confidant. For "Martel's" articles, see McAvoy, *Great Crisis,* 189–199.

19. ASV-SdiS 249 (1901): fasc. 4, Rampolla to Keane, the Vatican, March 27, 1898 (draft).

20. Storer and his wife had been in Rome only a few weeks before and had had a private audience with Leo XIII. See JIP, roll 6, Keane to Ireland, Rome, March 14, 1898.

21. JIP, Keane to Ireland, Rome, March 27, 29, and 30 (cables); ASV-SdiS 249 (1901): fasc. 3, Ireland to Keane, St. Paul, March 29, 1898 (cable).

22. On the war, here and below, see Philip S. Foner, *The Spanish-Cuban War and the Birth of American Imperialism, 1895–1902,* 2 vols. (New York: Monthly Review Press, 1972), and John Offner, "Washington Mission: Archbishop Ireland on the Eve of the Spanish-American War," *Catholic Historical Review* 73 (October 1987): 562–575.

23. JIP, roll 5, John Ireland "Patriotism, Its Duty and Value" (New York: Columbus Press, 1894), 12 p. This was a speech delivered to a veterans' group in New York on April 14, 1894. Theodore Roosevelt regularly read and applauded Ireland's discourses. "I count the opportunity of becoming friends with [Ireland] one of the great benefits I have derived from being in Washington." Roosevelt to O'Gorman, Washington, March 1, 1895.

24. ASV-SdiS 249 (1901): fasc. 3, Rampolla to Satolli, the Vatican, June 15, 1895, and Rampolla to Nava, the Vatican, December 15, 1897. The last date is significant, because Ireland always maintained that had he been called upon earlier he might have succeeded in helping to avert the war. Nava was the nuncio to Madrid.

25. "Tra [Fra?] due anni io e Lei governeremo gli Stati Uniti." Satolli used quotation marks. ASV-SdiS 280 (1897): fasc. 2, Satolli to Rampolla, Washington, April 13, 1894.

26. JJHP, g.c., Ireland to Hill, New York, February 26, 1898.

27. For Storer's presence, see JIP, roll 6, Storer to Ireland, Washington, April 14, 1898. Secretary of State John Sherman, ill and practically senile, played no part in the negotiations and resigned on April 25.

28. For Ireland's cables, as well as Rampolla's replies and exchanges with the nuncio in Madrid, see ASV-SdiS 249 (1901): fasc. 5 and 6. The cables were in code, transcribed into Italian. Typed copies of Ireland/Rampolla cables are in JIP, roll 6. Rampolla's cables were usually sent to the delegate, Martinelli, for transmission to Ireland, but the delegation itself was not formally involved in the negotiations.

29. Rampolla's understanding of the American Constitution was hazy, and Ireland had to explain to him that Congress, not the president, declared war.

30. Elkins kept a diary of the events of April 1898, an entry every day from April 3 through April 12, and a summary of events after April 12 on April 20. See the typed copy (54 p.) in JIP, roll 6. Unless otherwise noted, what follows is drawn from this diary and from the collection of cables, io as note 28, above.

31. *Washington Times,* April 4, 1898.

32. Frederick Rooker, speaking for the apostolic delegation, also denied to the press any knowledge of Ireland's presence.

33. JIP, roll 6, Storer to Ireland, Brussels, May 11 [1898]. Storer left Washington on April 15 to return to his post in Belgium. In Paris he met Woodford, who gave him this account.

34. See Leach, *Days of McKinley,* 182–183.

35. JIP, roll 6, Storer to Ireland, Brussels, May 11 [1898].

36. ASV-SdiS 249 (1901): fasc. 6, Keane to Rampolla, Anzio, April 14, 1898.

37. JIP, roll 6, Rooker to Elkins, Washington, April 17, 1898.

38. Rampolla replied (to Martinelli): "In my name thank Archbishop Ireland for all he has done." A useful narrative of these events is Thomas E. Cusack, "Archbishop John Ireland and the Spanish-American War: Peacemaker or Bungler" (Master's thesis, Univer-

sity of Notre Dame, 1974). See also John T. Farrell, "Archbishop Ireland and Manifest Destiny," *Catholic Historical Review* 33 (1947): 269–301, and the authorities cited there.

39. JIP, roll 6, Ireland to the editor of *Donahue's Magazine,* St. Paul, May 11, 1898 (copy).

40. ADR-UND, Ireland to O'Connell, St. Paul, May 2 and 11, 1898.

41. ASV-SdiS 249 (1901): fasc. 6, Ireland to Rampolla, St. Paul, April 29, 1898.

42. Francis A. MacNutt, *Six Decades of My Life,* 2 vols. (Brixen: Wegers Press, 1927), 2:82. For this reference to a very rare book I am grateful to Alexandra MacNutt Usher and Francis MacNutt, the grand-niece and grand-nephew of the author, and to Father Thomas Donlan, O.P.

43. JIP, roll 6, Keane to Ireland, Rome, June 19 [1898].

44. ADR-UND, Ireland to Keane, St. Paul, May 11 and 28, 1898.

45. JIP, roll 6, Rooker to Ireland, Washington, June 1, 1898.

46. ASV-SdiS 249 (1901): fasc. 6, Cambon to Maria Storer, Washington, May 9, 1898.

47. ASV-SdiS 249 (1901): fasc. 5, Keane to Rampolla, Rome, April 28, 1898, quoting verbatim Bellamy Storer's letter of a few days earlier. Keane and the Storers took on the task of gathering the testimonials.

48. JIP, roll 6, Davis to Maria Storer, n.p., May 17, 1898 (copy).

49. JIP, roll 6, Rooker to Ireland, Washington, May 16, 1898.

50. ASV-SdiS 249 (1901): fasc. 4, Ireland to Rampolla, St. Paul, May 28, 1898.

51. JIP, roll 6, O'Connell to Ireland, Rome, May 24, 1898.

52. See Klein, *Phantom Heresy,* 118–151.

53. JIP, roll 6, Keane to Ireland, Rome, June 19 [1898], and Houlgahe-Calvados (France), July 16 [1898]. Keane's two letters to Rampolla, June 2 and 13, 1898, are in ASV-SdiS 280 (1900): fasc. 2.

54. JIP, roll 6, O'Connell to Ireland, Rome, July 20, 1898.

55. Fogarty, *Vatican,* 170–171.

56. JIP, roll 6, O'Connell to Ireland, Freiburg im Breisgau, August 28, 1898.

57. Ralph E. Weber, *Notre Dame's John Zahm* (Notre Dame: University of Notre Dame Press, 1961), 129–131.

58. The book, *Evolution and Dogma,* appeared in 1896. See Weber, *Zahm,* 72–82, 106–111. For Zahm's gratitude to Ireland see JIP, roll 6, Zahm to Ireland, Notre Dame, November 11, 1898.

59. For a helpful discussion of the terminological problem, see Philip Gleason, "Coming to Terms with American Catholic History," *Societas* 3 (1973): especially p. 292–295 and 301–305.

60. ASV-SdiS 280 (1900): fasc. 2, Ireland to Ledochowski [*sic;* an error for Rampolla], St. Paul, July 11, 1898.

61. JIP, roll 6, Rooker to Ireland, Washington, June 1, 1898, with a reference to an article in the *New York Herald,* May 22.

62. Curran, *Corrigan,* 490–491. Ireland came to believe later that Corrigan had congratulated Lepidi for granting the imprimatur. See note 79, below.

63. AAB, Ireland to Gibbons, St. Paul, September 13, 1898.

64. JIP, roll 6, Touchet to Ireland, Orléans, July 24, 1898. See prologue, above.

65. JIP, roll 6, Infanta Maria de la Paz, n.p. [August, 1898].

66. See note 7, above, and JIP, roll 6, O'Connell to Ireland, n.p., June 25, 1898.

67. JIP, roll 6, Roosevelt to Ireland, Oyster Bay, September 19, 1898.

68. The Loras article appeared in the September and October 1898 numbers of the *Catholic World.* See chapter 2, note 20, above.

69. JIP, roll 6, O'Connell to Ireland, Freiburg im Breisgau, September 2, 1898.

70. ADR-UND, Ireland to O'Connell, St. Paul, October 27, 1898, in which Ireland says he was in Chicago giving a speech. The speech, "War and Peace," was actually deliv-

ered on October 18. Moynihan, *Life of Ireland,* 119, says, without citation, that Ireland was "detained by engagements" in Loretto, Pennsylvania.

71. Text in McAvoy, *Great Crisis,* 266–268.

72. JIP, roll 6, Keane to Ireland, Washington, October 18, 1898.

73. Ireland to Elliott, St. Paul, November 6, 1898, quoted in Ahern, *Life of Keane,* 271.

74. ACUA, Bouquillon papers, Ireland to Magnien, St. Paul, November 6, 1898. Gibbons had written six weeks after Ireland to protest the Lepidi imprimatur. See ASV-SdiS 280 (1900): fasc. 2.

75. ASV-SdiS 280 (1900): fasc. 2, Keane to Leo XIII, Rome, December 6, 1898.

76. ASV-DASU, St. Paul, fasc. 22, Rampolla to Martinelli, the Vatican, January 2, 1899, and Martinelli to Rampolla, Washington, January 17, 1899.

77. ASV-DASU, St. Paul, fasc. 23, Assumption parishioners to Martinelli, St. Paul, January 14, 1899; Abbot Engel to Martinelli, St. Paul, February 2, 1899; Martinelli to "Dear Sir," Washington, February 5, 1899 (copy). Some documents spell the monk's name "Meyer."

78. See the evidence cited by Ahern, *Life of Keane,* 275.

79. Ireland to Deshon, Rome, February 24, 1899, quoted in McAvoy, *Great Crisis,* 281. George Deshon was the Paulist superior. Although Ireland told Deshon "I read the letter!" he may have been exaggerating; he did not claim to have actually *seen* the original of Corrigan's letter to Lepidi, and there is no other evidence that such a letter exists. See note 62, above.

80. Full English text in McAvoy, *Great Crisis,* 379–391.

81. *London Tablet,* March 18, 1899, quoted in Vincent Holden, "A Myth in 'L'Américanisme,' " *Catholic Historical Review* 31 (1945): 157. See an analysis of Klein's preface in McAvoy, *Great Crisis,* 166–168, and Klein's own rebuttal to his critics, *Phantom Heresy,* 8–17. In the very large literature on Americanism, McAvoy remains fundamental; see especially his "Essay on Sources," 367–378. For an account of the controversy in France, written by a contemporary observer, see Houtin, *L'Américanisme,* 265–318.

82. See the comparison in Fogarty, *Vatican,* 172–173, 178–179.

83. This summary taken from David Killen, "Americanism Revisited: John Spalding and *Testem Benevolentiae,*" *Harvard Theological Review* 66 (1973): 420–421.

84. Text in *NC,* March 3, 1899.

85. Quoted in Ellis, *Life of Gibbons,* 2:71.

86. See Fogarty, *O'Connell,* 285, 291; notes 55 and 56, above.

87. Ireland to Deshon, Rome, March 16, 1899, quoted in McAvoy, *Great Crisis,* 285.

88. APF-NS, 147:86, Horstmann to Ledochowski, Cleveland, March 7, 1899.

89. ASV-SdiS 280 (1900): fasc. 3, Corrigan to Leo XIII, New York, March 10, 1899, and APF-NS, 147:144–146, Katzer et al. to Ledochowski, Milwaukee, "Pentecost," 1899. For English texts see McAvoy, *Great Crisis,* 292–293, 296–297. In the seventeenth century the French Jansenists accepted a papal condemnation, but denied that it applied to their views.

90. ADR-UND, Ireland to O'Connell, Naples, March 23, and Turin, April 17, 1899.

91. In the spring of 1899 Leo XIII, though in relatively good health, was in his eighty-ninth year.

92. As described at the beginning of this chapter.

93. For the Kraus connection see the provocative treatment in Ayers, "Kraus," 228–242, and the correspondence quoted and cited there.

94. ADR-UND, Ireland to O'Connell, the ocean, July 24, 1899.

95. See prologue, note 1, above.

96. ADR-UND, Ireland to O'Connell, Brussels, May 18, 1899.

97. Directly quoted in Baroness Eichtal to Kraus, Rome, May 29, 1899, quoted in Ayers, "Kraus," 241.

98. For O'Connell and O'Gorman at Avignon, see chapter 16, above.

99. ASV-SdiS 248 (1900): fasc. 15, O'Gorman to Rampolla, Paris, June 23, 1899. This exceedingly long letter also contained the strongest possible attack, filled with sarcasm, upon Périès and Satolli, both of whom O'Gorman knew well.

100. ADR-UND, Ireland to O'Connell, the ocean, July 24, 1899.

101. See note 97, above.

102. See the comments of Fogarty, *O'Connell,* 293–295.

103. Printed (English) minutes in APF-NS, 171:254–255. See also Curran, *Corrigan,* 501–502.

104. ADR-UND, Ireland to O'Connell, St. Paul, October 21, 1899.

105. ADR-UND, Ireland to O'Connell, St. Paul, October 21 and December 23, 1899.

106. "H.M." in *NC,* August 25, 1899, and J. St. Clair Etheridge, "The Genesis of 'Americanism,' " *North American Review* 170 (May, 1900): 679–693. Ireland's authorship of this latter piece (from which the quotation is taken, 693) is disputed. See McAvoy, *Great Crisis,* 335–336, and Ellis, *Life of Gibbons,* 2:75. Félix Klein believed Ireland was the author. For the best exposition of the American versus the European mind-set as displayed in *Testem Benevolentiae,* see Margaret Rehr, "Pope Leo XIII and 'Americanism,' " *Theological Studies* 34 (1973): 679–689.

107. AUND, Hudson papers, Spalding to Hudson, Peoria, March 1, 1899. The same day Maria Storer wrote the Vatican urging a red hat for Ireland. See ASV-SdiS 280 (1900): fasc. 3, Maria Storer to Rampolla, Brussels, March 1, 1899.

108. See Sweeney, *Life of Spalding,* 262–265.

109. JIP, roll 7, O'Connell to Ireland, Rome, March 23, 1900.

110. See Houtin, *L'Américanisme,* 435–437.

111. JIP, roll 7, O'Connell to Ireland, Rome, March 23, 1900.

112. For Caldwell and Spalding, see chapters 9, above, and 20, below.

113. Sweeney, *Life of Spalding,* 273–275, seems better informed that Ayers, "Kraus," 260, in placing the meeting in Florence rather than in Rome.

114. ASV-SdiS 248, no. 1526, Lorenzelli to Rampolla, Paris, December 8, 1902.

115. Sweeney, *Life of Spalding,* 277.

116. JIP, roll 7, McKinley to Ireland, Washington, June 11, 1900.

117. JIP, roll 7, John Ireland, *America and France* (New York: Columbia Press, 1900), 31 p. There is also here a typed version in French. Reprinted in *Church and Modern Society,* 1:9–30.

118. ASV-SdiS 248 (1901): fasc. 1, Lorenzelli to Rampolla, Paris, July 4, 1900, and (1900): fasc. 3, Lorenzelli to Rampolla, Paris, May 24 and July 21, 1900.

119. August 16, feast of St. Joachim, patron of Joachim Pecci.

120. The words quoted are from a signed article titled "The Pope's Civil Princedom," which appeared in the *North American Review* (March 1901) and was reprinted in *Church and Modern Society,* 2:195–218. Ireland spoke ex tempore at the consistory, but the article was written close enough to the event to warrant the assumption that its thesis was the same.

121. JIP, roll 8, Gibbons to Ireland, Rome, June 20, 1901, and roll 7, Lorenzelli to Ireland, Finistère, August 25, 1900. "Oration in the circle" refers to the circle of cardinals at the consistory.

122. See the correspondence quoted in Ayers, "Kraus," 262–273.

123. See, for example, ADR-UND, Rooker to O'Connell, Washington, October 22, 1900.

124. See chapter 12, especially note 39, and chapter 14, above.

125. See, for example, AAB, Ireland to Gibbons, St. Paul, October 27, November 23 and 28, 1888, and January 11, 1889.

126. Compare APF-SOCG 1042 (1892): 706–707, Ireland to Simeoni, St. Paul, [De-

cember 1891], with ASV-SdiS 280 (1900): fasc. 3, Ireland to Rampolla, St. Paul, May 25, 1900. See also John Ireland, "La Souveraineté temporelle du pape," *La Papauté et les peuples* 2 (1900): 177–188, translation of a speech delivered in Washington, December 5, 1899. "Temporal independence" was the phrase Ireland invoked as early as 1867. See chapter 5, above.

127. JIP, roll 7, Cambon to "Monsieur" [Denaro], August 29, 1900. Jules Cambon, French ambassador to Washington, nominated Ireland for the award. The certificate is also filed here. See also ASV-SdiS 248 (1901): fasc. 1, Lorenzelli to Rampolla, Paris, September 17 [or 7], 1900.

Notes to Chapter XIX, The Lady and the Hat

1. For the best example, see chapter 13, above.

2. See *St. Paul Dispatch,* May 31, 1875, reporting on Rupert Seidenbusch's episcopal consecration: "We cannot conclude this brief notice . . . without returning our thanks to the Rev. John Ireland for the courtesies extended to the reporters generally."

3. Ireland was still in England in early October. See JIP, roll 7, Halifax to Ireland, Doncaster, October 3, 1900. Lord Halifax, the famous ecumenist, wanted to meet with Ireland sometime within the following week.

4. Lincoln Steffens, *The Autobiography of Lincoln Steffens* (New York: Harcourt, Brace, 1931), 322. Steffens was at the time city editor of the *Commercial Advertiser,* and Hovey was his star reporter. I owe this reference to my friend and colleague, Professor Ronald Weber.

5. See the printed circular in JIP, roll 7, New York, October 20, 1890, citing "New York papers."

6. ASV-SdiS 280 (1900): fasc. 3, Lorenzelli to Rampolla, Paris, July 21, 1900.

7. See McAvoy, *Great Crisis,* 329.

8. MacNutt, *Six Decades,* 1:89–91.

9. JIP, roll 7, O'Gorman to Ireland, Rome, October 16 [1900].

10. JIP, roll 7, O'Gorman to Ireland, [Rome], October 20 and 23 [1900], and Maule, October 30 [1900]. For Ireland's reaction to this advice, see chapter 18, note 120, above.

11. JIP, roll 7, O'Connell to Ireland, Sorrento, December 19, 1900, and Rome, February 2 and 8, 1901.

12. JIP, roll 7, O'Gorman to Ireland, [Rome], October 20 [1900].

13. APF-NS, 194:846–862, "Relatio Archdiocesis Sancti Pauli, Anno Sancto M.C.M." This document, not in Ireland's hand but clearly in his style, has several marginal notes. For example, the $20,000 income figure is a marginal correction for $14,000. The most curious number in the document is 11,000 pupils in parochial schools. This was the same figure advanced eight years before, by both Ireland and Gibbons, at the height of the school controversy, when the Catholic population of the archdiocese had been a mere 155,000. In the interval Ireland had founded twenty-two new parishes. See Reardon, *Diocese of St.Paul,* 588–643, and chapter 14, especially note 74, above.

14. JIP, roll 7, Keane to Ireland, Dubuque, October 29, 1900.

15. ASV-SdiS 280 (1900): fasc. 1, Gibbons to Rampolla, Baltimore, April 17, 1900.

16. APF-NS, 194:727–728, Ireland to Ledochowski, St. Paul, April 29, 1900.

17. Summary in APF-NS, 194:723–725 and 735–738. Three years earlier Corrigan had similarly posed no objection to Keane's appointment to New Orleans. See APF-NS, 120:221–222, Corrigan to Martinelli, Beckmantown [N.Y.], August 9, 1897.

18. Ahern, *Life of Keane,* 301–309.

19. JIP, roll 7, Keane to Ireland, Dubuque, October 29, 1900.

20. A point astutely made by Fogarty, *Vatican,* 179.

21. Quoted in Ahern, *Life of Keane,* 315–316.

22. JIP, roll 8, Taft to M. Storer, Manila, May 19, 1901, and roll 7, December 4, 1900 (copies).

23. Quoted in Henry F. Pringle, *The Life and Times of William Howard Taft,* 2 vols. (New York: Farrar, 1939), 1:221–222.

24. JIP, roll 7, Taft to M. Storer, Manila, December 4, 1900 (copy).

25. *Reports of the Taft Philippine Commission,* 56th Cong., 2d sess., 1900–01, S. Doc. 112 (serial 4040), 30.

26. See Ireland's comments on the terna for New Orleans, APF-NS, 120:219–220, Ireland to Martinelli, St. Paul, August 20, 1897.

27. The Recollects were a canonically independent offshoot of the Augustinians.

28. This was Ireland's attitude toward the Spanish friars, an attitude derived mostly from informants on the scene. See, for example, JIP, roll 9, Smith to Ireland, May 7, 1903. James F. Smith was a lawyer-soldier who fought in the Philippines campaigns and later served as justice of the Filipino Supreme Court. He was governor-general from 1906 to 1909.

29. See Frank T. Reuter, *Catholic Influence on American Colonial Policies, 1898–1904* (Austin: University of Texas Press, 1967), 69, 82, 90.

30. ASV-SdiS 249 (1901): fasc. 4, Ireland to Rampolla, St. Paul, May 28, 1898.

31. JIP, roll 7, Taft to M. Storer, Manila, December 4, 1900 (copy).

32. JIP, roll 8, Rampolla to Ireland, the Vatican, May 2, 1901.

33. JIP, roll 8, Ireland to Rampolla, St. Paul, June 16, 1901 (copy). For the contact with Root, see Oscar M. Alfonso, *Theodore Roosevelt and the Philippines, 1897–1909* (New York: Oriole, 1970), 147.

34. JIP, roll 8, Rampolla to Ireland, the Vatican, July 2, 1901.

35. See ADR-UND, Ireland to O'Connell, New York, June 7, 1901; AAB, Ireland to Gibbons, St. Paul, August 25, 1901; and JIP, roll 8, O'Connell to Ireland, Rome, June 6, 1901.

36. See JIP, roll 8, John Ireland, "50 Years of Catholicity in the Northwest," n.p., n.d., 16 p., and *Church and Modern Society,* 2:253–278.

37. AAB, Ireland to Gibbons, St. Paul, August 25, 1901.

38. Taft papers, University of Notre Dame microfilm, Ireland to Taft, St. Paul, September 19, 1901; JIP, roll 8, Taft to Ireland, Manila, October 15, 1901.

39. Archives of the Josephite Fathers, Baltimore, Ireland to J.R. Slattery, St. Paul, June 18, 1901. Slattery, a Josephite, shared with Ireland a deep interest in the amelioration and evangelization of American blacks. I owe this reference to Professor William L. Portier.

40. JIP, roll 8, Schurman to Ireland, Ithaca, February 6, 1902. Schurman had chaired the first fact-finding commission to the Philippines in 1899. See Reuter, *Catholic Influence,* 68. The Taft Commission followed and evolved into the civil government of the islands. The phrase "Taft Commission" is therefore ambiguous, because it was also applied to the delegation Taft headed in the direct negotiations with the Vatican, as below.

41. JIP, roll 8, O'Connell to Ireland, Rome, November 25, 1901. Keane's lecture at Harvard took place in 1890. See Ahern, *Life of Keane,* 105.

42. AAB, Ireland to Gibbons, Washington, November 7, 1901.

43. AAB, Ireland to Gibbons, [Washington], December 15, 1901. See also JIP, roll 8, William H. Ward to Ireland, New York, March 7, 1902. Ward was editor of *The Independent.*

44. APF-NS, 215:131–133, "Minutes" (printed), November 21 and 22, 1901. The specific matter addressed by Corrigan was the provision and training of priests to serve Croatian immigrants, a task, he said, in which Ireland's seminary excelled.

45. AAB, Ireland to Gibbons, [Washington], December 15, 1901.

46. Ireland to B. Storer, Washington, November 3 and December 3, 1901, in Maria

Longworth Storer, *In Memoriam: Bellamy Storer, with Personal Reminiscences of President McKinley, President Roosevelt and John Ireland, Archbishop of St. Paul* (Boston: M. L. Storer, 1923), 57–59.

47. Storer, *In Memoriam*, 18.

48. See Mark Sullivan, *Our Times: The United States, 1900–1925*, 6 vols. (New York: Scribner's, 1926–35), 3:99–128, for the best treatment of the Storer-Roosevelt-Ireland affair. See also Moynihan, *Life of Ireland*, 345–355.

49. JIP, roll 7, M. Storer to Ireland, Barcelona, October 8, 1900. For some reason this letter was written in French.

50. Storer, *In Memoriam*, 21.

51. The earliest surviving letter to Ireland from Maria Storer is dated March 8, 1896. It may have been before that, however, that she contributed $10,000 to Ireland's real estate syndicate (see chapter 16, note 29, above).

52. ASV-SdiS 43 (1903): fasc. 1, M. Storer to Rampolla, Cincinnati, October 5, 1896.

53. See Morris, *Rise of Roosevelt*, 440–433, and Storer, *In Memoriam*, 35–36.

54. During this time the letters from the Storers to Ireland came from Deauville, San Sebastian, Biarritz, and Paris. See JIP, roll 8.

55. JIP, roll 8, M. Storer to Rampolla, n.p., n.d., and to Leo XIII, Biarritz, October 19, 1901 (copies). She quoted specifically Roosevelt's letter of April 30, 1900, to Bellamy. See Storer, *In Memoriam*, 42–43.

56. See the correspondence quoted in Sullivan, *Our Times*, 105–106.

57. Quoted in Ireland to B. Storer, in Storer, *In Memoriam*, 59.

58. The year before she had tried to intrude herself into the church-state negotiations in Cuba. See ASV-SdiS 249 (1901): fasc. 5, M. Storer to Rampolla, Madrid, March 14, 1900, Leonard Wood to M. Storer, Havana, February 21, 1900, and Rampolla to M. Storer, the Vatican, March 23, 1900 (draft).

59. JIP, roll 8, M. Storer to Ireland, New York, March 26, 1902, and n.p., [April 14, 1902].

60. Quoted in Storer, *In Memoriam*, 69.

61. Both Root's dislike and the curia's favor sprang from the same source, Sbarretti's strong papal and anti-masonic stance as temporary archbishop of Havana immediately after the American occupation of Cuba. See Reuter, *Catholic Influence*, 48, 52–54. The quotation is from JIP, roll 8, O'Gorman to Ireland, Rome, May 7 [1902].

62. See quotations in Storer, *In Memoriam*, 64.

63. Quoted in Storer, *In Memoriam*, 69.

64. Curran, *Corrigan*, 512, says Corrigan died on May 2, while Cohalan, *New York*, 174, says May 5.

65. JIP, roll 8, O'Gorman to Ireland, Rome, May 7 [1902].

66. JIP, roll 8, O'Gorman to Ireland, Rome, May 14 and 24 [1902].

67. JIP, roll 8, O'Gorman to Ireland, July 8, 1902. See also Ireland to Oster, November 6, 1902. John N. Stariha was appointed bishop of Lead, a new diocese comprising the western half of South Dakota, and James J. Keane went to Cheyenne. The latter was no kin to John J. Keane.

68. JIP, roll 8, O'Gorman to Ireland, Rome, May 24 and June 1 [1902].

69. JIP, roll 8, O'Gorman to Ireland, Rome, June 5 [1902]. The gift was eight volumes of Roosevelt's literary work.

70. Taft to Helen Taft, June 7, 1902, quoted in Pringle, *Life of Taft*, 1:228.

71. JIP, roll 8, O'Gorman to Ireland, Rome, June 5 [1902].

72. JIP, roll 8, O'Gorman to Ireland, June 5 and 17 [1902].

73. For copies of this and other relevant documents, see JIP, roll 8. They are printed in "Papers Relating to Friars' Land Negotiations," *Annual Reports of the War Department*

for the Fiscal Year Ended June 30, 1902, 57th Cong., 2d sess., 1902–03, H. Doc. 2 (serial 4443), 233–256.

74. See Ireland to M. Storer, St. Paul, March 29, 1902, quoted in Storer, *In Memoriam,* 66–67.

75. The number of Spanish friars in the Philippines declined from 1,013 in 1898 to 216 at the end of 1903. See Reuter, *Catholic Influence,* 155.

76. Taft to Roosevelt, Manila, September 13, 1902, quoted in Reuter, *Catholic Influence,* 147. See also JIP, roll 8, Taft to O'Gorman, Manila, October 17, 1902.

77. JIP, roll 8, Roosevelt to Ireland, Oyster Bay, July 23, 1902. See also the letter of August 8, 1902.

78. ACUA, O'Connell papers, Ireland to O'Connell, St. Paul, June 28, 1903.

79. See, for example, *Catholic Universe* (Cleveland), July 25, 1902; *Freeman's Journal* (New York), July 26, 1902; and the clippings in JIP, roll 8.

80. Interview with the Associated Press, *The New Century* (Washington), July 26, 1902. In the same issue the death of Cardinal Ledochowski in Rome was announced.

81. See, for example, JIP, roll 9, Hennessy to Ireland, Pagsanghan, June 27, and Campbell to Ireland, Manila, January 25, 1904.

82. Reuter, *Catholic Influence,* 153–155.

83. JIP, roll 9, Roosevelt to Ireland, Washington, June 3, 1904.

84. Ireland to M. Storer, St. Paul, September 28, 1902, quoted in Storer, *In Memoriam,* 73.

85. Ireland to B. Storer, St. Paul, January 5, 1904, quoted in Storer, *In Memoriam,* 92.

86. Sullivan, *Our Times,* 115–116.

87. JIP, roll 8, O'Connell to Ireland, Rome, October 6, 1902. On Ledochowski's death see note 80, above.

88. ADR-UND, Ireland to O'Connell, St. Paul, January 14, 1903.

89. See Fogarty, *O'Connell,* 294, 298, 300.

90. Ireland to M. Storer, St. Paul, January 9, 1904, in Storer, *In Memoriam,* 95–96.

91. See Storer, *In Memoriam,* 96, 106–107.

92. JIP, roll 21, Roosevelt to Ireland, Washington, February 21, 1906. Also here are typed copies of Storer's side of the correspondence. See also Sullivan, *Our Times,* 119–121.

93. See note 55, above.

94. Ireland to M. Storer, Rome, April 6, 1906, quoted in Storer, *In Memoriam,* 117.

95. Here and below, see Sullivan, *Our Times,* 121–124.

96. JIP, roll 11, M. Storer to Ireland, Saranac Lake, N.Y., January 4 and February 3, 1907. Some years later there were brief gestures of reconciliation. See chapter 20, below.

Notes to Chapter XX, "Evening Is Coming On"

1. Reardon, *Diocese of St. Paul,* 376–378, and Alan K. Lathrop, "Emmanuel L. Masqueray, 1861–1917," *Minnesota History* 7 (Summer 1980): 43. Lathrop says it was raining, but Reardon, who was present, says not. The fullest account, unsigned but Irelandian in its style, is *A&D* 1 (1907): 99–151. On the building of the Cathedral, here and below, see Reardon, *Diocese of St. Paul,* 372–381.

2. Strictly speaking, the term "pro-cathedral" is restricted to the church in a see city that for some reason has no proper cathedral. Minneapolis was not a see city until 1966, and since then the church Ireland built has been designated a "co-cathedral." See Reardon, *Diocese of St. Paul,* 382. I have used the more familiar term "Basilica of St. Mary," of which Reardon himself was the pastor for many years.

3. Hill explicitly denied a press report that he had contributed anything to the cathedral. It is possible, however, that the $15,000 he gave Ireland in January 1907 was intended for

this purpose, since this gift was separated from the other recorded ones by eight or nine years. See chapter 16, especially note 26. On the other hand, there was an economic recession in 1907, and Ireland may have needed aid similar to what he had received from Hill in the past.

4. See, for example, Archives of the Cathedral of St. Paul, Smith to Ireland, St. Paul, July 28, 1908, and Ireland to Smith, St. Paul, August 1, 1908. I owe copies of this material to my friend the present rector of the cathedral, Monsignor Ambrose V. Hayden.

5. Archives of the Cathedral of St. Paul, Ireland to Esther O'Connor, St. Paul, September 25, 1905.

6. Personal interview with Enous Gallagher, Burnsville, April 18, 1980, tape at MHS. I owe this reference to the kindness of Ann Regan, the interviewer.

7. Archives of the Cathedral of St. Paul, Ireland to Smith, St. Paul, September 1, 1906.

8. AAB, Ireland to Gibbons, St. Paul, April 8, 1911.

9. JIP, roll 11, Ireland to pastors, St. Paul, May 20, 1911 (printed).

10. Compare the figures in Reardon, *Diocese of St. Paul*, 378–379, 385–386. By 1911 the cost had risen to $2,750,000 (see note 8, above).

11. See JIP, roll 9, for the correspondence in 1905.

12. Lathrop, "Masqueray," 45–56. Masqueray was born in Dieppe and raised in Rouen and Paris.

13. On the controversy, here and below, see JIP, roll 11, "Apostolic Delegation, Washington, D.C., Record in the Matter of the Appeal of the Reverend John T. Harrison against the Most Reverend John Ireland, Archbishop of St. Paul," 1911 (75 printed p.), for the relevant documents, most of them notarized.

14. Ireland to M. Storer, Rome, April 6, 1906, in Storer, *In Memoriam*, 116. On the banquet, see newspaper clippings, Ireland papers, Archdiocesan Chancery, St. Paul, folder 1.

15. McNamara, *American College*, 386, 747. Though he had occasionally corresponded with Alfred Loisy and was friendly with one or two "progressive" Italians, Ireland had no interest in — nor, probably, any understanding of — the issues raised by Modernism. Loisy himself is the best witness to this: see *Mémoires pour servir à l'histoire religieuse de notre temps*, 3 vols. (Paris: Nourry, 1930–31), 1:547. Ireland wrote several articles in the *North American Review* (April 1907 and January, February, and April 1908) in support of Pius X's policies vis-à-vis Modernism. None of these pieces was theologically significant. See also JIP, roll 21, Merry del Val to Ireland, the Vatican, February 7, 1908.

16. AUND, Klein papers, Ireland to Klein, St. Paul, December 7, 1911, and JIP, roll 11 (partial copy).

17. Hurley, *On Good Ground*, 228–240.

18. See, for example, JIP, roll 7, Ireland to Howe, St. Paul, June 10, 1900, thanking her for a copy of her *Reminiscences* and for her recent visit. See also JJHP, g.c., Ireland to Hill, January 6, 1897, inviting Hill to tea in order to meet Crawford. Ireland acted as "godfather" to Crawford's eldest son at the latter's confirmation and first communion (JIP, roll 6, Crawford to Ireland, Mentone, March 16, 1899).

19. See especially JIP, roll 12, "Notes," January 4, 1912, taken by one of the seminary professors on a monologue given by Ireland on the Corinth campaign.

20. See *A&D* 1 (1907): 2–6 for Ireland's graceful "Introduction" to the journal.

21. JIP, roll 13, Falconio to Ireland, Rome, February 12, 1916.

22. AAB, Ireland to Gibbons, St. Paul, May 1, 1910. For an account of the consecration, see *Minneapolis Tribune*, May 20, 1910. The bishops consecrated were James O'Reilly for Fargo, Patrick Heffron for Winona, Timothy Corbett for Crookston, Joseph Busch for Lead, Vincent Wehrle for Bismarck, and John Lawler as auxiliary to Ireland.

23. The service was Henry Romeike, Inc., 110–112 West Twenty-sixth Street, New York; the clippings are in scrapbooks at ACHS.

24. JIP, rolls 11, 12, 13, and 21. See, for example, Leslie to Ireland, London, December 23, 1913, and Port Washington, November 4, 1915.

25. JIP, roll 21, Ireland to Benedict XV, n.p., [September 1914] (copy).

26. JIP, roll 12, Gibbons to Ireland, Baltimore, September 30, 1914.

27. JIP, roll 12, O'Gorman to Ireland, Naples, November [sic; for December] 5 [1914], and B. Storer to Ireland, Rome, November 29, 1914. Two years later Maria Storer attempted to resurrect the former chatty correspondence with Ireland; see roll 13, M. Storer to Ireland, Cincinnati, December 13 [1916].

28. JIP, roll 12, O'Gorman to Ireland, Rome, November 16 [1914]. In addition to Gibbons the American cardinals were John Farley of New York and William O'Connell of Boston, who had both been elevated in 1911.

29. AAB, Ireland to Gibbons, St. Paul, September 27, 1914.

30. JIP, roll 11, Roosevelt to Ireland, Washington, November 20, 1908, and Taft to Ireland, Cincinnati, November 21, 1908.

31. See JIP, roll 12, Taft to Ireland, New Haven, n.d. [1914]. "I cherish our friendship and our common view of many, many things."

32. JIP, roll 21, Merry del Val to Ireland, April 24 and May 26, 1910.

33. *New York Herald,* February 8 and April 10, 1910.

34. JIP, roll 11, Roosevelt to Ireland, July 27 [1910], and Egan to Ireland, Copenhagen, May 16, 1910.

35. JIP, roll 11, Ireland to Falconio, St. Paul, July 27, 1908 (copy). Diomede Falconio was then apostolic delegate.

36. Zwierlein, *Life of McQuaid,* 3:251.

37. JIP, roll 11, O'Connell to Ireland, San Francisco, July 10, 1910, and roll 12, Richmond, September 8, 1915.

38. JIP, roll 11, Keane to Ireland, Dubuque, December 19, 1911.

39. JIP, roll 11, Gibbons to Ireland, n.p., September 13, 1909.

40. Ahern, *Life of Keane,* 354–363.

41. Instances in Sweeney, *Life of Spalding,* 313, 315.

42. APF-NS, 264:632–633, Ireland to Gotti, St. Paul, August 5, 1902. Cardinal Gotti was Ledochowski's successor as prefect of Propaganda.

43. APF-NS, 264:612–613, Riordan to Satolli, Maynooth, November 15, 1902. The baroness claimed the intimacy had occurred between Spalding and her sister, Mary Gwendolen—"Mamie"—now the Marchise des Monstiers-Merinville. "The intimacy between the two," Riordan wrote, "continued for nearly twenty years. That is, whenever they met or travelled together. . . . I confide this letter to your sacred honor, and ask you to destroy it and give its contents only to Cardinal Gotti." There was a double irony in that Riordan, Spalding's oldest friend and the one most certain of his innocence, should have made the discovery, and that Satolli, Spalding's long-time opponent, should have been, as a matter of routine, in charge of the case within Propaganda. There is no evidence that Satolli fulfilled his duties in any biased way, though of course he did not destroy Riordan's letter. The rumors about Spalding and Mamie Caldwell went back many years; see, for example, chapter 9, note 52, above. See also Sweeney, *Life of Spalding,* 308–312, 347–352.

44. ADR-UND, Ireland to O'Connell, St. Paul, August 7, 1908.

45. JIP, roll 21, Falconio to Ireland, Washington, September 23, 1908.

46. JIP, roll 12, Riordan to Ireland, San Francisco, December 17, 1913.

47. AAB, Ireland to Gibbons, St. Paul, December 23, 1912.

48. JIP, roll 11, Gibbons to Ireland, Baltimore, January 2, 1908.

49. Hurley, *On Good Ground,* 228–238.

50. JIP, roll 21, Ireland to Welch, St. Augustine, January 21, 1918.

51. Quoted in Sampson, "The Ireland Connection," 15.

52. "Introduction" in Elliott, *Life of Hecker*, xv.

53. JIP, roll 13, "Last Will and Testament," September 27, 1916 (amended 1918). About one-quarter of Ireland's estate had been bequeathed to him by Bishop McGolrick of Duluth who predeceased him by some months.

54. JIP, roll 12, Ford to Ireland, New York, November 28, 1915. For the "peace ship," see Robert Lacey, *Ford: The Men and the Machine* (Boston: Little, Brown, 1986), 137–147.

55. Copy, dated April 18, 1917, in JIP, roll 13.

56. JIP, roll 13, Ireland to Schaefer, Washington, April 24, 1917 (telegram).

57. JIP, roll 13, Ireland to Sister St. Rose, St. Augustine, January 26, 1918.

58. The cause of death was given as chronic myocarditis, complicated by arteriosclerosis. I owe a copy of the death certificate to the kindness of Professor Joseph Connors.

59. JIP, roll 13, Larpenteur to O'Gorman, St. Paul, September 30, 1918.

60. Quoted in Ellis, *Life of Gibbons*, 2:432–433.

Bibliography

This partial bibliography includes references to works cited in more than one chapter of this book, to major works by John Ireland, and to works about John Ireland.

Acta et Decreta Concilii Plenarii Baltimorensis Tertii in Ecclesia Metropolitana Baltimorensi a die IX. Novembris usque ad diem VII. Decembris A. D. MDCCCLXXXIV. Baltimore: John Murphy, 1884.

Acta et Decreta Concilii Plenarii Baltimorensis Tertii; A. D. MDCCCLXXXIV. Baltimore: John Murphy, 1886.

Ahern, Patrick H. *The Catholic University of America, 1887–1896: The Rectorship of John J. Keane.* Washington: Catholic University of America Press, 1948.

Ahern, Patrick H. *The Life of John J. Keane, Educator and Archbishop, 1839–1918.* Milwaukee: Bruce, 1954.

Allong, Louis. "Monseigneur Ireland," *Revue d'histoire ecclésiastique et d'archéologie religieuse du diocèse de Belley* 15 (1923): 42–60.

Aubert, Roger. *Le Pontificat de Pie IX (1846–1878).* Paris: Bloud & Gay, 1951.

———. "L'Église catholique de la crise de 1848 à la première guerre mondiale." In *Nouvelle histoire de l'église,* 5 vols. Paris: Éditions de Seuil, 1975.

Ayers, Robert C. "The Americanists and Franz Xaver Kraus: An Historical Analysis of an International Liberal Catholic Combination, 1897–1898." Ph.D. diss., Syracuse University, 1981.

Barry, Colman J. *The Catholic Church and German Americans.* Milwaukee: Bruce, 1953.

———. *Worship and Work.* St. Paul: North Central Publishing Co., 1956.

Bland, Joan. *Hibernian Crusade.* Washington: Catholic University of America Press, 1951.

Browne, Henry J. *The Catholic Church and the Knights of Labor.* Washington: Catholic University of America Press, 1949.

Callahan, Nelson J., ed. *The Diary of Richard L. Burtsell, Priest of New York: The Early Years, 1865–1868.* New York: Arno Press, 1978.

Carlen, Claudia, ed. *The Papal Encyclicals, 1878–1903.* [Saginaw, Mich.]: McGrath Publishing Company, 1981.

Carmody, Charles J. "Rechabites in Purple: A History of the Catholic Temperance Movement in the Northwest." Master's thesis, St. Paul Seminary, 1953.

The Catholic Encyclopedia. 15 vols. New York: Robert Appleton, 1911.

Clapesattle, Helen. *The Doctors Mayo.* Minneapolis: University of Minnesota Press, 1941.

Cohalan, Florence D. *A Popular History of the Archdiocese of New York.* Yonkers, N.Y.: United States Catholic Historical Society, 1983.

Connors, Joseph B. *Journey Toward Fulfillment: A History of the College of St. Thomas.* St. Paul: College of St. Thomas, 1986.

Curran, Robert Emmett. *Michael Augustine Corrigan and the Shaping of Conservative Catholicism in America, 1878–1902.* New York: Arno Press, 1978.

Cusack, Thomas E. "Archbishop John Ireland and the Spanish-American War: Peacemaker or Bungler." Master's thesis, University of Notre Dame, 1974.

Dease, Dennis J. "The Theological Influence of Orestes Brownson and Isaac Hecker on John Ireland's Americanist Ecclesiology." Ph.D. diss., Catholic University of America, 1978.

Dolan, Jay P. *The American Catholic Experience: A History from Colonial Times to the Present.* New York: Doubleday & Company, 1985.

———. *Catholic Revivalism: The American Experience, 1830–1900.* Notre Dame, Ind.: University of Notre Dame Press, 1978.

Duggan, John F. "The Education of a Priest: Archbishop Ireland's Talks to Seminarians." *American Ecclesiastical Review* 51 (1939): 289–300, 385–398, 494–504.

Egan, Maurice Francis. "The Most Reverend John Ireland, D.D. Archbishop of St. Paul." *The Pilgrim,* May 1906, p. 6.

———. *Recollections of a Happy Life.* New York: George H. Doran, 1924.

Elliott, Walter. *The Life of Father Hecker.* New York: Columbus Press, 1891.

———. *Le père Hecker, fondateur des "Paulists" américains, 1819–1888.* Traduit et adapté de l'Anglais avec authorisation de l'auteur. Introduction par Mgr. Ireland. Préface par l'Abbé Félix Klein. Paris: Lecoffre, 1897.

Ellis, John Tracy. "Episcopal Vision in 1884 and Thereafter." *U.S. Catholic Historian* 4 (1985): 197–222.

———. *The Formative Years of the Catholic University of America.* Washington: American Catholic Historical Association, 1946.

———. *The Life of James Cardinal Gibbons,* 2 vols. Milwaukee: Bruce, 1952.

Fahey, Charles J. "Gibbons, Ireland, Keane: The Evolution of a Liberal Catholic Rhetoric in America." Ph.D. diss., University of Minnesota, 1980.

Farrell, John T. "Archbishop Ireland and Manifest Destiny." *Catholic Historical Review* 33 (1947): 269–301.

Fogarty, Gerald P. *The Vatican and the American Hierarchy from 1870 to 1965.* Stuttgart: Anton Hiersemann, 1982.

———. *The Vatican and the Americanist Crisis: Denis J. O'Connell, American Agent in Rome, 1885–1903.* Roma: Università Gregoriana, 1974.

Folwell, William W. *A History of Minnesota,* 4 vols. St. Paul: Minnesota Historical Society, 1921–1930.

Gleason, Philip. "Baltimore III and Education." *U.S. Catholic Historian* 4 (1985): 273–306.

———. *The Conservative Reformers: German-American Catholics and the Social Order.* Notre Dame: University of Notre Dame Press, 1968.

Hennesey, James. *American Catholics: A History of the Roman Catholic Community in the Unites States.* New York: Oxford University Press, 1981.

Hogan, Peter E. *The Catholic University of America—1896–1903: The Rectorship of Thomas J. Conaty.* Washington: Catholic University of America Press, 1949.

Houtin, Albert. *L'americanisme.* Paris: Émile Nourry, 1904.

Hubbard, Lucius F. "Narrative of the Fifth Regiment." *Minnesota in the Civil and Indian Wars, 1861–1865,* 2 vols. St. Paul: Pioneer Press, 1890.

Hurley, Helen Angela. "John of St. Paul: The Making of Archbishop Ireland." Typescript in Hurley papers, Minnesota Historical Society, 1959.

———. *On Good Ground.* Minneapolis: University of Minnesota Press, 1951.

Ireland, John. "Introduction." In Samuel Mazzuchelli, *Memoirs of a Missionary Apostolic.* Chicago: W. F. Hull, 1915.

———. "Introduction." In Walter Elliott, *The Life of Father Hecker.* New York: Columbus Press, 1891. Also published in *Catholic World* 51 (June 1890): 285–293.

———. "Life of Bishop Cretin." *Acta et Dicta* 4 (1916): 187–218 and 5 (1917): 3–66.

———. *Mathias Loras, the First Bishop of Dubuque.* St. Paul: n.p. 1898. Also published in *The Catholic World* 67 (September 1897): 721–731 and 68 (October 1897): 1–12.

———. "Memoir of Rev. Lucian [*sic*] Galtier, the First Catholic Priest of St. Paul." *Collections of the Minnesota Historical Society* 3 (1870–1880): 222–230.

———. *Patriotism, Its Duty and Value.* New York: Columbus Press, 1894.

———. "Theobald Mathew." *Catholic World* 52 (October 1890): 1–8.

———. *America and France.* New York: Columbia Press, 1900.

———. "Bishop Ireland's Address." *Collections of the Minnesota Historical Society* 6 (1894): 65–73.

———. *The Church and Modern Society,* 2 vols. St. Paul: Pioneer Press, 1904.

———. "Response to Hubbard." *Collections of the Minnesota Historical Society* 12 (1908): 546.

Johnston, Patricia Condon. "Reflected Glory: The Story of Ellen Ireland." *Minnesota History* 48 (Spring 1982): 13–23.

Klein, Félix. *Americanism: A Phantom Heresy.* n.p.: Klein, 1951.

Kunz, Virginia B. *St. Paul: Saga of an American City.* Woodland Hills, Calif.: Windsor Publications, 1977.

Leach, Margaret. *In the Days of McKinley.* New York: Harper & Brothers, 1959.

MacNutt, Francis A. *Six Decades of My Life*, 2 vols. Brixen: Wegers Press, 1927.

Martin, Albro. *James J. Hill and the Opening of the Northwest*. New York: Oxford University Press, 1976.

McAvoy, Thomas T. *The Great Crisis in American Catholic History*. Chicago: Henry Regnery, 1957.

Marx, M. Seraphica. "The Life of Thomas O'Gorman, Bishop of Sioux Falls." Master's thesis, University of South Dakota, 1959.

McNamara, Robert F. *The American College in Rome, 1855–1955*. New York: Christopher Press, 1956.

The Memorial Volume: A History of the Third Plenary Council of Baltimore, November 9–December 7, 1884. Baltimore: Baltimore Publishing, 1885.

Morris, Edmund. *The Rise of Theodore Roosevelt*. New York: Coward, McCann, & Geoghegan, 1979.

Morrissey, Timothy H. "Archbishop John Ireland and the Faribault-Stillwater School Plan of the 1890's: A Reappraisal." Ph.D. diss., University of Notre Dame, 1975.

Moudry, Richard P. "The Chapel of St. Paul." Master's thesis, St. Paul Seminary, 1950.

Moynihan, Humphrey. "Archbishop Ireland's Colonies." *Acta et Dicta* 6 (1934): 212–231.

Moynihan, James H. *The Life of Archbishop Ireland*. New York: Harper & Brothers, 1953.

O'Brien, Thomas D. "Dillon O'Brien." *Acta et Dicta* 6 (1933): 35–53.

O'Connell, Marvin R. "Duchesne and Loisy on the Rue de Vaugirard." In *Studies in Catholic History in Honor of John Tracy Ellis*, edited by Nelson H. Minnich et al., p. 589–616. Wilmington: Michael Glazier, 1985.

———. "Montalembert at Mechlin: A Reprise of 1830." *Journal of Church and State* 26 (1984): 515–536.

———. "Ultramontanism and Dupanloup: The Compromise of 1865." *Church History* 53 (1984): 200–217.

———. *The Counter Reformation, 1559–1610*. New York: Harper & Row, 1974.

———. *The Oxford Conspirators*. New York: Macmillan, 1969.

O'Neill, Daniel P. "The Development of an American Priesthood: Archbishop John Ireland and the Saint Paul Diocesan Clergy, 1884–1918." *Journal of American Ethnic History* 4 (1985): 33–52.

Offner, John. "Washington Mission: Archbishop Ireland on the Eve of the Spanish-American War." *The Catholic Historical Review* 73 (October 1987), 562–575.

Oster, Anatole. "Personal Reminiscences of Bishop Cretin." *Acta et Dicta* 1 (1907): 73–88.

Pahorezki, M. Sevina. *The Social and Political Activities of William James Onahan*. Washington: Catholic University Press, 1942.

Pyle, Joseph G. *The Life of James J. Hill*, 2 vols. New York: Peter Smith, 1936.

Ravoux, Augustin. *Reminiscences, Memoirs and Lectures* (St. Paul: Brown, Treacy and Co., 1890).

Reardon, James M. "The Beginning of the Catholic Total Abstinence Movement in Minnesota." *Acta et Dicta* 1 (1908): 199–209.

———. "The Catholic Total Abstinence Movement in Minnesota." *Acta et Dicta* 2 (1909): 44–93.

———. *The Catholic Church in the Diocese of St. Paul.* St. Paul: North Central Publishing Co. 1952.

Regan, Ann. "The Irish." In *They Chose Minnesota: A Survey of the State's Ethnic Groups,* edited by June D. Holmquist. St. Paul: Minnesota Historical Society Press, 1981.

Reilly, Daniel F. *The School Controversy (1891–1893).* Washington, D.C.: Catholic University of America Press, 1943.

Sampson, Ann Thomasine, ed. "The Ireland Connection." Reminiscences based upon the Oral History Project, Sisters of St. Joseph, St. Paul, 1982. St. Joseph's Provincial House, St. Paul.

Shannon, James P. *Catholic Colonization on the Western Frontier.* New Haven: Yale University Press, 1957.

———, ed. "Archbishop Ireland's Experiences as a Civil War Chaplain." *Catholic Historical Review* 39 (1953): 298–305.

Shea, John Gilmary. *The Hierarchy of the Catholic Church in the United States.* New York: Office of Catholic Publications, 1886.

Storer, Maria Longworth. *In Memoriam: Bellamy Storer, with Personal Reminiscences of President McKinley, President Roosevelt and John Ireland, Archbishop of St. Paul.* Boston: M. L. Storer, 1923.

Sweeney, David Francis. *The Life of John Lancaster Spalding.* New York: Herder and Herder, 1965.

Trisco, Robert. "Bishops and Their Priests in the United States." In *The Catholic Priest in the United States: Historical Investigations,* edited by John Tracy Ellis. Collegeville, Minn.: St. John's University Press, 1971.

Wangler, Thomas E. "John Ireland and the Origins of Liberal Catholicism in the United States." *Catholic Historical Review* 56 (1971): 617–629.

———. "The Ecclesiology of Archbishop John Ireland." Ph.D. diss., Marquette University, 1968.

———. "The Birth of Americanism: 'Westward the Apocalyptic Candlestick.'" *Harvard Theological Review* 65 (1972): 425–431.

Williams, J. Fletcher. *A History of the City of St. Paul to 1875.* 1876. Reprint. St. Paul: Minnesota Historical Society Press, Borealis Book, 1983.

Wister, Robert James. *The Establishment of the Apostolic Delegation in the United States of America: The Satolli Mission, 1892–1896.* Roma: Pontificia Universitas Gregoriana, 1981.

———. "The Establishment of the Apostolic Delegation in Washington: The Pastoral and Political Motivations." *U.S. Catholic Historian* 3 (1983): 115–128.

Wittke, Carl. *The Irish in America.* Baton Rouge: Louisiana State University Press, 1956.

Zwierlein, Frederick J. *Letters of Archbishop Corrigan to Bishop McQuaid and Allied Documents.* Rochester: The Art Print Shop, 1946.

———. *The Life and Letters of Bishop McQuaid,* 3 vols. Rome: Desclee, 1925.

Index

John Ireland is abbreviated JI; Catholic University of America is abbreviated CUA

The text and display type in this book is Bembo, cut for the Venetian printer Aldus Manutius by Francesco Griffo in 1495. That first appearance of the typeface occured in *De Aetna*, an account of a visit to Mt. Etna by Cardinal Bembo. The face was revived in 1929 by Stanley Morison of the English Monotype Corporation. This book is composed on a Compugraphic digital typesetting machine in an adaptation of that face for modern printing technology.